The Structure of American Industry

WALTER ADAMS
MICHIGAN STATE UNIVERSITY
editor

Seventh Edition

MACMILLAN PUBLISHING COMPANY
New York

COLLIER MACMILLAN PUBLISHERS
London

Copyright © 1986, Walter Adams

Printed in the United States of America

All rights reserved. No part of this book may be reproduced or transmitted in any form or by any means, electronic or mechanical, including photocopying, recording, or any information storage and retrieval system, without permission in writing from the publisher.

Earlier editions copyright © 1950, 1954, 1961, 1971, 1977, and 1982 by Macmillan Publishing Co., Inc.

Macmillan Publishing Company
866 Third Avenue, New York, New York 10022

Collier Macmillan Canada, Inc.

Library of Congress Cataloging in Publication Data

Main entry under title:

The Structure of American industry.

Includes index.
1. United States—Industries—Addresses, essays, lectures. I. Adams, Walter.
HC106.8.S78 1986 338.6′0973 85-11533
ISBN 0-02-300770-2

Printings: 3 4 5 6 7 8 Year: 6 7 8 9 0 1 2 3 4 5

ISBN 0-02-300770-2

For “Janie”

Preface

One of the major transformations in political economy since the first edition of this book appeared in 1950 is a renewed awareness that the power relationships in society—and especially the role of the state—are a matter of profound social concern and require continuing confrontation by public policy makers.

In the aftermath of Watergate and related revelations, it has become less fashionable to dismiss the Founding Fathers as anachronistic philosophers or to ridicule Lord Acton's warning about the consequences of concentrated power. The excesses of the "imperial" presidency, and the abuse of executive authority to harass and oppress individual citizens, have underscored the importance of a decentralized power structure within a framework of checks and balances. As Madison put it in *The Federalist,* No. 51, "If men were angels, no government would be necessary. If angels were to govern men, neither external nor internal controls on government would be necessary. In framing a government which is to be administered by men over men, the great difficulty lies in this: You must first enable the government to control the governed; and in the next place oblige it to control itself. A dependence on the people is, no doubt, the primary control on the government; but experience has taught mankind the necessity of auxiliary precautions . . ." And these auxiliary precautions, said Madison, require primarily a separation of power between the different branches of government, and secondarily a dispersion of power among the citizenry. The underlying purpose, he wrote, is to prevent the rulers from oppressing the ruled, and to render it improbable, if not impracticable, for one segment of society to oppress another.

This traditional, peculiarly American distrust of concentrated power is, of course, relevant not only to political but also to economic institutions. Despite the recent reemergence of Social Darwinism, there is a persistent recognition that economic power is not merely a decorative status symbol to be passively enjoyed in the counting houses and country clubs. Economic power, we are constantly reminded, may be used with statesmanlike forbearance and diplomatic skill. It may be used only where circumstances absolutely demand it, or when the political climate is particularly propitious. It may be accompanied by sophisticated public relations campaigns to purify its venality or sanitize the corporate image. But the fact remains that, in the long run, the possession of great power and the exercise of such power tend to coalesce. Wherever economic power exists it tends eventually to be used, and for ends chosen by those who control it.

With the election of President Reagan there was a renewed emphasis on the decentralization of economic power. Competition was touted as an instrument for achieving "the best allocation of resources, the lowest prices, the highest quality, and the greatest material progress"; a device to be used by society for social purposes; a blueprint for limited power operating in a comprehensive framework of checks and balances; a network of safeguards against the abuse of power to the detriment of the public; and, perhaps, above all, a regulatory system for the economy which obviates intervention and control by an all-pervasive state.

Unfortunately, the Administration's rhetoric has not always been matched by concrete action. "Deregulation" has often meant the curtailment of government regulations with respect to clean air, pure water, automotive safety, and fuel efficiency rather than the economic deregulation of inherently competitive industries. "Free trade" has meant resistance against the crasser forms of protectionism (e.g., for roses and water beds) but has not been considered inconsistent with "voluntary" import restraints negotiated on a bilateral or multilateral basis (e.g., for steel, textiles, and automobiles). "Antitrust policy" has not been mobilized to stem a rising tide of mega-mergers and joint ventures which are structurally transforming our industrial landscape. Government still seems content to protect, subsidize, and bail out vested interests which ought to be compelled to live by the Darwinist survival principles they preach to others.

In the context of the current debate over the proper role of government, the virtues of the competitive market, the challenge of international competition, and the need to "reindustrialize" America, the seventh edition of this book seems felicitously timed. It offers a kaleidoscopic view of American industry—a collection of case studies illustrating different types of structural organization, different behavior patterns, and different performance records—with an emphasis on international comparisons, where relevant, with industries in Japan and the European Economic Community. Although each industry is, of course, an "individual," the case studies offer to the student of industrial organization a "live" laboratory for clinical examination, comparative analysis, and the evaluation of public policy alternatives. For that reason the book, I hope, constitutes a useful supplement, if not a necessary antidote, to the economist's penchant for the abstractions of theoretical model building.

East Lansing, Michigan *Walter Adams*

Contributors

WALTER ADAMS is Distinguished University Professor, Professor of Economics, and Past President of Michigan State University. A member of the Attorney General's National Committee to Study the Antitrust Laws (1953–55), he has been an expert witness before Congressional Committees and the International Trade Commission as well as in antitrust proceedings.

GERALD W. BROCK is an economist in the Office of Plans and Policy of the Federal Communications Commission. He previously served as a consultant to the Department of Justice and to private firms in matters related to their antitrust suits against IBM.

JAMES W. BROCK is Associate Professor of Economics at Miami University (Ohio). He has served as a consultant on antitrust matters.

KENNETH G. ELZINGA is Professor of Economics at the University of Virginia. He served as Special Economic Assistant to the Chief of Antitrust Division and is co-author (with William Breit) of *The Antitrust Penalties, Murder at the Margin,* and *The Fatal Equilibrium*.

ARNOLD A. HEGGESTAD is William H. Dial Professor of Banking and Chairman of the Department of Finance, Insurance, and Real Estate at the University of Florida. He has previously served as financial economist, Board of Governors of the Federal Reserve System, specializing in public policy issues regarding the banking structure.

MANLEY R. IRWIN is Professor of Economics in the Whittemore School of Business and Economics at the University of New Hampshire. He has served as Chief, Western Electric Investigation, Federal Communications Commission (1972–74). He has also appeared as an expert witness in several antitrust proceedings.

JAMES V. KOCH is Professor of Economics and Provost, Ball State University.

STEPHEN MARTIN is Associate Professor of Economics at Michigan State University. He has served as an economic expert in antitrust proceedings.

WALTER S. MEASDAY formerly served as economist (1957–74) and chief economist (1974–80) of the U.S. Senate Antitrust and Monopoly Subcommittee. He also taught at the University of Maryland from 1950–1978.

HANS MUELLER is Professor of Economics and Finance, Middle Tennessee State University. He has been a consultant on steel industry problems to the World Bank, the Federal Trade Commission, and various private organizations. He has also appeared as an expert witness before Congressional committees and the U.S. International Trade Commission.

WILLARD F. MUELLER is William F. Vilas Research Professor of Agricultural Economics, Professor of Economics, and Professor in the Law School, University of Wisconsin-Madison. He served as Chief Economist and Director of the Bureau of Economics, Federal Trade Commission (1961–68) and Executive Director of the President's Cabinet Committee on Price Stability (1968–69).

FREDERIC M. SCHERER is Joseph Wharton Professor of Political Economy at Swarthmore College. From 1974 to 1976 he was director of the Federal Trade Commission's Bureau of Economics. He has also served as a consultant in diverse antitrust, international trade, and defense economics matters.

WILLIAM G. SHEPHERD is Professor of Economics at The University of Michigan. The economic advisor to the Chief of the Antitrust Division (1967–68), he has also been an expert witness in several antitrust proceedings.

DANIEL B. SUITS is Professor of Economics at Michigan State University and Fellow of the East-West Population Institute. He has served as consultant to the U.S. Secretary of the Treasury (1961–70) and to a number of other federal and state agencies.

Contents

1

Agriculture

Daniel B. Suits

I. INTRODUCTION

As supplier of most of the food we eat and of raw materials for many industrial processes, agriculture is clearly an important sector of the economy. But the importance of the industrial performance of agriculture transcends even this function. In nations where the productivity of farmers is low, most of the working population is needed to raise food and few people are available for production of investment goods or for other activities required for economic growth. Indeed, one of the factors that correlates most closely with the per capita income of a nation is the decline in the fraction of its population that is engaged in farming. In the poorest nations of the world, more than half of the population lives on farms, as compared to less than 10 percent in Western Europe and less than 4 percent in the United States.

In short, the course of economic development in general depends in a fundamental way on the performance of farmers. This performance, in turn, depends on how agriculture is organized and on the economic context, or market structure, within which agriculture functions. In this chapter, the performance of American agriculture is examined, beginning with a consideration of its market structure.

II. MARKET STRUCTURE AND COMPETITION

Number and Size of Farms

There are about 2,241,000 farms in the United States today. This is roughly 40 percent of the peak reached sixty years ago, and as the number of farms has declined, the average size has risen. Farms in the United States still average fewer than 460 acres, but this average can be misleading. In fact, modern American agriculture is characterized by large-scale operations. Although only 162,000 farms—5.5 percent of the total—are as large as 1,000 acres or more, they include more than 40 percent of total farm acreage. Nearly a quarter of all wheat, for example, is grown on farms of 2,000 acres or more, and the top 2.6 percent of wheat growers raise roughly 50 percent of our wheat.

Sizes of farms vary widely by product, but even where typical acreage is small, production is concentrated. Nearly 65 percent of our tomato crop is grown on farms smaller than 500 acres, but the remaining 35 percent is marketed by the largest 9 percent of tomato growers. Broiler chickens are raised on still smaller farms, with 55 percent coming from farms with fewer than 100 acres. However, more than 70 percent of all broiler chickens are raised by the largest 2 percent of growers.

Size of farm also varies with production technique as this is affected by region, climate, and other factors. In the southern United States, 60 percent of cotton output comes from farms of fewer than 1,000 acres, whereas farms that small produce only a third of cotton grown in the more capital-intensive western states. Over all, however, the largest 3 percent of all cotton growers produced 40 percent of all cotton and cotton seed in the United States.

With the advent of large-scale commercial agriculture, the family farm, long the American ideal, is no longer characteristic. Only about half of all present-day farmers earn their livelihood entirely from farm operations. The others must supplement farm income with industrial jobs or other off-farm employment. Moreover, large-scale agriculture is increasingly characterized by corporate operations. Although only 2 percent of all farms are incorporated, corporations own 12 percent of all land in U.S. farms and market 22 percent of the total value of all farm crops.

Corporate farms are especially important in states like California, where they operate a quarter of all acreage in farms and market 40 percent of the value of all farm crops (including almost 60 percent of all California sweet corn, melons and vegetables). But even in a state like Kansas, over a third of all farm products are marketed by corporate farms.

Competition in Agriculture

Despite the scale and concentration of production, however, modern agriculture remains an industry whose behavior and performance are best understood in terms of the theory of pure competition. Although agricultural production is concentrated in the hands of a relatively small percentage of growers, total numbers are so large that the largest 2 or 3 percent of the growers of any given product still constitute a substantial number of independent firms. For example, although only 2 percent of grain growers produce about 50 percent of all grain in the United States, this 2 percent consists of 27,000 firms. Numbers like this are a far cry from those for manufacturing. The largest number of firms of all sizes found in any one manufacturing industry are the 10,000 sawmills and planning mills engaged in the production of lumber. However, manufacturing industries typically have many fewer firms—even industries like men's work clothing (277 firms) and cotton-weaving mills (218 firms), which are widely recognized as highly competitive. Thus, even if we ignore the competitive influence exerted by the thousands of smaller farms in each line of production and look only at the very largest, we are still talking about nearly 100 times as many independent firms as are found in the most competitive manufacturing industries.

In any event, the number and size of existing firms are only partial measures of the competitiveness of market structure. An important additional consideration is the extent to which ease of entry generates potential competition beyond the firms engaged in production at any given moment. Not only do the many smaller farms produce and sell in the same market with the larger ones, but there are no special barriers to entry into agriculture. Moreover, many existing farms are adapted to the production of a variety of products and can shift output from crop to crop on the basis of the outlook for prices and costs.

As a result of this structure, even large modern farms are powerless to exert any appreciable individual influence on total output or prices through their own economic behavior. They can only plan production schedules on the basis of their own best expectations, with the knowledge that the ultimate price will be virtually unaltered by anything they might decide. Plans for how much of which crops to grow and by which methods are arrived at on the basis of price and cost expectations. The resulting crop comes on the market and sells at prices that are determined by total volume in conjunction with existing demand.

Demand for Farm Products

Another important element in the structure of agriculture markets is the nature of the demand for farm products. Before exploring farm products in particular, however, it is useful to review some of the properties of demand curves in general. Potatoes are fairly typical farm products and can be used as a convenient illustration.

Demand for Potatoes. In Figure 1, the average farm price of potatoes in the United States is plotted vertically against the annual per capita consumption of potatoes, measured horizontally. Each point represents data for a recent year. The downward drift of the scatter of points from upper left to lower right confirms the everyday observation that people tend to buy more at low than at high prices. At the high price of $2.57 for example, average consumption of potatoes in the United States shrank to 133 pounds per person in 1980, whereas at the low price of $1.46, consumption reached 152 pounds per person in 1979. Of course, as a glance at the chart reveals, price is not the sole influence on buying habits. Consumption during 1981 was somewhat greater, and that during 1979 somewhat less than would have been expected from the price of potatoes alone. Part of this variation can be traced to changes in buyers' incomes, and part to changes in the prices of other foods that can substitute for potatoes in the diet. Some of the variation is associated with changes in consumer tastes for potatoes, connected

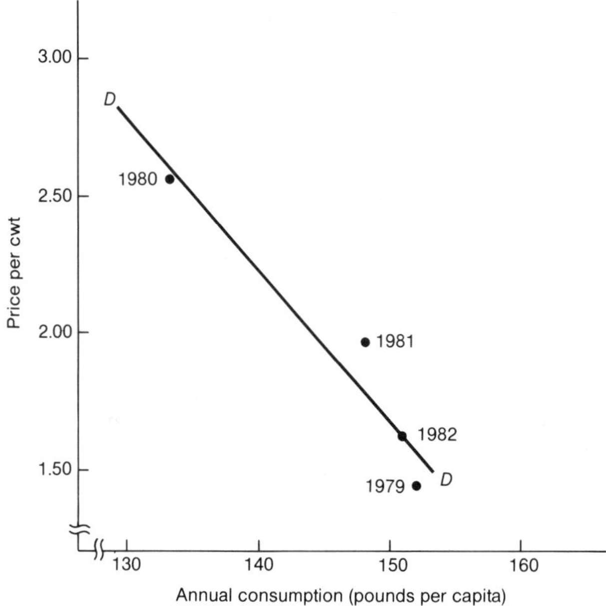

FIGURE 1. Demand for potatoes. *Source:* Data from the U.S. Department of Agriculture, *Agricultural Statistics,* various issues. Prices have been divided by the consumer price index to adjust for inflation.

with the shifting popularity of such things as packaged mashed potatoes, or "fries" at fast-food outlets.

By the use of appropriate statistical procedures it is possible to allow for the effects of many of these other influences and to estimate the effect of price alone on potato purchases. The result is shown by the curve *DD*, drawn through the midst of the observations. Such a curve, called a *demand curve,* represents the quantity of potatoes buyers would be expected to purchase at each price, other influences being held constant.

Demand Elasticity

Elasticity Defined. The responses of buyers to changes in price are measured by the *elasticity of demand* which expresses the percentage change in quantity purchased to be expected in response to a 1 percent change in price. For example, if a 1 percent price increase induced the buyers of a product to cut their purchases by 2 percent, the elasticity of demand for the product would be expressed as -2 to indicate that percentage changes in quantity purchased tend to be double the percentage change in price. The negative sign reminds us that quantity is altered in the opposite direction to the change in price, a rise in price being accompanied by a reduction in quantity, and vice versa. In a similar fashion, elasticity of $-.7$ would characterize the demand for a product when a reduction of only .7 percent in purchases would occur in response to a 1 percent price increase. An elasticity of −1 would indicate that percentage changes in quantity and price tend to be equal, and so on.

The elasticity of demand for particular products is readily estimated from fitted demand curves by selecting two prices close together and reading the corresponding quantities shown by the curve. The elasticity is then calculated as the ratio of the percentage difference in the two quantities to the percentage difference in the two prices. For example, careful measurement on the demand curve *DD* indicates that purchasers would be ready to buy about 142 pounds per year at a price of $2.10, but if the price were lowered to $2.00, purchases would expand to about 144 pounds. The price reduction from $2.10 to $2.00 is a change of −5 percent, whereas the increase in purchased quantity from 142 to 144 pounds is a change of about 1.4 percent. This yields an estimated elasticity of demand for potatoes of about 1.4/−5, or about −.3.

We are rarely interested in such exact measurement of elasticity, but we do need a general idea of how elastic the demand for a given product is. For this purpose it is convenient to classify demand curves into broad categories, using elasticity of −1, called *unit* elasticity, as the dividing point. Demand curves with elasticity smaller than 1 (in absolute value) are then referred to as *inelastic* demands. In these terms, the demand for potatoes with an elasticity of −.3 would be classified as *inelastic*.

Demand curves with elasticity greater than 1 in absolute value are termed *relatively elastic*. The demand for lettuce—estimated to have an elasticity of −2.8—is classified as relatively elastic.

Causes of Differences in Elasticity. Because elasticity measures buyer response to price, it varies widely among products, depending in each case on the characteristics of the product and on buyers' attitudes toward it. Products like potatoes, which many people view as necessities, or food staples, have inelastic demands. Buyers feel that they need a certain amount in their diet and are reluctant to cut back on their use of the commodity as its price rises. By the same token, because buyers are already consuming about as much of it as they feel they need, they have use for only little more when prices fall.

In contrast, products that are viewed as luxuries exhibit relatively elastic demands, for their consumption can be reduced almost painlessly when prices rise, yet buyers are delighted at the chance to enjoy them when lower prices place them within reach of the budget. Among farm products, demands for fruits and fresh vegetables tend to be relatively elastic. The demand for peaches, for example, has been estimated to have an elasticity of −1.49, five times that of potatoes. The high elasticity reflects the ease with which households can do without peaches when the price rises, and the welcome accorded the fruit when it becomes cheap.

The elasticity of demand also depends on the relationship the product

Table 1: Elasticity of Demand for Selected Farm Products

Product	Elasticity of Demand: Price	Elasticity of Demand: Income
Cabbage	−.25	n.a.[a]
Potatoes	−.27	.15
Wool	−.33	.27
Peanuts	−.38	.44
Eggs	−.43	.57
Onions	−.44	.58
Milk	−.49	.50
Butter	−.62	.37
Oranges	−.62	.83
Corn	−.63	n.a.
Cream	−.69	1.72
Fresh cucumbers	−.7	.7
Apples	−1.27	1.32
Peaches	−1.49	1.43
Fresh tomatoes	−2.22	.24
Lettuce	−2.58	.88
Fresh peas	−2.83	1.05

[a]Not available.

Source: Estimated by the U.S. Department of Agriculture.

bears to others. In particular, products that have good substitutes to which buyers can turn as alternatives tend to have relatively elastic demands. Even small percentage changes in price lead large numbers of buyers to choose the cheaper substitute. This is probably one of the reasons that demands for fresh vegetables tend to be relatively elastic. The elasticity of demand for fresh tomatoes, for example, has been estimated at −2.2, and that of fresh peas at −2.8, largely because many other fresh vegetables can be used instead of these if the price is right.

Price elasticities of demand for a number of farm products are given in Table 1. Note that demands for basic commodities like potatoes and corn tend to be inelastic, as might be expected from their nature. On the other hand, many individual fresh fruits and vegetables have highly elastic demands, partly because of their less basic character and partly because of the availability of many close substitutes to which consumers can turn.

Elasticity of Derived Demands. A particularly important aspect of demand for farm products is that most are purchased from the farm by canners, millers, and other manufacturers who process the raw product before selling it to final consumers. Wheat is milled into flour and baked into bread before it is purchased for the table; meat is butchered and packaged before con-

Table 2: Shares in Final Retail Value of Food Products

	Billions of Dollars	*Percent*
Final retail value	$297.6	100
Processing and marketing costs		
Labor	95.5	32
Rail and truck transportation	14.7	5
Power, containers, and other costs	90.8	31
Corporate profit (before taxes)	13.1	4
Farm value of products	83.5	28

Source: U.S. Department of Agriculture, *Agricultural Statistics,* 1983 (Washington, D.C.: U.S. Government Printing Office, 1983).

sumers buy it; and most fruit and vegetables are canned or frozen before consumers buy them. Even those to be sold fresh require transportation, packaging, and other retailing costs before they can be delivered to the table.

As shown in Table 2, only 28 percent of the retail value of food items purchased in the United States consists of their original value on the farm; 72 percent consists of value added by processing and marketing. These percentages vary widely among different farm products. Because of the lengthy production line required for bread and cereal products to reach the final consumer, farm value constitutes only 22 percent of the retail price. The value of the barley, rice, hops, and other farm products in the retail price of a can of beer is even smaller. In contrast, the farm share is 65 percent of the retail price of meat, poultry, and eggs that reach the table more directly.

Because of the value added by processing and marketing, the value of the farm product represents a small percentage of the retail price paid by ultimate buyers, and this tends to make the demand for raw farm products even less elastic. To make clear why this is so, let us consider a processed product with a relatively elastic demand—frozen peas with a demand elasticity of about -2. This elasticity would mean that a 5 percent reduction in the price of frozen peas would tend to increase consumption by about 10 percent. But if frozen peas are typical of other vegetables, farm value constitutes only about 30 percent of the final retail price, so a 5 percent reduction in the farm price of peas would result in no more than 1.5 percent reduction in retail prices for frozen peas. Given the elasticity of -2, this lower price would stimulate only 3 percent greater sales of frozen peas, and only a 3 percent increase in the purchase of raw peas to freeze. In consequence, then, a 5 percent price reduction at the farm level stimulates only a 3 percent increase in the quantity of peas bought from farmers, and this gives demand for peas an elasticity of only $-.6$ at the farm level, despite the highly elastic demand for frozen peas by consumers.

The relationship demonstrated for frozen peas holds for all derived demands. In general, the smaller the farm share in retail price, the lower the elasticity of derived demand for the product tends to be at the farm level. Because farm value is only 38 percent of the retail value of foods and other farm products, demand at the farm level would tend to be inelastic even if retail demands for final products were relatively quite elastic. In fact, however, because retail demands for most food products are inelastic even at the consumer level, the small farm share in retail price tends to make demand at the farm level very inelastic indeed.

Commodities with Several Uses. As we have seen, the elasticity of demand for a product depends on what it is used for, but many commodities are used for more than one purpose. In such cases, demand elasticity varies among the different uses, depending on the degree to which each particular use is viewed as "necessity" or "luxury," and depending on the availability of substitutes to replace the commodity for each purpose. Wheat, for example, has two important uses. It is used not only to make bread and bakery products for the table, but also as a feed grain for poultry and livestock. As a component of bread, wheat is generally viewed as a basic necessity; moreover, because of its gluten content, wheat flour has no good substitutes in baking. Indeed, wheat is so outstanding in this regard that most recipes for "rye" bread, "corn" bread, and other "nonwheat" bakery products call for the addition of wheat flour to the other grain in order to impart cohesiveness to the dough. As a result, the demand for wheat to make into bakery products is quite inelastic. As a feed grain, however, wheat has many fine substitutes in corn, oats, sorghum grains, and other commodities, so that the demand for wheat as feed grain in relatively elastic.

Statistical measurement by the U.S. Department of Agriculture bears out these differences in elasticity. The demand for wheat destined to be made into flour has an elasticity of only $-.2$, whereas the demand for wheat to be used as a feed grain has an elasticity of -3.

Taking all the uses together, the overall elasticity of demand for a product having several uses is the weighted average of elasticities of demand in the different uses, with weights proportional to the quantity consumed in each use. Because wheat is used overwhelmingly for flour, its overall demand is highly inelastic, despite the high elasticity of demand in one of its uses.

Elasticity and Allocation of Available Crop. Differences in elasticity play an important role in the allocation of farm products among different uses. When supplies are short, the consumption of products must be cut back. Generally, there is some reduction in all uses, but the greatest reduction is in less essential uses, or uses for which the product can readily be replaced by close substitutes. These are, of course, the uses in which demand elasticity is high. Rising prices curtail consumption in these areas, leaving proportionally more for essential uses where replacement is difficult. Response to increased supply is the opposite. As price falls, more of the product is devoted

Table 3: Tons of Wheat Consumed in the United States (in Millions) in Two Selected Years

	Human Food	*Animal Feed*
High supply	515.1	154.2
Low supply	503.3	20.2

Source: Adapted from data in U.S. Department of Agriculture, *Agricultural Statistics, 1983* (Washington, D.C.: U.S. Government Printing Office, 1983).

to all uses, but consumption expands proportionally more in the uses that are less essential, or where the cheaper product can replace substitutes.

The operation of this principle can be seen in Table 3, which shows uses of wheat during a year of high supply and during a year of lower supply. During the year of low supply, wheat consumption for human food was maintained at 98 percent of its higher level, whereas only 13 percent as much wheat was consumed for animal feed. These proportions are about what would be expected from the difference in demand elasticity in the two uses.

Other Factors Affecting Demand

In addition to price, the quantity purchased is affected by income, population, prices of substitute products, consumer tastes, and—for products like soybeans, which have important industrial uses—the state of industrial technology. The influence of change in these factors is generally represented by shifts in position of the demand curve. When, for any reason, consumers begin to buy more of a commodity than formerly at given prices, this fact is represented by a bodily shift of the demand curve to the right. Reduced purchases at given prices are represented by a shift of the demand curve to the left. Curve *DD* in Figure 1, for example, shows the location of potato demand when real per capita income stood at the average for the period. The point representing purchases during 1981, however, lies on a curve shifted slightly to the right by the high level of income in that year, whereas the dot corresponding to 1979 lies on a curve shifted to the left.

Income Elasticity. As with prices, the effects of income on buying are expressed in terms of elasticities. The income elasticity of demand is the percentage increase in quantity bought at given prices that occurs in response to a 1 percent increase in income. For example, calculation with potato data indicates that a 1 percent rise in real per capita income increases the volume of potatoes purchased by only .15 percent, and this is expressed as an income elasticity of .15. (Unlike price elasticity, most income elasticities are positive because the consumption of most commodities rises as income increases.)

An income elasticity of 1 characterizes a commodity whose consumption tends to rise in proportion to income. An income elasticity of less than 1 indicates that the quantity purchased grows less than in proportion to income. This is generally characteristic of staples and basic commodities, like potatoes, that even low-income families consume in quantity. An income elasticity greater than 1 characterizes products favored by rich people that poorer buyers cannot afford.

Income elasticity is given for most of the farm products in Table 2. As can be seen, basic staples like potatoes and onions have low income elasticities, whereas cream, fruit, and fresh vegetables are characterized by high income elasticities. The latter represent more expensive, preferred items whose consumption rises more than in proportion to income.

Commodities like cabbage and dried beans are characterized by negative income elasticity. That is, these are *inferior goods* that form an important part of the diet of poor people but are readily abandoned in favor of preferred, but more expensive, substitutes as income rises.

Because of wide differences in the income elasticities of different products, rising income does more to change the composition of demand than it does to increase the total amount of food consumed. That is, rising income increases the demand for more expensive, preferred foods, but it does so largely at the expense of reduced demand for other products. For example, families with incomes exceeding $15,000 (1973 prices) tend to eat, on the average, nearly three times as much sirloin steak as do families with incomes in the $5,000 to $6,000 bracket, but they eat only 20 percent more meat of all kinds, and the difference in total food consumption is even less. Richer families merely eat steak instead of other meat, and eat meat instead of other food. In addition, rich families consume a great deal less of such inferior foods as dried beans and cabbage than poor people do.

Prices of Other Products and Cross Elasticity of Demand. The purchase of products that have good substitutes is strongly influenced by the price of the substitute. A rise in the price of beef, for example, stimulates the demand for pork, and vice versa. This influence is measured by what is called the *cross elasticity* of demand; it is calculated by the percentage change that occurs in the quantity of the item purchased, given its own price, in response to a 1 percent change in the price of its substitute. Research into the demand for meat indicates, for example, that a 1 percent increase in the price of beef tends to increase the purchase of pork by about one quarter of 1 percent. This response is represented by a cross elasticity of .25 between the demand for pork and the price of beef. Cross elasticities are a good index of how closely two products substitute for each other in the buyer's consumption pattern. Low cross elasticity indicates products that are only poor substitutes, for a change in the price of one has little effect on the quantitity of the other that is purchased. The more readily products can be interchanged, the higher their cross elasticities tend to become. In the extreme case of perfect substitutes, any difference in price would lead to consumption of only the cheaper

Table 4: Elasticities of Demand for Beef, Pork, and Chicken

	Elasticity of Demand with Respect to			
Product	*Price of Beef*	*Price of Pork*	*Price of Chicken*	*Income*
Beef	−.65	.01	.20	1.05
Pork	.25	−.45	.16	.14
Chicken	.12	.20	−.65	.28

Source: Calculated for the author by students in Economics 835 at Michigan State University.

of thc two products, a situation that would be represented by an infinitely large cross elasticity.

In Table 4, estimated demand elasticities are given for three kinds of meat. As would be expected, a rise in the price of any one kind of meat reduces its consumption but increases the consumption of its substitutes. Thus, a 10 percent increase in the price of beef tends to reduce beef consumption about 6.5 percent (in keeping with its price elasticity of demand of −.65) but increases the purchase of pork by 2.5 percent and the purchase of chicken by 1.2 percent.

Individual Commodities Versus Commodity Groups. Demands for individual commodities with close substitutes have high price and high cross elasticities, so any change in prices causes a substantial change in the proportions in which consumers purchase the several products. When we consider the entire bundle of products as a group, however, we find a much lower response to price changes when the prices of all substitutes change together. For example, the demand for beef has an elasticity of −.65 in response to changes in its own price, and cross elasticities of .01 and .20 in response to changes in prices of pork and chicken, respectively. But when all meat prices change together, the buyer's response is measured not by these individual elasticities but by their algebraic sum. Thus, in response to a 10 percent increase in the prices of all three meats, consumption of beef would show an elasticity of $-.65+.01+.20=-.44$ and would decline only 4.4 percent. Similarly, a 10 percent rise in all meat prices would reduce pork consumption by only 4 percent and chicken by only 3.3 percent. In other words, when commodities are considered in groups, the demand elasticity for the group as a whole is substantially lower than the elasticities of demand for individual members of the group. The demand for feed grains as a whole is much less elastic than the demand for corn, oats, or sorghum grains taken individually, and the demand for fresh vegetables is much less elastic than the demands for tomatoes, fresh peas, or green beans taken individually.

Demand Elasticity and Farm Incomes

The general inelasticity of the demand for farm products, especially when major commodity groups are considered as a whole, has important consequences for the behavior of farm incomes. Unlike most manufactured goods, which are priced first with production adjusted to whatever sales materialize, farm crops are grown first and then are placed on the market for whatever price they will bring. Because these prices reflect the size of the crop, normal year-to-year variation in weather, insect pests, and other growing conditions generate year-to-year price fluctuations, the magnitude of which depend on demand elasticity.

The prices of products with inelastic demands fall more than in proportion to increased output, and total dollar value is smaller for a larger crop than it is for a smaller crop. This can be tested in terms of the demand for potatoes illustrated in Figure 1. According to the demand curve *DD*, the production of 130 pounds of potatoes per capita leads to a price of about \$2.75 per hundred pounds, or a crop worth about \$358 per consumer. In a nation of 230 million consumers, the total crop would be worth about \$823 million. Increasing production to 140 pounds per person, however, reduces the price to about \$2.21 per hundred pounds, making the larger crop worth about \$711 million all told. In short, an increase of less than 8 percent in the size of the crop reduces its total value by 14 percent.

Because most farm products—particularly when major commodity groups are considered as a whole—have inelastic demands, it follows that expanded production brings in fewer dollars and reduces farm incomes, whereas contracted production brings in more dollars and raises farm incomes. For this reason, natural year-to-year fluctuations in growing conditions make farming very much a "boom-or-bust" proposition. Poor growing conditions or crop failure in one part of the market mean severe losses to the farms affected but high incomes and prosperity for the other farms. Good growing conditions yield bumper crops but also result in low prices and reduced incomes for everybody.

Beyond the short-run fluctuations, demand exerts important long-run influences on farm incomes. Because demand is inelastic, a rising trend of farm yields means falling dollar receipts and a downward trend of farm income unless demand is expanded by enough to absorb the additional production. Two principal factors operate to expand farm demand. Demand tends to grow in proportion to the number of consumers and also expands as real per capita incomes rise. But growth in population raises demand only in proportion to the number of people (we might say that the "population elasticity" of farm demand is unity), whereas the income elasticity of demand for farm products is considerably less than unity. It thus follows that periods like the last fifty years, in which agricultural productivity grew much more rapidly than population, would also be periods of falling farm prices, diminishing farm incomes, and serious problems for the agricultural community.

The performance of agriculture is not exclusively a matter of demand, however, and before we can explore these problems further, we must turn to an analysis of agricultural supply.

III. SUPPLY AND THE PERFORMANCE OF AGRICULTURE

Just as demand represents the behavior of buyers in relation to prices, incomes, and other factors, *supply* represents the behavior of producers in response to prices and costs. Like demand, supply can be represented by a curve displaying the relationship between prices and quantities, and the response of quantity to changes in price can be expressed as an elasticity of supply. But there is an important difference between demand and supply, for although buyers tend to adapt promptly to new conditions, producers often require time to revise plans and production schedules or even to acquire new facilities and equipment. For this reason, it is useful to distinguish three different supply situations according to the scope afforded producers to respond to new information about prices and costs.

Harvest Supply—The Very Short Run

Once crops are mature and ready for market, the total quantity available is fixed and no action on the part of farmers can generate output beyond that total. Nevertheless, the total available is rarely harvested, for it seldom pays to strip fields so carefully that every last particle is collected. Some crops mature over periods of several weeks and growers must decide when the time is best for harvest and whether it is worthwhile to return to the fields for a second harvest a week or so later. Some crops can be harvested cheaply and quickly, but with greater loss of product than would be true of a slower, more expensive harvest. Clearly, high prices at harvest time make it profitable to harvest a larger proportion of the potential crop, whereas low prices make it unprofitable to take great care with picking, and this often results in the outright abandonment of low-yield acreage that would be too expensive to harvest.

Although there is some flexibility in the quantity produced from a given crop, the physical limitation to what can be harvested and the relatively low cost of harvesting (roughly 20 percent of variable cost) severely limit the extent to which output from a mature crop can be varied. Once crops are ready for market, harvest supply is extremely inelastic.

Short-Run Supply and Production Costs

Because the quantity that producers plan to grow depends on expected price in relation to production costs, the properties of short-run supply depend on the structure of costs.

Cost Structure. Production costs for farmers—like those of any other business firm—are of two general types. Some costs are fixed regardless of output, whereas others vary with the level of production. *Fixed costs* include taxes, interest on the farm mortgage, depreciation of equipment, and similar expenses that must be incurred whether production is undertaken or not, and that do not vary in magnitude as production rises and falls. *Variable costs* are zero as long as nothing is produced, but they rise sharply when production is initiated. The initial increase in variable cost is associated with planning, acquisition of materials, and other general costs that would not be incurred at all if nothing were produced. An important element of this start-up cost consists of the labor of the farm owner and family members, or the salary of managers of corporate farms.

Once start-up costs have been incurred, output can be expanded with relatively small increases in outlays for seed, fertilizer, herbicides, labor, power, and other variable costs; in this range, cost rises slowly as more bushels are produced. There is, however, a limit to the output available from given facilities, and as this capacity limit is approached, variable cost rises more and more sharply. Additional output can be had only by extra care, additional fertilizer, or other inputs to increase yield per acre.

Costs of a Corn Grower. Variable costs per acre of corn raised on central Iowa farms are given in Table 5. In keeping with modern farming methods, labor cost is low, with chemical herbicides employed in place of labor-in-

Table 5: Variable Costs per Acre of Corn Production, Central Iowa Farms

Costs	*Quantity*	*Costs per Acre (in $)*
Preharvest Costs		
Labor (including owners)	3.78 h	5.82
Seed	.23 bu	3.22
Fertilizer and lime		
nitrogen	100 lb	5.40
phosphorus	22 lb	4.58
potassium	19 lb	.99
lime	.23 ton	.91
Fuel, lubricants, repairs		3.95
Insecticides		2.18
Herbicides		2.24
Custom work		.85
Hail insurance		.30
Interest on operating expenses		1.01
Total preharvest cost		31.45
Harvest Costs		
Labor	2h	3.08
Fuel, lubricants, repairs		1.81
Custom hired harvesting and trucking		2.85
Other harvest expenses		1.98
Total harvest cost per harvested acre		9.72
Total harvest cost per planted acre		9.62
Variable cost per planted acre		41.07

Source: U.S. Department of Agriculture, Economic Research Service, *Selected U.S. Crop Budgets, Yields, Outputs, and Variable Costs: North Central Region,* Vol. 2, (Washington, D.C.: U.S. Government Printing Office, 1971).

tensive cultivation for weed control. Extensive use is made of commercial fertilizer to maintain high yields with little or no crop rotation. All together, variable cost amounted to $41.07 per acre planted. The sources from which the data were taken gave no indication of fixed costs; however, on a national average, fixed costs for farming—largely depreciation of buildings and equipment, interest on farm debt, and taxes—amount to about a third of variable cost. On this basis, we can estimate the total cost of corn grown in central Iowa at about $62.50 per acre.

Average and Marginal Costs. Total costs are translated into average and marginal costs in Figure 2. Marginal cost (MC) is the rate at which total cost rises as production is increased. Once start-up costs have been incurred and production is under way, additional corn can be raised for little more than the cost of the seed and materials needed to cultivate additional acreage. This keeps marginal cost low until production approaches the physical limits of the farm. As this capacity is approached, greater and greater outlays are needed to extract additional output, and marginal cost rises more and more sharply.

FIGURE 2. *Average and marginal costs of a corn grower.*

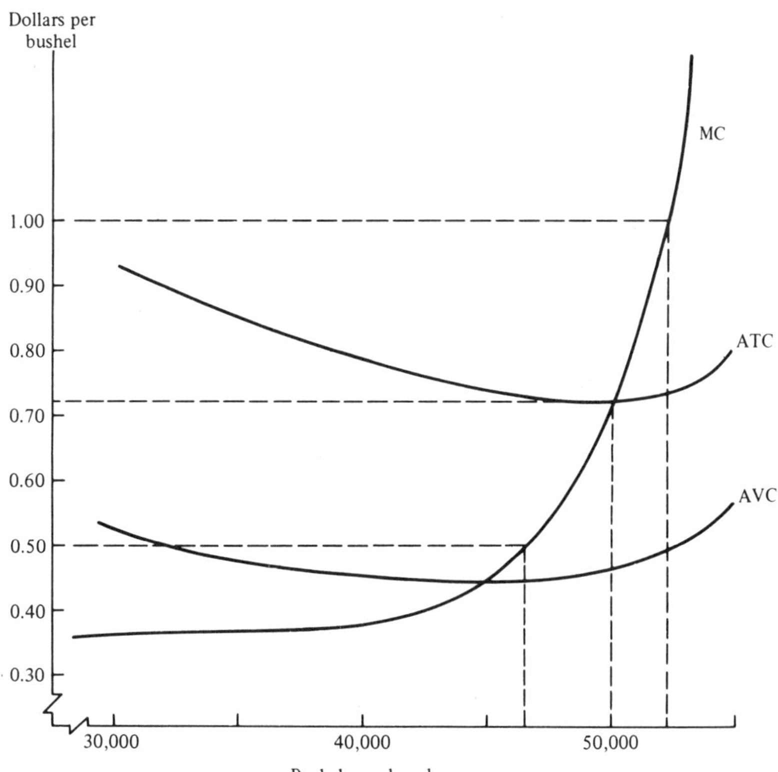

Average variable cost (AVC) is high at low levels of production because start-up costs are spread over limited output. As production expands, start-up costs are spread over more and more bushels of corn, pulling down the average variable cost per bushel. As production approaches the capacity of the farm, however, marginal cost begins to rise more than the average start-up cost declines, and at this point average variable cost stops falling and begins to rise.

Because fixed costs are unchanged as output expands, average fixed cost is inversely proportional to output regardless of production. Average total cost is merely the sum of average variable and average fixed costs.

Profit Maximization and Supply Elasticity. By a familiar proposition in competitive theory, output that brings marginal cost into equality with expected price is the most profitable production plan for a competitive firm—provided only that the expected price is high enough to cover the minimum average variable cost at which the firm can operate. At an expected price of 50 cents per bushel, the farm of Figure 2 would plan to raise about 46,500 bushels. If a price of 72 cents per bushel were expected, production would be increased to 50,000 bushels, and a price of $1.00 per bushel would raise the most profitable production to 52,300 bushels.

The cost curves shown are consistent with the cost data of Table 5 and are typical of agricultural production. Marginal cost rises so sharply near capacity output that even wide price variations exert little influence on the output of any individual grower, at least as long as he continues in operation. In other words, if a farm operates at all, it functions very nearly at the capacity output afforded by available land and facilities. As Figure 2 shows, even a 100 percent price increase—from 50 cents to $1.00 would induce the farmer to add only about 12.5 percent to planned production. This output response corresponds to a supply elasticity of only about .1.

But growers will continue to produce only so long as they expect prices that will cover their average variable costs. Fixed costs are already sunk in the business; they will continue whether anything is planted or not, and the only way to recover them is to operate the farm. Variable costs, on the other hand, are not incurred until the farmer decides to make the outlays; if there is no prospect of recovering variable costs, it is better to keep the money. To operate at all under these circumstances would result in losing not only fixed costs, but also some part of the variable cost in addition.

This proposition can be tested in terms of Figure 2. The 52,300 bushels produced at a price of $1.00 would entail an average total cost of about 74 cents per bushel and would leave nearly $13,600 as profit above cost. But production of 46,500 bushels at a price of 50 cents would involve an average total cost of about 73 cents per bushel, so the farm would sustain a loss of about $10,700 for the year. Even so, this would be better than shutting down the farm, for with no production at all, the farm would lose its entire $13,500 fixed cost. Because the 50-cent price is above the minimum average variable cost at which the farm can operate (about 44 cents per bushel) the farm is $2,800 better off when it produces at a loss than when it shuts down.

If, however, the price of corn should fall below the 44-cent minimum average variable cost to, say, 40 cents per bushel, marginal cost would be equated to price at an output of about 43,000 bushels. At this level of production, average total cost would be about 76 cents per bushel, and the operation would generate a loss of nearly $15,500. This would be about $2,000 more than the farm would lose if it simply stopped production and settled for the loss of all fixed costs.

Because farms in operation tend to operate very close to capacity regardless of price, the principal supply response to falling price occurs when farmers find it no longer profitable to produce the crop. Similarly, the principal supply response to rising prices comes when farmers find prices moving back into the profitable range and again take up production of the crop.

Variable costs differ widely among growers, depending on soil type, climate, length of growing season, and skill of the producer. During the same year that growers in central Iowa incurred an average variable cost of 47 cents per bushel of corn, Nebraska farmers produced corn at an average variable cost ranging from 49 cents per bushel in the lowest-cost district to 71 cents in the highest-cost area, and similar cost differences are characteristic of all other crops.

Figure 3 shows the striking variation in average costs among cotton growers in the United States. The curve shows the percentage of cotton production that was produced by cotton growers whose average costs were lower than those indicated on the vertical axis. For example, the average variable cost line indicates that whereas practically all cotton growers had an average variable cost below 39 cents per pound, only about 75 percent of cotton was grown by farmers with an average variable cost below 24 cents, and barely more than a third of all cotton was produced at an average variable cost below 18 cents.

Because no grower will plant cotton unless he expects price to cover at least his average variable cost, the distribution of average variable costs among growers gives a good indication of the elasticity of the short-run supply of cotton. For example, because practically all cotton grown in the United States was produced by growers with an average variable cost below 40 cents, but only about 92 percent by growers with an average variable cost below $.30, a 25 percent reduction of price from 40 cents to 30 cents would cause about an 8 percent reduction in cotton output, corresponding to a supply elasticity of about .3 for the short term.

Still another source contributing to the elasticity of short-run supply is the shifting composition of the output of multiple-product farms. For several reasons, many farms produce several different crops. Hog farmers, cattle feeders, and poultry growers need grain for feed, and it is natural for them to raise some of their own feed requirements. Other farmers raise crops that ripen at different times in order to spread harvesting over a longer period.

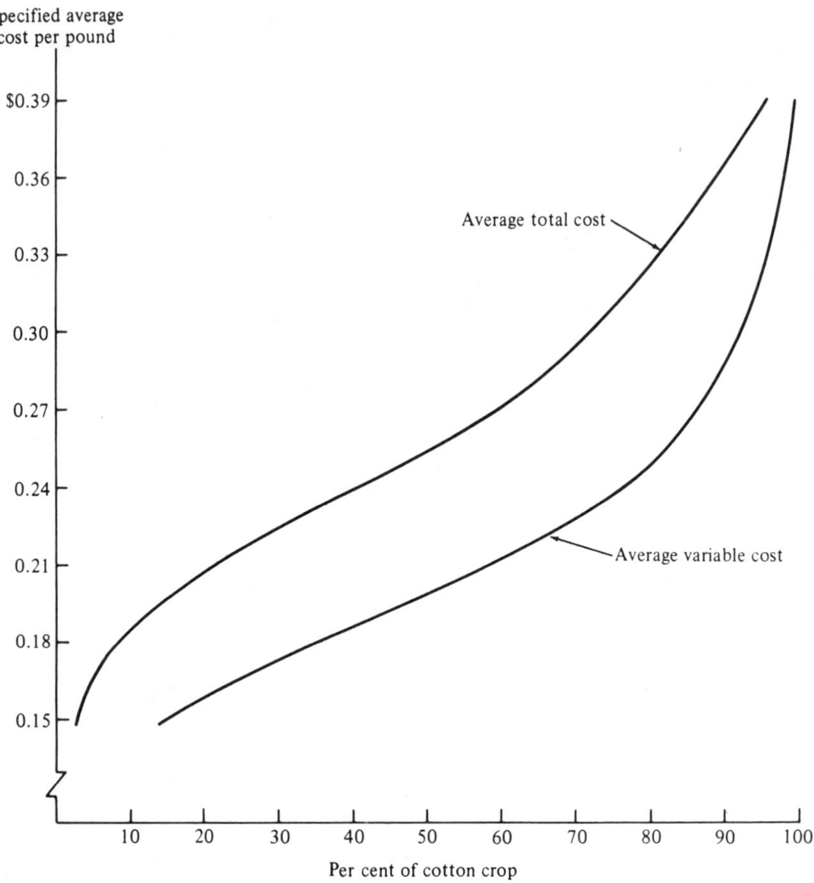

FIGURE 3. *Percentage of total U.S. upland cotton crop raised by growers with average costs below those specified.* Each point on the curve represents the percentage of U.S. cotton production (on the horizontal axis) raised by growers whose average costs were below the figure given on the vertical axis. *Source:* U.S. Department of Agriculture, *Costs of Producing Upland Cotton in the United States,* Economic Research Service, 1967.

This avoids the high harvesting costs that would be incurred if the entire crop had to be brought in within a few days, and reduces fixed cost by employing a smaller investment in harvesting equipment operated over a longer period, rather than a large investment that is used only briefly each year. Although it is less significant in these days of commercial fertilizer than it once was, crop rotation is another reason for multiple-product farms. Finally, producing several crops provides some degree of insurance against such natural calamities as blight, which can ruin yields for any one crop, and against the economic calamities that can result from unfavorable marketing conditions for any one particular commodity.

Regardless of the reason, however, the proportions in which different crops are grown are not fixed but vary in response to expected prices. The expectation of cheap corn and high-priced hogs, for example, leads hog raisers to increase the number of hogs, while planning to buy, rather than raise, extra feed requirements. Expectation of high prices for corn and low-priced hogs, on the other hand, induces growers to reduce hog production, while planning to sell, rather than feed, some of the high-priced corn. In a similar fashion, a division of acreage between corn and soybeans, the choice between planting more tomatoes or more sweet corn, and other planting decisions depend on expectations about the relative prices of alternative crops and therefore contribute to their supply elasticities.

Market Equilibrium and Adjustment Cycles

The interaction of short-run supply with demand for farm products governs the year-to-year behavior of production and prices. This interaction is depicted in Figure 4, where supply, *SS*, and demand, *DD*, determine a market equilibrium represented by price P^* and quantity Q^*. The P^* and Q^* values are equilibrium values in the familiar sense that no other combination of price and output could simultaneously satisfy the desire of consumers to buy—as indicated by the demand curve—and conform to the production plans of growers—as shown by the supply curve. At any price higher than

FIGURE 4. *Short-run market equilibrium.*

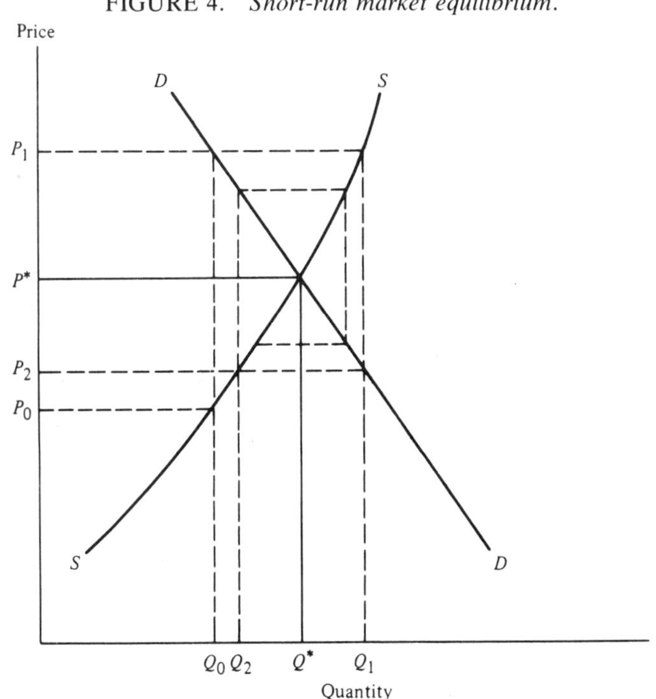

P^*—at P_1, for example—farms would expand planting in keeping with the supply curve and would bring to market a total output equal to Q_1, greater than Q^*. Yet, consumers, faced by a high price like P_1, would purchase only Q_0, an amount smaller than the equilibrium quantity, and considerably less than the amount farmers would be bringing to market. Resulting unsold surpluses would make it impossible to maintain the higher price, and the market would be forced back toward equilibrium. By the same token, any price below P*—say, P_2—would lead farmers to cut production back to Q_2, whereas the lower price would induce consumers to try to purchase a larger quantity, Q_1. The resulting inability of the market to satisfy demand would drive price and production upward toward the equilibrium values.

Equilibrium price and quantity comprise a kind of "target" for the market, marking values toward which actual price and output are continually being pushed, but it should be understood that day-to-day price and quantity are rarely observed at their equilibrium values. For one thing, supply deals with production *plans* rather than actual outcome. The most a farmer can do is to plant and tend his crop in a manner calculated to yield the most profit under normally expected conditions. Actual output invariably depends on vagaries of weather, insect damage, blight, and other factors that affect yields.

In addition, supply relates production plans to *expected* prices, and grower's expectations are not always exact. Indeed, the fact that they must plant for next season on the basis of price expectations derived from last season's experience sometimes leads to a systematic cycling of prices and output around equilibrium. For example, suppose farmers initially expect the low price P_0 and, consequently, plant the restricted output Q_0, in keeping with short-run supply. When this limited quantity reaches market, however, price would be driven up to P_1, in keeping with demand. But on the basis of the high price P_1, growers would be induced to plant Q_1 for the next season, and price subsequently would fall to P_2. The producer response to this would be an output of Q_2, which would again force price up. Under these circumstances, as can be seen in Figure 4, price and output would be observed to perform a series of diminishing cycles as they approached equilibrium. The spiral adjustment path marked out by the dotted lines in Figure 4 reminds some people of a cobweb, and for this reason the cycles of price and output observed in such markets are called *cobweb cycles*. Figure 4 is a highly simplified version of what actually happens. In the first place, production is not neatly divided into discrete stages but is subject to more or less continuous adjustment. Crops once planted can be cultivated or sprayed more intensively when prices are observed to be rising, improving yields beyond what had initially been planned, or acreage can be abandoned before maturity if it appears that low prices will make it impossible to recover the additional costs that otherwise would be invested in it over the remainder of the growing season.

The length of time between high and low prices or between low and

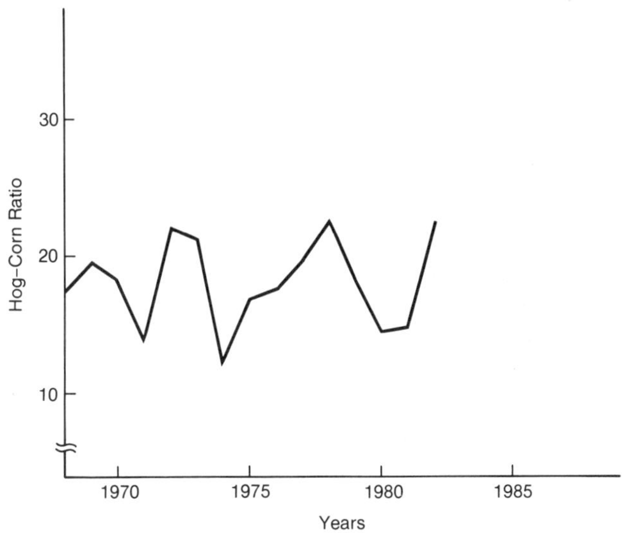

FIGURE 5. U.S. hog prices, 1968–1982. *Source:* U.S. Department of Agriculture, *Agricultural Statistics,* selected issues.

high prices in the cobweb cycle depends on the length of time between the initial planning and the marketing of the finished product. Crops such as onions and potatoes that have annual growing seasons also tend to have prices that oscillate annually, whereas products such as hogs that take longer to raise have prices that oscillate more slowly.

The history of hog prices in the United States exhibits cycles that are readily apparent in Figure 5. Because corn is the principal variable cost of hog production, the price of hogs is shown divided by the price of corn. The figure shows three complete price cycles in the 13-year period, beginning with the peak in 1969. This works out to an average of roughly four years for the price of hogs to complete a cycle from high to low and back again. The relatively long period of this cobweb cycle reflects the time required for hog raisers to respond to high prices by building up their herds of broodsows, and the additional time that must elapse after the sows are bred before mature hogs are available for market.

Ironing Out Price Fluctuations. The basic cause of systematic cycles in price and production is that farmers are forced to formulate production plans on the basis of past conditions, rather than on the basis of conditions at the time the crop will be ready for harvest. When farmers have advance information about market conditions, cycles are much less severe or are eliminated entirely. One way growers can obtain such information is by contracting with buyers in advance about prices and quantities, and this is common in many lines of agriculture. For example, 98 percent of all sugar beets, 85 percent of vegetables grown for processing, and 95 percent of all fluid-grade milk are sold to processors under contract. Contract marketing also covers 90 percent of all broiler chickens, 55 percent of citrus fruit, 45 percent of potatoes, and 42 percent of turkeys. This contrasts with barely 1 percent of hog production sold in advance.

A second way to iron out price fluctuations is by vertically integrating farming into the food-processing industry. Integrated farms are not independent producers at all, but operate as subsidiaries of food-processing firms. Vertical integration is especially common in cane sugar, where 60 percent of all cane grown comes from acreage owned by sugar-manufacturing firms. (The other 40 percent is grown under contract.) Similarly, 30 percent of citrus is grown in groves operated by processors, 35 percent of potatoes are grown on processor-owned farms, and 30 percent of vegetables commercially grown for fresh market are grown by subsidiaries of supermarket chains.

A third way to eliminate cycles in price and production is government action to stabilize prices by means of price-support programs. Essentially, these programs provide an advance guarantee to farmers that prices will not fall below a specified minimum, regardless of market conditions at time of harvest. The most important purpose of government agricultural price supports, however, is not to smooth out fluctuations, but, rather, as the term suggests, to maintain a level of farm prices higher than market equilibrium. We explore the operation of these programs at a later point.

Long-Run Supply

The Role of Average Total Cost. Farms that cover variable costs but fail to recover all their fixed costs can remain in business for short periods by allowing buildings and equipment to go unrepaired and by digging into savings to meet family living costs. Sooner or later, however, a time arrives when buildings become unusable or equipment must be replaced. At this point, farmers must decide whether to continue in operation. Unless prospects are so strong that additional investment will not only be recovered but will yield a profit, it is obviously better to shut down rather than invest more money in what is already a losing proposition. In the long run, in other words, supply depends on the ability of farmers to cover not just variable costs but total cost of production. The long-run elasticity of supply, then, depends on the distribution of average total costs among growers. For cotton production, this distribution is shown by the average total cost curve in Figure 3, each point on which indicates the percentage of total cotton production (on the horizontal axis) grown in the United States by producers whose average total costs are less than the figure indicated on the vertical axis. For example, 92 percent of all cotton was grown by farms with an average total cost below 39 cents, 88.2 percent was grown by those with an average total cost below 36 cents, and so on.

Naturally, the quantity of cotton that could be grown by farms that can cover average total cost at any given price is considerably smaller than what can be grown by those farms that could temporarily stay in production by covering average variable costs. The chart shows, for example, that whereas growers of 95 percent of the cotton in the United States could cover average variable cost at a price of 33 cents, growers of only 81 percent of the cotton could cover average total cost at that price. If price persisted at 33 cents, output would immediately fall to 95 percent; however, in the long run, producers of only 81 percent could afford to stay in operation. This greater long-run responsiveness of production is reflected in supply elasticity. Whereas practically all growers had an average total cost below 40 cents per pound, growers of only 73 percent of the cotton had an average total cost below 30 cents. Thus, the long-run effect of a 25 percent decline in price from 40 cents to 30 cents would be accompanied by a 27 percent decline in output, corresponding to a long-run supply elasticity of about 1.

Although supply in Figure 3 is treated only at prices below 39 cents per pound, similar relationships hold for supply at higher prices. Prices above 39 cents attract higher-cost growers to production, resulting in a larger long-run response to price than that obtained in the short run.

Long-Run Adjustments to Shifts in Demand. An important aspect of the performance of any industry is how effectively output is adjusted to shifts in demand. But because of the three different supply situations, adjustment of price and output is not a once-and-for-all process; it is a sequence of events that may require many years for completion. Buyers whose demand has risen, for example, find themselves initially confronted by a very inelastic harvest supply. Although rising prices signal a greater demand for the product, growers have little power to satisfy it, for they are locked into the results of production plans laid many months previously and can harvest no more than has been grown. The most they can do to satisfy increased demand is to strip fields with greater care than would have been profitable at lower prices and to harvest low-yield acreage that would otherwise have been abandoned.

Although rising prices do little to elicit additional output, they nevertheless perform two important functions. In the first place, rising prices reallocate available supplies among alternative demands. Buyers who are in a position to do so are forced to resort to (now) cheaper substitutes, or to go without the product entirely. The reduction of purchases by these buyers, in keeping with their highly elastic demand for the crop, leaves a larger quantity available for uses in which it is essential or for which satisfactory substitutes are unavailable.

Second, higher prices for the harvest encourage growers to plan a greater output in planting for the next season and to shift some of their fields from other crops to the more profitable use. By the time of the next harvest, these efforts will have expanded output, and prices will decline somewhat from the initial peak reached just after the upsurge in demand.

In the still longer run, as higher prices persist over the next several years, production is expanded further as farmers invest in additional equipment and as new farms are attracted to the profitable crop. This long-run expansion of output is accompanied by a gradual decline in price, but so long as the price remains high enough to attract new capacity, expansion continues. Expansion slows, however, and approaches a halt as prices approach levels that just cover average total costs of the least efficient, highest-cost farms engaged in production.

This adjustment mechanism has profound economic significance. The production of crops requires that resources be diverted from other uses and devoted to the purpose. Consumers who want the crop signal their willingness to provide the required resources by their willingness to pay prices. But time is required to transfer resources from one employment to another. At harvest time, the most producers can do is to apply a few extra labor-and machine-hours and a little extra gasoline and other costs to increase recovery of the crops already in the fields and thus squeeze out as much as possible for the consumer. Even so, the resources needed to do this raise harvest costs sharply.

Given more time, growers can plan expanded production and bring prices down from the peak reached at harvest. In the longer run, resources can be shifted in a more efficient way and equilibrium price will settle to the lowest level that will permit all growers of the new equilibrium quantity to cover the average total costs of operation.

The response to a reduction in demand would be the reverse. Reduced consumer desire for the crop would be signaled by sharply falling prices, indicating that consumers would prefer fewer resources devoted to production of this crop. But because most resources have already been irretrievably sunk in production, the most growers can do at harvest time is to divert some small amount of resources away from the harvest by the abandonment of low-yield acreage and by a less intensive harvest of the remainder. Output declines but little, and few resources are saved. In planning for the next season, however, growers who find they can no longer expect to cover average variable costs shift labor, fuel, and materials to other crops or release them for employment elsewhere in the economy. At this point, however, nothing can be done about the resources already sunk in farm equipment and buildings. In the long run, however, as capital equipment wears out, it is not replaced and labor and other resources that would otherwise be devoted to the production of farm machinery and buildings are freed for employment elsewhere.

IV. IMPROVEMENT IN TECHNOLOGY

It is not enough for an industry merely to move resources around in response to consumer demand. It also must see that the productivity of those resources is kept as high as possible. One way to raise the productivity of resources in use is by the introduction of new, more efficient methods of production, and an important criterion of the performance of any industry is the rapidity with which it improves its technology.

In analyzing the behavior of agriculture in this regard, however, we must remember that there are two distinct aspects to the problem. One question is how fast the industry itself originates and develops new methods of operation. The other question is how rapidly the industry adopts and puts into use new methods as they become available, regardless of where the ideas originated.

On the first count, the record of agriculture has been rather poor. The intensively competitive structure and the relatively small scale of operation characteristic of farming simply do not lend themselves to the research and development of new ideas. The expensive laboratories and large research budgets that are commonplace in many large industrial firms could not be supported by even the largest wheat or cotton farm, hog grower, or cattle raiser. If improvements in agricultural technology had to wait until they could be developed on the farm, agricultural productivity today would be little ahead of what it was a century ago.

Fortunately, however, we have not had to depend on the farm to develop its own technical improvements, for the job has been undertaken by others. One major source of new technology has been the government-subsidized laboratories of state universities and agricultural experiment stations. To a far greater extent, however, improvements have originated in agricultural equipment firms, chemical firms, and in other industries that supply input to modern agriculture. For, if farmers have done little themselves to raise their own productivity, they have provided a ready market for any improvement in method, once it has been developed and demonstrated. The result has been a rate of growth in productivity that has outstripped the rest of industry.

The Profit Incentive

The strong incentive to adopt better methods derives from the profits that are available to the first growers to implement them. A grower who can reduce the cost of his 30,000 bushels of corn from $28,000 to $23,000 immediately adds $5,000 to his annual income. His individual behavior cannot affect the price of corn, for his individual contribution to total supply is insignificant. Until others take up the new method, the entire $5,000 is pure profit.

Innovation and Prices

Unfortunately for the grower, however, the new profitable situation carries within it the germ of its own destruction. For, when other growers see this demonstration of the cheaper method, their own eagerness for greater profit leads them to imitate it. The spread of the new method produces a general increase in supply with a consequent fall in price to a new equilibrium level commensurate with the new lower cost of production.

This fall in price, which is the long-run consequence of technical innovation, has a number of important effects. In the first place, it means that exceptional profits are received only temporarily by the first growers to put the new methods into practice. As other farmers follow suit, extra gains from the lower-cost methods are wiped out as price is reduced by the rising supply of the product.

Falling prices also mean that in the long run growers have no effective choice about whether or not to adopt the new methods. As prices approach the new lower-cost levels, farmers still using the old, higher-cost methods are no longer able to cover the average total costs of production and are compelled to adopt the new methods if they are to survive. Those farmers who hold back too long are simply driven out of business.

Above all, as prices fall to the lower-cost levels, the entire gain from the new method is passed on to consumers. Growers who first adopted the method for the sake of extra profits, and those who followed along later in self-defense, have combined in an action that has not only increased the productivity of resources but also has passed the cost saving onto society at large in the form of lower prices.

Broiler Chickens—An Example of Innovations

The continual improvement of production methods is one of the most striking features of American agriculture. A good example is the revolution in the production of broiler chickens, shown in Table 6. Forty years ago, broiler chickens were raised commercially on farms where they ran at large in yards, competing with one another for food, with heavy loses from accident and disease and heavy labor costs for care. In those days, it took 16 weeks and 12 pounds of feed to raise one 3½-pound chicken, and labor cost ran as

Table 6: Production Cost, Output, and Price of U.S. Broiler Chicken, 1934–1980

	Production Cost per 100 lb of Chicken			
Year	*Feed (lb)*	*Worker-Hours*	*Production (lb per Capita)*	*Relative Price per Pound ($)*[a]
1934	n.a.[b]	n.a.	.76	.457
1940	420	8.5	3.13	.394
1950	330	5.1	12.82	.342
1960	250	1.3	32.76	.164
1970	219	.5	52.27	.135
1980	192	.1	68.48	.109

[a]Price of chicken divided by Consumer Price Index to adjust for inflation.
[b]Not available.

Source: U.S. Department of Agriculture, Economic Research Services, and *Agricultural Statistics, 1983* (Washington, D.C.: U.S. Government Printing Office).

high as 8.5 hours per 100 pounds of chicken raised. It is probably difficult for modern readers to realize that in those days chicken was too expensive for everyday use and generally was served only on holidays and other special occasions.

In about 1950, a revolution began in commercial broiler production: the chickens were raised indoors in individual cages. This eliminated wasteful competition among birds for feed, greatly reduced losses, permitted automated delivery of feed, and lowered labor costs. By 1960, a 3½-pound chicken could be raised in only 8 weeks on 7.5 pounds of feed and at labor cost of only 1.3 worker-hours per 100 pounds. By 1980, labor costs had been cut to barely 1 percent of their level of 40 years earlier, and birds were ready to market in 47 days.

As a result of this great increase in supply, prices of broilers, adjusted for changes in the Consumer Price Index, declined from 46 cents per pound in 1934 to 10 cents per pound by 1980. The fall in price, partly assisted by

Table 7: Productivity of Labor and Land in U.S. Agriculture: Selected Crops and Livestock, 1910–1982

Crop	*1910–1914*	*1935–1939*	*1945–1949*	*1955–1959*	*1965–1969*	*1978–1982*
Corn						
worker-hr per acre	35.2	28.1	19.2	9.9	6.1	3.4
bu per acre	26.0	26.1	36.1	48.7	71.1	105.3
Wheat						
worker-hr per acre	15.2	8.8	5.7	3.8	2.9	2.7
bu per acre	14.4	13.2	16.9	22.3	25.9	34.0
Potatoes						
worker-hr per acre	76.0	69.7	68.5	53.1	45.9	35.4
cwt per acre	59.8	70.3	117.8	178.1	205.2	269.4
Sugar beets						
worker-hr per acre	128.0	98.0	85.0	51.0	35.0	23.0
tons per acre	10.6	11.6	13.6	17.4	17.4	20.6
Cotton						
Worker-hr per acre	116.0	99.0	83.0	66.0	38.0	6.0
lb per acre	201.0	226.0	273.0	428.0	505.0	496.0
Soybeans						
worker-hr per acre	n.a.[a]	11.8	8.0	5.2	4.8	3.5
bu per acre	n.a.	18.5	19.6	22.7	24.2	30.1
Milk						
worker-hr per cow	146.0	148.0	129.0	109.0	84.0	35.0
cwt per cow	38.4	44.0	49.9	63.1	82.6	118.2
Hogs						
worker-hr per cwt	3.6	3.2	3.0	2.4	1.6	0.4
Turkeys						
worker-hr per cwt	31.4	23.7	13.1	4.4	1.6	0.3

[a]Not available.

Source: U.S. Department of Agriculture, *Agricultural Statistics* (Washington, D.C.: U.S. Government Printing Office, appropriate issues).

the increased demand arising out of growing population and income, resulted in a one hundred-fold increase in consumption of commercial broilers. Chicken is no longer a special holiday dish, but has become the cheapest meat in the store; outside the home, chicken sold in franchise outlets has become a rival of the hamburger.

Table 7 emphasizes that the story of commercial broiler chicken is by no means unusual. The continual search for a more profitable operation has sharply reduced production costs in virtually every line of agriculture. It takes only 10 percent as much labor per acre of corn today as it did 70 years ago, yet output per acre has quadrupled. Three times as much wheat can be raised per acre with one-sixth the labor, and a worker-hour of effort produces nine times as many pounds of hogs, thirteen times as much milk, and one hundred times as many pounds of turkeys as could be produced 70 years ago.

Technology and Scale of Operation

Most modern technical innovations have reduced farming costs by replacing labor with mechanization or other capital-intensive methods. Innovations of this kind reduce variable costs of operation at the expense of higher interest, depreciation, taxes, and other fixed costs. As a result, they generally require greater output than less capital-intensive methods if they are to realize their potential for lower average total cost.

Techniques of broiler production in general use in 1960 reached a minimum average total cost of 16.4 cents a pound at an annual output of 20,000 birds per farm. Subsequent technical improvements permitted cost to fall to 10.9 cents, but only if growers could produce and market an annual output of 116,000 birds each. If the improved methods were used to grow the same number of broilers per farm as in 1960, the average total cost would be considerably higher than even the 1960 level. Thus, the same forces that press for innovation and lower cost also bring irresistible pressure for larger-scale output.

When farms get larger, what happens to the total number in operation depends on demand. Falling prices expand total consumption in keeping with demand elasticity, and demand itself rises with population and income. When demand is sufficiently elastic, or rises sufficiently rapidly, markets for output may expand enough to maintain or even to increase the number of farms in operation, despite larger scale. But inelastic demand that rises only slowly results in a smaller number of farms as size increases. The trend toward a smaller number of larger-scale producers in the broiler industry is evident in Table 8. During the period 1959–1982, the average output per farm rose nearly ten-fold, but total sales only tripled, reducing the number of farms by half. Even this remarkable performance understates the effect of technology on farm numbers and size, for it is estimated that the largest five producers ship 40 percent of all birds marketed.

Growth in the average size of farms has been continuous throughout

Table 8: Number, Size, and Output of U.S. Broiler Producers

Year	*Number of Farms*	*Average Output per Farm (Number of Chickens)*	*Total Production (Millions)*
1959	65,314	18,985	1,240
1964	41,778	45,193	1,888
1978	31,743	96,462	3,062
1982	30,104	116,596	3,510

Source: U.S. Department of Commerce, *Census of Agriculture* (Washington, D.C.: U.S. Government Printing Office, appropriate issues).

the history of the United States. Some idea of the development can be had from the trend in number and average acreage of farms shown in Table 9. Improvements in agriculture came slowly during the first 40 years of the period shown, and average farms were only 11 percent larger in 1920 than they had been in 1880. Moreover, growth in demand had greatly exceeded the rate of growth in farm productivity, and there were more farms in 1920 than there had been 40 years earlier. The high point in number of farms occurred in 1920. In more recent decades, the tempo of technical improvement has greatly accelerated, but the rate of population growth has slowed, leading to a rapid rise in average farm size accompanied by rapidly falling numbers. In the period 1960–1982, the average size of farms in the United States doubled but the total number was reduced 60 percent.

Technology and the Displacement of Farm Labor

The same forces that affect the size and number of farms also affect labor cost and the number of people engaged in agriculture. When new technology raises the productivity of farm labor, any given quantity of farm product can be produced with fewer people than before. As a result, unless

Table 9: Number and Size of Farms, and U.S. Farm Employment, 1880–1982

Year	*Number of Farms*	*Average Acreage per Farm*	*Farm Employment (Thousands)*
1880	4,008,00	133.7	10,100
1900	5,740,000	146.6	12,800
1920	6,453,000	148.5	13,400
1940	6,104,000	174.5	11,000
1960	5,388,000	215.5	7,100
1970	2,730,000	389.5	4,200
1982	2,241,000	439.0	4,043

Source: U.S. Department of Commerce, *Census of Agriculture* (Washington, D.C.: U.S. Government Printing Office, appropriate issues).

consumption expands in proportion, rising productivity reduces the number of people needed. Higher productivity increases the supply of farm products, and the resulting decline in prices automatically expands consumption, but because of the very low demand elasticity for farm products, consumption will increase much less than in proportion to the productivity increase. The net result of the increase in productivity, therefore, is a reduction in the demand for farm labor.

It is the market that keeps the number of people engaged in agriculture in balance with demand. Reduction of demand cuts earnings of farm labor below what could be earned in other industries, and farm people with the necessary skills leave for more promising jobs in other industries. Those farm laborers without alternative employment for their skills find themselves trapped in low-paying farm occupations, or are forced off the farm into the city where, without marketable skills, they are added to the welfare roles.

The fate of farm labor is an excellent illustration of two important aspects of the operation of competitive markets. Competition generates inexorable pressure to extract greater output from available resources and passes the gains of this greater productivity onto the consumer in the form of lower prices and higher standards of living. But, in so doing, the market operates without regard to the fate or feelings of the people involved. The supply and demand for farm labor are rigorously balanced by the competitive market, regardless of what happens to farm families who are caught in the adjustment.

Other Social Costs of Modern Agriculture

The increasing scale of operations needed to apply modern farming methods has brought other profound changes to agriculture. Considerably more farming is being undertaken by large corporations, and commercial farming of specialized crops is replacing the more diversified agriculture of the family farm.

Moreover, modern agricultural methods are seen by some people as leading to an overspecialization in production, which increases the danger of soil exhaustion as single-crop agriculture replaces crop rotation. In addition, heavy reliance on chemical fertilizers puts water tables in danger of contamination, and the intensive use of sprays increases risks to consumers. Crop varieties are also being adapted to the requirements of mechanical harvest, storage, and shipping rather than to improved flavor and nutritional value.

Some of these objections reflect more on the tastes and preferences of American consumers than they do on farm technology. If people are willing to buy cheap tomatoes with the flavor and consistency of red baseballs rather than pay more for flavorful tomatoes that are too delicate for anything but hand harvest, competitive agriculture will provide for their preferences.

Others of these concerns, however, derive from problems that are fundamental to competition. The most important deficiency of competitive industry is that no account is taken of social costs that are external to the accounts of the individual firm. In the struggle to cut cost, the individual firm evaluates only its own costs. If reduction of costs of the firm also result in the imposition of higher costs on society as a whole, the competitive market provides no mechanism to balance one against the other.

The adoption of circular irrigation systems provides, in some areas at least, an example of this kind of problem. These irrigation systems enhance crop yields by doing for the fields what a lawn sprinkler does for a home garden. Hence, the adoption of the system is highly profitable to the individual farm. Yet widespread adoption of the technique has serious detrimental effects on the water table, which may even raise the long-run cost of agriculture in the area. None of the unfavorable wider consequences is directly presented to individual firms as part of the cost of irrigation, with the result that the individual farmer sees only the short-run profit potential of circular irrigation. The result is that pursuit of profit by individual farms can yield severe environmental impacts as well as cheaper food.

Similar external costs arise when insecticides and chemical fertilizers run off the fields to pollute streams and endanger water tables, or when antibiotics used in animal feeds create serious health problems for meat consumers. If the farm industry is to be properly regulated by the forces of competition, these costs must be somehow taken into account. Some part of the answer lies in action by government to limit the type and amount of spray that can be applied, and to monitor the use of the common water table. Thus, the environmental impact of DDT has resulted in laws forbidding its use for most agricultural purposes.

A thorough assessment of the problem of environmental pollution goes far beyond the scope of this chapter, but it is important to recognize that one important aspect of the behavior of any industry is its impact on the environment. In this respect, unmodified competition as exemplified by agriculture has a poor record.

V. EVALUATION OF AGRICULTURAL PERFORMANCE

Left to itself, agriculture is a highly competitive industry. As such, its performance is, in many respects, almost ideal. Indeed, it is difficult to imagine a system better adapted to carry out the purely technical functions of production and allocation of products:

1. Although harvest is subject to the vagaries of random events, available supplies are rationed among competing uses in accordance with consumer priorities as expressed by demand elasticities.
2. At each stage of production, the most is extracted from available resources. In the very short run, when most costs have been already sunk into crops, relatively little can be done to adapt to consumer desires; however, given time, the investment in production closely follows up demand, with matching shifts in output.

3. In addition, the industry has demonstrated a remarkable history of rapidly increasing the productivity of the resources it employs and of passing this increase on to consumers in terms of lower relative prices and increased standards of living; at the same time land, labor and other resources have been released for the production of other products.
4. All of this has been accomplished with virtually no conscious collective planning, administrative direction, or political processes. Competitive pressure toward improvement in inexorable. It is unnecessary to debate new methods; they simply impose themselves.
5. The same competitive process, however, appears inexorably to move along its own way regardless of the fates of the people involved. When productivity grows more rapidly than the demand for farm products, people who have devoted their lives to agriculture are driven off the farm to fend for themselves, as best they can, in urban areas.
6. By the same token, the absence of social costs from the accounts of the individual farm, in the search for cheaper farming methods, can result in the destruction of the environment.

VI. GOVERNMENT POLICY TOWARD AGRICULTURE

Price Supports

The severe dislocation wrought in agriculture by untrammeled technical innovation proceeding in the face of slowly increasing demand has generated overwhelming pressure for governmental intervention. This intervention has largely been directed toward efforts to hold up farm prices. Price-support programs were initiated during the New Deal of the early 1930s and, although repeatedly modified as to detail, they have maintained much the same general character.

Any program to support prices must somehow define a target level at which to support them and then devise methods for enforcing the supports. Support levels for farm prices are usually defined in terms of "parity" prices. These are prices that are calculated for each commodity; they bear the same relationship to the average price of things that farmers buy (the "prices-paid" index) that the price of that same commodity did during some base period.

As originally defined, parity prices were to bear the same ratio to the average prices-paid index that they had during the base period 1910–1914. For example, if the price of cabbage had been $1.10 per hundredweight as an average during 1910–1914, when the index of prices paid by farmers averaged 100, then the parity price of cabbage would be defined for any later year by multiplying the prices-paid index during that year by .011. Many years later, when the prices-paid index reached 350, this calculation would yield a parity price for cabbage of $3.85 per hundredweight. In subsequent legislation, definitions of parity have been altered to refer to more recent

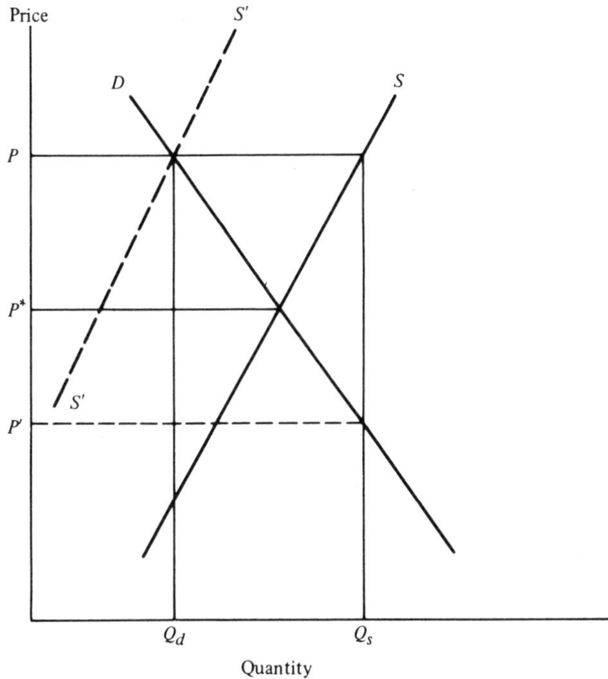

FIGURE 6. *Problems of price supports.*

base periods, and more complicated formulas are applied in the calculation of parity prices for individual commodities.

Once parity prices are defined, government policy then undertakes to support the prices of a number of key commodities at a specified fraction of their parity price. The fraction at which prices are supported varies from commodity to commodity and from time to time. Regardless of the level of support, however, one difficulty is encountered, for when prices are supported at levels higher than market equilibrium, government must somehow contend with the resulting gap between supply and demand. The problem is illustrated in Figure 6. Because the support price P exceeds the equilibrium price P^*, farmers tend to produce and bring to market a total quantity Q_s that exceeds the amount Q_d that consumers are willing to buy at that price. If market price is to be maintained at P, something must be done about this gap.

Restriction of Supply

There are three alternatives: (1) government might induce farmers to restrict supply to $S'S'$ so that the desired support price becomes the new market equilibrium, (2) government might purchase the output (Q_s-Q_d) which farmers cannot sell at the support price; or (3) the entire output might be sold on the market at whatever price it would bring (P'), and government make up the difference between *P'* and *P* by a subsidy paid directly to growers.

Historically, government price-support programs have involved a mixture of the three techniques. Supply has been restricted, usually by paying farmers to "set aside" part of their acreage, or to divert part of their acreage into "soil-conserving" crops, or to place acreage in a "soil bank." In the early years of price supports, acreage diversion was the most important weapon of government policy. At its peak in 1966, a total of 63.3 million acres were diverted from cultivation. This amounted to nearly 6 percent of all farm land in the United States and entitled farmers to more than $1 billion in government payments. More recently, however, outright payments to farmers for acreage diverted have been replaced increasingly by the use of acreage limitation as a criterion for receipt of other price-support payments.

The Commodity Credit Corporation

Any surpluses that remain after supply has been reduced have generally been dealt with by crop loans issued to farmers by the Commodity Credit Corporation (CCC). The CCC is a government agency that, under the direction of the secretary of Agriculture, each year designates a loan rate on each commodity to be supported. The loan rate is the amount per unit that the CCC stands ready to lend to farmers in good standing with the price-control program who want to borrow on their crops. For example, when the loan rate for corn is $2.65, farmers are entitled to borrow $2.65 for each bushel of corn they grow, regardless of its actual market value. Now, if too much corn is grown and the market price begins to sink below the $2.65 loan rate, the farmers are privileged to default on their loans, letting the CCC take the corn. On the other hand, if the market price should rise above the loan rate, the farmer can reclaim the crop, repay the loan, and sell the corn at the higher market price. Although the CCC is set up as a lending organization, its principal function is to provide a roundabout way for farmers to sell to the government any output that cannot be sold on the market at the price defined by the loan rate.

The Commodity Credit Corporation must, by law, extend loans on six "basic" commodities: corn, cotton, peanuts, rice, tobacco, and wheat, and on a group of designated "nonbasic" commodities that includes, among other things, butter, honey, tung oil, rye, and wool. In addition, from time to time, as directed by the Secretary of Agriculture, the CCC extends price-support loans on an extensive and diverse list of crops ranging from staples such as dry peas, soybeans, and potatoes to such things as almonds, cotton seed, and olive oil.

The volume of crops acquired depends on loan rates in relation to production and demand levels. Huge bumper crops harvested in the face of recession-level demand can leave large, unsold surpluses in government hands. During the recession of 1958–1959, the CCC spent nearly $2 billion to acquire unsold commodities, including more than 25 percent of the wheat crop for that year. From 1959–1963, the CCC owned an entire year's production of wheat.

Agricultural Subsidies

The third method of price support involves direct subsidy payments to growers of corn, wheat, cotton, sugar, wool, and a number of other commodities to make up the difference between market price and support level. In terms of Figure 6, for example, support of the price at *P* would induce farmers to grow Q_s bushels. When this output arrived on the market, the market price would be driven down to *P'*, but the price difference would be made up by payment to growers of a subsidy equal to (*P*-*P'*) dollars per bushel.

In their current versions, most price-support programs integrate direct subsidies with acreage limitation and CCC loans in a rather complicated package. In general, farmers who agree to limit their acreage are offered price-support subsidies designed to bring the prices they will receive for only a designated portion of their output up to the full support level. Beyond this specified portion, production is subject to support at CCC loan rates set below the full support level. For example, in recent years, the support price of corn has been $2.86 per bushel, and the CCC loan rate has been $2.65. This has meant that farmers participating in the corn-production program were guaranteed a price of $2.86 on a specified number of bushels, whereas the remainder of their crop was supported by the CCC loan rate, at a minimum price of $2.65. Similar programs have been in force for wheat, cotton, barley, and grain sorghum.

Because price supports of any kind make it difficult for farm products in the United States to compete in foreign markets, the government sometimes pays special export subsidies on commodities shipped abroad. In 1973, payments under the export program included, among others, subsidies of 34 cents per bushel for exported wheat, $1.75 per hundredweight of rice, 13 cents per pound of chicken, and 14 cents per pound of butter. In total, the U.S. government spent $405 million to subsidize exports of farm products during 1973. In 1985, the government embarked on a new Bonus Incentive Commodity Export Program, whereby some foreign buyers of grain from U.S. farmers were given free additional grain from CCC holdings. This is another way to raise the prices farmers receive above prices in the export market.

All told, the several price-support programs have absorbed huge government outlays. The cost of price-support to the American taxpayer was over $17 billion during fiscal year 1982, and rose to almost $20 billion during 1983. But a national spirit is moving in the direction of free markets, and this, combined with pressure to reduce federal deficits, will probably result in a reduction of these outlays; however, the farmers who now benefit are difficult to mollify, and it remains to be seen how much reduction can be accomplished.

Other Price-Support Measures

Not all prices are supported by direct governmental action. Prices of a broad array of commodities, ranging from citrus fruit to nuts, are set by *marketing orders* issued by the Secretary of Agriculture. These orders enable producers to organize *marketing boards*, which are given wide powers to control the production and marketing of designated commodities. Aside from certain professional sports, marketing boards are the only unregulated legal monopolies permitted in the U.S. The boards limit production, sometimes by restricting the quality or sizes of product that can be shipped. Some boards prop up prices by assigning quotas to individual producers and by requiring that any additional output be placed "in reserve," usually to be disposed of by exporting at low prices.

The price of milk is supported by a combination of marketing order and CCC intervention. A marketing order by the Secretary of Agriculture sets the prices that dairies must pay farmers for fluid milk destined for human consumption. Because demand is elastic, the higher this price is raised, the less milk the dairies will buy, but the marketing order cannot control production. To deal with this problem, all milk that farmers cannot sell at the price established by the order is marketed as "manufacturing-grade" milk and is sold at whatever price the market will bring. The demand for manufacturing-grade milk is supported, however, by means of CCC loans extended on such manufactured dairy products as dry milk, butter, and cheese.

The government accumulated so much cheese, butter, and dried milk that in 1982, 1983, and 1984 it became necessary to pass it out to poor recipients to forestall extensive spoilage. The milk program has recently been modified to compensate dairy farmers who agree to reduce production below their normal rate of output.

Who Benefits from Price Supports?

Because the clear result of agricultural price-support programs has been higher prices to consumers and higher taxes for taxpayers, one might well ask who benefits from these programs? Presumably, the rationale for farm policy has been to relieve some of the suffering that resulted from rapidly rising agricultural productivity. Yet, oddly enough, practically nothing about government farm policy has benefited the people who need it the most.

The history of agriculture has been a continuous story of small farmers driven out and people pushed off the farm. But even most farmers who remain on the farm get few benefits from farm programs. In fact, the very nature of price supports concentrates the benefits among the largest, most powerful growers, rather than among the poor and weak who really need help.

In 1982, the smallest 50 percent of farms received less than 8 percent of total government price-support payments. This amounted to an average of only $250 per farm. In contrast, the largest 12 percent of all farms received 48 percent of all government payments. The largest 5 percent of all farms received 24 percent of all payments, with an average receipt of almost $7,000 per farm. Payments to the few very largest farms ran to millions of dollars each!

This highly unequal distribution of benefits is a direct consequence of programs that pay for acreage diverted, buy up surpluses, and subsidize production. When farmers are paid to divert acreage, the farms with the largest acreage receive the largest payments. When price-support subsidies are paid, those with the largest output receive the most support. In short, all price-support benefits are inevitably distributed in direct proportion to the size of the operation, which, in the very nature of things, is inversely in proportion to human need. Moreover, this is only part of the picture, for gains to farmers extend beyond what they receive directly from the government. When acreage is restricted, farmers not only receive payments for that reason but the products that they grow on their remaining acreage sell at higher prices, providing a second benefit; but nobody knows how large this part of the benefit from the government program is. It has been estimated at many times the value of the direct payments, but—whatever it is—it is distributed in proportion to the size of the operation and is concentrated in the hands of the largest producers.

Rapidly rising agricultural productivity has generated a serious problem of human displacement and has been associated with serious human suffering. Public policy toward agriculture, however, has done practically nothing about this problem. It has, instead, subsidized the largest farms. It is the ultimate irony that agriculture, the industry whose operation is best understood in terms of purely competitive behavior, is subject to expensive governmental intervention to forestall the benefits of that very competition, and to protect the revenues of large corporate growers.

SUGGESTED READINGS

Heady, Earl O. *A Primer on Food, Agriculture, and Public Policy*. New York: Random House, Inc., 1967.

Lin, William, James Johnson, and Linda Calvin. *Farm Commodity Programs: Who Participates and Who Benefits?* U.S. Department of Agriculture, Agricultural Economic Report No. 474, Washington, D.C., 1981.

Roy, Ewell P., Floyd L. Cortz, and Gene D. Sullivan. *Economics: Applications to Agriculture and Agribusiness* Danville, Ill.: The Interstate Publishers, 1971.

Ruttan, Vernon W., Arley D. Waldo, and James P. Houck, eds. *Agricultural Policy in an Affluent Society*. New York: W. W. Norton & Co., Inc., 1969.

Schultz, Theodore W. *Transforming Traditional Agriculture*. New Haven, Conn.: Yale University Press, 1964.

2

The Petroleum Industry

Walter S. Measday and Stephen Martin

I. INTRODUCTION

The general chronology of events in the world oil industry since 1973 is well-known. Table 1, which shows the official price of Saudi Arabian light (so-called "marker") crude oil over that period, dramatically illustrates the consequences over time of shifts in the control of supply and demand of crude oil. The traces of major political events can be seen in Table 1: the Arab-Israeli War of October 1973, the fall of the Shah of Iran in January 1979. Economic changes, which occur more gradually, also leave their mark: the shift of ownership and control over Mideast crude-oil reserves from vertically integrated, Western-based international oil companies to local governments; the subsequent reduction in the growth of energy demand; and the shift in the composition of demand—away from petroleum and toward other primary sources of energy.

We will examine the political and economic forces that have determined the performance of the world oil market and the U.S. oil submarket. Some of the questions we shall answer are: What industry characteristics have allowed the exercise of market power, and by whom? What structural characteristics limit the exercise of market power? What has been the role of the major oil companies in the market, and what has been the role of smaller, independent companies? How have the policies of governments of consuming nations affected the market? What can we say, as economists, about likely market performance in the future?

II. STRUCTURE

The petroleum industry includes four distinct vertical levels: *production, refining, marketing,* and *transportation.* Production involves the location and extraction of oil and natural gas from underground reservoir formations. These formations may be so close to the surface that their oil seeps up through the ground, or they may require extensive drilling, from platforms located

Table 1: Official Price of Saudi Arabian Light (34°) Crude Oil (dollars per barrel)

1972	Jan.	1.79
	Jan. 20	1.91
1973	Jan.	2.05
	April	2.17
	May	2.55
	June	2.70
	July	2.75
	Aug.	2.85
	Sept.	2.86
	Oct.	2.80
	Oct. 16	4.76
	Nov.	4.81
	Dec.	4.68
1974	Jan.	10.84
	Nov.	10.46
1975	Oct.	11.51
1977	Jan.	12.09
	July	12.70
1979	Jan.	13.34
	April	14.55
	June	18.00
	Nov.	24.00
1980	Jan.	26.00
	April	28.00
	Aug.	30.00
	Nov.	32.00
1981	Oct.	34.00
1983	Feb.	30.00
	March 15	29.00

Note: Changes effective on the first of the month unless otherwise indicated.

Source: Petroleum Economist (April 1983), p. 141.

miles offshore. The refinery industry manufactures a wide range of finished products from crude oil—from petroleum coke to motor gasoline and jet fuel. Wholesale and retail marketers distribute these products to consumers. Connecting these three vertical levels is a specialized transportation industry, including pipelines, tankers, barges, and trucks, which moves crude oil from fields to refineries and finished products from refineries to marketers. We shall consider each vertical segment in turn.

Crude-Oil Production

The U.S. Market. Government policy has long been a major influence in the U.S. oil market. Until recently, it was government policy that separated the United States from the world oil market.

From the 1930s until the 1950s, controls on oil production by state governments (importantly, the Texas Railroad Commission) held crude-oil prices in the United States at artificially high levels.[1] These prices proved attractive to foreign suppliers, and the United States became a net importer of refined-oil products by 1948. Three congressional investigations of the matter in 1950 conveyed to the oil companies a congressional preference for low imports.[2] When domestic oil producers raised the price of U.S. crude oil in June 1950, the U.S. coal industry, with the support of the petroleum industry, sponsored a bill to place import quotas on petroleum.[3] The Eisenhower Administration set up "voluntary" import-restraint programs in 1954 and 1958, and when these proved ineffective, imposed mandatory quotas in 1959.[4]

These formal and informal restrictions on the flow of oil had numerous consequences. Prices for U.S. consumers were, of course, higher, perhaps by as much as $3 to $4 billion a year.[5] At a time when the price of 30-degree crude oil on the Eastern seaboard was about $3.75 per barrel, a Cabinet task force estimated that elimination of oil-import controls would reduce the price of crude oil by $1.30 per barrel.[6] Although the quotas had been justified on national security grounds, the effect of high U.S. prices in a shielded market was to encourage the extraction of relatively high-cost U.S. crude, accelerating the depletion in U.S. reserves and conserving lower-cost reserves elsewhere in the world. It became clear, in 1973, that national security would have been better served if the pattern of extraction had been reversed. In addition, it was these import restrictions that split the U.S. oil market from the world oil market.

United States crude-oil production, just over 60 percent of the world total in 1947,[7] fell to 13.7 percent of world output in 1977, and recovered slightly (to 16.1 percent of world output) during the first six months of 1984.[8] Major new production in the "Lower 48" states is unlikely, partly because they have been thoroughly explored and partly because of restrictions on development, based on concern about the environment. Geologists now estimate that half of future discoveries of U.S. oil and gas fields will be offshore,[9] and that the most promising regions are off the Alaskan shore.[10]

In comparison with other industries, concentration of United States oil production appears to be in the low-to-moderate range (Table 2). The most recent concentration figures available are for 1982. A wave of mergers among

Table 2: Concentration of Crude Oil Production, United States

	1979	*1980*	*1981*	*1982*
Top 8	48.8	51.1	49.6	49.5
Top 16	69.7	69.6	67.4	66.6

Source: U.S. Department of Commerce Bureau of the Census, Annual Survey of Oil and Gas. U.S. Government Printing Office, Washington, D.C., various years.

Table 3: Major U.S. Oil Companies

	1983 Revenues ($ Billions)
Exxon	94.6
Mobil + Superior[1]	60.3
Chevron + Gulf[2]	58.1
Texaco + Getty[3]	53.1
Standard Oil (Indiana)	29.5
Arco	26.3
Shell Oil[4]	20.7
Occidental Petroleum + Cities Service[5]	18.2
Phillips Petroleum	15.5
Sun	15.3

1. Mobil acquired Superior during March & April 1984.
2. Chevron (formerly Standard Oil of California) acquired Gulf in April 1984.
3. Texaco acquired Getty Oil in January 1984.
4. 69% of Shell Oil is owned by Royal Dutch/Shell, which is seeking complete control at this writing.
5. Occidental acquired Cities Service on December 3, 1982.

Source: The New York Times, March 21, 1984, p. 29; *Fortune* (May 2, 1983), p. 228.

large oil companies since 1982 has undoubtedly increased concentration since that time (Table 3).

Students of industrial organization justify their interest in market-concentration figures on the ground that such figures provide information on the likelihood that leading firms will come to recognize their mutual interdependence and act in a way that is likely to maximize joint profit. The common use of joint ventures in the oil industry makes the degree of effective concentration much higher than the figures reported in Table 2 suggest.

Adams,[11] for example, documents the extensive use of joint bidding for federal offshore leases. From 1970 to 1972, 4 of 16 U.S. major oil companies made no independent bids for offshore oil leases, but submitted a total of 863 joint bids with 14 alternative partners. Chevron submitted 79 individual bids and 108 joint bids with 9 alternative partners; Cities Service made 7 independent bids and 372 joint bids with 4 alternative partners. Among the 16 majors, only Exxon made no joint bids during this period, although it made 80 independent bids. A similar pattern of joint ventures occurs abroad (Table 5) and in pipelines.[12]

The partners in this overlapping network of joint ventures, to the extent that they profit from the same enterprises, have incentives to avoid competition. The operation of the network of joint ventures provides each company with myriad bits and pieces of information about the market strategies of its fellows. No single firm could contemplate noncooperative behavior without knowing that this behavior would be detected by other firms.

At the same time, since the lifting of U.S. import controls in 1973[13] and

Table 4: The World Oil Majors (1970)

	Gross Crude Production	Refinery Runs	Production As % of Runs	Product Sales
Exxon	6093	5270	115	$5684
Texaco	3228	2719	121	2917
Gulf	3050	1591	192	1545
Chevron	2558	1741	147	2421
Mobil	2083	2004	104	2145
Royal Dutch/Shell	5135	5042	98	5198
British Petroleum	3720	2260	164	2118

Output data in thousand barrels per day; product sales in million dollars.
Note: In 1984, Chevron acquired Gulf in the largest merger in American industrial history.

Source: Petroleum Press Service, May 1971, p. 166.

the deregulation of U.S. oil prices in 1979,[14] the U.S. market for crude oil has been integrated into the world oil market. Concentration of production among U.S. producers is, in and of itself, of little interest from the point of view of understanding the price of crude oil. Our interest in concentration at the crude level in the U.S. market is justified by the facts that the major U.S. producers also operate on the world stage (compare Tables 3 and 4) and are integrated forward into refining, transportation, and marketing.

The World Market

From the end of World War II until a transition period beginning in the early 1970s, the international oil industry was dominated by seven vertically integrated companies,[15] five of which were based in the United States. Their operations are described (for 1970) in Table 4. Adelman[16] estimates that the combined share of non-Communist crude-oil production outside of North America of the seven firms listed in Table 4, along with Compagnie Française des Petroles, fell from 100 percent in 1950 to 80.8 percent in the first half of 1969.

In one sense, the basis for this dominance was because the major oil companies operated under the system of joint ventures. Joint ventures for the richest oil fields in the world, in the Middle East, are described in Table 5. As we mentioned, continual contacts through joint ventures result in a sharing of information, which is not characteristic of "arm's length" competition:[17]

> Every major company was linked to practically every other one through a series of joint producing and refining ventures, long-term bulk purchase agreements, and long-term reciprocal supply arrangements. Where joint facilities existed, they normally required joint operating decisions; the output of Aramco in Saudi Arabia, for instance, as well as that of the Iraq Petroleum Company, was partly determined by an intricate bargaining process among the major companies.

The major oil companies owed their position in the world market to their control of Middle East oil, but what factor or factors allowed them to

Table 5: Ownership Shares in Major Middle East Joint Ventures (Percent)

	Iranian Consortium	*Iraq Petroleum Company*	*Aramco*	*Kuwait Oil Company*
Exxon	7	11.875	30	
Texaco	7		30	
Gulf	7			50
Chevron	7		30	
Mobil	7	11.875	10	
Royal Dutch/Shell	14	23.75		
British Petroleum	40	23.75		50
CFP	6	23.75		
Others	5	5		

Note: CFP = Compagnie Française des Petroles.

Source: S. A. Schneider, *The Oil Price Revolution*. Baltimore: Johns Hopkins, 1983, p. 40.

gain control? Turner[18] believes that it was the result of political support of the home governments of the major companies, especially in the immediate postwar period. To insure that the U.S. had access to Middle East oil was perceived as a national security issue. State Department policy was mentioned explicitly when the Justice Department waived antitrust objections to the participation of American firms in the Aramco (Saudi Arabia) joint venture. The Iranian consortium was established after a CIA-backed coup returned the Shah of Iran to power in August 1953 (reversing the nationalization of Iranian oil by the Mossadegh government).[19]

The majors had assets that went beyond political support. They were able to marshall the financial capital necessary for exploration and development. They controlled the refineries through which crude oil had to pass on the way to the final consumer. They were masters of the technology needed to make crude-oil production work; even today, this is an advantage to the major companies for production "on the margin"—offshore drilling and secondary and tertiary recovery.

In addition, as shown in Table 5, each major international company had access to reserves in at least two major Middle East areas. By judicious rearrangement of production, it was possible for the companies to resist pressure from the host countries. Blair[20] shows that aggregate production of eleven Organization of Petroleum Exporting Countries (OPEC) members, from 1950 to 1972, grew at essentially a constant rate of 9.55 percent per year, even though the output of individual countries fluctuated wildly. During the postwar era, the international majors controlled production, and they were able to maintain steady growth in overall production by reallocating production among producing nations.

The majors were producers and sales agents for the host countries. As a group, they lifted more crude oil than they required for their own substantial refining interests (see column three of Table 4). This excess crude was sold

Table 6: Ownership and Marketing of OPEC Oil

		1970	*1973*	*1978*	*1979*	*1980**
Producer Government Ownership (Entitlement)	%	2	20	75	80	80
Direct Exports By OPEC National Companies	%	0	5	36	46	50+

*Trend in Second Quarter.

Source: Jochen H. Mohnfeld, *Petroleum Economist,* August 1980, p. 329.

to independent refiners, generally under long-term contracts.[21] Relatively little crude oil—about 5 percent[22]—was traded on a short-term basis on the spot market.

The structure of world crude-petroleum production is vastly different today. As indicated in Table 6, the international majors have lost their position of control in the Middle East. OPEC-member nations now control their own oil reserves; national oil companies directly market the major portion of crude-oil output. To be sure, some of this oil is marketed to the international majors, but on terms significantly less advantageous than those that obtained when the majors lifted oil on a concessionary basis.

Table 7 shows the decline in the crude-oil supply to the international majors. Sales by the majors to independents have virtually ended:[23]

> Faced with heavy losses of Iranian oil in early 1979, the major companies cancelled or reduced most of their remaining third party contracts . . . The affected

Table 7: Crude Supply: The Seven World Majors

Year	*Crude Supply (Thousand b/d)*
1972	30,353
1973	32,161
1974	30,208
1975	24,712
1976	25,362
1977	24,501
1978	23,904
1979	23,031
1980	19,647
1981	18,659
1982	16,306
1983	14,715

Note: Crude oil and natural gas liquids, production and purchases, for the 7 firms listed in Table 2.

Source: Petroleum Economist, various issues.

customers were forced to look for new supply channels, thereby increasing the competition in world oil markets.

Current estimates are that 40 to 50 percent of world oil trade takes place on the spot market.[24] As suggested by Table 6, many spot-market sales are made by the national oil companies of the producing nations. When spot-market prices have been above the official prices at which long-term trade takes place, some producing countries have diverted supplies from long-term customers to the spot market.[25]

How did this massive alteration in the structure of the world crude-oil industry come about? How were the host countries able to wrest effective control of oil production from the international majors? To answer this question, it is useful to examine the background of the two worst oil shocks of the 1970s—the price increases at the end of 1973 and at the end of 1979.

As we have indicated, during the postwar period the international majors gave up to independent producers about 20 percent of the non-Communist world market (excluding North America). For the first time, the independents gained a foothold—some would say a toehold—in the Middle East when Iranian oil fields reopened in 1954.[26] The industry became less homogeneous, and more competitive.[27] Just as the majors had once been able to play host nation against host nation by shifting production, so host nations gradually gained the option of playing independent companies against the major companies.

During the postwar period, the exploration and development policy of the majors tended to concentrate supply in the Middle East. As shown in Table 4, the world majors had access to more than enough crude oil to satisfy their own needs. Throughout this period, the majors' biggest problem in the crude-oil market was not the location of additional sources of oil but that of resisting pressure from host countries to increase production.[28] Independents had little incentive to secure their own reserves because supplies were available from the majors under long-term contracts. Behind the shield of import quotas, the United States was thoroughly explored, but little attention was paid to potential reserves in Africa, Latin America, or the Far East.[29]

The development activities of the majors were concentrating the supply of oil in the Middle East. At the same time, the demand for oil was increasing throughout the industrialized world. The first column in Table 8 shows the growth of the U.S. market in the 1960s and early 1970s. Similar growth took place in Europe and Japan. In 1973, with simultaneous booms in North America, Europe, and Japan, world demand for energy—and for oil—was at an all-time high.[30]

In previous periods of peak demand (or supply interruptions, such as the 1967 Arab-Israeli War), Western nations had been able to expand production without substantial cost increases.[31] Spare capacity was sufficient to match supply with demand, which sharply reduced the bargaining strength of OPEC member nations. But[32]

Table 8: Import and OPEC Shares of U.S. Market

	U.S. Market* (Thousand b/d)	Import Share Of U.S. Market (Percent)	OPEC Share Of U.S. Market (Percent)
1960	9577	19.0	12.1
1961	9917	19.3	11.8
1962	10267	20.3	12.7
1963	10555	20.1	12.1
1964	10826	20.9	12.4
1965	11295	21.9	12.7
1966	11954	21.5	12.1
1967	12450	20.4	10.0
1968	13208	21.5	9.8
1969	13760	23.0	9.4
1970	14457	23.6	8.9
1971	14857	26.4	11.2
1972	15704	30.2	13.0
1973	16971	36.9	17.6
1974	16353	37.4	20.0
1975	15854	38.2	22.7
1976	16826	43.5	30.1
1977	17526	50.3	35.3
1978	18276	45.8	31.5
1979	18120	46.7	31.1
1980	16535	41.8	26.0
1981	15581	38.5	21.3
1982	14497	35.3	14.8
1983	14559	34.7	12.8
1984**	15068	36.3	13.6

*U.S. Production, plus Imports, Minus Exports, of crude oil plus natural gas liquid. Figures after 1977 include imports into Strategic Petroleum Reserve.
**First six months.

Sources: Authors' calculations, from data contained in *U.S. Petroleum Data Book,* 3:2 (Sept. 1983) and *Monthly Energy Review* (June 1984).

the margin of spare oil-producing capacity present in the United States, Canada, and Venezuela vanished during 1971 and 1972, leaving most of the world's quickly expansible oil production concentrated in the Middle East, and particularly in the Persian Gulf.

The result was a vast improvement in the bargaining position of OPEC nations vis-à-vis the international majors and vis-à-vis the oil-consuming countries. OPEC members were well on the way to achieving control of their crude reserves when the Egypt–Israeli War of October 1973 triggered the Arab embargo of Western nations and accelerated the transfer of control over crude-oil reserves from the international majors to the host countries. This also initiated the steady climb in the price of oil, which is shown in Table 1.

The course of the oil-price increase was influenced by the nature of the spot market. As the crude supplies of the majors were cut back by OPEC member nations (Table 7), the majors cut back supplies to independents. The independents, with survival at stake, turned to the relatively narrow spot market and bid prices up to ever higher levels. Where the spot market led, official OPEC prices soon followed.

The role of the international majors during this period is not without interest. They served as handmaidens to OPEC, administering the embargo in accordance with OPEC directives, even when this required conduct that was, arguably, in conflict with the national security interests of their home governments.[33] Turner[34] notes that the long-run effect of this compliance may have been permanent damage to the relationship between the international majors and their home governments. Except for this, the conduct of the international majors during this period probably had little influence on the structure of the industry in the long run. (The reader is referred elsewhere[35] for a comprehensive discussion.)

What changes were induced by the first oil-price revolution? There were some institutional changes: Western nations established the International Energy Agency, in November 1974. There were a number of changes in international financial institutions, designed to ease the recycling of "petrodollars" from oil-producing nations, through the Western banking system and back to oil-consuming countries (especially less-developed countries).

However, aside from the shift in control of production, there were remarkably few structural changes during the period following the first price increase. As shown in Table 8, the size of the U.S. market fell slightly in 1974 and 1975, but then rose to new heights by 1979. The share of imports in the U.S. market, and specifically imports from OPEC, peaked in 1977 but remained higher in 1979 than in 1973. The pattern of consumption and supply was much the same in other industrialized countries. As shown in Figure 1, OPEC's share of world crude-oil production fell only about 5 percent over the period 1973 to 1979. World production of crude oil grew throughout this period; but OPEC's production in 1979 was 61,000 barrels per day less than in 1973.[36] The underlying market conditions that greeted the fall of the Shah of Iran in January 1979 were essentially the same as those that had greeted the Arab-Israeli War of 1973: peak demand, concentration of supply in the Middle East, and absence of spare capacity in the West.

The impact of the course of events on the market was also similar. Supply was disrupted. Independent refiners had their supplies of crude cut off. They turned to the spot market, desperate for crude oil. The spot-market price shot up; the official price followed. This, too, can be seen in Table 1.

Table 8 and Figure 1 suggest that the response to the second oil-price shock was substantially different from the response to the first oil-price shock. The U.S. petroleum market, during the first six months of 1984, was smaller than it was in 1972. The share of the market provided by imports is less than in 1973; the same is true of the share provided by OPEC-member nations.

Similar patterns emerge in other industrialized nations. World production

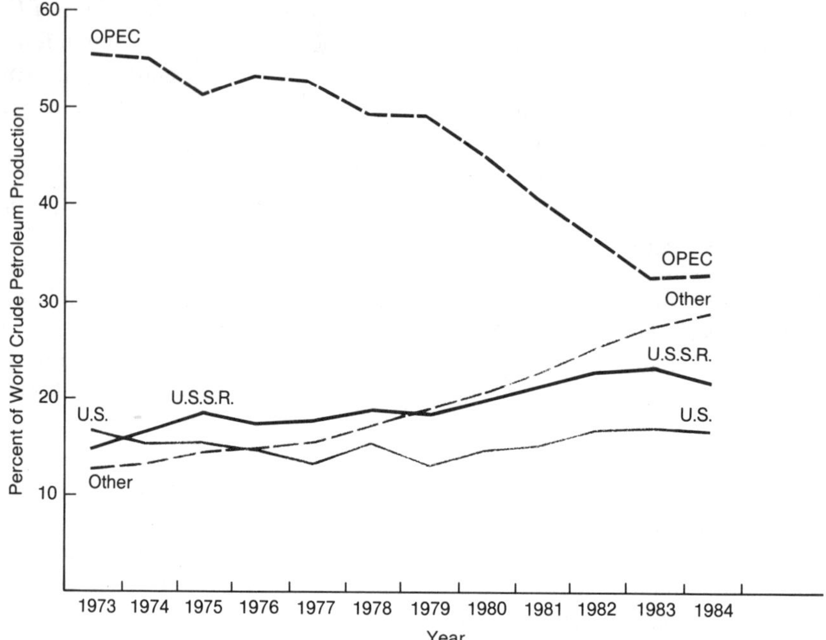

FIGURE 1. Percent of world crude petroleum production.

of crude oil has fallen from the 1979 peak to pre-1973 levels.[37] As shown in Figure 1, OPEC's share of world production has fallen precipitously since 1979.

The underlying cause for the substantial difference in responses to the two oil-price shocks is the long response time required to realize changes in the demand for and supply of energy resources. For example, at the time of the first oil-price shock, the electric power-generation industry was a major U.S. purchaser of petroleum, which was used as an intermediate product for generating electricity. It is, of course, possible to substitute other fuels for petroleum (i.e., coal). But the lead time for construction of a fossil-fuel electric power plant can be five years.[38] Many petroleum-fired power plants came on line in the period following the first price shock, simply because they had been planned during the period of cheap oil. Substantial reductions in petroleum consumption by the U.S. electric-power-generation sector did not begin until 1980—after the *second* oil-price shock. There is every reason to believe that the decline in demand for energy is a permanent change. The full effects of the installation of energy-saving equipment (and insulation in homes) has yet to be felt.[39]

There is a matching effect on the supply side of the market. Figure 1 divides the world production of petroleum into four sources. The United States, we have said, has been throughly explored; large future increases in output are unlikely. The Soviet Union will sell oil to the West so long as it has a need for hard currency, which is to say for the foreseeable future. There are, however, indications that future Soviet production will come only at higher cost per barrel (Siberia is no more hospitable to industrial activity than the North Slope of Alaska), and increases in oil supplies from this source ought not to be expected.[40]

But the share of other producing nations has increased rapidly throughout the post-1973 period. Mexico replaced Saudi Arabia as the leading U.S. source of imported oil in the second quarter of 1982.[41] British production of North Sea oil began in June 1975, but did not hit full stride until after the second oil-price shock.[42] At current world prices, oil reserves which are marginal, from a relative-cost point of view, are highly profitable to develop. Over time, more and more such reserves will be developed. As that happens, the share of OPEC in world production must continue to fall, if the OPEC official price for crude oil is to be maintained.

We can best illustrate the fundamental changes in supply-demand relationships by considering the third shock to world oil markets since 1973—the war between Iran and Iraq, begun in September 1980. An immediate consequence of the outbreak of war was a reduction in oil supplies from the two countries, which was equal to about 6 percent of world output. But production at that time exceeded the quantity demanded at official OPEC prices: the shortfall in production was made up largely by drawing upon inventories in consuming countries.[43] In the words of an industry analyst,[44] "The ultimate comment is that fact that Iran and Iraq hit tankers and prices go down, not up."

Refining

The refining segment of the petroleum industry transforms crude oil into a variety of final products, ranging from gasoline and liquified petroleum gases to residual fuel oil and petroleum coke. Refining involves not only the distillation of crude petroleum into refined products, but a number of upgrading processes by which lower-value refined products can be transformed into higher-value products (lead-free gasoline, for example).

In the U.S. market, concentration in refining is similar to concentration in production. In 1980, the eight largest U.S. firms operated 52 percent of the U.S. refining capacity.[45]

Engineering estimates place minimum-efficient scale in refining at around 200,000 barrels per day. A large number of refineries with less than this capacity have operated in the United States (Table 9), although the share of smaller refineries in total U.S. capacity is declining. Savings in transportation cost may enable small refineries to serve nearby markets in competition with larger, but more distant, refineries. As environmental regulations on the lead-content of gasoline tighten, the share of smaller refineries in total United States capacity will probably decline even more. Small refineries are not well-suited to the installation of the sort of upgrading equipment needed to produce lead-free gasoline.[46] In evaluating the minimum-efficient scale of

Table 9: Size Distribution of U.S. Refineries, 1980–1984

Crude Distillation Capacity (Barrels Per Day)	*1980*	*1981*	*1982*	*1983*	*1984*
Less Than 10,000	102	91	82	67	63
10,001–30,000	83	93	80	59	55
30,001–50,000	39	42	44	40	41
50,001–100,000	44	44	43	44	41
100,001–175,000	25	27	30	27	25
Over 175,000	26	27	22	22	21
Total	319	324	301	258	246

Note: Capacity as of January 1.

Source: Department of Energy, Energy Information Administration, *Petroleum Supply Annual 1983,* Vol. 1 (June 1984), p. 75.

refinery operation, it is worth noting that refineries in Europe are on average 70 percent larger than refineries in the United States.[47]

This suggests that entry into the refining industry is becoming more difficult. Exit has always been difficult; there is very little one can do with an oil refinery except refine oil. In contrast to capital assets in industries like airlines or trucking, investments in oil refining are largely *sunk costs,* costs which cannot be recovered once the entry decision is made.

Table 9 shows a decline in the number of U.S. plants of all sizes. This is typical of refining capacity throughout the industrialized world, and reflects worldwide overcapacity in refining (Table 10).

One obvious cause of refining overcapacity is the structural decline in the demand for oil products, a result of the 1973 and 1979 increases in the price of crude oil. A refining capacity adequate for world production of some 62,500 thousand barrels per day is bound to be excessive when world production is only 54,000 thousand barrels per day (first six months of 1984).

There is also excess capacity at the refining level. Oil-producing nations, through their national oil companies and often in joint ventures with the international majors, are integrating forward from production into refining. The motives for this integration are partly political and partly economic. A move forward into refining is a way of broadening the local industrial base while capitalizing on existing assets and skills. At the same time, a refinery associated with the national oil company of an oil-producing state has an almost insuperable advantage when compared with an independent refiner: the real cost of crude oil to the integrated refiner is the cost of crude production (regardless of the transfer price from the crude division to the refinery division); but the cost of crude oil to a nonintegrated refiner is the much higher market price for crude oil. Even though the international majors have some access to crude oil at better-than-market terms, they do not have access to crude oil at the cost of production. Ironically enough, this will place the international majors in a position very similar to that occupied by independent U. S. refiners before 1973. Integration forward into refining is a logical step

Table 10: Worldwide Refining Capacity (Thousand Barrels Per Day)

Year	*United States*	*Other Western Hemisphere*	*Middle East*	*Africa*	*Asia–Pacific*	*Europe*	*Sino–Soviet Bloc*	*World*
1973	13,671	8,176	2,758	825	7,916	16,827	9,110	59,282
1974	14,362	9,053	2,882	1,092	8,933	18,110	9,686	64,119
1975	14,961	9,536	3,281	1,083	9,397	18,718	10,575	67,551
1976	15,237	9,713	3,285	1,328	9,868	19,972	12,406	71,810
1977	16,398	10,015	3,348	1,444	10,048	20,859	13,068	75,181
1978	17,048	10,592	3,507	1,467	10,177	20,728	13,938	77,291
1979	17,441	10,273	3,546	1,668	10,285	20,329	14,748	78,289
1980	17,988	10,684	3,518	1,666	10,386	20,243	15,346	79,832
1981	18,621	10,717	3,730	1,698	10,555	20,206	16,037	81,562
1982	17,890	10,720	3,312	1,762	10,967	19,445	16,533	80,628
1983	16,800	9,874	3,685	1,882	10,902	17,125	16,873	77,141
Demand (1982)	15,296	6,480	1,720	1,635	8,495	12,455	12,820	58,901

Note: ''Demand'' is estimated demand for refined petroleum products.

Source: Basic Petroleum Data Book, Vol. 3, No. 3 (Sept. 1983), Section VII, Table 2a, Section VIII, Table 1.

for producing countries. It will pay them to do so, even if the refining capacity they build is excessive, from a world point of view.

Construction costs are somewhat higher in the Middle East and Africa than in the United States. This fact, and the transportaion cost involved in shipment from the Middle East to North America, suggests that products refined by oil-producing nations will have a more direct impact in Europe and the Far East than in the United States.[48] Nonetheless, as we will see, such forward integration provides a discreet way for oil producers to shade the price of oil below the official OPEC level, which can indirectly affect the U.S. petroleum market.

There is another development at the refining level that has consequences for crude-oil production. Before the 1973 crisis, refineries were generally designed to process relatively specific types of crude oil. U.S. refineries, for example, were largely designed to handle low-sulfur, "sweet" African crudes, which could be refined into motor gasoline at a relatively low cost.[49] When the supply of oil tightened, such refineries had few alternative sources of supply. Since that time, Western refineries in general, and especially those in the United States,[50] have adopted extensive upgrading equipment, which allows them to process heavier, high-sulfur ("sour") crudes in a cost-effective way. This too tends to put downward pressure on crude-oil prices.

Pipelines

Pipelines are the most important mode of oil transportation in the United States, where large volumes of oil must be moved overland.[51] In any oil field, a network of small-diameter "gathering lines" collect crude oil from individual wells in an oil field and transmit the field's output to a larger-diameter "trunk line" for shipment to a refinery. Pipelines will then move refined products to marketing centers.

Bulk shipment of oil in trunk lines provides a classroom example of decreasing cost per unit of output, based on physical economies of scale. Pipeline construction cost is roughly proportional to radius, and capacity is proportional to the square of the radius. If the pipeline radius is doubled, costs double, but capacity increases by a factor of four. Therefore, the construction and operating costs per unit of capacity decline, over virtually the entire range of technically feasible pipelines. Petroleum shipment over pipelines is for this reason a *natural monopoly*.

Major oil companies dominate pipeline transportation. As shown in Table 11, nearly 90 percent of crude-oil pipeline shipments reported to the Interstate Commerce Commission during 1976 originated in lines that were owned or controlled by the 16 major, vertically integrated, U.S. oil companies.[52]

At the same time, nearly 75 percent of refined-product shipments that originated in refineries (in contrast to those received from connecting carriers) went into pipelines owned by the major companies.

These figures give some idea of the degree of national concentration at

Table 11: Shipments Originated in Major Oil Company Pipelines, 1976

	Millions of Barrels	*Share Of Total (Percent)*
Crude-Oil Lines		
8 largest majors	1799.3	61.5
8 other majors	438.6	15.0
Joint ventures[a]	405.7	11.8
Total, 16 majors	2643.6	88.3
U.S. total	2925.7	100.0
Refined Product Lines		
8 largest majors	805.6	24.9
8 other majors	446.7	13.8
Joint ventures[a]	1144.0	35.4
Total, 16 majors	2396.6	74.2
U.S. total	3229.8	100.0

[a]Lines owned or controlled by groups of two or more major companies

Notes: Eight largest majors are Exxon, Chevron, Standard Oil (Indiana), Shell Oil (U.S.), Texaco, Gulf Oil, Mobil, and Atlantic Richfield. Eight other majors are Union Oil of California, Sun Oil, Standard Oil (Ohio), Phillips Petroleum, Conoco, Cities Service, and Getty Oil.

Source: U.S. Department of Commerce, ICC.

the pipeline level. But transportation is inherently local: oil moves from point *A* to point *B*:[53]

> Concentration in major crude oil transport corridors (i.e., specific pipeline markets) is extremely high. In the Texas–Cushing, Oklahoma, corridor for example, the four largest pipeline companies together account for 76% of total crude carried. Three pipeline companies control all crude oil shipments in the Gulf Coast–Upper Mid-Continent corridor . . . in 1979, the four-firm concentration ratio for pipeline shipments in the nation's major crude corridors averaged 91%.

This high degree of concentration is made worse by the common use of joint ventures in pipeline management. Institutionally, such joint ventures take two forms. A pipeline may be run as a separate corporation, with each parent firm owning stock in the subsidiary (and usually entitled to ship over the line in proportion to shares held). Alternatively, a pipeline may be run on an "undivided interest" basis, which means that it has no distinct corporate existence. Each owner operates the pipeline exclusively for periods of time, which are proportional to his capital contribution. Regardless of form, such joint ventures are not conducive to "arm's length" competition.

The implications of this concentration of pipeline ownership and control for the strategy of vertically integrated firms vis-à-vis independents are clear:[54]

> A pipeline rate set well above the competitive cost of transporting crude oil . . . imposes no burden on the majors who own the pipeline. For them, the high price is simply a transfer of funds from the refinery operation to the pipeline operation. To the nonintegrated refiner, however, an excessive pipeline charge is a real cost increase that he cannot recoup elsewhere and that places him at a competitive disadvantage vis-à-vis his integrated competitors.

Vertical integration from refining into transportation allows U.S. majors to apply a vertical price squeeze to refiners who are not integrated forward, much as vertical integration forward into refining allows crude-oil-producing countries to apply a price squeeze to refiners who are not integrated backward into production.

Marketing

Descriptions of the petroleum marketing structure generally focus on the 40 percent of the total product market that is represented by gasoline. This occurs because of both consumer familiarity with the local gas station and because of a shortage of data regarding most other products.[55] Nearly all jet fuel (95 percent, in the first half of 1980) is sold by refining companies directly to their customers, who are principally the Department of Defense and the commercial airlines. Most refiner sales of residual fuel oil (75 percent, in the first half of 1980) are made directly to large utility and industrial customers, with the remainder going to large terminal operators and dealers who are equipped to handle this product.

On the other hand, no more than one-third of distillate fuel-oil sales (33 percent for No. 2 and other distillate fuel, in the first half of 1980) is made directly to customers from refiner-owned facilities, whereas two-thirds goes through independent marketers. An even smaller percentage of gasoline sales (17 percent, in the first half of 1980) is made directly by refiners to bulk

Table 12: Combined Market Share of Eleven Largest Motor Gasoline Marketers: 1977–1983

Year	*Combined Share*
1977	58.80
1978	58.87
1979	59.12
1980	58.44
1981	55.57
1982	56.12
1983	56.44

Note: Combined share of Amoco, Shell, Exxon, Texaco, Mobil, Gulf, Chevron, Arco, Union, Phillips, and Sun.

Source: National Petroleum News Factbook Issue, 1984, p. 117.

buyers or through company-owned stations to retail buyers, compared with 83 percent sold through independent brand or nonbrand stations.[56]

We now turn to the market for retail gasoline, which, like all levels of the petroleum industry, has been severely affected by the structural changes that have occurred since 1973. In 1973, there were some 216,000 gasoline service stations in the United States; in 1984 there were only 130,000.[57] Branded gasolines have about 55 percent of the national market (Table 12), down from much higher levels (80 percent) in the mid-1960s. Still, gasoline distribution is inherently local in nature. Table 13 shows that the largest four firms in typical metropolitan markets generally have a substantial combined share of the market. This reflects a consolidation by major firms of the geographic scope of retail operations, since the 1970s. Table 13 also shows that the largest firms in local markets are the vertically integrated majors.[58]

Table 13: Market Shares by Metropolitan Area: Motor Gasoline

Area	*CR4*	*All Majors*
Boston, Mass. (1st Half 1983)	39	46
Camden, N.J. (1st Half 1984)	50	50
Philadelphia, Pa. (1st Half 1984)	53	61
Wilmington, Del. (1st Half 1984)	59	73
Washington, D.C. (1st Half 1984)	58	65
Miami, Fla. (2nd Half 1983)	44	50
Chicago, Ill. (2nd Half 1983)	56	56
Denver, Col. (2nd Half 1983)	31	31
New Orleans, La. (2nd Half 1983)	57	76
Houston, Tex. (1st Half 1984)	54	54

Note: Major brands represented are Mobil, Arco, Sun, Shell, Exxon, Texaco, Amoco, Gulf, Chevron, Citgo, Conoco, Phillips, Tenneco; "CR4," the "four-firm seller concentration ratio," is the combined market share of the four largest brands in the metropolitan area.

Source: National Petroleum News Factbook Issue, 1984, p. 119.

The reduction in the number of outlets seems to signal a change in the scale of operation:[59]

> The stations that are disappearing are generally on the smaller side—30,000 to 40,000 gal./month. In their places are being built the big superstations—the 100,000- to 200,000-gal./month-plus pumpers that are more economical to operate and frequently are on a seven-day, 24-hour basis.

This bodes ill for the independent retail outlet. To the extent that changes in refining eliminate independent refiners (see the foregoing discussion of the effects of the shift to more flexible refining techniques and stricter pollution controls), independent retailers will lose one of their usual sources of supply.[60]

Competition from the independent sector has been an important factor at the retail level. Because independent distributors are always vulnerable to cutoffs of supply, continued competition at the retail level depends in large measure on the survival of independents at the refining level. As we have already mentioned, the continuation of this competition is far from certain.

III. CONDUCT AND PERFORMANCE

The World Market

Most analyses of events in the crude-petroleum world market concur in the view that OPEC has acted as a cartel. Beyond that, there are important differences.

Some economists view the world oil industry as an industry with a single dominant firm: Saudi Arabia. Table 14 shows that Saudi Arabia owns one-quarter of the world's proven reserves, far more than any other single producer. This is enough to establish that Saudi Arabia will be a factor in the

Table 14: Estimated Proven Reserves of World Oil, 1983

Area	*Reserves (Million Barrels)*
United States	29,785
Canada	7,020
Latin America	78,482
Saudi Arabia	164,500
Other Middle East	204,786
Africa	57,822
Asia–Pacific	19,756
Western Europe	22,924
Communist Nations	85,115
World	670,189

Source: Basic Petroleum Data Book, Vol. 3, No. 3 (Sept. 1983), Section II.

world oil market for so long as oil is consumed. If Saudi Arabia were to act as a wealth-maximizing dominant firm, one would expect them to restrict output and to raise the price above the cost of production. Saudi Arabia would then gradually give up its share of the market to other producers, as the other producers expand output to take advantage of the opportunity for profit created by the price increase.

A variation on this analysis suggests that although no single OPEC member has sufficient control of resources to exercise control over price, OPEC, as a group, is able to act as a collusive price leader. The predicted performance is much the same as under the foregoing dominant-firm model. The OPEC share of the market should decline over time as independent producers respond to the incentive created by a price above the cost of production.

Figure 1 suggests that these models have a certain degree of explanatory power. The share of OPEC output in world crude-oil production fell very slowly from 1973 to 1979 (as noted before, this is a reflection of the long lead times in the discovery and development of oil reserves), and very rapidly since then. The dominant-firm/group model also predicts a gradual decline in price over time[61] as market share is given up to fringe producers. Table 1 suggests that this process has begun.

To the extent that OPEC is a cartel, it faces the problems that confront every cartel.[62] When price is raised above the cost of production, individual OPEC-member nations (not just independent producers) have an incentive to increase their own output. The essential fungibility of oil makes it difficult to keep track of the production of individual national oil companies. Vertical integration forward from production into refining provides a way of indirectly cutting the price of crude oil. For instance, instead of selling crude oil below the official OPEC price, an OPEC member can sell products refined from crude oil below the price of refined products which is possible for those independent refiners who purchase crude oil at the market price. Because independent refiners do not want to continue to lose money, they will turn away from purchases of OPEC crude at official prices and seek the best price they can get on the spot market. In the words of the president of Shell International Trading Company, "It is no good having security of supply if it drives you into bankruptcy . . . The narrowness of downstream margins . . . simply does not allow for term contracts with prices established by governments unrelated to market conditions."[63]

In an industry that produces a differentiated product, a successful cartel must confront the problem of controlling differentials between the prices of alternative varieties, as well as the general price level. Light, low-sulfur fuel has traditionally sold at a premium compared with heavier, higher-sulfur fuel, because it yields a more valuable mix of refined products to the refinery, at lower cost and with less depreciation. However, as refiners around the world have upgraded their facilities, demand for heavier oil has grown, at the expense of the demand for light oils. Negotiations within OPEC to readjust official price differentials will be difficult.[64] It is no surprise that the two OPEC members (Algeria and Nigeria) who refused to go along with OPEC's late-1984 attempt to revise price differentials are the OPEC members that produce primarily light oil, and which compete most directly with non-OPEC North Sea oil.[65]

Refinery upgrading when there is excess capacity has another indirect effect on the crude market, one which works down from the retail level:[66]

> With distillation processes losing money, few refiners with upgrading facilities have been able to resist the lure of marginal-cost processing—understandably, in view of the huge cost of cracking plant. Cracking the marginal barrel is attractive from the viewpoint of the individual refiner for as long as the additional revenue outweighs the resulting fall . . . in gasoline prices, but ultimately will lead to lower returns for all if gasoline moves significantly into surplus.

Downward pressure on price at the retail level will exert downward pressure, all the way down the vertical chain to the crude level.

These interactions between retail, refining, and production levels demonstrate an important point: it is not possible to understand structure-conduct-performance relationships in the petroleum industry without taking into account vertical relationships.

The problem of setting price differentials is one aspect of a broader cartel problem: OPEC-member nations have differing long-term interests. Although it is fair to say that the ability of OPEC members to absorb petrodollars has expanded far more rapidly than Western experts would have considered possible in 1973,[67] there remain substantial differences in the urgency with which OPEC members desire revenue from oil sales. Countries such as Saudi Arabia, Kuwait, and the United Arab Emirates have small populations, high GNPs per capita, and a political situation that is well served by industrialization at a slow pace. Their massive oil reserves insure that they will earn oil revenues for the foreseeable future. Other countries, such as Indonesia, Nigeria, and Algeria, have larger populations, smaller GNPs per capita, and fewer oil reserves. Their only prospect for development is through the maximization of oil revenues in the short run. Political pressures will sometimes reenforce this economic incentive: the current (at this writing) military government in Nigeria came into power as a result of mismanagement of oil revenues by the previous, civilian, government.[68,69] Such governments are subject to competitive pressures of a kind that do not affect the managements of major companies.

Analysis of OPEC as a cartel suggests that the exercise of market power in the crude-oil market will not be a long-run phenomenon. In fact, the events of late 1984 and early 1985 (OPEC meetings to lower quotas of individual countries, even though all individual countries are exceeding their current quotas, and refusal of the largest single producer to accept as large a cut in production as had been expected) appear to be the beginning of cartel collapse:[70]

> The classic breakdown sequence is (1) incremental sales at less than the collusive price, with incremental revenues for the cheaters; (2) matching of price cuts, with the bigger cartelists, reluctant to cut, losing market shares to the smaller; (3) accusations, confrontations; and then (4) renewed agreements among the cartelists, but with mutual suspicion and readiness to retaliate.

Even if this turns out to be correct, however, the short run in the oil industry can turn out to be an uncomfortably long time.

Cartel analyses may not capture all aspects of OPEC behavior. Evans[71] suggests that OPEC be viewed not as a cartel but as a union formed to break up the exercise of oligopsony power on the buying side of the crude-oil market by the international majors. The main predictions of the union model—increasing price of oil and increasing sales by OPEC—are indeed consistent with market behavior in the years immediately following the first oil-price shock (which is the period that Evans focuses on in his analyses). Later evidence (noted in Table 1 and Figure 1) seems more consistent with the notion of OPEC as a cartel. But Evans' work does emphasize an important point: OPEC does not face the problem of acting collusively in a market with many small purchasers. In the market in which OPEC sells its product there is an oligopoly on the supply side, an oligopsonistic core of international majors on the demand side, and a fringe of growing independents at various levels.

The interaction between these two sides of the market is complex. Although the interests of independent refiners are clearly opposed to the interests of oil producers (a higher price for crude oil, which is what producers seek, is a higher cost to the independent), the interests of vertically integrated majors are less clear-cut.

When OPEC raises the price of crude oil, it increases the value of oil in the ground everywhere, including oil in the ground that is owned or controlled by vertically integrated majors. To this extent, the majors have interests in common with the OPEC cartel. Table 15 demonstrates that the five U.S.-based international majors enjoyed sharp increases in net income after each of the price shocks of the 1970s. It also shows a decline in net income as the OPEC official price falls.

This explains the cooperation of the major oil companies with oil-producing countries during the 1973 embargo. Indeed, in times of excess supply at official prices, the majors, in a system of informal prorationing, have allocated output among OPEC members. Describing the slack market of early 1975, Schneider[72] says, "the oil companies allocated crude supplies by responding to adjustments that individual OPEC members made for the prices of their crudes." In terms of the success of OPEC as a cartel, "This ad hoc move and countermove by the exporting countries and the companies had one great advantage over formal prorationing: it gave the exporting countries great flexibility and thereby enabled adaptations to the needs of particular countries, which, probably, OPEC would never have agreed to as part of a

Table 15: Net Income, Five U.S. Majors

Year	*Net Income (Million Dollars).*
1970	3620
1971	3979
1972	3739
1973	6228
1974	7657
1975	5617
1976	6150
1977	6088
1978	6621
1979	11168
1980	14511
1981	13180
1982	8957
1983	10282

Note: Exxon, Gulf, Mobil, Chevron, Texaco.

Source: Petroleum Economist, various issues.

formal prorationing system.'' Similar behavior may well have taken place during the slack market of late 1984.[73]

But the majors also have an interest in replacing the supply of crude to which they lost access in the early 1970s (Table 7) by developing new crude reserves. Especially to the extent that this would result in excess capacity at the crude level, the interests of the majors do not coincide with the interests of oil-producing nations.

In the United States, there has been extensive exploratory and developmental activity (Table 16) in spite of declining prospects for large finds. The prospect of modest discoveries in parts of the world where property rights are respected is no doubt more alluring than the prospect of large finds in parts of the world where contracts are subject to continual revision.

The world majors have sought secure crude supplies elsewhere—among the assets of their competitors. Much of the net income that accrued to the majors as a result of the price increases of the 1970s (Table 15) was diverted away from exploration and development into a frenzy of mergers within the industry, some of which are indicated in Table 3.

Oil companies have also diversified their operations. Mobil Oil purchased Montgomery Ward (a department store chain) in 1976; Exxon purchased a producer of motors (Reliance Electric) in 1979. Neither acquisition has been a financial success.

Some oil companies have disappeared into firms based in other industries. DuPont acquired Conoco (in 1980, the fourteenth largest U.S. oil firm) in September 1981. U.S. Steel acquired Marathon Oil (in 1980, the ninth largest U.S. oil firm and the largest independent) in 1982.

Table 16: Exploratory and Development Wells Drilled, United States

Year	*Oil*	*Gas*	*Dry*	*Total*
1973	9,902	6,385	10,305	26,592
1974	12,784	7,240	11,674	31,698
1975	16,408	7,580	13,247	37,235
1976	17,059	9,085	13,621	39,765
1977	18,912	11,378	14,692	44,982
1978	17,775	13,064	16,218	47,057
1979	19,383	14,681	15,752	49,816
1980	27,026	15,730	18,089	60,845
1981	37,671	17,894	22,973	78,538
1982	40,301	18,952	26,542	85,795
1983	37,207	15,628	23,494	76,329

Source: Monthly Energy Review, June 1984, p. 68.

As is generally the case, there are various views about the implications of this merger movement for the development of new oil and gas reserves, a critical element of market performance. One argument suggests that the result will be more successful exploration:[74]

> all major oil companies have separate lists of exploration prospects, separate banks of proprietary geological data and separate holdings in land and offshore drilling leases. Thus, when these separate resources are thrown together in a merger . . . the company that emerges can select its drilling prospects from a richer list using the combined and presumably enhanced expertise that results.

Others suggest, however, that bigger might not necessarily be better. In the words of Walter J. Levy:[75]

> Instead of having 20 people deciding whether we should explore here or there, it will all become more centralized. That's dangerous because no one knows for sure where oil is. We want varied judgments applied in the search for oil. That's how great oil fields have been found.

Considering that the direct effect of a large merger is to commit liquid assets of the acquiring firm, which would otherwise be available for exploration and development, it seems doubtful that the net effect of the current merger movement will be to increase the development of new reserves. It would certainly reduce the odds of arm's-length competition.

Perhaps more important is the diversification of major U.S. oil companies into the production of alternative energy sources: coal, uranium, and solar technology. Especially in the long run, such fuels compete with oil. If energy users substitute away from oil and toward alternative energy sources, then the value of oil in the ground—the principal asset of the major oil companies—is reduced. By the nature of the investments they make in the development of alternative energy sources, major oil companies influence the value of their oil reserves.[76]

Coal competes with oil and gas as an input for electric power-generation. Oil and gas companies produced 225 million tons of coal in 1980, more than a quarter of the coal industry's output. Eight of the 16 firms listed at the foot of Table 11 had a combined coal production in 1980 of 142 million tons, one-sixth of total output.

Uranium also competes with oil and gas in fueling electric power plants. Most of the major oil companies and a few independents are involved in uranium ore exploration and development. Kerr-McGee, an integrated independent oil company, is the largest holder of uranium reserves; Gulf Oil is second, and Conoco (now part of DuPont) is fourth.[77] Four other major oil companies are among the ten leading holders of uranium reserves.

The development of other alternative energy sources (such as solar power, and the extraction of oil from shale) will involve massive investments in research and development. If such research and development programs are successful, the value of oil reserves will be reduced. In 1980, oil companies owned, in whole or in part, more than half of the firms involved in the development of solar power.[78] Here again, the relevant question seems to be: "Can we really expect these giant firms to undermine their stake in depletable oil and gas resources (the value and profitability of which are enhanced by their progressive scarcity) by investing the huge sums required to promote the rapid development of economically viable substitutes?"[79]

IV. GOVERNMENT POLICY

U.S. Antitrust Policy

Antitrust policy has been the traditional approach to the preservation of competition in the United States. In 1911, the Supreme Court upheld a finding that the Standard Oil Company, the giant of the industry, had violated the Sherman Antitrust Act in achieving monopoly power in the refining, marketing, and transportation of petroleum. A structural remedy was imposed when the parent holding company was ordered to divest itself of controlling stock interests in 33 subsidiaries. This first case was also the last successful big case involving the oil industry.

In 1940, another structural attack was launched, this time so broad in scope that it became known as the "Mother Hubbard Case."[80] Twenty-two major oil companies, 344 subsidiary and secondary companies, and the American Petroleum Institute were charged, in a Justice Department civil suit, with violating both the Sherman and Clayton acts. The case was postponed because of the onset of World War II, and thereafter languished until, in 1951, it was dismissed, without prosecution, at the Justice Department's request.

In the closing days of the Truman Administration, the government accused the five U.S.-based international majors (along with British Petroleum and Royal Dutch Shell) of seeking to restrain and monopolize crude oil and refined petroleum products, in violation of the Sherman Antitrust Act. Foreign policy considerations caused the proceedings to be dragged out; the last parts of the case were dropped by the Justice Department in 1968.[81]

A number of antitrust cases relating to the conduct of the oil industry have been brought successfully. Here, "successfully" means that the government won the cases and that legal principles were established, not that they were successful in making any real changes in industry conduct. Thus, the California Stations Case (1949)[82] established the principle that a refiner may not require his dealers to carry his brand of gasoline exclusively. Although this decision was reached in 1949, a major class-action suit involving the same questions was settled, the week before trial, in September 1984. In the settlement,[83] "The nation's major oil companies . . . agreed to allow more than 50,000 service station operators to sell any brand of gasoline they choose, even though their neon signs and franchise agreements identify them with a single brand." Whether any substantial change in behavior will occur remains to be seen.

Although recent federal antitrust actions involving the oil industry seem singularly ineffective, private (at least, non-federal) antitrust cases suggest that this is not because of an outbreak of arm's-length competition among major American oil companies. Documents released during the course of an antitrust suit initiated by the state of California and the city of Long Beach show that[84]

> Regular exchanges of price information and sensitive marketing data were a way of life in the oil business from the late 1950s into the early 1970s. . . . The federal court records . . . depict major oil companies working in concert to prop up retail prices of gasoline in several states at the expense of consumers and cut-rate independent marketers; the records also show the companies cooperating to preserve the bargain prices they were paying for supplies of heavy crude in California. While the defendant companies deny violating any laws, the documents portray an industry so clubby and inbred that executives considered it bad manners to compete too aggressively with each other on price.

Although one of the defendant companies has reached a settlement with the plaintiffs, the remaining companies continue their defense, and this private antitrust case could well remain in litigation for years.

Government Policy Responses to OPEC

The fact that the oil crisis of 1973 was repeated just six years later suggests that Western governments generally were unable to develop adequate energy policies. Schneider[85] identifies five weaknesses in governments' energy policies:

> the rise in U.S. oil imports; the lack of consuming-country cooperation; overemphasis on nuclear power, despite its inability to keep pace with the expectations of energy planners; the corresponding neglect of alternative energy sources; and inadequate effort to find and develop additional sources of oil and natural gas.

These criticisms apply to the United States and to other Western governments. In many cases, governments did take action on these matters, but very slowly. It was not until April 1979 that President Carter deregulated U.S. oil prices, allowing them to rise to the world level (giving maximum incentive to conserve energy and reduce oil imports).

The founding of the International Energy Agency (IEA), in November 1974, suggests a recognition of the importance of cooperation among consuming countries. However, France refused to join the IEA, apparently preferring bilateral government-to-government negotiations with oil-producing nations. Such government-to-government negotiations grew rapidly in the tight crude markets of 1978–1980, when security of supply was a matter of concern. Since that time, with crude oil in excess supply at official OPEC price levels, sales with government involvement have declined; supplies can be acquired on the spot market, and often at prices below the official OPEC levels.[86]

Optimal government policy, of course, may not lead to lower oil prices. It is *higher* prices which induce conservation, as well as the discovery of new reserves, and the development of new energy technologies. It is for these reasons that Hogan[87] has advocated a collective consuming-country import tariff on petroleum. Others[88] have suggested an increase in the federal tax on gasoline, which would have similar effects. These plans would maintain the sort of price incentives that will encourage the development of energy sources outside OPEC control, and divert revenue from OPEC treasuries to those of the consuming governments.

There is much to be said for these proposals. At the same time, the current merger movement among oil companies is evidence that resources directed toward the energy sector by the price system are not always applied to the development of new resources within the energy sector. In any event, Western countries lacked the political will to implement a very similar price support scheme which was proposed in the early years of OPEC[89], and there is little reason to think they would do so now.

V. CONCLUSION: PUBLIC POLICY FOR THE FUTURE

The decade of the 1970s saw momentous changes in the structure of the world's oil industry, changes that are still evolving in the mid-1980s. In 1970, the "Seven Sisters" (identified in Table 4) dominated the world oil market. They owned or controlled most of the world's reserves and production outside the Soviet bloc and North America. Their position abroad had been actively supported for nearly half a century by the governments of the United States, the United Kingdom, and the Netherlands. With a network of joint ventures, particularly in the Mid-east, the Seven Sisters were able to adjust the levels of foreign production to changes in demand, and in a way that maintained price stability over long periods of time.

The same seven companies, with a handful of other domestic majors, also dominated the oil industry in the United States. The Mandatory Oil Import Control program was still, in 1970, insulating the U.S. market from the rest of the world. Within this market, state regulatory agencies controlled production to preserve the level of posted prices, which were determined primarily by the major companies. Regardless of demand fluctuations, prices were virtually constant for years at a time.[90] In short, on a worldwide basis, production was responsive to price rather than vice versa. Here again, the major companies, in their capacities as the largest *buyers* of domestic crude oil, played a pivotal role.[91] Their monthly nominations to state prorationing agencies, regarding their intentions to purchase crude in the various states, was the most important factor in the agencies' decisions as to allowable production rates.

The stability of the system was shattered soon after 1970. Shortages of crude oil within the United States (as a result of the rising demand for products) led state regulatory agencies to raise allowable production to 100 percent of effective capacity in 1972, and to a suspension of import limitations at the federal level. Events abroad were even more dramatic. Nationalization sharply reduced the reserves of the international majors.[92] They have become net buyers of crude instead of net sellers. State-owned national oil companies have taken over the center of the stage in foreign oil sales. They are willing to sell to independent refiners directly or through brokers, and on government-to-government deals, as well as to major integrated companies. In short, something like a true intermediate crude-oil market is now emerging, beyond the control of the traditional international majors.

It is true that OPEC still exists. But with several years of slow growth worldwide, a vigorous international conservation effort, and the proliferation of non-OPEC crude sources, the cartel has been hard-pressed to preserve its status. Output has been slashed from 31 million barrels a day in 1980 to only 16 million in early 1985. The market price for Arabian light crude oil was cut from $34 to $29 a barrel in early 1983, with a reduction in quality differentials in January 1985, representing even greater cuts for the highest-quality OPEC oils. Despite these actions, there is evidence, in early 1985, that some members, pressed for foreign exchange, are cheating both on production quotas and price.

In 1979, the panic with which the rest of the world regarded OPEC (panic that enabled the OPEC nations to raise prices as far as they did) has abated, with the oil surpluses of the mid-1980s. It may have been succeeded by a smug complacency, which can be as dangerous as the earlier panic. In 1975, Congress established a Strategic Petroleum Reserve as insurance against future interruptions in foreign supplies. Targets, set in later detailed plans, were for 500 million barrels in storage by 1980 and a billion barrels by 1985. Early in 1985, President Reagan proposed a moratorium on further purchases of oil for storage beyond the following September, at which time the Reserve was projected to reach 489 million barrels—below even the original 1980 target.[93] Optimistic expectations for the development of alternative liquid fuel sources, such as shale oil, synthetic oils from coal, and methanol from agricultural products, among others, have evaporated as federal support for these initiatives has been scaled back or eliminated in the face of apparently ample crude-oil supplies from abroad. There is little chance that any of these alternatives will make a significant contribution before the year 2000. Conservation, including improvements in the efficiency with which fuels are used, has made a major contribution toward holding down demand for petroleum products. But the more we accomplish in this area, the more difficult it becomes to achieve further improvements at the margin.

In short, economic growth will raise the demand for petroleum products, albeit somewhat more slowly than the growth rate in GNP. There is virtually no chance at all that domestic production will grow; indeed, the odds are considerably greater that production of crude oil will decline, rather than be maintained at present levels. The reality, therefore, is that the United States will become increasingly dependent upon foreign oil through the rest of the century. One reasonable forecast is that 45 percent of our crude-oil demand by the year 2000 will be filled by imports, and most of the oil will come from OPEC suppliers.[94] If there is a worldwide recovery from the economic stagnation of the early 1980s, there can be a very rapid rise in the demand for OPEC oil. It is not likely that non-OPEC oil-producing countries will be able to expand output to any great extent.

In other words, it is premature to assume that OPEC has suffered any permanent loss in power, or that oil shortages are a thing of the past. Saudi Arabia's oil minister, Sheik Ahmed Zaki Yamani, has remarked, with respect to OPEC customers, "They think that they can live without a crisis because they think there is plenty of oil around. Well, I hope they will not be disappointed because if it happens it will be rather serious."[95] A new dimension has been added to the supply risks since 1970. Regardless of anything else one may say about the Seven Sisters, they were studiously apolitical in distributing concession oil; seldom, if ever, did they allow the foreign policies of their home countries to influence their deliveries to customers. The new national oil companies, on the other hand, may be used as instruments of foreign policy by their parent governments, particularly if world consumption rises significantly. Supply interruptions could come as a result of foreign policy disputes between OPEC suppliers and non-OPEC oil-consuming countries, or because of conflict among OPEC members themselves, such as the Iran-Iraq war. (Currently, there are growing tensions between moderate and radical Arab governments.)

The nation's experiences over the past 15 years should provide some sense of urgency to the problem of developing a coherent public policy in the energy field, one that can be effective over a long period of time. This is an inherently difficult problem, given (1) the political realities of changing Administrations; (2) changes in the composition of successive Congresses; and (3) the brevity of the public's memory, once an obvious crisis has passed.[96] Nevertheless, it is worth considering some of the areas that might be included in such a policy.

The output of the petroleum industry (including natural gas as well as oil products) will have to fill more than half of the country's primary energy needs—into the early twenty-first century, at least. Thus, securing the continuity of supply is of paramount importance. Proved reserves of U.S. crude oil dropped precipitously—by 30 percent—from 1970 to 1979. Increased exploratory and developmental drilling in response to higher prices, however, may have halted this slide, with proved reserves (crude oil alone) remaining somewhat above 27 million barrels through 1983. Clearly, it will pay to maintain a climate that will support a continued high level of drilling activity.

In addition to drilling activity to maintain proved reserves (insofar as possible), improvement in the recovery rate from known fields would also be helpful. It has been estimated that, across the United States (with considerable variation from field to field), less than one-third of the oil originally in place in known reservoirs will ever be produced.[97] A policy that would support improvements in the average recovery rate would pay huge dividends in terms of additions to usable reserves. The processes employed to enhance recovery (tertiary recovery) are costly, therefore a system of price guarantees for this oil would probably be necessary, to provide producers with some insurance if oil prices should decline sharply.

And, of course, along with this we would need a long-term program to support conservation, and to improve efficiency in the utilization of the oil that is available to us. The problem here is to ensure the same attention to conservation practices during periods when oil and gas are in ample supply as during times of acute crisis.

A second area of public policy would involve actions to minimize the risks of an import interruption. Certainly, every effort should be made to increase the number of suppliers to the U.S. market. Government-to-government arrangements (which many importing countries other than the United States have negotiated with exporting nations) might be considered, in order to assure the contracting suppliers of a reasonably stable position in this market.

Still, despite our best efforts, we shall continue to be heavily dependent upon the Mideastern OPEC nations, which have exhibited a certain amount of volatility as supply sources over the past 15 years. This is the reason for building up the Strategic Petroleum Reserve. The original billion-barrel target would have replaced an import cutoff of more than 2.5 million barrels a day for a full year. It may be that a lower target would be sufficient, but such a decision should be made on the basis of strategic probabilities, not on the basis of short-term political expediency.

Given the likelihood of declining domestic oil and gas production, and of increasing reliance on imports in coming decades, it is rational to intensify the effort to find alternatives to conventional oil and natural gas—shale oil, coal gasification, coal liquefaction, solar power, nuclear fusion, and others. This is not an area of activity that can be left completely to "market forces." We know now that the costs for commercial-scale plants are far higher, and development times far longer, than anyone would have anticipated even a decade ago. Private firms are unwilling to engage in this development without long-term commitments in the form of price guarantees, loan guarantees, and perhaps direct subsidization. This in turn requires a stable, long-term government policy, which recognizes that project lead times may range anywhere from five to ten years for commercial-scale coal gasification and perhaps fifty years for nuclear fusion. An important reason for moving ahead steadily, however, is that these alternatives promise ample supplies of energy for a future in which our reserves of oil and gas will have been completely exhausted.

A third important area of public policy should be activity to foster and protect competition in the oil industry and in potentially competitive alternative fuel industries. In a perverse way, OPEC nationalization has accomplished something that our antitrust agencies have never even attempted. The once powerful international majors now buy their imported crude oil at approximately the same prices as their nonintegrated competitors in the U.S. market. The advantage enjoyed by the former concession companies has now largely evaporated.[98] This development should be supported by antitrust law-enforcement, which would preserve an independent crude-oil-production sector that is willing to supply nonintegrated suppliers, and to ensure that access to pipeline transportation is available on a nondiscriminatory basis to anyone who wishes to tender crude oil or products for shipment.

It is important also to preserve competition between the oil and gas industry and any alternative energy industries that may develop. It may not be necessary to prohibit major oil companies from entering the coal or uranium industries, for example, but it is absolutely necessary to prevent the major oil companies from dominating an alternative-energy industry. Much can be accomplished with respect to coal and uranium by a government leasing policy for federal lands which avoids domination by major oil companies.

In short, it is important that government policy be carefully structured to provide an adequate supply of energy to the economy for the foreseeable future, and that this supply be available on competitive terms, both within the petroleum industry and between the petroleum industry and alternative-energy industries. For those of us who can hear the bell tolling, it seems clear that the nation cannot afford further delay in implementing the policies to achieve these goals.

NOTES

1. M. A. Adelman, *The World Petroleum Market* (Baltimore: Johns Hopkins, 1972), p. 148.

2. Ibid., p. 151.

3. L. Turner, *Oil Companies in the International System* (London: Allen & Unwin, 1983), p. 50.

4. Ibid., p. 51.

5. S. A. Schneider, *The Oil Price Revolution* (Baltimore: Johns Hopkins, 1983), p. 46.

6. Subcommittee on Antitrust and Monopoly, Committee on the Judiciary, United States Senate, *The Petroleum Industry: Part 4, The Cabinet Task Force on Oil Import Control* (Washington, D.C.: U.S. Government Printing Office, March 1970).

7. American Petroleum Institute, *Basic Petroleum Data Book,* Vol. 3, No. 3 (Sept. 1983), Sec. IV, Table 2.

8. U.S. Department of Energy, Energy Information Administration, *Monthly Energy Review* (June 1984), p. 117.

9. *The New York Times,* Oct. 23, 1984, p. 41.

10. F. E. Niering, "Alaska, Key to Future Oil Supply," *Petroleum Economist,* (July 1984), pp. 259–265.

11. W. Adams, "Vertical Divestiture of the Petroleum Majors: An Affirmative Case," *Vanderbilt Law Review,* **30:** 122–123 (Nov. 1977).

12. Ibid., pp. 124–125.

13. Schneider, op. cit, p. 196.

14. Turner, op. cit., p. 208.

15. An eighth firm, Compagnie Française des Pétroles, is sometimes included among the majors.

16. M. A. Adelman, *The World Petroleum Market* (Baltimore: Johns Hopkins, 1972), p. 81.

17. R. Vernon, "An Interpretation," *Daedalus,* **104:**7 (Fall 1975).

18. Turner op. cit., Chap. 3.

19. Schneider, op. cit. pp. 32–33.

20. J. M. Blair, "The Implementation of Oligopolistic Interdependence: International Oil, a Case Study," *Journal of Economic Issues,* **9:**299–302 (June 1975).

21. J. H. Mohnfeld, "Implications of Structural Change," *Petroleum Economist* (July 1982), pp. 269–272.

22. F. E. Niering, "Oil Industry's Changing Structure," *Petroleum Economist* (Jan. 1984), p. 14.

23. Mohnfeld, op. cit. p. 269.

24. Niering, op. cit., Jan. 1984, p. 9.

25. J. H. Mohnfeld, "Changing Patterns of Trade," *Petroleum Economist* (Aug. 1980), p. 330.

26. Vernon, op. cit., p. 4.

27. N. H. Jacoby, *Multinational Oil* (New York: Macmillan, 1974), pp. 294–301. For a general but illuminating discussion of the effect of heterogeneity of firm goals on industry performance, see H. H. Newman, "Strategic Groups and the Structure-Performance Relationship," *Review of Economics and Statistics,***60:**417–427 (Aug. 1978).

28. M. A. Adelman, "OPEC As a Cartel," in J. M. Griffin, and D. J. Teece, (eds.) *OPEC Behavior and World Oil Prices* (London; Boston: Allen & Unwin, 1982), pp. 37–63.

29. Schneider, op. cit., p. 67.

30. J. Darmstadter and H. H. Landsberg, "The Economic Background," *Daedalus,* **104:**17–18 (Fall 1975).

31. Schneider, op. cit., p. 118.

32. Jacoby, op. cit., p. 270.

33. Turner, op. cit., p. 136. Turner describes an incident in which Exxon used its influence to provide Saudi Arabia with information on the shipment of refined oil products to U.S. military bases.

34. Turner, ibid., p. 136.

35. Schneider, op. cit; Turner, op. cit.

36. U.S. Department of Energy, op. cit., p. 117.

37. U.S. Department of Energy, op. cit., p. 117.

38. R. L. Gordon, *U.S. Coal and the Electric Power Industry* (Washington, D.C.: Resources for the Future, Inc., 1975), p. 143.

39. F. E. Niering, "Long-Term Effects of Conservation," *Petroleum Economist* (August 1983), pp. 308–309.

40. I. Gorst, "Big Boost to Offshore Oil Search," *Petroleum Economist* (April 1984), pp. 145–147.

41. *Petroleum Economist* (Sept. 1982), p. 352.

42. Schneider, op. cit., p. 372, p. 484.

43. Ibid., p. 451.

44. *The New York Times,* Oct. 28, 1984, Sec. 3, p. 1.

45. W. S. Measday, "The Petroleum Industry," in W. Adams, (ed.) *The Structure of American Industry,* 6th ed. (New York: Macmillan, 1982), p. 46, fn. 16.

46. D. O. Croll, "Sustained Rise in First Half," *Petroleum Economist* (Sept. 1984), p. 322.

47. M. Quinlan, "Gathering Pace of Plant Closures," *Petroleum Economist* (Oct. 1983), p. 373.

48. *Petroleum Economist* (Nov. 1983), p. 411.

49. F. E. Niering, "Shifting Patterns of Demand," *Petroleum Economist* (Dec. 1982), p. 501.

50. M. Quinlan "Impact of OPEC Product Exports," *Petroleum Economist* (Sept. 1984), p. 319.

51. In some areas, pipelines face competition from other modes of transportation. See B. T. Allen, "Structure and Stability in Gasoline Markets," *Journal of Economic Issues,* **15:**(March 1981), fn. 8: ". . . states between the Rockies and Appalachians were open to uncontrollable transporation: river barge, independently owned pipelines, and (. . .) trucks."

52. Three pipelines are excluded. Trans-Mountain and Lakehead move Canadian oil to Northern Tier refineries, and Portland transports foreign oil in bond from Portland, Maine, to Montreal refiners.

53. W. Adams and J. W. Brock, "Deregulation or Divestiture: The Case of Petroleum Refineries," *Wake Forest Law Review,* **19:**711–712 (Oct. 1983).

54. Adams and Brock, op. cit., pp. 1134–1135.

55. Measday, op. cit., p. 49.

56. Ibid., p. 50.

57. National Petroleum News, *1984 Factbook Issue,* 1984, p. 103.

58. Allen, op. cit., shows that vertically integrated firms are able to stabilize their market shares.

59. National Petroleum News, op. cit., *1984 Factbook Issue,* 1984, p. 103.

60. *National Petroleum News* (June 1984), p. 33.

61. D. W., Gaskins, Jr., "Dynamic Limit Pricing," *Journal of Economic Theory,* **3**:306–322 (Sept. 1971); N. J. Ireland, "Concentration and the Growth of Market Demand," *Journal of Economic Theory,* **5**:303–305 (Oct. 1972).

62. F. M. Scherer, *Industrial Market Structure and Economic Performance,* 2nd ed. (Chicago: Rand McNally, 1980), Chap. 7.

63. Niering, op. cit. (Jan. 1984), p. 13.

64. D. Martin, "The Troubling Economics of Oil," *The New York Times,* Oct. 28, 1984, Sec. 3, p. 1.

65. Y. M. Ibrahim, "Algeria and Nigeria Refuse to Endorse Internal Pricing Pact Reached by OPEC," *The Wall Street Journal,* Dec. 31, 1984, p. 3.

66. Quinlan, op. cit. (Sept. 1984), p. 320.

67. *Business Week* (Nov. 12, 1984), pp. 36–37; *The Wall Street Journal,* July 31, 1984, p. 2.

68. M. Quinlan, "Oil Policy Under the Generals," *Petroleum Economist* (Feb. 1984), pp. 55–57.

69. For both sides in the debate between "target revenue" modelers and "wealth maximizer" modelers, see J. M. Griffin and D. J. Teece, (eds.) *OPEC Behavior and World Oil Prices* (London; Boston: Allen & Unwin, 1982).

70. M. A. Adelman, "Oil Import Quota Auctions," *Challenge* (Jan.–Feb. 1976), pp. 17–22.

71. R. D. Evans, "An Exercise in OPEC Taxonomy," *Antitrust Bulletin* (Fall 1983), pp. 653–667.

72. Schneider, op. cit., pp. 394–396.

73. E. Rothschild and S. Emerson, "Born Again Cartel," *The New Republic* (Nov. 5, 1984), pp. 20–25.

74. T. J. Lueck, "Benefits for New Oil Giants," *The New York Times,* March 21, 1984, p. 29.

75. *The New York Times,* March 11, 1984, Sec. 3, p. 12.

76. This argument depends on the depletable nature of natural resources, and supposes that there is a rising supply price of production. See D. W. Gaskins, Jr., "Comment," in Edward J. Mitchell (ed.), *Horizontal Divestiture in the Oil Industry* (Washington, D.C.: American Enterprise Institute for Public Policy Research, 1977), pp. 31–34.

77. Data as of 1976, reported by Professor Duane Chapman in U.S. Senate, Subcommittee on Antitrust, Monopoly, and Business Rights, Hearings on S. 1246, Part 1, p. 430, July 20, 1979.

78. "Big Oil's Push into Solar Power Irks Independents," *The Wall Street Journal,* Dec. 8, 1980, p. 31.

79. W. Adams, "Horizontal Divestiture in the Petroleum Industry: An Affirmative Case," in Edward J. Mitchell (ed.), *Horizontal Divestiture in the Oil Industry* (Washington, D.C.: American Enterprise Institute for Public Policy Research, 1977), p. 14.

80. *U.S. v. American Petroleum Institute et al.,* Civil No. 8524 (D.D.C., October 1940).

81. B. I. Kaufman, "Oil and Antitrust: The Oil Cartel Case and the Cold War," *Business History Review,***51**:37 (Spring 1977).

82. *Standard Oil of California and Standard Stations v. U.S.*, 337 U.S. 293 (1949).

83. *The New York Times,* Sept. 25, 1984, p. 1.

84. B. Jackson and A. Pasztor, "Court Records Show Big Oil Companies Exchanged Price Data," *The Wall Street Journal,* Dec. 17, 1984, p. 1. In June 1985, most of the charges in this case were dismissed; see K. A. Hughes, "Oil Price-Fixing Counts Dropped by U.S. Judge," *The Wall Street Journal,* June 21, 1985, p. 2. A related suit remains in the courts.

85. Schneider, op. cit., p. 324.

86. Mohnfeld, op. cit., (Aug. 1980; July 1982).

87. Hogan, W. W., "Policies for Oil Importers," in J. M. Griffin and D. J. Teece, eds. *OPEC Behavior and World Oil Prices* (London; Boston: Allen & Unwin, 1982), pp. 186–206.

88. "Bust OPEC Now," *The New Republic,* Feb. 11, 1985, pp. 5–6.

89. M. A. Adelman, "Oil Import Quota Auctions," *Challenge* (Jan–Feb. 1976), pp. 17–22.

90. There was practically no spot market. The appearance of spot bids either above or below posted prices for a field was a signal to agencies, such as the Texas Railroad Commission, to either increase or decrease production "allowables" for the following month.

91. Note that an integrated oil company does not simply move crude oil from its oil fields to its refineries. Rather, the company's production department sells oil to its refining department at the same posted prices that it charges to anyone else. An important reason for this is that the tax code (as it applied to integrated major companies for fifty years, through 1974) allowed producers to deduct depletion from income as a generous percentage of the selling price of crude oil.

92. Exxon, for example, reported the loss of some 38 billion barrels of proved reserves (1979 *Annual Report*, "Financial and Statistical Supplement," pp. 28–29), an amount that is substantially greater than total proved reserves of crude oil and natural gas liquids in the United States today.

93. In addition, private stocks of crude oil held by refineries have been reduced to record low levels, relative to refinery output, to minimize carrying charges on expensive inventories.

94. "World Energy Outlook Through 2000," Coordinating and Planning Department, Conoco, Inc., April 1984, p. 10.

95. *The Washington Post,* Jan. 31, 1985.

96. In 1974, consumers, jolted by high gasoline prices and service station waiting lines turned to smaller cars. As soon as the lines disappeared and the new price level was accepted as "normal," consumers shifted back to larger cars, and by 1978, motor-gasoline consumption set an all-time record. In 1979, consumers were again shocked by a doubling of gasoline prices and began to buy compact cars in record numbers. By 1985, with the new level of gasoline prices accepted, sales of large models were rising sharply once again.

97. See American Petroleum Institute, *Reserves of Crude Oil, Natural Gas Liquids, and Natural Gas in the United States and Canada as of December 31, 1979,* p. 10.

98. In this connection, see the fascinating article by John C. Sawhill, former U.S. energy czar, "Break Up the Oil Companies!" *The Wall Street Journal,* Feb. 21, 1985, p. 30.

SUGGESTED READING

BOOKS AND ARTICLES

Adams, Walter. "Vertical Divestiture of the Petroleum Majors: An Affirmative Case." *Vanderbilt Law Review,* Vol. 30, No. 6 (Nov. 1977).

Adams, William J. "Selective Selling in the Petroleum Industry," *Zeitschrift für die Gesamte Staatswissenschaft,* Vol. 136, No. 3 (Sept. 1980).

Adelman, M. A. *The World Petroleum Market*. Baltimore: The Johns Hopkins University Press, 1972.

Allvine, Fred C., and James M. Patterson. *Competition, Ltd.: The Marketing of Gasoline*. Bloomington, Ind.: Indiana University Press, 1972.

Blair, John M. *The Control of Oil*. New York: Pantheon Books, 1976.

DeChazeau, Melvin G., and Alfred E. Kahn. *Integration and Competition in the Petroleum Industry*. New Haven, Conn.: Yale University Press, 1959.

Engler, Robert. *The Brotherhood of Oil*. Chicago: University of Chicago Press, 1979.

Frankel, Paul H. *The Essentials of Petroleum,* New ed. London: Frank Cass and Co., Ltd., 1969.

Schneider, Steven A. *The Oil Price Revolution*. Baltimore: The Johns Hopkins University Press, 1983.

Turner, Louis. *Oil Companies in the International System,* 3rd ed. London: George Allen & Unwin, Ltd., 1983.

GOVERNMENT PUBLICATIONS

Federal Trade Commission, Staff Report. *Concentration Levels and Trends in the Energy Sector of the U.S. Economy*. Washington: D.C.: U.S. Government Printing Office, 1974.

——— *In the Matter of Exxon Corporation, et al.* Docket 8934, "Complaint Counsel's First Statement of Issues, Factual Contentions and Proof," October 31, 1980.

U.S. Comptroller General, Report to the Congress. *Petroleum Pipeline Rates and Competition—Issues Long Neglected by Federal Regulators and in Need of Attention*. Washington, D.C.: General Accounting Office, July 13, 1979.

U.S. Congress, Senate Committee on Interior and Insular Affairs. *Measurement of Corporate Profits,* 93rd Cong., 2nd sess., 1974.

U.S. Congress, Senate Committee on Foreign Relations, Subcommittee on Multinational Corporations. *Multinational Oil Companies and U.S. Foreign Policy,* 93rd Cong, 2nd sess. Report, 1975.

U.S. Congress, Senate Committee on Energy and Natural Resources. Staff Report. *The Geopolitics of Oil,* 96th Cong, 2nd sess., November 1980.

3

The Steel Industry

Walter Adams and Hans Mueller

I. INTRODUCTION

In 1950, America's steel industry was the most powerful in the world. Accounting for nearly one half of global steel output, it produced more steel than all of Europe combined, nearly three times as much as the Communist bloc, and almost twenty times as much as Japan. Moreover, the large American steel firms enjoyed an undisputed position of world leadership in technology and in plant-scale, a position that had gone virtually unchallenged by foreign competitors during the preceding five decades.

Today the situation is radically different. The United States accounts for less than 12 percent of the world's steel output and is now the fourth largest steel producer—behind the Soviet Union, the European Community (EC), and Japan (see Table 1). More significantly, the trade position of the United States has changed from a leading exporter to the world's largest importer of steel, and our once dominant integrated steel giants are constantly clamoring for government protection from foreign competition.

A brief look at the industry's history throws some light on these dramatic changes.

History

Prior to the formation of the U.S. Steel Corporation in 1901, the industry was the scene of active and, at times, destructive competition. Competition for market shares was vigorous, often taking the form of aggressive price cutting. Companies that failed to adopt the best technology or anticipate market shifts fell by the wayside. Unlike the British steel industry, which was becoming conservative and defensive, innovative American managers and an industrious work force were creating a dynamic industry that was highly cost-competitive in international markets.

In this early period, various gentlemen's agreements and pools were organized in an effort to control the production of steel rails, billets, wire, nails, and other products, but the outstanding characteristic of these agree-

Table 1: The Changing International Position of the U.S. Steel Industry

	United States			European Community			Japan			World
	Output[a]	*Percent of World Total*	*Net*[b] *Exp.*	*Output*[a]	*Percent of World Total*	*Net*[b] *Exp.*	*Output*[a]	*Percent of World Total*	*Net*[b] *Exp.*	*Output*[a]
1870	1.8	16.2%	−.7	7.5	69.2%	1.2	—	—	—	10.8
1900	14.6	34.2	.9	20.3	49.4	5.0	—	—	—	41.1
1920	49.2	59.8	2.2	27.8	33.7	8.0	.9	1.1%	—	82.3
1950	96.8	48.4	1.6	53.2	25.6	9.0	5.3	2.6	.4	200.0
1960	99.3	27.6	−.2	107.8	29.6	9.7	24.4	6.7	2.5	360.3
1970	131.5	21.6	−6.3	151.6	23.8	7.4	102.9	16.1	22.3	637.8
1980	111.8	14.1	−12.4	140.1	17.8	15.0	122.8	15.5	34.7	792.2
1984	91.5	11.7	−22.9	132.5	16.9	11.3	116.4	14.9	31.8	783.0

[a]In million net (or short) tons of raw steel.
[b]Exports minus imports, in million net tons of steel products. (One product ton is roughly equivalent to 1.25 tons of raw steel.)

Sources: American Iron and Steel Institute, *Annual Statistical Report,* various years; European Community, Eurostat, *Iron and Steel,* Yearbook, various years; *Tekko Nenkan,* various years.

ments was the "frequency with which they collapsed."[1] Their weakness was that inherent in any pool or gentlemen's agreement: "60 per cent of the agreers are gentlemen, 30 per cent just act like gentlemen, and 10 per cent neither are nor act like gentlemen."

With the birth of U.S. Steel, these loosely knit agreements were superseded by a more stable form of organization. In the "combination of combinations," U.S. Steel merged more than 65 percent of the nation's steel-producing capacity into a single entity. Under the leadership of Judge Gary, its first president, it inaugurated the famous "Gary Dinners," which were a transparent form of collusion among competitors.[2] Cooperation replaced competition, and U.S. Steel held a price umbrella over the industry, which was high enough to accommodate its much smaller, even marginal rivals.[3]

This policy of "friendly competition," of course, was not without cost. It permitted the Corporation's rivals to expand and to gain an increasing share of the market. But the corporation seemed content with this trade-off between high and stable prices in exchange for loss of market share. Over time, this policy led to the transformation of an asymmetrical oligopoly, dominated by a giant firm, into an industry with a more balanced oligopolistic structure. Friendly competition had one other fundamental consequence. Eventually, when the oligopoly felt entrenched enough to pursue a policy of constant price escalation—in good times and bad, in periods of declining as well as rising costs—it attracted newcomers.

The challenge to the steel oligopoly, starting in the 1960s, came from two principal sources: foreign competition and the appearance of the minimills. Against the former, the industry's primary defense was to plead for government protection in the form of a variety of trade restraints. Against the latter, the primary response was the gradual abandonment of industry segments in which the minimills had established themselves as the low-cost producers.

By the 1980s, the steel oligopoly seemed moribund—a collection of helpless giants begging for government relief from self-inflicted injury.

II. MARKET STRUCTURE

In economics textbooks, the steel market of the United States is often described as having a purely oligopolistic structure. This means that a few large firms sell a homogeneous product in a market surrounded by high barriers to the entry of new competitors.

The simplistic notion of a pure oligopoly ignores several important characteristics of the steel market. First, there are about 10,000 distinct iron and steel products: the most crude is pig iron; other products include semi-finished steel (billets, blooms, and slabs); rolled products (bars, rods, structurals, hot- and cold-rolled sheets, coated sheets, and plates); and steel products with a very high unit value—forgings and castings.

Second, even very narrowly defined products are often further differentiated according to metallurgy, physical properties, and surface conditions. Thus, it matters to some buyers whether otherwise identical steel products are made from scrap or iron ore, are processed via the ingot or the continuous-casting route, are rolled on recent-vintage or older rolling mills, or whether they are annealed by the batch or the continuous method. In addition, differences in quality of the more sophisticated products (such as cold-rolled and coated sheets) have become important enough to make steel buyers quite selective concerning the reputation of their suppliers, both domestic and foreign.[4]

Third, the term *market* connotes the interaction of buyers and sellers, demand and supply, in a geographical trading area. In a pure oligopoly, theory tells us, a slight difference in price can cause a sale to be switched from one producer to another. But in the vast expanse of the North American continent, steel—a relatively heavy good—is also differentiated by the location where it is offered for sale. Because of high freight costs, the supply potential in one part of the country may have little relevance to demand conditions in another, except perhaps in wartime or other emergencies, when costs do not matter. A steel user in San Francisco is economically (that is, in terms of freight costs) much closer to Japan than to Pittsburgh.[5] No matter how identical in other respects, tonnages of steel in those two cities are not homogeneous. The geographical area of the United States is, therefore, not necessarily synonymous with the "home market" of the American steel industry.

Changes in Demand. If regional markets are lumped together, the American steel market is by far the largest in the Free World. It even exceeds that of the European Community (EC), which includes the markets of ten member countries. In the late 1920s, and again in the early 1950s, the United States produced almost one-half of all the steel consumed in the entire world. In the post-World War II period, "apparent" consumption[6] reached an all-time peak of 123 million short tons (mt) in 1973 but declined to 76 mt in 1982. Although consumption has revived somewhat since then (reaching 93 mt in 1983 and 98 mt in 1984), it is not expected to move significantly beyond the 100 mt mark in the foreseeable future.

Significantly, relatively weak steel demand after 1974 has been a phenomenon common to other industrialized areas of the Western world as well. It appears that after most of the investment was made to furnish people with homes, automobiles, and the supporting infrastructure, less steel was needed to maintain economic growth. Other reasons for weak steel demand include the development of lighter, stronger steels, and, in the transportation sector, more emphasis on lighter, more energy-efficient vehicles.[7] Population growth will have a positive effect on steel demand in future years, but this may be more than offset by a decline in exports of steel and, especially, exports of steel-containing goods to Third World countries, as these countries become more self-sufficient in manufactured products.[8]

Moreover, given the recent proliferation of automated machinery in manufacturing industries, steel users are likely to require finer-gauge tolerances, greater uniformity, and better surface quality of steel products, in order to prevent jamming of sophisticated, high-speed equipment. This means that, in many applications, steel demand will shift toward a more refined, higher-value product mix—in other words, that steel will cease to be a "tonnage" product.

Much has been written about the substitution of other materials—such as aluminum, plastics, cement, and lumber—for steel.[9] However, except for one specific niche of the market, beverage containers, there has been no conclusive evidence that substitution occurred in one direction only, i.e., against steel. Casual observation indicates that many structures that years ago were built with bricks, cement blocks, and lumber (small factories, warehouses, and school gyms) are now usually made from steel.

Regional Market Shifts. Historically, steel demand in the United States has moved toward the West and the South. This tendency was reinforced during World War II by the construction of shipyards and manufacturing plants in those regions.

The trend continued in the postwar period. According to a study by the Commerce Department, in the 1960s and 1970s, steel demand increased relatively faster in the "newer" regional markets of the West, Southwest, and the South than in the traditional markets of the Great Lakes area and the Northeast.[10]

There has also been a shift in regional markets relative to the location of steel suppliers. Transoceanic freight costs have increased less over the long term than overland freight costs, and (as the result of the Jones Act) less than shipping rates from one American port to another. As a result, many American steel users in the Pacific, Gulf, and South Atlantic regions can buy certain flat-rolled products from foreign suppliers at a lower (delivered) cost than from American producers located in the steel-producing centers in the Northeastern section of the country.

The Changing Supply Side of the U.S. Steel Market

The steel market in the United States is supplied by four groups of producers—integrated companies, minimills, specialty steel firms, and foreign steel mills. Integrated companies produce most of their steel from iron ore smelted in blast furnaces.[11] For technological reasons, most integrated plants have a capacity in excess of three million tons of raw steel a year.[12] The staple products of these mills are plates, hot- and cold-rolled sheets, coated (e.g., galvanized) sheets, and heavy structurals (e.g., large I-beams). Some also produce pipes and tubes, rails, pilings, and a variety of other products.

Minimills are relatively small steelmaking operations, which produce steel from scrap and roll it into nonflat (or "long") products, such as reinforcing bars, wire rods, and light structural products.[13] The chief economic advantage of these mills is that they can be operated efficiently on a small scale. With capacities ranging from 150,000 to 800,000 tons a year, their size is only a fraction of that of most integrated plants. Because investment requirements per ton of capacity are also much lower, total construction costs for minimills producing simple bars and light shapes may be less than $50 million (compared with more than $5 *billion* for a new, integrated plant).[14]

The specialty-steel segment of the industry produces primarily alloy, stainless, and tool steels. Most of the 35 small firms in this area rely on scrap, rather than iron ore, as their ferrous input. However, several of the integrated companies also produce specialty steels.

As for imports, it is noteworthy that (1) virtually every steel product made in the United States must compete with imports; (2) the bulk of imports consists of steels produced by integrated mills; and (3) nearly every nation producing more than insignificant amounts of steel also exports some quantities to the United States. The largest among them (in 1984) were Japan, the European Community, Canada, South Korea, Brazil, and Spain.[15]

Changes in Structure and Organization

The supply side of the steel market has experienced significant structural changes in the last thirty years. In the mid-1950s, approximately 92 percent of the market was supplied by the large, integrated producers. Minimills accounted for less than 2 percent, a motley of specialty firms for about 4 percent, and imports for just over 1 percent. By 1984, the share of the large mills had shrunk to 53 percent, minimills had moved up to 16 percent, specialty mills to 5 percent, and imports to 26 percent.[16] In the following section, we shall focus primarily on the integrated producers and the extent to which they have become subject to effective competition from minimills and imports.

Waning Market Power of the Integrated Steel Mills. When it was created in 1901, the U.S. Steel Corporation accounted for 65 percent of all the steel produced in this country; by 1938, its share had dropped to approximately one half of that (see Table 2) and, by 1984, its share of raw steel output had dwindled to 16.6 percent (13.4 percent of total steel consumption in this country).[17]

Several factors contributed to the relative decline of the U.S. Steel Corporation. One was a shift of the market away from the heavy products in which the company was strong (such as rails, plates, and structural shapes) to sheet and strip. What made this shift in demand even more painful for the Corporation was the geographic source of the new demand—especially that of the growing auto industry—which was often located at a considerable distance from the Corporation's main plants.

Another factor was the impact of changing technology, in which U.S. Steel lagged significantly behind its integrated rivals. For example, in 1926, Armco bought the patents for the continuous-rolling mill process, which was the major American advance in steel technology during the period between

Table 2: Concentration of Raw Steel Production Shares

	U.S. Steel	*4 Largest Firms*	*8 Largest Firms*
1904	60.8	74.2	83.5
1920	45.8	58.5[a]	65.7[a]
1938	33.1	62.0	79.0
1947	33.7	63.5	79.9[b]
1961	25.7	54.6	75.5[b]
1976	22.1	52.8	73.4
1984	16.6	46.6	65.0

[a]Shares of firms 2 to 8 computed from capacity data.
[b]National's share was estimated.

Sources: Federal Trade Commission, *The United States Steel Industry and Its International Rivals* (Washington, D.C., 1977), p. 157; and International Iron and Steel Institute, *World Steel in Figures* (1985), p. 2.

the two World Wars. Republic Steel became the leader in the growing alloy-steel field.

A third factor was a number of horizontal mergers involving other integrated firms. Starting in the 1920s, the "independents" in the industry took part in an aggressive consolidation movement. In 1922, Bethlehem Steel acquired all the properties of the large Lackawanna Steel Company near Buffalo, New York; it erected extensive facilities at Sparrows Point, Maryland; it acquired the large Cambria Steel Company (1923); and, in 1930, it bought the assets of the Pacific Coast Steel Company and the Southern California Iron and Steel Company. In 1930, another powerful independent arose when a merger combined the Republic Iron and Steel Company, the Central Alloy Steel Corporation, the Corner Steel Company, and the Bourne Fuller Company. A third important merger that occurred during this period resulted in the formation of the National Steel Corporation (1929), which united steel plants in the West Virginia and Detroit areas and the blast furnace properties of the M. A. Hanna Company of Cleveland.[18]

In the period after World War II, the merger trend was temporarily stalled by government antitrust objections to Bethlehem's acquisition of Youngstown, a merger that would have combined the second and sixth largest steel producers. In the late 1960s, however, when the merger movement resumed momentum, several integrated firms began to buttress their positions through horizontal consolidations. The following combinations took place:

1. 1968—Wheeling Steel (10th largest) and Pittsburgh Steel (16th largest).
2. 1971—National Steel (4th largest) and Granite City Steel (13th largest).
3. 1978—Jones & Laughlin (7th largest) and Youngstown (8th largest).
4. 1983—Jones & Laughlin (3rd largest) and Republic (4th largest).[19]

The two mergers involving Jones & Laughlin (J & L) also had conglomerate aspects. In 1968, both J & L and Youngstown were taken over by conglomerates, the former by Ling-Temco-Vaught (LTV), which had aerospace, meatpacking, and sporting-goods operations, and the latter by Lykes, which was primarily active in ocean shipping. Neither LTV nor Lykes infused badly needed capital into their steel properties. Ten years later, both companies were in a precarious financial condition and the Attorney General felt compelled to approve the merger of the two conglomerates and their sizable steel subsidiaries by relying on the "failing company" exception under the antimerger law.

The 1983 merger of the enlarged LTV company with Republic Steel was at first rejected because, in the view of the Justice Department, the new company would obtain unacceptably high market shares in two important product lines, sheet-steel products and specialty steel.[20] Eventually, the merger was approved on the condition that Republic's alloy-steel plant in Massillon, Ohio, and its carbon-steel plant near Birmingham, Alabama, would be sold within a fixed time period. This was the first major case in which international competition was an important consideration in the government's enforcement of the antimerger law.

Upon consummation of the merger, the new LTV became the second largest steel producer in the United States. With a capacity of about 22 mt, it follows U.S. Steel (26 mt), and leads Bethlehem (17 mt). Table 3 shows the rank of other major steel producers.

Thus, the integrated segment of the American steel industry has greatly changed from its previously very lopsided oligopolistic structure. The two outstanding modifications are, first, that the towering dominance of the U.S. Steel Corporation has dwindled considerably. U.S. Steel is now only one of three large steel companies. Because both U.S. Steel and LTV are candidates for more trimming of obsolete capacity, the size differential between the leading steel producers is likely to shrink further. Second, the market share of the entire integrated segment has declined as more and more sales have been lost to aggressively competitive minimills and foreign producers.

Other Structural Changes in the Integrated Segment. There have been a number of other changes that affected the structure of the integrated steel companies. One is a diversification movement that began in the 1960s and led to these acquisitions: a chemical firm (by U.S. Steel); a large nonmetallic composite firm (by Armco); a builder of prefabricated homes (by Inland); an aluminum firm (by National); and a producer of plastic products (by Bethlehem). More recent acquisitions included a California Savings & Loan Association (by National); an insurance holding company (by Armco); and—the largest of all—Marathon Oil Company (by U.S. Steel). Its ownership of Marathon Oil meant that U.S. Steel now derives more revenues from petroleum than from steel.[21] Several of these acquisitions have been unprofitable, if not disastrous (e.g., Armco's venture into the reinsurance business) and a few have subsequently been spun off.

Recently, the environment of weak demand, rising costs, and increas-

Table 3: The Largest Steel Firms in the United States

	Raw Steel Capacity, 1984		*Shipments, 1984*			
	Millions of Tons	*Percent of Total*	*Millions of Tons of Steel Products*	*Percent of Total*	*Profits (Losses) Mill. $ 1984*	*Net Profit as Percent of Equity Average of 1980–1984*
1. U.S. Steel	26.0	18.3	12.1	16.6	142	1.1
2. LTV	22.2	15.6	8.1	11.1	(217)	14.4
3. Bethlehem	16.8	11.8	8.9	12.2	(95)	deficit
4. Inland	9.3	6.5	5.0	6.8	(41)	deficit
TOP 4	74.3	52.3	34.1	46.7		
5. Armco	8.1	5.7	4.6	6.3	(26)	deficit
6. National Intercorp	5.8	4.1	4.5	6.2	(21)	deficit
7. Wheeling-Pittsburgh	4.4	3.1	2.2	3.0	(52)	deficit
8. Weirton	4.0	2.8	2.1	2.9	60	na
TOP 8	96.6	68.9	47.5	65.1	Percent of Equity	
Steel Industry Total	142.0	100.0	73.0	100.0	Median 1.5	Median 7.9
All U.S. Industries					Median 13.4	Median 15.1

Sources: Capacities are authors' estimates; Shipment figures are from company reports; Profit figures are from *Forbes* (Jan. 14, 1985), p. 171.

ingly intensive competition from minimills and foreign producers has generated a so-called *restructuring* of several integrated companies. This restructuring, which began in 1977, involved the closure of facilities that should have been shut down during the 1950s, or, at the latest, in the 1960s. Some of the plants that were partially or completely closed were originally built in the last century. Although their technology and scale had been updated to some extent, many of their structural features—such as location and the flow of materials—reflected the best-practice standards of a bygone era.

Many of these closures occurred in the eastern Ohio–western Pennsylvania area, between Youngstown, Pittsburgh, and Johnstown. Others affected primarily northern New York (Buffalo and Lackawanna) and South Chicago.[22] The suddenness of these closures wrought a great deal of hardship on communities and workers in these regions. Much of this harm could have been avoided had these plants been phased out during the growth stage of the industry, when workers would have had little difficulty finding employment in an expanding steel industry, or in other manufacturing industries. One company, National Steel, attempted to shed all of its steel operations. It managed to sell its largest steelworks at Weirton, West Virginia, to the employees of that plant. The company decided that the future earnings potential did not justify large investments to replace worn equipment. The independent Weirton Plant has since become marginally profitable, largely as a result of significant voluntary wage cuts and tightened work rules.[23] But there is some question, whether the workers will eventually be able to raise hundreds of millions of dollars to finance the needed replacement of major facilities.

Finally, there are two recent developments that will have a substantial, but as yet unpredictable, impact on the configuration of the integrated steel industry. First, major Japanese steel producers have acquired equity shares in several integrated American steel firms. Second, joint ventures have been organized to build and operate new steel installations.

All of the Japanese participations were negotiated in 1984. First, Nisshin, Japan's sixth largest steel producer, bought a 10 percent interest in Wheeling-Pittsburgh, one of the smaller integrated firms. Then Nippon Kokan (NKK), the second largest Japanese steel company, bought a 50 percent share in National Steel (after a proposal by U.S. Steel to acquire National had been withdrawn because of opposition by the Justice Department). And Kawasaki, the fourth largest Japanese producer, acquired a 25 percent share of a new company, California Steel Industries, which was formed to reactivate the rolling facilities of the former Kaiser integrated steelworks near Los Angeles.[24]

The joint ventures were formed (also in 1984) for the purpose of adding continuous electro-galvanizing capacity in order to produce rust-resistant coated steel sheets for the automotive industry. They took the form of partnerships between Bethlehem and Inland, U.S. Steel and Rouge (the Ford

Motor Company steel plant), and LTV and Sumitomo (the third largest Japanese steel producer).

Both of these developments—financial and managerial participation by Japanese firms, as well as joint ventures—can be expected to lead to new alliances and, probably, to greater cohesiveness in the conduct of the integrated firms. However, it remains to be seen whether they will add to or detract from the monolithic structure of the integrated segment, and what their lasting effect will be on the industry's competitive behavior.

The Rise of American Minimills. New entry into the domestic steel industry during the postwar period has been exclusively in the minimill category—primarily because of the relatively modest amounts of capital required for operating a minimill.[25] Furthermore, as a result of the ubiquitous availability of scrap in this country, many electric-furnace mills have been located in areas that were shunned by the large steel companies, especially in the western and southern states. Low transportation costs for both raw-material input and finished products, low overhead, availability of nonunion labor, and efficient management have made these mills formidable competitors of the larger companies.[26] In such product lines as wire rods, bars, and light shapes the minimills have greatly reduced the market share of both the large mills and imports. They have gained a market share at the expense of their integrated rivals, in part because of their lower costs, but also because they rapidly adopted new technology and were generally more flexible in their pricing and production policies.

Minimills have sprung up throughout the United States since the early 1950s. As of December 1984, there were 43 such firms, operating a total of 53 plants.[27] Initially, the technological basis of this development was the adaptation of scrap-using electric furnaces for the mass production of carbon (i.e., nonalloy) steels. Beginning with the 1960s, the growth of minimills was further stimulated by the introduction of the cost-saving continuous billet caster and the construction of a new generation of small rod-and-bar mills.

Whether or not the minimills will attain (as currently predicted) a market share in excess of 30 percent by the end of this decade will depend on their ability to overcome their technological limitations and to expand their traditional product mix. The limitations are, first, the metallurgical pollution of their ferrous raw material (scrap) by ineradicable, harmful trace elements (such as copper and zinc) and, second, the present requirement of very large-scale facilities to roll thick slabs into high-grade sheets.[28]

A great deal of progress is being made in developing new methods that may significantly reduce the minimum efficient scale of producing metallurgically pure iron and of rolling high-quality sheet products. One necessary step to bring down the scale of a sheet-rolling mill, or the continuous casting of thin slabs, was developed in 1985 for Nucor, one of the leading minimill operators in the United States. Should these advances enable minimills to

Table 4: United States Steel Consumption and Imports, 1960–1984

	Consumption (million net product tons)	Imports (million net product tons)	Share of Total U.S. Imports (percent): Japan	Others: EC	Others: Canada	Others: Rest	Import Share of U.S. market (percent)
1960	71.5	3.4	17.9	62.4	6.3	7.4	4.7
1965	100.6	10.3	42.5	47.3	6.2	4.0	10.3
1968	107.6	18.0	40.6	46.8	6.9	5.7	16.7
1971	102.5	18.3	37.7	46.5	7.0	8.8	17.9
1975	89.0	34.3	12.0	48.6	8.4	8.7	13.5
1978	116.6	21.1	30.7	35.3	11.2	22.8	18.1
1981	105.4	19.9	31.3	32.6	14.6	21.6	18.9
1983	83.5	17.1	24.8	24.1	13.9	37.1	20.5
1984	98.2	26.2	25.3	24.2	12.1	38.4	26.6

Source: AISI, *Annual Statistical Report,* various years.

invade the sizable sheet market on a wide front, the integrated mills would have to face yet another major battle for market share, if not for survival.

Imported Steel—Functions and Structure. Steel imports increased from a trickle of mostly low-quality products in the 1950s to a flood of high-grade steel in the mid-1960s. From 1968 to 1980 imports fluctuated widely around an almost stationary long-term average share of roughly 16.5 percent of the U.S. market. (See Table 4 and Figure 1.) Several developments contributed to the growing market share of imports in subsequent years. One was the

FIGURE 1. Amount of steel imported by the United States, 1968–1984. Lower figures over each bar show millions of net tons. Figures in parentheses show import volume as a percent of apparent supply. (U.S. Commerce Department)

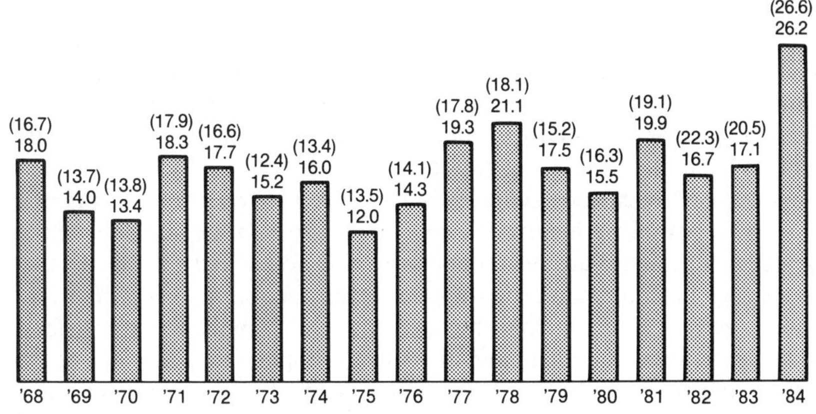

rising international value of the dollar which widened the cost and price gap between domestic and foreign steel. Another was the "oil shock" of 1979 and its impact on several newly industrializing nations. Faced with domestic recession and enormous foreign debts, these nations were desperately trying to increase their exports in order to earn foreign currency. Some (notably South Korea, Brazil, and Argentina) managed to turn abruptly from being net steel importers to becoming major steel exporters. A considerable portion of their exports entered the U.S. market, often at very low prices. A third development was a significant increase in the purchase of imported semi-finished steel (slabs) by the integrated American steel producers, and a temporary shortage (1980 and 1981) of domestic capacity to produce tubular products for the oil industry.

The function of imports in the American steel market is well described in a study by the Department of Commerce: "Imports serve to meet shortfalls in the U.S. capacity for particular regions, products, and time periods. They are largest relative to demand in regions where there are capacity shortfalls. For those regions with capacity overhangs, import penetration is typically well below national averages."[29] A comparison of import statistics by destination bears out those conclusions. In 1968, two-thirds of all imported steel came into ports on the East Coast and the Great Lakes and only one-third into Gulf and Pacific ports. By 1982, shipments of imported steel to Gulf and Pacific ports had increased to 60 percent of total imports while shipments to other ports had declined correspondingly.[30] With respect to products sold primarily by integrated mills (sheet, plate, heavy structurals, and pipes), the import dependence of Western and Southwestern regions has grown even more, largely because the integrated domestic producers do not have much (efficient) capacity in those regions.

Imports also meet shortfalls in particular products. A 1980 survey by the International Trade Commission showed that customers had switched from domestic to foreign suppliers in nearly half of all the instances because domestic supply was not available.[31] More than 13 percent did so because they could not find domestic products of the required quality, and 7 percent preferred multiple sourcing. Only 28 percent switched to imports because of price considerations. In the same year, a General Accounting Office survey of domestic-steel users found that, for products other than those supplied by minimills, salient motives for buying imported steel were better quality, assured availability, and marketing help.[32]

On several occasions, imports surged when temporary shortages, indicated by rapidly lengthening delivery times, arose in the domestic market. From August 1983 to May 1984, imports of cold-rolled and galvanized sheets rose sharply because domestic suppliers were unable to keep up with an unusually strong demand from the automotive and appliance industries.[33]

Table 4 shows the changing structure of imports. As a result of trade litigation and pressure by the U.S. government, the share of steel imports from the European Community and Japan declined between 1964 and 1984, but Canada, Spain, South Korea, South Africa, a multitude of nations from the Third World, and even Eastern Europe began to ship significant amounts of steel into the U.S. market. In addition, the product mix of imports has changed over the long run, in the direction of higher-value products (such as cold-rolled and coated sheets, as well as tubular products), because foreign mills have an incentive to increase the value-added content of their exports.

Some International Comparisons

1. Firm Size and Concentration. An international comparison of firm size and concentration lends some perspective to our discussion of market structure. In 1984, the four largest steel firms in Japan annually produced 71 million tons compared to 44 million tons by the four largest producers in the United States and 53 million tons by the four largest producers in the European Community. The eight largest firms produced 61 million tons in the United States, 77 millions tons in the European Community, and 87 million tons in Japan. (See Table 5.) It is evident that the international differences are greater for the four largest firms than for the eight largest firms.

There is also a marked contrast in the concentration ratios of the three steel producing industries. Thus, the four-firm concentration ratio in Japan (61.2 percent) is larger than that in the United States (48.4 percent), and substantially larger than that in the European Community (40.0 percent). Indeed, the four-firm ratio in Japan exceeds the eight-firm ratio in the European Community. The eight-firm ratios for Japan and the United States are much closer.

2. Plant Size and Economies of Scale. An international comparison of firm size and concentration in different countries may provide some clues about the degree of competition in their home markets. Taken by itself, however, such comparisons yield little information about industrial efficiency, because in an industry like steel the primary unit of efficiency is the individual plant rather than the firm, and the largest firms do not necessarily operate the largest plants.

Of the 29 integrated plants operating in this country in 1983, 23 (or 79 percent) had an annual raw-steel capacity of less than 4 million tons—the capacity generally considered to be the minimum efficient scale for a plant with a narrow product range. Indeed, 15 of those plants could not have produced 3 million tons at full capacity.[34]

The Japanese industry, in particular, has led the world in the construction of large-scale steel plants, followed by the European Community. (See Tables 6 and 7.) Large plants have also been built in Canada, Eastern Europe, and in several developing countries (South Korea, Taiwan, Brazil, India, and China).

Large plants do not necessarily make good use of best-practice economies of scale. The efficiency of a steel-making operation is also influenced by the location of the plant, the size, layout, and flexibility of the various

Table 5: The Largest Steel Producers in the United States, the European Community, and Japan, 1984

U.S.			EC			JAPAN		
Firm	Output (mNT)[a]	World Rank[b]	Firm	Output (mNT)[a]	World Rank[b]	Firm	Output (mNT)[a]	World Rank[b]
U.S. Steel	15.8	2	Finsider (It.)	14.9	3	Nippon Steel	32.4	1
Bethlehem	12.1	9	BSC (U.K.)	14.0	4	Nippon Kokan	13.8	5
LTV	9.9	12	Thyssen (G.)	12.9	6	Sumitomo	12.5	7
Inland	6.5	17	Usinor (Fr.)	11.2	10	Kawasaki	12.5	8
Top 4	44.3		Top 4	53.0		Top 4	71.2	
Armco	6.2	19	Sacilor (Fr.)	7.6	13	Kobe	7.3	14
National	4.9	25	Hoogovens (Neth.)	6.1	20	Nisshin	3.3	36
Wheeling-Pittsburgh	2.8	40	Cockerill-Sambre			Tokyo	3.2	38
Weirton	2.4	44	(Belg.)	5.3	21	Daido	1.9	54
			Krupp (G.)	4.9	24			
Top 8	60.6		Top 8	76.9		Top 8	86.9	
Total Output	91.5		Total Output	132.5		Total Output	116.4	
Share of Top 4 Comp.	48.4%		Share of Top 4 Comp.	40.0%		Share of Top 4 Comp.	61.2%	
Share of Top 8 Comp.	66.8%		Share of Top 8 Comp.	58.0%		Share of Top 8 Comp.	74.7%	

[a]Million net tons of raw steel.
[b]Excluding steel firms in the Communist bloc.

Sources: Metal Bulletin, June 11, 1985, p. 27; *Tekko Nenkan,* 1985, pp. 610–613.

Table 6: The Largest Ten Steel Plants in the United States, the European Community (of Nine), and Japan, 1984 (Million net tons of raw steel capacity)

U.S.		EC (9)		Japan	
1. Inland Steel, East Chicago, Ind.	9.30	Italsider, Taranto, It.	12.60	NKK[b], Fukuyama	15.00
2. USS, Gary, Ind.	8.00	Thyssen, Duisburg, Germany	11.60	Kawasaki, Mizushima	12.90
3. Bethl., Sparrows Point, Md.	7.00	Usinor, Dunkirk, France	8.80	Sumitomo, Kashima	12.70
4. Bethl., Burns Harbor, Ind.	5.30	Hoogovens Ijmuiden, Neth.	7.70	NSC[c], Kimitsu	10.40
5. USS, Fairless, Pa.	4.00	Salzgitter, Germany	5.90	Sumitomo, Wakayama	9.90
6. Weirton, W.V.	4.00	Kloeckner, Germany	5.70	NSC, Yawata	9.70
7. Rouge Steel, Mich. (Ford Motor Co.)	3.80	Hoesch, Germany	5.10	Kawasaki, Chiba	9.00
8. National, Great Lakes, Mich.	3.60	Mannesmann, Germany	4.70	NSC, Oita	8.80
9. J & L, East Chicago, Ind.	3.60	Scunthorpe, U.K.	4.60	NSC, Nagoya	8.20
10. Republic, Cleveland, Ohio	3.50	Teeside, U.K.	4.20	Kobe, Kakogawa	6.60
Total	52.10[a]		70.90[a]		103.20[a]

[a]The cumulative size of the largest five plants is as follows: U.S., 33.6 mnt; EC, 46.6 mnt; Japan, 60.90 mnt.
[b]NKK = Nippon Kokan Kaisha.
[c]NSC = Nippon Steel Corporation.

Sources: Authors' estimates based on Metal Bulletin, *Iron and Steel Works of the World,* 8th ed. (1983), company annual reports, and announcements in *American Metal Market, Metal Bulletin,* and *Stahl und Eisen.*

Table 7: Changes in the Plant Size of Integrated Steel Producers

	1952			1960			1984		
Plant Size	*U.S.*	*EC*	*Japan*	*U.S.*	*EC*	*Japan*	*U.S.*	*EC*	*Japan*
above 6 mNT	—	—	—	3	—	—	3	4	12
4 to 6 mNT	4	—	—	6	—	—	3	8	3
2 to 4 mNT	7	—	—	18	4	3	17	18	2
1 to 2 mNT	20	7	2	23	16	6	12	9	2

Sources: William Haller, "Technological Change in Primary Steelmaking in the United States, 1947–64," *Hearings,* Subcommittee on Antitrust and Monopoly, Committee on the Judiciary, September-October 1967, pp. 3186–3197. Louis Lister, *Europe's Coal and Steel Community* (Twentieth Century Fund, 1960), Appendix E; Eurostat, *Iron and Steel,* 1970 yearbook, Table 11-8; Institute for Iron and Steel Studies, *Commentary* (Jan. 1983); Metal Bulletin, *Iron and Steel Works of the World,* 8th ed. (1983), updated from company annual reports and reports in the trade press.

Table 8: Plant and Equipment Economies of Scale

	Equipment	*U.S.*	*EC*	*Japan*
Plants (1984)	Capacity of the 5 largest plants (Max. raw steel production potential)	34	47	61
	Capacity of the 10 largest plants	52	71	103
	Number of plants with a raw steel capacity in excess of 6 million NT	3	4	12
Blast Furnaces (1984)	No. of blast furnaces with an inner volume in excess of 70,629 cubic feet (2,000 cubic meters)	6	19	39
Steelshops (1982)	No. of oxygen converters 220 NT or larger (charge weight)	31	39	32
	Average annual capacity of oxygen steelshops, million NT	2.4	2.8	3.5
	Capacity-weighted ave. converter size	225	240	218
Hot Wide Strip Mills (1982)	No. of mills			
	a. fully continuous	21	11	9
	b. semi continuous	14	14	8
	Average rated annual capacity, million NT	2.4	3.1	3.5
Plate Mills (1982)	No. of mills (only heavy and medium reversing, except two and three high)	18	34	16
	Average total annual capacity, million NT	.67	.62	1.68

Sources: Institute for Iron and Steel Studies, *Commentary* (January 1983); Metal Bulletin, *Iron and Steelworks of the World* (1983), updated by the authors; Jonathan Aylen, "Size and Efficiency in the Steel Industry: An International Comparison," *National Institute of Economics Review* (May 1982), pp. 65–76.

interrelated processes, and the degree of product specialization. Comparative information concerning these factors is difficult to obtain, but some of the relevant data are listed in Table 8.

Summary

Summarizing the discussion of market structure, we may conclude that, not only has the power of a single firm, which once dominated the U.S. market, greatly diminished, but the entire integrated segment of the industry has become subject to effective competitive checks from a group of small domestic producers and (in the absence of interventions) from imported steel.

The implications of these structural changes for market conduct and public policy will be examined in the following sections.

III. MARKET CONDUCT

Business conduct or behavior is closely related to industry structure. A tight, oligopolistic structure is generally expected to lead to nonaggressive pricing behavior.[35] An absence of competitive pressures may also lead to a lack of progressiveness which over the longer term will cause severe inefficiencies in the industry's structure and performance.

Administered Pricing under U.S. Steel's Leadership

From the turn of the century until the early 1960s, the U.S. Steel Corporation was the acknowledged price leader of the steel industry and, for the most part, the other oligopolists followed in lockstep. Prices were generally uniform, rigid, and, over the years, steadily escalating. The pricing discipline observed by the large American steel producers, even during severe recessions, became the envy of foreign steel producers, who often experienced great price instability during periods of weak demand. Although this "administered pricing" helped to create an environment of stability and predictability, it had harmful effects over the longer term. It exposed the industry to external challenges that eventually resulted in a significant erosion of its oligopoly power.

External Threats to Administered Pricing

Government "Oversight." After World War II, the remarkable insensitivity of steel prices to market conditions, and their escalation in a pattern of unbroken regularity, naturally attracted the attention of both Congress and the President. The government could not ignore reports like that of the Council of Economic Advisors, which concluded that

> Steel prices played an important role in the general price increases of the 1950s. Between 1947 and 1951, the average increase in the price of basic steel products was 9 percent per year, twice the average increase of all wholesale prices. The unique behavior of steel prices was most pronounced in the mid-1950s. While the wholesale price index was falling an average of 0.9 percent annually from

> 1951 to 1955, the price index for steel was rising an average of 4.8 percent per year. From 1955 to 1958, steel prices were increasing 7.1 percent annually, or almost three times as fast as wholesale prices generally. No other major sector shows a similar record.[36]

Periodic investigations by Congressional committees condemned the price policy of the steel oligopolists. The Kefauver Committee, for example, charged that "no matter what the change in cost or in demand, steel prices since 1947 have moved steadily and regularly in only one direction, upward." The fact that these increases could be "made to stick," even in periods of general recession, said the Committee, was a further "tribute to the perfection with which price leadership in the steel industry maintains price rigidity."[37]

Over the years, there were hearings and investigations by Congress, presidential confrontations with steel leaders (such as the Kennedy-Blough face-off in 1962), pressure from the Council on Wage and Price Stability, and other forms of jaw-boning, moral suasion, and wage-price guidelines; there was even a temporary imposition of wage-price controls during the Nixon administration—but nothing seemed to have any lasting effect. Any resulting influence was largely cosmetic, and the essence of oligopoly power, as manifested in price policy, was left largely undisturbed.

However, since the mid-1960s, when imports began to make significant inroads into the domestic market, the government's posture has changed radically. Instead of focusing on the persistent steel price increases, government became increasingly concerned with the "deleterious" effect of imports on domestic production and employment, and with the declining health of the steel oligopoly.[38]

In sum, it seems that government policy has seldom had more than a marginal, transitory effect when attempting to moderate the market power of the domestic oligopoly.

Minimills. Minimills have posed a far more effective challenge to the integrated steel oligopoly than government "oversight." Although their production was largely confined to particular product lines—viz., reinforcing bars, wire rods, and some light structurals—these nonintegrated producers have expanded their share of domestic shipments from a mere 3 percent in 1960 to 20 percent in 1984. Applying strategies of targeted, low-cost, and modern production, they have grown at an annual rate of 10 percent while many of their integrated rivals were contracting.

In wire rods, for example, the International Trade Commission found "that in 1979 integrated producers accounted for 68 percent of U.S. production and 74 percent of producers' open-market shipments. These producers utilized 63 percent of their capacity in 1979. Nonintegrated producers, mostly operating independent mini-mills, had only 32 percent of production and 26 percent of open market shipments while utilizing 83 percent of their capacity."[39] By 1983, however, the situation "showed a near complete reversal. In that year, the *integrated* producers' share of both U.S. production and producers' open market shipments had fallen to 39 percent of the totals and *nonintegrated* firms had the remaining 61 percent. While integrated firms suffered with capacity utilization at only 35 percent, nonintegrated firms had actually increased their capacity by 56 percent and in spite of this were able to utilize over 78 percent of it." "It is clear," concluded Commissioner Paula Stern, "that the nonintegrated producers are largely responsible for the decline in shipments suffered by the integrated producers."

Moreover, Commissioner Stern observed:

> It is also obvious why the integrated producers lost so much of the market to the mini-mills. The latter are modern and efficient mills dedicated to the production of one or two products. The efficiency of their technology, management, and cost control techniques enable mini-mills to keep their prices low. . . . Price data show that the average delivered price paid for rod from nonintegrated firms was well below that price paid for rod from integrated firms in most regions and in most of the period of investigation. But even more significant is the fact that these efficient U.S. mills were able to sell wire rod at a price that, on average, was below the average price of imported wire rod.[40]

Thus, in 1983, in the Detroit market, minimills *under*sold imported wire rod by an average of about fifty dollars (15 percent) per ton, whereas the integrated producers charged an average price of twenty-five dollars (5.7 percent) *above* that of the imported product. Similar pricing patterns prevailed in other product categories in which minimills were preeminent.

In sum, minimills have eroded the erstwhile oligopoly power of the integrated producers in selected product markets. They have captured substantial market shares at the expense of the integrated producers and, in some cases, forced them to abandon the field altogether. Their success was the result of efficient production, high-quality products, good customer service, and, above all, old-fashioned price competition.

Imports. Starting in 1960, imports have captured a growing share of the U.S. domestic market and, inevitably, have had a moderating influence on the administered pricing policy of the domestic oligopoly. Thus, the Council on Wage & Price Stability found that, between 1959 and 1969, "mill prices of steel and all industrial commodities moved very similarly. . . . They were level in the first half of the period, and increased slightly in the second half. In approximately the same overall period, steel profits on equity fell substantially from the rates which steel had enjoyed previously." In interpreting this phenomenon, the Council stated: "Apparently there were limiting forces which operated to prevent U.S. steel companies from increasing prices and maintaining the previous higher profit levels. *Chief* among these was import competition."[41]

The Federal Trade Commission came to the same conclusion. It also found that, after 1960, the industry's pricing changed from "administered price leadership" to "barometric price leadership"—i.e., even though the structure of the steel industry continued to be an oligopoly, its prices were not sustained above competitive levels and changed in a pattern that mimicked a competitive industry. The Commission concluded that an important element in this transformation was "the role of imports."[42]

Predictably, the domestic oligopoly did not view this trend with complacency, and launched an orchestrated political campaign to recapture its erstwhile control over prices. It launched a succession of antidumping complaints and countervailing-duty charges before the U.S. Tariff Commission (now the International Trade Commission), and lobbied Congress for the imposition of a variety of import restraints to neutralize the threat of foreign competition. The result was a succession of "voluntary" import quotas imposed on foreign producers.

1. The Voluntary Restraint Agreement (VRA), 1969–1974. Under this Voluntary Restraint Agreement, steel imports from Japan and from the European Community were each limited to 5.8 million tons annually, compared with their then current levels of 7.5 million and 7.3 million tons, respectively. The Agreement also provided for an annual growth factor of 5 percent in the allowable quotas.[43]

The price effects of the VRA were dramatic. According to one study, between January 1960 and December 1968, a period of nine years, the composite steel price index rose 4.1 points—or 0.45 points per year—indicating the moderating effects that surging imports had on domestic prices. In the four years between January 1969 and December 1972, while the VRA was in effect, the steel price index rose 26.7 points—or 6.67 points per year—which was twice as much as the index for all industrial products (including steel). Put differently, since the import quotas went into effect, steel prices increased at an annual rate 14 times greater than in the nine years prior thereto.[44]

Another study showed that the products that had been subjected to particularly hard import pressure prior to the VRA evidenced greater price increases than other steel products after the VRA became effective, again highlighting the anticompetitive effects of the quotas.[45]

Yet another study estimated that the VRA caused steel prices to increase by $26 to $39 per ton, meaning that the price of steel would have been 13 to 15 percent lower in the absence of the VRA.[46]

2. The Trigger Price System, 1978–1982. After the lapse of the VRA in 1974, and after a plethora of complaints by the domestic oligopoly before the International Trade Commission, the Carter Administration granted the industry a novel form of protection in the form of the Trigger Price Mechanism (TPM). For all practical purposes, the TPM set minimum prices for all carbon-steel products imported into the United States.[47] The "trigger prices" (so-called because undercutting by foreign suppliers was to trigger antidumping proceedings by U.S. authorities) were based on estimated Japanese production costs plus freight costs from Japan. In exchange for administrative protection, the steel industry agreed to refrain from filing antidumping, subsidy, or import-injury complaints before the International Trade Commission. Domestic steel prices began to rise immediately upon the application of the trigger price minimums.[48]

Because the trigger prices were set at a level close to domestic list prices, they precipitated a two-pronged upward pressure on the price level: (a) importers could now raise prices (which formerly reflected world market conditions) to the higher level dictated by trigger prices; and (b) domestic producers could and did raise actual prices to at least the list price, thus wiping out the discounts from list which market conditions formerly compelled them to grant to their customers. Furthermore, domestic producers, protected by the minimum prices established under the trigger price system, were now free to raise list prices so that they would be higher than import prices—at least to the extent of the accustomed differential between domestic and foreign prices.

The TPM not only maintained American steel prices significantly above world market levels. It also distorted patterns of steel pricing and consumption in the United States. Traditionally, domestic steel prices had been low in the Great Lakes region, where the most efficient American integrated plants are located, and high on the West Coast, which lacks adequate domestic capacity. Trigger prices, however, because they were calculated on the basis of Japanese production and freight costs, were lowest in the Western states and highest in the Great Lakes region. The distribution pattern of steel imports changed accordingly, as foreign producers—even remote British, German, and Brazilian suppliers—shipped more to the West Coast and less to the northeastern states.[49]

Other distortions generated by the TPM affected the competitiveness of American steel distributors and steel-using manufacturers. The basic cause of these distortions was the large difference between the protected prices in the U.S. market and prices in the world market. This permitted some importers to market their steel at very low prices through offshore affiliates. By selling the steel in the United States at trigger prices but without markup (all profits were assigned to the affiliate), the firms were able to undercut distributors lacking such offshore connections.[50] American steel-using manufacturers and fabricators were injured by the TPM because they paid considerably higher prices for their steel than most of their foreign competitors. By raising American steel prices to an artificial level, the TPM tended to shift imports from steel products to fabricated steel and other steel-containing products. Especially hard-hit were firms producing items for which the cost of steel amounted to a significant portion of total production costs, such as wire rope, fasteners, large containers, transmission towers, bridge components, and oil rigs.

It is noteworthy that the impact of the TPM system was intimately linked to exchange-rate fluctuations, and that this eventually caused the system's demise. In fact, the entire episode serves as an excellent illustration of the effect that currency relations have on the international competitiveness of national industries. Increases in trigger prices in 1978 and in the first half of 1979 were attributable primarily to a fall in the dollar–yen exchange rate. Japanese production costs rose only when measured in dollars; in terms of their own currency, those costs hardly changed. But when the dollar ceased to fall, trigger prices ceased to rise. Because the TPM in effect set not only a price floor for imports but also a ceiling for domestic prices, American steel producers grew dissatisfied, and, in March 1980, brought the system down with a volley of trade cases aimed chiefly at European exporters.[51] These proceedings became moot when the TPM was restored at a higher level of trigger prices in October 1980. It continued its precarious existence against the backdrop of a rising dollar in international markets, until January 1982. American steel producers, chagrined by government inaction in the face of open undercutting of trigger prices by some foreign suppliers, caused the final demise of the system. When they again breached their agreement to refrain from trade litigation while the TPM was in force, and filed another broadside of antidumping and antisubsidy cases against European and South American steel exporters, the government promptly suspended the TPM.

3. The "Reagan" Quotas, 1984–. It soon became clear that the industry, led by U.S. Steel, had been rash and ill-advised in destroying the TPM. The industry had hoped that massive trade litigation would choke off sufficient quantities of foreign steel to compensate for the elimination of minimum import prices. Yet, January 1982 was the worst possible time for demolishing the shield against foreign price competition which the government had been willing to provide. Demand for steel was falling precipitously—to its lowest level since the recession of the early 1960s. To make things worse, steep increases in crude-oil prices had paralyzed economic expansion in several newly industrializing countries, which found themselves with large amounts of excess steelmaking capacity. In desperation, they produced steel that found its way into the United States, usually at prices well below those of the traditional steel exporters from the European Community, Japan, and Canada, and far below the prices charged by the integrated American producers.

Trade litigation did force the European Community to agree to a new quota arrangement in October 1982, but the nontraditional steel exporters soon filled the market share conceded by the EC producers. Despite a continuing barrage of antidumping and antisubsidy complaints filed (for the most part, successfully) by the domestic producers, the import share of the market rose in 1983 and 1984, primarily owing to greater penetration by those new steel exporters. In addition, price discounting by domestic firms became so severe that the difference between realized and list prices for major carbon-steel products reached $100 per ton.[52]

To remedy this situation, the Reagan Administration, in 1984, began to negotiate a set of voluntary restraint agreements with a large number of countries. Many foreign-steel exporters agreed to quantitative restraints because the alternative would have been stiff penalties, which had been assessed against them by the Commerce Department for having violated U.S. trade laws. Others, such exporters as from Japan and South Korea, yielded to open threats of economic sanctions. By March 1985, American negotiators had concluded quota agreements—most of them for a period of five years—with nearly every major steel-exporting nation in the world, including Brazil, Mexico, Argentina, Poland, and Rumania.[53] As a result of these agreements, the total market share of imports is expected to decline from 26.6 percent in 1984 to about 21 percent during the remainder of the 1980s.

Assigning quantitative limits to troublesome foreign competitors will facilitate pricing coordination among the domestic suppliers, if only by making it easier for them to read each other's signals. Except in those product markets where they compete against efficient American minimills, the integrated producers are likely to achieve the main objective of their intensive trade litigation and political lobbying: to stabilize and, ultimately, raise steel prices.

Price Policies of European and Japanese Producers

Unlike the U.S. steel industry, European and Japanese producers depend for a large part of their sales on the international market. In 1983, the European Community exported 29 percent of its total steel production, and Japan, 36 percent. To compete successfully in export markets, sellers must be flexible in their price policy and stay in the forefront of product development. In addition, they must respond quickly to the wishes of their customers and the changing strategies of their foreign rivals.

In the EC, price competition has been active—at times, aggressive—ever since the common steel market was inaugurated in 1953. Despite rising industry concentration, EC steel executives were never quite successful in coordinating their price policies or in maintaining desired price levels.[54] In 1977, partly owing to low-priced imports from Eastern Europe, price-cutting became so severe that the EC Commission instituted a system of output reductions and minimum prices for some steel products (Davignon Plan).[55] At the same time, the Commission negotiated quotas with foreign suppliers, which reduced the price-cutting by importers and arrested the sharply rising trend of imports (from 4 percent in 1965 to 13 percent in 1977). In a further effort to keep steel prices in the Community from falling to world-market levels, the Commission added tight production controls to these measures in 1981. Simultaneously, it directed EC steel producers to reduce capacity by a prescribed ratio in order to lessen the downward pressure of excess capacity on prices.[56]

The pricing structure in the Japanese steel market is characterized by a two-tier system: the big-buyer prices and the dealer prices. Big-buyer prices used to be charged for about 90 percent of all home-market sales. But the long recession and increased competition, in part from imported steel, has reduced this ratio to approximately 70 percent of the total.

Big-buyer prices are negotiated among the largest steel consumers and producers (usually Toyota and Nippon Steel, respectively). Judging by the losses suffered by the steel industry on home-market sales during several years in the 1970s and 1980s, it appears that the tight, oligopolistic structure of Japanese steel producers was not solid enough to impose "administered" prices on Japanese steel users. Big-buyer prices usually remain fairly constant over a period of several years; dealer prices fluctuate with market conditions. Also, as a consequence of rising import competition, dealer prices have had a growing influence on the Japanese steel market.[57]

Of total steel consumption in Japan, the share of steel imports has increased from 1 percent in 1978 to 4 percent in 1984. However, in some product lines (e.g., hot-rolled coils), imports took 25 percent of the Japanese market in 1984.[58] Because most of the imports originate in developing countries, especially South Korea, Taiwan, and Brazil, the large Japanese steel producers have urged their government to tighten the rules on steel imports from Third World steel industries.

Summary

Price policy, especially in a basic industry like steel, is of crucial importance to the firms that depend on this product as a major input. Many American steel-using firms (e.g., automobile manufacturers) are engaged in a relentless battle with aggressive foreign rivals for market share. The price of the steel products available to them may determine the outcome of this competition. In recent years, steel-using firms in Europe and Japan have been able to buy steel at considerably lower prices than could their American counterparts—a fact that obviously jeopardizes this nation's traditional position of leadership in such areas as engineering and equipment construction.

From the viewpoint of the large domestic steel companies, the remedy for their "profitability" problem seems to be further price increases, but implemented with a shield to protect home markets against further erosion by imports. This need explains the persistent and unrelenting pressure of the large steel companies on the government to give protection through "voluntary" or mandatory quotas, countervailing tariffs, antidumping measures, or "buy-American" policies. From the viewpoint of the sizable American steel-using sector, however, the remedy consists of stimulating steel-industry efficiency, performance, and competitive pricing. Otherwise, the much-vaunted reindustrialization of the United States will have to draw heavily on foreign engineering and the use of imported equipment.

IV. MARKET PERFORMANCE

An industry's performance is nothing more than the product of its structure and conduct. It is a measure of how well—how efficiently—it functions to serve consumer needs and contributes to the welfare of the national economy. Obviously, a precise quantitative assessment of performance is difficult, if not impossible, but international comparisons of an industry's performance with that of its counterparts in other nations can yield valuable insights and guidelines for public policy.

For more than six decades, the American steel industry was a tight oligopoly, a structure that encouraged a cost-plus, target-rate-of-return pricing policy. Largely as a result of these antecedents, the steel industry—or rather, the integrated and concentrated segment of the industry—finds itself, in the 1980s, with a number of deep-rooted problems. First, despite the many closures of marginal facilities since 1977, several large firms are still saddled with plants that are suboptimal in size and not well located with respect to markets. Second, much of the integrated capacity—which accounts for nearly all the industry's output of flat-rolled products—is clustered in a few Midwestern states, whereas other regions, notably the South and the West, are deficient in this type of capacity. Third, the integrated firms find themselves in this predicament even though they have outspent their foreign rivals (per ton of capacity replaced or added), and, in doing so, have significantly increased their debt burden.

Before examining these problems further, we first turn our attention to an index of performance that has been the focus of professional discussion since the early 1960s—technological progressiveness. This index measures an industry's ability to keep up with the latest advances in "best practice" operations, or to be in the forefront of such advances. Judged by this criterion, the U.S. steel industry, except for its minimill and specialty-steel segments, has lagged rather than led in the post-World War II period. Consequently, it has suffered serious erosion of its cost-competitiveness, not only in world markets but even in its domestic market.

Technical Progressiveness

Historically, according to the American Iron and Steel Institute, "the steel industry in this country has adopted most new technologies, wherever they were developed, at least as rapidly and probably more rapidly than steel industries in other parts of the world."[59] The industry's spokesmen were quick to label anyone who dissented from this view as "simply misinformed."[60]

Today, the technological lethargy of the U.S. steel industry is hardly a matter of dispute. It is recognized not only by the industry's academic critics but also by financial analysts, and even some steel company executives. One steel company president puts it this way:

> For many generations a continuing stream of new inventions and manufacturing techniques allowed us to far outpace the rest of the world in both volume and efficiency of production. In many areas this is no longer true. . . Beset by labor featherbedding and restrictions, with tremendous investments in outmoded plants, with huge staffs and complex corporate structures, our larger steel companies have not quickly accepted technological advances and in some cases have adopted new techniques only when the economic evidence was overwhelming.[61]

The validity of such criticisms can be evaluated by a comparison of the innovative efforts of the U.S., European Community, and Japanese steel industries, which are not too dissimilar in size and the ratio of factor costs.[62]

R&D Expenditures

In a study released in 1980, the Congressional Office for Technology Assessment (OTA) reported that "the number of R&D scientists and engineers per 1,000 employees is smaller for steel than for any other industry except for textiles and apparel, about 15 percent of the average for all reported industries."[63] The OTA also noted that "foreign steel producers spend more on R&D than those in the United States. The U.S. steel industry's steel-related R&D expenditures have been about 0.5 to 0.6 percent of sales in recent years; in Japan, they are slightly more than 1 percent. Furthermore, Japanese steel-related R&D expenditures have grown gradually but steadily over time . . . even though Japanese steel sales and profits have declined since 1974. In 1974, steel R&D occupied 3 percent of the total number of researchers in Japanese industry, and accounted for 5 percent of total industry R&D spending; in 1973–75, the equivalent figures for U.S. steel R&D were 0.9 and 1.3 percent, respectively."[64] In 1983, the expenditure on research and development as a percent of sales revenue was 0.6 in the United States, and 1.5 in Japan.[65]

Process Innovation

Among the large number of process improvements that have been made in basic steelmaking during the last 30 years, two undoubtedly deserve to be characterized as technological breakthroughs: the *basic oxygen furnace* (BOF), a fast technique for converting iron to steel, and the *continuous caster,* a process that bypasses both the laborious ingot-pouring process and the energy-intensive reheating of ingots and primary rolling. Other major developments during this period were an environmentally clean (but capital-intensive) method for quenching coke; new blast-furnace tops, which permit operations at higher pressure; and computer-controlled strip and plate mills, which allow rolling to finer tolerances and, hence, the production of higher-quality material.

The Basic Oxygen Furnace (BOF). The oxygen furnace was first put into commercial use in a small Austrian steel plant in 1950. It was first installed in the United States in 1954, by a small company (McLouth), but was not adopted by the steel giants until more than a decade later: U.S. Steel in December 1963; Bethlehem in 1964; and Republic in 1965. As of September 1963, several of the largest steel companies, together operating more than 50 percent of basic steel capacity, had not installed a single BOF furnace, whereas smaller companies, operating only 7 percent of the nation's steel capacity, accounted for almost half of the BOF installations in the United States.

The large American steel producers have defended their late start in the use of BOF's by pointing out that their major program of capacity expansion was already under way when the Austrian converters came on stream, and that the scale of the first converters was too small for American mass-production conditions.[66] The first of these "alibis" may have a certain validity, because the American steel market was buoyant at the time. In a situation in which they could sell all the steel they produced, the large firms preferred "off-the-shelf," or well-proven techniques rather than new, and possibly risky, techniques. Nevertheless, had the large integrated producers at least kept abreast of this new development, they would have had a pilot plant in operation about the time the Austrians initiated commercial production with the new furnace. In that case, they could immediately have begun the upscaling of the process and would have been ready with larger versions of the BOF by the mid-1950s, at the latest.

As for the second reason for postponing the adoption of the new process, it is true that the earliest converters had capacity limitations. But several of the large steel companies were operating many integrated plants that were even smaller than those of the first North American companies (Dofasco in Canada and McLouth in the United States) that had adopted the new converter. It was thus not unreasonable to expect the large American companies to take a chance with the new method in at least some of their small plants,

FIGURE 2. Comparative adoption rates of basic oxygen furnace (BOF) and continuous casting (CC) technology in various countries. *Source:* IISI, *Statistical Yearbook Steel,* various years; IISI, *World Steel in Figures* (1984), pp. 6–7; German Iron and Steel Federation, *Statistical Yearbook,* various years.

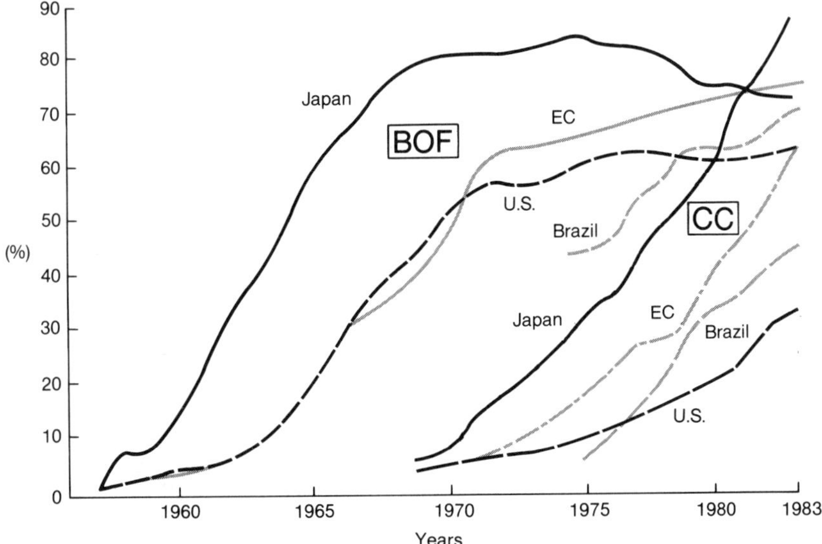

especially because American iron ores were well suited for the BOF, unlike the phosphorous ores used by many European producers.[67]

The most likely explanation of the hesitant adoption of the Austrian converter by the large American firms is that their managements were still imbued with Andrew Carnegie's motto: "invention don't pay."[68] Let others first assume the cost and risk of research and development, and of breaking in a new process, then we'll decide.[69] The result was that during the 1950s, the American steel industry installed 40 million tons of melting capacity which, as *Fortune* observed, "was obsolete when it was built."[70]

Continuous Casting. The belated adoption of continuous casting by the American steel giants is a further illustration of their technological lethargy. Again, it was a small company (Roanoke Electric), with an annual capacity of 100,000 tons, that pioneered in introducing this European invention in the United States, in 1962. Other small steel companies followed, so that by 1968, firms with roughly 3 percent of the nation's steel capacity accounted for 90 percent of continuous-casting production in the United States.

By 1978, the U.S. steel industry (taken as a whole) was continuously casting 15.2 percent of its steel, less than one half the 46.2 percent achieved in Japan. But these totals conceal a curious fact: the American minimills, with a rate of 51.2 percent, were already ahead of the Japanese average, whereas the integrated U.S. mills were producing only 11 percent of their output by the continuous-casting method.[71] The latter managed to boost their average to 30 percent by the end of 1984, but by that time Japanese producers and U.S. minimills were already achieving rates of 90 percent.

Other Processes. The quantitative information that is available on other aspects of steel technology and innovation tends to reinforce the impression that the integrated segment of the U.S. steel industry has fallen behind the standards achieved elsewhere in the world, especially in Japan. Thus, at the

Table 9: Continuous-Casting Adoption Rates, 1969–1984
(in percent of steel production)

Year	*U.S.*	*EC*	*Japan*	*Brazil*	*South Korea*
1969	2.9	3.3	4.0	0.1	na
1971	4.8	4.8	11.2	0.8	na
1973	6.8	9.4	20.7	3.2	na
1975	9.1	16.5	31.1	5.7	19.7
1977	11.8	25.4	40.8	17.4	32.0
1979	16.9	30.9	52.0	27.6	30.4
1981	20.3	45.1	70.7	36.6	44.3
1983	31.2	60.4	86.3	44.4	56.6
1984	39.6	65.4	89.1	41.3	60.6

Sources: International Iron and Steel Institute, *Steel, Statistical Yearbook,* 1978 and 1982; IISI, *World Steel in Figures,* 1985.

"hot stage," front end of steelmaking (i.e., the coking and blast-furnace stage) many installations in the United States suffer from old age, suboptimal economies of scale, and obsolescent technology. There are only 6 blast furnaces of minimum-efficient size in this country, compared with 19 in the European Community and 39 in Japan. The new bell-less top system, which was also developed in Europe, is just beginning to be applied in the U.S. (see Table 10), and American smelting practice has fallen behind in the use of high pressures and high temperatures. As a result, fuel-consumption rates are considerably higher in this country than in Europe and Japan.

Much the same is true of U.S. rolling mills. Rolling technology has undergone substantial progress in the 1960s and 1970s, with respect to speed of operation, gauge control, and the improvement of surface quality. A considerable portion of the rolling equipment operated by the integrated domestic steel companies is often unable to meet the increasingly exacting standards of quality and tolerances demanded by American steel consumers. This is all the more surprising, in view of the enormous sums that the large U.S. producers have invested in the construction of new rolling mills and in the modernization of old ones during the last twenty-five years.

The Problem of Organic Technological Progress

Technological progressiveness is an organic rather than a piecemeal process. It is not enough simply to add a modern continuous caster to an antiquated open-hearth furnace or to install a new BOF in a plant that is poorly located with respect to raw material sources or markets. Efficiency, in the best-practice sense, requires a coordinated approach to modernization.

Some of the defects afflicting many of the integrated American steel companies can be traced to the manner in which they were created: independent firms were combined into a few large empires by multiple, often helter-skelter, mergers. Unfortunately, the absence of the sharp wind of aggressive competition made it unnecessary for those empires to apply rigorous standards of evaluation to the many plants they inherited or acquired.[72] The adverse effects of the long noncompetitive era (a management attitude of cautiousness toward future market opportunities, and an aloofness toward innovations developed abroad) had not yet begun to take its toll.

After the treaty that formed a common European coal and steel market was signed in 1951, and after the Japanese launched their first "greenfield" (i.e., brand new) steel plant in 1952, American steel producers—after a long debate and much procrastination—finally embarked upon a major expansion program. But they seemed to take little notice of the growing foreign competition, that is, the new technologies and new concepts of plant design that were already clearly discernible in the early 1950s. Enormous amounts were spent by U.S. firms on the piecemeal expansion of many poorly located and poorly laid out plants. Some of the older steelworks were so hemmed in by hills, rivers, or urban growth that large-scale installations had to be custom-

Table 10: A Comparison of Technology and Performance (for 1984, unless indicated otherwise)

Blast Furnaces	*U.S.*	*EC*	*Japan*	*Canada*	*Brazil*	*S. Korea*
Bell-less systems (best practice: 100%)	12%	46%	23%	51%	37%	20%
Fuel Rate, 1980 (best practice: .460–.480)	.596	.538	.466	.546	.506	na
Steel Melting						
BOF	57.1%	74.3%	72.3%	73.0%	69.7%	70.5%
Electric Furnace	33.9%	25.7%	27.7%	27.0%	25.9%	29.5%
Obsolete (OH)	9.0%	—	—	—	4.4%	—
Continuous Casting (best practice: 90%)	39.6%	65.4%	89.1%	38.5%	41.3%	60.6%
Yield Estimates						
(Finished steel per net ton of raw steel, adjusted for product mix and imported slabs and billets)	78%	78%	88%	78%	79%	82%
Energy Use, 1978, per net ton finished steel, in mill. Btu's	29.98	24.9	20.4	24.8	25.6	na
Scrap ratios, 1978 (the greater the use of scrap, the less should be the energy use)	51.5%	43.8%	31.9%	47.4%	42.2%	na
Labor Productivity						
Man-Hours per net ton of finished steel (incl. both white- and blue-collar employees as well as contract workers)	8.0	8.9	7.8	8.2	18.0	11.0

Sources: International Iron and Steel Institute (IISI), *World Steel in Figures,* 1985; IISI, *Statistical Yearbook Steel,* 1982; Bureau of Labor Statistics, U.S. Department of Commerce, "International Comparisons of Productivity and Labor Costs in the Steel Industry, Jan. 1984; *Siderurgia Latinoamericana* (May, 1985), pp. 22–32; information obtained from the Brazilian Steel Institute, and the Paul Wurth Co., Luxembourg.

designed and shoe-horned into existing sites. The patterns of location of raw-material resources had changed to such an extent since the time when many of the plants were first constructed that iron ore had to be hauled over much longer distances, and frequently had to be reloaded several times when changing from one mode of transportation to another. The transfer of materials and semifinished products inside the plants often followed zigzag patterns because new units could not be installed in line with complementary production stages. As a result of differences in efficient size, work speed, and quality standards, the grafting of new equipment onto an old process rarely made for a good fit.[73]

When the expansion ended in the late 1950s, the U.S. industry found itself in a worse competitive position than at the beginning of the decade. Meltshops that had just been constructed were already outmoded; only modest improvements in labor productivity had been achieved; and most of the large multiplant steel companies had missed the opportunity for tidying up their empires.

The acid test came in the mid-1960s, when the industry's hold on the American steel market was seriously challenged by less conservative, less disciplined competitors. Japanese and, in some degree, European companies were fielding new capacity that had been specifically designed for all-out competition in the world market.

In the 1960s and 1970s, the U.S. steel industry launched expensive modernization programs. Measured in 1978 dollars, investments on steel-related operations amounted to more than $40 billion in the 1960–1978 period.[74] However, at the end of this period the industry found itself with integrated-mill capacity that was still generally older and less efficient than that of its chief foreign rivals. Rather than concentrating its funds on plants that held promise of being transformed into world-class operations, the industry spread available funds over too many plants, many of them of marginal efficiency. (There was, for example, too much duplicate investment in expensive installations, such as hot-strip mills.)[75] At the same time, insufficient funds were invested in modern blast-furnace technology, a mistake that eventually cost the industry dearly in higher energy use after this resource had greatly risen in price.

What is remarkable about these efforts is that, per ton of steel capacity installed or replaced, the industry had outspent its European and Japanese rivals.[76] Clearly, the lag in the industry's performance cannot be attributed to insufficient spending on plants and equipment. And, in view of the high level of investments in nonsteel operations, this lag can be blamed with even less justification on inadequate financial resources.[77] A more plausible explanation is that the costly investment effort made by the U.S. steel industry foundered on the lack of integrated, organic company planning with respect to plant structure and organization—a deficiency that continues to plague the majority of integrated steel companies in this country.

An International Comparison of Production Costs

The finding that the chief foreign competitors of the U.S. steel industry have demonstrated superior performance in the areas of technology and plant structure is corroborated by several comparisons of average costs, e.g., costs per ton of steel shipped. These costs are a function of two influences: the prices paid for inputs and the efficiency with which management and labor are able to turn inputs into products. Management and labor efficiency depend in turn on skill levels, discipline, and cooperativeness of all employees, but also on the characteristics of plant and equipment. Together, these are reflected in the rates, or intensity, with which inputs are used. Foreign costs expressed in dollars are also a function of prevailing exchange rates. After 1973, these rates began to fluctuate widely. As a result, European and Japanese costs rose sharply from 1977 to 1980, but then began to fall again, relative to American costs.

Major Input Costs. These costs comprise the chief raw materials (iron ore and coking coal), fuel oil and electricity, labor, and capital. Relatively easy access to data makes it possible to observe changes in costs over the longer term.

The United States had a clear advantage in the 1960s with respect to the delivered prices of raw materials. Coking coal prices have remained lower here than in Europe and Japan, but high wages and, to some extent, Occupational Safety and Health Administration (OSHA) regulations have caused this gap to dwindle in recent years, and it may disappear entirely before long. As to iron ore, the ability of foreign producers to shop around the globe for the cheapest and highest-grade ores is a greater advantage now than the ownership of captive mines.[78]

In 1960, hourly employment costs (wages plus fringe benefits) were $4.12 in the United States versus 54 cents in Japan. American labor cost was in part offset by a low use-rate (high productivity) of labor. Whereas the American steel industry required 17 employee hours in 1960 per ton of steel shipped, 56 hours were needed in Japan. By 1984, the hourly employment cost of the U.S. steel industry had risen to $21.30 and that of the Japanese industry had risen to $10.45. But, in the mid-1970s, largely as a result of their modern plants, the Japanese had begun to surpass their American competitors in labor productivity. Average employment costs in the more heterogeneous EC steel industry were about $10.90 in 1984; in some countries (Germany and Holland) labor productivity was approximately the same as in the U.S. industry, whereas in others (England) it was 20 percent lower.[79]

In 1983, hourly employment costs of American steel producers were 75 percent higher than the average for the American manufacturing sector. In Japan and the European Community, the differences were 44 and 15 percent, respectively.[80]

Capital costs (interest and depreciation only) in 1984 were $55 in the

Table 11: An International Comparison of Employment Costs (1960–1984)

	Hourly Employment Costs		*Hours per Net Ton of Steel Shipped*		*Unit Labor Cost*	
	(blue and white collar employees, including contract workers)					
	1960	*1984*	*1960*	*1984*	*1960*	*1984*
U.S.	$4.12	$21.30	17	8.0	$70	$170
EC	1.16	10.90	21	8.9	24	97
Japan	.54	10.45	51	7.8	28	82
Brazil	.60	2.45	na	18.0	na	44
South Korea	na	2.20	na	11.0	na	24

Sources: Bureau of Labor Statistics, unpublished data; AISI, *Annual Statistical Report,* various issues (white-collar employee differential estimated); Eurostat, *Wages and Incomes,* various issues; Ministry of Labor, Japan, *Monthly Survey of Labor Statistics;* Japanese Steelworkers Union, Tekko Roren, *Rodo Handbook,* 1984, and information obtained from the Instituto Brasileiro de Siderurgia.

United States, per ton of steel shipped; from $54 (Germany) to $80 (France and Italy) in the EC; and $77 in Japan. This difference is owing to the fact that foreign steel companies are generally more *leveraged,* i.e., financed with long-term loans rather than equity investments.[81]

The Sum of Major Input Costs. The data in Table 12 reflect primarily the costs of integrated steel producers. In the majority of countries, integrated firms account for 70 to 80 percent of total steel output. The cost of scrap,

Table 12: An International Comparison of Major Input Costs, 1984
(in dollars per net ton shipped)

	Labor	*Coal & Ore*	*Energy*	*Capital*	*Total*	*Difference from U.S. Cost*
U.S.	170	102	76	55	403	zero
EC	97	102	48	67	314	89
Japan	82	97	46	77	302	101
Brazil	44	86	50	114	296	126
South Korea	24	97	48	85	256	166

Note: Product mix of steel output, i.e., the proportion of high and low value steel products, is similar for the steel industries of the United States, the Europen Community, and Japan. The steel industries of Brazil and South Korea produce a higher proportion of less sophisticated products, which causes the differential between their cost and that of the U.S. industry to be overstated by $15 to $25 per net ton shipped.

Sources: Table 11 for labor costs; for material, energy, and capital costs see AISI, *Annual Statistical Report,* 1985, pp. 86–97; Charles A. Bradford, Merrill Lynch, *Steel Industry Quarterly,* April 1985, pp. 54–58, 87–90; and Peter Marcus and Karlis Kirsis, Paine Webber, *Major Country Carbon Steel Price/Cost Models,* Cost Monitor No. 6, November 1984, unpaged.

the chief raw material used by minimills, does not vary significantly among the industrialized countries, although it is usually higher in developing countries.

Distorted exchange rates account for some of the high costs of American steel firms. For instance, at 1980 exchange rates EC employment costs would be $178 per ton of steel shipped and Japanese costs would be $135 (rather than the $116 and $89 respectively, as shown in Table 12). But the strong dollar had only minor distorting effects on the prices of raw materials and energy because most of them are internationally negotiated in dollar terms.

Continued efforts by the integrated U.S. firms to reduce labor and energy costs (primarily by further closures of obsolete capacity and productivity-raising investments), combined with some normalization of dollar exchange rates, might well make U.S. producers competitive again in their home markets, at least vis-à-vis their traditional international rivals. However, short of government protection, they will find it difficult to compete in regions where they neglected to build efficient capacity (as in the West and the Southwest of the United States), and with new steel-producing nations, such as South Korea and Taiwan.

Product Quality, Product Availability, and Customer Service

Serving customers' needs requires not only that sellers remain cost-competitive, but that they maintain high-quality standards for their products, and make certain that they are able to meet demand in all regions of the country, and for all product types. Moreover, to compete successfully, steel producers must deliver their product on time, and they must show an interest in technical problems their customers might encounter.

In 1980, the General Accounting Office conducted a survey of over 100 American steel-buying firms, "to gain insights as to why foreign-made steel is purchased." The agency found that

> decisions to purchase foreign steel not only depend upon price considerations but also on quality, supply protection and marketing services and attitudes. In cases where consumers bought foreign steel, it was frequently because foreign mills performed better in many or all of these areas. . . . Most companies who criticized domestic steel quality pointed to Japanese steel as exemplary. The officials, however, identified high-quality steel purchased from mills in 14 other countries. As a rule, the high quality was derived from more modern plants regardless of the country in which located.[82]
>
> West Coast companies explained that some mill products not available from western steel mills are produced elsewhere in the United States; however, freight costs preclude their purchase from midwestern or eastern steel mills.[83]

Furthermore, domestic steel producers were said to be less responsive than foreign companies to customers' needs for new types of steel. In one instance, the technology capable of turning out formable, high-strength steel was originally developed by an American company, but was then perfected and produced by a Japanese steel firm.

Steel buyers also complained about undependable delivery from domestic firms. They indicated "that imported steel must generally be ordered further in advance but is delivered more consistently on time."

Finally, many buyers were critical of "the U.S. integrated producers' marketing attitudes" and their " 'take it or leave it' sales philosophy." Foreign mills were said to be more willing "to work with customers in solving problems [and] to tailor products to customer specifications or perform additional manufacturing operations at the mill before shipment." By contrast, domestic minimills were given high marks for their customer service.

Other Factors Affecting International Competition

There have been allegations that the domestic steel industry's competitive position has been adversely affected by the high level of expenditures required for environmental protection, and by direct and indirect subsidies received by foreign suppliers of steel to the American market.

The Burden of Environmental Protection. Although the integrated American steel producers have been forced to divert large investments for the purpose of cleaning up the environment, there is evidence that foreign competitors were equally burdened by such requirements.[84] One major difference is that many foreign producers were able to design antipollution measures directly into their new plants, which is generally less expensive than the retrofitting of old installations with such devices. In addition, just as in production, there are also economies of scale in environmental protection.[85] For example, the cost of fitting a single large blast furnace with antipollution equipment is less, per ton of pig iron, than similarly equipping several smaller blast furnaces. In other words, a given outlay for this purpose can be stretched further where facilities are of recent design and large scale, as in Japan.[86]

Dumping and Subsidies. Spokesmen for the domestic steel industry are wont to blame plant closures and the layoff of employees on unfair competition by foreign suppliers. They maintain that, in their home markets at least, the integrated steel companies could compete successfully "on a level playing field," i.e., if all market participants observed the rules of "fair" competition.[87]

Such complaints fail to take note of the following facts. First, since the early 1970s, the integrated mills lost more market share to aggressive domestic minimills (about 15 percent) than to imports (8 percent until 1984). Second, there has been no significant finding of unfair competition regarding the largest steel exporters to the United States, i.e., Japan, Canada, West Germany, and South Korea, which traditionally account for nearly 60 percent of all imports. These exporters possess sufficient steelmaking capacity to make up for any reduction in shipments by foreign suppliers who, without quota agreements, might be forced to withdraw from the U.S. market following the imposition of stiff antidumping and antisubsidy penalties.

Although the U.S. law is couched in arcane language, its purpose is essentially to protect domestic companies from injury by foreign producers who either practice unfair pricing methods (dumping) or receive subsidies from their governments. With respect to dumping, the law used to deal only with international price discrimination, i.e., where a foreign supplier charged a lower price in the United States (on an f.o.b. basis) than in its home market. But the law was written at a time when fixed exchange rates were the rule. Since then, fluctuating exchange rates have turned the determination of "fair" export prices into a complex issue. Thus, a sudden rise of an exporter's home currency in terms of the dollar will, *ceteris paribus,* raise its prices in the home market (in terms of dollars). The firm would then face a Hobson's choice: to expose itself to charges of "dumping" or to raise its prices in the U.S. market, and, if its competitors refuse to match the increase, price itself out of the U.S. market.

Moreover, after 1974, when Congress expanded the definition of *dumping,* foreign firms could also face dumping charges if, during a prolonged market downturn, they incurred losses and sold their products below average cost both in their domestic markets and in the United States.[88] Yet, American firms competing against these same foreign suppliers in the U.S. market were not subjected to a similar cost-plus pricing rule. The legality of selling below cost was made to depend entirely on whether the seller was of domestic or foreign origin.

With respect to subsidization, it is indisputable that all national steel industries are subject to a variety of government policies that affect their ability to compete in international markets. On one hand, some have benefited from direct government contributions to operating funds, loans at reduced interest rates, loan guarantees, area-redevelopment programs, manpower training programs, investment tax incentives, buy-domestic rules, and import quotas. On the other, they have been injured by price controls, the overvaluation of their country's currency, interference with decisions on investments and on plant location, denials of permission to close obsolete plants or to lay off redundant employees, as well as by the uncertain enforcement of environmental regulations. Obviously, it is only the *net* effect of both the favorable and the burdensome interventions that can modify an industry's comparative advantage and hence distort its competitive position vis-à-vis other national steel industries.[89]

According to some observers, the American antisubsidy (countervailing duty) law was aimed only at those subsidies that help foreign competitors to gain an advantage over American firms, and not those that left the allocation of resources unchanged. However, the Department of Commerce interpreted a congressional limitation on "offsets" (for negative effects of intervention) to mean that penalties must reflect *all* the assistance received by a foreign supplier and not merely its trade-distorting effects.

Moreover, in recent cases, the International Trade Commission has found subsidization to violate American law even where the subsidy margin was clearly negligible and where it clearly did not distort the competitive advantage of foreign over domestic producers. In *Certain Carbon-Steel Products from Belgium, France, Italy, the United Kingdom, and the Federal Republic of Germany,* for example, the evidence with respect to hot-rolled carbon-steel plate showed that:

1. Belgium benefited from a weighted average subsidy margin well under 2 percent, but undersold domestic producers by 5 to 15 percent.
2. Germany enjoyed a subsidy evaluated by Commerce at 0.000, but undersold domestic products by 10 to 15 percent.

With respect to carbon-steel structural shapes, the evidence showed that:

1. Luxembourg benefited from a subsidy ranging in size from 0.5 to 1.5 percent, with a weighted average of about 0.5, but undersold domestic producers by generally wide margins, ranging from 2 to 38 percent.
2. One German exporter was deemed to benefit from a subsidy of 1.131 percent, but another's was officially listed as 0.000, with a weighted average of 1981 exports to the U.S. of 0.0 percent. The margin by which these German exporters undersold their U.S. rivals ranged from 1 to 28 percent.[90]

Despite these facts, the exporters in question were found to have benefited from unlawful subsidization and were penalized. Clearly, such decisions go far beyond protection of domestic producers against trade-distorting policies by foreign governments. They constitute protection of domestic producers from foreign competition.

Historical Roots of the U.S. Steel Industry's Lagging Performance

The investment effort made by the integrated American steel companies during the last two decades was apparently not sufficient to achieve a degree of modernization comparable to that of their foreign competitors, and to fend off growing competition from the minimills. The official American Iron & Steel Institute (AISI) explanation has been that those investments were still less than what was required to stay abreast of the progress made abroad.[91]

An alternative explanation is that many of the large American steel companies suffer a congenital defect that can be traced back to their heritage and to the noncompetitive environment they had created for themselves before the arrival of imports and minimills. Born of multiple mergers, the large steel companies managed to foster a system of coordinated pricing and orderly growth. There were no unforgiving rivals to force them to remain in the forefront of organizational and technological efficiency. Circumstances were usually such that a chief executive could avoid the ordeal of closing down a poorly located or inefficient steel plant and, with few exceptions, to feel comfortable with the endless "rounding out" of existing plants. Hardly any new mills were constructed and, until recently, few were shut down. As a result, there was also little rejuvenation of the infrastructure that had to serve as the base for subsequent capacity expansions. In short, the majority of the large steel companies were plagued by a managerial rigidity that precluded a fundamental reassessment of corporate plans when the external environment was undergoing rapid change. When that change occurred in the 1960s, the industry found itself "with enormous capacity, much of it recently built and very little of it embodying new technology."[92] A history of concentrated market structure, nonaggressive conduct, and technological lethargy had left the industry vulnerable to attack by new rivals.

V. PUBLIC POLICY

Given the lackluster performance of the integrated steel producers, what direction should public policy take? Specifically, should antitrust enforcement be relaxed in order to facilitate mergers and encourage a "rationalization" movement among the integrated giants? Should the government—in the national interest—maintain its import-restraint policy in order to assure the survival of an integrated steel sector in the American economy? We now turn to a brief examination of these issues.

Antitrust Policy

In examining the application of the antitrust laws to the steel industry from 1890 to the present, it is fair to say that the law has had a minor impact on the structure and the conduct of the industry. The Sherman Act did not block the formation of U.S. Steel and its achievement of market dominance in 1901; it did not result in the dissolution of U.S. Steel in 1920; it did not block the emergence of a tight oligopoly through a series of mergers among the erstwhile "independents"; it did not interdict the recent mega-mergers between LTV and Youngstown or LTV/Youngstown and Republic;[93] and it did not prevent oligopolistic coordination among the leading firms of the industry, either under the conspiratorial basing-point system or other mechanisms designed to ensure collective action among ostensible competitors. The outstanding antitrust success in the steel industry was prevention of the proposed merger between Bethlehem (then the industry's second largest firm) with Youngstown Sheet and Tube (then the industry's sixth largest firm) in the mid-1950s. The net result of this action was that Bethlehem decided to build a modern greenfield plant at Burns Harbor, Indiana, in order to compete more effectively in the Chicago market. In other words, the law forced Bethlehem to expand by "building" rather than by "buying"; to expand without substantially lessening competition in an already overly concentrated industry. Incidentally, the law "forced" the corporation to build a plant that even today still ranks as the most modern and efficient steel-producing unit in the Bethlehem empire. One can only speculate whether a tougher antitrust stance, especially toward acquisitions and mergers, would not have helped the industry avoid some of its current difficulties in trying to remain internationally competitive, and thus obviated its dependence on government protection.

Import Policy

The major stimulus to competition in steel has come not from antitrust but from import competition and, to some extent, from the appearance of the minimills. Not surprisingly, therefore, the major public policy battles, at least since 1960, have revolved around the industry's efforts to obtain protection from import competition. These efforts consisted of political lobbying and intensive trade litigation. As a rule, the industry argued that it needed import restraints because unfairly traded (dumped and subsidized) imports had deprived it of an opportunity to modernize as rapidly as its foreign rivals. Such restraints were to provide the breathing space for the industry to raise its efficiency and regain its former cost competitiveness. The idea was simple: limit imports in order to permit the industry to raise prices, so that it can earn higher profits, and so that it has more investment funds to put into new, modern facilities, which will enable it to stand on its own feet and compete effectively with best-practice firms around the world. Critics of the industry argued that the high costs and technological backwardness of the large domestic steel firms were not attributable to a lack of funds, but to poor investment decisions and the diversion of funds into nonsteel activities; that much of the imported steel was neither dumped nor subsidized; and that protection of steel would place a heavy burden on American steel-using industries.

Nevertheless, with strong political support from the United Steelworkers Union, the industry prevailed. Since the late 1960s, successive administrations have granted it protection by means of import quotas, increased tariffs on specific products, and minimum import prices. If one had to summarize the effect of these measures on the American economy, what conclusions would one have to draw?

The Impact of Trade Restrictions on the Economy. As already mentioned, the cost burden on the economy of such protectionist measures as the VRA and the first TPM is significant. According to Robert Crandall, both interventions "have yielded remarkably similar results. Import prices have been raised substantially with most of the gain going to exporters." Estimates of the annual cost burden of the VRA range from $386 million to $1 billion.[94] For the year 1978 alone, the total cost of the TPM to consumers has been put at $1.1 billion.[95] The burden increased significantly by 1981 (the last full TPM year), when changing currency relations created a rapidly widening gap between trigger prices and world-market prices for steel.

The Reagan quota system will probably not have a noticeable effect on domestic steel prices until dealers have had a chance to reduce the inventories that were built up in 1984 in anticipation of trade restrictions. Nevertheless, the eventual cost of these quotas to the American economy is likely to be substantial, and in all likelihood larger than that of the TPM. Even before the latest trade intervention became effective, domestic steel prices exceeded world-market prices by about 20 percent. The rising strength of the dollar, a VRA concluded with the European Community in October 1982, voluntary export restrictions by Japanese steel exporters, and a number of unfavorable antidumping and antisubsidy decisions against Third World and East European steel producers had already insulated the U.S. market from some of the rigors of international competition. The Reagan quotas will only serve to increase the degree of insulation.

Trade restrictions in steel are particularly harmful to "downstream" manufacturing, i.e., industries for which steel is a major input.[96] (For the wire-drawing industry, the cost of steel amounts to 60 to 70 percent of total production costs; for heavy-equipment makers, it is about 25 percent.) A significant rise in steel prices—the usual consequence of quota restrictions—will force some of these firms to abandon certain product lines to foreign suppliers, or to relocate their businesses to countries where steel is available at lower cost. Ultimately, the decline in steel imports resulting from the restrictions will largely be offset by rising imports of steel-containing goods. Thus, the steel-trade balance of the United States will improve whereas the balance of the "indirect steel trade" will deteriorate.

The Effect of Trade Restrictions on the Domestic Steel Industry. The basic policy dilemma is that import restraints may give an industry the larger profits to finance investment in new facilities, but at the same time will remove the competitive pressure that would *compel* the industry to make such investments. Import restraints are essentially a price-support program for the domestic industry and, like any such program, *permits,* but does not *compel,* the industry to do what it should do to assure its competitive viability and survival. Price supports seldom achieve the objectives that were originally proclaimed to justify them. As J. Paul McGrath, the Chief of the Antitrust Division, told a Congressional Committee in 1984:

> Despite the existence of import restraints during most of the 1970s, integrated steel producers did very little to reduce their costs, to improve their product mix and to modernize and consolidate their facilities. It has only been with the competitive pressures of the marketplace during the last two or three years that integrated steel producers began to consider truly significant changes in their operations.[97]

He advised Congress that to "remove those pressures now would be to ensure a return of the policies of the past that are largely responsible for many of the problems that currently face the industry."

Furthermore, it is doubtful that the Reagan quota will lead to increased employment of steelworkers. As the Congressional Budget Office recognized in a report published in 1984, quotas raise domestic prices which, in turn, result in diminished consumption. Moreover, the trade-off between direct and indirect steel imports will eventually lead to a contraction of demand for steel and, hence, of demand for steelworkers.

Conclusion

Our analysis of the U.S. steel industry has, we believe, illustrated the beneficial effects of competition on industrial performance. It has also documented the high cost of the erstwhile oligopoly structure and of oligopolistic behavior, not only to the national economy but to the industry itself. It would be prudent, therefore, to make competition the lodestar of public policy regarding the steel industry. Once competition is abandoned or seriously crippled—and this is the necessary consequence of import restrictions and large-scale intraindustry mergers—a surrogate for the competitive process will have to be devised. Some new regulatory device will have to be invented to assure efficient performance and to induce technological progressiveness. Such a *deus ex machina* is not yet on the drawing boards.

NOTES

1. H. R. Seager and C. A. Gulick, *Trusts and Corporation Problems* (New York: Harper, 1929), p. 216. This book is an excellent source on the early history of U.S. Steel.

2. Ida M. Tarbell, *The Life of Elbert H. Gary* (New York: Appleton, 1930), p. 205.

3. *Fortune,* **13:**157(March 1936).

4. International Trade Commission (ITC), *Carbon Steel Wire Rod from Argentina and Spain,* Publication 1598 (Nov. 1984), pp. A5–A6; General Accounting Office, *Report by the Comptroller General, New Strategy Required for Aiding Distressed Steel Industry* (Jan. 8, 1981), Chap. 3 (hereunder, GAO Steel Report).

5. ITC, *Transportation Costs of U.S. Imports,* Publication 1375 (April 1983), pp. 6, 43; and information obtained by the authors from Conrail and from the Santa Fe Railroad Company.

6. Apparent consumption (or apparent supply) is composed of domestic shipments plus imports minus exports. It does not take into account the often sizable changes that occur from one year to the next in inventories held by steel mills and steel-using companies.

7. The Economist Intelligence Unit, Special Report 128, *The World Steel Industry—Structure and Prospects in the 1980s,* London, 1982, pp. 15–17.

8. Ibid., pp. 18–23.

9. Ibid., p. 17; Office of Technology Assessment (OTA), *Technology and Steel Industry Competitiveness* (June 1980), pp. 156–179 (hereunder, OTA Steel Report); Charles A. Bradford, Merrill Lynch, *Steel Industry Quarterly* (June 1984), pp. 11–12 (aluminum vs. steel); *Metal Bulletin* (Jan. 25, 1985), p. 23 (on plastics vs. steel), and Feb. 12, 1985 (reinforced concrete vs. steel).

10. U.S. Department of Commerce, *The Structure of Steel Markets in the United States* (unpublished study, 1979).

11. American Iron and Steel Institute (AISI), *The Making of Steel* (undated).

12. A. Cockerill, *The Steel Industry* (Cambridge, Mass.: Cambridge U.P., 1974), Chap. 5.

13. Jack Robert Miller, "Steel Minimills," *Scientific American* (May 1984), pp. 33–39; OTA Steel Report, op. cit., pp. 251–252.

14. OTA Steel Report, op. cit., pp. 257–262.

15. AISI, *Steel Import News* (Jan. 31, 1985).

16. Estimated from AISI, *Annual Statistical Report,* 1983, p. 8; Charles A. Bradford, *Steel Industry Quarterly* (Jan. 1985), pp. 19, 85–90; and Institute for Iron and Steel Studies (IISS), *Commentary* (Jan. 1983), *pass.*

17. Federal Trade Commission, *The United States Steel Industry and Its International Rivals* (Washington, D. C., 1977), p. 158 (hereunder, FTC Steel Study).

18. For a history of the early merger movement in the steel industry, see U.S. Congress, House, *Hearings Before the Committee on Small Business, Steel Acquisitions, Mergers, and Expansion of 12 Major Companies, 1900–1950,* 81st Cong., 2d sess., 1950.

19. This ordering pertains to the capacity of these companies. In terms of output, Jones & Laughlin was in third position but Republic only in the fifth position in 1983 (after National and Inland). For a description of these mergers, see William T. Hogan, *The 1970s: Critical Years for Steel* (Lexington, Mass., 1972), pp. 23–25, and 28–32; *Steel in the United States: Restructuring to Compete* (Lexington, Mass.), pp. 59–65, 70–72.

20. J. Innace, "Reshaping Domestic Steel," *33 Metal Producing* (Nov. 1983), pp. 47–52; George McManus, "LTV-Republic Merger Heralds Major Changes for Steel Industry," *Iron Age* (Oct. 21, 1983), pp. 56–59.

21. Charles A. Bradford, *Steel Industry Quarterly,* Merrill Lynch (Sept. 1983), pp. 2–3; "The Recovery is Over Already for Steel," *Business Week* (Feb. 25, 1985), pp. 50–56.

22. *U.S. Steel News* (July 1982), pp. 18–23; *News from U.S. Steel* (Jan. 17, 1984).

23. "Making Money and History at Weirton," *Business Week* (Nov. 12, 1984), p. 46; Hogan, op. cit.(1984), pp. 51–54; *Metal Bulletin* (Feb. 8, 1985), p. 27.

24. Hogan, op. cit.(1984), pp. 56–57, 139; *The Wall Street Journal,* Jan. 8, 1985, p. 5.

25. According to Kenneth Iverson, president of NUCOR, one of the most successful minimill companies in the United States, "to put up a new, integrated facility costs about $1,000 a ton of annual capacity. We've never put one up for more than $100 a ton." The *Forbes* article (Dec. 11, 1978, p. 115), which quoted Iverson, pointed out that the key to NUCOR's profitability was its high labor productivity resulting from its reliance on nonunion labor and, hence, the avoidance of union-imposed work rules.

26. Donald F. Barnett and Louis Schorsch, *Steel—Upheaval in a Basic Industry* (Cambridge, Mass.: Ballinger, 1983), pp. 86–96; Jack Robert Miller, op. cit., pp. 37–38; *The Wall Street Journal,* Jan. 12, 1981, p. 1.

27. *Metal Bulletin Monthly* (March 1984), pp. 47–49 (updated by the authors).

28. Scott Laufenschlager, "Iverson Sees Thin Slabs Boon to Minimills," *American Metal Market* (Dec. 11, 1984), p. 1.

29. U.S. Department of Commerce, op. cit., p. 2.

30. AISI, *Annual Statistical Report,* 1968 and 1982.

31. ITC, *Certain Carbon Steel Products from Belgium, the Federal Republic of Germany, France, Italy, Luxembourg, the Netherlands, and the United Kingdom,* Publication 1064 (May 1980), pp. A-81, A-96, A-111, A-124, and A-138.

32. GAO Steel Report, Chap. 3, pp. 4-11.

33. Peter Marcus, *Carbon Steel Price Track,* Paine Webber. Jan. 27, 1984, p. 2; *Metal Bulletin* (May 9, 1984), p. 29.

34. Institute for Iron and Steel Studies (IISS), *Commentary* (Jan. 1983), pp. 3–5; Metal Bulletin, *Iron and Steel Works for the World,* 8th ed. (London: 1983), pp. 573–666. For differences in the scale of major equipment (blast furnaces, meltshops, and several types of rolling mills), see Barnett and Schorsch, op. cit., pp. 160–166; and Jonathan Aylen, "Plant Size and Efficiency in the Steel Industry: An International Comparison," *National Institute Economic Review* (May 1982), pp. 65–76.

35. According to Carl Kaysen and Donald F. Turner, the links between certain lines of conduct and certain structural features of the market are so strong that a sharp separation between them is artificial. Thus, oligopolistic price leadership "may be classified as 'conduct' or viewed simply as a correlate of the structural features of small numbers and closely similar products." See Carl Kaysen and Donald F. Turner, *Antitrust Policy* (Cambridge, Mass.: Harvard U. P., 1959), p. 60. Another author actually includes certain behavioral characteristics, such as hindrance to access and coercion, in the description of market structure. See Corwin D. Edwards, *Maintaining Competition* (New York: McGraw-Hill, 1949), pp. 9–10.

36. Council of Economic Advisors, *Report to the President on Steel Prices* (Washington, D.C.: U.S. Government Printing Office, April 1965), pp. 8–9.

37. U.S. Congress, Senate, Subcommittee on Antitrust and Monopoly, *Administered Prices in Steel,* S. Report no. 1387, 85th Cong., 2nd sess., 1985, p. 129. Again, it should be noted that those prices subject to more intense competition or buyer pressures increased less than others, but the composite index for all steel products clearly rose.

38. See, for example, Hearings before the Committee on Finance, United States Senate, *Import Quotas Legislation,* 89th Cong., 1st sess., October 20, 1967, pp. 818–978.

39. ITC, *Carbon and Certain Steel Products,* Publication 1553 (July 1984), vol. 1, p. 109.

40. *Ibid.,* p. 110.

41. Council on Wage and Price Stability, *A Study in Steel Prices* (July 1975), pp. 9–10 (emphasis supplied).

42. FTC Steel Study, pp. 168, 240, 524.

43. Kent Jones, *Impasse and Crisis in Steel Trade Policy* (London: Trade Policy Research Center, 1983), p. 9.

44. Cited in Comptroller General of the United States, *Economic and Foreign Policy Effects of Voluntary Restraint Agreements on Textiles and Steel,* Report B-179342 (Wash., D.C., 1974) p. 23.

45. See testimony by Walter Adams in ITC, Stainless Steel and Alloy Tool Steel, Investigation No. TA-203-3 (Wash., D.C., Sept. 1977) p. 11 (mimeo).

46. Ibid., pp. 11–12.

47. Kent Jones, op. cit., Chap. 4; Richard Carbaugh, "A Trigger to Limit Dumping," *Business Economics* (Jan. 1982), pp. 42–46.

48. In the first year of the TPM's operation, the government raised trigger prices by 10.6 percent. Steel buyers, however, reported that the prices they had to pay were actually 15 percent higher because, as *The Wall Street Journal* noted, "last fall's widespread discounting has evaporated."

49. AISI, *Annual Statistical Report,* 1978, 1979, and 1980; Joel B. Dirlam and Hans Mueller, "Import Restraints and Reindustrialization: The Cast of the U.S. Steel Industry," *Journal of International Law* **14:**427–428 (Summer 1982).

50. *American Metal Market* (Oct. 8, 1981), p. 1; *Metal Bulletin* (Oct. 13, 1981), p. 35.

51. *Federal Register,* vol. 45, no. 76, (April 17, 1980), pp. 26109–26115; ITC, op. cit., (May 1980), passim.

52. Peter Marcus, *Carbon Steel Price Track,* Paine Webber (Oct. 31, 1983), pp. 2, 7; (May 25, 1984), p. 2.

53. *Metal Bulletin* (Dec. 21, 1984), p. 23; *33 Metal Producing* (Jan. 1985), p. 9. By December 1984, the following quotas had been negotiated (expressed as a percentage of total U.S. Steel consumption): Japan 5.8 percent, South Korea 1.9 percent, Brazil 0.8 percent, Spain 0.67 percent, South Africa 0.42 percent, Mexico 0.3 percent, and Australia 0.18 percent. The European Community had been allowed a quota of 5.4 percent in October 1982, and Canada, which did not participate in any negotiations, was conceded 3.0 percent. The total of all these quotas, 18.47 percent, was already very close to the 18.5 limit that the Reagan Administration originally established (somewhat in excess of 20 percent if separately negotiated quotas for semi-finished steel products, especially slabs, are included). However, as of March, many of the smaller steel-exporting nations—among them Argentina, Venezuela, and Taiwan, as well as Scandinavian, East European, North African, and Arab countries—had still not concluded any quota agreements with the U.S. Trade Representative. Perhaps to placate American steel producers, the Trade Representative indicated that the quotas would have to include not only "steel-mill products" but also some fabricated steel products.

54. Klaus Stegemann, *Price Competition and Output Adjustment in the European Steel Market* (Tubingen, Germany: Mohr, 1977), Chap. 3; Hans Mueller, "The Prohibition of Price Discrimination in the European Coal and Steel Community: The Rules and Their Enforcement," *Antitrust Bulletin* (July–August 1966), pp. 738–765; *Metal Bulletin* (Aug. 1, 1978), p. 33.

55. Kent Jones, op. cit., pp. 32–33, and Chap. 5; Commission of the European Community, "A Steel Policy for Europe," *European File* (March 1979).

56. *Official Journal of the European Community,* No. L-180 (July 1, 1981), and L-184 (July 4, 1981); *Metal Bulletin* (June 11, 1982), p. 9.

57. Kiyoshi Kawahito, "Relative Profitability of the U.S. and Japanese Steel Industries," *The Columbia Journal of World Business* (Fall 1984), pp. 13–17; Peter Marcus, *Carbon Steel Price Track,* Paine Webber (Jan. 27), p. 8; *Peter Marcus, The Steel Strategist,* Paine Webber (Dec. 1984), pp. 19–20; *Metal Bulletin* (July 27, 1984), p. 19.

58. *Metal Bulletin* (July 27, 1984), p. 19.

59. *U.S. Steel News* (Dec. 1980), p. 15.

60. Luc Kiers, *The American Steel Industry: Problems, Challenges, Perspectives* (Boulder, Colo.: Westview, 1980), p. 67 (citing Fred Langenberg, former president of the AISI). See also "The Myth of the Steel Technology Gap," *U.S. Steel News* (Dec. 1980), pp. 14–17.

61. Remarks by Kenneth Iverson, president of NUCOR Corporation, to the Association of Steel Distributors in Portland, Oregon, reprinted in *American Metal Market* (Dec. 13, 1978).

62. Steel industries producing for a very small market and having access to low-cost energy or labor might be expected to pursue a different direction in their innovative efforts than that of the United States. For example, steel firms in developing nations, where capital costs are relatively much higher than in advanced countries, sometimes buy equipment discarded by firms as obsolete, in Japan or the United States. Steel firms in countries with cheap natural gas or electricity are likely to adopt different steelmaking methods than those that are able to draw on relatively low-cost coking coal.

63. OTA Steel Report, p. 275.

64. Ibid., pp. 277–278. For the Japanese data, the OTA cited the Agency for Industrial Science and Technology, and for the U.S. data, the National Science Foundation.

65. Calculated from OECD data presented in Jonathan Aylen, "Innovation in the British Steel Industry," in Keith Pavitt, ed., *Technical Innovation and British Economic Performance* (London: Macmillan, 1980), p. 206.

66. See, for example, David R. Dilley and David L. McBride, "Oxygen Steelmaking, Fact vs. Folklore," *Iron and Steel Engineer* (Oct. 1967) pp. 3–24.

67. It was only by 1957, or five years after the Austrian converter began operating, that the process was modified sufficiently for use of the high-phosphorous Lorraine and Luxembourg iron ores, which were to some extent also exported to Belgium and Germany. See Walter Adams and Joel B. Dirlam, "Big Steel, Invention, and Innovation," *Quarterly Journal of Economics* (May 1966) pp. 170–71; and Louis Lister, *Europe's Coal and Steel Community* (New York: Twentieth Century Fund, 1960), pp. 53–54.

68. Henry W. Broude, *Steel Decisions and the National Economy* (New Haven, Conn.: Yale U.P., 1963), p. 165.

69. Even defenders of the American steel giants concede that it was the cold winds of competition rather than the sheltered atmosphere of protectionism that ultimately forced the domestic majors (belatedly) to follow the path of technological progress. Thus, Alan McAdams admits that by "1962 it appears that the costs to United States producers for not innovating were significantly raised by actual and threatened competition from both domestic and foreign oxygen steelmakers." Competition, not protection, broke down the industry's habitual lethargy and resistance to change. See Alan McAdams, "Big Steel, Invention, and Innovation: Rejoinder," *Quarterly Journal of Economics,* **81:**473 (Aug. 1967). For a more recent analysis, see Sharon Oster, "The Diffusion of Innovation among Steel Firms," *The Bell Journal of Economics* (Spring 1982), pp. 45–56; and Leonard Lynn, "New Data on the Diffusion of the Basic Oxygen Furnace in the U.S. and Japan," *Journal of Industrial Economics* (Dec. 1981), pp. 123–135.

70. *Fortune,* **74:**135(Oct. 1966).

71. "Continuous Casting," *Iron and Steel Engineer,* **33:**52(May 1968); OTA Steel Report, p. 290. Technical executives were acutely aware of this uneven progress in the adoption of the continuous-casting method. For example, in 1966, William P. Hill, engineering executive of National Steel, observed:

> There were eight companies operating continuous-casting machines before 1965 handling small tonnage. The outstanding thing was all of these companies were small, independent companies. They are competing by continous casting their entire tonnage. These companies are demanding the low cost, low operating, and fixed cost in order to produce small tonnage. It is a little embarassing to some of us when we see this.

(Quoted in R. Easton and J. W. Donaldson, "Continuous Casting," *Iron and Steel Engineer,* **43:**80(Oct. 1966).

See also D. Ault, "The Continued Deterioration of the Competitive Ability of the U.S. Steel Industry: The Development of Continuous Casting," *Western Economic Journal,* **11**:89–97(Mar. 1973).

72. The lack of such standards on the part of the largest American steel producer, U.S. Steel, was confirmed by a management firm as early as the 1930s. The findings of this firm, as summarized by the late Professor George W. Stocking, pictured the corporation as "a big sprawling inert giant, whose production operations were inadequately coordinated; suffering from a lack of a long-run planning agency; relying on an antiquated system of cost accounting; with an inadequate knowledge of the costs or of the relative profitability of the many thousands of items it sold; with production and cost standards generally below those considered everyday practice in other industries; with inadequate knowledge of its domestic markets and no clear appreciation of its opportunities in foreign markets; with less efficient production facilities than its rivals had; slow in introducing new processes and new products."

Specifically, according to the engineers, U.S. Steel "was slow in introducing the continuous-rolling mill; slow in getting into production of cold-rolled steel products; slow in recognizing the potentials of the wire business; slow to adopt the heat-treating process for the production of sheets; slow in getting into stainless steel products; slow in producing cold-rolled sheets; slow in tinplate developments; slow in utilizing waste gases; slow in utilizing low-cost water transportation because of its consideration for the railroads; in short, slow to grasp the remarkable business opportunities that a dynamic America offered it. The corporation was apparently a follower, not a leader, in industrial efficiency." (George W. Stocking, testifying before the *Subcommittee on Study of Monopoly Power:* 81st Cong., 2nd sess., 1950, Part 4A, p. 967).

73. In the words of a steel consultant at Arthur D. Little [in many steel mills] "you've got a mishmash—100-year-old stuff fitted into two-year-old stuff." *The Wall Street Journal,* April 4, 1983, p. 11.

In 1979 Norman Robins, research manager of Inland Steel, gave the following report after a visit to Japan ["Steel Industry Research and Technology," *American Steel Industry Economics Journal* (AISI) (April 1979) pp. 49–58]:

> I was in the Fukuyama plant last year, and one of the most impressive things about it was the lack of truck and train traffic. Inland's plant, on the other hand, was begun in 1902 and undoubtedly was not conceived at that point in time to grow to the size that it has since become. Presently, there are blast furnaces in two locations and a new one being built in a third location, steelmaking at four different locations and a great deal of material handling and transportation required to move steel through the finishing facilities.

74. According to D. F. Barnett, formerly an economist with the American Iron and Steel Institute, the entire industry invested $45 billion (measured in constant 1978 dollars), exclusive of expenditures on nonsteel operations and pollution-control expenditures for the 1960–78 period. (See OTA Steel Report, p. 123.)

We adjusted this figure to include 1979 investments as well as pollution-control expenditures (also in 1978 dollars) and obtained an estimate for total steel-related investments of $52 billion. From this amount we subtracted $6 billion for the construction of about 12 million tons of minimill capacity, from 1960 to 1979, and an equal amount for investments by the specialty-steel sector, leaving $40 billion for the blast-furnace based (or "integrated") sector.

75. Hogan, op. cit., 1972, p.34; and 1983, p. 126; *Iron Age* (Oct. 1978), p. MP-21.

76. According to our estimates, the sustainable U.S. raw-steel capacity (which can be maintained for at least one year) was 99 million tons in 1950, 143 million tons in 1965, and 150 million tons in 1979. Because from 1965 to 1979 at least 12 million tons of new minimill capacity was installed, integrated capacity actually declined by several million tons (as the result of plant closures).

After reducing reported investment figures for the U.S. steel industry by 40 percent (in order to correct for nonsteel investments and for higher construction costs relative to Europe and Japan) the following estimates were obtained for amounts invested, per ton of capacity added or replaced, from 1965 to 1979 (in constant 1978 dollars): U.S., $525; EC ("The Six"), $353; Japan, $414. For the 1950–1979 period, the estimates were U.S., $448, EC (6), $387; Japan, $337. The amount of replaced capacity was estimated in each case on the basis of a 25-year life span for plant and equipment. (See Hans Mueller, *Protection and Competition in the U.S. Steel Market: A Study of Managerial Decision Making in Transition,* Monograph No. 30, Business and Economic Research Center, Middle Tennessee State Univ., Murfreesboro, TN, 1984, pp. 133–147.)

77. GAO Steel Report, pp. 2–17.

78. Charles A. Bradford, *Steel Industry Quarterly,* Merrill Lynch (Jan. 1985), p. 46; Peter Marcus, *The Steel Strategist,* Paine Webber (Dec. 1984), pp. 30–31.

79. U.S. Department of Labor, Bureau of Labor Statistics, unpublished data; Charles Bradford, *Steel Industry Quarterly,* Merrill Lynch (Jan. 1985), pp. 12–13.

80. Japan Ministry of Labor, *Monthly Survey of Labor Statistics* (Nov. 1983), pp. 16, 20; U.S. Department of Labor, Bureau of Labor Statistics (unpublished data).

81. Peter Marcus, *The Steel Strategist* (Dec. 1984), Table 6.

82. GAO Steel Report, Chap. 3, pp. 1 and 6–11.

83. The U.S. company is Inland Steel, the Japanese firm is Nippon Kokan, and the product is dual-phase steel. (GAO Steel Report, pp. 3–8.)

84. Tabulations of antipollution expenditures are only available for the United States and Japan. Sporadic information indicates that expenditures by European Community steel producers are similar to those of U.S. firms. According to the Organization for Economic Cooperation and Development *(Emission-Control Costs in the Iron and Steel Industry,* 1977, p. 133), the German steel industry's antipollution expenditures absorbed about 14 percent of total investments in 1972 and 1973.

Environmental standards seem to be more rigorous in Japan than in the United States and Europe. (IISI meeting in Tokyo, May 19, 1980; the data were reproduced in Hans Mueller, op. cit., 1984, p. 121.)

In the past decade, the antipollution expenditures of the U.S. and Japanese steel industries were as follows (in million dollars and percent of total investments):

	1983	*1982*	*1981*	*1980*	*1979*	*1978*	*1977*	*1976*	*1971–75*
U.S.	$140	262	489	511	651	458	535	489	1,116
Japan	215	286	201	180	321	304	444	920	2,111
U.S. (%)	4.3	6.2	14.5	15.4	19.3	18.0	19.7	15.0	12.0
Japan (%)	5.6	6.3	5.4	6.3	11.5	15.2	20.6	18.4	15.7

Sources: AISI, *Annual Statistical Report,* various Japan years; Tekko Tokei Yoran, various years; Tenko Nenkan, 1983, p. 128.

85. Arthur D. Little, *Steel and the Environment, A Cost-Impact Analysis* (Boston, 1975), Part 4, pp. 26–34.

86. The Japanese have also made a greater effort to combine environmental efforts with measures designed to save energy, for instance, by recycling BOF gases for generating electricity rather than flaring them, as is done by the integrated American producers.

87. David M. Roderick, "Interview with David Roderick: Embattled Steel," *Challenge* (May–June, 1978), p. 22; and "The Need for Steel Import Quotas," Statement before the Subcommittee on Trade, Committee on Ways and Means, U.S. House of Representatives, April 26, 1984. See also, AISI, *Steel at the Crossroads: The American Steel Industry in the 1980s* (Jan. 1980), pp. 1 and 7.

88. According to Robert Crandall of the Brookings Institution, "all world trade will come to a halt," if the cost-plus pricing rules were to be uniformly enforced during recessions. *American Metal Market,* (Dec. 8, 1978), p. 1. Elsewhere, Crandall observed: "It would be obvious folly to say that Chrysler has been engaging in unfair competition because it has been losing money. It would be similarly absurd to say that steel producers in Germany, Japan, or France have been behaving unfairly because they find the world steel market so weak that they have to offer prices below their full unit costs in order to make a sale." *Regulation* (July–Aug. 1980) p. 21.

See also, Kiyoshi Kawahito, "Steel and the Anti-Dumping Statutes," *Journal of World Trade Law* (March–April, 1982), pp. 152–164; and Kawahito, "Japanese Steel in the American Market: Conflict and Causes," *The World Economy* (Sept. 1981), pp. 229–250.

89. Federal Trade Commission, "Comment in the Matter of Certain Steel Products from Belgium, Brazil, the Federal Republic of Germany, France, Italy, Luxembourg, the Netherlands, Romania, South Africa, Spain, and the United Kingdom," (mimeograph, 1982), p. 8; Hans Mueller and Hans van der Ven, "Perils in the Brussels–Washington Steel Pact of 1982," *The World Economy* (Nov. 1982), p. 265.

90. ITC, op. cit., Publication 1064 (1980). For an economic analysis concerning the effects of subsidies on prices, see John Mutti, "Subsidized Production, World Steel Trade, and Countervailing Duties," *Southern Economic Journal* (Jan. 1984), pp. 871–880.

91. AISI, *Steel at the Crossroads: The American Industry in the 1980s* (Washington, D.C.: AISI), pp. 2-e and Chap. 6.

92. Laurence Fenninger, Bethlehem Steel Corporation, paper presented at the AISI Economic Seminar, Chicago, Aug. 25, 1966, p. 6.

93. The Department of Justice did, however, block an intended acquisition of the National Steel Corporation by the U.S. Steel Corporation in 1984.

94. Stephen P. Magee, "The Welfare Effects of Restrictions on U.S. Trade," *Brookings Papers* (1972) pp. 645–701 [$386 million]; Comptroller General of the United States, "Economic and Foreign Policy Effects of Voluntary Restraint Agreements on Textiles and Steel," Report B-179342 at 23(1974) [up to $1 billion].

95. Robert W. Crandall, Statement before the Commerce, Consumer, and Monetary Affairs Subcommittee, Committee on Government Operations, U.S. House of Representatives, Dec. 20, 1979, p. 10. For a detailed discussion of this cost, see Robert W. Crandall, *Steel in Recurrent Crisis* (Washington, D.C.: Brookings, 1981), Chap. 7.

96. R. Crandall, op. cit., (1981), pp. 148–150.

97. Statement before the Subcommittee on Trade, House Committee on Ways and Means, "Problems Facing the U.S. Steel Industry and H.R. 5081, the 'Fair Trade in Steel Act of 1984,' " May 2, 1984.

SUGGESTED READINGS

BOOKS AND PAMPHLETS

Acs, Z. J., *The Changing Structure of the U.S. Economy: Lessons from the Steel Industry*. New York: Praeger, 1984.

Barnett, D. F. and L. Schorsch, *Steel—Upheaval in a Basic Industry*. Cambridge, Mass.: Ballinger Publishing Co., 1983.

Cockerill, A. *The Steel Industry: International Comparisons of Industrial Structure and Performance*. New York: Cambridge University Press, 1974.

Crandall, R. W. *The United States Steel Industry in Recurrent Crisis: Policy Options in a Competitive World*. Washington, D.C.: Brookings Institution, 1981.

Friden, L. *Instability in the International Steel Market: A Study of Import and Export Fluctuation*. Stockholm, Sweden: Beckmans, 1972.

Harris, A. W. *U.S. Trade Problems in Steel—Japan, West Germany, & Italy*. New York: Praeger Pubs., 1983.

Hogan, W. T. *Economic History of the Iron and Steel Industry in the United States*. 5 vols. Lexington, Mass.: D.C. Heath Co., 1971.

———*The 1970's: Critical Years for Steel*. Lexington, Mass: D.C. Heath Co., 1972.

———*World Steel in the 1980s—A Case of Survival*. Lexington, Mass.: D.C. Heath Co., 1983.

———*Steel in the United States: Restructuring to Compete*. Lexington, Mass.: D.C. Heath Co., 1984.

Jones, K. *Impasse and Crisis in Steel Trade Policy*. London: Trade Policy Research Center, 1983.

Kawahito, K. *The Japanese Steel Industry: With an Analysis of the U.S. Steel Import Problem*. New York: Praeger Pubs., 1972.

Kiers, L. *The American Steel Industry: Problems, Challenges, Perspectives*. Boulder, Colo.: Westview Press, 1980.

Mueller, H. and K. Kawahito. *Steel Industry Economics: A Comparative Analysis of Structure, Conduct and Performance*. New York: Japan Steel Information Center, 1978.

Rieben, H. *La Bataille de l'Acier*. Lausanne: Center de Recherches Européennes, 1977.

Stegemann, K. *Price Competition and Output Adjustment in the European Steel Market, 1954–75*. Tübingen, Germany: J.C. Mohr, 1977.

GOVERNMENT PUBLICATIONS

Congressional Budget Office. *The Effects of Import Quotas on the Steel Industry*. Washington, D.C., July 1984.

Council of Economic Advisors. *Report to the President on Steel Prices*. Washington, D.C.: U.S. Government Printing Office, April 1965.

Council on Wage and Price Stability, Staff Report. *A Study of Steel Prices*. Washington, D.C.: U.S. Government Printing Office, July 1975.

———*Report to the President on Prices and Costs in the United States Steel Industry*. Washington, D.C.: U.S. Government Printing Office, October 1977.

Federal Trade Commission. *Staff Report on the United States Steel Industry and Its International Rivals: Trends and Factors Determining International Competitiveness*. Washington, D.C.: U.S. Government Printing Office, November 1977.

General Accounting Office. *Report to the Congress of the United States by the Comptroller General: New Strategy Required for Aiding Distressed U.S. Steel Industry*. Washington, D.C.: U.S. Government Printing Office, January 1981.

United Nations. Industrial Development Organization. *Technological Profiles on the Iron and Steel Industry,* New York, 1978.
U.S. Congress. Office of Technology Assessment. *Technology and Steel Industry Competitiveness.* Washington, D.C.: U.S. Government Printing Office, June 1980.

JOURNAL AND MAGAZINE ARTICLES

Adams, W. "Import Restraints and Industrial Performance: The Dilemma of Protectionism." *Michigan Yearbook of International Legal Studies,* **1**:34–52 (1979).
———and J. B. Dirlam. "Steel Imports and Vertical Oligopoly Power." *American Economic Review,* **54**:626 (Sep. 1964).
———and J. B. Dirlam. "Big Steel, Invention, and Innovation." *Quarterly Journal of Economics,* **80**:167 (May 1966).
———and J. B. Dirlam. "The Trade Laws and Their Enforcement by the International Trade Commission," in *Recent Issues and Initiatives in U.S. Trade Policy,* R. E. Baldwin (ed.). National Bureau of Economic Research, 1984.
Ault, D. "The Continued Deterioration of the Competitive Ability of the U.S. Steel Industry: The Development of Continuous Casting." *Western Economic Journal,* **11**:89–97 (March 1973).
Aylen, J. "Innovation in the British Steel Industry," in *Technical Innovation and British Performance,* K. Pavitt (ed.). London: Macmillan & Company Ltd., 1980.
Bradford. C. A., *Japanese Steel Industry: A Comparison With Its United States Counterpart.* Merrill Lynch, Pierce, Fenner and Smith, Inc., Securities Research Division, 1977.
Bright, S. L., and J. A. McKinney. "The Economics of the Steel Trigger Price Mechanism." *Business Economics,* **16**:40–46 (July 1984).
Carbaugh, R. "A Trigger Limit to Dumping." *Business Economics,* **12**:42–46 (Jan. 1982).
Crandall, R. W. "Competition and 'Dumping' in the U.S. Steel Market." *Challenge,* **21**:13–20 (July–Aug. 1978).
———"Steel Imports—Dumping or Competition." *Regulation,* **4**:17–24(July–Aug. 1980).
Dielmann, H. J. "U.S. Response to Foreign Steel: Returning to Trigger Prices." *Columbia Journal of World Business,* **16**:32–42(Fall 1981).
Dirlam, J. B., and H. Mueller. "Protectionism and Steel: The Case of the U.S. Steel Industry." *Journal of International Law,* **14**:419–445(Summer 1982).
Ignatius, D. "Who Killed the Steel Industry?" *The Washington Monthly,* **11**:9–19(March 1979).
Imai, K. "Iron and Steel: Industrial Organization." *Japanese Economics Studies,* **3**:3–67(Winter 1974–75).
Kawahito, K. "Relative Profitability of the U.S. and Japanese Steel Industries." *The Columbia Journal of World Business,* **19**:13–17(Fall 1984).
Lynn, L. "New Data on the Diffusion of the Basic Oxygen Furnace in the U.S. and Japan." *Journal of Industrial Economics,* **30**:123–135(Dec. 1981).
Mancke, R. B. "Iron Ore and Steel: A Case Study of the Causes and Consequences of Vertical Integration." *Journal of Industrial Economics,* **20**:220–29 (July 1972).
Marks, M. "Remedies to Unfair Trade: American Action Against Steel Imports." *World Economy,* **1**:223–237 (Jan. 1978).
Martin, D. D. "The Davignon Plan: Whither Competition Policy in the ECSC?" *Antitrust Bulletin,* **24**:837–887(Winter 1979).
McAdams, A. K. "Big Steel, Invention and Innovation, Reconsidered." *Quarterly Journal of Economics,* **81**:457–474(Aug. 1967).
McCormack, G. P., "The Reinstated Steel Trigger Price Mechanism: Reinforced Barrier to Import Competition." *Fordham International Law Journal,* **4**:289–339(1980–1981).

Mueller, H., and K. Kawahito. "An Examination of Recent Allegations of Japanese Steel Dumping." *Journal of Economics,* **5**:77–81(1979).

———and H. van der Ven. "Perils in the Brussels-Washington Steel Pact of 1982." *World Economy,* **5**:259–278(Nov. 1982).

Mutti, J. "Subsidized Production, World Steel Trade and Countervailing Duties." *Southern Economic Journal,* **51**:871–880(Jan. 1984).

Parsons, D., and E. Ray. "The United States Steel Consolidation: The Creation of Market Control." *Journal of Law and Economics,* **18**:181–218 (April 1975).

Rippe, R. D. "Wages, Prices, and Imports in the American Steel Industry." *Review of Economics and Statistics,* **52**:34–46(Feb. 1970).

Rosegger, G. "Trigger Prices Under Floating Exchange Rates: A Dubious Experiment in Trade Policy." *Journal of International Law,* **14**:493–507(Summer 1982).

Rowley, C. K., and G. K. Yarrow. "Property Rights, Regulation and Public Enterprise: The Case of the British Steel Industry 1957–1975." *International Review of Law and Economics,* **1**: 63–96(1981).

Scheuermann, "The Political Economy of Steel Imports: The Crisis in Law." *Economic Forum,* **13**:25–47(Winter 1982–1983).

Stevens, R. G. "Measuring the Imaginary: The Employment Effect of Imported Steel Revisited." *Industrial Labor Relations Review,* **29**:97–106(Oct. 1975).

Walter, I. "Protection of Industries in Trouble—The Case of Iron and Steel." *World Economy,* **2**:155–187(May 1979).

4

The Automobile Industry

Walter Adams and James W. Brock

I. INTRODUCTION

The automobile industry and its products have an important impact on American life and culture. Sizable quantities of plastics, steel, machine tools, lead, and rubber are used in automobile production, and one out of six jobs in the U.S. are directly or indirectly related to the manufacture, distribution, repair, or use of motor vehicles. Motor vehicles have provided Americans with a personal mobility that was unimaginable 80 years ago. But motor vehicles also are involved in 50,000 traffic-accident deaths a year, are an important source of air pollution in urban areas, and account for a large fraction of the country's petroleum consumption. The automobile has been an important influence on the shape and structure of metropolitan areas.[1]

It is this sizable impact on American society that has led to an increased public-policy focus by government on the automobile industry, regarding safety, air-pollutant emissions, fuel consumption and, more recently, the ability of the industry to withstand foreign competition.

The history of the industry can be divided into the following fairly distinct periods: the era of the independents; the emergence of the Ford Motor Company as the dominant producer; the shift of dominance to General Motors and progressive industry concentration; and, finally, the era of foreign competition.

The automobile, as we know it today, first took shape in the 1890s. Gasoline engines, steam engines, and electric motors were all tried as sources of propulsion. By 1900, more than 4,000 cars had been sold.

During the next decade, production expanded rapidly, and by 1910, 187,000 automobiles were sold annually. Entry into the industry was comparatively easy. The manufacturer of automobiles was largely an assembler of parts. The new entrepreneur needed only to design a vehicle, announce to the public its imminent appearance, and contract with machine shops and carriage makers for the engines, wheels, bodies, and other components. The assembled autos could be sold for cash to dealers, or directly to customers.

The capital requirements for a new company were not steep. Prices varied widely (from $650 up), and both entry and exit rates were high.

The next decade marked the emergence of the Ford Motor Company as the dominant producer. Henry Ford's goal was to provide an inexpensive car that would reach a large market. Standardization, specialization, and mass production, he felt, were the keys to lowering manufacturing costs, and constant price reduction the key to tapping additional layers of demand. "Every time I reduce the charge for our car by one dollar, I get a thousand new buyers," Ford said. His strategy seemed simple enough: to take lower profits on each vehicle, and thereby achieve larger volume. According to his biographer, successive "price reductions meant new enlargements of the market, and acceleration of mass production's larger economies, and greater aggregate profits. The company's firm grasp of this principle . . . was its unique element of strength, just as failure to grasp it had been one of the weaknesses of rival car makers. As profits per car had gone down and down, net earnings had gone up and up."[2] Not surprisingly, by 1921, Ford's Model T alone (which remained largely unchanged for 19 years) had more than 50 percent of the market.

The 1920s marked a shift of preeminence from Ford to General Motors. The latter's success was built on a two-pronged strategy. First, contrary to Ford's emphasis on a single model, GM decided on a broad range of products that would blanket all market segments. Its motto was "a car for *every* purse and purpose." Second, again contrary to Ford's strategy, GM decided to modify its cars each year, with a combination of engineering advances, convenience improvements, and styling changes. GM felt that annual model changes, despite the sacrifice of cost savings, would stimulate replacement demand and increase sales—enough to compensate for the higher costs. GM's strategy succeeded and catapulted the company into industry leadership, which it did not relinquish from 1931 on.

In the new era, the groundwork was also laid for the concentration that is the hallmark of today's auto industry. Figure 1 depicts the successive acquisitions and mergers that have produced the triopoly that dominates domestic auto production in the United States.

A final observation: Starting in the mid-1950s, successive waves of imports have challenged the domestic oligopoly. By the mid-1970s, imports had captured more than 25 percent of the U.S. market and triggered repeated efforts by the Big Three—in collaboration with the U.A.W.—to obtain government protection from foreign competition. Today, the question of foreign competition is perhaps the prime public-policy issue in this industry.

II. INDUSTRY STRUCTURE

The most important structural features of the U.S. automobile industry will be discussed under four headings: (1) buyer demand and the nature of the product; (2) the number of competing sellers and their relative size (con-

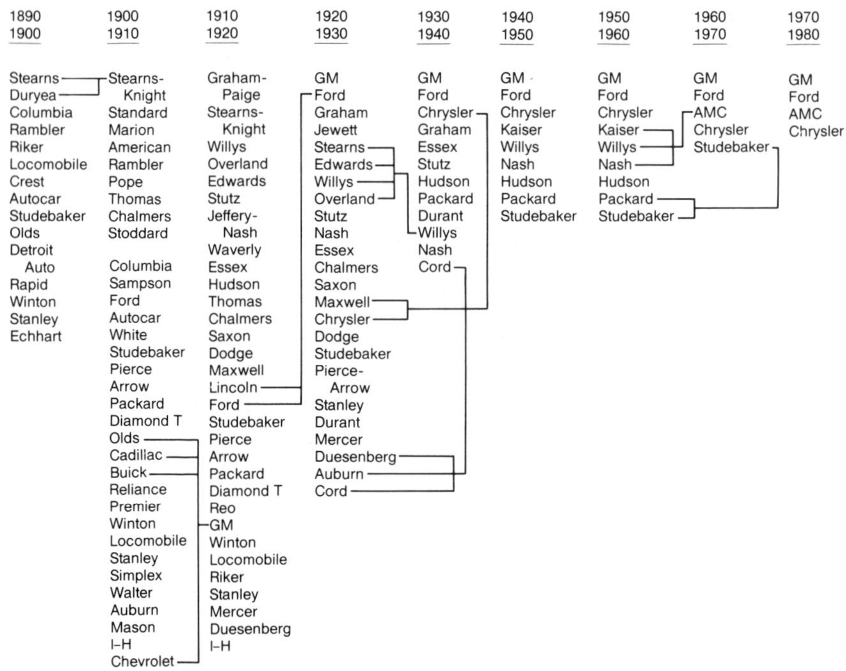

FIGURE 1. *Historical evolution of auto industry structure. Source:* U.S. Congress, House, Subcommittee on Economic Stabilization, Committee on Banking, Finance and Urban Affairs, *The Chrysler Corporation Financial Situation, Hearings,* part 1A, 96th Cong., 1st sess., 1979, p. 474.

centration); (3) the extent of economies of scale; and (4) barriers to the entry of new competitors.

Demand and the Nature of the Product

The automobile is an expensive, technically complex, durable good. During its useful life, it provides a variety of transportation services. For some, the automobile's role is limited solely to this utilitarian purpose. For others, an automobile also projects an image—that of power, prestige, personality, and/or wealth. Its physical appearance is susceptible to seemingly unlimited combinations and permutations of features. For these reasons, then, the demand for new cars is a multifaceted phenomenon, one that is influenced by a variety of factors.

First, the buyer side of the market comprises two numerically and behaviorally disparate groups: private individuals (who purchase a new car for their personal use, and who collectively account for two-thirds of new-car registrations); and fleet buyers, including rental-car agencies, business firms, and local, state, and federal governments. In contrast to fleet buyers, private consumers typically have neither the resources nor the capability to acquire extensive technical acumen, and for this reason are more susceptible to advertising claims and brand loyalty.[3] Moreover, private owners expect repair services and parts to be available from dealers, gasoline stations, and repair shops.

Second, the demand for new cars in the United States is predominantly a *replacement* demand. The acquisition of a new car can therefore be deferred simply by keeping an old car longer, and this characteristic of demand (in conjunction with the absolute expense involved) injects a considerable element of volatility into the market.

Third, an important determinant of demand, of course, is price. Although exact estimates of the price elasticity of the aggregate demand for all new cars vary, they tend to cluster in the range −1.0 to −1.5.[4] Thus, the demand for *all new cars considered together* is slightly price-elastic. Yet, as economic theory would predict, the demand for a *particular make of car* is much more price-sensitive because of the general availability of close substitutes. This prediction has been confirmed by Frank Irvine; he found the demand for particular car makes to be extremely sensitive to price, with price elasticities ranging from − 4.59 (Chrysler, Plymouth Fury) to − 16.99 (GM, Pontiac Catalina), and averaging − 10.42 for the makes covered. These findings are significant, for they suggest that price could be a potentially strong basis for competition.

Fourth, because an automobile involves a large outlay of funds (after a house, a new car is the second most expensive item that most families buy), the demand for new cars is significantly influenced by macroeconomic conditions, including employment, income, and interest rates. Researchers have found new-car demand to be highly sensitive to income, with the income elasticity of demand estimated to lie in the 1.0 to 4.0 range.[5] Additionally, the majority of new automobiles (two-thirds) are bought on credit, and the availability and cost of financing, including interest rates, importantly affect the price paid by consumers and, hence, the demand for new cars.[6]

Fifth, a long-term shift in the composition of new-car demand has taken place, in favor of small cars and away from large cars. Although the precise proportions vary from year to year, Table 1 shows that the share of small cars (compacts and subcompacts) rose, from 25 percent of all new-car sales in 1967 to 52.4 percent by 1984; over the same period, the share of large cars declined from 51 to 21.4 percent. This shift to smaller, more fuel-efficient cars doubtless is owing in part to the shortages and skyrocketing price of gasoline in the 1970s. Yet, a closer inspection of Table 1 shows that the trend in demand toward small cars began well before the first oil embargo in 1973. Gasoline supplies and prices may have amplified this trend, but other factors have been exerting a long-run influence, such as smaller family size and the growing prevalence of multiple-car households, whose second car is generally smaller and more utilitarian in purpose.[7]

Table 1: New-Car Sales by Auto-Size Segment[1]

Year	*Small*[2]	*Intermediate*	*Large*[3]
1967	25.0%	23.6%	51.0%
1968	25.0	26.2	48.5
1969	27.2	25.1	47.3
1970	36.3	23.8	40.0
1971	38.5	20.3	40.5
1972	38.1	21.7	39.5
1973	42.6	23.0	33.6
1974	48.4	24.2	26.3
1975	52.7	24.1	21.9
1976	38.4	27.3	23.1
1977	48.3	26.9	24.0
1978	48.0	26.8	23.9
1979	54.0	24.2	20.8
1980	62.2	20.6	17.2
1981	51.3	28.1	20.6
1982	49.4	28.1	22.5
1983	43.6	33.1	23.4
1984	52.4	26.2	21.4

[1]Excludes sales of imports.
[2]Compact, subcompact, and minicompact.
[3]Full-size plus luxury.
Sources: J. A. Hunker, *Structural Change in the U.S. Automobile Industry* (Lexington, Mass.: Heath, 1983), p. 18; *Ward's Automotive Yearbook*, 1982, 1984, and 1985.

Industry Concentration

Automobile manufacturing is one of the most structurally concentrated of all major American industries. Domestic *production* is dominated by a tight triopoly, but domestic *sales* are less concentrated, because of growing import competition in recent years. In analyzing the industry's structure, therefore, it is imperative to understand (1) the pattern of domestic concentration; (2) the role of import competition; and (3) the trend toward cross-national ownership positions and joint ventures.

1. Concentration of Domestic Production. The manufacture of automobiles in the United States is, as Table 2 shows, a stable and tight triopoly. From a high of 88 firms in the early 1920s, the number of domestic producers dwindled to six. Since the 1950s, the three largest firms have dominated more than 90 percent of the domestic industry; in 1984, their collective share stood at 94.7 percent.

General Motors is, and has long been, the largest firm in the industry, accounting for 50–60 percent of all automobiles manufactured in the U.S. in recent years, and producing more cars than the remainder of the domestic

Table 2: U.S. Auto Production: Market Shares and Concentration, 1913–1984

Year	General Motors	Ford	Chrysler	Other U.S. Producers	Share of Top Three
1913	12.2%	39.5%	(a)	48.3%	
1923	20.2	46.0	1.9%	31.9	68.1%
1929	32.3	31.3	8.2	28.2	71.8
1933	41.4	20.7	25.4	12.5	87.5
1937	41.8	21.4	25.4	11.4	88.6
1946–1955	45.2	24.4	19.4	11.0	89.0
1956–1965	50.9	28.6	14.3	6.2	93.8
1966–1975	54.1	27.1	16.5	2.3	97.7
1976–1983	59.6	24.2	12.6	3.5	96.4
1984	55.9	22.8	16.1	5.3	94.7

[a]Chrysler not yet in existence.
Sources: L. J. White, *The Automobile Industry Since 1945* (Cambridge, Mass.: Harvard U. P. 1971), Appendix; L. J. White, "The Automobile Industry," in W. Adams (ed.), *The Structure of American Industry*, 6th ed. (New York: Macmillan, 1982), p. 147; *Ward's Automotive Yearbook*, 1985.

industry combined. (Its share of intermediate- and large-car production approaches 80 percent.) Ford is the second largest producer, with a 23 percent share of domestic production; and the third largest firm, Chrysler, accounts for approximately 16 percent. The remainder of the field includes AMC, in which the French Renault firm owns a 46 percent equity interest, and two established foreign producers, Volkswagen and Honda, which inaugurated U.S. production in 1978 and 1982, respectively.[8] Other Japanese producers have announced plans to follow suit. Nevertheless, the Big Three collectively dominate the industry. Moreover, they are extensively integrated—horizontally, vertically, and internationally.

They are horizontally integrated, not only in terms of high relative shares of domestic production, but also because they assemble automobiles in more than 30 plants dispersed throughout the nation. General Motors assembles automobiles in 19 plants, Ford in 10, and Chrysler in 4.

The Big Three are also integrated vertically, and produce a substantial proportion of the parts and components from which automobiles are assembled. One analyst estimates that GM produces 85 to 90 percent of the parts and components it uses; in-house parts-production at Ford ranges from 50 to 60 percent; and Chrysler's internal supply of parts and components fluctuates sharply, varying from 0 to 100 percent in any particular year.[9] The remainder of the Big Three's parts needs are met by approximately 40,000 domestic supplier firms and, increasingly, by foreign ("offshore") sourcing. (Offshore sourcing differs by make and manufacturer, and industry experts estimate that foreign sourcing accounts for approximately 5 percent of domestic producers' parts-consumption.)[10]

GM, Ford, and Chrysler are also extensively integrated internationally.

For example, Ford is the largest auto company in Australia; the second largest in Canada and England; and the third largest manufacturer of autos in Brazil, Mexico, Spain, and West Germany. Similarly, GM and (to a lesser degree) Chrysler rank among the largest automobile producers in a number of countries around the world.[11]

Finally, the Big Three recently have made a number of large conglomerate acquisitions: General Motors expended $2.5 billion to acquire Electronic Data Systems (EDS) in 1984, and outbid Ford in 1985 to acquire Hughes Aircraft Company (a leading defense contractor) for $5 billion. Chrysler, too, has joined the acquisition game, disclosing plans to acquire Gulfstream Aerospace ($636.5 million) and credit operations of E.F. Hutton ($125 million). Meanwhile, Ford has disclosed plans to buy the First Nationwide Financial Corporation (the nation's 9th largest savings and loan association) for $493 million.

2. Foreign Competition. Foreign-produced imports have steadily increased in competitive importance over recent decades. As shown in Table 3, the import share of U.S. auto sales has grown from 0.4 percent in the immediate post-World War II decade, to 21.2 percent in the years 1976–1983. In 1984, imports accounted for 23.4 percent of new-car sales in the U.S. The relative share of imports is somewhat overstated because of "captive" imports, brought into the U.S. by American producers (such as Chrysler's importation of Mitsubishi small cars); these captive imports totalled 764,000 cars in 1982.[12] Nevertheless, foreign producers have been a critical, if not the only, source of effective competition for the U.S. oligopoly in the post-World War II period. Japanese companies provide the single most important source of competition; collectively, they accounted for approximately

Table 3: Import Share of New-Car Sales

Year	*Import Share*
1946–1955	.4%
1956–1965	5.9
1966–1975	13.1
1976–1983	21.2
1984	23.4

Note: For 1966–1983, domestic producers' shares include captive imports. For 1983, imported Hondas and Volkswagens are included in imports.
Sources: L. J. White, *The Automobile Industry Since 1945* (Cambridge, Mass.: Harvard U. P., 1971), Appendix; *Ward's Automotive Yearbook*, 1985.

20 percent of new-car sales in the U.S., and 70 percent of all U.S. imports, in 1983.[13]

The competitive success of foreign producers in the U.S. market has been especially significant in a structural sense, for it has served as the most important force for deconcentration of the domestic industry in the postwar period. Thus, although GM, Ford, and Chrysler together accounted for 94.7 percent of U.S. *production* in 1983, import competition reduced their collective share of *sales* by 23 percentage points, i.e., to 71.6 percent on the U.S. market. In particular, foreign competitors have focused on the small-car segment of the market, and it is in this field that their deconcentrating impact has been greatest: imports account for more than 50 percent of subcompact sales in the U.S., but have a negligible share of the intermediate- and large-car segments.[14]

However, the salutary structural impact of imports in lessening concentration in the U.S. market has been abated since 1981 by "voluntary" import quotas, which limited the number of Japanese automobiles permitted to enter the U.S. We shall return to this point in our discussion of public policy.

*3. **Cross-Ownership and Joint Ventures.*** Another significant feature of concentration in the industry is the recent, increasingly intricate latticework of cross-ownership positions and joint ventures between U.S. and foreign automakers. The extent and nature of this web of intercompany coordination is illustrated in Figure 2. These burgeoning cross-ownership positions and cooperative agreements—which are now becoming trilateral in nature, conjoining U.S., Japanese, and Korean producers—are structurally significant, because they extend the degree of interfirm coordination and cooperation. Consequently, they tend to aggravate concentration and constrict autonomous, independent decision making. Given the important competitive role that imports have played in lessening concentration in the U.S. market, these cross-ownerships and joint ventures between U.S. firms and their potential—or actual—foreign rivals are of particular concern.

The Question of Economies of Scale

To what extent is the observed level of concentration in U.S. automobile production the consequence of efficiencies of large-scale operation? Are the gains and efficiencies of large scale in automobile manufacturing and assembly so great as to necessitate a triopoly structure for the industry?

Drawing on interviews and visits to U.S. auto plants, a team of manufacturing engineers recently prepared estimates of economies of scale in automobile assembly, as well as in the production of principal automotive components (body units, engines, frames, transmissions), for four different car sizes. These estimates of the minimum efficient scale (i.e., the output level at which the gains from large-scale production are exhausted) are shown in Table 4. According to these estimates, minimum efficient scales of pro-

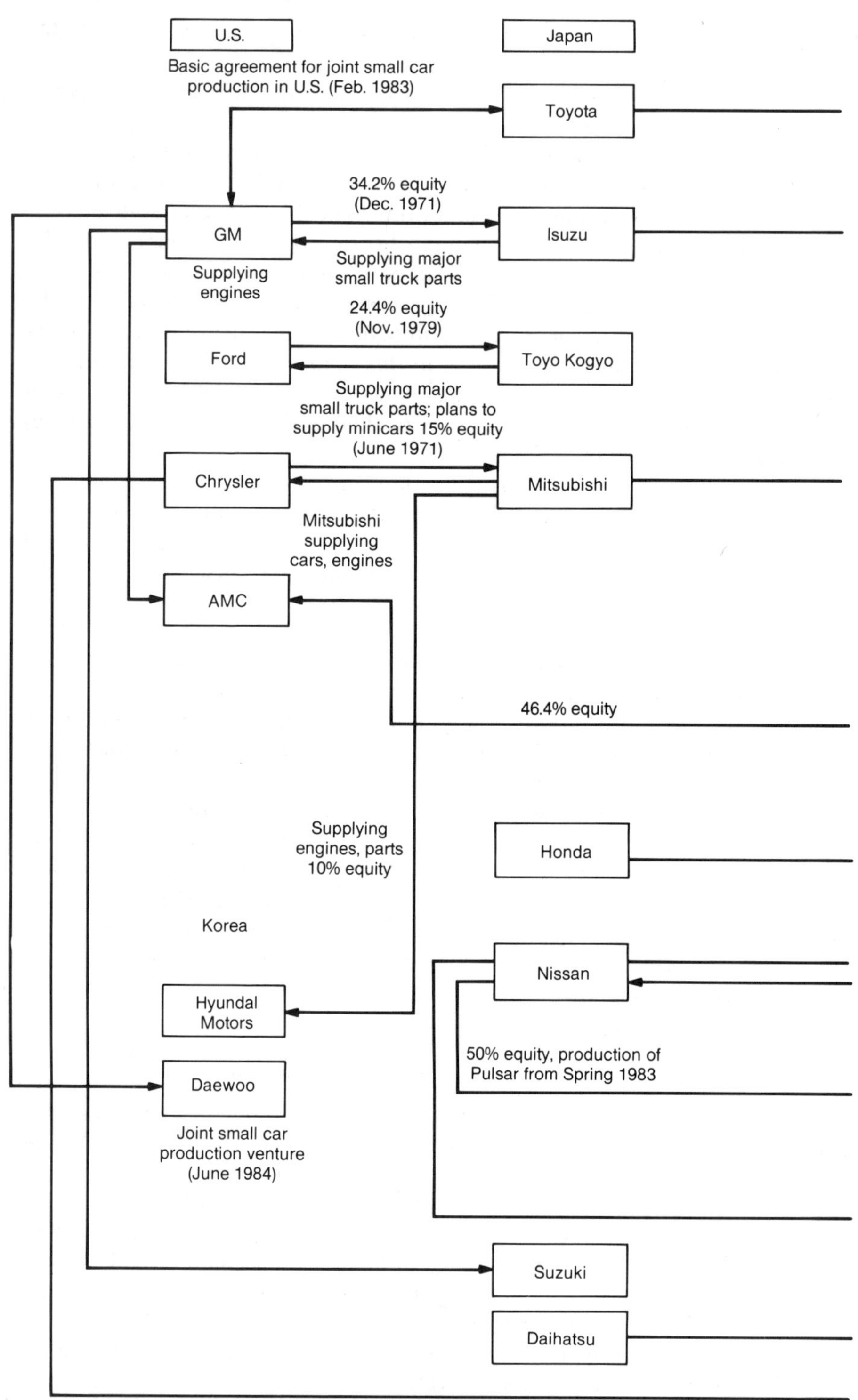

FIGURE 2. *Cooperation between World Auto Manufacturers. Sources: Ward's Automotive Yearbook*, 1984, p. 52; *The Wall Street Journal*, June 15, 1984, p. 4.

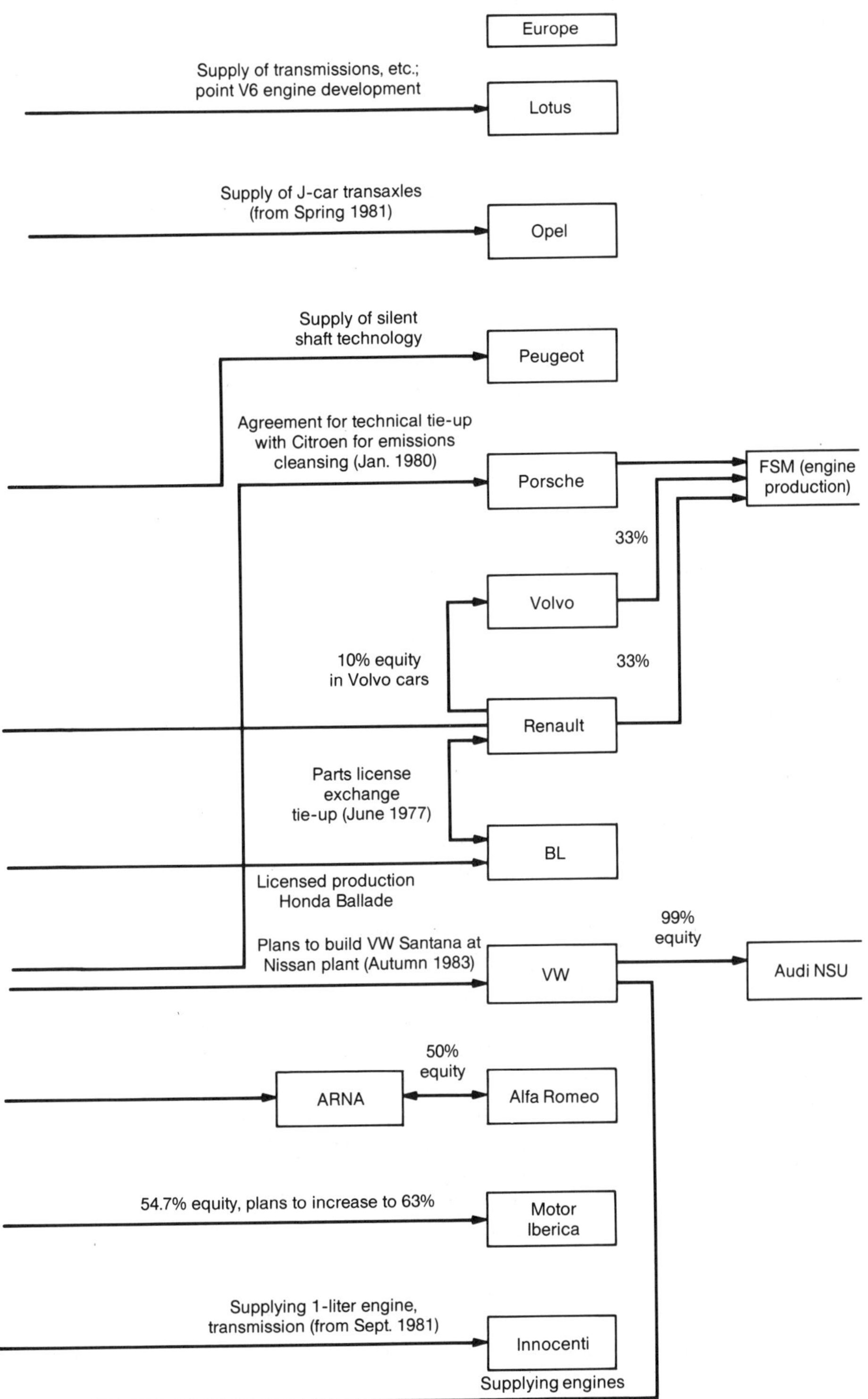

Europe
Supply of transmissions, etc.;
point V6 engine development
Lotus
Supply of J-car transaxles
(from Spring 1981)
Opel
Supply of silent
shaft technology
Peugeot
Agreement for technical tie-up
with Citroen for emissions
cleansing (Jan. 1980)
Porsche
FSM (engine
production)
33%
Volvo
10% equity
in Volvo cars
33%
Renault
Parts license
exchange
tie-up (June 1977)
BL
Licensed production
Honda Ballade
99%
equity
Plans to build VW Santana at
Nissan plant (Autumn 1983)
VW
Audi NSU
50%
equity
ARNA
Alfa Romeo
54.7% equity, plans to increase to 63%
Motor
Iberica
Supplying 1-liter engine,
transmission (from Sept. 1981)
Innocenti
Supplying engines

Table 4: Minimum Efficient Scale for Automobile Production (thousands of automobiles per year)

	Type of Automobile			
Cost Element	*Mini*	*Compact*	*Intermediate*	*Standard/Luxury*
Automotive assembly	400	300	250	200
Body unit	400	300	250	200
Engine	400	400	350	250
Frame	200	200	200	206
Transmission	317	317	317	317

Note: Assumes two-shift, five-day work-week production.
Source: E. J. Toder, *Trade Policy and the U.S. Automobile Industry* (New York: Praeger, 1978), p. 133.

duction occur at annual output levels in the 200,000–400,000 unit range, depending on the particular size of automobile and component. Though large in an absolute sense, these production levels imply that a firm with a 3–6 percent share of U.S. auto production would be big enough to benefit from all significant economies of scale, or, conversely, that the industry could conceivably support 17 to 33 efficient producers (at 1983 productions levels). Another industry expert, Lawrence J. White, suggests that the risks and vagaries of the market might require a viable firm to produce two distinct lines of automobiles, rather than one, thereby approximately doubling minimum efficient scale estimates.[15]

Actual plant output levels in the industry provide additional insight into the extent—and limits—of economies of scale in auto production. Because the Big Three firms assemble cars in *multiple* plants rather than concentrating all assembly in one or two giant plants, they appear to recognize that there are limits to the gains obtained from ever larger plant installations. An analysis of the size distribution of assembly plants operated by the Big Three reveals that they produce 60 percent of their total output in plant sizes of 200,000 units or less, and 84 percent of their total output in plants equal to, or smaller than, 300,000 units per year.[16] Thus, it would appear that optimum assembly-plant scale lies between 200,000 and 300,000 units per year—a figure quite comparable with the foregoing minimum efficient scale estimates.

There is a glaring divergence, then, between optimal *plant* scale and the size of *firms* in the industry, a difference that cannot be explained on the basis of economies of scale in production at the plant level.[17] Perhaps this divergence is owing to economies of scale in marketing (i.e., advertising, promotion, brand identification, and so on). Or perhaps it stems from a non-economic advantage of large firm size, such as an enhanced capacity to influence government decision making and public policy regarding antitrust (joint ventures), international trade (import quotas), safety (airbags), or pollution controls.

Barriers to Entry

Barriers to the entry of new competition (another important element of industry structure) are substantial in the automobile industry. Indeed, according to one economist, they are "very high and perhaps insuperable."[18] These barriers include the costs of constructing optimally sized production facilities, advertising expenses and brand loyalty, and access to dealers.

1. Capital Costs of Production Facilities. Costs to construct a new auto assembly plant, as well as plants to produce major components and parts, recently have been estimated by the Department of Transportation. According to the Department's figures, an assembly plant alone would cost more than $200 million to build. Production of major components and parts, of course, would drive capital costs significantly higher for a new entrant; the total costs to construct four basic types of facilities (engine plant, transmission plant, parts and components plant, and assembly plant) would be $1.2 to 1.4 billion.[19] For example, Volkswagen has invested more than $1 billion in its U.S. production facilities, which are limited to an assembly plant and two allied component-production plants.[20] One industry expert contends that the capital needed by a new firm entering the industry on a vertically integrated basis could reach as high as $3 billion.[21] Clearly, then, the magnitude of these costs, and the difficulty of raising such sums, are important obstacles to the entry of new competitors.

2. Advertising Expenses and Brand Loyalty A new entrant must not only produce automobiles; it must *promote* and *sell* them to consumers. This is another barrier to new competition, for two reasons. First, established automobile companies expend enormous amounts on advertising and promotion each year. In 1982, the Big Three together spent nearly a half billion dollars advertising their automobiles; General Motors alone spent in excess of $200 million.[22] With these levels of advertising by established firms, a new entrant would have to incur heavy expenses merely to inform consumers of its existence. Second, consumer loyalty and attachment to established producers in the industry is substantial.[23] If a new entrant attempted to break these bonds of buyer loyalty and to offset the sustained, heavy advertising by the Big Three, it would be forced to spend proportionately greater amounts on advertising per car than established firms.

3. Access To Dealers. Finally, in addition to producing and advertising its cars, a new entrant would have to assemble a dealer system to distribute, retail, and service its automobiles. Given the extensive dealer systems developed by the Big Three firms, this would be a difficult, costly task. The magnitude of this is evident in Table 5, which shows the number of dealers handling cars sold in the U.S. by various manufacturers. According to one

Table 5: U.S. Dealer Outlets 1983

	Number of Dealers
Big Three:	
General Motors	10,040
Ford	5,508
Chrysler	3,864
Selected Others:	
AMC/Renault	1,526
Nissan (Datsun)	1,093
Toyota	1,089
Volkswagen	942
Honda	809

Source: Ward's Automotive Yearbook, 1984.

analyst, "developing a dealer network to provide sales and service is both expensive and time-consuming and serves as a major barrier to entry into the market."[24]

Taken together, then, capital costs to construct production and assembly facilities of economical scale, advertising expenses and brand loyalty, and the expense and difficulty of building a dealer network are imposing barriers to the entry of new competition in the U.S. auto industry. As of 1985, only three firms have commenced domestic production of automobiles since the early-1950s. These "new" producers, it should be noted, are Volkswagen, Honda, and Nissan—established companies that had produced cars abroad and imported them into the U.S. for a number of years. These companies rank among the world's largest automobile producers, and among the largest industrial corporations outside the U.S.[25]

III. INDUSTRY CONDUCT

Industry conduct comprises the tactics adopted by firms in their efforts to compete, or refrain from competing, with one another. Primarily shaped by industry structure, conduct comprises two major categories—pricing behavior, and nonprice behavior.

Pricing

As economic theory would predict, the general pricing pattern in automobiles is one of oligopolistic interdependence among a few large firms. It reflects a recognition by the Big Three that their interest as a group is best served by avoiding serious price competition among themselves. *The Wall Street Journal* explains: "Auto makers can maximize profits because in the oligopolistic domestic auto industry the three major producers tend to copy each other's price moves. One auto executive notes that if one company lowered prices, the others would follow immediately . . . As a result, price cuts wouldn't increase anybody's market share, and 'everybody would be worse off,' he says."[26]

Specifically, pricing conduct in automobiles is distinctive in at least four important respects: (1) GM's role as price leader; (2) the tacitly collusive way in which domestic firms generally arrive at prices; (3) the uniformity among domestic producers' prices; and (4) the impact of foreign competition in the small-car segment of the market.

1. Price Leadership. General Motors is clearly the price leader in the industry. It initiates general rounds of price increases; it can, by refusing to follow, prevent either of its two main rivals from leading price alterations; and, finally, its price changes establish de facto price ceilings for Ford and Chrysler. An inspection of Table 6 will show that GM initiated every one of the nine rounds of general price increases that occurred during the period surveyed. GM not only initiates price changes, it controls price changes through its pricing actions or, alternatively, through its refusal to follow the lead of others. For example, GM surprised its two main rivals when, in the fall of 1981, it disclosed price increases averaging a sharp 6 percent; although Ford and Chrysler had already planned price boosts of only 4 percent to their dealers, both firms quickly fell in line with General Motors' higher prices.[27]

2. Communication, Price Signalling, and Tacit Collusion. The prices actually adopted by the Big Three appear at times to represent a tacit mutual agreement arrived at through a process of subtle communication and signalling. The machinations of the Big Three during the summer and fall of 1983, as they prepared for their 1984-model lines, provide an example of this process at work. General Motors led off by communicating its "preliminary," planned price increase of 2 percent. Chrysler followed, signalling its "tentative" consideration of a 1.4 percent price rise; and Ford communicated "expected" price increases of 2.3 percent. With all of the main players' hands, intentions, and contemplations thus exposed, GM then raised prices by an average of 2.4 percent—an increase matched shortly thereafter by Ford and Chrysler.[28]

3. Price Uniformity. Parallelism and uniformity in pricing among the Big Three is strikingly—and at times, astonishingly—close. For most of the rounds covered in Table 6, for example, price increases adopted by Ford and Chrysler were virtually identical with those disclosed by General Motors. Of course, automobiles are highly differentiated products, and for this reason it is difficult to make direct comparisons between models produced by different firms. In addition, a certain amount of price flexibility occurs at the retail level, where buyers dicker with dealers. Nonetheless, substantial price uniformity exists for comparable models offered by different manufacturers, which limits price differentials up and down the chain of manufacturing and

Table 6: Pricing by the Big Three Auto Companies

Company	*Date*	*Price Change*	*Description*
GM	5/1/78	+ 1.4%	Average across 1978 line.
Chrysler	5/8/78	+ 1.4%	"
Ford	5/10/78	+ 1.3%	"
GM	8/21/78	+ 4.1%	Average across 1979 line.
Ford	9/7/78	+ 4.4% to 6.6%	"Tentative" increase for 1979 line, varying by models.
GM	9/14/78		Prices reduced for four sporty car models.
Ford	9/20/78	+ 4.2%	Average actually adopted across 1979 line.
Chrysler	10/3/78	+ 4.2%	Average across 1979 line.
GM	12/6/78	+ 0.5%	Average across 1979 line.
Ford	12/13/78	+ 0.5%	"
Chrysler	12/15/78	+ 0.4%	"
GM	12/22/78	+ 1.7%	Average across 1979 line.
Chrysler	1/2/79	+ 1.2%	"
Ford	1/5/79	+ 1.7%	"
Chrysler	1/29/79	slight increase	Glass-belted radial tires made standard equipment.
GM	2/14/79	+ $15	Increase across 1979 line.
Ford	2/14/79	+ $15	"
Chrysler	2/28/79	+ $13	"
GM	4/2/79	+ 2.1%	Average across 1979 line.
Chrysler	4/5/79	+ 2.4%	"
Ford	4/6/79	+ 2.1%	"
GM, Ford	6/21/79		Dealers notified of average price increases of 3.5%.
GM	7/2/79	+ 0.9%	Average actually adopted across 1979 line.
Ford	7/5/79	+ 1.2%	"
Chrysler	7/6/79	+ 1.8%	"
GM	9/4/79	+ 3.6%	Average for some 1980 models; further pricing due.
GM	10/2/79	+ 4.6%	Average actually adopted across 1980 line.
Ford	10/11/79	more than 3.8%	Price changes plus changes in standard equipment.
Chrysler	10/15/79	+ 5.2%	"
GM	12/24/79	+ 1.6%	Average across 1980 line.
Ford	1/2/80	+ 1.9%	"
Chrysler	1/7/80	approx. + 2.0%	"

Sources: The Wall Street Journal, various issues, 1978–1980.

distribution. According to the results of one statistical study, "if actual prices are adjusted for . . . standard indexes of comfort and quality, no [statistically] significant differences exist between the prices of the different cars produced by American firms."[29]

4. Foreign Competition and the Small-Car Segment. We have seen that the small-car segment is different, in important structural aspects, from other segments of the market. It is on this particular segment that foreign competitors have focused; and, until the imposition of import restrictions in 1981, they suceeded in capturing nearly 40 percent of the field. Thus, a significantly greater number of independent producers compete in the small-car segment than in the intermediate- and large-car segments. Economic theory predicts, and experience confirms, that pricing conduct regarding small cars would differ in a number of ways from conduct in the rest of the industry.

First, there is no clear price leader in the small-car field. Although some evidence indicates that Toyota was the price leader in small cars in the U.S. in the 1970s,[30] an examination of recent small-car pricing behavior reveals no single, distinct leadership role for Toyota or for any other firm. Second, no rigid pattern of leadership-followership governs relations among the Big Three in the pricing of their small cars—a sharp contrast to their monotonously regular "1–2–3" relationship in other segments of the market. Third, the pricing of small cars displays a measure of the variability, unpredictability, divergence, and disorganization characteristic of a structurally more competitive market, a pattern very different from that in the portions of the market dominated primarily by the Big Three. (Of course, the imposition in 1981 of numerical import quotas on Japanese firms—the main competitors in the small-car field—destroyed their incentive to use price as a way to gain market share, and, as a result, undermined price competition in this segment of the market.) Finally, sharply divergent profit margins in the sale of small versus large cars attest to structurally based differences in market power and price control between these two segments of the market. Industry observers estimate that per-car profits on large cars may reach as high as $6,000, but profits on small cars may by only $200 to $300 per car.[31] Differences in market structure appear to underlie these profit differentials: "The subcompact and compact models have historically earned a proportionately smaller share of the total corporate [profit] contribution," government experts conclude. "This is the result of low retail prices caused by stiff import competition."[32]

Nonprice Rivalry

With price competition eschewed in all but the small-car segment of the market, rivalry in the domestic automobile industry perforce is channelled into nonprice areas. Most prominent among these are styling and annual model changes, and advertising. Yet, nonprice conduct, too, is marked by an important element of mutual oligopolistic interdependence and tacit collusion, both generally (in terms of the degree of product uniformity among producers) and specifically (in mutual restraint by the Big Three in entering the small-car field). And, as in the case of pricing, foreign competition has imparted an invigorating impact on product design, engineering, and (genuine) product variety.

1. Styling and Annual Model Changes. Product styling and annual model changes are the predominant bases of rivalry in the domestic automobile industry. For the most part, these changes are cosmetic style variations rather than technological breakthroughs. From the industry's viewpoint, they have the virtue of stimulating the replacement demand for automobiles while avoiding the competitive uncertainty and possible "market disruption" that aggressive technological rivalry would entail. Alfred Sloan, Jr. (G.M.'s former Board Chairman) realized this, and urged General Motors to take the lead in consciously avoiding "radical" product innovation and "the risk of untried experiment."[33] Eventually, after other companies had adopted the GM strategy, styling, frequent model changes, and the marketing of "new" models became the principal arena for interfirm rivalry in the industry.

The typical pattern is for a producer to market major restylings of models every few years, and offering minor "face-lifting" variations in exterior sheet metal, grills, chrome adornments, and the like in the interim years. As J. Keats describes it: "The basic shell is bent a little bit this way, this year, and is bent slightly that way next year. The headlights are higher one year, lower the next, or grow in double . . . The door knobs are hidden, or recessed, or turned into buttons or bars . . . Tail fins grow higher, or maybe grow in sideways."[34] Styling was geared to a three-year cycle prior to the 1960s, quickened to a two-year pace in the 1960s, and more recently has lengthened to three, four, and, in some cases, as much as seven years.

The styling and style-change game in autos is significant in two further respects. First, it is extremely costly, necessitating large outlays on tools, dies, and the like. Representatives of GM, Ford, and Chrysler estimated their *annual* styling costs in the 1950s to be $500 million, $350 million, and $200 million, respectively, making for a combined total yearly outlay of nearly $1 billion.[35] Economists Franklin M. Fisher, Zvi Griliches, and Carl Kaysen estimated total combined retooling costs owing to style changes during the period 1950–1960 to be approximately $4 billion.[36] Extrapolating these estimates, the annual cost of the style-change game today amounts to more than $300 per car produced by the Big Three. Indeed, since the mid-1960s, the costs of annual model changes have reportedly exceeded their economic value, which may in part explain producers' decisions to stretch out styling cycles in recent years.[37]

Second, despite the industry's emphasis on styling, risk-averse behavior—in the form of leadership-followership and "protective styling imitation"—results in a surprising degree of *uniformity* in the offerings of the Big Three. "There are indeed perceptible differences among competing products at most times," Joe S. Bain has observed. "But the fact that all sellers generally follow product policies of protective imitation of their competitors has generally kept these differences within a rather narrow range, and on a superficial rather than a fundamental level. Thus, at most times, the similarity among competing brands in appearance, engine design, power, and the like is, from a technical standpoint, perhaps more striking than the difference, considering the almost unlimited variety of design alternatives open to automobile manufacturers.''[38] Likewise, F. M. Scherer points to ''the absolutely remarkable parallelism of the Big Three in terms of model sizes, design concepts, mechanical features, and other qualitative features,'' and concludes: ''Historically, Detroit has offered Americans nothing like the diversity of technical approaches in Europe and Japan.''[39]

2. Advertising. Advertising constitutes a second feature of nonprice rivalry in the automobile industry, with the Big Three ranked among the largest advertisers in the country. In part, heavy advertising may be a necessary corollary of the styling and annual style-change strategy, with producers ''compelled to undertake annual advertising campaigns to impress consumers with the unique appearance of annually altered automobiles.''[40] Heavy advertising may also be a means of reinforcing brand loyalty and thereby maintaining barriers to new competition. As Table 7 shows, GM is the industry's largest advertiser, having spent $202 million advertising its passenger cars in 1982; Ford and Chrysler are the second and third largest advertisers in the field, respectively. But as Table 7 further reveals, the *rates* of advertising expenditures, calculated on a per-car basis, vary substantially among firms. In particular, although the absolute amount of GM's expenditures exceeds that for any other firm, GM's advertising *rate* of $57.45 per car is far less than that for any other firm shown in Table 7. This pattern reflects an im-

Table 7: Automobile Advertising Expenditures (1982)

Company	*Passenger Car Advertising (millions) (a)*	*Advertising Per New Car Sold in U.S.*
1. General Motors	$202	$ 57.45
2. Ford	175	130.01
3. Chrysler	79	99.50
4. Toyota	56	105.66
5. Nissan/Datsun	49	104.26
6. Volkswagen	45	281.25
7. Renault[b]	31	206.67
8. Mazda[c]	28	176.10
9. Honda	25	68.31

[a]Advertising in U.S. market.
[b]Advertising by Renault; new-car sales include AMC and Renault.
[c]New cars registered in U.S. used as proxy for new-car sales.
Sources: LNA, *Ad $ Summary (Jan.–Dec. 1982)*, p. 53; *Ward's Automotive Yearbook*, 1984.

portant nonproduction economy of scale: given GM's larger size, it can spend a larger total amount on advertising; yet, by spreading its expenditures over an even larger volume of sales, it can reduce its per-car rate of spending. In attempting to match GM, however, its rivals must spend proportionately more per car.

*3. **Mutual Interdependence and Oligopolistic Restraint: The Case of Small Cars.*** We have seen that high market concentration in autos militates toward a recognition by the Big Three of mutual interdependence and the advantages of tacit collusion in pricing. Another manifestation of this oligopolistic rationality is the historic resistance by the Big Three to the introduction of small cars.[41]

At the conclusion of World War II the small, light-weight, inexpensive automobile was seen as the means for expanding the postwar urban car market in a manner analogous to Henry Ford's Model T decades earlier. The United Auto Workers, for example, urged Detroit to build a small car, citing an opinion survey conducted by the Society of Automotive Engineers, which revealed that 60 percent of the public wanted the industry to produce a small car.[42] In May 1945, General Motors and Ford disclosed that they were considering the production of small cars. The following year, Chrysler announced that "if the market exists and if other companies have a low-priced car, Chrysler will be ready with something competitive."

However, the Big Three did not seriously undertake to produce and market such a car until the 1970s, at least for the American market.[43] Attempts were made to meet successive import surges with the introduction of the "compact" car in the late 1950s and the "subcompacts" in the 1960s. But these efforts were, at best, half-hearted and dilatory. In 1962, for example, Ford cancelled the planned introduction of its "Cardinal," which featured a front-mounted, four-cylinder engine and front-wheel drive—a compact car quite similar to the X-cars, the Escort, and Omni of the 1980s.

Lawrence White explains this antipathy to small cars in terms of oligopolistic firm behavior. General Motors, Ford, and Chrysler, he writes, each seemed to recognize that vigorous entry into small cars by any one of them would trigger entry into the field by the others. Further, each firm seemed to believe that the demand for small cars was not great enough to permit profits acceptable to the group if all of them should simultaneously decide to enter this part of the market. "Twice, one or two of the Big Three pulled back from plunging ahead with a small car when the market did not look large enough for all three . . . A sizable niche might well have been carved out at the bottom of the market by a Big Three producer in 1950, or again, with a 'sub compact' in 1962 or 1963. Room-for-all considerations, however, appeared to rule this out."[44] Reinforcing the "room-for-all" *Weltanschauung* was the apparent desire by each of the Big Three to protect group profits in large cars by withholding the small car as an inexpensive substitute. "In this behavior, the Big Three definitely recognized their mutual interdependence, since in the absence of retaliation by rivals a single firm contemplating the production of a small car should have expected to gain more profits from stealing the dissatisfied customers from other firms than he would lose from dissatisfied customers of his own large cars . . . But the Big Three mutually contemplating a small car could only see lost profits from reduced sales of large cars.''[45]

Independents and foreign competitors, of course, were not immobilized by such considerations, because they had no vested interests and no established positions to protect. For these reasons, they were able to break through the logjam of tacit restraint and force the domestic oligopoly to confront the challenge of building small, light-weight, fuel-efficient automobiles. As White puts it, ''reduced profits on small car sales were better for the Big Three than no profits on lost sales to imports . . . In the absence of the press of competition from imports,'' he concludes, ''it is likely that the Big Three might never have provided small cars to the market.''[46]

4. The Impact of Foreign Competition. Evidently foreign competitors explored, exploited, and promoted small cars—a segment of the market that was neglected by the domestic oligopoly in the interest of short-run, joint profit maximization. But the invigorating impact of foreign competition in product design, quality, and engineering reaches considerably beyond small cars.

First, foreign competitors now lead the market in styling and design. As summarized by one research group, ''American producers are now imitating Europeans in designs for sporty and touring/luxury versions of mass-market models and imitating the Japanese in designs emphasizing economy and utility.''[47] Second, the advent of foreign competition has injected a degree of genuine product variety into the market, which had not been seen since the earliest days of the industry, when it was populated by a multitude of producers. ''Whether in terms of size, performance, or quality,'' the Automobile Panel of the National Academy of Engineering reports, ''foreign firms have sought an advantage by creating products that were different from the standard or traditional [U.S.] products.''[48] Finally, foreign competitors now lead not only in styling and variety, but in quality and engineering, as well. This is especially the case with respect to Japanese producers, as regards workmanship, defects, body and mechanical reliability, and design.

Perhaps the most insightful characterization of the domestic industry's conduct over the post-World War II era has been provided by H. Ross Perot, founder of the EDS Corporation recently acquired by GM. ''General Motors and the entire American automobile industry had a big respite from competition,'' Mr. Perot explains. ''[I]t got so bad that [U.S. auto companies] tried to get divisions to compete with one another—Chevrolet compete with Pontiac, Oldsmobile with Buick, and so on . . . Now we've got a whole generation of people who think that's what competition is. And I don't like that, and I say 'Fellows, that's intramural sports.' I said 'you don't even tackle there, you just touch the guy . . . you don't even play with pads . . . Now the Japanese have showed up, and they're competing professionally' . . . First board meeting . . . I gave 'em my immigrant's view of General Motors. And I said 'you don't understand competition . . .' "[49]

IV. INDUSTRY PERFORMANCE

Industry performance concerns the end results, or consequences, of firms' conduct and requires an evaluation of how well or how poorly an industry functions. Relevant performance dimensions in the automobile industry include: (1) efficiency in production; (2) pricing and profitability over the long and short run; (3) the quality of the product; (4) technological progress (dynamic efficiency); and (5) the industry's impact in creating or exacerbating broader social problems (social efficiency).

Production Efficiency

Do American automobile firms produce cars at the lowest possible cost, or is there excess "slack" (in economic jargon, "X-inefficiency")? Is the concentrated structure of the domestic industry conducive to efficient production, or has it militated toward waste and inefficiency? What impact has foreign competition had on production efficiency in the industry?

Available evidence indicates that, on at least five fronts, the U.S. auto industry has performed poorly in terms of production efficiency. However, under the impact of foreign competition, the Big Three have recently initiated some notable changes in production, organization, and management practices.

1. Raw-Materials Procurement Practices. One aspect of inefficiency in the industry is lax raw-materials procurement practices. For example, because steel is the major raw material used in the manufacture of automobiles, one would assume that auto companies bargain vigorously to reduce the cost of their steel requirements. Yet, *Fortune* recently described what it characterizes as a "stunning complacency" on the part of General Motors in its procurement of steel.[50] Only in 1982, and only when pressed by foreign competition, did GM take the "radical" step of requiring suppliers to bid competitively among one another for the firm's steel requirements. Astonishingly, GM's reformed buying practice appears to have marked a startling "new" departure among the Big Three firms.[51]

2. Excessive Overhead. Recent, sizable reductions in fixed costs and overhead expenses by the Big Three—again, forced by foreign competition—further attest to production inefficiencies built up in the industry.[52] Bloated salaries and redundant white-collar positions have been one source of excessive overhead expenses.[53] Inefficient utilization of existing equipment has also artificially raised fixed costs in the industry. Presumably in contrast to traditional practice, for example, Ford now has "recycled old tooling for a new four-cylinder engine and a new automatic transmission—saving $506 million compared with the cost of new tooling.''[54] Furthermore, recent efforts by domestic firms to reduce the extent to which they internally manufacture parts and components strongly suggest that the industry has heretofore operated with excessive levels of vertical integration.[55]

3. Tacit Vertical Collusion and the Labor–Management Complex. Excessive labor compensation constitutes a third major source of production inefficiency in the industry. Of course, this source of inflated manufacturing costs has not been unilaterally imposed by the United Auto Workers union; instead, excessive labor costs are the result of what is perhaps most accurately described as *vertical collusion,* or ''coalescence of power,'' between organized labor and the management of the Big Three companies.[56] On the one hand, the union has demanded wages far in excess of labor productivity gains; on the other hand, oligopoly in the product market has rendered the management of the Big Three firms quite compliant with union wage demands. Until the advent of foreign competition, higher labor costs could easily be passed on to buyers merely by raising car prices. Thus, although labor productivity in autos rose 39 percent over the years 1967–1980, labor compensation in the industry rose *five and one-half* times faster (214 percent). As a result, unit labor costs escalated sharply.

Recently, foreign competition has moderated this cost-price spiral; the three-year contract negotiated between GM, Ford, and the union in the fall of 1984 calls for wage increases approximately half those negotiated in 1979, and lower than the wage increases bargained for in other manufacturing industries.[57] It is too early to say whether such ''moderate'' settlements will set a pattern for the future. Chrysler's deal with the UAW in 1985 would seem to indicate a return to business as usual.[58]

4. Poor Management and Organization of Production. Comparative analyses of production costs for small cars in the U.S. and Japan indicate that another source of production inefficiency in the U.S. industry lies in poor organization and management of manufacturing processes. Table 8 lays bare the differential in production efficiency between U.S. auto companies and their Japanese competitors.

In analyzing these figures, it is important at the outset to note four factors that do *not* contribute to greater Japanese production efficiency. First, Japanese auto companies appear *not* to use more capital-intensive manufacturing methods.[59] And the Japanese advantage is not the result of utilizing ultrasophisticated, ultramodern plant and equipment.[60] Greater Japanese operating efficiency is *not* the result of an undervalued yen manipulated by the Japanese government to artificially reduce costs of production. Automotive consultant Martin Anderson points out that ''the Japanese pay tariffs and buy the bulk of their raw materials and their most costly services—including transportation and marketing—in currencies other than yen (U.S. dollars, for example) . . .

Table 8: Japanese Production-Cost Advantage for a Typical Subcompact Car

Technology	= $ 73	
		Subtotal = $ 73
Management Systems and Techniques		
Quality-Control Systems	= 329	
• manpower • scrap • warranty savings		
Just-in-Time Production	= 550	
• smaller plants • plant complexes • fewer people • utility savings • interest savings • in-bound freight savings		
Material Handling Engineering	= 41	
Other Productivity Improvements	= 478	
• quality circles • job classification		
		Subtotal = $1,398
Union-Management Relations		
Absenteeism (unscheduled) (6–8% U.S. vs. 2% Japan)	= 81	
Relief Systems and Allowances	= 89	
Union Representatives	= 12	
		Subtotal = $ 182
Wage and Fringe Rates (Total hours Japan *X* Difference in Weighted-Average Wage Rate)	= 550	
		Subtotal = $ 550
Total Manufacturing-Cost Advantage		*Total* = $2,203
Japanese Ocean Freight, Duty, and Port Cost		= $ (485)
Net Japanese Landed Cost Advantage		*Net* = $1,718

rce: U.S., Department of Transportation, *The U.S. Automobile Industry, 1981* (Washington, , 1982), p. 15.

A big chunk of Japanese expenses . . . is not in yen and has nothing to do with the yen.''[61] And finally, although excessive labor costs in the U.S. are not insignificant (as we have just seen), they are *not* the primary cause of the relative inefficiency of the U.S. industry. The data in Table 8 show that the wage differential is almost completely offset by the costs of transporting Japanese autos to the U.S. market.

Rather than any of the foregoing, superior Japanese efficiency appears to be grounded in greater attention to, and more effective organization and management of, manufacturing and production processes. ''The Japanese work smarter. Manufacturing techniques and methods, ranging from materials-handling systems to maintenance procedures, all reflect the careful attention of both management and workers to the details of production.''[62] In a profound way, Japanese managers have been far more astute students of the father of automotive mass production, Henry Ford, than the chieftains of the U.S. industry. Unlike the domestic oligopoly, which has grown complacent, and is wed to the status quo, the Japanese follow Henry Ford by viewing the plant as a laboratory and production as a never-ending experiment.[63]

*5. **The Crush of Bureaucracy.*** Inefficiency in the U.S. auto industry is further compounded by the crush of bureaucracy born of elephantine size. A former GM official provides the following inside view of Chevrolet, GM's largest operating division: ''One of the biggest . . . problems was in the manufacturing staff. It was overburdened with layers upon layers of management. Between a plant manager and my office there were no less than five levels of management.''[64] Similarly, former GM president, Elliott M. Estes, once candidly confided: ''Chevrolet is such a big monster that you twist its tail and nothing happens at the other end for months and months. It is so gigantic that there isn't any way to really run it. You just sort of try to keep track of it.''[65] Inefficiency bred of large-scale bureaucracy afflicts Ford and Chrysler as well.[66]

Recent efforts to enhance production efficiency and pare waste, triggered by foreign competition and the 1981–83 recession, have somewhat reduced the magnitude of this problem—most significantly by reducing the size of the Big Three.

Pricing and Profitability

Pricing and profitability constitute a second dimension of industry performance. Are automobile profits, and hence, prices, excessive? How have automobile prices behaved over the long run? Does the short-run behavior of auto prices dampen or aggravate cyclical fluctuations in the industry, and, given the industry's strategic place at the heart of the industrial sector, in the American economy?

1. Industry Profitability. Profitability provides one perspective on industry performance. But profitability must be carefully interpreted. On the one hand, "normal" profit rates comparable to those in other manufacturing sectors do not necessarily imply good economic performance; profit rates may only appear normal because costs are higher than they would be under conditions of effective competition. On the other hand, low profits or losses can reflect deficient industry performance in other respects (i.e., inefficiency in production or failure to innovate).

With these provisos in mind, we turn to Table 9, which depicts profit rates (expressed as after-tax net income as a percent of stockholder equity) for the auto industry and for all U.S. manufacturing corporations, over the years 1947–1984. These data are significant for a number of reasons. First, profit rates, and thus prices in the industry, historically have been excessive when evaluated against profit rates for all manufacturing corporations.

Second, profitability varies among the Big Three producers. General Motors' long-run average profit rate of 19.5 percent is quite close to the firm's traditionally targeted rate of return of 20 percent, and is more than one and one-half times greater than the profit rate recorded in manufacturing generally. Ford's long-term profit rate, although less than that for GM, still exceeds the rate for all U.S. manufacturing corporations by 11 percent. Chrysler historically has obtained a rate of return below that for GM and Ford, and below the rate in industry generally.

Third, historically excessive rates of return in the automobile industry cannot be attributed to relatively greater risk; the variance of rates of return for GM and Ford are one-quarter to one-third of the variance in rates of return for all U.S. manufacturing corporations over the years 1947–1983.

Fourth, the fortunes of U.S. automakers have fluctuated dramatically since the late-1970s. Chrysler faced imminent bankruptcy in 1979, and was saved only by a government bailout. Then, in 1980, the industry recorded a loss of more than $4 billion—a 9-billion-dollar swing in profits from the previous year, and the worst one-year performance ever turned in by any U.S. industry. By 1983, the Big Three again reaped record profits. However, this does not necessarily reflect an increase in efficiency or competitiveness; instead, this may be the result of restraints on Japanese competition. According to one financial analyst, "without the quotas, there would not be any record earnings, because the Japanese would be pursuing their usual volume-based strategy and holding down prices."[67]

2. Long-Run Price Behavior. The long-run record of automobile prices is one of sustained, sizable price escalation. The average selling price of new cars in the U.S. more than *tripled* over the 18-year period, from 1967 to 1984, rising from $3,200 in 1967 to $11,100 in 1984. Put differently, new-car prices during this period were raised at an average annual rate more than 18 percent greater than the rate of inflation in the consumer price-index. The gap between auto price increases and increases in the consumer price-index

Table 9: Profitability in the U.S. Auto Industry: Net Income After Taxes, Divided by Stockholders' Equity

	1947–1977	*1978*	*1979*	*1980*	*1981*	*1982*	*1983*	*1984*
Big Three producers:[a]	14.3%	9.8%	13.2%	−11.1%	−6.3%	−2.8%	31.3%	40.1%
General Motors:	19.5	20.0	15.1	−4.3	1.9	5.3	18.0	18.9
Ford:	13.1	16.4	11.2	−18.0	−14.4	−10.8	24.7	29.5
Chrysler[b]:	10.2	−7.0	—	—	—	—	51.3	72.0
All U.S. manufacturing corps.:	11.8	15.0	16.4	13.9	13.6	9.2	10.6	12.9[c]

[a]Arithmetic average; GM and Ford only, for 1979–82.
[b]1979–1982 data not meaningful owing to federally guaranteed loans and government stock-ownership program.
[c]Average for first three quarters of 1984.
Sources: Moody's Industrial Manual, various years; U.S. Congress, Senate, Subcommittee on Antitrust, Committee on the Judiciary, *A Reorganization of the U.S. Automobile Industry,* Committee Print, 93rd Cong., 2nd sess., 1974, p. 234; *Economic Report of the President,* 1985.

has grown even larger in more recent years: average new-car selling prices were raised 44 percent between 1977 and 1983—a rate more than two and one-half times greater than the rise in the consumer price index over the same period.[68] As a result, new cars have become significantly more expensive, and less affordable commodities.

Two other observations are relevant. First, the rapid rise in new-car prices *cannot* be attributed to costs of government regulation of automobile safety and pollution. According to the Bureau of Labor Statistics, costs incurred by auto producers to comply with government regulations in these areas accounted for less than 12 percent of the total increase in automobile prices between 1975 and 1979.[69] Second, auto companies have *raised* their prices at an accelerating rate, even as they boasted about efficiency gains and productivity improvements. Here again, import quotas and the elimination of foreign competition appear to play a key role. "The quotas raised the general level of automobile prices in this country so that today those prices are very high," one financial analyst concludes. "It's a common theme for the auto makers to talk about how they've lowered their break-even point, but they didn't pass the break on to the consumer."[70]

3. Cyclical Price Behavior. The cyclical behavior of auto prices is shown in Figure 3. It is significant in two important respects. First, automobile prices are seen to be rigid in a downward direction, despite large short-run declines in new-car sales. (In recent years, this tendency has been counteracted somewhat by the price rebates and subsidization of interest rates, sporadically instituted by auto manufacturers in periods of slack demand.) Second, new-car prices not only fail to decline in response to large drops in demand and sales, but they behave in a highly perverse fashion, i.e., they are consistently *raised* in the face of sales declines. Perverse short-run pricing was especially marked in the early 1980s. In 1980, on the eve of what would prove to be the worst national recession since the Great Depression of the 1930s, and with an unemployment rate of 26 percent in the motor vehicle sector, the domestic auto oligopoly announced price increases which *The Wall Street Journal* described as "rivaling anything in modern Detroit history."[71] Another round of price increases, engineered by the industry shortly thereafter, prompted one exasperated dealer to exclaim that the auto companies "don't know what's going on in the market. They defy the law of supply and demand."[72] As the recession deepened throughout 1981, and as automobile sales and production continued to fall, "General Motors Corp. slapped an exceptionally steep price boost on its 1982 models"—a boost matched by Ford and Chrysler.[73] Such downward price rigidity and perverse price increases in the face of declining demand, of course, exacerbate instability in autos and in the economy at large.

Product Quality

Product quality is a third dimension of industry performance. Ford Motor Company now tells us that "Quality is Job 1," and GM proclaims its "Com-

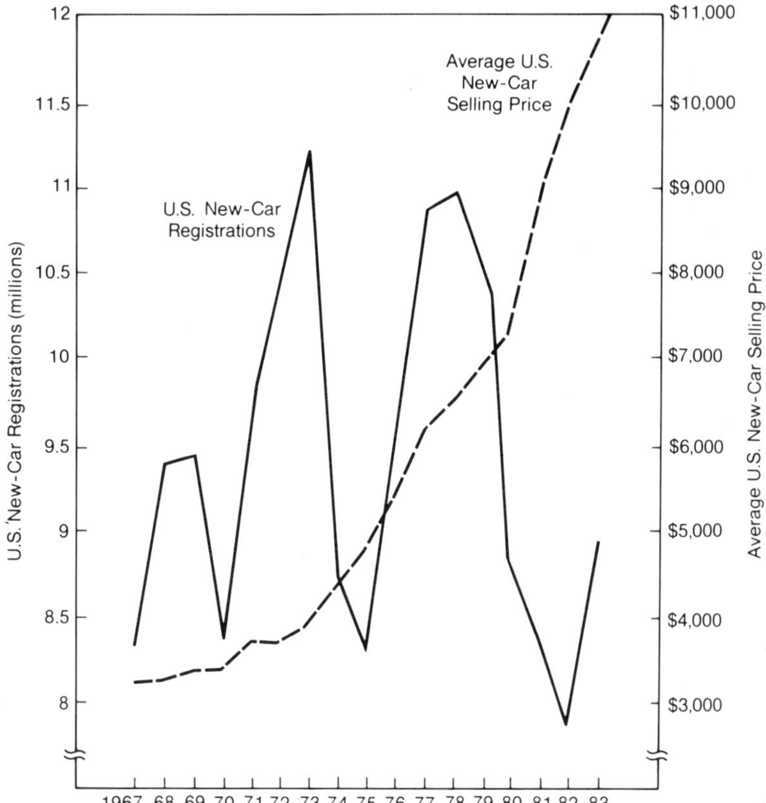

FIGURE 3. *Prices and new-car registrations. Source:* Automotive News, *Market Data Book Issue,* 1984.

mitment to Excellence." But how well built are American cars when compared to foreign competitors?

One measure of product quality is the extent to which new cars are plagued with defects upon receipt by buyers. According to J. D. Power & Associates, "While less than half (48%) of the domestically produced cars are problem-free on delivery, two-thirds of the Japanese-built imports are trouble-free when buyers receive them."[74]

Another measure of quality is the number of recalls of defective new cars ordered by the Government. The evidence here is equally unflattering for the American automobile oligopoly; after examining recent recall rates for foreign and domestic cars, Commissioner Paula Stern, of the International Trade Commission, found "none of the four largest-selling Japanese makers had a recall rate higher than one-third the *lowest* rate shown by a U.S. producer."[75]

Additionally, foreign-produced automobiles require significantly fewer repairs as compared with domestic cars. Robert W. Crandall finds: "In 1970 . . . the repair records of U.S. cars were only marginally worse than the records of Japanese imports in the first few years of service. These differences may have narrowed or disappeared in later years of service. By 1976, however, Japanese cars had much better repair records than their American counterparts—and this gap has persisted and even widened in the years since then.''[76] As *Fortune* points out, Japanese firms ''have found that high quality and low [production] costs are not incompatible goals that can be resolved only through trade-offs—generally the view in the U.S.—but are linked and complementary objectives.''[77]

Dynamic Efficiency

Another component of industry performance is dynamic efficiency, which encompasses product innovation (the development and commercialization of product improvements) and process innovation (the adoption of new, more efficient methods of production). How aggressively do firms in the industry explore, develop, and commercialize product innovations? How vigorously do they pursue and adopt more efficient production techniques? More importantly, does the industry's structure *compel* the firms to be competitive by innovating and taking risks? Or does it permit firms to enjoy the quiet life, complacent with the status quo and free of the competitive compunction to innovate?

The rate and the breadth of product innovation in the U.S. automobile industry were greatest in the decades preceding World War II, when the field was populated by a large number of independent producers. Competition was intense, and new people with new ideas could put their ideas (the bad along with the good) into practice. The independents were a particularly fertile source of product innovation.[78] To be sure, GM, Ford, and Chrysler introduced product innovations during this period as well, but owing to what Donald A. Moore has described as ''competitive vigor born of necessity,'' the contributions of the independents far exceeded their share of the market.[79]

With the demise of the independents and the increase in industry concentration, the pace of product innovation slackened. ''I believe that the amount of product innovation successfully introduced into the automobile is smaller today than in previous times, and is still falling,'' a Ford vice president told a gathering of auto engineers in 1964. ''The automatic transmission was the last major innovation of the industry.''[80] Lawrence White confirmed this assessment a decade later: ''The major features of today's automobiles—V-8 engines, automatic transmissions, power steering, and power brakes—are all pre-war innovations. These have been considerably improved and refined over the past twenty-five years, but still the industry has been uninterested in pursuing alternatives. The suspension, ignition, carburetion, and exhaust systems are fundamentally the same. Only the pressure of Federal legislation on air pollution has effected any change in these last three systems.''[81]

This diagnosis is still valid. According to John De Lorean:

> Today's transverse engine front-wheel-drive layouts differ little from the British Leyland mini of 25 years ago. . . .
>
> I remember my first visit to the G.M. proving ground in October 1956. I rode in a 1956 Chevrolet with John Dolza, G.M.'s noted engine engineer. In this particular car, he had rigged the V-8 engine to run on all eight cylinders when maximum power was required and to cruise at highway speeds on only four cylinders to save fuel. That was 24 years ago. A Cadillac advertisement recently touted that a V-8 that accelerates on eight cylinders and cruises on four is 1981's hottest feature.[82]

Apparently, as one U.S. Senator observed, "back garage inventors and operators have done more, far more in the way of innovative research and development than has Detroit."[83]

In fact, the Big Three firms have relied heavily on their suppliers for technological advances: "The parts suppliers—for example, Bendix, Budd, Kelsey-Hayes, Wagner Electric, Borg-Warner, Dana, Thompson Products (now TRW), Motorola, and Electric Auto-Lite—did much of the pioneering development work on new items like power steering, power brakes, ball joints, alternators, transistorized ignition, and others . . . Similarly, the materials suppliers—steel, aluminum, glass, plastics, and paint companies—have provided much of the development work on new uses of materials. Effectively, the auto companies have allowed their suppliers to take the risks and absorb the initial costs of developing new technology."[84]

The domestic industry's record in the area of process innovation and adoption of more efficient production methods is hardly more reassuring. Here, too, the Japanese have aggressively sought out, experimented with, and adopted new production and management methods. Significantly, an important part of superior Japanese process innovation is attributable to the deployment of *American* tools and equipment marketed by *American* equipment manufacturers from the 1950s onward—tools and equipment ignored by the U.S. auto companies.[85] It is supremely ironic, then, as well as an indictment of the technological delinquency of the U.S. auto giants, that the Big Three are now turning to Japanese auto companies for joint production ventures in order to learn how to manufacture cars efficiently.[86] Although GM has recently disclosed its "Saturn" project (a $5 billion state-of-the-art small-car operation), the project is only in the planning stage and therefore cannot be evaluated at this time.

Thus, the U.S. automobile industry's performance in terms of dynamic efficiency has been poor. Although the Big Three annually spend vast sums for research and development ($4.7 billion in 1983), outcomes and results—not dollar expenditures—are the relevant measures of dynamic efficiency. Judged on this basis, the industry's record of product and process innovation has not been impressive. Its technological somnambulence seemed deeply rooted in its oligopolistic, noncompetitive structure, until foreign competition forced the U.S. giants to awaken from their postwar lethargy.

Social Efficiency

"Social" efficiency is the last dimension of industry performance that we shall consider, albeit briefly. We shall discuss how well or how poorly the industry has served the public interest in three areas: pollution control, auto safety, and fuel efficiency.

1. Smog and Automotive Air Pollution. By the early-1960s, the typical American automobile spewed approximately one ton of pollutants per year into the nation's atmosphere, and motor vehicles accounted for an estimated 60 percent of all air pollution.[87] Yet the industry confronted this fact with remarkable equanimity.

At first, the industry simply denied the existence of the problem—observation and its own internal research results to the contrary notwithstanding.[88] "[W]aste vapors are dissipated in the atmosphere quickly and do not present an air-pollution problem," Ford Motor Company told the Los Angeles County supervisors in 1953. "The fine automotive powerplants which modern-day engineers design do not 'smoke.' "[89]

Later, as automotive air pollution worsened, and as national concern about the problem increased, the automobile companies decided to eliminate rivalry in the development and commercialization of pollution-control technology. In an antitrust suit against the industry, filed in 1969 and not contested by the industry, the Justice Department found that domestic auto producers "conspired not to compete in research, development, manufacture, and installation of [pollution] control devices, and did all in their power to delay such research, development, manufacturing, and installation."[90]

In the 1970s, under intense public pressure, the industry hastily seized on the catalytic converter as a pollution-control device, a device that the National Academy of Science characterized as "the most disadvantageous with respect to first cost, fuel economy, maintainability, and durability." Said the Academy: "it is unfortunate that the automobile industry did not seriously undertake such a [pollution control] program on its own volition until it was subjected to governmental pressure. A relatively modest investment, over the past decade, in developmental programs related to emission control could have precluded the crisis that now prevails in the industry and the nation. The current crash programs of the major manufacturers have turned out to be expensive and, in retrospect, not well planned."[91]

2. Automotive Safety. "In 1965," the Senate Commerce Committee reported, "49,000 persons lost their lives in highway accidents, 1,500,000 suffered disabling injuries, and an equal number suffered non-disabling injuries. Economic costs of highway accidents which can be tabulated for the same year aggregated $8.5 billion. Since the introduction of the automobile in the United States, more Americans have lost their lives from highway accidents than all the combat deaths suffered by America in all our wars."[92]

Although a variety of factors (road design, weather conditions, reckless and drunk driving) influence automobile safety, it is incontrovertible that the design of the automobile itself plays a major role in the carnage on the nation's roads and highways.[93] Nevertheless, the industry seemed casually indifferent to this national problem. Patents awarded to the auto companies in the 1920s and 1930s for such safety features as padded dashboards and collapsible steering wheels were shelved for decades, until their incorporation in automobiles was mandated by government decree.[94] As automobiles became progressively more dangerous in design over the postwar period,[95] the industry insisted that safety should be optional, supplied in response to consumer demand and preference (or the lack thereof). Yet it steadfastly refused to make available the safety information essential to informed, rational consumer choice and decision making.[96] At the same time, safety features such as seatbelts were deliberately made more expensive and troublesome to install, and (until recently) were rarely advertised or merchandised.[97] The industry spent hundreds of millions of dollars extolling raw horsepower and rocket acceleration, and then disingenuously hid behind its slogan, "safety don't sell"—despite evidence to the contrary.[98] The explanation, once again, may be found in the recognition of mutual interdependence among the Big Three. As former GM president Alfred Sloan put it, "I feel that General Motors should not adopt safety glass for its cars. I can only see competition being forced into the same position. Our gain would be purely a temporary one and the net result would be that both competition and ourselves would have reduced the return on our capital and the public would have obtained still more value per dollar expended."[99]

3. Automotive Fuel Consumption. The fuel economy of automobiles decisively affects the nation's overall level of petroleum consumption, and thereby significantly determines national dependence on geopolitically volatile foreign petroleum supplies.

In characteristic fashion, the industry did not consider either the fuel efficiency of its products, or limited domestic petroleum supplies, to be pressing concerns. It ignored warnings, even when sounded by responsible officials within the industry itself.[100] Instead, the industry proceeded to absolve itself of any particular responsibility as it had done in pollution and safety matters. The general manager of GM's Buick division was asked, in 1958, what steps his division was taking in the area of fuel efficiency. "Oh," he flippantly replied, "we're helping the gas companies, the same as our competitors."[101] Likewise, the domestic oligopoly seemed uninterested in engine innovations (including alternative powerplants) capable of enhancing fuel economy. During Congressional hearings conducted in 1973, a parade of inventors, scientists, and engineers testified to the companies' indifference. "I was assured in the first meetings with the Big Four in Detroit that what they would like to do with this is put it into a 20- or 30-year development program," said one. "I told them I would rather do it next year in Japan, and I meant that very seriously."[102]

As a consequence of the industry's nonchalant attitude, the fuel efficiency of U.S. automobiles steadily worsened from 1958 to 1973. In part, this decline was attributable to the installation of pollution controls, but the principal cause was the bloated size and weight of the cars the industry chose to produce in its race for styling supremacy.[103] Ironically, this made the industry vulnerable to the flood of fuel-efficient imports that swamped the American market in the wake of periodic gasoline shortages and skyrocketing fuel prices. Had the Government not acted to impose fuel-economy standards on the industry, "the auto companies, especially Chrysler, might have been even less prepared than they were for the . . . swing in customer preferences to small cars."[104]

In sum, the performance of the American automobile industry in terms of social efficiency must be adjudged as unsatisfactory, if not deplorable. Perhaps such problems as air pollution, safety, and fuel consumption are not susceptible to market solutions and therefore require some measure of governmental intervention and regulation.

V. PUBLIC POLICY

In this final section we shall examine public policy in the automobile industry in three major areas: antitrust, protection from foreign competition, and government efforts to regulate automotive air pollution, safety, and fuel economy.

Antitrust Policy

The bulk of the antitrust suits in this industry have been altogether tangential and peripheral in nature; they have never challenged the structurally rooted market power of the automobile oligopoly. Thus, in 1972, antitrust forced Ford to divest itself of Electric Auto-Lite (a spark plug and electrical components producer, which Ford had acquired in 1961); in 1968, it required General Motors to divest itself of the Euclid Road Machinery Company (a producer of heavy, off-the-road trucks, which GM had acquired fifteen years earlier); in 1957, it forced duPont (a major supplier of fabrics and paints to GM) to sell its large holding of GM stock; in 1964, it blocked an attempted merger between Chrysler and Mack Truck; and, in the 1960s, it charged General Motors with monopolization, but only in its bus and locomotive operations. In fact, the only structural antitrust case to be brought against GM's automotive operations was filed forty years ago, and was directed against the firm's GMAC new-car financing subsidiary.

Other antitrust cases have dealt with only isolated aspects of noncompetitive conduct in the industry. For example, the Government charged GM and Ford with noncompetitive pricing, but only in the fleet market for new cars sold to businesses and rental car agencies.[105] It charged the auto companies with unlawfully conspiring to eliminate competition, but only in the pollution-control field.[106] Of late, however, the Government has sought to vacate this and other past antitrust settlements;[107] it has even encouraged a rash of joint ventures and cross-ownership arrangements between the domestic oligopoly and its foreign rivals (such as GM-Toyota) which, as we have seen, poses serious anticompetitive problems.[108] Finally, in what might be considered "failing company" antitrust, the Government engineered the Chrysler bailout to prevent the automobile triopoly from degenerating into a duopoly.

The antitrust record in autos thus seems to confirm J. K. Galbraith's charge that American antitrust is a "charade" which fosters the illusion of competition and thereby legitimates the power actually wielded by firms that are free from effectively competitive checks and balances.

Protection from Foreign Competition

As we have seen, in the post-World War II period, a recognition of, and respect for, the mutual oligopolistic interdependence between the domestic auto companies became solidified. This, together with the protection afforded by well-nigh impenetrable entry barriers, insulated the domestic industry from effective competition. Noncompetitive conduct, including tacit vertical collusion between management and organized labor, and steady price-wage-price escalation, flourished in this cozy noncompetitive environment.

Only foreign competition tended to disturb this oligopolistic *bonhomie*, and this made it imperative for the domestic producers to obtain government protection from imports. Accordingly, starting in 1974, management and labor began to seek such protection. Their efforts were crowned with success when the Government persuaded the Japanese to accept voluntary import quotas, starting in 1981. These "temporary" quotas, designed to give domestic producers "breathing space," were renewed in 1983, and formally expired in March 1985. (However, the Japanese government has replaced them with its own quota system—in part to protect the high profits which the restraints provide Japanese auto companies in the U.S. market.)

The quotas were imposed in spite of an early warning by the U.S. Council on Wage & Price Stability that the most important reasons for the increased market share of foreign automobiles were "the pricing policies of domestic producers and the inability of domestic manufacturers to respond rapidly to changing market conditions"; that import restraints "would likely result in an immediate increase in the price of automobiles to the American consumer"; that such restraints, or the mere threat of restraints, "could substantially check the single most effective spur to competition in this highly concentrated industry"; and that this, "in turn, could lead to less competitive prices and a reduced level of innovation."[109]

These dire predictions came to pass. By creating an artificial scarcity, the "voluntary" quotas have dramatically driven up the prices of Japanese cars. The rise in Japanese prices, in turn, has permitted domestic producers to push through sizable price boosts of their own. According to industry experts, 1983 new-car prices (both foreign and domestic) rose $800 to $1,000 on average, as a direct consequence of import quotas; and "additional dealer markups" on some Japanese models reportedly have risen as much as $2,600.[110] In the aggregate, "protection" from foreign competition is estimated to have cost American car buyers $15.7 billion in artificially inflated new-car prices.[111] In addition, the quotas have effectively cartelized Japanese exports to the U.S. by forcing the Japanese government to allocate quota shares among its exporters to the U.S. market.

This raises a number of public-policy questions: Is protection from foreign competition necessary (as management and labor contend) in order to counteract the alleged "Japan, Inc." juggernaut of state-industry collaboration? Or, have the U.S. auto industry's travails been largely self-inflicted—the result of decades of noncompetitive conduct and performance, compounded by an industrial-labor complex, and aggravated by severe recessionary/depressionary macroeconomic conditions?[112] Does protectionism encourage the domestic oligopoly to do anything that it would not have been forced to do by the press of foreign competition?[113] Or, does it merely give the Big Three time to arrange joint ventures with foreign manufacturers for the production abroad of small cars,[114] and to redirect resources to the production of large luxury cars?[115] More importantly, have the quotas served to *strengthen* Japanese auto producers by vastly improving their profitability, thereby compounding the competitive disabilities of the American industry and making continued protectionism necessary?[116] Finally, is the domestic industry's drive for continued restraints on foreign competition more than a little hypocritical when, at the same time, U.S. car companies are themselves increasingly turning to foreign sources for parts and components?[117]

Regulation: Safety, Pollution, and Fuel Economy

Have the government's attempts to regulate automobile safety, pollution, and fuel consumption been too costly in comparison with the benefits obtained? Is it true, as the industry generally maintains, that "excessive" regulation "adds unnecessary costs for consumers, lowers profits, diverts manpower from research and development programs, and reduces productivity—all at a time when our resources are desperately needed to meet the stiff competition from abroad?"[118] Or is it a fact, as Henry Ford II has conceded, that "we wouldn't have had the kinds of safety built into automobiles that we have had unless there had been a Federal law. We wouldn't have had the fuel economy unless there had been a Federal law, and there wouldn't have been the emission control unless there had been a Federal law."[119]

Regulation of safety is prototypical of the problem. In 1964, Congress directed the General Services Administration to specify safety equipment and safety features for automobiles purchased for the government's sizable fleet. Two years later, responding to the "grim roll of Americans lost and maimed on the nation's highways"; disturbed by "evidence of the automobile industry's chronic subordination of safe design to promotional styling," as well as the industry's "laxity in furnishing adequate notification to car owners of latent defects which had crept into the manufacturing process—defects frequently directly related to safety," Congress concluded that "the promotion of motor vehicle safety through voluntary standards has largely failed. The unconditional imposition of mandatory standards at the earliest practicable date is the only course commensurate with the highway death and injury toll."[120] Congress therefore enacted the Motor Safety Act of 1966, which directed the Secretary of Commerce (and later, the Secretary of Transportation), in conjunction with what would become the National Highway Traffic Safety Administration (NHTSA), to research, devise, administer, and enforce motor vehicle safety standards. The Act prohibits the sale of any vehicle not in conformity with these standards; it provides penalties in the form of fines of up to $1,000 per violation and per car; it provides for the recall and repair by the manufacturer of cars later determined to be unsafe in operation; and it mandates that producers maintain records and information necessary to determine compliance with the standards promulgated.[121]

Air-pollution and fuel-economy regulations are based on a similar rationale—i.e., the finding that voluntary industry efforts are inadequate for the task at hand. Nevertheless, some have argued that less direct forms of regulation—for example, "incentive-based" measures, featuring taxes or "fees" imposed on the sale of unsafe, polluting, gas-guzzling cars—would be preferable and equally effective. Such proposals are attractive to economists who are almost congenitally sympathetic to market-oriented solutions. But is it realistic to assume that government would impose penalties, fines, or mass recalls if to do so would jeopardize the financial viability of a General Motors, a Ford, or a Chrysler? Would the government ever consider shutting down GM, for example, if the firm failed—or refused—to meet emission standards, safety requirements, or fuel-economy regulations? Given the economic importance and political power of the Big Three, would the government not grant delays, extensions, exemptions, and so on, whenever its regulations threatened to exact a significant toll from its regulatees? In short, direct or indirect government regulation is bedeviled by the same problem: the labor-industrial complex that dominates the U.S. auto industry.

VI. CONCLUSION

The American automobile industry affords a unique laboratory for studying the dynamic interaction of industry structure, conduct, and performance in a tightly knit oligopoly. Beyond this, it highlights the critical role that industry structure plays in determining the convergence or divergence of private advantage and the public interest. The public-policy challenge is to decide whether (to borrow a phrase from Charles E. Wilson, former president of General Motors and former Secretary of Defense) what is good for G.M. is necessarily good for the country.

NOTES

1. The material in this section is taken largely from Lawrence J. White, "The Automobile Industry," in Walter Adams (ed.), *The Structure of American Industry,* 6th ed., (New York: Macmillan, 1982).

2. Allan Nevins, *Ford: The Times, the Man, the Company.* (New York: Scribner, 1954), p. 493.

3. A vice president of Ford Motor Company admits: "It isn't always a rational decision that is going on out in the world of car buying." U.S. Congress, Senate, Subcommittee on International Trade, Committee on Finance, *Issues Relating to the Domestic Auto Industry, Hearings,* Part 2, 97th Cong., 1st sess., 1981, p. 211.

4. See the surveys of price elasticities in F. O. Irvine, "Demand Equations for Individual New Car Models Estimated Using Transactions Prices with Implications for Regulatory Issues," *Southern Economic Journal,* 49: 766(1983); L. J. White, *The Automobile Industry Since 1945* (Cambridge, Mass.: Harvard U. P., 1971), pp. 94–95.

5. White, op. cit., pp. 94–95.

6. U.S. Congress, Office of Technology Assessment, *U.S. Industrial Competitiveness: A Comparison of Steel, Electronics, and Automobiles* (Washington, D.C., 1981), p. 44.

7. J. A. Hunker, *Structural Change in the U.S. Automobile Industry* (Lexington, Mass.: Heath, 1983), p. 17; National Academy of Engineering, *The Competitive Status of the U.S. Auto Industry* (Washington, D.C.: National Academy Press, 1982), pp. 20, 70.

8. U.S. Congress, House, Subcommittee on Economic Stabilization, Committee on Banking, Finance and Urban Affairs, *Findings of the Chrysler Corporation Loan Guarantee Board,* 96th Cong., 2nd sess., 1980, p. 150.

The expansion of Volkswagen, Honda, and Nissan into the U.S. appears to have arrested and mildly reversed the secular rise in domestic concentration. However, these firms continue to import a substantial proportion of the automobiles that they sell in the U.S., with imported cars representing 40 percent of total U.S. Volkswagen sales, and 86 percent of Honda's total sales in the American market. See *Ward's Automotive Yearbook,* 1984, pp. 81, 101.

9. Hunker, op. cit., p. 31.

10. U.S. Congressional Budget Office, "The Fair Practices in Automotive Products Act (H.R. 5133): An Economic Assessment," reprinted in U.S. Congress, House, Trade Subcommittee, House Committee on Ways and Means, *Domestic Content Legislation and the U.S. Automobile Industry,* Committee Print, 97th Cong., 2nd sess., 1982, p. 22.

11. *Ward's Automotive Yearbook,* 1984, pp. 48–50.

12. U.S. International Trade Commission, *The U.S. Auto Industry: U.S. Factory Sales, Retail Sales, Imports, Exports, Apparent Consumption, Suggested Retail Prices, and Trade Balances with Selected Countries for Motor Vehicles, 1964–82* (Washington, D.C.: 1983), pp. 11–23.

13. *Ward's Automotive Yearbook,* 1984, pp. 101, 110.

14. *Findings of the Chrysler Corporation Loan Guarantee Board,* Committee Print, op. cit., p. 150.

15. Adams, *Structure of American Industry,* 6th ed., op. cit., p. 150. However, another research group concludes that evolving manufacturing systems "reduce dramatically the volume required for many components and most car models in order to gain full-scale economies," and thus, "automobiles can be produced competitively by organizations of widely varying forms and sizes." *The Future of the Automobile,* Report of MIT's International Automobile Program (Cambridge, Mass.: MIT Press, 1984), p. 248.

16. *Ward's Automotive Yearbook,* 1984, p. 74.

17. It is relevant to note that, although GM and Ford produce a significantly greater number of motor vehicles than do any of the four largest Japanese car manufacturers, the latter produce their cars in vastly larger *plants* than do GM and Ford. The average plant operated by the four largest Japanese firms has an annual output of approximately 460,000 cars; the comparable average U.S. plant size for GM and Ford (considered together) is on the order of 182,000 cars per year. Though smaller in overall *firm* size, then, the Japanese enjoy greater economies of scale at the *plant* level. Conversely, economies of scale at the *plant* level need not necessitate gigantic *firm* size on the order of GM or Ford. Japan Automobile Manufacturers Association, *Motor Vehicle Statistics of Japan,* 1984, pp. 14–15; Japan Motor Industrial Federation, *Guide to the Motor Industry of Japan,* 1983, pp. 28–42; Automotive News, *Market Data Book Issue,* 1984, p. 4; *Ward's Automotive Yearbook,* 1984, p. 74.

18. J. S. Bain, *Industrial Organization,* 2nd ed. (New York: Wiley, 1968), p. 287.

19. U.S. Department of Transportation, *The U.S. Automobile Industry, 1980* (Washington, D.C., 1981), p. 66.

20. *Issues Relating to the U.S. Auto Industry, Hearings,* op. cit., Part 1, p. 201; Hunker, op. cit., pp. 26–27.

21. Adams, *Structure of American Industry,* 6th ed., op. cit., p. 151.

22. Leading National Advertisers, Inc., *Ad $ Summary (Jan.–Dec. 1982),* p. 53.

23. National Academy of Engineering, op. cit., p. 99; Hunker, op. cit., p. 45; Department of Transportation, op. cit., p. 48.

24. Hunker, op. cit., p. 32. Access to an established dealer distribution and service system may have played an important role in Renault's acquisition of controlling interest in AMC. See National Academy of Engineering, op. cit., p. 64.

25. Automotive News, *Market Data Book Issue,* 1984, p. 4; *Fortune* (Aug. 20, 1984).

26. *The Wall Street Journal,* Aug. 3, 1983, p. 1.

27. *The Wall Street Journal,* Aug. 10, 1981, p. 2; *The Wall Street Journal,* Aug. 11, 1981, p. 2; *The Wall Street Journal,* Sept. 1, 1981, p. 2.

28. *The Wall Street Journal,* July 6, 1983, p. 3; *The Wall Street Journal,* July 22, 1983, p. 7; *The Wall Street Journal,* Sept. 14, 1983, p. 2; *The Wall Street Journal,* Sept. 27, 1983, p. 11.

29. U.S. Congress, Senate, Subcommittee on Antitrust, Committee on the Judiciary, *A Reorganization of the U.S. Automobile Industry,* 93rd Cong., 2nd sess., 1974, p. 235. See also, S. E. Boyle and T. F. Hogarty, "Pricing Behavior in the American Automobile Industry, 1957–71," *Journal of Industrial Economics,* 24:81(1975).

30. J. E. Kwoka, "Market Power and Market Change in the U.S. Automobile Industry," *Journal of Industrial Economics,* 32:512–515(1984).

31. *Business Week* (March 24, 1980), p. 79; *Fortune* (June 25, 1984), p. 24.

32. *Findings of the Chrysler Corporation Loan Guarantee Board,* op. cit., p. 165.

33. Quoted in National Academy of Engineering, op. cit., p. 29. Compare with Henry Ford's philosophy:

> It is considered good manufacturing practice, and not bad ethics, occasionally to change designs so that old models will become obsolete and new ones will have to be bought either because repair parts for the old cannot be had, or because the new model offers a new sales argument which can be used to persuade a customer to scrap what he has and buy something new. We have been told that this is good business, and that the object of business ought to be to get people to buy frequently, and that it is bad business to try to make anything that will last forever, because when once a man is sold he will not buy again.
>
> Our principle of business is precisely to the contrary. We cannot conceive how to serve the customer unless we make him something that, as far as we can provide, will last forever. . . . It does not please us to have the buyer's car wear out or become obsolete. We want the man who buys one of our products never to have to buy another. We never make an improvement that renders any previous model obsolete.

Quoted in J. M. Blair, *Economic Concentration* (New York: Harcourt, 1972), p. 335.

34. J. Keats, *The Insolent Chariots* (New York: Lippincott, 1958), pp. 54–55.

35. U.S. Congress, Senate, Subcommittee on Antitrust, Committee on the Judiciary, *Administered Prices: Automobiles, Report,* 85th Cong., 2nd sess., 1958, pp. 79–80.

36. F. M. Fisher, Z. Griliches, and C. Kaysen, "The Costs of Automobile Model Changes Since 1949," *Journal of Political Economy,* 70:448(1962).

37. W. Abernathy, *The Productivity Dilemma* (Baltimore: Johns Hopkins, 1978), pp. 46–47, 127–128.

38. Bain, op. cit., p. 241.

39. U.S. Congress, House, Subcommittee on Monopolies and Commercial Law, Committee on the Judiciary, *Corporate Initiative, Hearings,* 97th Cong., 1st sess., 1982, pp. 40–41.

40. Note, "Annual Style Change in the Automobile Industry as an Unfair Method of Competition," *Yale Law Journal,* 80:583(1971).

41. Except where indicated, the following account draws primarily from L. J. White, "The American Automobile Industry and the Small Car, 1945–70," *Journal of Industrial Economics,* 20:179(1972).

42. P. Blumberg, "Snarling Cars," *The New Republic* (Jan. 24, 1983), p. 12.

43. A small, light-weight car developed by GM was marketed in Australia in 1948 by a GM subsidiary; Ford's light car appeared the same year as the French Ford Vedette. White, "American Automobile Industry and the Small Car," op. cit.

44. Ibid., p. 191.

45. Ibid., p. 180.

46. U.S. Congress, Senate, Subcommittee on Antitrust, Committee on the Judiciary, *The Industrial Reorganization Act, Hearings on S.1167,* Part 3, 93rd Cong., 2nd sess., 1974, pp. 1954, 1957. It might be argued that in marketing large rather than small cars, the domestic oligopoly was merely following the dictates of consumers' preference for large cars. But as Paul Blumberg points out, this argument "overlooks the fact that consumer taste does not develop in a vacuum but is shaped by manufacturers through massive advertising. . . . Throughout the postwar years Detroit spent . . . billions fashioning public taste for the gas guzzlers, and then proceeded to satisfy that taste." Blumberg, op. cit., p. 12.

47. Report of MIT's International Automobile Program, op. cit., p. 174.

48. National Academy of Engineering, op. cit., p. 30.

49. Perot quoted in *The Washington Post,* July 7, 1985. On engineering quality, see W. J. Abernathy, K. B. Clark, and A. M. Kantrow, *Industrial Renaissance* (New York: Basic, 1983), pp. 65–66; U.S., Congressional Budget Office, *Current Problems of the U.S. Automobile Industry and Policies to Address Them* (Staff Working Paper, July 1980), p. 17.

50. S. Flax, "How Detroit Is Reforming the Steelmakers," *Fortune* (May 16, 1983), p. 126.

51. *The Wall Street Journal,* March 23, 1982, p. 3.

52. See *Business Week* (June 21, 1982), p. 82.

53. *The Wall Street Journal,* Dec. 19, 1983, p. 10.

54. Ibid.

55. Ibid. Also see *The Wall Street Journal,* Oct. 27, 1980, p. 8.

56. For a detailed treatment of tacit vertical collusion between management and organized labor in autos and other industries, see W. Adams and J. W. Brock, "Tacit Vertical Collusion and the Labor-Industrial Complex," *Nebraska Law Review,* 62:621(1983).

57. *The Wall Street Journal,* Sept. 24, 1984, p. 1.

58. For a comment on the Chrysler settlement and its implications, see Paul A. London, "Car Bomb," *The New Republic,* Nov. 25, 1985, pp. 14–15.

59. Abernathy et al., op. cit., p. 62.

60. See U.S. Congress, House, Subcommittee on Economic Stabilization, Committee on Banking, Finance and Urban Affairs, *To Determine the Impact of Foreign Sourcing on Industry and Communities, Hearing,* 97th Cong., 1st sess., 1981, p. 25.

61. Quoted in *Fortune* (June 25, 1984), p. 22.

62. *Fortune,* (Feb. 8, 1982), p. 35.

63. Abernathy et al., op. cit., pp. 79–80.

64. J. P. Wright, *On a Clear Day You Can See General Motors* (Grosse Point, Mich.: Wright Enterprises, 1979), pp. 114–115.

65. Ibid., p. 100.

66. See *Business Week* (Sept. 14, 1980), p. 97.

67. Quoted in *The New York Times,* Feb. 8, 1984, p. 31.

68. Automotive News, *Market Data Book Issue,* 1984, p. 59; *Economic Report of the President,* 1984.

69. U.S. Congress, House, Subcommittee on Economic Stabilization, Committee on Banking, Finance and Urban Affairs, *The Chrysler Corporation Financial Situation, Hearings,* Part 1A, 96th Cong., 1st sess., 1979, p. 557.

70. Quoted in *The New York Times,* April 8, 1984, sec. 3, p. 1. Economist John Kwoka contends that, lacking a competitive advantage, domestic producers have raised small-car prices sharply and conceded this segment of the market to foreign producers. See Kwoka, "Market Power and Market Change in the U.S. Automobile Industry," op. cit., pp. 512–515.

71. Department of Transportation, op. cit., pp. 83–85; *The Wall Street Journal,* Oct. 3, 1980, p. 1.

72. *The Wall Street Journal,* Jan. 5, 1981, p. 5.

73. *The Wall Street Journal,* Aug. 10, 1981, p. 2; *The Wall Street Journal,* Sept. 1, 1981, p. 2.

74. U.S. Congress, House, Subcommittee on Trade, Committee on Ways and Means, *Fair Practices in Automotive Products Act, Hearings on H.R. 5133,* 97th Cong., 2nd sess., 1982, p. 271.

75. U.S., International Trade Commission, *Certain Motor Vehicles and Certain Chassis and Bodies Therefor,* Dec. 1980, p. 145.

76. R. W. Crandall, "Import Quotas and the Automobile Industry: The Costs of Protectionism," *The Brookings Review* (Summer 1984), p. 10.

77. *Fortune* (Feb. 8, 1982), p. 36.

78. U.S. Congress, Senate, Subcommittee on Antitrust, Committee on the Judiciary, *Economic Concentration, Hearings Pursuant to S. Res. 40,* Part 3, 89th Cong., 1st sess., 1965, p. 1123.

79. D. A. Moore, "The Automobile Industry," in W. Adams (ed.), *The Structure of American Industry,* rev. ed. (New York: Macmillan, 1954), p. 303.

80. Quoted in U.S. Congress, Senate, Subcommittee on Executive Reorganization, Committee on Government Operations, *Federal Role in Traffic Safety, Hearings,* Part 3, 89th Cong., 2nd sess., 1966, p. 1266.

81. *Industrial Reorganization Act, Hearings,* op. cit., p. 1954. For example, domestic auto companies were forced to incorporate microelectronic circuitry in their cars in order to meet government fuel economy and pollution regulations. Now, the industry proclaims microelectronics to mark a revolutionary new departure in automotive design and engineering. See *Business Week* (Feb. 11., 1985), p. 114; *Fortune* (July 8, 1985), p. 26.

82. *The New York Times,* April 26, 1981, sec. 3, p. 3.

83. U.S. Congress, Senate, Committee on Commerce, *Automotive Research and Development and Fuel Economy, Hearings,* 93rd Cong., 1st sess., 1973, p. 369.

84. L. J. White, "The Automobile Industry," in W. Adams (ed.), *The Structure of American Industry,* 5th ed. (New York: Macmillan, 1977), p. 195.

85. *Impact of Foreign Sourcing on Industries and Communities, Hearing,* op. cit., p. 54.

86. The most important justification offered in defense of GM's joint California production venture with Toyota, according to Federal Trade Commission Chairman James Miller III, is that "the venture offers a valuable opportunity for GM to complete its learning of the more efficient Japanese manufacturing and management methods." U.S. Congress, House, Subcommittee on Commerce, Transportation, and Tourism, Committee on Energy and Commerce, *Future of the Automobile Industry, Hearing,* 98th Cong., 2nd sess., 1984, p. 500.

87. White, *The Automobile Industry Since 1945,* op. cit., pp. 228–29.

88. See *Automotive Research and Development and Fuel Economy, Hearings,* op. cit., p. 619. Indeed, GM was sufficiently concerned about automotive air pollution to begin researching the problem as early as 1938. See Smog-Control Antitrust Case, *Congressional Record,* May 18, 1971, pp. 15626–27 (House edition).

89. U.S. Congress, Senate, Subcommittee on Air and Water Pollution, Committee on Public Works, *Air Pollution—1967 (Automotive Air Pollution), Hearings,* Part 1, 90th Cong., 1st sess., 1967, p. 158.

90. Smog-Control Antitrust Case, op cit., p. 15627. As recorded in the minutes of a 1958 meeting, each participant understood that "no company should expect to take advantage competitively by being the first, or claiming to be the first, to offer such a device." Ibid., p. 15630.

91. National Academy of Sciences, Report by the Committee on Motor Vehicle Emissions, February 12, 1973, reprinted in *Congressional Record,* February 28, 1973, pp. 5832, 5849 (Senate edition).

92. U.S. Congress, Senate, Committee on Public Works, *Highway Safety Act of 1966, Report,* 89th Cong., 2nd sess., 1966, p. 3.

93. U.S. Congress, Senate, Committee on Commerce, *Traffic Safety Act of 1966, Report,* 89th Cong., 2nd sess., 1966, pp. 2–3.

94. *Federal Role in Traffic Safety, Hearings,* op. cit., Part 3, pp. 1319–21; R. Nader, *Unsafe at Any Speed* (New York: Grossman, 1965), pp. 92–93.

95. See Nader, op. cit., p. 134. The industry's disregard for safety at times can be ludicrous; in 1983, for example, *The Wall Street Journal* reported on General Motors' efforts "to persuade the federal government that it isn't dangerous for a car's rear-wheel axle to fall off." *The Wall Street Journal,* March 8, 1983, p. 44.

96. See, *Federal Role in Traffic Safety, Hearings,* op. cit., Part 3, p. 1279.

97. White, *The Automobile Industry Since 1945,* op. cit., p. 241.

98. John Jerome found in his study of the industry that Ford could not meet the unexpectedly strong demand for safety options offered in some of its 1956 car models. J. Jerome, *The Death of the Automobile* (New York: Norton 1972), p. 273. Yet, the president of Ford, Robert S. McNamara, abruptly cancelled the safety package the same year in which it was first offered—perhaps, some suggest, because of pressure exerted by GM. See L. Iacocca, *Iacocca* (New York: Bantam, 1984), p. 296.

99. U.S. Congress, Senate, Select Committee on Small Business, *Planning, Regulation, and Competition: Automobile Industry—1968, Hearings,* 90th Cong., 2nd sess., 1968, p. 967. In like fashion, Ford remained silent after discovering (through its own internal testing) the dangerous design of GM's infamous Corvair; Ford's reticence appears to have been motivated largely by a desire to maintain cordial relations with its dominant rival. See E. Cray, *Chrome Colossus* (New York: McGraw-Hill, 1980), p. 409. For charges of tacit collusion in the provision of seat belts, see *Federal Role in Traffic Safety, Hearings,* op. cit., Part 3, p. 1302.

100. See S. Melman, *Profits Without Production* (New York: Knopf, 1983), p. 41.

101. Cited in Keats, op. cit., p. 14. Just months before the first OPEC oil embargo of 1973, GM's chairman advocated more rapid licensing of nuclear power plants as an important means for resolving the nation's energy problem; one month before the overthrow of the Shah of Iran in 1979, and the onset of the nation's second energy crisis in six years, GM assured the American public that "fuel-economy standards are not necessary and they are not good for America." *Automotive Research and Development and Fuel Economy, Hearings,* op. cit., p. 564; Cray, op. cit., p. 524.

102. *Automotive Research and Development and Fuel Economy, Hearings,* op. cit., p. 70.

103. According to research conducted by the Environmental Protection Agency, "the increase in average vehicle weight (more than 350 pounds) and the associated changes in engine size over the total 12-year-period [1962–1973] alone have accounted for about ½ of the total loss" in automotive fuel economy. U.S., Environmental Protection Agency, *A Report on Automobile Fuel Economy,* October 1973, p. 32. See also Fisher et al. op. cit.

104. *Fortune* (Oct. 22, 1979), p. 48.

105. These suits were eventually decided in favor of the firms. See *United States v. General Motors Corp. and Ford Motor Co.*, 1974–2 Trade Cases, No. 75, 253.

106. *United States v. Automobile Manufacturers Association, Inc.*, 1969 Trade Cases, No. 72, 907.

107. See *Issues Relating to the Domestic Auto Industry, Hearings,* op. cit., Part 3, p. 49.

108. For a detailed discussion of the serious anticompetitive problems posed by the GM–Toyota joint venture, see *Future of the Automobile Industry, Hearing,* op. cit., pp. 277–291.

109. Comments of the Staff of the Council on Wage and Price Stability: Before the U.S. International Trade Commission, September 5, 1975, pp. 4–5.

110. See Crandall, op. cit., pp. 13–15; *The New York Times,* April 8, 1984, sec. 3, p. 1; *The Wall Street Journal,* Dec. 3, 1984, p. 33.

111. U.S., International Trade Commission, *A Review of Recent Developments in the U.S. Automobile Industry, Including An Assessment of the Japanese Voluntary Restraint Agreements* (Washington, D.C.: USITC Pub. No. 1648, February 1985), p. ix.

112. Carefully conducted research raises serious questions regarding the image of "Japan, Inc.," which has become part of the popular mythology. See G. R. Saxonhouse, "What Is All This About 'Industrial Targeting' in Japan?" *The World Economy,* 6:253(1983); W. Duncan, *U.S.–Japan Automobile Diplomacy,*(Cambridge, Mass.: Ballinger, 1973), pp. 53–113. *The Wall Street Journal,* too, casts doubt on the conventional wisdom regarding government–industry collaboration in Japan. "A generation ago," the Journal recently editorialized, "Mr. Honda wanted to expand his motorcycle company by making cars. But the planners at Japan's Ministry of International Trade and Industry (MITI) didn't like the idea. They wanted only two companies—Toyota and Nissan . . . But Japan is a free country, so Mr. Honda went ahead. Today Honda Motor is universally respected for making excellent cars—and selling an extraordinarily large number of them. What's more, other upstarts followed Mr. Honda and Japan now has nine successful and hotly competitive automakers." *The Wall Street Journal,* Dec. 11, 1984, p. 32.

113. As Crandall points out, the new product offerings and manufacturing-process developments now being put into place by the domestic industry were already underway prior to the advent of the import-quota program. Crandall, op. cit., pp. 12–13.

114. See *Fortune* (Dec. 10, 1984), p. 172; *The Wall Street Journal,* Jan. 24, 1984, p. 28. It is interesting that General Motors petitioned Congress to raise the Japanese import ceiling in order to "accommodate" the small cars that it has arranged to produce jointly in Japan. See U.S. Congress, Joint Economic Committee, *Japanese Voluntary Auto Export Limits, Hearing,* 98th Cong., 1st sess., 1984, p. 70.

115. "Privately," *The Wall Street Journal* reported, "high Cabinet officials are angry that U.S. auto makers haven't used the restraints on the Japanese to successfully develop and manufacture small cars, as was the intention of the breathing period. Instead, the domestic auto makers have been diverting their resources to building bigger cars, which are more profitable, and asserting that consumers are 'demanding' big cars." *The Wall Street Journal,* Oct. 17, 1983, p. 34.

116. See *The Wall Street Journal,* April 28, 1983, p. 30. In 1980, for example, Chrysler Chairman Lee Iacocca stressed the temporary nature of the then-proposed import restraints: "We need a sunset law to get us to the fall of 1982 and let us get some blood back," he said. (*Business Week,* Oct. 20, 1980, p. 43.) Two years later, however, the industry's position began to change as auto executives pointed to continuing poor car sales to justify an extension of the quotas beyond their original termination date. (See *The Wall Street Journal,* Oct. 18, 1982, p. 4.) By 1983, Ford, Chrysler, and the United Auto Workers openly suggested that long-term protection might be needed to offset permanent "unfair" Japanese cost advantages. (See *The New York Times,* Nov. 2, 1983, p. 25.)

117. See *The Wall Street Journal,* May 14, 1980, p. 1.

118. U.S. Congress, House, Committee on Government Operations, *The Administration's Proposals to Help the U.S. Auto Industry, Hearings,* 97th Cong., 1st sess., 1981, p. 129. A compendium of the industry's criticisms of air pollution, safety, and fuel-economy regulations is contained in U.S. Congress, Senate, Subcommittee on Economic Stabilization, Committee on Banking, Housing, and Urban Affairs, *Government Regulation of the Automobile Industry, Hearing,* 96th Cong., 1st sess., 1979. Detailed rebuttals to the industry's charges may be found in *Chrysler Corporation Financial Situation, Hearings,* op. cit., pp. 447–565, and in U.S. Congress, House, Subcommittee on Telecommunications, Consumer Protection, and Finance, Committee on Energy and Commerce, *National Highway Traffic Safety Administration; Oversight Hearing,* 97th Cong., 2nd sess., 1982, pp. 618–76.

119. Quoted in U.S. Congress, Senate, Subcommittee for Consumers, Committee on Commerce, Science and Transportation, *Cost of Government Regulations to the Consumer, Hearings,* 95th Cong., 2nd sess., 1978, p. 87.

120. *Traffic Safety Act of 1966, Report,* op. cit., pp. 1–4.

121. P. L. 89-563; 80 Stat. 718.

SUGGESTED READINGS

BOOKS:

Abernathy, W. J. *The Productivity Dilemma.* Baltimore: Johns Hopkins University Press, 1978.

———K. Clark, and A. Kantrow. *Industrial Renaissance.* New York: Basic Books, 1983.

Cray, E. *Chrome Colossus.* New York: McGraw-Hill Book Co., 1980.

Duncan, W. *U.S.–Japan Automobile Diplomacy.* Cambridge, Mass.: Ballinger Publishing Co., 1973.

Flink, J. J. *The Car Culture.* Cambridge, Mass.: MIT Press, 1975.

Hunker, J. A. *Structural Change in the U.S. Automobile Industry.* Lexington, Mass.: D.C. Heath and Co., 1983.

Iacocca, L. *Iacocca.* New York: Bantam Books, 1984.

Keats, J. *The Insolent Chariots.* New York: J. B. Lippincott Company, 1958.

Leavitt, H. *Superhighway—Superhoax.* New York: Doubleday & Co., 1970.

Nader, R. *Unsafe At Any Speed.* New York: Grossman Publishers, 1965.

National Academy of Engineering. *The Competitive Status of the U.S. Auto Industry.* Washington, D.C.: National Academy Press, 1982.

National Academy of Sciences. *Report by the Committee on Motor Vehicle Emissions.* Printed in *Congressional Record,* February 28, 1973, pp. 5831–52 (Senate edition).

Nevins, A. *Ford: The Times, The Man, The Company.* New York: Charles Scribner's Sons, 1954.

Owen, N. *Economies of Scale, Competitiveness, and Trade Patterns Within the European Community.* Oxford: Clarendon Press, 1983.

Owen, W. *The Accessible City.* Washington, D.C.: Brookings Institution, 1972.

Reich, R. B. and J. D. Donahue. *New Deals: The Chrysler Revival and the American System.* New York: Times Books, 1985.

Report of MIT's International Automobile Program. *The Future of the Automobile*. Cambridge, Mass.: MIT Press, 1984.

Sloan, A. P. *My Years With General Motors*. New York: Doubleday & Co., 1965.

Toder, E. J. *Trade Policy and the U.S. Automobile Industry*. New York: Praeger, 1978.

White, L. J. *The Automobile Industry Since 1945*. Cambridge, Mass.: Harvard University Press, 1971.

———*The Regulation of Air-Pollutant Emissions from Motor Vehicles*. Washington, D.C.: American Enterprise Institute, 1982.

Wright, J. P. *On a Clear Day You Can See General Motors*. Grosse Point, Mich.: Wright Enterprises, 1979.

GOVERNMENT PUBLICATIONS:

Department of Transportation. *Automotive Fuel Economy Program: Fifth Annual Report to the Congress*. Washington, D.C.: U.S. Government Printing Office, 1981.

———*The U.S. Automobile Industry, 1980*. Washington, D.C.: U.S. Government Printing Office, 1981.

———*The U.S. Automobile Industry, 1981*. Washington, D.C.: U.S. Government Printing Office, 1982.

Federal Trade Commission. *Report on the Motor Vehicle Industry*. Washington, D.C.: U.S. Government Printing Office, 1939.

International Trade Commission. *Certain Motor Vehicles and Certain Chassis and Bodies Therefor*. Washington, D.C.: USITC Pub. No. 1110, 1980.

———*The U.S. Auto Industry: U.S. Factory Sales, Retail Sales, Imports, Exports, Apparent Consumption, Suggested Retail Prices, and Trade Balances with Selected Countries for Motor Vehicles, 1964–82*. Washington, D.C.: USITC Pub. No. 1419, 1983.

Smog-Control Antitrust Case, *Congressional Record*, May 18, 1971, pp. 15626–37 (House edition).

U.S. Congress, Office of Technology Assessment. *U.S. Industrial Competitiveness: A Comparison of Steel, Electronics, and Automobiles*. Washington, D.C.: U.S. Government Printing Office, 1981.

U.S. Congress, House, Subcommittee on Economic Stabilization. *Findings of the Chrysler Corporation Loan Guarantee Board, Committee Print*, 96th Cong. 2nd sess., 1980.

———*The Chrysler Corporation Financial Situation, Hearings*, Parts 1–2, 96th Cong. 1st sess., 1979.

———*To Determine the Impact of Foreign Sourcing on Industry and Communities, Hearing*, 97th Cong. 1st sess., 1981.

———*Government Regulation of the Automobile Industry, Hearing*, 96th Cong. 1st sess., 1979.

U.S. Congress, House, Subcommittee on Trade. *Domestic Content Legislation and the U.S. Automobile Industry*, 97th Cong. 2nd sess., 1982.

———*Fair Practices in Automotive Products Act, Hearings*, 97th Cong. 2nd sess., 1982.

U.S. Congress, House, Subcommittee on Commerce, Transportation, and Tourism. *Future of the Automobile Industry, Hearing*, 98th Cong. 2nd sess., 1984.

U.S. Congress, House, Subcommittee on Transportation, Aviation and Materials. *H.R. 5880—Automobile Research Competition Act, Hearing*, 97th Cong. 2nd sess., 1982.

U.S. Congress, House, Subcommittee on Telecommunications, Consumer Protection, and Finance. *National Highway Traffic Safety Administration, Oversight Hearings*, 97th Cong. 2nd sess., 1982.

U.S. Congress, Joint Economic Committee. *Japanese Voluntary Export Limits, Hearing,* 98th Cong. 1st sess., 1984.

U.S. Congress, Senate, Subcommittee on Antitrust and Monopoly. *A Reorganization of the U.S. Automobile Industry,* 93d Cong. 2nd sess., 1974.

———*Administered Prices: Automobiles, Report,* 85th Cong. 2nd sess., 1958.

———*Bigness and Concentration of Economic Power—A Case Study of General Motors Corporation, Report,* 84th Cong. 2nd sess., 1956.

———*The Industrial Reorganization Act, Hearings,* Parts 3–4A, 93d Cong. 2nd sess., 1974.

U.S. Congress, Senate, Subcommittee on Executive Reorganization. *Federal Role in Traffic Safety, Hearings,* Parts 1–3, 89th Cong. 1st and 2nd sess., 1965–66.

U.S. Congress, Senate, Subcommittee on International Trade. *Issues Relating to the Domestic Auto Industry, Hearings,* Parts 1–3, 97th Cong., 1st sess., 1981–82.

U.S. Congress, Senate, Committee on Commerce. *Automotive Research and Development and Fuel Economy, Hearings,* 93d Cong., 1st sess., 1973.

U.S. Congress, Senate, Select Committee on Small Business. *Planning, Regulation, and Competition: Automobile Industry—1968, Hearings,* 90th Cong. 2nd sess., 1968.

U.S. Congress, Senate, Subcommittee on Surface Transportation. *Motor Vehicle Safety and the Marketplace, Hearings,* 98th Cong., 1st sess., 1983.

ARTICLES:

Adams, W., and J. W. Brock. "Tacit Vertical Collusion and the Labor–Industrial Complex," *Nebraska Law Review,* **62** (Fall 1983).

Blumberg, P. "Snarling Cars," *The New Republic* (Jan. 24, 1983).

Boyle, S. E., and T. F. Hogarty. "Pricing Behavior in the American Automobile Industry, 1957–71," *Journal of Industrial Economics,* **24** (Dec. 1975).

Burck, C. "Can Detroit Catch Up?" *Fortune* (Feb. 8, 1982).

Business Week. Various issues.

Crandall, R. W. "Import Quotas and the Automobile Industry: The Costs of Protectionism," *Brookings Review* (Summer 1984).

Fisher, F. M., Z. Griliches, and C. Kaysen. "The Costs of Automobile Model Changes Since 1949," *Journal of Political Economy,* **70** (Oct. 1962).

Flax, S. "How Detroit Is Reforming the Steelmakers," *Fortune* (May 16, 1983).

Irvine, F. O. "Demand Equations for Individual New Car Models Estimated Using Transactions Prices with Implications for Regulatory Issues," *Southern Economic Journal,* **49** (Jan. 1983).

Kraar, L. "Detroit's New Asian Car Strategy," *Fortune* (Dec. 10, 1984).

Kwoka, J. E. "Market Power and Market Change in the U.S. Automobile Industry," *Journal of Industrial Economics,* **32** (June, 1984).

Note: "Annual Style Change in the Automobile Industry As an Unfair Method of Competition," *Yale Law Journal,* **80** (Jan. 1971).

Peltzman, S. "The Effects of Automobile Safety Regulation," *Journal of Political Economy,* **83** (Aug. 1975).

Robertson, L. "A Critical Analysis of Peltzman's 'The Effects of Automobile Safety Regulation' ", *Journal of Economic Issues,* **11** (Sept. 1977).

Stokes, H. S. "Honda, the Market Guzzler," *Fortune* (Feb. 20, 1984).

Ward's Automotive Reports. Various issues.

The Wall Street Journal. Various issues.

White, L. J. "The American Automobile Industry and the Small Car, 1945–70," *Journal of Industrial Economics,* **20** (April 1972).

Wichlein, J. "Whitewashing Detroit's Dirty Engines," *Washington Monthly* (June 1970).

5

The Breakfast Cereal Industry

F. M. Scherer

INTRODUCTION

Western cultures have become more homogeneous, but intercultural distinctions remain. In Germany, breakfast is hardly anything without freshly baked Brötchen, and the French savor their croissants. The great North American breakfast institution is the ready-to-eat (RTE) cereal, served with milk in a dazzling variety of grains, shapes, and flavors. In 1971, a marketing research survey revealed, the average American consumed 90 servings of RTE-cereal per year.

Cereals date back in history to the days when humans began to supplement hunting and gathering with the systematic cultivation of grain crops. A porridge made from cooked cereal grains is the simplest of processed foods, and its widespread use preceded in time the making of flat, and then leavened, bread. Yet cereal eaten as porridge is an inferior good—its consumption is reduced as real income rises. Outside Asia, consumers have shown a definite proclivity to abandon porridge for bread products made from wheat or rye when their means permitted.[1] Samuel Johnson, indulging the English penchant for ridiculing Scotland as a land of primitives, defined "oats" in his *Dictionary* (1755) as "a grain which in England is generally given to horses, but in Scotland supports the people."[2] The negative income elasticity of its oatmeal porridge staple was clearly recognized by the Quaker Oats Company in its annual report for 1907, a year of recession: "When people are forced to economize, and count the dollars and pennies, they naturally turn to cereals, which are always relatively the cheapest and most nutritious of foods."

The appearance of ready-to-eat breakfast cereals did much to ward off the consequences of inferior-good status for cereals in the increasingly prosperous American economy. The first recorded step was Dr. James C. Jackson's "Granula," which was offered in New York during the 1860s as a health food. Its economic impact was modest, but growing interest in processed ready-to-eat cereals as health foods induced a wave of parallel innovations during the 1890s. Leading the way to mass production and distribution was Henry D. Perky's shredded wheat, exhibited in 1884 at the World's Food Fair in Boston. Perky promoted his product on the lecture circuit, proclaiming among other things that:

> From the most abject physical wreck, I have succeeded by the use of naturally organized food, in reorganizing my body into perfectly healthy condition . . . I am fifty-five years of age and feel younger than twenty years ago.[3]

Although strong acceptance in the market enabled Perky's Shredded Wheat Company (sold in 1928 to the National Biscuit Company) to erect a world-famous factory at Niagara Falls, the center of the newly emerging RTE-cereal industry shifted to Battle Creek, Michigan, where Dr. J. H. Kellogg operated a sanitarium emphasizing vegetarian nutrition as a path to good health. During the 1880s and 1890s, Kellogg experimented with various prepared cereal products, sending them by mail to his patients after they left the sanitarium. One patient, C. W. Post, went on to found his own cereal foods clinic and sales company. In 1898, Post's Grape Nuts cereal was introduced, and in 1904 it was followed by a corn flake product, first called Elijah's Manna, but three years later renamed Post Toasties. Post recognized that his RTE-cereals had a potential appeal much broader than health foods devotees, so he embarked upon nationwide advertising campaigns to stimulate sales. After observing Post's endeavors, J. H. Kellogg's brother, W. K. Kellogg, founded his own cereal company in 1906 and began the production of Kellogg's Toasted Corn Flakes. To spur demand, Kellogg committed a third of his new company's working capital to a full-page advertisement in the *Ladies Home Journal,* in which he offerred a season's supply of corn flakes free to any woman who persuaded her grocer to stock the Kellogg product. In its first year, the Kellogg Company distributed four million free samples. Attracted by the success of the Perky, Post, and Kellogg ventures, dozens of other cereal-production enterprises were founded, many of them in Battle Creek. The RTE-cereal industry was off and running, led by three of the companies that in 1980 would continue to be among its top six sellers.

In 1905 the Quaker Oats Company, a leader in the more traditional hot-cereal (i.e., porridge) market, branched out into the RTE-cereal business by acquiring the puffed wheat and puffed rice patents of a smaller firm. Thus, four of the five principal RTE-cereal production methods—granulation, flaking, shredding, and puffing—were already in use by 1905. Only the extrusion method, first successfully demonstrated by General Mills with the introduction of Cheerios in 1941, remained to be developed. Quaker also commenced the production of a corn-flake product, and won a law suit in 1914, in which Kellogg sought to block Quaker's use of the name Toasted Corn Flakes.

Ready-to-eat cereals steadily gained over hot cereals in consumer favor. In 1939, as shown in Table 1, RTEs accounted for approximately 65 percent of combined hot and ready-to-eat-cereal output (excluding baby cereals) by dollar volume, and 45 percent by poundage. (RTEs require more processing

Table 1: Sales of Hot and RTE Cereals, 1939–1982

	"To Be Cooked" Cereal Sales		RET-Cereal Sales		RTE-Cereals As a Percent of Total Sales	
Year	*Million Pounds*	*Million $*	*Million Pounds*	*Million $*	*Pounds*	*Dollars*
1939	712.1	36.4	576.5	67.1	44.7	64.8
1947	773.1	69.7	713.1	148.1	48.0	68.0
1954	630.6	74.2	926.1	246.0	59.5	76.8
1958	612.4	83.3[a]	1043.6	341.1	63.0	80.4
1967	420.2	62.2	1600.2[a]	616.4[a]	79.2	90.8
1977	782.5[a]	226.0[a]	1910.5[a]	1477.4[a]	70.9	86.7
1982	n.a.	270.0[a]	2080.0[a]	2531.0[a]	n.a.	89.1

[a]Some figures for 1958 and later years are estimates using brand-share data to disaggregate product subclasses combined or suppressed in Census reports.
Source: U.S. Bureau of the Census, *Census of Manufactures*, for the years given.

than rolled oats, farina, and other hot cereals; they therefore typically cost more per pound, and hence have higher sales-dollar shares than poundage shares.) By 1954, the RTEs had pulled ahead in pound sales as well as in dollar volume. By 1967, the output of hot cereals had fallen to 420 million pounds, from a 1947 Census-year high of 773 million pounds. During the next decade, the "hots" staged a modest recovery. It is not clear whether this was a result of the introduction of new and more convenient instant-oatmeal products, the stagnation of real-income growth during the 1970s (bringing into play the negative income elasticity effect that has historically been associated with hot cereals), or some combination of these and other influences.

The output of RTE-cereals meanwhile grew more rapidly than population, rising from 577 million pounds in 1939 to roughly 1.9 million pounds in 1977 and 2.1 million pounds in 1982. Among the factors that influenced this growth were several other product developments. One was presweetening, which was pioneered by a small firm in 1939 and brought to large-scale commercial success when General Foods (successor to the Post Company) introduced its Sugar Crisp product in 1950. Because of their special appeal to children, the "presweets" have been widely imitated. Second, although RTE-cereals were originally promoted as health foods, their nutritional value actually left much to be desired. The processing of grain into RTE-cereals removes important nutrients. It was not until the early 1940s, when wartime food shortages aroused concern over nutritional value, that the federal government induced RTE-cereal producers to add sufficient vitamins and iron to restore their cereals to preprocessing whole-grain levels. Further vitamin and mineral fortification steps followed during the next three decades, which permitted cereal makers again to emphasize the nutritional quality of their offerings. A third noteworthy development was the modest renaissance of granola-type cereals in the 1970s, as a result of a surge of interest in "natural" foods not unlike that which spurred the original appearance of RTEs during the 1890s.

The main focus in this chapter is on ready-to-eat cereals, which are distinct in their appeal and marketing methods, and which, at least since the 1940s, have accounted for the lion's share of breakfast-cereal production. Only peripheral attention is devoted to the much smaller hot-cereal market.

II. MARKET STRUCTURE

By any definition, the breakfast cereal industry is a tight oligopoly—one of the most highly concentrated industries in the U.S. manufacturing sector. Census data on seller concentration exist only for the four-digit industry defined as "cereal preparations," which includes three main components—RTE-cereals, hot cereals, and infant cereals. In 1977, the four-firm seller concentration index for cereal preparations was 89 percent, and the top eight sellers originated 98 percent of industry sales. Of the 449 manufacturing industries for which 1977 concentration ratios are published or can be imputed, only seven had higher four-firm indices than cereal preparations.

Not surprisingly, the principal components of the cereal preparations category are also highly concentrated. In 1982, the four leading producers accounted for 84.5 percent of total RTE-cereal pound sales.[4] Kellogg was in first place, with a market share of 39 percent. General Mills (which entered the business in 1928 by purchasing the company making Wheaties) was second, with 21 percent; General Foods (Post) was third, with 16 percent; Quaker was fourth, with 9 percent; and Ralston was fifth, with 6 percent. The hot-cereal market was dominated by Quaker, with a market share of 65 to 70 percent in 1970, and Nabisco (maker of Cream of Wheat), with a market share on the order of 20 percent. Two companies, Gerber and Heinz, account for the preponderance of infant cereal sales.

Statistical research has shown that above-average concentration ratios have a tendency to decline over time. This has not been the case for cereals. Table 2 reveals that the leading four sellers' share of all cereal-preparation sales rose from 68 percent in 1935 (the first year for which Census data are available) to 90 percent in 1972. RTE-cereal concentration exhibits a more gradual increase, from 84 percent in 1937 to 89 percent in 1972. The four-percentage-point decline thereafter is largely attributable to the growth of private-label and natural cereal sales, pioneered by non-Big Four members.

The lack of comparable data makes it difficult to reconstruct what happened to concentration in earlier stages of the cereal industry's history. High concentration was apparently a characteristic of the hot-cereal industry after several companies, which had previously collaborated in a cartel, merged

Table 2: Seller Concentration Statistics, All Cereal Preparations and RTE-Cereals, 1935–1982

	All Cereal Preparations			
Year	*Number of Sellers*	*Four-Firm Concentration Ratio*	*Eight-Firm Concentration Ratio*	*RTE-Cereals: Four-Firm Ratio*
1935	n.a.	68	82	n.a.
1937	n.a.	n.a.	n.a.	84
1947	55	79	91	88
1958	34	83	95	91
1967	30	88	97	89
1972	34	90	98	89
1977	32	89	98	85
1982	31	n.a.	n.a.	85

Sources: U.S. Bureau of the Census, *1977 Census of Manufactures*, "Concentration Ratios in Manufacturing," MC77-SR-9 (Washington, D.C.: May 1981); Federal Trade Commission, *In re Kellogg Co. et al.*, CX-106-A and GFX-1366; and issues of *Advertising Age*, cited in Note no. 15. The "all cereal preparations" ratios are for dollar value of shipments; those for RTE-cereals are for pounds.

to form the American Cereal Company, which later became Quaker Oats. Quaker's oatmeal market share was raised from 55 to 70 or 75 percent when it acquired the assets of the Great Western Cereal Company, makers of Mother's Oats, in 1911. Early accounts suggest that the number of RTE-cereal makers may have come close to 100 during the first decade of the twentieth century. Census records show that there were 137 plants that specialized in the production of various cereals, hot or cold, in 1914. The number of plants fell during the Great Depression from 121 in 1929 to 70 in 1939, with a further decline to 46 in 1954, after which there was a modest increase to 51 in 1982. From the available qualitative evidence, it would appear that the RTE market leaders of the 1980s pulled ahead relatively early in the game through the use of aggressive advertising and marketing techniques aimed at achieving a large nationwide sales volume.

Economies of Scale

When an industry is as highly concentrated as breakfast cereals or RTE-cereals, one is compelled to ask why. Mergers, as we have seen, played an important role in the development of the oatmeal market structure, but in most respects they had little impact on the RTE-cereal market structure. Another possible explanation might be economies of large-scale operation, which must be explored more fully.

RTE-cereal production processes involve machines of characteristically modest scale. According to a study conducted in the mid-1960s, the most expensive (and also the highest-capacity) single item of equipment used in RTE-cereal production was a packaging line, which cost $150,000.[5] On two-shift operation, such a line could package 14 million pounds of cereal per year, or about 1.1 percent of the total 1966 RTE-cereal output. There are scheduling flexibility advantages in having several production lines, including linked packaging lines, within a single plant; and multiline plants also achieve somewhat more economical utilization of raw grain handling and other plant overhead facilities. These considerations lead to the conclusion that, although it is possible to operate fully equipped cereal plants with a capacity of 20 million pounds per year, plant scale economy advantages persisted during the 1960s out to capacities of 50 or 60 million pounds per year, or 4 to 6 percent of industry output at the time. A new plant of that size cost roughly $25 million during the mid-1960s, and $100 million in the late 1970s.[6]

That these "engineering estimates" accurately characterize the plant size required to take advantage of all appreciable scale economies is attested to by the fact that the leading sellers, Kellogg and General Mills, chose to operate multiple plants (as of 1978, five each) rather than concentrate their output at a single larger plant. When new plants have been constructed by the leading cereal makers, they have tended to be in the 40–60-million-pound capacity range. Companies such as Kellogg and General Mills, with multiple, geographically decentralized plants, probably realize an advantage in being nearer their customers; they incur lower outbound freight costs, which, for the industry as a whole, amounted to approximately 5 percent of sales during the 1970s. However, an internal study by the General Foods Corporation in 1967 concluded that the transportation-cost disadvantage of operating (as it did at the time) from a single Battle Creek plant was not competitively important.[7] Thus, it seems reasonable to conclude that economies of scale in production and physical distribution are not sufficiently compelling to explain the leading sellers' large market shares. Kellogg in particular was seven to ten times as large in 1978 as it needed to be to realize the principal production-scale economies.

Economies of scale in marketing require a somewhat different and more complex explanation. Since the early experience of Messrs. Post and Kellogg, the cereal makers have placed great stress on selling their products through advertising. During the mid-1970s, the cereal makers devoted 9 to 11 percent of their sales revenues to media advertising. There are definite advantages in mounting a large rather than a small advertising campaign, especially via television.[8] Discounts can be obtained by buying network insertions rather than a multiplicity of spot messages. Also, on a per-second basis, it is cheaper to buy a 40-second commercial slot (e.g., covering two brands) rather than one lasting 20 seconds.

Perhaps more important, a certain amount of repetition is required before consumers react to one's message. The need for achieving this threshold-level of recognition is so great that the cost of mounting an effective network advertising campaign can be viewed as almost fixed, i.e., invariant with respect to actual or prospective market penetration. During the early 1960s, the "fixed" advertising cost of launching a new RTE-cereal brand appeared to be on the order of $3.2 million in the first year of sales.[9] Outlays in the third year averaged $1.16 million. To match the industry-wide advertising/sales ratio under these circumstances, a product would have to achieve sales of between $7 and $20 million, or from 1.3 to 3.6 percent of total RTE-cereal *industry* sales at the time. Considerations of this kind led industry participants to believe that a brand had to achieve a market share of 1 or 2 percent to be viable over the long pull. Popular brands such as General Mills' Cheerios and Kellogg's Sugar Frosted Flakes are probably able to sustain consumer interest through advertising outlays that are smaller in proportion to sales than those required by brands with only 1 or 2 percent of the market. In this sense, there are definite advantages of size in having substantial sales of any single brand, which is the relevant unit of analysis in advertising campaigns.

None of this, however, is enough to explain whether there are significant advantages to being as large as Kellogg or General Mills, who each have more than a dozen brands in distribution. That the advantages of size diminish at a sales volume not greatly in excess of a single efficient plant's output (i.e., 3 percent of the 1977 market) or the best-selling brand (e.g., in 1982, Kellogg's Corn Flakes, at 6.8 percent of poundage) is suggested by the fact that the cereal profit margins of General Mills were larger than those of Kellogg, with twice General Mills' market share. Moreover, Ralston, the sixth largest seller at the time, with a market share of only 4 or 5 percent, enjoyed net-profit margins about as large as those of Kellogg during the 1958–70 period, for which detailed data are available.[10] Although economies of scale definitely exist, they are not enough to explain why the cereal industry became, and remained, so highly concentrated.

Product Proliferation and Barriers to Entry

The answer probably lies in a complex interaction between scale economies in the advertising and promotion of individual brands, plant-scale economies, and the leading sellers' practice of proliferating new brands to cover all niches in the spectrum of product characteristics.[11] Consumers' demands for cereals vary greatly. Some like it hot, some like it cold; some prefer highly sweetened products, others prefer cereals that are unsweetened; some are indifferent to shapes, whereas others favor an animal configuration or an intricately woven biscuit, and so on. The RTE-cereal producers' response has been to launch many new and differentiated brands. At the beginning of 1950, as shown in Table 3, the six industry leaders had a total of 26 brands in distribution beyond the test stage. During the next 23 years, 84 brands were introduced, and although many dropped by the wayside, a total of 80 brands remained in distribution at the start of 1973. One consequence was that the market share enjoyed by individual brands tended to fall. In 1950, the best-selling brand was Kellogg's Corn Flakes, with a poundage market share of 16 percent.[12] Wheaties were second, with 10 percent, and Cheerios were third, with 7.5 percent. By 1978, Kellogg's Corn Flakes had fallen to 7.1 percent, Cheerios were second, at 5.8 percent, and Kellogg's Sugar Frosted Flakes were third, at 5.4 percent.

Viewed in isolation, these developments might be characterized as nothing more than an admirable responsiveness to consumer wants. However, there are other less favorable ramifications, one of which we shall consider now, and another later.

As brands proliferated, it became increasingly difficult for yet another brand to find a sizable niche in the market. Among the new brands launched during the 1950s, only three held market shares in excess of 2 percent three years after national distribution began. Kellogg's Special K fared best, with a 3.9 percent share of the market. But of the brands introduced in the 1960s, only Cap'n Crunch passed the 2 percent mark (with 2.1 percent). The more fragmented the market became, the poorer were the prospects of an additional brand capturing a significant market share.

Consider now the strategy problem of an outsider contemplating entry into the RTE-cereal market through product innovation. The potential entrant could not realistically expect its new brand to gain much more than 1 percent of the market, and it might do considerably worse. Yet, to establish a least-cost production and distribution operation, the outsider would need to obtain enough business to load a plant capable of producing 3 to 6 percent of total industry output. Somewhere between a half dozen to a dozen product

Table 3: RTE Brand Introductions and Brands in Distribution: 1950–1973

Year	New Brands Introduced	Total Brands: Six Leading Sellers	Total Brands: Individual Sellers					
			Kellogg	General Mills	General Foods	Quaker	Nabisco	Ralston
1950		26	9	3	6	3	2	3
	7							
1955		33	12	4	8	3	2	4
	14							
1960		44	15	8	9	3	5	4
	13							
1965		55	18	11	12	4	6	4
	28							
1970		69	20	15	12	10	6	6
	22							
1973		80	20	19	15	11	7	8

Source: Federal Trade Commission, *In re Kellogg et al.*, CX-409.

launches of average success would be required. The outsider could possibly have succeeded, but after carefully considering the difficulties, the would-be entrant was likely to seek less problematic fields in which to invest its funds.[13] For established sellers, on the other hand, brand space "crowding" posed no special critical-mass problem. If sales prospects for any single contemplated brand justified the investment of several million dollars in an advertising campaign, the new product could be accommodated within existing or planned production facilities. Thus, the proliferation of cereal products became a barrier to the entry of newcomers without symmetrically affecting the new-product launching activities of insiders.

Two other factors made new entry even more difficult. For one, good shelf position in supermarkets is vital to the sales of food products, and especially to the sale of RTE-cereals, many of which are purchased on impulse. Virtually every supermarket has its "cereal aisle." Marketing studies suggest that shoppers make more eye contact with products shelved near the middle of the aisle than with those at the ends of the aisle. To maximize the probability of impulse purchases, the leading RTE-cereal sellers have encouraged grocers, both through formal "shelf space" plans and regular salespersons' visits, to stock Big Three products in the center positions, relegating smaller companies' brands to the flanks.

Also, shelf space is limited, and, with 50 to 80 brands jostling for position, some brands have to be left off the shelf. The cereal that is not on the grocer's shelf does not get purchased. The shelf-space plans that retailers were urged to adopt by Kellogg and its closest rivals allocated space in proportion to historical sales volume. This, plus the "what's on the shelf gets sold" tendency and the eye-contact/impulse-purchase phenomenon, impart a considerable degree of inertia to company market-share movements. To be sure, it is not impossible for smaller producers to obtain preferred shelf placement. The usual vehicle for doing so is to offer retailers a special discount (e.g., 10 percent off the normal wholesale price) for favorable shelf position. This is costly, but it is a cost the larger firms do not have to incur for their established brands. It therefore adds differentially to the cost of smaller companies, and as such, it is a barrier to their entry or expansion.

The Natural Cereals Boom

All this implies that new entry into the RTE-cereal industry is quite difficult. This inference is consistent with most of the historical record. Between 1940 and 1970, there was no sizable new entrant into the business. Nevertheless, the early part of the 1970s proved to be an exception, and it is instructive to see what happened.

During this period, the array of products confronting consumers—which was seemingly so tightly crowded with brands as to defy any successful outside penetration—suddenly proved to have a gaping hole. "Natural" granola-type cereals were hardly new; variants had been produced by, among others, Dr. J. H. Kellogg, in the 1890s, but they had fallen out of favor. The renaissance of natural cereals began in the back rooms of California health foods stores during the 1960s. What at first was an isolated fad then turned into a nationwide passion. The first to tap this opportunity on more than a back-room scale were small or little-known companies such as Sovex, Organic Milling, and Niblack Foods. Their entry into the cereals market was facilitated by the relative simplicity of granola-making processes, but they found it difficult to assemble the combination of capital, management, and access to high-volume distribution channels needed to expand sales rapidly. Overextended logistic systems, and hence weak inventory control, coupled with the absence of preservatives in natural cereals, caused rancidity problems, which alienated consumers. Some but not all of these handicaps were avoided by the next round of entrants, which included such well-known national food-products manufacturers as Pet, Inc., Pillsbury, and Colgate.

By late 1972, the established cereal companies recognized that they had overlooked a potentially large market. They embarked upon a "fast-second" campaign: they developed their own natural cereal products, marketed them on an accelerated timetable, and supported the launches with a multimedia advertising barrage.[14] Quaker was the first of the Big Four, introducing its 100% Natural brand in March of 1973. General Mills followed with Nature Valley in August, and in October, Kellogg introduced Country Morning. The interlopers were effectively halted, and Pillsbury and Colgate withdrew. The most successful of the new entrants, Pet, saw the market share of its Heartland cereal fall from a peak of 1.8 percent in 1974 to 0.2 percent in 1978 and to 0.1 percent in 1980. As is often the case, the first firm to combine an established market position and heavy marketing artillery with a "new" product—in this instance, Quaker—experienced the greatest market success, retaining a 1.8 percent market share for its 100% Natural in 1978. As the natural cereal boom ebbed, Kellogg's Country Morning faded to a 0.2 percent market share in 1978, and had disappeared from the published tallies by 1980. A similar fate befell General Mills' Nature Valley.[15]

Thus, the exception to the conclusion that new entry into the RTE-cereal industry is difficult turns out, in the end, to reinforce that conclusion.

III. CONDUCT

In a tightly oligopolistic market, economic theory indicates, sellers should be acutely conscious of the fact that their business fortunes are interdependent. A policy of cooperation can lead to high profits, especially when barriers to new entry are appreciable. A policy of all-out rivalry can undermine profits. This generalization holds true for pricing, product policy, advertising, and other aspects of sellers' conduct. The RTE-cereal companies have exhibited considerable respect for their mutual interdependence in many, though not all, facets of conduct.

Pricing

Although the evidence is sparse, there apparently was a period following World War II when the leading cereal makers did not pursue pricing policies that could be deemed cooperative. A General Foods Corporation task force wrote, in 1967, of "the highly price-competitive nature of the cereal market in the early 1950s."[16] In 1966, a study for the National Commission on Food Marketing observed that "Prior to World War II, distribution of free samples and the use of prices as a lure to consumers, which in many cases took the form of price battles, were prevalent, especially for Kellogg and General Foods."[17] It stated further that "The move to deemphasize price competition has come within the past 25 years." The change in industry behavior was sufficiently dramatic to prompt a high-ranking Kellogg executive to boast at the annual meeting of his sales managers in 1966:

> [L]et me pass along to you the remark made by an advertising executive with many years of experience among leading companies of the food industry. The remark . . . is one which I consider a true compliment from a qualified observer who had no obligation whatsoever to our Company. He said this: "In my judgment there is no area in the food business today in which the true qualities of industry leadership are more aptly displayed than in the cereal industry where Kellogg provides strong and consistent leadership in building and expanding the profitable climate of true growth, virtually free from destructive pricing and promotional practices that—in many similar product categories—have undermined the vitality that is so necessary to their industry's continued progress."[18]

Similarly, two economists commissioned by the cereal makers to write a report on the industry concluded in 1966 that "Active price competition in cereals is low relative to some grocery product categories such as soaps and detergents, coffee, margarine, and others. . . ."[19]

How was this change accomplished? We do not know entirely, because time has obliterated many memories and documents, and those who know what happened may have good reason not to tell. Nevertheless, there are some clues.

One instrument with an apparently important role was price leadership. Company memoranda reveal a consensus among Big Three members that Kellogg was the price leader. The Kellogg executive quoted above emphasized in the same speech Kellogg's contribution as a leader in maintaining industry pricing discipline:

> A leader should do all in its power to build and expand its industry sales and avoid any steps which will drag the industry down. (A leader must maintain a profitable price structure within the industry—both for its members and distributors.)
>
> Kellogg has a long history of consistently *resisting* price cutting and gimmicks and withstanding competitive pressure in these arenas with notable restraint—up to the point where it was necessary to participate—overwhelmingly—in order to put an end to destructive practices. We intend to maintain this patience and

> restraint in the future—but—we will also be just as determined not to allow competitors to take an advantage beyond the point where the best interests of Kellogg are involved. There must always be a point at which we must protect ourselves at the sacrifice of a steady industry.
>
> Only a strong company can afford to exercise restraint when it is needed to keep an irritable condition from deteriorating into a war that no one wins. Only a strong company can set the pace that provides a favorable climate for a strong and growing industry. Only by disciplining ourselves can we set the example for a disciplined industry.[20]

There is also evidence that employees of the leading companies talked to one another with some frequency, e.g., at meetings of the Cereal Institute and in the various sales districts, and perhaps also at social occasions in Battle Creek, where Kellogg has its headquarters and General Foods and Ralston had major plants. What they talked about can only be speculated. *If* the other companies understood Kellogg's leadership policy, as articulated by Mr. Tornabene, the likelihood of cooperative pricing behavior in an industry as highly concentrated as cereals had to be enhanced.

In most respects, the cereal industry has all the earmarks of one in which price leadership can facilitate monopolistic pricing.[21] But product differentiation complicates matters. Some products, such as the various brands of corn flakes and raisin bran, are perceived by consumers to be close substitutes. Recognizing that a retail price differential of one or two cents per package could lead quickly to appreciable market-share transfers, the makers of those products maintained virtual price identity at most times, and General Foods in particular followed Kellogg's lead closely. But for cereals such as General Mills' Trix, Kellogg's Froot Loops, and GF's Sugar Crisps, there was sufficient differentiation so that prices could deviate by several cents before a significant movement toward the lower-priced brand took place. Differentiation complicates price leadership by making it unclear exactly at what level any specific brand should be priced in order to be "competitive" with its rivals. But at the same time, it slows down the transfer of customers between brands, rendering precise parity-pricing less essential. The price leadership institutions that evolved under these conditions were therefore rather different from those one might observe for steel, autos, or banking.

Kellogg normally led list-price changes in "rounds" covering many but not all the products in its line. Out of fifteen unambiguous price-increase rounds between 1965 and 1970 (for which period the documentary evidence is reasonably complete), Kellogg led twelve of the rounds. Kellogg's price increase was followed nine times by General Mills and ten times by General Foods; on only one occasion did neither follow. General Mills led once and was followed by the other Big Three members; General Foods led twice, and was followed once. Quaker tended to pursue a more independent policy; it seldom followed Kellogg's lead in pricing directly but, in periodic price moves, paid close attention to the relationship between its prices and those of other industry members. The price leader did not rescind its price increases when others failed to follow; instead, it relied upon its product differentiation to prevent a sudden loss of business, and waited until parity was restored in a subsequent round. When General Mills or Post failed to follow Kellogg on a round, they tended to make up for the failure by raising prices on a disproportionate share of their product line in a subsequent round. All in all, the price-leadership pattern showed more flexibility than in highly disciplined industries with more homogeneous products. Yet leadership was sufficiently robust to permit price increases in times of both booming and stagnant demand. With a change for each product and package size counted separately, "Big Six" cereal producers effected a total of 1,122 list-price changes, uncomplicated by package-size changes, between 1950 and 1972.[22] Of these, only 17, or 1.5 percent, were list-price reductions, and half of the decreases occurred in a single incident, when Kellogg's Corn Flakes experienced unusually severe competition from a private-label producer. Completely absent were the kinds of secret price cuts that characterize weak price leadership in other industries. Between 1962 and 1970, although raw-grain prices oscillated and the wholesale price index for processed foods rose by 23 percent, the average price per pound of RTE-cereals rose by 39 percent. This occurred even though there was almost no growth of cereal consumption between 1965 and 1970.

Private-Label Competition

In many food-products lines, private-label products (those on which the supermarket affixes its own company imprint) contribute a significant element of price competition. Because they are sold at lower prices, without the benefit of extensive advertising and other differentiation, their presence limits the extent to which nationally branded marketers can elevate prices. During the 1930s, private-label cereals reportedly accounted for 15 to 20 percent of total industry sales.[23] However, by 1966 the supply of private-label cereals had dwindled so much that a National Commission on Food Marketing study found, for a sample of 212 food products, that RTE-cereals had exceptionally low private-label availability. Fewer than 6 percent of the 147 retailers surveyed carried private-label RTE-cereal products.[24]

The Kellogg Company has long had a stated policy of declining to supply private-label cereal products. In 1943, Kellogg took over the Miller Cereal Company, which had been one of the three leading private-label manufacturers. It converted Miller's production to Kellogg branded items, and, in effect, permanently removed Miller from the private-label scene. During the 1960s, Kellogg was approached by a number of food retailing chains and asked to supply private-label cereals, but it consistently declined. On occasion, Kellogg attempted to persuade the retailers of the "folly" of their private-label plans.[25] General Mills similarly shunned all private-label production.

The General Foods story is different but more interesting. In 1943, General Foods acquired the Jersey Cereal Company, another of the three leading private labelers. Unlike Kellogg, it continued Jersey's private-label sales.

However, during the 1960s General Foods let Jersey's private-label business atrophy. It was asked by several sizable retailing chains to expand its private-label activity into such popular lines as presweetened cereals. The manager of General Foods' private-label sales found that doing so would be profitable. For example, a private-label brand requested by A&P would have yielded a gross profit margin of 47 percent.[26] At the time, GF was suffering from stagnant sales of its regular cereals and was operating its plant at 61 percent of capacity. Nevertheless, each such request for a private-label brand was turned down by higher management. The most plausible interpretation of General Foods' behavior is that the company was willing to accept direct profit sacrifices "in the small" in order to serve the broader objective of not disturbing the industry's price competition-avoiding consensus.

There was, however, one maverick in the picture. Ralston, now the fifth largest cereal maker, was another of the three leading private-labelers during the 1930s. It had not been acquired by its larger rivals, and it continued to offer private-label cereals. And in the 1960s, when it found that the sales of its branded products were slipping, Ralston intensified its efforts to win private-label business. Its private-label corn flakes—which a General Foods technical research group found to be "without doubt better" than the Post Toasties flake and "equal to or better than Kellogg corn flake quality—"[27] were priced to give consumers a 10 percent price saving and retailers a 6 percent larger gross margin than on branded corn flakes.[28] Ralston began making inroads into Kellogg's Corn Flakes sales, leading Kellogg to deviate from its normal policy and offer retailers special month-long case-price discounts in 1968 and 1969. Still Ralston continued to advance, and after Ralston won another large private-label account, Kellogg in July 1971 cut its wholesale Corn Flakes price to equality with Ralston's. Shortly thereafter, Ralston answered the Kellogg move with its own price reduction, but the resulting price differential was narrowed from its "pre-price-war" 16 percent value to only 10 percent. Whether this was attributable to cost pressures on Ralston, to the chastening effect of Kellogg's decision "to participate—overwhelmingly" in a disciplinary action,[29] or to some combination of the two, is uncertain.

Ralston's private-label cereals nevertheless continued to be a thorn in Kellogg's side. Private-label inroads were partly responsible for a seven-point decline in Kellogg's market share during the 1970s and Ralston's displacement of Nabisco as the fifth-largest RTE-cereal producer. In 1982, Kellogg again acted, cutting its Corn Flakes price by 8 percent. Ralston responded with a reduction of 5.5 percent.[30] A year later, Kellogg tried a different tactic: it introduced a "new" product, Crispix, which was virtually identical to Ralston's best-selling branded cereal, Chex. According to an industry analyst, Kellogg's action was taken to "[get] back at Ralston" for its successful private-label emulation of Kellogg products.[31] How this set of moves and countermoves will affect the intensity of private-label competition remains to be seen.

Quasi-Price Competition

There are many ways to engage in price competition without attempting to undercut list prices. Three forms of "quasi-price competition" in the cereal industry deserve attention.

One form is the use of "in-pack premiums"—trinkets, baseball cards, and the like, which are packed into the cereal box to induce purchase. Cereal makers found in-pack premiums to be a potent selling tool, but one that could readily be matched by rivals, leaving no one cereal maker with an advantage, but with everyone incurring higher costs. Despite this, rivalry in the use of "in-packs" was vigorous during the late 1940s and much of the 1950s. Usage rates of "in-packs" ran between 6 and 22 percent of packages sold during 1955 and 1956. Then, in the summer of 1957, "Big Three" usage abruptly fell below 1 percent and remained there for a decade. Several months earlier, a leading trade journal had reported that "The great tide of premiums offered by cereal manufacturers may be stemmed shortly. Several trade sources said last week that major cereal suppliers are formulating an agreement to drop package inserts.The reason given was excessive package breakage."[32] Ten years later, General Foods staff analysts, evaluating a rumor that rivals might break "the industry guideline," recounted the history of in-pack premium usage, as follows:

> To date, the three major manufacturers in the cereal business have been respecting an "unwritten rule," stemming from fierce and unprofitable competition in the early and middle '50s, that they have retail exposure with only one pack-in premium in one brand at a given time.[33]

Premium usage did escalate in 1968, showing that even in a tight-knit oligopoly, agreements can break down. In 1980, the rivalry was extended by all Big Four members to the use of in-pack lottery games.[34]

Another institution common in the food manufacturing industry is *trade dealing*—that is, giving retailers a sizable percentage or dollar discount for a limited period of time to promote some product particularly vigorously. There are various types of trade deals, which are also called *trade allowances*. One kind of allowance used frequently in the cereal industry is granting a discount during the first few weeks after a new product is introduced in order to encourage the retailer to stock the new product and give it favorable shelf placement. These discounts compensate the retailer for changing its stocking pattern; they are seldom if ever passed on to the consumer. At the other extreme is the *straight trade deal,* in which a discount is given with the explicit understanding that it will be passed on to the consumer to enhance an existing product's price competitiveness on the shelf. Deals of this sort were employed by Kellogg in 1968 and 1969 to combat Ralston's private-label corn flakes, and they occurred frequently in the late 1940s and early 1950s. But during the late 1950s, the use of such deals dried up almost completely for a decade. Exactly how this change took place is unknown. Whatever the explanation, it is clear that the leading cereal producers had a strong aversion to trade dealing. According to a General Mills advertising agency analysis:

> Historically, the cereal category has resisted pressures to enter into the allowance battles which most other package goods categories wage continuously. The reason has been that once this type of activation is made to work to one company's overall advantage . . . competition must retaliate and it soon becomes more of a defensive than offensive marketing device. . . . [W]hen discounting of products becomes widespread, the atmosphere of the marketplace changes.[35]

The analysis went on to recommend alternative strategies "with less chance of the spiraling effects of straight trade activation," such as giving retailers a discount to have them feature cereal *with* milk and having the discount passed on to the consumer in the form of a lower milk price. This sort of "we shouldn't do it, because if we do, the other guy will too, and we'll all be worse off" reasoning epitomizes the interdependence that draws oligopolists toward either cooperative policies (e.g., avoiding all straight trade dealing) or strategies that minimize the possibility of quid pro quo retaliation and spiraling.

A third kind of quasi-price competition cereal makers often use—and without apparent inhibition—is *couponing*. A coupon is inserted into a package, newspaper, or direct-mail brochure, and the consumer who presents it at the retail checkout counter is given, say, a 15-cent discount on the product mentioned. From the manufacturer's perspective, couponing has three advantages over straight price cutting. First, it is selective, since discounts are only taken by price-sensitive customers—those who will go to the bother of collecting and redeeming coupons—while others pay the full price. Second, it permits precision targeting. For example, repeat purchasing can be encouraged by enclosing in one box of a product a coupon offering a discount on the next box, with the expectation that a continued string of purchases is more likely to follow from two purchases than one. Third, couponing is less likely to spiral because the practice is expensive. The retailer must be paid several cents per redeemed coupon to cover processing costs, and during the 1970s, a central clearing house was paid roughly 2 cents per coupon for its handling services. However, from a broader perspective, this third advantage is a disadvantage, for couponing is a form of price competition with unusually high transactions costs. According to an official of the Nielsen Company, the leading coupon clearing house, in 1976, the average redemption value of coupons for all grocery products (not just cereals) was 14.2 cents, and the average handling cost was 6 cents.[36]

New Product and Advertising Competition

It has often been said that even though oligopolists refrain from pricing rivalry, they may compete vigorously in such nonprice areas as advertising and the introduction of new products.[37] This is so in part because it is more difficult to retaliate in kind to a new product or a clever advertising campaign.

Also, even the most industry welfare-minded executives have competitive juices, and if their instinct to compete is blunted on one dimension it may spill over into another. A more analytical variant of this notion will be presented shortly. For the moment, it suffices to say that the cereal industry's conduct fits well the model of price competition-avoiding, nonprice competition-prone oligopoly.

New products and product variants have typically been launched with a vengeance. Despite unusual data-exchange arrangements among the leading companies, advertising rivalry has also been fierce. Statistics on 1967 comparable advertising expenditures as a percentage of sales are available for 324 more or less narrowly defined manufacturing industries.[38] Among them, cereal preparations had (at 18.5 percent) the second highest figure, surpassed only by toiletries (perfumes, cosmetics, dentifrices, and the like), at 30 percent. The average for all consumer-goods industries was 3.8 percent. In the following decade, there may have been some decline in the cereal makers' advertising proclivities. A different and more accurate source shows cereals to have had only the seventh highest advertising/sales ratio (10.5 percent) of 237 industry groups in 1975 and 1976.[39] The pace-setters were proprietary drugs (19.6 percent) and toiletries (14 percent). High rates of product introduction and high advertising/sales ratios are related to some extent, because the advertising of new products is particularly intense. Even most older brands of cereal products, however, are heavily advertised compared with the norm for all consumer goods.

This emphasis on advertising and new products is accompanied by considerable sophistication in the use of modern marketing methods, both within the cereal firms and in their advertising agencies. The basic objective is *market segmentation*. Through market research, one attempts to identify particular niches in the market, those that are associated with physical differences in consumer tastes, or psychological themes that will elicit a unique consumer response. Products are designed to fill the niches; and advertising campaigns are tailored both to inform consumers that the product satisfying their wants is available for trial and to persuade them of its uniqueness. If the effort is successful, the seller wins repeat purchases on a product that has a little monopoly with respect to its specialized clientele. Among other things, this gives the cereal maker a margin of discretion in pricing its product, subject, of course, to the constraints imposed by the prices of imperfect substitutes.

An example of how this strategy can work is provided by Kellogg's Sugar Frosted Flakes (SFF), the fourth-best selling RTE-cereal (in terms of pounds) in 1970 and the third-best seller in 1982.[40] The product is made by applying a sugar frosting to Kellogg's Corn Flakes (KCF). It is advertised heavily as a presweetened product of broad appeal, with special targeting for children through the brand "spokesman," Tony the Tiger. The main physical difference between KCF and SFF is that the sucrose content of Corn Flakes is approximately 7.8 percent, whereas it is 29 percent for Sugar

Frosted Flakes. To make a pound of SFF, one in effect adds 0.23 pounds of sugar to 0.77 pounds of Corn Flakes. Following an increase in the price of KCF in July 1970, and before the Corn Flakes price war of 1971, the wholesale list price of KCF in an 18 ounce package was 34.44 cents per pound, whereas the price of SFF was 44.67 cents per pound. The corn flakes portion of a pound of SFF had an equivalent price of $0.77 \times 34.44 = 26.52$ cents, so the premium associated with SFF was $44.67 - 26.52 = 18.15$ cents. The 0.23 pounds of refined cane sugar used to effect this transformation cost 2.55 cents at the time. If one deducts a small amount to cover spraying-process costs, the rest of the price premium (i.e., something on the order of 14 or 15 cents) is attributable to subjective differentiation or "image."

A 1963 General Foods marketing plan provides more general insight into the cereal makers' pricing strategy.[41] On products with direct competitors, such as Post Toasties, parity with the rival's price was maintained. Five years later, after some inflation, this meant a gross profit realization of 13 cents per pound.[42] For established products on which General Foods had an exclusive position, such as Grape Nuts, the 1963 gross profit target was 16 cents per pound. For exclusive *new* products, the target was a minimum of 21 cents gross profit per pound. These goals were not always attained, but to the extent that market segmentation worked as intended, higher prices and profit margins were the result.

Nutrition and Product Fortification

Market segmentation also helps explain the cereal companies' otherwise puzzling conduct in the realm of product nutritional quality. As we saw earlier, during World War II, most RTE-cereal products were fortified with thiamine (vitamin B1), niacin, and iron, up to whole-grain levels prior to processing. But more could be done. Kellogg led the way in 1956, with its Special K, which featured substantially enhanced protein content. Other high-nutrient cereals followed. In 1961, General Mills offered Total, the first cereal brand that was fortified to 100 percent of minimum daily requirements for iron and nine vitamins. Each company developed its own set of fortified cereals and promoted them to consumers who were especially interested in nutrition.

The question then arose, what about "regular" products? The Post cereals marketing plan for 1960 observed:

> Inherent in this trend toward more nutritional new cereals is a risk toward the sales of old established cereals which research indicates are in general felt to be of less if not of questionable nutritive value. To counteract this consumer attitude and in order to more effectively compete, we are exploring the possible addition of key vitamins and minerals to enhance or strengthen existing product copy platforms.[43]

1966, Kellogg fortified its 40% Bran Flakes to 100 percent of minimum daily iron requirements. In its comparable product, Post promptly matched the increase. In May 1967, Post fortified its presweetened Sugar Crisp, a children's cereal, to 33 percent of minimum daily vitamin requirements, and Kellogg retaliated by fortifying its Sugar Smacks to the same level. After analyzing whether Kellogg should initiate further moves on the nutrition front, a staff member noted that retaliatory action had already neutralized the innovator's advantage, and concluded:

> The experiences of a few brands seems [sic] to indicate that fortification should be considered a promotional tool and not a long-term product improvement. Similarly to buying allowances and inserts, a fortification story will stimulate sales temporarily. But, after the news of fortification becomes old and no longer has promotional and advertising value, the sales volume tends to return to the pre-fortification level. . . . Certainly, in some countries, fortification could cause good sales increases; but the long-term results would probably be influenced by competitive reactions and the general awareness of the consumer for the need of vitamins.[44]

And so, between 1968 and 1970, not much happened.

These internal analyses make clear the companies' consciousness of oligopolistic interdependence, and the belief that feasible nutrient enhancements were not worth making unless they conferred a marketing advantage. However, it is less than obvious why the cereal makers vigorously pushed a few high-nutrient brands and left the rest at the nutritive value of wholegrains. The answer seems likely to be found in the logic of market segmentation. In their purchasing decisions, only a subset of consumers were sensitive to nutrient content. Their demands were met by the special nutritional cereals. Fortifying *all* RTE-cereals would undermine the uniqueness of the nutritional cereals and cause a flow of nutrition-conscious consumers' purchases from high-profit-margin specialties to lower-margin staples. This was plainly undesirable, and so, for those who were insensitive to nutritional features or were unwilling to pay the higher price of specialty brands, the solution was, "Let them eat (unfortified) corn flakes."

There has been, and continues to be, considerable controversy over the nutritional benefits from vitamin and mineral fortification of cereals.[45] During the 1960s, the Food and Drug Administration was considering a rule that would have limited cereal makers' fortification steps. But the tide of opinion soon changed. In 1969, a White House Conference on Nutrition successfully urged that the FDA drop its proposed rule; and in 1970, testimony before a Congressional committee concerning the low nutrient content of 60 RTE-cereals received extensive publicity.[46] These events precipitated a crash program by the major RTE-cereal producers to fortify their entire line of products to 25 or 33 percent of the minimum daily requirements in eight nutrient categories.

IV. PERFORMANCE

Values differ. Some people believe that the ready-to-eat cereal industry has exhibited outstanding economic performance, epitomizing modern marketing management's responsiveness to consumer wants. This author respectfully disagrees.

To a securities analyst or marketing professor, high profits are the hallmark of good performance.[47] To an economist, persistently high profits that are not attributable to unique and nonreplicable efficiency or resource endowments reflect resource misallocation and the unnecessary redistribution of income from consumers to investors. Profits in the RTE-cereal industry have in fact been unusually high. Average after-tax accounting returns on the cereal division assets of five leading producers for the 13-year-period 1958–1970 were as follows:[48]

Kellogg	18.9%
General Mills	29.5
General Foods (Post)	15.1
Quaker	9.0
Ralston	20.5
Weighted average	19.8%

The comparable figure for all manufacturing industry was 8.9 percent, or less than half the cereal firms' weighted-average return. Only the profit margin at Quaker was near the all-manufacturing average. General Foods' relatively low profit return is probably attributable to acknowledged inefficiencies.[40]

The industry's profits remained high in times of both buoyant demand and during the late 1960s, when the end of the U.S. "baby boom" brought demand growth to a virtual halt. Data that were assembled through a survey which disaggregated corporate financial performance information by line of business show that these high returns persisted.[50] Of 237 manufacturing industries for which such information was available, the cereal industry ranked third or fourth in terms of 1974–76 operating income before taxes as a percentage of assets. Its pre-tax annual returns were in the range of 38 to 40 percent. No other industry consistently exceeded cereals' returns.

Another way of looking at the industry's performance is to consider how much prices deviate from manufacturing costs. Because one needs a benchmark, the best approach is to analyze the so-called price-cost margin (PCM), which is defined as

$$PCM = \frac{\text{Sales (less freight)} - \text{Materials Costs} - \text{in-Plant Payrolls}}{\text{Sales}}$$

Comparable 1972 PCM data are available for 451 U.S. manufacturing industries. The PCM of the cereal preparations industry (including hot cereals) for 1972 was 0.48 (For 1967, 1977, and 1982, the comparable figures were 0.47, 0.46, and 0.53 respectively.) This means, in effect, that after products that were sold for a dollar left a cereal factory's shipping door, the maker had approximately 48 cents left to cover marketing expense, research, corporate overhead, taxes, interest, and profit. For all manufacturing industry combined, the comparable figures were 24 cents in 1972, 23 cents in 1967, and 24 cents in 1977. Only eight of 451 industries in 1972 (or nine of 449 in 1977) had higher price-cost margins than cereals. In this respect, as in others, the cereal industry is extreme among American industries.

These price-cost margin data provide an approximation to the surplus of price over marginal cost, which is widely accepted as an index of monopoly power.[51] Of course, other bills must be paid after production costs are covered. One of the largest, in cereals, is for advertising, which for the six leading sellers together ranged from 12 to 19 percent of sales over the 1950–1972 interval, and (using different data sources) from 9 to 11 percent in 1974–76.[52] Here too, as we have seen, the cereal industry is an outlier among American industries. But now we can advance a step farther. Cereal's performance in terms of price-cost margins and its extreme advertising expenditures are causally linked. The Dorfman-Steiner theorem[53] demonstrates that if sales rise with increasing advertising outlays, more will be spent on advertising, the higher price-cost margins are. The logic behind this theorem is simple: It pays to push one's advertising farther into the stage of diminishing marginal returns if the extra dollar of sales gained through advertising brings a gross profit margin of 50 cents than if it yields only 25 cents.

That the theorem holds for cereal is shown by the history of corn flakes advertising. In 1966 and 1967, Kellogg's Corn Flakes advertising outlays averaged 16.5 percent of its sales of those products. In 1968, Ralston began making significant inroads into Kellogg's corn flake sales, and Kellogg initiated two month-long straight trade deals that provided discounts of roughly 10 percent. With its price-cost margins squeezed by these deals, and unable to raise prices because Ralston had not followed its price lead in late 1966, Kellogg reduced its Corn Flakes advertising to 11.2 percent of sales. The advertising/sales ratio remained in this range until 1971, when Kellogg effected its unusual Corn Flakes list-price reductions at midyear. With its margins squeezed still more tightly, Kellogg's advertising/sales ratio on Corn Flakes was reduced to 8.6 percent in 1971 and to 5.8 percent in 1972. Post Toasties advertising followed an identical pattern. The more price-competitive the situation became, the less incentive there was to support high levels of advertising.

It follows that for the vast majority of products, on which price competition was at best blunted, high price-cost margins stimulated high advertising outlays. In this respect, much cereal advertising is seen to be a social waste: it is an expenditure that would not have occurred if price competition had been more vigorous.

A similar, but more complex, logic applies to the cereal industry's record of product proliferation. For consumers, a greater variety from which to choose is obviously better, all else being equal. But all else is not equal. The launching of additional products consumes substantial resources, and, as the resulting market segmentation increases, monopoly power is enhanced. Economic analysis reveals that market processes can lead to too little product variety, to too much variety, or to the socially optimal amount.[54] There are two main observable indicia by which one can discern whether the tendency is toward too much variety. One is the degree to which new products "cannibalize" the sales of existing products. If most sales of a new product come at the expense of products already in the marketplace, new-product competition is likely to lead to too much variety. If, on the other hand, the overall market is appreciably expanded by a new product, it is reasonable to presume, as a first approximation, that social benefits exceed costs and that the innovation is desirable. Second, for a given, substantial amount of cannibalization, excessive product proliferation is more likely to occur when price-manufacturing cost margins are higher. This is so because when the sales one manufacturer takes from its rivals carry a generous margin, there is a heightened incentive to launch a new product and attempt the capture.

We have already seen that price-cost margins in cereal have been extraordinarily high. There is also abundant evidence concerning cannibalization. Many memoranda and statements by cereal company executives reveal a belief that extensive cannibalization had occurred. Two examples must suffice.[55] In 1966, a Kellogg vice president lamented the appearance of "so many meaningless new products" and "the futility and wastefulness of having *too* much of a good thing."[56] Three years later, this executive observed that "for the past several years, our individual company growth has come out of the other fellow's hide."[57] Other cereal company statements point with pride to the substantial poundage growth of cereal sales and attribute a good deal of that growth to new product development. There is undoubtedly some truth in the linkage. But it is also true that, on closer analysis, one finds that 57.5 percent of the cereal industry's pound output growth between 1954 and 1972 consisted of sugar. If this sugar increment is deducted on the assumption that without presweetening, consumers would simply have dipped on their own into their sugar bowls, the industry's output growth rate turns out to be no more rapid than the growth of the consuming population. From this perspective, the industry's record in stimulating real growth through new products is unimpressive, strengthening the inference of extensive cannibalization, which in turn supports the inference that the industry proliferated products to a socially wasteful degree. This conclusion does not mean that all new cereal products failed a "social benefits vs. costs" test. Some new products clearly passed the test. But there were also many failures—the marginal entries that producers knew contributed little or nothing to expanding the market. Again, the waste, which flowed in the first instance from a breakdown of price competition and high price-cost margins, was sizable.

Much of the indictment for the poor performance of the cereal industry rests then upon the premise that cereal prices have been noncompetitively high. Industry defenders counter this allegation by arguing that even though price-cost margins may have been high, RTE-cereals are nevertheless a bargain because they are less costly per ounce than most alternative breakfast foods. The argument is specious. It is exactly analogous to an argument by OPEC ministers that their cartel was innocuous because even after they quadrupled crude-oil prices in 1973 and 1974, oil continued to be a bargain relative to alternative energy sources such as shale oil, nuclear power, and solar heating. The appropriate benchmark is the price of a product that free competition would set. Nature endowed the cereal makers with an unusually economical means of providing nutrition. If they have abused that endowment by charging prices well above the competitive level, they have performed badly.

V. PUBLIC POLICY

A number of public policy measures have been directed toward the activities of the cereal industry. The most ambitious step was a major antitrust suit by the Federal Trade Commission against Kellogg, General Mills, General Foods, and Quaker. (Quaker was dropped from the suit in 1978). Much of the evidence analyzed in this chapter stems from that proceeding. The suit was unusual in a number of ways, two of which warrant special mention. First, the FTC charged monopolization of the industry not by a single dominant seller (which had been the emphasis in nearly all prior monopolization suits), but collectively by the four (later three) leading sellers. Second, proceeding on the assumption that the cereal problem was a lack of price competition, which followed in turn from the company and brand structure of the market, the FTC staff sought a structural remedy that was unprecedented in antitrust annals. Splitting off three new competitive firms from Kellogg, and one each from General Mills and General Foods, was not an unusual request. But the FTC also asked that each of these prospective, newly created companies be given exclusive branded and trademarked products to make up 3 percent of industry sales—not enough to use their capacity fully. The remaining trademarks and formulas of the Big Three were to be made available for nonexclusive licensing to the newly founded firms, so that they could enter into competitive production, pitting, say, the ABC Cereal Company's Cheerios against General Mills' (previously exclusively trademarked) Cheerios. The FTC staff hoped that in this way genuine competition that stressed price as well as image could be fostered.[58]

The FTC suit, commenced in 1972, was fought bitterly on a multiplicity of fronts. Testimony was taken at a hearing that lasted from 1976 to 1980. The transcript without exhibits totaled some 41,000 pages, and the battle did not remain in the courtroom. Kellogg dismissed its original team of lawyers in mid-trial. A new team took over and enlisted the support of the AFL-CIO with a consultant's study alleging that union workers would lose their jobs if the government prevailed. Cereal company lobbyists spilled over onto Capitol Hill, securing bills (eventually dropped) that would have halted the case or removed the FTC's power to impose a divestiture remedy. During the week before he was elected President of the United States, Ronald Reagan released a letter written to the president of Kellogg, observing, "It is clear to me that the [cereal] case under consideration has very little basis in fact and that a favorable ruling on behalf of the FTC would have a chilling effect on American industry."[59] A similar statement was made by then-President Carter while he was campaigning in Michigan.

The case was also marked by significant procedural errors. For one, at its outset, FTC lawyers waived any claim that the cereal makers had engaged in an overt conspiracy. After circumstantial evidence of collusion was presented in later testimony, cereal company attorneys objected to its consideration. Also, as the trial neared completion, the presiding Administrative Law Judge (ALJ) was removed, following a cereal company protest that he had lost his independence by entering semiretirement and accepting a consulting contract to see the case through to its conclusion. The replacement judge heard the last tenth of the case record, drew the threads together, and gave an initial decision.[60]

In it, the new ALJ acquitted the cereal companies and ordered that the case be dismissed. Except for viewing RTE-cereals as a relevant market and finding that market to be highly concentrated, he resolved virtually every contested issue of fact in favor of the companies. Conflicting evidence on such matters as the existence of collusion, the nature and effectiveness of price leadership, accounting adjustments required to assess profitability accurately, entry barriers, and even the applicability of the Dorfman-Steiner theorem, was simply ignored or dismissed.[61] Indeed, the imbalance of findings on a complex case, which all agreed had been closely contested, recalls the analysis of Professor (later Harvard president) Derek Bok, citing an earlier FTC case:

> the task of weighing conflicting pieces of evidence is necessarily formidable. It was perhaps to avoid these complications that the Commission felt impelled to find that *each* of the relevant matters weighed against the defendant in *Brillo*, just as the hearing examiner [i.e., ALJ], in order to reach a contrary result, had to resolve each in the company's favor.[62]
>
> [B]y increasing the complexity of our proceedings, we may increase the impact of certain nonrational tendencies upon the thought processes of the judge. . . . Nonlogical processes at least afford a means by which problems can be resolved; and if care is not taken to provide a method and a basis for deciding cases under section 7 that lie within normal intellectual capacities, less rational influences are bound in one way or another to fill the void. For example, it has been demonstrated that when it becomes very complicated to resolve a problem in terms of one criterion, there is a marked tendency to shift imperceptibly to some other criterion that seems more amenable to judgment.[63]

What followed was even more unprecedented. As is common in important FTC proceedings, the losing side (i.e., the FTC enforcement staff) sought to appeal to the Commission as a whole. But their superiors, chosen by Reagan Administration appointees, refused to transmit the appeal. The staff then bypassed their bureau directors and appealed directly to the Commission. Under a cloud of continuing Congressional criticism concerning both the case's substance and its alleged procedural irregularities, the Commission elected to receive the appeal but dismiss it without addressing its factual merits.[64] Speaking for a divided majority, Commissioner Patricia Bailey cited "congressional stormwaters of imposing magnitude" and concluded:

> The paradox we are left with is that while there may be a legitimate concern about the anticompetitive effects of the exercise of oligopoly power, it is rarely true that these concerns will mandate an administrative agency to restructure an industry, short of a legislative warrant to that effect. Therefore, I will vote that this appeal be terminated, not for the reasons relied upon by the Administrative Law Judge, but because the promulgation of relief by this agency will not, in any eventuality , conceivably lead to a restructuring of the cereal firms.[65]

Recognizing that without a full appeal process the Federal Trade Commission could not determine whether or not the ALJ's decision was "riddled . . . with major procedural errors, and does not fairly give weight to certain of the evidence," Commissioner Bailey ordered that the ALJ's decision be vacated, with "no precedential or even persuasive authority for any proposition whatsoever." Thus ended one of the most ambitious cases in American antitrust history: not with a bang but a whimper.

An earlier federal antitrust suit, alleging that the Quaker Oats Company monopolized the oatmeal industry through its acquisition of the Great Western Cereal Company's rolled oats trademarks and other assets, was terminated in a 1916 judgment favoring Quaker.[66] In a two-to-one split decision, the majority opinion, which typified the generally weak state of merger law at the time, stressed Quaker's failure to gain complete control of the oatmeal market and the ease of entry into unbranded oatmeal production. The dissenting judge argued that the highly advertised products of Quaker and Great Western were significantly differentiated from unbranded rolled oats, that the merger eliminated competition among the two main branded-oats makers, and that it strengthened Quaker's "already strong grasp upon the entire industry."

Other governmental actions have been aimed at improving the nutritional quality of ready-to-eat cereals. As noted earlier, World War II measures led to the fortification of RTE-cereals to whole-grain levels; and Senate hearings in 1970 spurred further fortification with vitamins and minerals. Along with other food products manufacturers, the cereal companies have also been affected by Food and Drug Administration regulations, which require the disclosure (on the package) of product ingredients, and, more recently, nutrient content.

A different approach to the nutrition problem nearly proved to be the Federal Trade Commission's undoing. Following petitions by diverse consumer groups expressing concern over the intensive advertising of heavily sugared products, including presweetened cereals, on children's television shows, the FTC in 1978 instituted a rule-making proceeding to consider, among other things, a proposed prohibition of television advertising directed toward children "too young to understand the selling purpose of . . . or evaluate the advertising."[67] This so-called "kid vid" proceeding triggered a storm of protest from the media, cereal companies, toy makers, and others with a stake in the $600 million per year children's advertising business. Making common cause with business interests angered by other FTC consumer protection initiatives, the Washington advocates of these groups secured in the House of Representatives passage of appropriation bills curbing the FTC's rule-making powers.[68] When these measures were repeatedly rejected by the Senate, the FTC was forced for more than two years to operate without a formal budgetary appropriation. On two separate occasions in 1980, the FTC's operations were shut down when interim funds ran out. Finally, a compromise was reached. Among other things, it suspended (and later abandoned) the long-delayed "kid vid" proceeding.

In this experience, there are clear implications for policy makers, even if not for public policy. Advertising, which enjoys important constitutional freedom-of-speech guarantees and a strong lobby to make the most of them, is best approached by government reformers according to the rules of the minuet. Sending a fullback into the line of scrimmage is for another game.

NOTES

1. See Naum Jasny, *Competition Among Grains* (Stanford, Cal.: Food Research Institute, 1940), pp. 35–37.

2. To which a canny Scot is said to have replied, "And England is known for the excellence of her horses, Scotland for the excellence of her men."

3. William Cahn, *Out of the Cracker Barrel* (New York: Simon & Schuster, 1969), p. 211. Perky died at age 62.

4. In this chapter, the market-share data for recent years are from *Advertising Age* (May 28, 1984), p. 32; (May 25, 1981), p. 62; and (July 9, 1979), p. 49. For earlier years, they are from Exhibit CX-106D in the Federal Trade Commission antitrust proceeding *In re Kellogg Company et al,* Docket No. 8883. The author appeared as a witness on behalf of the Federal Trade Commission.

5. Louis W. Stern, Technical Study No. 6, *Studies of Organization and Competition in Grocery Manufacturing* (Washington, D.C.: National Commission on Food Marketing, June 1966), p. 97.

6. See Stern, op. cit.; Robert S. Headen and James W. McKie, *The Structure, Conduct, and Performance of the Breakfast Cereal Industry: 1954–1964* (Cambridge, Mass: Arthur D. Little, March 1966); and the testimony of Michael Glassman *In re Kellogg et al.,* transcript pp. 26319–26372. In most industries, technological change raises over time the absolute amount of output associated with the minimum optimal scale of production. See F. M. Scherer, *Industrial Market Structure and Economic Performance,* 2nd ed. (Boston: Houghton-Mifflin 1980), pp. 98–99. It is unclear whether this has happened in cereals.

7. *In re Kellogg et al.,* CX-GF-4039Z90.

8. See Scherer, op. cit., pp. 108–112.

9. See the analysis in F. M. Scherer, "The Welfare Economics of Product Variety: An Application to the Ready-to-Eat Cereals Industry," *Journal of Industrial Eco-*

nomics, **28:**122(Dec. 1979), which drew upon a Quaker Oats survey. By the early 1980s, advertising expenditures for a new children's cereal "launch" had mounted into the $20–$25 million range. See "Quaker 'Ts' Up Newest Cereal," *Advertising Age* (June 25, 1984), p. 116; and "Move Over, Cap'N Crunch: Pac-Man and His Pals Are Taking Over," *Business Week* (July 18, 1983), p. 174.

10. *In re Kellogg et al.,* CX-701A and CX-106A.

11. For a more rigorous and complete analysis, see Richard Schmalensee, "Entry Deterrence in the Ready-to-Eat Breakfast Cereal Industry," *Bell Journal of Economics,* **9:**(Autumn 1978), pp. 305–327.

12. The United Kingdom market was much less fragmented. In 1959, Kellogg's corn flakes alone had a 37 percent market share, which fell to 31 percent in 1971. U.K. Monopolies Commission, *Report on the Supply of Ready Cooked Breakfast Cereals* (London: HMSO, Feb. 1973), p. 35.

13. See the testimony of Procter & Gamble's Owen B. Butler, *In re Kellogg et al.,* transcript pp. 25820–25859.

14. See W. L. Baldwin and G. L. Childs, "The Fast Second and Rivalry in Research and Development," *Southern Economic Journal,* **36:**(July 1969), pp. 18–24; and Scherer, *Industrial Market Structure and Economic Performance,* pp. 427–432.

15. See *Advertising Age* (July 9, 1979), p. 49; and *Advertising Age* (May 25, 1981), p. 62.

16. *In re Kellogg et al.,* CX-GF-4039Z108.

17. Stern, op. cit., p. 177.

18. Speech text of C. A. Tornabene, December 1966, appearing as exhibit CX-K-549P of *In re Kellogg et al.*

19. Headen and McKie, op. cit., pp. 75–76.

20. Speech text of C. A. Tornabene, CX-K-549M and Q (emphasis in original).

21. See Jesse W. Markham, "The Nature and Significance of Price Leadership," *American Economic Review,* 41:(Dec. 1951), pp. 891–905; and Scherer, *Industrial Market Structure and Economic Performance,* pp. 176–182, from which this account is adapted in part.

22. See the author's testimony *In re Kellogg et al.,* transcript pp. 27728–27753.

23. Testimony of Michael Glassman *In re Kellogg et al.,* transcript p. 26347.

24. National Commission on Food Marketing, *Special Studies in Food Marketing,* Technical Study No. 10, "Private Label Products in Food Retailing" (Washington, D.C.: June 1966), pp. 89–91.

25. See CX-K-7054 and CX-K-7148, *In re Kellogg et al.*

26. *In re Kellogg et al.,* CX-GF-123 (Jan. 1967). For a more extensive analysis, see the author's testimony at transcript pp. 27927–27936.

27. *In re Kellogg et al.,* CX-GF-604 (Sept. 1966).

28. Testimony of Ralston's Donald Schnitz, *In re Kellogg et al.,* at transcript pp. 17509 ff.

29. Cf, p. 183 *supra.*

30. See "Aggressive New Cold Cereals Seen in '82," *Advertising Age* (June 14, 1982), p. 62; "Outlook Brightens for Profitable Kellogg," *The New York Times,* March 25, 1982, Sec. IV, p. 1; and "Who's Afraid of Generic Cereals?" *Industry Week* (May 16, 1983), pp. 33–36.

31. "Kellogg Co. Rolls Crispix," *Advertising Age* (April 25, 1983), pp. 2, 72.

32. "Cereal Makers' Agreement May Stem Premium Tide," *Supermarket News* March 11, 1957, p. 4.

33. *In re Kellogg et al.*, CX-GF-76A (Aug. 1967).

34. "Cereal Makers Ready Games," *Advertising Age* (Nov. 24, 1980), pp. 2, 70.

35. *In re Kellogg et al.*, CX-GMI-16B (Dec. 1970).

36. Speech text of Richard H. Aycrigg on "Current Couponing Trends," Couponing Workshop of the Association of National Advertisers, May 24, 1977, pp. 20 and 25. By 1983, the processing fee paid retailers had increased to seven cents. See "Retailing May Have Overdosed on Coupons," *Business Week* (June 13, 1983), p. 147.

37. For an early statement, see William Fellner, *Competition among the Few* (New York: Knopf, 1949), pp. 183–191.

38. Stanley I. Ornstein, *Industrial Concentration and Advertising Intensity* (Washington, D.C.: American Enterprise Institute, 1977), pp. 81–85.

39. Federal Trade Commission, *Statistical Report: Annual Line of Business Report, 1975 and 1976* (Washington, D.C.: Sept. 1981 and May 1982), Table 2-3.

40. This example is drawn from Scherer, "The Welfare Economics of Product Variety," p. 127. For another example, see "Monopoly on the Cereal Shelves," *Consumer Reports* (Feb. 1981), p. 79.

41. *In re Kellogg et al.*, CX-GF-17L (fiscal year 1963 Marketing Plan Summary).

42. *In re Kellogg et al.*, CX-GF-4341, presenting fiscal year 1968 margin data. Earlier figures are not available.

43. *In re Kellogg et al.*, CX-GF-16N (1959).

44. *In re Kellogg et al.*, CX-K-487 (July 1969).

45. See "Which Cereal for Breakfast?" *Consumer Reports* (Feb. 1981), pp. 68–75, which reports *inter alia* on an experiment with rats showing little correlation between the level of vitamin fortification and growth experiences.

46. U.S. Senate, Committee on Commerce, Subcommittee for Consumers, Hearings, *Dry Cereals* (Washington, D.C.: U.S. Government Printing Office, 1970), especially pp. 2–43.

47. See Steven R. Cox, "An Industrial Performance Evaluation Experiment," *Journal of Industrial Economics*, **22:**(March 1974), pp. 199–214, who found that marketing professors and business journal writers tended to rate the performance of high-advertising, high-profit industries much more favorably than did academic economists.

48. *In re Kellogg et al.*, CX-701A. Comparable data for Nabisco were unavailable. There is reason to believe Nabisco's returns were well below the industry average.

49. See for example the 134-page internal task-force report analyzing General Foods' problems, *In re Kellogg et al.*, CX-GF-4039 (1967).

50. Federal Trade Commission, *Statistical Report: Annual Line of Business Report, 1974, 1975, and 1976* (Washington, D.C.: Sept. 1981 and May 1983), Table 2-1.

51. A. P. Lerner, "The Concept of Monopoly and the Measurement of Monopoly Power," *Review of Economic Studies*, **1:**(June 1934), pp. 157–175. In 1935, 1947, and 1954, when price competition in cereals was said to be more intense, price-cost margins ranged from 0.35 to 0.36.

52. *In re Kellogg et al.*, CX-513. See also note 39 *supra*.

53. Robert Dorfman and Peter O. Steiner, "Optimal Advertising and Optimal Quality," *American Economic Review*, **44:**(Dec. 1954), pp. 835–836.

54. The analysis here is adapted from Scherer, "The Welfare Economics of Product Variety."

55. For a proliferation of citations, see Scherer, "The Welfare Economics of Product Variety," p. 123.

56. *In re Kellogg et al.,* CX-K-549Q and R.

57. *In re Kellogg et al.,* CX-K-744B.

58. For more skeptical views, see Brian F. Harris, *Shared Monopoly and the Cereal Industry* (East Lansing: Michigan State University Graduate School of Business Administration, Division of Research, 1979); and Dominick T. Armentano, *Antitrust and Monopoly: Anatomy of a Policy Failure* (New York: Wiley, 1982, pp. 127–131.

59. "Candidates Hit FTC Cereal Action," *Washington Post,* Nov. 4, 1980, p. D7.

60. Initial Decision dated Sept. 1, 1981, reprinted in 99 *Federal Trade Commission Reports* 16–269 (1982).

61. Thus, dismissing much evidence to the contrary, the ALJ accepted as valid an effective half-life of seven years for cereal advertising's impact on consumption decisions (p. 225). This assumption was crucial to his conclusion that cereal firms were not enjoying supra-competitive returns on investment. Given the conclusion that profit returns were not unusually high, he then dismissed (p. 243) the relevance of price-cost margin data. But under Dorfman-Steiner, or alternative "rent-seeking" theories of investment, high price-cost margins *cause* high advertising outlays, which (by the judge's reasoning) pulled down profit returns. Even if profit returns were normal, that finding could not logically exclude the causal role of high price-cost margins.

62. Derek C. Bok, "Section 7 of the Clayton Act and the Merging of Law and Economics," *Harvard Law Review,* **74:**(Dec. 1960), p. 270.

63. Ibid., p. 296. On p. 290 of the same analysis, Bok provides a prophetic examination of the difficulties in assessing the relative importance of price leadership—a key point of contention in the cereals case.

64. Dismissal order dated January 15, 1982, 99 *Federal Trade Commission Reports,* pp. 8, 269–290 (1982).

65. Ibid., p. 289.

66. *U.S. v. Quaker Oats Co. et al.,* 232 Fed. 499 (1916). See also *Tilden et al. v. Quaker Oats Co. et al.,* 1 F. 2d 160 (1924).

67. Federal Trade Commission, Proposed Trade Regulation Rulemaking and Public Hearing, "Children's Advertising," 43 *Federal Register* 17967 (April 27, 1978).

68. For differing views, see Robert Sherrill, "Jousting on the Hill: Skewering the Consumer's Defender," *Saturday Review* (March 29, 1980), pp. 17–22; Ernest Gellhorn, "The Wages of Zealotry: The FTC Under Siege," *Regulation* (Jan.–Feb. 1980), pp. 33–40; and, from the incumbent FTC chairman's perspective, Michael Pertschuk, *Revolt Against Regulation* (Berkeley: U. of California Press, 1982), Chap. 3.

SUGGESTED READINGS

BOOKS AND PAMPHLETS

Cahn, William. *Out of the Cracker Barrel.* New York: Simon & Schuster, 1969.

Harris, Brian F. *Shared Monopoly and the Cereal Industry: An Empirical Investigation of the Effects of the FTC's Antitrust Proposals.* East Lansing: Michigan State University Graduate School of Business Administration, Division of Research, 1979.

Headen, Robert S., and James W. McKie. "The Structure, Conduct, and Performance of the Breakfast Cereal Industry: 1954–1964." Cambridge, Mass.: Arthur D. Little, March 1966.

GOVERNMENT PUBLICATIONS

Stern, Louis W. Technical Study No. 6, *Studies of Organization and Competition in Grocery Manufacturing*. Washington, D.C.: National Commission on Food Marketing, June 1966.

United Kingdom, Monopolies Commission. *Report on the Supply of Ready-Cooked Breakfast Cereals*. London: Her Majesty's Stationery Office, Feb. 1973.

U.S. Council on Wage and Price Stability. "Interim Report on Breakfast Cereals and Bakery Products." Washington, D.C.: Jan. 1976.

U.S. National Commission on Food Marketing, Technical Study No. 10, *Special Studies in Food Marketing*, "Private Label Products in Food Retailing." Washington, D.C.: June 1966.

ARTICLES

Scherer, F. M. "The Welfare Economics of Product Variety: An Application to the Ready-to-Eat Cereals Industry." *Journal of Industrial Economics*, **28:**113–134 (Dec. 1979).

Schmalensee, Richard. "Entry Deterrence in the Ready-to-Eat Breakfast Cereals Industry." *Bell Journal of Economics*, **9:**305–327 (Autumn 1978).

6

The Beer Industry

Kenneth G. Elzinga

I. INTRODUCTION

In 1620, as every youngster knows, the Pilgrims landed at Plymouth Rock. What is not commonly known is that the Pilgrims had originally planned to end their voyage in Virginia, not in Massachusetts. What led them to change their minds? One of the voyagers recorded the following entry in his diary: "Our victuals are being much spente, especially our beere." One can only speculate about the effect of the Mayflower's dwindling beer inventory on the course of American history. Speculation is not required, however, in ascertaining the structure and level of competition in the beer industry today. Here economic analysis reduces the need for conjecture.

Definition of the Industry

Beer is a potable product with four main ingredients.

1. Malt, which is simply barley (or some grain) that has been allowed to germinate in water and is then dried.
2. Flavoring adjuncts, usually hops and corn or rice, which give beer its lightness and provide the starch that the enzymes in the malt convert to sugar.
3. Cultured yeast, which ferments the beverage and feeds on the sugar content of the malt to produce alcohol and carbonic acid.
4. Water, which acts as a solvent for the other ingredients.

Because the process of brewing (or boiling) is intrinsic to the making of beer, the industry often is called the *brewing industry*.

Brewing beer does not produce a perfectly homogeneous product. The white beverage (spiced with a little raspberry syrup) that is favored in Berlin, the warm, dark-colored drink served by the English publican, and the amber liquid, kept at near-freezing temperatures in the cooler of the American convenience store, are all beer. Generically, the term *beer* means any beverage brewed from a starch (or farinaceous) grain. Because the grain is made into a malt that becomes the main substance of the beverage, another term for beer is *malt liquor,* or malt beverage. In this study, the terms *beer, malt liquor,* and *malt beverage* are used broadly and interchangeably, to include all such products as beer, ale, light beer, porter, stout, and malt liquor. For this study, then, beer includes a variety of products: those branded as beer as well as products branded as ale and malt liquor. The factor common to the beverages of this industry, and that which differentiates them from other alcoholic and nonalcoholic beverages, is that they are brewed by a process of fermentation applied to a basic grain ingredient.

A unique production process is not, however, the key to defining an industry. The concept of an industry implies a group of firms (or conceivably, one firm) which supplies a set of products that consumers, voting in the marketplace, find close substitutes for each other. Some avid drinkers of the product beer may not prefer to substitute, say, the product ale; but they would prefer to substitute milk even less. The cross-elasticity of demand is high between malt beverages, and the cross-elasticity of demand between beer and other alcoholic beverages, for most customers, is lower.[1] It is this fungibility characteristic that enables the distinction of malt beverages as a separate industry to be made. The delineation is supported, moreover, by the high cross-elasticity of supply between the separate products of this industry and the low cross-elasticity of supply between malt beverages and all other beverages, including wine and distilled spirits.

Early History

Beer was a very common beverage in England in the 1600s, and the early settlers in America had not only a taste for beer but also a supply of it on the ships that brought them. According to the records, the first public brewery was established, in New Amsterdam, in 1625. Other commercial brewing followed, although considerable brewing was done in homes in seventeenth-century America. At the time, all that was needed in the way of equipment were a few vats, one for mashing, one for cooling, and one for fermenting. The resulting product would be scarcely recognizable (or consumed) as beer today. The process was very crude, and the end result was uncertain. It is not surprising that brewing was referred to as "an art and mystery."

Brewing was often publicly encouraged in early America. For example, the General Court of Massachusetts passed an act, in 1789, to support the brewing of beer "as an important means of preserving the health of the citizens . . . and of preventing the pernicious effects of spiritous liquors." James Oglethorpe, trustee of the colony of Georgia, was even blunter: "Cheap beer is the only means to keep rum out."

Lager Beer: The Jumping-Off Point

The 1840s and 1850s were important decades in the American brewing industry. The product beer, in the basic form that is consumed today, was introduced in the 1840s with the brewing of lager beer.[2] Prior to the introduction of lager beers, malt beverage consumption in America resembled English tastes—heavily oriented toward ale, porter, and stout. Lager beer represented the influence of German tastes and brewing skills. The influx of German immigrants provided not only skillful brewers but also eager customers for this type of beer. At the start of the decade in 1850, there were 431 brewers in the United States producing 750,000 barrels of beer annually.[3] By the end of that decade, 1,269 brewers produced more than a million barrels annually, evidence of the high expectations of the future held by many in this industry.

The latter half of the nineteenth century saw not only the successful introduction of lager beer in America but also the adoption of technological advances that affected the production and marketing of malt beverages. Mechanical refrigeration greatly aided the production process as well as the storage of beer. Prior to this development, beer production was partly dependent on the amount of ice that could be cut from lakes and rivers in the winter. Cities such as St. Louis, which had underground caves where beer could be kept cool while aging, lost this (truly natural) advantage with the advent of mechanical refrigeration. Pasteurization, a process originally devised to preserve wine and beer, was adopted during this period. Beer no longer had to be kept cold; it could be shipped into hot areas and stored for a longer period of time without refermenting. Once the stability of beer was secured through pasteurization, the way was opened for wide-scale bottling and the off-premise consumption of beer. In addition, developments in transportation technology enabled brewers to expand their production beyond their local markets. The twentieth century saw the rise of the "national" brewer.

Prohibition

The twentieth century also saw the legal banning of beer sales. The temperance movement, which began by promoting voluntary moderation and abstention from hard liquors, veered toward a goal of universal compulsory abstention from all alcoholic beverages. The beer industry seemed blissfully ignorant of this. Many brewers thought (or hoped) the temperance movement would ban only liquor.

In 1919, 36 states ratified the Eighteenth Amendment to enact the national prohibition of alcoholic beverages. This led many brewers simply to close up shop; some produced products such as candy and ice cream. Anheuser-Busch and others built a profitable business selling malt syrup, which was used to make "home brew." Because a firm could not lawfully state what the ultimate purpose of malt syrup would be, the product was marketed as an ingredient for making baked goods, such as cookies.

Prohibition lasted until April 1933, and the rapidity with which brewers reopened after repeal was amazing. By June 1933, 31 brewers were in operation; in another year, the number of brewers had risen to 756.

The Demand for Beer in the Post-World War II Period

Nationally, the market demand for beer began a slow decline in 1948, from a 1947 record sale of 87.2 million barrels. The 1947 figure was never surpassed until 1959, which had sales of 87.6 million barrels. During this period, per capita consumption of beer fell from 18.5 gallons in 1947 to 15.0 gallons in 1958.

In the 1960s and 1970s, total demand began to grow again, at an average rate of better than 3 percent per year. The year 1965 marked the first year in which more than 100 million barrels were sold, and the figure for 1983 was 177.5 million barrels. Per capita consumption of beer in this country has increased from 1958's level of 15 gallons to a level of 23.6 gallons in 1983. The rightward shift in the demand curve for beer was the result of the increasing number of young people in the United States (the result of the post-World War II baby boom), the lowering of age requirements for drinking in many populous states, and the enhanced acceptability of beer among females. Moreover, the number of areas in the United States that are "dry" shrank considerably.

In the 1980s, the market demand for beer has been stable. Demographic patterns reversed themselves as the pool of young people (18–34 years of age) declined. Several states escalated their minimum age requirements for the purchase of alcoholic beverages, and for others such legislation is pending. Moreover, two factors have cut into demand: the pursuit of physical fitness and the increasing concern with alcohol abuse. Some brewers have reacted by introducing low-alcohol beer. Finally, in some states laws restraining the use of one-way containers have reduced consumption.

The total market demand for beer exhibits seasonal fluctuations, a result of greater thirsts during hot weather. The demand for beer in the United States also varies from region to region. The Mountain states and the west-south-central states show the highest per capita consumption; the east south-central and Middle Atlantic states show the lowest. By states, the demand for beer differs considerably. Alabama and Utah had per capita consumption of 17.7 and 13.5 gallons in 1983, respectively. Needless to say, with a national per capita consumption in 1983 of 23.6 gallons, some states must register a heavier consumption to offset the more moderate states. In fact, 13 states have per capita figures of beer consumption of more than 27 gallons; of these, Nevada leads all others with a per capita consumption of over 35 gallons.

Although economists are not able to measure price elasticity infallibly, statistical estimations indicate the market demand for beer to be inelastic, in the range of 0.7 to 0.9. However, for most beer drinkers, brand attachment is not so strong as to make the demand for any particular malt beverage inelastic. Indeed, the demand for individual brands of beer appears to be quite elastic.[4] This elasticity places an important limitation on the market power of domestic brewers.

One indication of how responsive beer consumers have been to price

Table 1: Percentage of the St. Louis Market Recorded by Anheuser-Busch

Brewer	*December 1953*	*June 1954*	*March 1955*	*July 1956*
Anheuser-Busch	12.5	16.6	39.3	21.0
Griesedieck Bros.	14.4	12.6	4.8	7.4
Falstaff	29.4	32.0	29.1	36.6
Griesedieck Western	38.9	33.0	23.1	27.8
Others	4.8	5.8	3.9	7.2

Source: Taken from *Federal Trade Commission v. Anheuser-Busch,* 363 U.S. 536 at 541. Subsequent evidence indicated that factors in addition to price accounted for the Griesedieck Bros.'s drop in market share.

changes is provided in the records of a price-discrimination case that will be discussed later in this chapter. Table 1 shows the percentage of the St. Louis market, supplied on various dates by Anheuser-Busch, three important rival brewers, and the combined total of the other brewers. At the close of 1953, Anheuser-Busch's Budweiser beer was selling for 58 cents per case more than the three rivals and had a 12.5 percent share of the market. Early in 1954, the price of Budweiser was cut 25 cents, but, because this was a wholesale price, it had only a small impact on the retail price. Still, the Anheuser-Busch market share increased.

In June 1954, Anheuser-Busch cut its price to $2.35 per case, the same price as its rivals. By early 1955, Budweiser was the largest beer seller in St. Louis. At that time, prices were increased by all the sellers in such a manner that Budweiser again sold at a differential of 30 cents per case. The Anheuser-Busch market share then dropped, evidence that consumers will shift brands in response to price incentives.

There are many contemporary illustrations of the high elasticity of demand for individual brands of beer. When Stroh cut the price of its Schaefer brand in Ohio, this provoked a sizable increase in the quantity demanded. Heileman had a similar experience in other parts of the country with price reductions on its Carling Black Label brand. But when Heileman attempted (unsuccessfully) to raise the price of its Old Style brand in the Midwest (where in some cities it is the leading seller), many of its customers switched to rival brands.

II. MARKET STRUCTURE

One general conclusion of economic analysis is that consumers are more likely to be able to buy the exact product they want at the lowest price when they face a number of independent rivals. When facing a monopolist (or tightly knit oligopoly), choice is reduced and the price is likely to be elevated. Because of this, the question of the total number and size distribution of firms is of economic importance. Is the beer industry unconcentrated, with its customers courted by many firms, or is it concentrated, leaving beer drinkers with little choice?

In the post-World War II period, two contrary trends have been at work in the industry, one leading to increased concentration, the other in the opposite direction. On the one hand, there has been a marked decline in the number of brewers in the United States. At the same time, there has been an increase in the size of the market area that is potentially served by existing brewers. We examine each of these trends in turn.

The Decline in Numbers

The decline in the number of individual plants and independent companies in the brewing industry has been dramatic. In 1935, shortly after repeal of the Eighteenth Amendment, 750 brewing plants were operating in the United States. Since that time the number of brewing plants has declined steadily to a total of 80 in 1983. Table 2 shows the decline in the number of beer companies and plants. In the period shown, the number of companies dropped 90 percent (although beer sales increased by some 90 million barrels). Few other American industries have undergone a similar structural shake-up.

Concomitant with the decline in the number of companies has been the increasing share of national business done by the largest brewers. As shown in Table 3, in 1947, the top five companies accounted for 19 percent of the

Table 2

Year	*Independent Companies*	*Separate Plants*
1947	404	465
1954	263	310
1958	211	252
1963	150	211
1967	125	154
1974	58	108
1978	44	96
1983	44	80

Source: Adapted from Breweries Authorized to Operate, Department of the Treasury, Bureau of Alcohol, Tobacco, and Firearms (Washington, D.C.: U.S. Government Printing Office, various years); Modern Brewery Age, Blue Book (Stamford, Conn.: Modern Brewery Age Pub., various years); and *The Brewing Industry*, Staff Report of the Federal Trade Commission, Bureau of Economics (Washington, D.C.: U.S. Government Printing Office, 1978).

Table 3: Concentration of Sales by Top Brewers

Year	*Five Largest*	*Ten Largest*	*Herfindahl Index*
1947	19.0%	28.2%	.013–.015
1954	24.9	38.3	.024
1958	28.5	45.2	.031
1964	39.0	58.2	.044
1968	47.6	63.2	.067–.071
1974	64.0	80.8	.108–.109
1978	74.3	92.3	.141–.149
1981	75.9	93.9	.1699
1983	83.5	94.0	.1944
1984	87.3	98.7	.2114

Source: Adapted from A. Horowitz and I. Horowitz, "The Beer Industry," *Business Horizons,* **10:**14(1967), and various issues of *Modern Brewery Age.*

industry's barrelage; in 1983 their share was over 83 percent. Another way of summarizing the distribution of firm size is shown in Table 3: the Herfindahl index. It is the sum of the individual sellers' market shares squared (its maximum value is *1,* with one firm in the market). The rising Herfindahl also testifies to the industry's structural transformation. Whereas some industry observers speak of the "Big Five" (Anheuser-Busch, Miller, Stroh, Heileman, and Coors, in 1983 order), one might more appropriately refer to the "Big Two," because the two leaders in 1983 shared over 53 percent of the national market.

The Widening of Markets

To understand the offsetting structural factor to this decline in the number of brewing companies, one must realize that, in the days of hundreds of brewing companies, most beer drinkers faced an actual choice of only a few brewers. The majority of brewers were small and the geographic market area they served was severely limited. Beer is an expensive product to ship, relative to its value, and few brewers could afford to compete in the "home markets" of distant brewers.

Thus, at one time it was very meaningful to speak of local, regional, and national brewers. Of these, the local brewer who brewed for a small market (perhaps smaller than a single state, and often only a single metropolitan area) was the most common. The regional brewer was multi-state, but usually encompassed no more than two or three states. The national brewers, those selling in all (or almost all) states, were very few in number. In addition, it was very uncommon for a firm to operate more than one plant.

Today, the terms *local, regional,* and *national* brewers are less meaningful than they were in the past. The average geographic market served by one brewer from one plant has widened because of the economies of large-scale production and, to some extent, marketing. With the average-size brewing plant much larger today, the brewing company may extend itself geographically to maintain capacity operations.[5] The premier example of this is the Adolph Coors Company, which reaches customers on the Eastern seaboard from its single brewing plant in Colorado. But it does so at a significant transportation cost disadvantage.

The second factor supporting the ability to serve new geographic regions is the propensity on the part of large sellers in the industry to operate more breweries. In 1959, the top 10 brewers operated 34 breweries. By 1961 the top 10 brewers operated 40 plants and, by 1983, they operated 46 plants. However, multiplant operation by leading brewers remains considerably less than is typical in the U.S. food and tobacco industries.

Size of the Market

The problem of determining the degree of market concentration in brewing is inextricably tied up with delineating just how wide the markets are for beer. If there is one market, a national one, then concentration statistics for the entire nation are relevant. But if brewing, like cement or milk, has regional markets, then delineating their boundaries is necessary before the industry's structure can be ascertained.

The federal courts have to solve this problem when deciding antimerger cases in the brewing industry.[6] A couple of examples of these attempts indicate that to understand the supply-and-demand forces in this industry, one must look to a wide geographic market, but possibly not so wide as to include the entire country.

In evaluating the merger of the Joseph Schlitz Brewing Company with a California brewer, and its stock control over another western brewer, a California district court, noted that freight rates were important in beer marketing, and singled out an eight-western-state area as a separate geographic market.[7] The judge was impressed by the fact that, in 1963, 80 percent of the beer sold in this area was also produced there, and that 94 percent of the beer produced in the area that year was sold there. The Continental Divide was seen as a transportation barrier of sorts from outside the area, as evidenced by those brewers who, having plants both in the eight-state area and outside, generally supplied the eight-state area from their western plants only.

Given these figures, many economists would agree that if one wants to see what determines the supply and demand for beer in this eight-state area, one need be concerned only slightly, if at all, by supply-and-demand conditions in the regions east of the Continental Divide. Even here, however, the geographic area is not perfectly clear-cut. Coors, located outside the eight-state area, was the leading seller of beer in the eight-state area in 1963, with 13.6 percent of the total sales. Some economists might well argue that any market area that overlooked this important seller neglected an important force on the supply side. Their argument would be even stronger today. In 1980, 38 percent of the beer consumed in the eight-state-western area was imported from outside. The market, in its economic sense, should include all buyers and sellers who are important in explaining the supply-and-demand conditions in any one place.

In another case, involving the merger of two brewers located in Wisconsin, the Antitrust Division asked an eminent economist at nearby Northwestern University to testify in support of the view that Wisconsin is a separate market for beer. The economics professor told the government lawyers that this position was economically untenable. Nevertheless, the lawyers persisted in this view and eventually persuaded the U.S. Supreme Court that Wisconsin, by itself, is "a distinguishable and economically significant market for the sale of beer."[8]

Although for legal purposes Wisconsin may have been a separate market, to single it out as a market in the economic sense is to draw the market boundaries too narrowly. In 1978, brewers in the state of Wisconsin sold 21.3 million barrels of beer; that year, consumers in Wisconsin bought 4.8 million barrels of beer.

Because beer is also "imported" into Wisconsin from brewers in other states, obviously more than three-fourths of Wisconsin beer is "exported" for sale outside the state. To say that Wisconsin is a separate geographic market is to overlook the impact of over three-fourths of the production of beer in that state, not to mention the impact of the supply of beer coming to Wisconsin and competing with the "home" brewers. In 1961, the time of the antitrust contest, roughly 25 percent of the beer consumed in Wisconsin was not produced there.[9]

Consequently, one cannot explain the price of beer in Wisconsin without looking at the supply-and-demand conditions in other states, which buy the bulk of Wisconsin's beer production. In this case, the court erred by singling out the state of Wisconsin as an economically meaningful market.

Despite the difficulties of ascertaining with numerical exactness the geographic scope of the brewing industry, brewing *is* a concentrated industry, more concentrated than the average food and tobacco industry.[10] In most states, the forces that work to widen markets have probably been more than offset by the forces that increase concentration.

Reasons for the Decline in the Number of Brewers

What are the reasons for the precipitous drop in the number of rival brewers? In a sense, each brewer's demise is unique, but many have common characteristics. In this section, two factors leading to the decline in brewers are considered: mergers and economies of scale. In a later section, the effect on the industry's structure of entry conditions, product differentiation, and the conglomerate nature of one leading brewer will be assessed.

Mergers

The conventional (and often accurate) explanation for an industry's oligopolization is a merger-acquisition trend among the industry's firms. Given the fact that in the period 1947–1979, the 25 leading brewers made approximately 100 acquisitions, it might seem that mergers are the primary cause of the rising concentration in this industry. But corporate marriages between rival brewers do not explain the increase in concentration by the largest firms. It will prove instructive to review the merger track record of the top five (as of this writing) brewers.

The first antimerger action by the Antitrust Division in the beer industry was taken in 1958, against the industry's leader, Anheuser-Busch. Anheuser-Busch had purchased the Miami brewery of American Brewing Company. The government successfully argued that this merger would eliminate American Brewing as an independent brewer and end its rivalry with Anheuser-Busch in Florida. The final judgment called for Anheuser-Busch to sell this brewery and refrain, for a period of 5 years, from buying any other breweries without court approval. As a result of this action, Anheuser-Busch forsook any policy of acquiring rival brewers and instead began an extensive program of building new plants in Florida and at other locations. Anheuser-Busch deviated from its internal-growth policy in 1980, when it purchased for $100 million the modern Baldwinsville, N.Y. brewing plant of the Schlitz Brewing Company. Schlitz's sales had declined so much that it did not need the brewery; the plant's capacity was so huge that only an industry leader could absorb its output.

The second largest brewer, Miller, purchased brewing plants in Texas and California, back in 1966, but has acquired no other breweries since. In 1972, Miller acquired three brand names from a bankrupt brewer, and in 1974, it bought the rights for the domestic manufacturing and marketing of a prominent German beer. The latter acquisition was unsuccessfully challenged by a private antitrust plaintiff, Miller's only encounter with the antimerger law. The Miller Brewing Company itself, however, was the subject of a conglomerate acquisition by the Philip Morris tobacco company, in 1970. The consequences of this merger are discussed in a later section.

The third-ranking firm, Stroh, acquired the F. M. Schaefer Brewing Company in 1980. This did not significantly affect its rank (it was then the seventh largest brewer). But in 1982, Stroh acquired the Joseph Schlitz Brewing Company, itself in a sales tailspin, and at the time the fourth largest brewer. This catapulted Stroh to number three in the industry. The Antitrust Division, in consenting to the merger, required Stroh to divest a brewery in the Southeast. Stroh complied by exchanging its Tampa plant for a brewery in St. Paul, Minnesota, owned by Pabst.

The G. Heileman Brewing Company, the industry's fourth-ranking firm, is the product of over a dozen acquisitions, from 1960 to 1980, notably Wiedemann, Associated Brewing, the Blatz brand, Rainier, and Carling. In 1960,

Heileman was the nation's 31st-ranking brewer. It is now number four, and has tried without success to expand further by absorbing all of Pabst, the sixth largest brewer. In 1981, Heileman was a rejected suitor for Schlitz (just prior to the Stroh-Schlitz amalgamation), and in 1982 it was a rejected suitor for Pabst. At that time, the Antitrust Division objected to both mergers. But Pabst and Heileman became substantially intertwined. Pabst, during this time frame, had purchased the Olympia Brewing Company (producer of the Olympia, Lone Star, and Hamm's brands) in a complex exchange that transferred its breweries in Georgia, Texas, and Oregon to rival Heileman, as well as the Lone Star, Red White and Blue, Blitz-Weinhard, and Burgermeister brands. This also entailed the obligation, on Heileman's part, to brew beer in the Southeast for Pabst, at the former Pabst brewery in Perry, Georgia, which Heileman had acquired. Recently, Heileman was thwarted in a private antitrust suit from acquiring the remainder of Pabst. Most of the Pabst assets now have been acquired by the owner of Falstaff.

Fifth-ranked Coors has never acquired another brewer. Its stated policy has been to brew its beer only in one location, Golden, Colorado; but Coors now plans to ship beer in bulk to a Virginia-based packaging plant for sale in the East.

The Antitrust Division's determination to stop the Heileman-Schlitz merger indicated the limits to which expansion by merger could take place in the beer industry. Heileman-Schlitz would have resulted in a firm with 16 percent of the national market (Heileman had 7.6 percent in 1980, Schlitz, 8.5 percent). The share of the top four brewers would have increased that year from 67 percent to almost 75 percent; the Herfindahl index would have jumped .0129, from a level of .1585 to .1714 (based on 1980 data). In the 13-state Great Lakes and North Central market for beer, the two firms combined would have had 24 percent of the market, with the Herfindahl index rising .0211, from .1449 to .1660. Independent rivalry between Heileman's premium-price Old Style and the Schlitz brand (which was often discounted below premium-price levels) would have ended. In addition to their market prominence as premium beer sellers in the Midwest, the Heileman and Schlitz companies were the two runaway leaders in malt liquor sales (with about 67 percent of that market segment in 1980), and Schlitz's Old Milwaukee brand (the nation's best-selling popular-price beer) was in head-to-head rivalry with a stable of Heileman's popular-price beers (such as Carling Black Label, Blatz, and Wiedemann). Independent rivalry in these segments would have been lost as a result of this merger. Strong rivalry in popular-price brands not only benefits consumers favoring that segment of the market but also those who purchase primarily premium brands, because competition at the popular-price level places a downward drag on premium prices. In assessing what would have been the largest merger in the history of the brewing industry, the Antitrust Division quite properly said no.

But most mergers in the beer industry have not involved firms of such stature. Generally, they represented the demise of an inefficient firm, which salvaged some remainder of its worth by selling out to another brewer. The acquiring brewer gained no market power but might have benefited by securing the barrelage to bring one plant to full capacity, or to gain access to an improved distribution network or new territory. Mergers such as these are not the cause of structural change; rather, they are the effect, as firms exit through the merger route. This type of merger should be allowed—even encouraged—for, in a roundabout way, easing the exit process facilitates the entry of new firms into the industry. If exit is difficult, potential aspirants will be unlikely to enter any industry.

Leonard Weiss developed a test for measuring the impact of mergers on an industry's structure, and found that in the period 1947–1958, only a small part of the increase in concentration in brewing was the result of mergers.[11] The same calculations for the period 1959–1972, when the share of the leading brewers almost doubled, indicates that, once again, mergers accounted for practically none of the increase. The two top firms, since 1972, have virtually refrained from growth via acquisition of rival firms, and yet their combined share of the market has continued to increase.

This is not to say that mergers have made no imprint on the structure of the brewing industry. The present stature of Stroh and Heileman, as just mentioned, is the result in part of important mergers. But the trend to concentration would have occurred even if all mergers had been prohibited. Indeed, the enforcement of the antimerger law against firms such as Pabst, Schlitz, Falstaff, and Anheuser-Busch was partly responsible for the emphasis on internal growth by most of the leading brewers. At this point, the application of the antimerger law can do little to stem the rising concentration—or the demise—of independent brewers. Although it did prevent the combination of Heileman and Schlitz, one of the few mergers stopped by the Antitrust Division in recent years, the antitrust authorities recognized, in the mid-1970s, that mergers they once would have attacked do not merit challenge, even if the merger involves sizable regional sellers.[12] One must look to factors other than mergers to explain the industry's structural shake-up.

Economies of Scale

Economies of scale pertain to the size of the plant needed to attain the lowest unit costs. Economies of scale exist if big plants produce at lower unit costs than small ones. When discussing economies of scale, economists generally plot a smooth, continuous average-cost curve, which is the envelope of a host of similarly curvaceous short-run average-cost curves, each one representing a different-size plant. What is seldom mentioned in the discussion of these curves, however, is that great confidence cannot be attached to the location of any point on these cost curves in spite of their appearance of a precise rendering.

With this caveat firmly in mind, Figure 1 is a representation of economies of scale in the brewing industry. The figure illustrates the fairly sharp decline

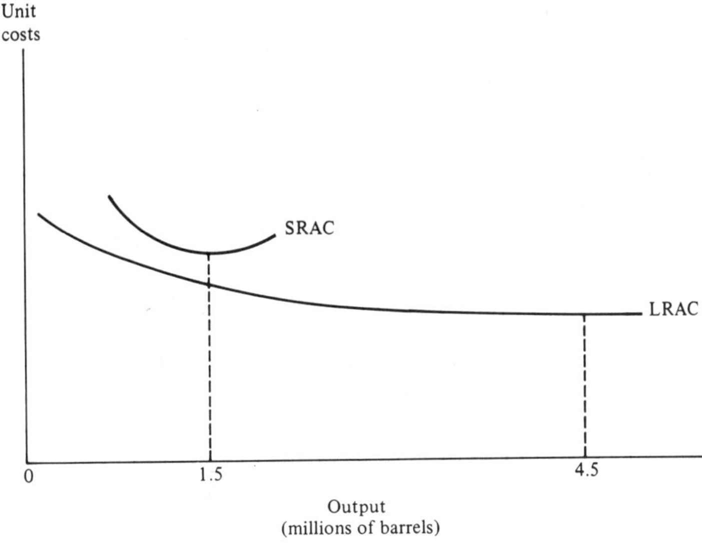

FIGURE 1. Economies of scale in brewing.

in long-run unit costs, until a plant size of 1.25 million barrels per year of capacity is reached. Beyond this capacity, costs continue to decline, but less sharply, until a capacity of 4.5 million barrels (an enormous brewery) is attained. Here, economies of large scale seem to be fully exploited.[13]

Table 4 shows one method used by economists to estimate the extent

Table 4: Surviving Breweries by Capacity: 1959–1983

Listed Capacity Barrels (thousands)	*1959*	*1963*	*1967*	*1971*	*1975*	*1979*	*1983*
0–25	11	8	3	2	2	2	12
26–100	57	46	33	19	9	8	9
101–250	51	39	26	19	9	6	5
251–500	40	33	18	14	10	7	7
501–750	14	13	13	12	4	3	2
751–1000	16	20	22	20	9	5	0
1001–1500	14	12	15	13	7	8	8
1501–2000	4	5	3	8	6	3	5
2001–3000	5	6	5	9	9	6	4
3001–4000	3	4	5	3	3	7	5
4000–	2	3	4	7	15	20	23

Source: Compiled from plant capacity figures listed in the *Modern Brewery Age Blue Book* (Stamford, Conn.: Modern Brewery Age Pub., various years); Charles W. Parker, "The Domestic Beer Industry" (1984), and industry trade sources. These figures do not include plants listed only on a company-consolidated basis (in the case of multiplant firms) or single-plant firms not reporting capacity in the Blue Book. Most plants list their capacity.

of economies of scale, the *survivor test,* which, like all techniques for estimating economies of scale, is not without its difficulties.[14] As its name implies, the survivor test distinguishes plants of a specific size that have survived over time. There has been a steady decline (dramatic in some cases) for breweries of under a 1-million-barrel capacity. Moreover, the truly large brewing operations are not only surviving but growing in number, prima facie evidence of their lower unit costs. One can better understand the concentration statistics in brewing if one knows that the 18 plants of the industry leaders (Anheuser-Busch and Miller) have an average capacity of 6.8 million barrels. There is a statistical oddity in Table 4, regarding very small brewers, those in the 0–25000 barrel capacity: an increase from 1979 to 1983. This reflects the opening of several small breweries—"minibreweries," or "boutique breweries," as they are called. But their total output and competitive significance are tiny.

Figure 1 also includes a single short-run average-cost curve above the long-run average-cost curve. A long-run cost-curve represents the envelope of different sized plants, each of which uses the latest in capital equipment and production techniques. The isolated, single curve portrays the situation of many breweries that have met (or will meet) their demise. These breweries were not only too small to exploit all the economies of scale, but their capital equipment was so outmoded that their costs were further elevated.

Some of the economies of larger operations are the result of packaging equipment. The newer bottling lines at the Anheuser-Busch Houston brewery have line speeds of 1,100 bottles per minute. Modern canning lines are even faster: 2,000 cans per minute. It takes a brewery of substantial size to utilize such equipment at capacity. Large plants also save on labor costs via the automation of brewing and warehousing, and on capital costs as well. Construction cost per barrel is cut by about one third for a 4.5-million-barrel plant, compared to a plant with a 1.5-million-barrel capacity.[15] However, in a study of multiplant economies of scale, no significant reduction in production costs was detected.[16]

In a real sense, economies of scale relate not only to some finite productive capacity but also to management's ability to use the capacity efficiently. Shortly after repeal in 1933, there was a flood of new entrants into the brewing industry, all expecting to slake the thirst of many customers. However, the demand for beer was unexpectedly low after repeal. From a high of 750 brewers operating in 1935, almost 100 were eliminated in but five years. Quite a few of these enterprises had operated before prohibition, but many were under new management. Some were family-owned firms, and heredity had been cruel to the second or third generations, by not endowing them with the brewing and/or managerial capabilities of their fathers or grandfathers. Competitive pressures, with no respect for nepotism, eliminated such breweries.[17]

In today's industry, a small brewer, producing a quality product and marketing it so as to keep transportation costs at a minimum, might survive by finding a special niche for itself. This seems to be the status, by way of examples, of San Francisco's tiny Anchor Steam Brewery, Wisconsin's Stevens Point Brewery, and the nation's oldest brewing firm, D. G. Yuengling & Son, in Pennsylvania. However, such cases are the exceptions that prove the rule. In brewing, unlike many manufacturing industries where optimum-sized plants seem to be getting smaller, large, capital-intensive plants are necessary to exploit economies of scale and survive in the industry.[18] In markets where vigorous competitive pressures exist, firms that do not exploit economies of scale or operate with internal efficiency will not survive. This has been the fate of many brewers; they have exited from the industry because of inefficient plants, poor management, or both.

The Condition of Entry

The ease with which outsiders can enter an industry is a structural characteristic of great importance in ensuring competitive performance. If entry is easy, if potential rivals are lurking in the wings, so to speak, existing firms will be reluctant to use what market power they may have to raise prices—lest they encourage an outbreak of fresh competition. On the other hand, if entry is barred, perhaps by a patent or government license, existing firms will find the potential for garnering monopoly gains greatly enhanced.

Entry into the beer industry is not hindered by the traditional barriers of patents and exclusive government grants. Nor is the monopolization of key resources or economies of scale so important that an efficient entrant would have to supply an enormous share of industry output. However, the sheer expense of entering the beer industry is considerable (although it would be less if profits were higher, thereby making credit easier to acquire). With the expiration of the small brewery has come the demise of the inexpensive brewery. The price of constructing a modern 4-million-barrel brewery is some $250 million. And once built, marketing the new brew also will be costly because entrants must introduce their products to consumers already smitten by vigorous advertising efforts.

A look at the record indicates the low probability of an entry threat to existing brewers from *de novo* aspirants. No firm of any significance in the brewing industry is a new entrant since World War II. This paucity of entry is explained by the relatively low profitability of the industry and the ominous fate of so many exiting firms. Moreover, the industry is risky because its plant facilities have few uses other than brewing beer. Finally, current demographic trends would not be encouraging to prospective entrants, especially given the abundance of existing capacity. Miller alone has 10 million barrels of unutilized capacity sitting in Trenton, Ohio, at a new brewery it has yet to open.

The beer industry has been classed as one with moderate, although increasing, barriers to entry.[19] Presently, the most promising source of new competition is that of an established brewer moving into a new geographic market, or the importation of foreign beer. Beer imports to the United States, most of which come from the Netherlands and Canada, have increased over 600 percent in the period 1970–1981. Imports represent only about 3 percent of domestic consumption, and most imports are expensive brands that sell in the superpremium category.[20] But imported beer has made inroads against domestic brands in on-premise consumption during recent years, and its presence no longer can be discounted as insignificant.

Product Differentiation

To the extent that customers are persuaded that the product of one firm is superior to that of others, the favored firm can raise its price somewhat without losing these customers. This phenomenon is called *product differentiation*. Several studies have revealed that, at least under test conditions, beer drinkers cannot always distinguish between brands of beer.[21] And there is little persuasive evidence that the more expensive brands cost proportionately more to produce. Yet, considerable talent and resources are devoted to publicizing real or imagined differences in beers, with the hope of producing product differentiation.

One indicator of the relative amount of advertising done by industries is the ratio of advertising expenditures to sales. For some companies in the soap, cosmetic, and drug industries, this ratio is greater than 10 percent. For the malt beverage industry, the ratio is notable but has modulated. In the years 1961–1965, this ratio was close to 7 percent; in 1976–1977, the figure fell below 4 percent; for 1977–1981, the latest dates for which data are available, the average was 4.3 percent.[22] This is less than the average of leading food and tobacco firms, and considerably less than is expended in such industries as soft drinks, candy, cigarettes, preserved fruits, and other alcoholic beverages.[23]

Although final industry data are not available, examination of the expenditures of various firms since 1975 reveals a sharp escalation in advertising, beginning in 1976–1977. For example, in 1974, Anheuser-Busch, Schlitz, and Pabst spent 52, 92 and 59 cents per barrel, respectively, on media advertising. In 1977, the figures for these companies were $1.60, $1.98, and 68 cents per barrel, respectively.[24] One explanation given for this increase is that it was a response to Miller's enormous promotional outlays following its affiliation with Philip Morris. One conclusion drawn is that this escalation in advertising has caused the increase in concentration taking place in the industry. Douglas F. Greer, Willard F. Mueller, and others have stressed that advertising, particularly television advertising, is a primary cause of increasing concentration in the industry.[25] But the facts do not permit any tidy explanations or conclusions.

First, Miller has long been a heavy advertiser; in the period 1967–1971, it spent generally twice as much per barrel as rival brewers. But Miller's market share did not expand, nor did other firms feel compelled then to emulate its sizable promotional outlays. Second, there is no hard-and-fast relationship between dollars spent on advertising and market share gained. Schlitz spent more on advertising in 1975 and 1976 than either Anheuser-Busch or Miller, and yet the Schlitz brand had declining sales in that time frame. Coors experienced expanding sales but with very small advertising expenditures; in 1968–1974, years of sizable growth, Coors spent only an average of 17 cents per barrel on media advertising. Coors' growing use of media advertising correlates with its declining growth in sales. Even Miller has not yet been able to secure more than a toehold in the superpremium segment of the market (one would think it would be the most image-conscious), notwithstanding extraordinary advertising expenditures per barrel. In 1980, Miller High Life was the most heavily advertised brand of beer in the United States. In that same year, its sales slowed down. On the other hand, General Brewing once had its sales decline reversed when it introduced, without media promotion, a low-price product in a white can, labeled simply "BEER!"

The amount spent on advertising beer is large, and this is not surprising. There are millions of actual and potential beer drinkers a brewer wants to inform of the quality and availability of its product. New beer customers come of age and producers seek to inform them; old customers may forget, and producers seek to remind them. Nevertheless, at some stage, massive advertising offers only inframarginal information and may have the effect of entrenching the industry leaders. Unfortunately, economic analysis does not provide a tool for determining at what stage advertising becomes redundant and wasteful.

The most absorbing aspect of product differentiation in this industry is associated with what is called *premium beer*. The phenomenon of premium beer began years ago, when a few brewers decided to attempt to sell their beer nationally and added a price premium to offset incremental transportation costs that were encountered in shipping greater distances. To secure the higher price, the beer was promoted as being superior in taste and quality, allegedly because of the brewing expertise found in their locations. At one time, the extra price was absorbed by higher shipping costs; but the construction of efficient, regionally dispersed breweries by most of the large shippers now eliminates the transportation disadvantage. Yet the premium image remains. Thus, with transportation costs equalized, and with production costs generally being lower, these firms can wage vigorous advertising (and price-cutting) campaigns in areas where regional and local brewers were once the largest sellers.

The national brewers also have two other advertising advantages: (1) none of their advertising is "wasted," whereas regional brewers do not always find media markets (especially in television) that coincide with their selling territories; and (2) their advertising investment is less likely to be lost when a customer moves to another part of the country.[26] Still, advertising presents no inevitable relationship between firm growth and promotion expenditures, and the concentration statistics for the industry cannot be explained facilely by the current trend in promotional expenditures because concentration also increased at a time of declining advertising-to-sales ratios.

Rising per capita income may also contribute to increasing concentration. Premium beer is what economists call a *normal good,* with a positive income elasticity. The brewers who came to be the major factors in the industry in the 1970s are, essentially, producers of premium brands. A reference to Table 1 will show that, not many years ago, producers of premium brands were not the major sellers in any given part of the country; the popular-price brands of regional producers were. This has changed. It has been estimated that the premium brands grew from 36 percent of the market to over 52 percent during the period 1970–1981.[27] Superpremium brands, also controlled largely by the top brewers, grew from 1 percent to over 6 percent during the same period. The loser: popular-price beer, which dropped from almost 60 percent in 1970 to less than 20 percent in 1981. In 1982 and 1983 the share of popular-price brands began to increase, at the expense of premiums. But by this time, most of the leading popular brands were marketed by the top four brewers, for example, Stroh's Old Milwaukee and Schaefer brands, which have led the resurgence of popular-price beer. Some popular-price beers for the first time now receive exposure through television advertising. Light beer, nonexistent in 1970, in 1981 had over 14 percent of the market, almost all of this being brewed by the top brewers and selling at premium prices. The downswing of Schlitz and Pabst in recent years is in part explained by their lack of success in the growing low-calorie segment of the market. In 1983, Miller's sales of its Lite brand actually exceeded the sales of its flagship brand, Miller High Life.

The Philip Morris–Miller Affiliation

In the decade of the 1970s, the most dramatic single factor in the brewing industry's structural change was the rise of the Miller Brewing Company from the seventh to the second largest seller. Miller's ascent involved far more than a mere reshuffling of ranking industry leaders. Its production capacity and marketing methods have added a new dimension to the industry, which will affect the industry's economic behavior throughout the 1980s.

The dates of two acquisitions are important in understanding the Miller phenomenon: 1970, when Miller's procurement by the Philip Morris Company was completed; and 1972, when Miller purchased the brand names of Meister Brau, Inc., a defunct Chicago brewing firm.

The 1970 date initiated the management takeover of Miller by Philip Morris personnel. The new management accomplished three master strokes with the Miller High Life brand. First, it was (in marketing parlance) *repositioned* to appeal to the blue-collar consumer, who may drink several beers a day. Previously, the brand promotion was directed at a group of consumers who rarely consumed more than one beer at a sitting. As one Miller advertising executive put it, the strategy was to "take Miller High

Life out of the champagne bucket and put it into the lunch bucket without spilling a drop."[28] The repositioning was effected by a very successful advertising campaign. Second, Miller improved the quality of its product; any of its beer not drunk within 120 days of its production was destroyed if not sold. Third, the company introduced a 7 oz. (pony) bottle that appealed both to infrequent beer drinkers with small capacities and to hearty drinkers, who found that the beer remained colder in the small receptacle. These three events alone yielded Miller enormous growth.

But Miller's adroit use of *amyloglucosidase*[29] amplified even more the company's ascendancy. The virtually unnoticed Miller purchase of the three Meister Brau trademarks included one called Lite, a brand of low-calorie beer that was brewed by the amyloglucosidase process, and which had been marketed locally by Meister Brau to upper-middle-class weight-conscious consumers. The Miller management became curious about the fact that Lite had once sold fairly well in Anderson, Indiana, a town with many blue-collar workers. In what is now a marketing classic, Miller zeroed in on "real" beer drinkers, claiming that its low-calorie beer allowed them to drink their beer with even less of a filled-up feeling. The upshot of this marketing campaign is evident to any grocery store shelf-stocker: Lite is the most popular new product in the history of the beer industry, and many brewers now have their own brand of light beer as competition. Parenthetically, one of the few failures of Miller was in its legal campaign to reserve not only Lite but even the term "light" to itself; the courts left the generic word in the public domain, and thereby allowed other brewers to use this term to describe their low-calorie emulations.

Miller's ascendancy has not been without its brickbats, which come generally in two forms. The first criticism is that Miller changed the *process* of beer rivalry, with the emphasis no longer on production economies but upon market segmentation and brand proliferation. If "beer is beer," then it is argued that consumers do not truly benefit by the product and packaging differentiation that is now extant in the industry. Economics as a science has little to contribute to the discussion of this issue.

But some economists are concerned that brand proliferation, and the advertising dollars needed to sustain it, can erect barriers to entry to smaller firms, thereby lessening competition. In response, the contrary argument has been made that Miller had to bear the financial burden of making its low-calorie beer palatable to consumers; having done this, Miller's rivals, producers both large and small, have been able to introduce their own light beers more easily.[30]

The second criticism of Miller is that it is owned by a conglomerate, and that Philip Morris's "deep pocket" provides unfair advantages to Miller vis-à-vis its rivals. For example, Robert A. Uihlein, formerly the chairman of Schlitz, was persuaded that Philip Morris "is definitely taking profits from one business and sticking them into another business to gain market share by selling below cost."[31] Professor Willard F. Mueller testified before a Senate committee that "Miller's record expansion after 1970 was made possible by Philip Morris' capacity and willingness to engage in deep and sustained subsidization of Miller's operations."[32] He cited Miller's media advertising budget and capital expansion program as evidence of this, arguing that Miller could not have raised such funds on its own. Mueller testified further that the operation of Miller makes no economic sense if the firm is viewed as an "autonomous profit center." He implicitly concluded that Philip Morris's behavior makes economic sense only if the upshot of its subsidization is a monopoly position for Miller (or shared monopoly with Anheuser-Busch) in the near future.

However, the matter of cross-subsidization is not a simple one to analyze. The detailed accounting records of the Miller subsidiary are not in the public domain. It is not clear, for example, whether a depreciation instead of expensing of Miller's advertising expenditure would reveal any sizable loss on the Miller operations. Moreover, even if Miller were a poor investment as a beer business, it is not clear now, more than a decade after the acquisition, how Philip Morris can expect to recoup these alleged losses by monopoly pricing its beer, given the sizable rivals still remaining and their intense rivalry with Miller.

III. CONDUCT

Pricing

Judging from the early records of the preprohibition beer industry, life in the industry was very competitive. Entry was easy and producers were many. Economic theory would predict a competitive industry, given these two characteristics, and the evidence bears this out. Some brewers made a fortune and perhaps held some market power; they were also the ones that pioneered new techniques for producing and marketing quality malt beverages.

In fact, the early beer industry offers a classic example of the predictions of price theory. Given the inelastic demand, brewers saw the obvious advantages of monopolizing the industry, raising prices, and gleaning high profits. Various types of both loose and tight-knit cartels were seen as advantageous, but the difficulty of coordinating so many brewers, and the lack of any barriers to entry, prevented any of these efforts from being successful, at least for long. The degree of competition is evident in this plea from Adolphus Busch to Captain Pabst:

> I hope also to be able to demonstrate to you that by the present way competition is running we are only hurting each other in a real foolish way. The traveling agents . . . always endeavor to reduce prices and send such reports to their respective home offices as are generally not correct and only tend to bring forth competition that helps to ruin the profits . . . all large manufacturing interests are now working in harmony . . . and only the brewers are behind as usual; instead of combining their efforts and securing their own interest, they are fighting

each other and running the profits down, so that the pleasures of managing a brewery have been diminished a good deal.[33]

This is the sort of letter vigorous market rivalry should elicit.

The beer industry also escaped the horizontal mergers that transformed the structure of so many industries—such as steel, whiskey, petroleum, tobacco, and farm equipment—during the first great merger movement. There were attempts, mostly by British businessmen, to combine the large brewers during this time. One attempt called for the amalgamation of Pabst, Schlitz, Miller, Anheuser-Busch, and Lemp into one company, a feat that, had it been successful, would have greatly altered the structure and degree of competition in the industry. But the attempt failed, and brewing entered the prohibition period with a competitive structure that responded with competitive pricing.

The Pricing Pattern

Basing-point pricing systems, which had been common in industries such as steel and cement, have never been representative of pricing in the beer industry. Instead, beer is generally sold FOB the brewery. Some brewers sell on a uniform FOB-mill basis, but most vary their prices, at times, to different customers, to reflect localized competitive conditions or to test perceived changes in the marketplace. For example, in 1980, Stroh's prices differed in the contiguous states of Illinois, Kentucky, and Indiana and its prices in Pennsylvania, a state with unusually vigorous price-cutting, were lower than in nearly all Midwestern states.

The present pattern of prices dates back to the turn of the century, with the introduction of premium beers, an aspect of the industry discussed earlier. These brands will generally be priced just above the price level of "popular"price beers, which will be above "local" (or "price" or "shelf") beer. A more contemporary category is the *superpremium,* a beer selling at a price above premium. A number of major brewers market their own brand of superpremiums, and most imported beers are in this price category.

The distinction between local, popular, and premium beers has become blurred in recent years, not only because of the introduction of the superpremium, but because the price differential between premium brands and popular-price brands has narrowed. At the same time, the distinction between local and popular beer (on the basis of price) has become murky because of pricing specials that regularly appear in both segments of the market. Of course, the demise of most local breweries has reduced the distinction further.

The pattern for beer prices is different from the price differentials that exist for various grades of lumber, steel, or aluminum. In these cases, the differential is attributable to some identifiable physical characteristic of the product. In the case of malt beverages, price differences are in part the result of customers' tastes and are thus subjective. Beer drinkers have not distinguished themselves by their ability to discern taste differences or brand identities when a beer's corporate genus is kept secret.

Price Discrimination

In 1955, the Federal Trade Commission (FTC) issued a complaint against Anheuser-Busch, charging it with unlawful price discrimination. Anheuser-Busch had dropped the price of its premium brand to all buyers in the St. Louis area, but it did not make this reduction in any other areas. The FTC maintained that this was price discrimination and the result would be to impair competition by diverting to Anheuser-Busch sales from regional rivals serving St. Louis.

The charge against Anheuser-Busch was brought under Section 2(a) of the Robinson-Patman Act. Proof of such a violation involves answering three questions:

1. Is there price discrimination?
2. If so, does the respondent have a defense?
3. If not, might the price discrimination lessen competition?

There was vigorous disagreement on the answer to each of these questions.

After the price cut, Anheuser-Busch's Budweiser-brand beer was selling for less money per case in St. Louis than anywhere in the country, and this differential could not be explained fully by the lower transportation costs from the Anheuser-Busch brewery in St. Louis. Query: Is this, automatically, price discrimination?

The U.S. Court of Appeals said no, and argued that price discrimination could not exist unless different prices were charged to *competing* purchasers. The Court put it this way:

> Anheuser-Busch did not thereby discriminate among its local competitors in the St. Louis area. By its cuts, Anheuser-Busch employed the same means of competition against all of them. Moreover, it did not discriminate among those who bought its beer in the St. Louis area; all could buy at the same price.[34]

The FTC, and ultimately the U.S. Supreme Court, disagreed with this interpretation. The Supreme Court said that price discrimination is "selling the same kind of goods cheaper to one purchaser than to another," and, thereby, overruled the court of appeals.[35]

Ever since the "Detroit case,"[36] a defense to a charge of price discrimination has been to show that one's lower price was offered to meet the equally low price of a rival. Prior to the FTC complaint, Budweiser was selling at $2.93 per case in St. Louis; its rivals were three regional brewers, who sold their beer at $2.35 per case. In two successive price cuts, Anheuser-Busch dropped its price to $2.35 per case. Query: Could not Anheuser-Busch argue that it was only meeting the equally low price of its rivals?

Anheuser-Busch did, but the FTC categorically rejected this defense. Note what this implies: Anheuser-Busch went on record, so to speak, that its premium beer is the same product as popular-price beer—that is, "beer is beer." The FTC, however, argued that, at $2.35 a case, Anheuser-Busch "was selling more value than its competitors were . . . the consumer has proved . . . that [he] will pay more for Budweiser than . . . for many other beers."[37] This statement comes very close to saying that Budweiser, because of its "superior public acceptance," should, and must, be priced at a differential above regional and local beers. After the Supreme Court ruled that Anheuser-Busch had priced in a discriminatory fashion, the U.S. Court of Appeals had to decide whether competition might be lessened by the company's pricing practice. The FTC (arguing from the figures given earlier on the changing market shares in St. Louis), said that this practice would give Anheuser-Busch market power in St. Louis by increasing its market share.

The Court of Appeals disagreed, ruling that the simple diversion of business was not an indication that competition in St. Louis was being lessened. In its decision, the Court pointed out that Anheuser-Busch was not subsidizing St. Louis with revenues from other markets, and that none of the rivals of Anheuser-Busch in St. Louis had felt so "pushed" as to lower its price in response to the Anheuser-Busch cut. The only result was that consumers of beer in St. Louis could buy Budweiser for less money, which, in the Court's opinion, is what market competition is all about.

If the FTC had won its case and Anheuser-Busch had been barred from making this price cut in St. Louis, one might argue that competition would be increased, for companies would be prevented from making selective price cuts to eliminate smaller rivals or to enforce price leadership. But there is another implication to consider. Barring selective price cuts may be the same as barring price competition. Anheuser-Busch could respond to the loss of sales in its own backyard by cutting its prices across the board all over the country. But, as one observer put it, "If a seller by law must lower all his prices or none, he will hesitate long to lower any."[38]

Charges of discriminatory price-cutting have been leveled against most of the national brewers, and several private antitrust suits were brought by local and regional brewers, alleging that national sellers were picking off regional sellers by discounting heavily in their areas, and making up for the losses by profits earned on sales in other parts of the country. The FTC was urged to enjoin the practice. However, no evidence surfaced that the national companies were pricing below cost; the regional brewers were the victims not of predatory pricing but of high-cost brewing operations.

One unfortunate response to the pricing practices of the national brewers was the installation in a number of states of price-posting laws. Basically, these laws provide that sellers must publicly post their wholesale prices, maintain them for some period of time, announce any price changes, and in some cases specify the retail price of the product as well. Although such legislation has the facade of protecting beer consumers against quick price increases, its impetus actually came from smaller brewers, who saw such laws as protection against competition from promotional price campaigns, and from wholesalers and retailers, who saw these as laws providing floors under their own price structure.

Questionable Payments

In the early 1970s, some brewers and beer wholesalers used "questionable payments" (or "blackbagging") in marketing their beer to selected retail accounts. This is a pricing practice that, depending upon one's point of view, could be dubbed either a bribe or a price cut. For example, a brewer might offer, through its distributor, a thousand dollars to a restaurant chain if that company would sell only that brewer's beer on tap at its outlets. If the payment went to a restaurant employee to secure the business, it would be a bribe, but if it went into the restaurant's till, it would be (from an economic standpoint) like a price cut, because other brewers also could make the restaurant as well off by reducing their price to gain its business. One reason why brewers would not simply cut their prices openly would be to avoid Robinson-Patman Act vulnerability; another would be to conceal the price cut from rivals (who might match it) or other customers (who might demand it too).

Whatever the rationale, such payments may violate certain tax and beer-marketing laws. Schlitz, for example, incurred a 747-count criminal indictment in 1978 for its questionable payments. In a 1984 consent decree, Anheuser-Busch agreed to pay a $2 million penalty to resolve such allegations against it.

Price-Affirmation Laws

One potential impairment to the competitive pricing of beer is the application of state price-affirmation laws to the brewing industry. Price-affirmation statutes require a firm to sell its product within a state at a price no higher than is charged in other states. Several states already require manufacturers of distilled spirits to notify the state alcoholic beverage authority of the prices they charge, and to "affirm" that lower prices for these products are not found anywhere else in the country. It is possible that these states and others will eventually include malt beverages within their affirmation requirements; two states already have done this.

On the face of it, these state regulations might seem beneficial, at least for the residents of those states that have enacted them. But economic theory teaches us to be skeptical of legislation that tampers with the nervous system of the marketplace, that is, price. Although the precise economic effects of price-affirmation laws are not known, the probable result of them will be to reduce price competition. Conceivably, these laws could even promote price-fixing, because the states, by publishing rivals' prices, will perform a "service" that rivals could not themselves perform for fear of violating the antitrust laws. Moreover, manufacturers will find it far more difficult to run specials and sales, for example those that are designed for events specific to a region or town, because a price cut could not be made in such an area without being applied in other price-affirmation states at the same time. In addition, sellers will be handicapped in testing the price-sensitivity of products in response to what they perceive as demand or supply changes; and firms will incur additional paperwork costs for compiling and submitting forms to the states in order to validate their various prices. All of these drawbacks ignore the difficult and technical task engendered by price-discrimination laws. It is no simple matter to make actual price comparisons in the face of the complex discount structures, rebates, allowances, and tax and transportation differentials that a brewer incurs when marketing in different states.

Marketing

Although all industries are subject to various federal and state laws that affect the marketing of the industry's product, the brewing industry faces an especially great variety of laws and regulations concerning labeling, advertising, credit, container characteristics, alcoholic content, tax rates, and litter assessments.

For example, Michigan does not permit a beer label to show alcoholic content; Minnesota requires an accurate statement of alcoholic content; in Indiana, advertising is strictly regulated; and Louisiana has no advertising restrictions. Some states require sales from the brewer to wholesaler to retailer to be only on a cash basis, whereas other states allow credit. The size of containers, both maximum and minimum, is stipulated in some states. Alabama permits no package-beer containers to be larger than 16 ounces, but Connecticut allows any size. States have varying requirements on the maximum and minimum permissable alcoholic content. In some states, alcoholic content may be different for different types of outlets.

The governmental involvement in the beer industry also includes taxation. The federal tax alone on a barrel of beer is $9.00; in 1982, the Treasury Department coffers received over $1.6 billion in beer taxes. The state taxes on beer vary substantially but average over $5.00 per barrel. In addition, brewers, wholesalers, and retail outlets pay federal, state, and sometimes local occupational taxes. Taxes represent the largest single-cost item in a glass of beer.

There is little forward integration by brewing firms into the marketing of beer. The possibilities would include the brewing firms' owning distributors and retail outlets. In England, the brewing industry has extensive holdings in the retailing of beer, owning more than half of all retail outlets, including about 80 percent of the public houses and hotels.[39] But in the United States, brewers are prohibited by law from owning any retail outlets, which means that the wholesale distribution of the product is the only legitimate forward vertical-integration route. The retailing of beer is done through two general types of independent outlets: those for on-premise consumption and those for off-premise consumption.

Most brewers rely on independent distributors to channel their product to these retail outlets. In 1984, there were approximately 4,000 wholesalers of beer, the vast majority being independent merchant wholesalers. Some brewers own a portion of their wholesale channel. For example, Anheuser-

Busch distributes about 75 percent of its beer through independent wholesalers; the remainder is marketed through branch offices in large metropolitan areas.

A brewer's keen financial interest in the distribution of its beer is self-evident: a disgruntled customer reads the brewer's name on the container, not the name of the wholesaler or retailer. Therefore brewers negotiate contracts with wholesalers as to the marketing obligations of each party, but not all areas of concern to the brewer are open for negotiation. For example, the determination of resale prices is not a matter for private agreement because, in this area, the antitrust laws limit the contractual opportunities of a brewer. The antitrust laws could make it potentially difficult for a brewer to prevent what in economics is called the *free-rider problem*. An example would be a distributor who trans-ships dated beer to a territory that has long been served by a distributor who, by careful stock rotation, had given that brand a reputation for freshness. On the other hand, territorial-exclusivity clauses give the distributor a reprieve from intrabrand competition.

Some large retail customers, notably chain stores, would prefer to purchase beer directly from brewers, eliminating the wholesale distributor. Or they prefer to bargain with different distributors of the same brand of beer (and possibly purchase from a price-cutting wholesaler in another area). But brewers almost unanimously market through a three-tier distribution system, and they support federal legislation that would immunize from antitrust attack a distributor's exclusive territorial limits (and would thereby prevent a distributor from shipping outside its "territory"). The beer industry has joined with the National Beer Wholesalers Association in championing legislation permitting exclusive territorial agreements similar to legislation secured earlier by the soft drink industry. Both the Department of Justice and the Federal Trade Commission have opposed this antitrust exemption.

Although this legislation has not been adopted by Congress (as of this writing), Anheuser-Busch recently proceeded with new wholesaler agreements that restrict a distributor's sales to only his own territory; a wholesaler who makes sales directly or indirectly to customers outside the assigned territory is subject to immediate termination.[40] Clauses of this character earlier had been illegal per se under the antitrust laws. But they are now scrutinized more permissively under the rule of reason. Other brewers have copied the Anheuser-Busch initiative.

The beer wholesaler at one time distributed mainly kegs of beer for on-premise draught consumption. In 1935, only 30 percent of beer sales were packaged—that is, in bottles or cans suitable for on- or off-premise consumption. Since that time there has been a shift to packaged beer relative to draught; in 1982, 87 percent of beer sales were packaged. The popularity of the can and the one-way bottle, the changing consumption habits of the male, the apparent loss of the "saloon habit" during prohibition, and the preferences of the female mean that the beer distributor, today, will make more delivery trips to the grocery store than to the tavern.

This trend in beer marketing works to the disadvantage of the small brewer. When beer sales were primarily by the keg for on-premise consumption, the small brewer could survive by selling to taverns in his immediate area. But packaged beer sales are primarily for off-premise consumption, and the distribution of packaged beer increases the importance of product differentiation and brand emphasis.

Profits

If an industry is effectively monopolized, one might expect to see this reflected in its profits. This is not necessarily so because (1) demand may not be sufficiently high to yield profits, in spite of monopoly; (2) the monopolists may be inefficient; or (3) the accounting records may not show the monopoly gains because accounting records often are imperfect measures of economic costs and profits. In spite of these difficulties, economists regularly look at profit data for some insight into an industry's performance.

On the whole, brewing firms have been less profitable than the average manufacturing firm in the post-World War II period. Profits in the industry were quite modest until 1967. During the three years 1968–1970, the industry's rate of return on net worth after taxes averaged 9.5 percent, as compared to the return for all manufacturing firms of 7.4 percent. However, in the most recent years for which data are available, 1979 through 1981, the beer industry tallied a return of only 4.9, 6.0, and 2.1 percent for each year, respectively, compared with 10.6, 8.7, and 6.7 percent, respectively, for all manufacturing.[41]

As one might expect from the earlier discussion on economies of scale, the largest brewers have done better than the industry average. Beginning in 1964, the top four companies began to outperform the rest of the brewing industry in terms of profits. Prior to that time, the profit record of the top four brewers approximated that of the rest of the industry, and was usually inferior to the firms ranked five through eight.[42]

Externalities

Externalities, or spillover effects, occur when transactions between parties (such as the simple sale of a product) have economic consequences on others who are not party to the transaction. These spillover effects can be positive or negative in value and, to the extent that an industry manifests externalities—either in the production process or in the consumption of its product—the social performance of that industry is likely to be affected.

The beer industry is remarkably free of the negative externalities in production that are commonly associated with manufacturing enterprises, that is, air and noise pollution. Brewing is a very *clean* industry (breweries must be more sanitary than hospitals, in fact), and, partly for this reason, brewing firms are often courted by areas seeking industry. The brewing industry performs well on this count.

The externality problems in brewing occur in the consumption of the product. True, there would be positive externalities for members of the Beer Can Collectors of America if they found along the roadside an empty can of Monticello beer (with its emblem of Mr. Jefferson's home) or Olde Frothingslosh (with its rather rotund female bathing-beauty trademark). However, most citizens are able to restrain their enthusiasm for the billions of beer cans and bottles that end up as litter. These negative externalities are imposed on them, even though they neither sold nor bought the beer.

Although legislation banning or restricting the sale of beer containers is commonly proposed, only a few states and localities actually have passed such laws. The most restrictive of these laws is in effect in the college town of Oberlin, Ohio, which simply outlawed the sale or possession of beer in nonreturnable containers. The most well-known of these laws is the Oregon "bottle bill," passed in 1971, which bans all cans with detachable pull tabs and places a compulsory 5-cent deposit on all beer and soft-drink containers. Because retail stores do not want to handle returned cans, there has been a drastic reduction in the sale of beverages in this container, and there is now an inducement to use returnable containers, or to consume draught beer on-premise. In Oregon and Vermont, mandatory-deposit legislation apparently led to reductions of 60 and 80 percent, respectively, of beverage-container litter on the roadside. However, the statewide (or local) approach cannot solve the problem (say, in Vermont) of customers going "over the line" (to New Hampshire) to avoid the deposit requirement and higher prices.

The United States Brewers Association (with the exception of Coors) opposes all taxes and bans on containers; instead, it stresses voluntary action and other litter-recovery programs. The latter program, if generously financed, could solve the litter problem, but partially at the expense of nonproducers and nonconsumers.

The economic question of where the liability for any externality (in this case, litter) should be placed depends on which party—the consumer, the producer, or a third party (or some combination of the three)—would be the most efficient at removing the externality. The evidence is not yet in on this complicated question. One study, done at the University of Iowa's Division of Energy Engineering, suggests that mandatory-deposit legislation is not the economical way to correct negative externalities in beer consumption.[43] Based on a cost-benefit study of one Iowa county's experience with such legislation, this conclusion was reached: the costs incurred by consumers and merchants who handled the returned beer containers would have paid for road crews to clean 2,000 miles of roads of *all* litter (the county has only 750 total miles of roadway).

Although data are being gathered on the relative cost of various remedial proposals, because of estimation difficulties, little is known about the size of the economic benefits to be derived from different levels of litter abatement. This makes cost-benefit calculations more than recondite. Efficiency questions aside, an equity standard would suggest that the burden for removing the externality should be borne by the consumers and the industry itself. A full discussion of the externality problem in brewing would require many pages, and should include what is also a significant externality: the economic and noneconomic costs imposed by behavior influenced by alcohol. To distinguish this negative externality in the consumption of beer from the concomitant externalities associated with distilled spirits—where the problem is undoubtedly of much greater magnitude—would also be a difficult task. This topic is one still in need of much research.

Competition

Increasing concentration at the national level, and the unlikely entrance of new rivals, pose a threat to the future level of competition in the beer industry. As the industry becomes populated by fewer companies, there is enhanced potential for their engaging in tacit or direct collusion (given the inelastic nature of demand) to establish a joint profit-maximizing price and output. One study argued that high two-firm concentration ratios constitute a critical measure of market power.[44] Similarly, with high concentration, the chances may be lessened that smaller firms will follow a truly independent price and production strategy. In an industry with only a few sellers, the normal result is an increased danger of a parallel business behavior.

However, the prospect of joint profit-maximizing behavior is not worrisome for the beer industry in the near future. Thus far, there is no evidence of collusion in the industry. Even with the increased demand for beer in the 1960s and 1970s, competition forced the exit of marginal firms. Moreover, Miller's increase in productive capacity prompted other rivals to follow suit in building or expanding plants. This capacity overhangs the industry, and now provokes the large brewers to battle even more amongst themselves instead of competing to take away market share from smaller firms. For example, it was Coors whose share of the market declined after Anheuser-Busch's recent California expansion, and it was Schlitz who lost considerable business in Texas as Coors entered that state. It is precisely this overhang of capacity that, barring collusion or government interference, should keep brewing firms from exercising harmful market power in future years, notwithstanding the relative increase in concentration the industry has experienced.

If the weapon of price-cutting is sheathed, a seller may select nonprice methods of gaining sales, for example advertising. As mentioned earlier, some economists are persuaded that in highly concentrated markets such rivalry can be economically harmful to the consumer. But thus far price competition has been a weapon of standard issue for the beer industry. During 1973–1984, the Producer Price Index for bottled beer went from 115 to 213, and the Producer Price Index for all commodities increased from 136 to 311 (June index). That is, the price index for beer has risen more slowly than the price index for all goods.[45] In 1973, when the industry had permission from the Cost of Living Council to raise prices (because of cost increases), competitive pressures prevented the price adjustment. As the FTC report on the brewing industry concluded:

> Costs in brewing may have risen less rapidly than the average because the industry is relatively capital-intensive. . . .However, the data on profits indicate that the industry was unable to retain the benefits of cost reductions for itself . . . thus, the implication is that competition forced any savings in cost to be passed on to consumers.[46]

One measure of an industry's rivalry is the extent of changes in market share or turnover in the ranking of its sellers. The beer industry exhibits high mobility in this regard. Schlitz, the nation's second-ranking firm in 1976, which brewed the "Beer That Made Milwaukee Famous," is no longer located in Milwaukee. Pabst was the third-leading seller as recently as 1975, ahead of Miller; it was even the subject of an Antitrust Division action, but is now a shell of its former self. In 1980–82, the company was diverted by a revolving-door management and several takeover bids, which resulted in bitter and costly litigation. Miller, number eight in 1968, has been number two since 1977. But Miller, the darling of the industry in the 1970s, thus far has experienced an absence of growth in the 1980s. Coors once "owned" Oklahoma and California, with 54 percent and 40 percent of the sales in these states, respectively. In 1983, these percentages had slipped to 35 and 16 percent.

The one constant in all this has been Anheuser-Busch: number one since 1957. In the period 1970–1983, the company has averaged a better than one percentage point increase in national market share, its portion increasing every year since 1976. Recall (from Table 1) that Anheuser-Busch has not always been the largest seller (even in its home town), and in the 1960s, many investors inaccurately predicted that Schlitz would someday be number one. In the 1970s, some predicted that Miller would become number one. It was the Miller competition that in 1976 provoked Anheuser-Busch to strengthen its organization; it improved its productivity and revised its marketing efforts.

Rivalry from foreign producers has never been a strong force in the beer industry. However, the amount of beer imported into the United States has been increasing and provides a modest source of rivalry to the high-priced brands. Presently, imported beer faces a tariff of approximately $1.86 per barrel. To preserve the present degree of competition, it is important that the threat of foreign rivalry remain. Therefore, the tariff on beer should not be increased; preferably, it should be removed.

Increases in concentration in brewing are neither the result nor the cause of market power. The reasons are benign: the exploitation of scale economies and the demise of suboptimal capacity; new or superior products; changes in packaging and marketing methods; poor management on the part of some firms; and product differentiation, which, if not unambiguously benign, is at least outside the pale of traditional antitrust concern.

The statistics on the structure of the beer industry, the pricing and marketing conduct of its members, and the profits it has received do not mark it as a monopolized industry. The extent of exits from brewing in the last two decades indicates that this is hardly an industry in which the inefficient producer is protected from the chilling winds of competition.

NOTES

1. For certain individuals this figure may be relatively high. Some Germans claim the reason Dinkelacker is such good beer is because it must compete with the fine wines also produced in the Stuttgart area.

2. Lager beer is aged (or "stored") to mellow. Also, it is bottom-fermented, that is, the yeast settles to the bottom during fermentation. The result is a lighter, more effervescent potation.

3. A barrel of beer contains 31 gallons, or 446 eight-ounce glasses (allowing for spillage), or almost 14 cases of 24 12-ounce bottles.

4. Thomas F. Hogarty and Kenneth G. Elzinga, "The Demand for Beer," *Review of Economics and Statistics,* **54:** 197(May 1972). Income elasticity is approximately 0.4.

5. Many brewers regularly ship distances of 300 to 500 miles. For example, one major brewer ships about 40 percent of its production 300 miles or more; but it ships less than 20 percent of its production more than 500 miles.

6. In order to determine the possible effect of a merger on competition, the relevant geographic market has to be determined.

7. See *United States v. Jos. Schlitz,* 253 F.Supp. 129 (1966); aff'd. 385 U.S. 37 (1966). The states were California, Oregon, Washington, Nevada, Idaho, Montana, Utah, and Arizona.

8. *United States v. Pabst,* 384 U.S. 546 (1966) at 559.

9. Ibid. Trial transcripts: testimony of M. A. Adelman, Vol. 15A, April 20, 1967, p. 2007.

10. John M. Connor, *The U.S. Food and Tobacco Manufacturing Industries,* U.S. Department of Agriculture Report No. 451, March, 1980, p. 11.

11. "An Evaluation of Mergers in Six Industries," *Review of Economics and Statistics,* **42:** 172(May 1965).

12. Such as Carling and National, Heileman and Rainier, Olympia and Lone Star, General Brewing and Pearl, Olympia and Hamm, Heileman and Carling, and Stroh and F. M. Schaefer.

13. See Kenneth G. Elzinga, "The Restructuring of the U.S. Brewing Industry," *Industrial Organization Review,* **1:** 105–109(1973), and the sources cited therein.

14. See William G. Shepherd, "What Does the Survivor Technique Show About Economies of Scale?" *Southern Economic Journal,* **34:** 113(July 1967).

15. *The Brewing Industry,* Staff Report of the Federal Trade Commission, Bureau of Economics (Washington, D.C.: U.S. Government Printing Office, 1978), pp. 48–49.

16. F. M. Scherer et al., *The Economics of Multi-Plant Operations: An International Comparisons Study* (Cambridge, Mass.: Harvard U.P., 1975), pp. 334–335.

17. Alfred Marshall saw this phenomenon as one of the important factors limiting the growth and size of firms, and an important determinant in the preservation of competition. See his *Principles of Economics,* C. W. Guillebaud (ed.) (New York: Macmillan, 1961), pp. 315–317.

18. See Anthony Cockerill, "Economies of Scale: Industrial Structure and Efficiency: The Brewing Industry in Nine Nations," in A. T. Jacquemin and H. W. DeJong (eds.), *Welfare Aspects of Industrial Markets* (Leiden: Martinus Nijhoff, 1977), pp. 273–301, for evidence that the phenomenon is not unique to the United States.

19. H. Michael Mann, "Seller Concentration, Barriers to Entry, and Rates of Return in Thirty Industries, 1950–1960," *Review of Economics and Statistics,* **48:** 299(Aug. 1966).

20. The United States exports much less beer than it imports.

21. For examples, see J. Douglas McConnell, "An Experimental Examination of the Price-Quantity Relationship," *Journal of Business,* **41:** 439(Oct. 1968); F. B. Meeker and R. D. Bettencourt, "Perceptual Learning of Discrimination in Beertasting: Effects of Ss' Belief in Their Ability to Discriminate" (Paper delivered at the Western Psychological Association Meeting, April 1973); and Ralph I. Ellison and Kenneth P. Uhl, "Influence of Beer Brand Identification on Taste Perception," *Journal of Marketing Research,* **1:** 36(Aug. 1964).

22. As calculated from the U.S. Department of the Treasury, *Corporation Source Book of Statistics of Income* (Washington, D.C.: U.S. Government Printing Office), various years. The Treasury data include figures for the malt industry as well. Because the product *malt* is not as extensively advertised as beer, this understates somewhat the actual ratio for brewing.

23. Connor, op. cit., p. 58.

24. Douglas F. Greer, "The Causes of Concentration in the Brewing Industry," *Quarterly Review of Economics and Business,* **21:** 100(Winter 1981).

25. Greer, ibid.; see also Greer, "Product Differentiation and Concentration in the Brewing Industry," *Journal of Industrial Economics,* **19:** 201–219(July 1971); John M. Connor, Richard T. Rogers, Bruce W. Marion, and Willard F. Mueller, *The Food Manufacturing Industries* (Lexington, Mass.: Lexington Books, 1985), pp. 244–259.

26. Yoram Peles, "Economies of Scale in Advertising Beer and Cigarettes," *Journal of Business,* **44:** 32(Jan. 1971).

27. "Product Segment Structure of Malt Beverages Entering the Domestic Market 1970–1981," by R. S. Weinberg, cited by Charles W. Parker in *The Domestic Beer Industry*. (Unpublished manuscript, 1984), p. 33.

28. "John Murphy of Miller is Adman of the Year," *Advertising Age* (Jan. 9, 1978), p. 86.

29. This is a natural enzyme that reduces the amount of carbohydrates (and therefore calories) in beer. The enzyme was commercially available in 1964.

30. Lutz Isslieb, a Pearl Brewing Company executive, stated, "It's no longer necessary to sell the idea of a light beer; the issue now is *which* light beer." *Modern Brewery Age* (April 21, 1980), p. 12.

31. "Miller's Fast Growth Upsets the Beer Industry," *Business Week* (Nov. 8, 1976), p. 61.

32. See Mergers and Industrial Concentration, Hearings, U.S. Senate, Committee on the Judiciary, Subcommittee on Antitrust & Monopoly, 95th Cong., 2nd sess., May 12, 1978, p. 99.

33. Thomas C. Cochran, *The Pabst Brewing Company* (New York: New York U.P., 1948), p. 151. (Letter of Jan. 3, 1889.)

34. *Anheuser-Busch, Inc. v. Federal Trade Commission,* 265 F.2d 677 (7th Cir. 1959) at 681.

35. *Federal Trade Commission v. Anheuser-Busch, Inc.,* 363 U.S. 536 (1960) at 549.

36. *Federal Trade Commission v. Standard Oil,* 355 U.S. 396 (1958).

37. *In the matter of Anheuser-Busch,* FTC, Docket no. 6331, p. 19. (Emphasis supplied.)

38. F. M. Rowe, "Price Discrimination, Competition, and Confusion: Another Look at Robinson-Patman," *Yale Law Journal,* **60:** 959(1951).

39. The British Monopolies Commission has investigated this vertical relationship in England, and concluded that such integration retards the efficient distribution of beer, raises the entry barriers in brewing, hinders price competition, and protects inefficient producers. But for a defense of the "tied house," see Kevin Hawkins and Rosemary Radcliffe, "Competition in the Brewing Industry," *Journal of Industrial Economics,* **20:** 20(Nov. 1971).

40. "A-B Wholesaler Contract Wins High Praise," *Modern Brewery Age* (Oct. 18, 1982), p. 1.

41. Compiled from U.S. Department of the Treasury, *Statistics of Income, Corporation Income Tax Returns* (Washington, D.C.: U.S. Government Printing Office, various years). The figures include the malt industry.

42. See FTC, *Report of the Federal Trade Commission on Rates of Return in Selected Manufacturing Industries, 1960–1969* (Washington, D.C.: U.S. Government Printing Office); FTC *Quarterly Financial Reports for Manufacturing Corps.* (Washington, D.C.: U.S. Government Printing Office, various years).

43. Gustave J. Fink and Richard R. Dague, "The Iowa Beverage Containers Deposit Law," College of Engineering, University of Iowa, Dec. 1979.

44. John E. Kwoka, "The Effect of Market Share Distribution on Industry Performance," *Review of Economics and Statistics,* **61:** 101(Feb. 1979). This scenario does not fit the brewing industry. See William J. Lynk, "Interpreting Rising Concentration: The Case of Beer," *Journal of Business,* **57:** 43(Jan. 1984).

45. But inflation has kicked up the nominal price, and the day will never return when the beer drinker in, say, Cincinnati can go to "Glossner's or Billiod's, where the bartender put a mug on a scale and then added beer until it weighed a pound more—at a cost of 3 cents." William L. Downward, *The Cincinnati Brewing Industry* (Athens: Ohio U.P., 1973), p. 6.

46. FTC, op. cit., p. 3.

SUGGESTED READINGS

BOOKS PAMPHLETS AND MONOGRAPHS

Arnold, John P., and Frank Penman. *History of the Brewing Industry and Brewing Science in America.* (Privately printed, Chicago, 1933.)

Baron, Stanley Wade. *Brewed in America.* Boston: Little, Brown and Company, 1962.

Brewers Almanac. Washington, D.C.: United States Brewers Association, an annual.

Cochran, Thomas C. *The Pabst Brewing Company.* New York: New York University Press, 1948.

Cockerill, Anthony. *Economies of Scale in the Brewing Industry: A Comparative Study.* Department of Economics. Cambridge University, England. (Private circulation.)

Connor, John M., Richard T. Rogers, Bruce W. Marion, and Willard F. Mueller. *The Food Manufacturing Industries*. Lexington, Mass.; Lexington Books, 1985.
Downward, William L. *The Cincinnati Brewing Industry*. Athens: Ohio University Press, 1973.
Fink, Gustave J., and Richard R. Dague, *The Iowa Beverage Containers Deposit Law*. University of Iowa College of Engineering, December 1979.
Friedrich, Manfred, and Donald Bull. *The Register of United States Breweries 1876–1976* (2 vols.) Stamford, Conn.: Holly Press, 1976.
Jacobson, Michael, George Hacker, and Robert Atkins. *The Booze Merchants*. Washington, D.C.: Center for Science in the Public Interest, 1983.
Modern Brewery Age: Blue Book. Stamford, Conn.: Modern Brewery Age Publishing Co., an annual.
Norman, Donald A. *Structural Change and Performance in The U.S. Brewing Industry*. Unpublished doctoral dissertation, UCLA, 1975.
Parker, Charles W. *The Domestic Beer Industry*. Unpublished manuscript, April 1, 1984.
Pluta, Joseph E. *Regional Change in the U.S. Brewing Industry*. Univ. of Texas Bureau of Business Research Industry Series No. 1, 1983.
Porter, John. *All About Beer*. Garden City, N.Y.: Doubleday & Co., 1975.
Robertson, James D. *The Great American Beer Book*. New York: Warner Books, 1978.
Scherer, F. M. et al. *The Economics of Multi-Plant Operations*. Cambridge, Mass.: Harvard University Press, 1975.
Shih, K. C., and C. Y. Shih. *American Brewing Industry and the Beer Market*. Brookfield, Wis.: W. A. Krueger, 1958.
Steinman, Jerry. *The Beer Industry*. 1982.
Thomann, Gallus. *American Beer*. New York: United States Brewers Foundation, 1949.

ARTICLES

"A–B Wholesaler Contract Wins High Praise." *Modern Brewery Age*, (Oct. 18, 1982), p. 1.
Ackoff, Russell L., and James R. Emshoff. "Advertising Research at Anheuser-Busch, Inc. (1963–1968)." *Sloan Management Review*, **16:** 1–15(Winter 1975).
"Advertising Research at Anheuser-Busch, Inc. (1968–74)." *Sloan Management Review*, **16:** 1–15 (Spring 1975).
"The Battle of the Beers." *Newsweek*. Sept. 4, 1978, pp. 60–71.
Branch, Ben. "Nonreturnable Containers and the Environment." *Atlanta Economic Review* (Sept.–Oct. 1973), pp. 49–52.
Burck, Charles G. "While the Big Brewers Quaff, the Little Ones Thirst." *Fortune* (Nov. 1972), pp. 103–107 ff.
Clements, Kenneth W., and Lester W. Johnson. "The Demand for Beer, Wine and Spirits: A Systemwide Analysis." *Journal of Business*, **56:** 273–304(1983).
Cockerill, Anthony. "Economies of Scale: Industrial Structure and Efficiency: The Brewing Industry in Nine Nations," in A. T. Jacquemin and H. W. DeJong (eds.). *Welfare Aspects of Industrial Markets*. Leiden: Martinus Nijhoff, 1977.
Elzinga, Kenneth G. "The Restructuring of the U.S. Brewing Industry." *Industrial Organization Review*, **1:** 101–114(1973).
Fraundorf, Kenneth C. "The Social Costs of Packaging Competition in the Beer and Soft Drink Industries." *Antitrust Bulletin*, **20**: 803–831(Winter 1975).
Greer, Douglas F. "Product Differentiation and Concentration in the Brewing Industry." *Journal of Industrial Economics*, **19**: 201–219(July 1971).

"The Causes of Concentration in the Brewing Industry." *Quarterly Review of Economics and Business,* **21**:100-117 (Winter, 1981).

Hawkins, Kevin, and Rosemary Radcliffe. "Competition in the Brewing Industry." *Journal of Industrial Economics,* **20**: 20–41(Nov. 1971).

Hogarty, Thomas F., and Kenneth G. Elzinga. "The Demand for Beer." *Review of Economics and Statistics,* **54**: 195–198(May 1972).

Horowitz, Ira, and Ann Horowitz. "Firms in a Declining Market: The Brewing Case." *Journal of Industrial Economics,* **13**: 129–153(March 1965).

"The Beer Industry." *Business Horizons,* **10**: 5–19(Spring 1967).

Kelton, Christina M. L., and W. David Kelton. "Advertising and Intraindustry Brand Shift In The U.S. Brewing Industry." *Journal of Industrial Economics,* **30**: 293–303(March 1982).

"The King Of Beers Still Rules." *Business Week* (July 12, 1982), pp. 50–54.

Kinkead, Gwen. "Heileman Toasts the Future with 34 Beers." *Fortune* (June 18, 1979), pp. 124–130.

Kwoka, John E. "The Effect of Market Share Distribution on Industry Performance." *Review of Economics and Statistics,* **61**: 101–109(Feb. 1979).

Lynk, William J. "Interpreting Rising Concentration: The Case Of Beer." *Journal of Business,* **57**: 43–55(1984).

McConnell, J. Douglas. "An Experimental Examination of the Price-Quality Relationship." *Journal of Business,* **41**: 439–444(Oct. 1968).

Modern Brewery Age. Stamford, Conn.: Modern Brewery Age Publishing Co., tabloid ed., 40 times a year.

Müller, Jürgen, and Joachim Schwalbach. "Structural Change in West Germany's Brewing Industry: Some Efficiency Considerations." *Journal of Industrial Economics,* **28**: 353–368(June 1980).

Ornstein, Stanley. "Antitrust Policy and Market Forces as Determinants of Industry Structure: Case Histories in Beer and Distilled Spirits." *Antitrust Bulletin,* **26**: 281–313(Summer 1981).

Ornstein, Stanley I., and Dominique M. Hanssens. "Alcohol Control Laws, Consumer Welfare, and the Demand for Distilled Spirits and Beer." UCLA Center for Marketing Studies, Working Paper No. 102, March 1981.

Peles, Yoram. "Economies of Scale in Advertising Beer and Cigarettes." *Journal of Business.* **44**: 32–37(Jan. 1971).

Santoni, Gary J., and T. N. Van Cott. "The Impact of Mandatory Bottle Deposit Legislation." *Social Science Quarterly,* **58**: 141–145(June 1977).

Scherer, F. M. "The Determinants of Industrial Plant Sizes in Six Nations." *Review of Economics and Statistics,* **55**: 135–145(May 1973).

Snider, Darryl L., and Dana L. Trier. "United States v. Falstaff Brewing Corporation: Potential Competition Re-Examined." *Michigan Law Review,* **72**: 837–868(March 1974).

Weiss, Leonard W. "An Evaluation of Mergers in Six Industries." *Review of Economics and Statistics,* **42**: 172–181(May 1965).

GOVERNMENT PUBLICATIONS

Adolph Coors Co. v. Federal Trade Commission, 497 F. 2nd 1182 (1974).

Anheuser Busch v. Federal Trade Commission, 265 F.2d 677 (1959); 363 U.S. 536 (1960); 289 F.2nd 835 (1961).

Connor, John M. *The U.S. Food and Tobacco Manufacturing Industries,* U.S. Dept. of Agriculture Report No. 451, March 1980.

Mueller, Willard F. Testimony in *Hearings, Mergers and Industrial Concentration,* U.S. Senate, Committee on the Judiciary, Subcommittee on Antitrust & Monopoly, 95th Cong., 2nd sess., May 12, 1978.

Staff Report of the Federal Trade Commission Bureau of Economics. *The Brewing Industry,* Dec. 1978.
United States v. Anheuser-Busch, 1960 C.C.H. Trade Cases, para. 69, 599.
United States v. Falstaff, 410 U.S. 526 (1973).
United States v. Jos. Schlitz, 253 F. Supp. 129 (1966); 385 U.S. 37(1966).
United States v. Pabst, 233 F. Supp. 475 (1964); 384 U.S. 546 (1966).

7

The Computer Industry

Gerald W. Brock[1]

I. INTRODUCTION

The computer industry traces its origin to Charles Babbage. Inspired by the punch card-controlled Jocquard Loom, Babbage began work on the Analytic Engine in 1833. The Analytic Engine was to be run by steam power, and to perform controlled-sequence calculations at the rate of sixty additions per minute. The basic architecture of Babbage's machine was to be similar to modern computers: the plans included an arithmetic unit, internal memory, external memory, punched card input, and conditional program transfer. Babbage worked on the machine until his death in 1871, but lacked both the financial resources and the technology to build a successful model.

A hundred years later, in 1937, a Harvard graduate student, Howard Aiken, conceived of a mechanical, automatic calculating machine similar to the Analytic Engine. Aiken began development of the Mark I with IBM engineering and financial support. IBM put a total of $500,000 into the project before its completion in 1944. The Mark I was made of electrically powered mechanical moving parts, and had a speed similar to that of the machine envisioned by Babbage. The program was stored externally, on paper tape, and could make a conditional transfer. Aiken conceived of the computer as a tool for calculating scientific tables, and predicted that six machines could fulfill the entire demand in the United States.

Development of the *electronic* computer was also begun in 1937, by John Atanasoff, professor of physics and mathematics at Iowa State College. Atanasoff's goal was a machine for the solution of large systems of simultaneous linear equations. Atanasoff completed his design in 1939 and began construction of a prototype machine, but a working model was not completed. Atanasoff shared his ideas with John Mauchley of the University of Pennsylvania, and Mauchley, together with John Eckert, continued development of the electronic computer.[2] In early 1943, the Army Ordnance Office was informed of the Eckert-Mauchley computing ideas. The Army was extremely interested because of the pressing need for better methods of calculating artillery flight paths. The Army awarded a contract to the University of Pennsylvania for the development of an electronic numerical integrator and computer (ENIAC). The ENIAC, generally recognized as the first electronic computer, was completed in late 1945.

The ENIAC was a monstrously large and unwieldy machine. It was two stories tall, weighted thirty tons, and covered 1,500 square feet of floor space. It contained 18,000 vacuum tubes, which required regular replacement, and consumed vast amounts of power. Its 700,000 resistors, 6,000 switches, and other components were held together with 500,000 soldered joints. It could only be reprogrammed by physically changing the complex wiring. However, it contained a unique computing capability, which allowed the numerical solution of complex differential equations that had previously daunted the most determined teams of mechanical calculator operators. Although the ENIAC was completed too late to contribute to the artillery duels of World War II, its first task—computing the solution to a set of differential equations which determined the feasibility of a hydrogen bomb—illustrated the crucial military significance of the new invention.

The early use of the ENIAC was indicative of the demand for the first crude computers. As the Cold War began, an intense demand for computing capacity developed. Many new companies were formed to develop new kinds of computers. Established research organizations, such as AT&T's Bell Laboratories and IBM, took an active role in defense-related computer work. Feasibility calculations and design work for the hydrogen bomb required enormous amounts of computational capacity and provided a ready market for computer innovations. At one point, hydrogen-bomb design calculations were being run on all twelve high-speed computers in the country.[3]

Eckert and Mauchley believed the computer could be a commercial success, and left the University of Pennsylvania to form a computer firm. They obtained a contract from the Census Bureau to design and build a large computer to process the 1950 census. The Eckert-Mauchley company merged with Remington Rand and completed its contract as the Univac division of Remington Rand. Univac delivered the Univac I to the Census Bureau in 1951, and sold five other Univacs to government agencies before making its first sale to a private company. The Univac I incorporated stored program control (that is, program instructions in memory instead of in the wiring, an innovation developed by mathematician John Von Neumann). Consequently, Univac I was far easier to use than the ENIAC.

The commercial age of computers began with the delivery of Remington Rand's Univac I in 1951 and IBM's 701 in 1953. Then, in 1954, IBM introduced the small-scale 650, which became the first commonly used computer. The 650 was an effective replacement for IBM's punched-card accounting machines. The 650 memory consisted of a small, rapidly rotating drum, which was far more reliable than the memory of earlier systems. More than 400 IBM 650s were installed in its first two years. The 650 stimulated widespread interest in a single model of a computer, and contributed to programming developments and other improvements which changed computer technology from the exclusive privilege of the specialist to a common business function. With improved models of the large-scale 701 and with the success of the 650, IBM established dominance in the emerging commercial computer market at a level almost equal to its 90 percent share of the tabulating-card machine market.

Despite the success of commercial vacuum-tube computers, the dominant market for computer technology in the 1950s remained defense business. Bomb-design calculations continued to require vast amounts of computational capacity because of the need to simulate interactions inside a hydrogen bomb. The two primary atomic weapons laboratories, Los Alamos and Lawrence Livermore, acquired reputations as automatic customers for any computer with a plausible claim to being faster than those currently on the market. The development of an elaborate air defense and early-warning system required extensive computer coordination. Control systems for new generations of airplanes and missiles required many computer innovations. In 1955, IBM received $10 million in revenue from its 650 and 700 series of commercial computers, far less than the $35 million it received for the B-52 bombing/navigation computer systems, or the $47 million it received for the SAGE air-defense computer system. IBM's revenue from SAGE computers peaked at $122 million in 1957 and remained near $100 million per year for the next two years.[4]

Beginning in 1958, commercial computers shifted from vacuum tubes to transistors. With transistors, much smaller and more reliable computers were possible. The "second generation" transistor-based computers were greatly reduced in price for a given computing capability; they had superior data storage and input-output facilities and improved program languages which greatly eased the cumbersome machine-language-programming procedures of the earliest computers. Many new companies entered the market, either as established electronics companies attempting to integrate forward into the computer market, or as completely new companies. The most successful were those which developed an innovative product for a market niche that was receiving insufficient attention from the established companies. Control Data's entry, with large-scale scientific machines, and Digital Equipment's entry, with minicomputers, were notably successful. The price reductions, technological innovations, and development of new uses for computers expanded the commercial industry dramatically during the second generation. The value of installed computers (excluding specialized military computers) skyrocketed, climbing from $1 billion in 1959 to $6 billion in 1965. Military computer use remained important but declined relative to commercial computer usage.

The pattern of expansion set during the transistor revolution has continued to the present time. Electronic-component advances have sparked new generations of computers. The increased capability has opened up new areas of application and expanded total sales, and has provided opportunities for new entrants who perceive a specialized application that is not adequately served by the established companies.

II. STRUCTURE

Concentration

In 1956, IBM had 75 percent of the installed base of commercial, general-purpose computers (commercial and scientific, excluding the specialized military). As the market expanded, IBM maintained its dominance and retained a market share in the 70 percent range for the "mainframe" segment of the market. Initially, "mainframe" and "general-purpose computers" were practically synonymous, but the growth of other segments relative to mainframes has reduced IBM's overall share of computing revenue. In the early 1960s, the industry was known as "Snow White and the Seven Dwarfs", because IBM held approximately 70 percent of the market, and the seven dwarfs (Honeywell, Univac, Burroughs, RCA, General Electric, NCR, and Control Data) divided the other 30 percent among themselves. In addition, there were several minicomputer companies, each of which was quite small, which made products not easily substitutable for mainframe computers. With the exit of RCA and General Electric from the market, the mainframe market acquired the designation of IBM and the BUNCH where the BUNCH was composed of the five remaining dwarfs.

Although IBM's share of the narrowly defined mainframe industry remained roughly constant, after 1970 its share of the entire computer market declined substantially because of rapid expansion of other segments of the market. Minicomputers gained much greater capacity and developed from specialized laboratory machines into substitutes for general-purpose machines. The primary enhancements were greater programming capabilities and greater input-output and data-storage capabilities. Communications applications became very significant. In the 1980s, rapid growth of personal computers (microcomputers) provided another alternative to the large mainframe computer structure. The growth of distributed networks caused terminals, communications processors, and similar equipment to increase in importance. Although IBM expanded into the new market segments, it did not attain the dominance that it had enjoyed in mainframe computers.

By 1983, IBM retained 64 percent of the revenue in the mainframe computer market, but the overall industry had expanded into so many other directions that IBM's share of the broadly defined "data processing" industry had dropped to 39 percent ($35.6 billion out of $91.8 billion total market). Although concentration is high in the mainframe market because of IBM's dominance, it is only moderate in the more broadly defined market. The top four had 52 percent of the broad market. The next four had 11 percent, and the four after that had 5 percent of the revenue. Ten companies had over a billion dollars in data-processing revenues.

The newest and fastest-growing sectors of the market have provided the greatest opportunities for new entrants and the least stability of market shares. Recently, the fastest-growing segment of the market has been the personal computer or microcomputer market, in which the basic processor consists of a single silicon chip. The "computer-on-a-chip" was first developed by the semiconductor maker Intel in 1971, but it did not achieve popularity as an independent personal computer until several years later, when it was made the basis of a small computer system containing data storage and input-output functions. The market has shown extraordinary growth and rapid changes in market shares. In 1982, Apple Computer was the leading company, with $664 million in sales, followed by IBM, with $500 million, Tandy Corp (Radio Shack), with $466 million, and Commodore, with $368 million. Combined sales of the top four zoomed from $2.0 billion in 1982 to $5.1 billion in 1983. Apple lost its first-place position with growth of "only" 63 percent as IBM took the lead with $2.6 billion in sales, more than the combined total of the first four the previous year.[5] Table 1 summarizes market shares and revenue for the broadly defined data-processing market and selected narrower markets in 1982 and 1983.

Barriers to Entry

A key issue in evaluating the barriers to entry is the compatibility of systems. In the early days of computers, systems from different manufacturers came as incompatible total systems. An IBM computer could not use programs written for a Honeywell, nor could the IBM read a disk written by a Honeywell. Consequently, customers tended to make long-term commitments to a manufacturer and expected to upgrade routinely with that manufacturer's products because a change would be too expensive. Even personnel were specialized to the products; a change from one manufacturer to another could mean not only replacing the machine but much of the software written for it, and also replacing or retraining the programmers. Consequently, there was a high degree of brand loyalty and a correspondingly high degree of barriers to entry. The barriers arose because customers were not free to try out a new manufacturer simply because it appeared to have a better-performing machine. Customers were purchasing a long-term relationship with a supplier, and planned to invest substantial capital in specialized programs to run on that machine. Regardless of the technical qualities of a particular machine, a new manufacturer would have trouble convincing potential customers of its staying power and its ability to provide adequate upgrades as the customer's requirements increased and as technological progress made improved machines possible.

In the traditional mainframe industry of the 1960s, entry was practically impossible because of the need to assemble a complete system, write a large library of software, and convince customers to pay the high costs of switching from their current supplier to the new entrant. Many companies entered,

Table 1: Market Shares

Company	1983 Revenue ($ millions)	Share (percent)	1982 Revenue ($ millions)	Share (percent)
Broadly Defined Data-Processing Market				
1. IBM	35,603	39	29,265	38
2. Digital Equipment	4,827	5	4,019	5
3. Burroughs	4,000	4	3,848	5
4. Control Data	3,500	4	3,301	4
Top 4	47,930	52	40,433	52
Mainframe Market				
1. IBM	11,444	64	10,662	63
2. Burroughs	2,000	11	2,000	12
3. Honeywell	1,020	6	1,060	6
4. NCR	1,000	6	1,100	6
Top 4	15,464	87	14,822	87
Minicomputer Market				
1. Digital Equipment	2,700	24	2,500	24
2. IBM	2,627	23	2,945	28
3. Burroughs	950	8	900	8
4. Wang	893	8	660	6
Top 4	7,170	63	7,005	66
Microcomputer Market				
1. IBM	2,600	41	500	19
2. Apple	1,085	17	664	25
3. Commodore	927	15	368	14
4. Tandy	598	9	466	17
Top 4	5,210	82	1,998	75

Source: Computed from revenue figures in "The Datamation 100" and Pamela Archbold, "Fathoming the Industry," *Datamation* (June 1, 1971), pp. 53–144.

but only in specialized segments of the industry, such as large-scale scientific computers, or minicomputers, which were not so tied to the commercial marketplace.

Several events have changed the industry and reduced the problems of entry. The first is the decreasing cost of computing power compared to software. In the early days of the industry, computing power and memory were very expensive. It was consequently worthwhile to use highly specialized programs to optimize the machine. Specialized programs took advantage of each machine's unique capabilities and consequently could not be used on another machine. Programs were frequently written in *assembly language,* a low-level language that was closely tied to the internal operations of the machine and therefore not usable on any other manufacturer's brand. As computer prices declined and programmers' wages rose, the benefits of specialized programs decreased. It became more worthwhile to write programs in high-level languages, such as Fortran and Cobol, which did not use the machine resources as efficiently as good assembly-language programs but were easier to write, to modify, and to transport from one machine to another. With a high-level language, the programmer statements are the same or similar regardless of the machine, and the computer compiler translates the statements into the code for the particular machine. Consequently, a Fortran program written for an IBM computer can be run on a Control Data computer with few changes if it is written in the standard form of the code and if the programmer refrains from using tricks or special features available only on one type of computer.

The second development was the increasing use of IBM standards for non-IBM computers. This is known as the *plug-compatible* approach, because the goal is to plug the new manufacturer's piece into an IBM system and have the system continue, with no need for further changes. This effort began with peripheral devices, such as tape drives and disk drives, around 1970, and then expanded into central processors in the mid-1970s. Entry is much easier with plug-compatible machines because the entrant need only develop a single piece of machinery rather than an entire system, and because the customer takes much less risk. If the manufacturer of the plug-compatible equipment fails to perform as expected, the customer need only reorder equipment from IBM because the programs and specifications remain those set by IBM. The disadvantage of entry through plug-compabitility is that it restricts the design freedom of the entrant and makes the entrant subject to retaliation by IBM for changing the interface specifications that are used to connect the entrant's equipment to the IBM system. Knowledge of the technical details of IBM's plans is a vital component of success in the plug-compatible business, and has been the subject of several highly publicized cases of industrial espionage.

Capital availability has varied with general stock market conditions but generally has not been a significant barrier to entry in the computer industry. In fact, stock market enthusiasm for new computer companies has been a positive spur to new entry. Many small groups of engineers or programmers have been induced to break away from an established company and form a new one by the lure of stock market wealth. In the late 1960s, vast profits to early stockholders in Control Data and Digital Equipment fueled a speculative bubble in new computer-company stocks. The most spectacular example of money-raising for a speculative new company is that of Viatron Computer Systems. Viatron raised $800,000 from the founders and their associates, $2 million from a private placement of stock, $12 million from a public stock offering, and $25 million from an offering of convertible debentures—all before the company began deliveries. At its height in 1969, as the financing phase was being completed but before deliveries began, the company had a stock market value of $217 million. As deliveries began in 1970, the company's total revenue was $2.5 million and net profit was a *negative* $7.6 million. In April 1971, after mounting debts had used up all reserve capital, the company was forced into bankruptcy and was later declared insolvent.[6]

Around 1970, the availability of funds for new computer companies began to diminish as general money conditions tightened, investor disillusionment with high-technology companies set in, and IBM's aggressive tactics created doubt about the viability of IBM competitors. Capital was hard to find, not only for speculative ventures such as Viatron, but also for solid innovative companies that needed substantial amounts of capital to bring a product to market. Despite his prestige as a principal designer of the IBM System 360, in the mid-1970s Gene Amdahl had difficulty raising capital to finance the research and development phase of his Amdahl Corporation.

By the end of the 1970s, capital again became freely available to new computer companies. Helped by a reduction in capital-gains tax rates and the emerging new market segment of microcomputers, money flowed rapidly into new computer companies. The success of Apple Computer's public offering inspired venture capitalists to invest in new computer-related companies. Increasing public fascination with high technology also contributed to a flood of venture capital into computer-related companies. According to one estimate, half of all venture capital placed in the early 1980's went into new computer-related companies.[7] Consequently, capital shortage was no barrier to entry. Instead, the spur of rapid profits was a positive incentive to entry because of the high valuation the public placed upon new high-technology companies.

Overall barriers to entry vary widely, according to the segment of the industry considered. Barriers remain high in general-purpose mainframe computers. If a potential entrant attempts to develop a computer not compatible with IBM, it continues to face the barriers of the 1960s—high customer risk, heavy expenses to convert software, a need for new or retrained personnel, and so forth. If a potential entrant attempts to produce machines compatible with those of IBM, it must overcome IBM's ability to use its control of the other system components for competitive advantage. Walter Adams and James Brock's study of competition in systems markets concluded that extensive market power results from control of system specifications:

> The essence of integrated monopoly power resides in the dominant system seller's dual capacity as rival and rule maker. By introducing incompatibilities, or undisclosed alterations in his components, the integrated monopolist can render the system—and the industry—"allergic" to rivals' components.[8]

In the computer-mainframe case, the potential entrant that attempts to remain compatible with IBM must be able to adjust to all the changes that IBM can make, and yet remain far enough below IBM's price to induce customers to accept the "imitation" product. The entrant also must forego opportunities for innovation that would violate IBM's system-interface standards. Thus, entry into the mainframe market is difficult, either with or without compabitility. Despite enormous total market growth and rapid technological change, the top six mainframe manufacturers in 1983 remained IBM and the BUNCH, all established computer manufacturers in the early years of the industry. Mainframe market shares have been far more stable over the years than market shares in other segments of the industry.

The lowest barriers to entry are in the applications-software (programming) market, in which a few capable programmers can produce a marketable product. One software-company executive described the optimal development team for a software product as "four super systems programmers and one documenter."[9] Effective software companies generally require enough people to maintain, support, and improve existing products while developing new ones, but the traditional barriers to entry—i. e., large capital requirements, patents, control of scarce resources, and large amounts of fixed plant—are absent.

Customized or special-purpose computers comprise another market segment with low barriers to entry. Many new companies have entered the market after discovering a specialized application for computers. They purchase minicomputers or microcomputers, write specialized software, and thereby turn the machine into a special-purpose processor. They then sell the package to the target customers. These companies have added value to basic machines via software, service, and information. They allow a small company to guarantee the solution to a particular problem for a fixed price, thus freeing the customer from concern over whether the appropriate pieces of the solution will be available at the expected price, or whether they will work properly together. As IBM discovered very early, many customers prefer to purchase a solution to a particular problem rather than buy specific pieces of computer equipment. This is because they are not certain the computer equipment will provide solutions to their business problems. Thus, the customization companies provide a valuable service, even if they only resell hardware and software components that are available separately.

In recent years, the easiest computer-manufacturing segment to enter was that of the microcomputer. The microcomputer segment has been characterized by *open architecture*, that is, the practice of designing the computer system to connect its components with a standard interface. Open architecture computer systems are meant to be flexible, allowing the easy attachment of devices from many different manufacturers. A microcomputer system consists of a central processing unit (CPU), a memory, a data-storage capability (generally *diskettes*), a monitor and keyboard, together with software for the operating system, language compilers, and applications programs. Each of the components can be purchased from independent suppliers and assembled into an effective package. Even the original IBM Personal Computer was produced in this way, in a dramatic departure from IBM's normal integrated-production methods. The existence of independent component suppliers makes barriers to entry much lower than if entry required the simultaneous entry into the manufacturing of all the components.

Although barriers to entry vary, from extremely low to very high (depending on the market segment of the broadly defined computer industry), an overall assessment is that they are low to moderate. The low-barrier segments provide an entry path into the segments with greater barriers to entry. A company that begins by assembling previously manufactured parts can then integrate into some of its own manufacturing without facing the full range of barriers to entry encountered by a start-up company.

III. CONDUCT

The early computer industry pattern was the development of full-scale systems and support from a single manufacturer for each customer. IBM was the premier developer and practitioner of this strategy, and because of its success, other manufacturers imitated it. The strategy was dictated by the fact that information was scarce in the early industry. Computers were complex, specialized machines which required a great deal of machine-specific knowledge. Capable professionals who were experienced with IBM equipment could not easily program a different machine, or even evaluate its capabilities. The decision to purchase a company's machine was a long-term relationship with the company rather than a specific equipment purchase; it included a commitment by the customer to invest in personnel and software specialized to that type of machine.

The undeveloped and rapidly growing computer industry of the 1960's allowed IBM to satisfy its customers' needs and to gain a great deal of market power by concentrating on total solutions. The IBM salesmen were renowned for their knowledge of a customer's business, and, in addition to selling, frequently acted as consultants about potential applications and necessary equipment. Close relationships were developed between technical and managerial personnel in each customer location and the IBM personnel. IBM systems engineers and salesmen were often key sources of information for evaluating the performance of their customer's personnel, and they assisted in recruitment efforts. Once an IBM system was ordered, vast amounts of support services (such as education and consulting) were provided "free" to the customer. IBM's approach is clearly stated in this exerpt from a report to the IBM Management Committee:

> The basic concept revolves around an in-depth planning session for each account initially involving only IBM personnel. The purpose will be to look at the account power structure and decision-making process, designing a data processing system as if we were board chairman, and developing an open item list with individual IBM responsibilities of all things necessary to sell the resultant system.[10]

As part of the account-control process, IBM emphasized leasing rather than selling. Leasing allowed IBM continued interaction with the customer and reduced the customer's risk when accepting a very expensive piece of capital equipment. IBM sold itself as the knowledgeable party which could provide a limited-risk solution to the customer's business problems for a fixed price per month. Considering the limited information possessed by top management regarding how to translate specific business problems into requirements for arithmetic speed and storage capacity, the IBM total-solution approach was very effective in attracting customers. It also limited competitive inroads, because the customer who depended heavily upon IBM advice and assistance lacked the ability to fully evaluate the alternative solutions offered by other manufacturers.

The total-solution strategy, with prices charged only for hardware, meant that prices for specific items were far above their manufacturing cost. Consequently, if another manufacturer could figure out a way to replace specific pieces of IBM equipment while the computer retained its IBM character and continued to receive IBM services, that manufacturer could undersell the IBM product. This led to the *plug-compatible* manufacturer, which produced some particular part of a computer system designed to be a substitute for the IBM part. There were several companies that were experienced at making peripheral equipment for resale to computer-systems companies. If one of those companies could produce equipment that would perform like an IBM piece of equipment, and sell it directly to the ultimate user, IBM's price structure would be in danger.

Prior to the introduction of IBM's System/360 in 1965, there was little incentive to replace individual peripherals because of the specialized interfaces between the peripheral equipment and the mainframe; consequently, the market for any particular piece of peripheral equipment was limited. If a potential competitor assumed that it would be limited to a small percentage of IBM's installations, either because of consumer resistance or because of IBM's countermeasures, then it was not worth the development cost to engineer a system prior to the 360. However, the System/360 had a standard interface between the various computer models and the peripheral equipment, which meant that a single tape-drive could be attached to various sizes of 360 computers rather than to only a single model. In addition, by the late 1960's, the market had expanded dramatically in total size, creating a huge target population of vulnerable peripheral equipment.

The first plug-compatible competition began in November 1967 with tape-drive replacements; this was followed by the entry of other competitors, with both tape- and disk-drive replacements in 1968. The Memorex replacement for IBM's popular 2311 disk-drive rented for $500 per month per drive, and also had slightly faster access times than IBM's $590-per-month drive. In 1968, at the time Memorex deliveries began, IBM had 19,000 of that type of disk-drive installed and 10,500 on order. Because of its own large demand backlog and the limited manufacturing capacity of the new entrants into the market, IBM considered the new companies to be no serious threat when its first study of their capabilities was made. IBM's 1968 study concluded that it was "too early to forecast effect" of the competition, and that "IBM strategy sound over plan period," and recommended improved products for later years.[11]

The absence of IBM reaction to the initial plug-compatible competition spurred the entry of many companies with a broad line of products. High initial profits and a booming stock market created great paper wealth for the pioneers of direct competition with IBM systems. Manufacturing capacity rapidly increased, and the competitors moved from the long-established products into the newer, more technologically advanced ones—those on which IBM counted for future revenue growth.

As the competition grew, IBM responded with three basic strategies. The first strategy was based on tying peripheral products to the CPU. Because the competitors were only replacing peripherals, tying the peripherals to the CPU protected them from competition. However, a formal tying strategy would have been a violation of the antitrust laws. Consequently, the strategy was based on pricing and product moves which could be defended against a tying charge but which would reduce the competitors' ability to attach their peripheral products to IBM CPUs.

In 1970 IBM announced the 2319A disk program (described by one IBM executive as "the plan we came up with to kludge three 2314's repriced into the NS 1"[12]) for its announced but undelivered System/370 computers. The 2319A program was a modified version of the popular 2314 large-scale disk drives for the System/360 computers, in which the controller was integrated into the central processing unit and the drives were cut in price. Integrating the controller protected it from competitive replacement, and also changed the interface.Two years later, a similar change was made: the controller for the high-capacity 3330 disk drives (for larger System/370 models) was integrated into the CPU as part of a set of product modifications known as the "SMASH program." The SMASH announcements also imposed minimum memory sizes for each CPU, in order to protect memory from competitive replacement. This was done despite the worries of an IBM analyst who was studying ways to protect memory from competitors. He wrote:

> I cannot think of a good rationale for drastically increasing memory minimums to provide a very limited performance increment . . . restricting PCMs from 60–70 percent of their market without price competition would almost certainly provoke legal consequences and I wonder what contingency I can provide against a civil triple damage suit.[13]

In lawsuits related to the effort to tie peripherals to the CPU, the competitors claimed that the changes were illegal attempts to tie the sale of peripherals to CPUs, and IBM claimed that the integration was a natural technological result of reductions in the size of components which allowed more to be packed into the same box than previously. The courts ruled in IBM's favor.

The second IBM strategy was the fixed-term plan, which gave a discount for one- and two-year leases, rather than IBM's standard monthly rental terms. The fixed-term plan was only available for peripheral equipment, not for CPUs. It was adopted after an IBM analysis indicated that if products could be protected for twenty months after introduction, the competitors could not make a profit on initial placements of peripheral equipment. The potential rent for competitive peripheral equipment was based on the IBM product cycle. From the time when an IBM computer was installed, the competitors needed some time to "reverse engineer" a product that would be competitive with the IBM product; the competing company could then receive full rental until a replacement IBM product was introduced. With monthly rental, customers could accept a new product from IBM, then replace it with a competitive product as soon as the competitive product was ready. With the fixed-term plan, the customer either had to retain the IBM product for the full term (and therefore reduce the effective life of the competitive product) or pay the higher monthly rental rate, in order to preserve flexibility. The IBM analysis of the potential benefits of a term-lease plan was quite optimistic regarding its effectiveness in protecting IBM from competitors. It concluded that, with a term-lease plan, "PCM corporate revenues lower—no funds for mfg., eng.—dying company!"[14]

The third strategy was to reduce prices, repackage products, and increase the rate of product improvement. When competitors began attacking the huge and highly profitable base of 2314 disk drives for the larger System/360 computers in 1970, IBM performed an analysis which concluded that the minimum break-even price for a competitor's drive was $381 per month.[15] IBM then repackaged the 2314 drive into a unit of three drives, priced at $1,000 per month ($333 per drive).

As competition increased for the high-performance IBM 2420-7 tape drive, introduced in January 1968, IBM was forced to revise its pricing policy. The company had used *functional pricing* rather than cost-based pricing. Functional pricing meant that different models of tape drives were priced according to their relative benefits to the customer rather than according to their relative costs to IBM. This practice put the highest profit margins on the fastest drives because high-speed drives of a particular family cost only a little more to manufacture than lower-speed drives. So long as IBM controlled the market for the drives attached to its computers, functional pricing produced the highest profits, but with competition, functional pricing only provided an attractive target for the competitors. An IBM analysis of tape-drive competition concluded:

> Due to the increased amount of competition, it is our belief that the concept of functional pricing is no longer the most suitable way to price in the magnetic-tape area. Apparently, manufacturing cost of high- and low-performance drives do not differ substantially and competition has concentrated in the higher-performance area and priced their drives very competitively . . . a continuation of this policy would contribute to future losses.[16]

IBM's price for the 2420-7 drive was $1,020 per month; its price for the half-speed version, known as the 2420-5, was $565 per month, in accordance with the functional-pricing policy. As a result of competition, IBM introduced a "new" series of tape drives. The 3420-5 (with the same performance as the 2420-5) was priced at $560 per month, almost identical to the $565 charged for the 2420-5. But the 3420-7 (with the same performance as the 2420-7) was priced at $670 per month, a 34 percent price cut, which signalled a move toward cost-based rather than functional pricing.[17]

IBM's reactions slowed the growth of the PCM competition and brought some companies close to bankruptcy, sparking several antitrust suits. But IBM's efforts to protect itself against the peripheral companies required a major change in the company's overall approach to the computer market. The IBM strategy of bundling items into the CPU was frustrated by Amdahl's entry, a plug-compatible CPU designed to run on IBM's software. With the plug-compatible CPU, it became theoretically possible to put together an "IBM system" using parts from a variety of manufacturers and getting only the free software from IBM. Obviously, this made untenable the strategy of charging only for hardware and providing free software and services. The fixed-term plan was a movement away from the leasing-control strategy. The customer was no longer free to upgrade to any IBM improvement. Although the term leases protected the installed base against PCM encroachment, they reduced account control. The strategy of reduced prices and improved products was the only viable long-term strategy, given the reduced barriers to entry faced by new companies after the plug-compatible movement. However, this was basically a strategy that involved full competition and it meant giving up part of the market control of the earlier days.

A further impetus toward a change in strategy came from antitrust pressure and the increasing sophistication of the computing community. The Department of Justice antitrust case, filed in January 1969, challenged the IBM practice of bundling free services with hardware, and IBM had responded with a partial unbundling. The increasing sophistication of computer personnel reduced IBM's account control. The growth of minicomputers and networks of computers made the pure IBM shop largely a relic of the past. The increasing sophistication of software and the large number of tools available to provide a bridge between the user and the actual machine functions allowed greater portability of skills among computer systems.

Because of the changes in the industry as a whole, as well as the growth of PCM competition, IBM's strategy evolved during the late 1970s into one based on technological progress and low prices rather than account control. IBM did not give up the advantages of size which allowed it to set standards in the industry, but it did begin to charge a relatively competitive price for each piece of equipment instead of assuming that customers would purchase entire IBM systems. The company began emphasizing outright sales of equipment rather than rental and also began cutting prices on existing products to keep them competitive. This was a change from earlier strategy in which rental levels generally remained constant throughout the life of a product even though prices for equivalent performance in newly introduced products were declining.

IBM's new strategy was most clearly illustrated by its Personal Computer. The Personal Computer was produced from parts manufactured by a variety of companies and was designed with an *open architecture,* which made it easy for others to produce software and enhancements for use with it. Despite a slow entry into a market segment pioneered by others, IBM's rapid introduction of several models of its Personal Computer established it as the standard. Aided by support from IBM for linking the small computers to mainframes, the IBM model soon became the standard choice for companies seeking networks of compatible microcomputers.

A related change in IBM's strategy is the company's recent emphasis on acquisitions and cooperative agreements. IBM has largely grown by its own sales efforts, and has remained a strongly independent company with integrated manufacturing and allegiance to the IBM way of doing things. After 1980, the company began actively pursuing agreements with others to expand its knowledge base in the broadly defined data-processing industry. The most significant of these were the purchase of a partial ownership in Intel and the acquisition of Rolm. Intel invented the microcomputer and remains a leader in semiconductor innovation. The partial ownership tied IBM into the competitive world of commercial semiconductor manufacturers and provided an outside window on significant innovations beyond those that occur in the IBM laboratories. The purchase of a partial interest, and then the purchase of the remainder of Rolm, put IBM into the private-branch exchange (PBX) market, and is expected to provide assistance in constructing integrated computer and communications systems of the future.

To summarize, IBM's strategy of total account control floundered on the twin problems of increasing customer sophistication and successful selective entry by competitors into overpriced IBM products. The strategy has been successfully changed into one based on traditional competitive criteria—technological innovation and low-cost manufacturing—along with emphasis on the advantages of dealing with a widely diversified IBM which can provide a solution for any computer problem. In more technical language, IBM is emphasizing economies of scale and economies of scope in its current strategy. Now, it is the largest player in a much broader data processing industry, rather than the dominant player in a mainframe computer industry. The success of the IBM Personal Computer (based on an open architecture) and the rash of its cooperative agreements, which position IBM in the communications industry, suggest a continuation of this strategy.

IV. PERFORMANCE

The three basic economic measures of performance are *allocative efficiency, technical efficiency,* and *dynamic efficiency.* Allocative efficiency refers to how well the price system allocates goods to supply user desires. It is high if prices are close to marginal costs, and progressively lower as prices depart from marginal costs. Technical efficiency refers to how close the actual costs of production are to the lowest possible costs of production, considering the product mix to be produced. Dynamic efficiency refers to the rate of technological progress compared with the optimal rate.

Allocative efficiency was relatively poor in the early days of the computer industry but has improved greatly in more recent years. Two sources of poor allocative efficiency existed. The first was IBM's control of the market that led to IBM's higher than normal profits. In a fully competitive system, the excess profits would have attracted additional entrants, bringing down the price and reducing profits to the normal level. However, the barriers to entry in the systems market prevented this from occurring and allowed IBM to make sustained profits of approximately twice the normal level. IBM's average after-tax profit on stockholder equity, between 1958 and 1973, was 17.5 percent, 64 percent higher than the average of all manufacturing corporations for the time period.[18]

The second source of poor allocative efficiency was the practice of selling the various components of a computer system as a single unit rather than charging separate prices directly related to the cost of each component. This practice overpriced hardware components, such as disk drives and tape drives, and underpriced service components, such as education, consulting, and software assistance.

Both of these sources of distortion declined in the 1970's. As IBM's control of the market declined, prices were placed closer to real costs because of the inability to prevent competitors from undercutting the prices on products designed to subsidize "free" services. Greater competition also brought IBM's profit rate closer to the average profit rate for other manufacturing companies.

Technical efficiency is difficult to measure because of the difficulty in ascertaining the minimum cost of production if existing companies are not operating at minimum costs. IBM appears to operate manufacturing facilities at a lower cost than other companies, which suggests that there is some technical inefficiency in the smaller companies. However, the amount of inefficiency is uncertain. A reasonable guess would be that overall technical efficiency is quite good in the industry. There are no obsolete plants or featherbedding labor agreements which lead to observable inefficiency.

Dynamic efficiency has been outstanding. The opportunity for technical progress has been at a high level throughout the life of the industry. Innovation has been the key to survival in the industry. Even IBM could not survive long without introducing new products with reduced prices.

Traditional industries with a single dominant firm often move toward price leadership strategies that prevent adjustment to new conditions and reduce competitive activity. There is often implicit oligopolistic coordination, which all companies in the industry see as being to their advantage to maintain. However, in the computer industry, the long tail of fringe companies prevents a cartel from controlling the market. Oligopolistic coordination depends upon stable prices and is infeasible in the context of the complex pricing adjustments necessary to keep up with technological progress in the industry.

The rate of price decline has been extraordinarily rapid in the industry.

For the years 1956 to 1965, a regression equation based on internal characteristics of computers shows a rate of price decline of about 25 percent per year.[19] For later years, the internal measurements become less meaningful because of the great significance of peripheral equipment and software for overall computer performance. However, the price declines have continued at a similarly rapid rate. For example, the large-scale IBM 3033 processor, with 16 million bytes of memory, sold for approximately $5 million when introduced in 1978; it was reduced to $3.8 million in 1979, then to $3.1 million in 1980, and to $2.2 million in 1982.[20]

The rapid price declines and the existence of large numbers of small firms have made the development of an oligopolistic cartel impossible. The fringe firms are too small to clearly influence the market and consequently have no incentive not to undercut IBM prices. IBM can retaliate by cutting prices itself, but cannot hope to drive the other firms out of the market and keep them out. The existence of potential new entrants, and the antitrust consequences of predatory action, make predatory action unlikely.

In summary, the current performance of the industry is very good. The structure balances the desire of some consumers for stability with enough competition to provide an incentive for IBM to remain efficient. The growth of non-IBM-dominated sectors of the market has made IBM's hold tenuous. Because of IBM's size, there is at least one company large enough to take advantage of economies of scale in manufacturing. IBM also provides a safe alternative for risk-averse customers, who are willing to pay for the increased probability that their supplier will provide compatible upgrades and improvements for their present equipment.

V. PUBLIC POLICY

Antitrust policy has played a major role in the industry. IBM's dominance of the industry has made it a natural target of antitrust suits. In a private suit brought by Control Data over the submarket for supercomputers (very large-scale scientific computers) IBM lost the first battle in its antitrust war. IBM's candidate for the most powerful computer of the early 1960's was the 7030 or Stretch computer. It failed to meet its performance specifications and sold only a few models, at a substantially reduced price from that originally announced. When Stretch was withdrawn, Control Data's 3600, first delivered in 1963, took the lead as the largest computer. In 1963, Control Data announced the 6600, a far more powerful machine than anything then on the market. In August 1964, just before the first 6600 deliveries, IBM announced the 360/91, a top-of-the-line machine competitive with the 6600. The 360/91 announcement reduced the demand for CDC's 6600 and forced CDC to take a price cut in order to continue selling the machines. However, IBM was not able to produce the 360/91 on schedule and eventually discontinued the line, with a substantial loss.

Because IBM's announcement of the 360/91 reduced CDC's profit on the 6600, and because IBM was not able to fulfill the 360/91 promises, CDC determined that the 360/91 program was a predatory action. After being rebuffed by the Justice Department, CDC filed a private suit and began discovery proceedings, in which each side gains access to internal documents of the other side. CDC examined 25 million IBM documents and found a number of potentially incriminating statements to the effect that the 360/91 program was aimed directly at CDC, and further, that it could not meet the normal IBM standards for profitability. IBM's defense was that even if the 360/91 was sold below full cost, the action was not predatory because it provided research that would benefit all future large-scale products.

In January 1973, prior to the beginning of the trial, IBM and CDC reached an out-of-court settlement in which CDC dropped the charges against IBM in return for IBM selling its Service Bureau Corporation subsidiary to CDC at book value, and an IBM payment of $101 million to CDC. The payment was designated as reimbursement for CDC's legal fees and expenses ($15 million), payment for research and development to be done by CDC and made available to IBM, and for fringe benefits for Service Bureau Corporation employees transferred to CDC. The net effect was a transfer of $75 to $125 million to CDC, depending upon the value assigned to the Service Bureau Corporation. A crucial feature of the settlement was that the index to IBM documents compiled by CDC in preparation for trial be destroyed. The Department of Justice had filed a government antitrust suit against IBM soon after the CDC suit, with many of the same allegations, and had planned to use CDC's discovery efforts and index of documents for its own suit.

IBM's efforts to protect its peripheral market from plug-compatible peripheral companies provoked strenuous protests from the companies involved, and led to a series of private antitrust actions. In January 1972, Telex charged IBM with monopolizing and attempting to monopolize the market for peripheral equipment plug-compatible with IBM CPUs. That IBM made a determined effort to protect those products from competition was undisputed; the legal question was whether such a narrowly defined "market" existed, and whether IBM's tactics were improper. IBM countersued with a claim that Telex had stolen IBM trade secrets in order to be able to manufacture plug-compatible equipment. At the conclusion of the trial in September 1973, the judge found both parties guilty of the respective charges. IBM was ordered to pay Telex $353 million in antitrust damages ($118 million actual damages, which are automatically tripled in an antitrust case) plus costs and attorneys' fees. Telex was ordered to pay IBM $22 million in trade-secret damages, plus costs and attorneys' fees. After some revisions, the award represented a net payment from IBM to Telex of $260 million.

The award was huge in relationship to the amount of the business done by the relatively small Telex company. In a company whose stock was selling for just over $3 per share, it represented $25 per share, or some eight times the stock-market value of the company. However, investors were apparently sceptical that the money would be paid because the Telex stock price was only about $1 per share higher three months after the original award than before the award. Attorneys for other peripheral companies were more optimistic and rushed to file copycat suits to cash in on the Telex bonanza. Following the September 1973 decision in favor of Telex, California Computer Products sued in October, asking $300 million in damages; Memorex sued in December, asking $3 billion in damages; and Marshall Industries sued in December, asking $108 million in damages.

The investors' scepticism was more justified than the lawyers' enthusiasm. When the Telex case was reviewed in the Appeals Court, the antitrust verdict against IBM was reversed, but the trade-secrets verdict against Telex was upheld. Suddenly, the minor offset against a massive antitrust award took on crucial significance. The trade-secrets payment threatened bankruptcy for Telex. Telex appealed to the U.S. Supreme Court. Just before the Supreme Court was scheduled to announce whether or not it would review the case, IBM offered to settle all disputes between the two companies with no payments on either side. Telex then faced the risk of bankruptcy if the Supreme Court refused to hear the case, or if after review, it upheld the Appeals Court decision. On the other hand, there was the possibility of a huge windfall if the Supreme Court should uphold the District Court. Telex management was not willing to bet the company's survival on the chance of a Supreme Court victory and settled the litigation.

Although the copycat private suits were inspired by the Telex victory, the preparations for trial were not stopped by the Telex reversal. Attorneys who had labored on briefs showing how similar their suits were to the Telex suit, and consequently why the Telex victory should apply to their companies, issued new briefs which distinguished their cases from Telex. Three related peripheral-company suits (California Computer Products, Memorex, and Transamerica Computer) went through long and expensive preparation and trial. IBM won all three trials, establishing several important legal precedents along the way regarding the actions that a dominant firm may take. The courts ruled that IBM's actions were an acceptable form of competitive action rather than illegal predatory practices designed to kill off competitors and maintain a dominant position in the industry.

Meanwhile, the Justice Department suit proceeded at a glacial pace. The suit was filed in January 1969—on the last day of the Johnson Administration. The original issues concerned IBM's dominance of the mainframe market, especially IBM's practice of bundling services with hardware, and IBM's aggressive tactics to deflect CDC's success in supercomputers. The suit was later amended to include the complaints of Telex and other peripheral companies regarding actions that occurred after the original suit was filed. Trial preparation was set back by the destruction of the CDC index to IBM documents in 1973. After slow preparations throughout the Nixon Administration, the trial finally began in the Ford Administration. The trial droned on through the Carter Administration, and the suit began to resemble the one portrayed by Dickens in *Bleak House*. While witnesses testified interminably and the judge insisted that all the minutia of the legal form to be followed, the computer industry changed dramatically. As the trial ground toward a conclusion, even Justice Department attorneys began to doubt that the relief originally proposed was necessary or appropriate for the emerging, more competitive industry. When the Reagan Administration took office in January 1981, the last witnesses had testified but no decision had been issued. The new Assistant Attorney General for Antitrust, William Baxter, conducted an extensive personal review of the case. His review included a mock trial, with himself as the judge and lawyers for IBM and the Justice Department trial staff representing the two parties. Baxter concluded that the case was without merit and dropped the charges without waiting for the judge's decision.

By the time the suit was dropped, many of the objectives of the original suit had been obtained. IBM's market share and dominance in the computer industry had declined. IBM no longer practiced bundled pricing. Control of a lease base was reduced because of the new IBM emphasis on outright purchase.

Legal developments also had been unfavorable to continuing the suit. The supercomputer attack on Control Data was an isolated incident rather than representative of a general attempt to drive competitors out of business. Control Data had collected private damages because of the incident, and it was unclear what public interest would be served by further restrictions on IBM's conduct. IBM's plug-compatible peripheral actions had been found acceptable in four different private actions, raising doubt about continuing to pursue them in the public suit.

A related reason for dropping the suit was the settlement on the same day of the Justice Department suit against AT&T. The AT&T settlement split the local monopoly telephone operating companies from the long-distance and equipment-manufacturing segments of AT&T. The remaining AT&T was freed from previous restrictions which had limited it to regulated businesses and had greatly restricted its freedom to compete in the computer industry. Technologically, the industries of communications and computers had been coming together. Both a computer system and a public telephone system are based on connecting various devices through communications paths and switching systems. There are many differences which had induced separate technologies in the earlier days, but those have been becoming less significant as semiconductor advances have made the use of standard computers efficient for switching telephone circuits. The settlement of the AT&T suit provided a major entrant with established research capabilities and computer experience useful for the commercial computer industry, further reducing IBM's ability to dominate the industry.

One lesson to be drawn from the very extensive IBM litigation is that of the need to examine the likely changes in an industry prior to prescribing policy remedies. As the suit was being prepared in 1968, by all the standard measures, the computer industry appeared to be an obvious candidate for antitrust action: one firm dominated the industry, barriers to entry were high, and there was evidence of conduct designed to maintain a monopolistic position. In retrospect, 1968 marked the high point of IBM's dominance of the industry. The extraordinary success of the System/360, then at its peak, provided a set of standards that were a natural target for fringe competitors. The heavy user investment in software for the System/360, which had tied customers to IBM, also restricted IBM's freedom to change the standards and allowed other companies to design products to replace the IBM models. IBM's practice of bundling services with hardware meant that hardware was overpriced and thus a natural target for companies who could replace individual pieces. As limitations on IBM's freedom became clear because of the events of the 1970s, the desirability of antitrust action to promote a competitive industry became far more questionable.

NOTES

1. This chapter does not necessarily reflect the views of the Federal Communications Commission or any member of its staff other than the author.

2. Atanasoff's role in the early development of computers is highly controversial. Mauchley denied gaining anything of value from Atanasoff, and Atanasoff's own computer model was never finished. The issue of who deserved credit was litigated after Eckert and Mauchley attempted to patent their invention. The judge ruled that Atanasoff deserved credit for the basic computer ideas. *Honeywell v. Sperry Rand,* (DC Minn. 1973), *1974 Trade Cases,* Number 74,874.

3. Fred Kaplan, *The Wizards of Armageddon* (New York: Simon & Schuster, 1983), p. 221.

4. IBM's revenues from each product for each year through 1970 were provided in a court-ordered census of the industry for the *Control Data v. IBM* litigation. Although the data was originally collected under strict nondisclosure requirements, it was introduced several years later into the trial record of *California Computer Products v. IBM,* and became a matter of public record.

5. Market shares are computed from revenue figures in "The Datamation 100" and Pamela Archbold, "Fathoming the Industry," *Datamation* (June 1, 1984), pp. 53–144.

6. W. David Gardner, "The Rise and Fall of Viatron," *Datamation* (May 15, 1971), pp. 38–40; (July 1, 1971), pp. 44–47.

7. John Verity, "Start-up Fever Is Spreading," *Datamation* (Sept. 1982), p. 180.

8. Walter Adams and James W. Brock, "Integrated Monopoly and Market Power: System Selling, Compatibility Standards, and Market Control," *Quarterly Review of Economics and Business,* **22:**29–42 (Winter 1982).

9. Curt Monash, "Software Strategies," *Datamation* (Feb. 1984), p. 172.

10. IBM, "Management Committee Minutes" (Jan. 6, 1972), released in *Telex v. IBM* as Plaintiff's Exhibit 387-066.

11. IBM, "Management Committee Minutes and Charts" (July 15, 1968), *Telex v. IBM,* Plaintiff's Exhibit 384B-035.

12. IBM, "Peripherals Study" (June 25, 1970), *Telex v. IBM,* Plaintiff's Exhibit 41.

13. IBM, "B. M. Hochfeld to D. J. Perry" (March 15, 1971), *Telex v. IBM,* Plaintiff's Exhibit 153.

14. IBM, "Lease Plan—Plug-Compatible Manufacturers," *Telex v. IBM,* Plaintiff's Exhibit 141A.

15. IBM, "Summary Comparison—IBM-Telex," *Telex v. IBM,* Plaintiff's Exhibit 280.

16. IBM, "Phase II Forecast, Aspen I, Monarch" (June 15, 1970), *Telex v. IBM,* Plaintiff's Exhibit 272, p. 9.

17. More extensive discussion of the competitive actions related to peripheral-company competition may be found in Gerald Brock, *The U.S. Computer Industry* (Cambridge, Mass.: Ballinger, 1975), Chap. 8.

18. Ibid., p. 221.

19. Ibid., p. 79.

20. Hesh Wiener, "Mainframe Maneuvers," *Datamation* (Feb. 1984), pp. 164–166.

SUGGESTED READING

BOOKS

Brock, Gerald W. *The U.S. Computer Industry: A Study of Market Power.* Cambridge, Mass.: Ballinger Publishing Co., 1975.

Feigenbaum, Edward A., and Pamela McCorduck. *The Fifth Generation: Artificial Intelligence and Japan's Computer Challenge to the World.* Reading, Mass.: Addison-Wesley Publishing Co., 1983.

Fisher, Franklin M., John J. Mcgowan and Joen E. Greenwood. *Folded, Spindled, and Mutilated: Economic Analysis and U.S. v. IBM.* Cambridge, Mass.: MIT Press, 1983.

Rogers, William. *Think: A Biography of the Watsons and IBM.* New York: Stein and Day Publishers, 1969.

Soma, John T. *The Computer Industry.* Lexington, Mass.: Lexington Books, 1976.

PERIODICALS

Datamation. Monthly magazine that provides extensive coverage of companies, products, and competitive issues in the computer industry.

Computerworld. Weekly newspaper that covers the industry in great detail.

Data Communications. Magazine that focuses on the communications aspect of the computer industry.

COURT DOCUMENTS

A vast amount of information on the industry is available through documents made public in the various cases. Although the documents are public, they are relatively inaccessible, except from participants in the cases. The huge amount of court records and exhibits makes standard procurement from court clerks, at high per-page fees, prohibitively expensive for most academic purposes. Two exceptions to the general inaccessibility of the documents are Fisher's book, listed above, which is based on economic testimony for IBM; and the *Telex v. IBM* exhibits, which were publicized by the Computer and Communications Industry Association, and are in some libraries.

8

The Telecommunications Industry

Manley R. Irwin

I. INTRODUCTION

U.S. industrial experience suggests that any transition from monopoly to competition is neither abrupt nor precipitous. Changes in market structure tend to be marginal, orderly, and discretionary. Over time, new generations of management are able to accommodate their decision-making process to the new reality of consumer choice and market entry. Nature indeed makes no leap.

Not so it is in U.S. telecommunications. On January 1, 1984, the largest private telephone company in the world ceased to exist. The American Telephone and Telegraph Company (AT&T), also called the Bell System, was dismantled and dissolved. AT&T forfeited ownership in 23 local Bell operating companies in one dramatic corporate divestiture. A natural monopoly ceased and a competitive firm commenced, which suggests that the U.S. telecommunication industry will never be the same again.

Historians will long debate whether AT&T can or will make this cultural leap into the competitive market with dispatch or success. It may be years, even decades, before a definitive answer is forthcoming. At the same time, a diminution of market power poses another question, equally vexing, regarding public policy. Will regulation, as an institution, also be eroded, and then dissolve? The recent actions of the FCC, the state utility commissions, the Justice Department, the federal court system, and the Defense Department suggest that, on the contrary, regulation is searching for a new mandate of legitimacy. "Natural monopoly" regulation has been replaced by matters of equity, subsidy, technological transfer, and national defense. All of this argues that the U.S. has yet to create a policy equivalent to private bankruptcy. Unlike old soldiers, once regulatory institutions are born, they seldom fade away.

II. MARKET STRUCTURE

History

What are the origins of the telephone in the U.S.? How did a monopoly commence, and endure? And who conceived of the institution—private monopoly with public oversight? The answer lies in an admixture of historical accident and entrepreneurial genius.

Telecommunications cannot be separated from the telephone patent. Once it was sanctioned by the U.S. Supreme Court in 1876, the Boston Bell Patent Association found itself in telephone service, after the Western Union Telegraph Company turned down an offer to purchase the patent for $100,000. The telegraph company soon realized its blunder and started its own telephone company.[1] From 1877 to 1879, the fledgling Bell company battled a telegraph collosus for customers, revenues, rights-of-way, and line interconnection. When Western Union retreated to telegraphy in 1879, the telephone industry marked that year as its own "Magna Carta." The U.S. telecommunications market was effectively cartelized.

Until the basic patents expired in 1894, the Bell Telephone Company was off and running as a corporate entity. Local franchises were issued in exchange for shareholder equity. A long-distance company was established in 1885 (AT&T); a manufacturer was acquired in 1882 (Western Electric). The components of what was later to be known as the *Bell System* were in place within a decade of the basic patent grant. The organizational genius behind the telephone company was an ex-Post Office employee, Theodore N. Vail.

The Bell patents expired in 1894, and competition in telephone services and equipment commenced at the turn of the century. Bell occupied the dense population centers, so independent telephone companies sprouted in the rural areas of the U.S. Non-Western electric plants sprang up to supply the needs of these new telephone companies. And predictably, as competition spread, telephone rates fell, productivity jumped, and phone service expanded accordingly.

Despite a near 50 percent penetration by the independents in 1908, the Bell System, now called AT&T, remained the dominant firm in the industry. The company occupied local sites, enjoyed a long-distance monopoly, and hooked its toll facilities to its own local companies exclusively. AT&T denied non-Bell companies access to the Bell long-distance network, thus isolating the independents geographically. AT&T assigned patents to Bell System companies exclusively, and Western Electric refused to sell equipment to independent telephone companies. A telephone patent was thus transformed into a corporate monopoly.

By the turn of the century, corporate trust-busting was no longer unthinkable as a policy remedy. AT&T, its organization, and market size were exposed, if not vulnerable, to the charge of monopoly power. It was then (circa 1907) that Theodore Vail, Bell's chief executive officer, declared unequivocably that competition in telephone service was tantamount to industrial warfare. Diversity, entry, and rivalry violated, he asserted, quality service, scale economies, and universal telephone service. Telephony, Vail argued, was a natural monopoly.

Unlike his contemporaries, Vail realized that proclamation of a monopoly privilege was hardly a sufficient policy prescription. Borrowing a concept from the railroad industry, Vail advocated regulatory oversight—private ownership, public regulation.[2] Bell's Chairman thus set in place an institution that was to serve as a unique response to the dilemma posed by a natural monopoly.

Vail lobbied for regulation at the state level in 1907 and 1908; and two years later, the Interstate Commerce Act, amended by the Mann-Elkins Act, extended federal jurisdiction ovr interstate telephone service. The passage of the Communication Act of 1934 merely formalized what Vail had begun twenty-seven years earlier.

At the time, the bargain struck between the telephone company and the public appeared eminently workable. In return for an exclusive franchise, the telephone company consented to submit its rates, earnings, and services to public scrutiny. Due process would protect the consumer from excessive rates, exorbitant profits, and indifferent service.

And government regulation had still another virtue: it could serve to hold the antitrust statutes at bay. After regulation, AT&T relaxed some of its policies. It permitted toll interconnection to telephone companies and agreed to sell telephone equipment to non-Bell carriers. Under regulation, the Bell System was to evolve into the world's largest corporation.

The industry prospered in the Roaring Twentes, weathered the Great Depression, and mobilized for World War II. But after the 1948 election of Truman (an upset), an antitrust crisis threatened Bell's structure of service and manufacturing. The Department of Justice alleged that Bell's telephone service monopoly had also foreclosed competition in equipment manufacturing.[3] The government proposed to divest Western Electric from AT&T, to split Western Electric into three separate entities, and to order the Bell companies to buy equipment on a competitive basis. Once again, vertical integration loomed as AT&T's Achilles' heel.

A 1956 agreement with the Department of Justice ended the 1949 antitrust suit. In return for a promise to make available its patents on a royalty-free basis, the Department of Justice dropped its suit, and AT&T agreed to confine itself to regulated communication services only.[4] The result meant that the structure of the Bell System was preserved and protected. At the time, the 1956 Agreement was hailed as a masterful exercise in management perspicacity.

If nothing else, the 1956 Decree reaffirmed two of Vail's basic tenets—integration of service and equipment, and commission regulatory oversight.

Other telephone companies soon patterned their own company organizations after AT&T's, and over the next two decades, the telephone holding company served as the industry's corporate model.

The late 1950s and 1960s appeared economically stable and promising. Electronic switching was soon to replace electromechanical switchboards and promised to provide customer services; Bell Telephone Laboratory was to receive a Nobel Prize for the transistor invention; direct distance-dialing was inaugurated on a national scale; and a video phone service held promise of eroding the revenues of the nation's airline carriers.

One small cloud hung over the future, however. A Bell Laboratory briefing to AT&T executives suggested that new technology might spawn new firms, products, systems, and hardware.[5] These companies, the Bell Laboratory contended, could generate rivalry in long-distance service and in equipment production. Perhaps natural monopoly would not reside in perpetuity.

But the year was 1961. Entry of other forms into telecommunication services, generally perceived as unthinkable, contradicted the premise of natural monopoly, fifty state public-utility commissions, and the FCC. Vail's strategy had withstood an exogenous shock, and Bell System policies appeared valid for the foreseeable future.

But entry of other firms indeed began in the late 1960s. The Federal Communications Commission encouraged selected access to peripheral telecommunication markets. The Commission's actions were hesitant and tentative. But from AT&T's perspective, competition, however slight, constituted a flagrant violation of scale economies. Bell's reaction to entry ignited the antitrust flames once again, and in 1974, the Department of Justice sought dissolution of Bell's vertical structure.

AT&T vigorously defended its policies and organization. It even took its case to Congress, but there was no legislative solution to this antitrust suit, which seemed interminable.

Negotiations finally commenced in 1981 with the Assistant Attorney General William Baxter, and a settlement was reached at the end of the year. AT&T formally agreed to spin off its 23 Bell operating companies. Some 800,000 employees found that they worked for a new employer. Breaking up the nation's largest corporation was a difficult task indeed.

Present Market Structure

The former 23 Bell operating companies are now reconstituted as seven regional Bell holding companies (Figure 1). They include Nynex, Bell Atlantic, Bell South, Ameritech, Southwestern Bell, Pacific Telesis, and U.S. West. Under the terms of the Justice Department's Consent Decree, the regional Bell operating companies (BOCs) would not engage in manufacturing telephone equipment, nor would they engage in interstate toll- or long-distance services. Competition would reign in the toll market—although individual state commissions would determine whether entry could occur within

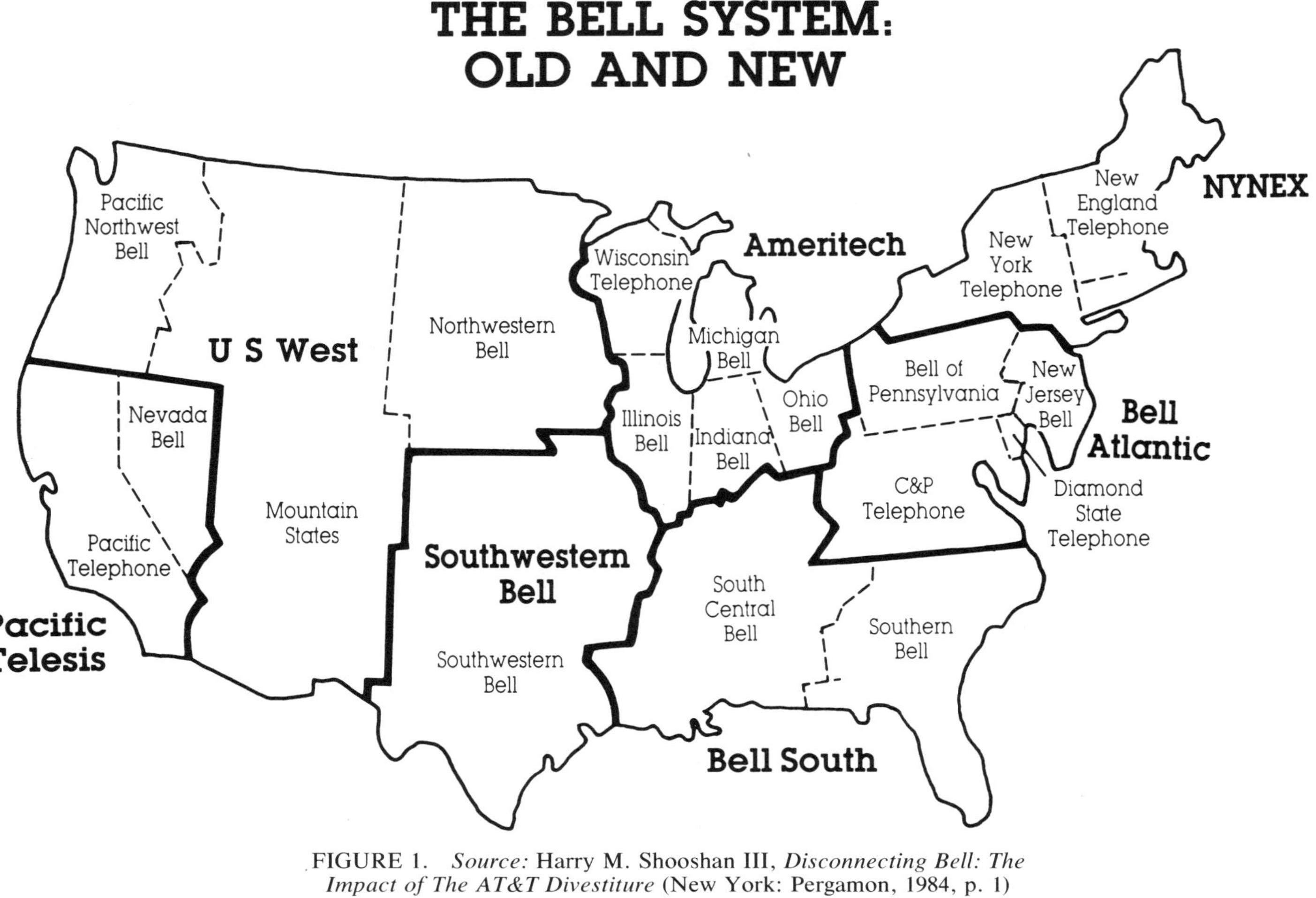

FIGURE 1. *Source:* Harry M. Shooshan III, *Disconnecting Bell: The Impact of The AT&T Divestiture* (New York: Pergamon, 1984, p. 1)

state jurisdictions—sometimes called *intra-lata* competition. (A lata, an acronym for local access transport area, is equivalent telephone area codes.)

The regional Bell operating companies retain the familiar Bell symbol; they may provide yellow page services, may sell telephone equipment to their customers, and must give equal local access to all long-distance competition. Presumably, the regional Bell operating companies enjoy the last vestige of "natural monopoly" in local exchange service.

For its part, AT&T has been released from the restraint of its 1956 Consent Agreement. The Company has created an unregulated affiliate (AT&T Information Systems), and its manufacturing affiliate—Western Electric—is now called AT&T Technologies. The Company is diversifying into office and factory automation, and has brokered joint ventures in Europe, Canada, and the Far East.

The independent or non-Bell companies continue to provide about a fifth of the nation's basic telephone service. Most of them remain associated with the telephone holding companies, such as GTE Inc., United Telecommunications, and Continental Telephone Company.

Now, a postdivestiture world is witnessing the entry and consolidation of families of specialized carriers, such as terrestrial microwave carriers, satellite carriers, value-added terrestrial firms, and value-added satellite carriers. Optical-fiber networks (Fiberoptics) are providing still more submarket access and diversity. Indeed, AT&T asserts that some 400 rivals have driven its market share from 90 percent to 57 percent in four years, and IBM has acquired MCI, AT&T's largest rival. The company has petitioned the FCC for permission to deregulate its long-distance prices and services. In an unprecedented transition in corporate organization, corporate culture, and corporate incentives, we are witnessing a company's recycling of itself—from the status of protected monopoly to private competition.

III. MARKET CONDUCT

Price/Nonprice Conduct

Conduct and structure are in counterpoint. Corporate conduct augments barriers to market entry; structure conditions the price and nonprice response of a firm. AT&T's corporate reaction to market entry precipitated a crisis in telecommunication policies. As in most events, market entry was incremental and undramatic. But as competitive firms gained momentum, their force became cumulative in three markets: customer telephone equipment, long-distance service, and equipment manufacturing.

1. Customer-Premise Equipment. The basic telephone instrument was owned by the telephone company, almost from the beginning of the industry. AT&T did not sell equipment, it provided a service—a policy that originated with Alexander Graham Bell's father-in-law, who once served on the Board of Directors of United Shoe Machinery Corporation. By custom, tradition, and habit, the company assumed responsibility for service, quality, innovation, repair, and equipment retirement. Customer ownership did not carry that service obligation. Indeed, ownership of equipment by the user was labeled "foreign." If a subscriber persisted in owning equipment, the user courted the ultimate penalty—loss of telephone service. And, in the name of "system integrity," state commissions even banned florists' plastic covers on telephone directories.

One small rupture occurred in the 1950s. A company marketed a unit that covered the telephone mouthpiece, to insure privacy. AT&T labeled the device a "foreign" attachment, and, supported by the FCC, banned the device on grounds of compromised telephone service. An appeals court overturned AT&T's policy, which proved to be a minor setback. But that ruling was of no great moment; Bell merely readjusted its tariffs to accommodate the Hush-a-phone device.[6]

A more unsettling event occurred when a Texan, Tom Carter, invented a device, the Carterfone, which linked an offshore oil rig to a land mobile unit. By its very application, the Carterfone device stood in violation of AT&T's equipment-ownership policy. The Company confiscated the unit.

Under regulation, telephone company policies, prices, and conditions of service were filed before state and federal commissions. If the agencies accepted company practices, they were embodied as "tariffs." (Violation of a tariff was almost tantamount to breaking the law.) When Bell confiscated Tom Carter's device, he filed an antitrust suit. The case eventually wound up before the Federal Communications Commission, and in June 1968, the FCC approved Tom Carter's device by an 8 to 0 vote.[7]

The Carterfone decision gave birth to what was to become known as the *interconnect industry*. Manufacturers supplied businesses with key telephone systems, station equipment, PBXs (office switchboards), automatic call directors, and data modems—all of which were located on the customer's premises, and all of which were competitive with Bell's equipment. The 1968 interconnect decision also encouraged entry into the manufacturing of telephone equipment.

AT&T fought the interconnect firms on grounds that customer equipment would harm the quality of its voice network. In fact, Bell imposed an interface device (a *coupler*) between the telephone instrument and its lines, which was accepted by both state and FCC commissions. The coupler not only raised the cost of buying telephone equipment, it started a controversy as to whether the device caused a diminution of telephone-voice quality.

Of course, Bell insisted that the coupler functioned as a protective fuse. But that position was not without challenge. Some claimed that the technical-harm issue was bogus; others contended that it was quite legitimate. The FCC asked Bell for documented data, but the available evidence proved thin and inconclusive. One AT&T officer was later to recall, "The plain fact of the matter is that studies of such rigor and continuity to support or rebut the harms argument were not carried out."[8]

In addition, AT&T opposed an FCC policy whereby approved customer equipment could be plugged directly into the telephone network. The interconnection industry supported this policy of certification; AT&T opposed it. When the FCC favored certification, the issue was taken into the courts. By the time due process had run its course and certification became national policy, ten years had elapsed since the FCC's 1968 Carterfone decision.

As customers examined the features, costs, and technical options of interconnect equipment, Western Electric began to feel competitive pressures. The Company introduced new PBXs to the market, and reexamined both its production costs and equipment prices.[9] Not only had interconnect suppliers challenged the basic assumptions of telephone costing, depreciation, and pricing, they also challenged Bell's performance in innovation and manufacturing.

With minor exceptions, state commissions tended to treat telephone companies as aggrieved parties. State agencies viewed interconnect suppliers as a threat to telephone revenues and attempted to ban interconnect practices outright. Failing that, public utility commissions (PUCs) tried to convert interconnect firms into public utilities. Nevertheless, entry into the customer-equipment market persisted, and so did casualties among independent equipment producers. A rash of antitrust suits were brought by these companies, each alleging that Bell was attempting to monopolize the customer-equipment market.[10]

2. Toll/Local Service. A second Bell policy had tied long-distance to local facilities. AT&T enjoyed a monopoly in the former; the Bell operating companies a monopoly in the latter. The nexus of local toll integration was under AT&T's ownership.

Over time, local telephone rates became dependent upon long-distance rates. Long-distance facilities tended to enjoy higher productivity, lower costs, and higher profits. Under a complex allocation formula, which was supported by state commissions, toll revenues were transferred to local rates.

Predictably, the spread between toll price and toll cost invited market entry. In 1969, the FCC permitted a firm to begin service in leased or dedicated circuits only. Then, to the consternation of AT&T and the FCC, specialized carriers began to offer dial-up toll telephone service, as well. The FCC, state PUCs, and AT&T united in opposition, insisting that the specialized carriers had jumped their assigned market boundaries. As punishment, the FCC ordered AT&T to deny MCI local telephone interconnection. MCI then took both AT&T and the FCC to court, and surprisingly won on a judicial appeal.[11]

Now the fat was in the fire. AT&T warned regulators that any unraveling of rate cross-subsidization would push up local telephone rates. The company strenuously fought entry of specialized carriers—whether microwave, satellite, or telephone resellers. Bell operating companies delayed local access to AT&T's long distance rivals, toll rates were cut, and the result was another rash of private antitrust suits.

3. Utilities/Manufacturing. Finally, in the 1970's, equipment suppliers began to challenge Western Electric's exclusive access to the Bell operating companies. For the most part, Bell's operations were self-sufficient: Bell Laboratory designed equipment, Western Electric manufactured it, and Bell incorporated hardware into their rate base; AT&T coordinated the integration process. An outside supplier might produce a piece of equipment that Bell Laboratory had not developed. And, on occasion, an operating company would express an interest in non-Western Electric hardware. But such departures from vertical integration were the exception.

In the 1970s, an FCC investigation documented the mechanics of a closed market. Western Electric would examine a rival's equipment, and would later introduce a similar product. AT&T would preannounce its product to the Bell operating companies. The Bell operating companies would order Western's product, even before they had firm price quotes.[12] Subsequent antitrust suits alleged that Bell's structure constituted an insurmountable barrier to market access in equipment supply.

Then, in November 1974, the Department of Justice struck. The department alleged that AT&T had engaged in anticompetitive activities in customer-premise equipment, had sought to maintain its monopoly in the intercity toll service market, and had monopolized telephone manufacturing. The Department of Justice sought a restructuring of Bell operating companies, Western Electric, and AT&T's Long-Distance affiliate.[13]

Diversification Problems of the Bell System

However controversial, the antitrust problem represented only one facet of the Bell System's strategy difficulties. Corporate diversification was another. The 1956 judgment was becoming an impediment to new markets, new products, and new services, because that decree allowed Bell to participate in regulated activities only.

Several developments underscored AT&T's problems under the 1956 Consent Decree. In the late 1970s, Bell Laboratory developed a telephone handset that accepted commercial credit cards (the transaction telephone), and soon AT&T announced a rudimentary form of an electronic funds-transfer system. AT&T's competitors alleged that Bell's funds-transfer service violated its 1956 Consent Decree. On the other hand, Bell insisted that its activities were subject to regulatory oversight. However, the regulatory issue faded away, because the transaction telephone service proved to be an unsuccessful marketing endeavor.

Then, in the early 1970s, Western Electric developed the Dataspeed 40—a new generation of teleprinter equipment, supplied by Teletype Corp., a Western Electric affiliate. The FCC agonized over the equipment and service. Was Bell's Dataspeed 40 service communications per se?[15] Was it data processing? Was it neither? AT&T insisted that it had long manufactured hard-copy devices, that its service was a natural progression into what it called *communication processing,* and that the service should be regulated.

IBM, on the other hand, asserted that Bell had developed a computer terminal, that computer terminals were unregulated, and that the FCC had no business approving the device in the first place. So insistent was IBM that it carried its appeal to the U.S. Supreme Court, where it lost on *certiorari.*[16]

Another problem was the new generation of office-switching equipment (PBXs) which offered cost accounting, least-toll routing, and other features. Although Bell Telephone Laboratory and Western Electric introduced these products into the marketplace, the computer industry insisted that Bell's office-switch incorporated software and data-processing features and therefore violated the 1956 Consent Decree.

But it took the State of Texas to deliver the cruelest blow of all. Southwestern Bell, a regional company, converted yellow pages into a data base available via a television set. A computerized data base was hardly an unprecedented development, given prototypes available in Canada, Japan, and Europe. However, the Texas Newspaper Association, joined by *The Washington Post,* alleged that AT&T was diversifying into electronic publishing.[17] Once again, the 1956 Consent Decree was cited as overriding and binding.

A disconcerting pattern began to emerge. Whenever AT&T sought to diversify into new services, the company found itself confronted by competitors who alleged that its 1956 agreement confined the company to regulated activities only. The problem was that information technology was obscuring a clear distinction between *voice* and *data*. Subtly, over time, due process was evolving into a telephone company nightmare.

In the late 1970s, the issue of antitrust and divestiture continued to plague the Bell System. In 1979, a new chairman of AT&T declared that Bell would seek to offer knowledge-intensive services in domestic and international markets. The objective may have been obvious, but the institutional means to achieve it were not.

In the meantime, the government's antitrust case continued, year after year. The Antitrust Division announced its intention to introduce one hundred witnesses. As noted, AT&T attempted to circumvent the judicial process through legislative changes in the 1934 Communication Act. Due process had proved to be ponderous, but for AT&T, the legislative process was a political quagmire. Failing to vacate the government suit via a Congressional mandate, AT&T apparently concluded that the suit by the Department of Justice was the only game in town. The rest—a consent decree mandating divestiture—is history.

IV. PERFORMANCE

Service/Choice

Any industry in transition provides clinical insights into the terms of economic performance. This is especially true in telecommunications. Consider services, rates, marketing, expenses, investment, return on investment, depreciation, manufacturing, and research before and after the advent of market rivalry. Prior to entry, telephone service in the U.S. was dominated by plain old telephone service (POTS). Telephone service, the central mandate of the industry, was relatively undifferentiated. The industry offered local residential, business service, and direct distance-dialing, as well as dedicated or private-line facilities to business users.

Today, subscribers are confronted with a broader range of options and services. Some carriers offer services via their own facilities, others secure bulk services from common carriers and pass discounts on to their customers. Satellite carriers, value-added carriers, and satellite resale carriers have developed a range of voice, data, and digital offerings. Today, segmentation is the hallmark of the telecommunication industry.

Telephone Rates

Prior to competition, telephone carriers posted either flat rates or time-distant-sensitive prices. Local telephone services illustrated the former; long distance, the latter. Because competition was deemed unworkable in local telephone service, telephone rates tended to be demand-oriented rather than cost-oriented. Business rates, for example, were posted higher than residential rates—presumably because of the greater value assigned to the business carrier. Rate disparities were not crucial so long as a company's total revenue covered its total cost.

Over time, rate cross-subsidies became an accepted practice. Conventional wisdom held that metropolitan areas subsidized rural users and business users subsidized residential subscribers. Without cost-accounting techniques, the direction and the amount of the subsidy remained somewhat of an unknown. Nevertheless, regulators and carriers acknowledged that particular telephone rates did not track unit costs.

Today, telephone company pricing is moving toward cost-base pricing. Predictably, rates in excess of costs attracted a host of entrants—specialized carriers, value-added carriers, satellite carriers, and satellite resellers. Long-distance rates and interexchange rates for the residential business are being discounted by either specialized carriers, telephone resellers, or AT&T itself. At the same time, local exchange rates are being increased.

Marketing

Competition has expedited telephone marketing activities. Under monopoly, price adjustments were confined to off-peak-time pricing as a device to utilize idle plant. Local-exchange marketing was driven by the need to "let your fingers do the walking" to encourage the use of basic exchange service. Today, telephone marketing is no longer solely a matter of taking orders. Competition has intensified advertising, and price discounts are now standard fare in the industry. Recently, AT&T introduced rate discounts and employed techniques quite similar to frequent-flyer airline programs. Some telephone resellers are giving away telephone sets as a bonus to initial customers. All in all, marketing is now a centerpiece in an industry that traditionally was guaranteed customer usage.

Operating Expenses

Under regulation, a carrier recovered operating expenses appropriate to the delivery of subscriber service, including labor, maintenance, depreciation, management salaries, advertising, and the like. If expenses were disallowed by the Commission, the telephone carrier was not permitted to include some costs in its telephone rates. But disallowance was rare. Operating expenses were driven by the mathematics of cost-plus.[18]

Today, competition has turned economic incentives upside down. Through a program of early retirement of management, personnel transfers, and layoffs, AT&T Communications and AT&T Technologies have undergone a massive personnel reassessment.[19] As AT&T Communications experiences intense rivalry from specialized carriers, downward-cost pressures can be expected to intensify in the future.

Cost-reduction pressures have also affected labor-wage rates. Contracts and work rules negotiated by the Communication Workers of America are under increased scrutiny.[20] AT&T Communications is experiencing competition that is not unlike airline carriers competing with the nonunion pilots of upstart carriers. Market entry, in short, has imposed standards of productivity and efficiency on a once quiet industry.

Investment

To the extent that nearly three dollars of capital is required for every dollar generated in revenue, telephony has traditionally been treated as a capital-intensive industry. Cost-plus rate of return dominated the investment decisions of the carriers. The larger the capital rate base, the higher the absolute level of earnings. Some critics allege that capital equipment reached excessive levels of redundancy in quality, and academics wrote volumes on the subject of rate-base-over-investment.

Though a prerogative of management, investment decisions are ultimately approved by regulatory agencies. It was Commission oversight that permitted the allocation of expenditures on customer-premise equipment, local distribution systems, copper-paired wire, telephone trunks, and switching and transmission facilities. The fact that commissions allocated $100 billion dollars of investment apparently did not seem to provoke widespread criticism.

Competition today has challenged the industry's investment decision making. AT&T Communications is no longer the only long-distance player in the field; rivals are not only employing alternative equipment and hardware, they are no longer constrained by fixed rates of return. If specialized carriers employ more efficient switches and transmission facilities, and if they expense rather than capitalize labor installation, AT&T Communications is bound to experience an ongoing reappraisal of its own costs.

In the past, investment tended to favor long-haul intercity rather than local-loop or rural facilities. Estimates were that about 50 percent of physical telephone plant was assigned to local-loop (the wire linking subscriber equipment to the central office exchange).[21] Today, market entry in toll facilities places emphasis on flexibility and efficiency, and the local distribution plant is being rejuvenated under fiberoptics, satellites, digital radio, data compression, and infrared transmission.

Competition has stimulated innovation in local-area networks, fiberoptic communication systems, digital-termination systems, (microwave) broadcast techniques, and direct-satellite broadcast services. And rivalry is especially keen in customer-premise equipment. Twenty years ago, customer equipment was dominated by the Bell System. Today, AT&T's market share has dropped two thirds as some 270 firms supply PBX equipment with over a hundred different features.[22] Pluralism is the hallmark of today's telephone plant.

Rate of Return/Risk

Rate-of-return regulation postulates that a firm generate an *opportunity cost* on its investment, that is, a weighted average of the firm's cost of capital. Telephone carriers in the U.S. treated profits as a markup on their invested capital, no matter how profits were derived. Ceiling-on-profit incentives resulted in predictable corporate behavior: carriers tended to be risk-averse. After all, what was the payoff for marketing risks if there was not a commensurate return to the shareholder. In the world of regulation, management stock options were an alien concept.

Regulatory constraint did not mean that telephone companies were technical Neanderthals. On the contrary, AT&T pushed developments in computer-switching and transmission, particularly in long-haul usage. And although Bell's Picturephone service was unsuccessful, this kind of innovation suggested that technical change could take place within a telephone company culture. Nevertheless, a profit ceiling did act to dampen enterprise as an ongoing process. One could say that the quality of telephone-company management ranked somewhere between IBM on one side and the U.S. Post Office on the other.

Deregulation, i.e., competition, has profoundly altered the innovation incentives. As new carriers enter existing markets, and as they develop enhanced data services, the incumbent carriers respond in kind. Whether the newcomers are specialized, value-added, satellite, terrestrial resellers, or satellite resellers, the new entrants are nothing if not unconventional and entrepreneurial. The pressure of competition, transmitted to the incumbent telephone carriers, has inspired them to respond with new pricing and marketing techniques, and with innovative services.

AT&T Communications has, through an unregulated subsidiary, introduced new products and new services. Since divestiture, AT&T's innovation record in PBXs, personal computers, minicomputers, local-area networks, digital switching, and teleconferencing techniques has been unprecedented. Even the regional Bell operating companies have become more entrepreneurial. The Southern New England Telephone Company has formed a joint venture with railroad companies for the purpose of laying fiberoptic cable along rights-of-way east of the Mississippi River. U.S. West, a regional Bell operating company, has established offices in major cities throughout the U.S., and Pacific Telesis attempted, unsuccessfully, to acquire a specialized carrier in Great Britain.

The relaxation of profit ceilings and the promotion of rivalry has encouraged firms to embrace rather than eschew risk-taking. The correlation is direct: the higher the risk, the greater the potential payoff. It is true that many companies continue to play it safe, but this is no longer standard policy. Telephone companies today view themselves as information entities, and the world replete with new opportunities for investment, service, growth, and earnings. The industry, in short, is experiencing a managerial renaissance.

Depreciation

Before competition, regulatory commissioners assigned extended periods of economic life to telephone equipment. In some cases, PBX life extended for twenty years, and central-office equipment was thought to last forty years. Longer write-off periods translated into reduced annual depreciation expense, which in turn held down local telephone rates—at least in the short run.

Such a write-off period postponed capital recovery and retarded technological innovation. To the extent that capital remained in a carrier's rate-base, and to the extent that new technology generated equipment with lower unit costs and greater capacity, carriers more often than not acknowledged that their equipment base was antiquated. So long as no prior market test existed, carriers continued to render service on equipment that was deemed used and useful.

Certainly, the old telephone equipment worked. A central-office-panel exchange, for example, installed in Brooklyn, N.Y., in the 1920s, was retired in the 1980s. The telephone companies expressed pride in equipment longevity and reliability, and were applauded by the regulatory commissions for the quality of their service. But today, competition has revolutionized the notion of product life cycles. As new firms enter the industry, the old carrier hardware, terminals, switching, software, and transmission are no longer deemed adequate in terms of cost, features, and state-of-the-art technology. Competition has added a sense of urgency to the innovation cycle.[23]

Equipment and Pricing

Two decades ago, the integration of service and equipment manufacturing was the order of the day. AT&T's ownership of Western Electric and the operating companies not only biased make/buy decisions, in favor of Western Electric, but also made it inevitable that the operating company purchase the bulk of its hardware in-house. Indeed, to buy equipment other than Western Electric's was equivalent to playing corporate Russian Roulette. Western Electric obviously enjoyed a privileged status in telephone manufacturing.

Equipment pricing was essentially a cost-plus endeavor. Profits included a markup on standard manufacturing costs and equipment. Given vertical integration, the utility concept translated into pricing and costing, on the manufacturing side; and integrated suppliers, though not public utilities, often acted as if they possessed an exclusive franchise.

For many years, vertical integration and the purchasing policies associated therewith not only cartelized manufacturing in the U.S. but imposed a unique burden upon regulation. How could any oversight commission insure that telephone rates were reasonably priced if equipment costs were not only unregulated but immune from the discipline of the marketplace? Obviously, the issue focused essentially on AT&T and Western Electric. The courts attempted to provide one answer by ruling that the burden of price reasonableness rested with the carrier. Since that decision in the 1920s, AT&T had undertaken a series of price-comparison studies, comparing Western Electric's prices with those of the general trade suppliers.[24] The studies invariably concluded that Western Electric was more efficient than other telephone manufacturers in the U.S.

One key to Western Electric's prices turned on its scale economies. Large production runs, captive telephone markets, and the absence of marketing costs permitted Western Electric to engage in continuous output to anticipate user demand, and to locate its plants near its customer base. All this was said to translate into lower telephone costs and into optimal rates for the telephone subscriber. Most state commissions accepted uncritically the premise of AT&T's price-comparison studies.

In the 1970s, the FCC ruled that AT&T's price-comparison studies failed to meet the test of economic efficiency.[25] Indeed, the FCC alleged that Bell's vertical structure potentially foreclosed the equipment market, to the ultimate detriment of the telephone user. In response, AT&T formed a procurement division, in order to broaden the opportunities of outside equipment suppliers.

After divestiture, the equipment market expanded and became more diversified. The development of station equipment, switching transmission, computer software, and fiberoptics, and satellites is driven not merely by the growth of user demand and private networks but also by the needs of specialized carriers, telephone resellers, and corporate networks. New entrants alone have generated a $2 billion equipment market.[26]

Some 380 firms supplied related telephone equipment in the U.S. in 1978. Four years later, the number of suppliers had increased to 550.[27] Regional Bell operating companies no longer confine their purchases to Western Electric exclusively, and are distributing their orders among a variety of North American and overseas suppliers.

The dynamics of the equipment market reinforce the dynamics of telecommunication services. Suppliers improve the state of the art of technical equipment, which enables carriers to offer new features to the user public. Thus, an innovative counterpoint has developed between service entry and equipment entry.

This reconfiguration has not been lost upon Western Electric (now AT&T Technologies.) Less than five years ago, Western Electric's plants were thought to enjoy the efficiencies of long production runs and economies of scale. Recently, AT&T Technologies announced the closing of the Hawthorne works, the Kearney works, the Indianapolis works, and the Baltimore plant, because of excess capacity, obsolete plant, or changing customer requirements.

V. RESEARCH

In a monopoly environment, a laboratory enjoys the luxury of the long view. Bell Telephone Laboratory (BTL), the research arm of AT&T, earned a reputation for research and development (R&D) excellence. The laboratory was funded from operating company revenues and Western Electric sales. As BTL's budget grew, so did its reputation and global stature.

Nevertheless, research budgets are not immune to the forces of economics. When is a budget too small, too large, or optimal in size? The answer proved elusive. An AT&T vice president, expressing concern over BTL's budget, observed that "apparently unstemmable growth of the Bell System's R&D outlays has, from time to time, given rise to a question whether Bell Laboratories is manageable—by AT&T, that is."[28]

Today, corporate divestiture has removed Bell Telephone Laboratory's assured source of revenue—at least the portion formerly derived from the operating companies. Indeed, Bell Telephone Laboratory is vulnerable to competitive market forces.[29] AT&T, nevertheless, appears committed to basic research; and Bell Telephone Laboratory's president has insisted that such endeavors are critical to AT&T's performance in a competitive environment.

How can one summarize telecommunications market performance? Under regulation, telephone services were undifferentiated, demand was perceived as being price inelastic, rates masked individual costs, and toll revenues subsidized local exchange rates. Telephone marketing was virtually nonexistent, operating expenses were passed forward to subscriber rates, investment was cost-plus oriented, profits were capped, risk-incentives were attenuated, manufacturing was cartelized, and the telephone research base was narrow.

Regulation policed the ground rules that, to a large degree, set the tone for the industry's performance. From the regulators' perspective, its track record was inspiring: rates were generally low, telephone service universally accepted, and telephone quality assured. Anyone questioning this regulatory symbiosis was asked, "Have you ever made a telephone call in Paris?"

Competition has interrupted this quiet world of economic incentives. Demand today is perceived as being price elastic; rate discounts are rampant; leased services are mushrooming; and toll prices are trending toward costs. Telephone companies are becoming cost-conscious and are aggressively embracing marketing as a new management tool. Risk-taking is endemic, and economic incentives drive the search for new products as life cycles contract. And the manufacturing and production base in the U.S. is expanding.

Beyond these developments, three additional observations should be noted. First, competition expedites the growth of markets and new services. Currently, the U.S. is experiencing a 4 percent growth in local telephone service, a 14 percent growth in long-distance telephone service, and a 20 percent growth in data-communication service.[30] The disparity in these growth rates must be assigned, in part, to the intensity of rivalry in each market.

Second, investment in local-area networks, customer-premise equipment, satellite–earth terminals, PBX's, and digital switching is increasing. Entry of new firms has generated $2 billion in telephone-equipment investment, in addition to that of the incumbent carriers. The ripple effect of that investment has spilled into critical sectors of the U.S., specifically, the semiconductor industry and solid-state electronics.

Third, a change in the incentive system is not without its employment consequences. From 1950 to 1970, most new jobs (three out of four in the U.S.) were generated by either the Fortune 1,000 Companies or the government sector.[31] From 1970 to 1980, most of the 20 million new jobs in the U.S. were generated by firms classified as *small business*. From 1981 to 1982, small firms—those with under 20 employees—generated most of the new jobs during that two-year recession; and during 1982–1983, more new firms sprang up in the deregulated sectors of the economy than in the rest of the economy.[32] In communications, employment rose by 15 percent compared with 13 percent for the economy as a whole. Indeed, a Bell System study asserted that a 10 percent reduction in long-distance prices would, over the next ten years, generate some 400,000 new jobs; a price cut of 20 percent would, by 1993, generate almost 900,000 new jobs.[33] The creation of jobs cannot be separated from the U.S. experience of deregulation.

VI. PUBLIC POLICY

The Short Run

Despite improvements in price, efficiency, productivity, investment, and employment, the transition from a monopoly to a competitive structure is not without its traumas. Since deregulation three issues have developed in the U.S. that are nothing if not controversial. They include (1) telephone bypass; (2) the price of basic telephone service; and (3) global-equipment competition.

Telephone Bypass. Perhaps no single issue is as politically explosive as the subject of telephone bypass. Bypass, usually defined from the perspective of the telephone industry, is nothing more or less than technological competition—the rivalry for long-distance facilities in the telephone industry or for local-loop distribution. The first affects AT&T investment; the second affects the facilities of the regional operating companies.

Toll bypass traces its roots to the basic telephone toll subsidy, discussed on pages 268-269. Since the 1930s, a portion of the local distribution plant —wires, loops, outside plant, and switching—have been assigned to interstate toll costs. Over the years, some 30 percent of toll costs carried the basic exchange cost, which was a form of toll subsidy for local exchange services.

The FCC, the state commissioners, and the independent telephone companies (as well as Bell) found this toll, and the settlement arrangement quite workable. Toll rates held down the cost of telephone rates and thus contributed to the universality of telephone service. But intercity competition disrupted this long-standing revenue flow. Prices in excess of costs attracted entry; prices fell, and the toll-subsidy loss portended increases in basic exchange rates. State commissions were concerned that rising rates would cause a drop-off in basic telephone service and would thus reverse what they perceived to be the goal of universal service.

The FCC was also apprehensive about what it termed *uneconomic bypass,* that is, firms circumventing toll facilities because the local subsidy inflated the long-haul costs. Having encouraged private microwave carriers, specialized carriers, resale carriers, and satellite entities, the FCC looked for ways for AT&T to retain competitive tariffs and pricing. The answer, according to the FCC, was to reverse the long-standing toll subsidy by imposing a local access fee on the residential and business user.

When the FCC proposed an access charge to replace a $9 billion subsidy, the prospects of exchange-rate increases hit the state commissions and spilled into Congress, in a move so emotional that the FCC delayed its expected proposal. Nevertheless, the access charge is expected to be phased in gradually.[34]

Local bypass has raised several intriguing policy questions. Did not regulation, through its subsidy program, set the stage for bypass in the first place? And, would not the technology that produced fiberoptics, satellites, and digital microwave ultimately threaten the investment strategy of the carriers? And will the establishment of a new subsidy—the universal telephone pool—effectively insulate rural telephone subscribers from potential rate increases? The point is that telephone bypass is nothing less than technological competition, and telephone companies must meet the challenge of rivalry by their own production and investment decisions.

Another problem is circumvention of the distribution loop, which is often referred to as the "last mile" of telephone plant. This circumvention occurs both because of price and nonprice factors. New technology, including cellular radio, digital-termination systems, broadcast satellites, and fiber-optics, offer cost advantages to users/extensive communication services. Nevertheless, if users bypass the local loop, one must look for the reason. Is it because regulation neglected to urge the carriers to excel in technology? Is it because artificial cost-price margins insulated the market from entry and thus discouraged an incentive to explore innovative engineering changes?

Whatever the answer, band-width capacity represents another dimension of the local-loop. Firms that generate large volumes of data transmission (computer to computer, video conferencing, facsimile, graphics, and computer-aided design) find that the twisted-wire-pair cannot easily accommodate the capacity for these new services. Large corporates who use these techniques search for a means to circumvent a telephone plant, essentially oriented toward voice or analogue services.

The threat of competitive bypass has generated a spirited debate in the U.S. AT&T has mounted a strenuous effort to replace the toll settlement with an access fee, and state commissions have opposed technical bypass in order to preserve what they perceive as the viability of telephone plant. Indeed, state commissions have tried to protect the investment in telephone facilities by proposing a tax on all competitive substitutes.

What makes bypass so critical is that some 50 percent of telephone plant is in the local loop, and a relatively small proportion of users account for a vast majority of telephone revenues. In some cases, 4 percent of the customers account for 62 percent of total revenues.[35]

Nevertheless, the economics of bypass continues to be explored. Many state agencies are building microwave or fiberoptic networks. Specialized carriers, large customers, and AT&T Communications itself are contemplating bypass. And Bell operating companies themselves are pursuing bypass in order to retain their customer base. Regional Bell operating companies are laying fiberoptic cable, are applying for microwave systems, and are introducing new generations of PBXs in response to shifting user needs. Some fourteen regional operating companies have applied for digital-termination systems licenses (microwave), and one regional Bell operating company is constructing a satellite teleport. So long as technological options proliferate (and there is no end in sight), efficiency and innovation will motivate both suppliers and users of telecommunication facilities.

Basic Telephone Rates/Universal Service. A second trauma since deregulation which cannot be separated from technological bypass is the issue of basic exchange rates and universal telephone service. State regulatory commissions are concerned that any loss of the toll-subscriber revenue would drive the price of basic telephone service beyond the reach of the average user. State commissions suggest that bypass will precipitate a domino effect, that is, it will lead to revenue losses, which will lead to higher rates and the start of another round of bypass. The fear is that ultimately, universal telephone service in the U.S. will erode.

Proponents of competition argue that exchange local loops are uneconomic precisely because under regulation there was minimum research, no market entry, long depreciation-life cycles, and rate-base economics. Moreover, proponents argue that the toll subsidy is indiscriminate if applied to all users, irrespective of income class.. Those who truly need a subsidy to keep the rates low might receive some form of telephone stamp as a direct receipt. And finally, subscriber costs are a mix of both local and toll rates. Local rates may rise, but toll rates will certainly decline. The question is, what is the proportion, what is the mix, what will be the net effect upon each subscriber?

Many observers of the industry are certain that telephone rivalry, divestiture, and toll repricing will cause an upward pressure on basic telephone rates in the short term. Yet few contemplate putting the technological genie back into the bottle, and no one, except perhaps the National Association of Regulatory Utility Commissioners (NARUC), seriously believes that technology can be policed or taxed effectively. Fifty years of rate subsidization have obviously created distortions, and subscribers of telephone service are enduring the withdrawal pains of an industry that is in transition from monopoly to competition. Some carriers are exploring the idea of combining cellular radio and satellite combinations as an alternative to poles and wires in the rural sections of the country. At the same time, user choices and options are becoming irrevocably broader over the long term.

Offshore Equipment. A third trauma since deregulation, i.e., the separation of the regional Bell operating companies from Western Electric, means that the equipment market is open to competitive bidding for apparatus and hardware. The beneficiaries of this procurement shift include general trade suppliers, both domestic and foreign. Japan has achieved notable success in selling a variety of hardware to the regional operating companies in the United States.

Changes in equipment procurement have not gone unnoticed. Some foreign suppliers have captured 19 percent of the customer-premise equipment market.[36] Congress, in observing the disparity between U.S. exports of equipment to Japan and vice versa, has threatened to impose import restrictions on the Japanese.

Access to the telephone equipment market has political and international implications. Several years ago, AT&T awarded a fiberoptic transmission system to its own affiliate, Western Electric, in the U.S. Northeastern corridor. However, the FCC pressured AT&T to solicit competitive bidding, and subsequently, Fujitsu, a Japanese company, submitted the low bid and received the award.[37] An outcry from Congress prompted AT&T to revoke that bid and reassign the contract to its own manufacturing affiliate.

How, then, can one summarize the issues that are essentially of short-term duration? First, so long as technology continues to be the driving force in telecommunications, prices will ultimately reflect that technology and confer on the user more options. Bypass represents one such option.

Second, technology is changing the perception of the telephone company itself. As carriers witness not merely the erosion of their markets, but more importantly, as they offer opportunities for new industries and new revenues, they will be under pressure to explore their own comparative advantage. Since divestiture, the attitude shift of both AT&T and the regional operating companies has been nothing less than phenomenal. The telephone franchise, once perceived as a protective license, is now viewed at least by some as an impediment to emerging opportunities. It is true that not all carriers manifest this change. But there is sufficient pluralism among telephone companies to suggest that some carriers are inexorably moving away from the sanctuary of due process.

The Long Run

First, the U.S. economy is in the midst of an ongoing technological explosion. It is a cliché to observe that the computer and the communications industries have been on a collision course for at least two decades. The reality is that several systems are intersecting simultaneously—fiberoptics, solid-state devices, digital microwave, satellite relay, optical memory, and so on. There appears to be no damper on the productivity growth of information technology (Figure 2).

Second, technology under the aegis of market competition alters the equation of supply, demand, price, and cost. Unprecedented productivity changes yield cost reductions that translate into lower unit prices, whether for integrated circuits, microprocessors, or computer memory. These products penetrate new markets and activate old ones.

Third, the diversity of technology permits the user to combine and blend various technologies on the basis of relative cost trade-offs. Newspaper articles, today, are transmitted by a combination of "smart" terminals, facsimile, fiberoptics, satellite relay, and broadcast techniques. Expanded technology invites and enlarges the range of user options.

Finally, technology knows few limits or boundaries—a pervasiveness that suggests that no one firm, industry, sector, indeed nation, possesses exclusivity in the state of the art. In the Far East, North America, and Europe, the diffusion of knowledge changes one's notions about a technological monopoly.

Information Infrastructure. Technology is the driving force in terminals, networks, and services—an information infrastructure. It is true that the

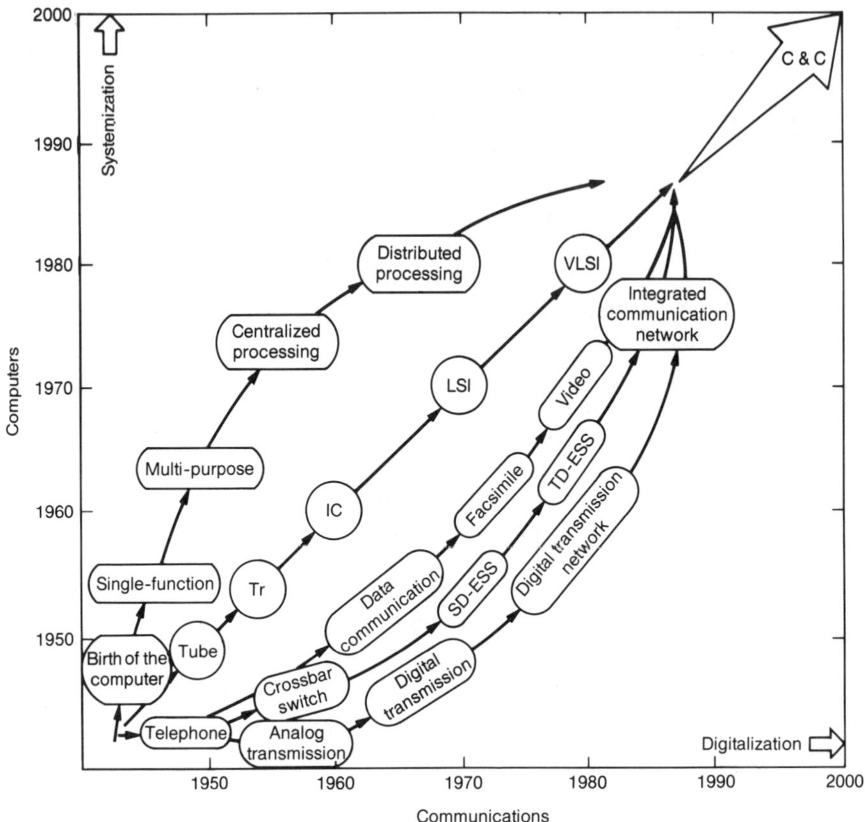

FIGURE 2. Technological confluence. *Source:* K. Kobayashi, "Telecommunications and Computers: An Inevitable Marriage," *Telephony* (Jan. 28, 1980).

U.S. investment in our present telephone system exceeds $200 billion. Nevertheless, the proliferation of work stations, PBXs, personal computers, and satellite dishes makes the word *terminal* a generic term, which means a device that receives, stores, and transmits information. According to this definition, a point-of-sales device, an ATM, or a gas pump qualifies as an information terminal. As microprocessors, fiber optics and satellites information relays, "intelligent" buildings may qualify as terminals, and might include shopping centers, science parks, university libraries, or satellite teleports.

Networks. A second component—voice, analog, or digital networks—is spreading within and between buildings, and among structures, regions, and nations. Networks may utilize fiberoptic cable, copper wire, coaxial cable, broad-band techniques, satellites, microwave systems, digital-termination systems, satellite master antenna systems, or cellular radio. And they may include a variety of switching techniques and protocols.

Although voice and telex still predominate in many nations, data, video, facsimile, and graphics transmission are increasingly being used in manufacturing, retailing, banking, schools, and offices. Their functions include computer-aided design, electronic funds-transfer, hotel-reservation systems, electronic mail, word processing, and the electronic newspaper. The potential of these new applications has yet to be exhausted.

Market Boundaries. Finally, a technological infrastructure erodes one's notion of market demarcations. Distinctions among firms, industries, customers, and suppliers, as well geographical boundaries are rapidly eroding. In fact, the *network* is emerging as a corporate strategy.[38]

Industry boundary lines are softening and overlapping; this is evident from recent corporate moves. The Ford Motor Company recently acquired an interest in a satellite reseller of voice and data services to 1,500 firms throughout the country.[39] General Motors recently acquired electronic data systems, and EDS is selling communication services to 20,000 customer on-line terminals.[40] McDonnell Douglas acquired a value-added carrier, and the company is heavily engaged in data processing via its McAuto subsidiary.[41] Boeing Computer Services won an $18 million award from the State of Pennsylvania, to install and operate a nationwide telephone network, and has submitted a proposal to NASA for integrating digital networks for voice, data, and facsimile.[42] Even Toyota Motor Car Company has formed a joint venture with Japan's national highway commission to construct a fiberoptics network.[43] Information is perceived by some firms as an alternative to the physical movement of people and goods.

Moreover, industry boundary lines are intersecting. The term *banking*, for example, may now be a misnomer, and the term *financial services* may be more appropriate, because now Sears Roebuck, Merrill Lynch, Prudential Bache, Household Finance, and General Motors all offer financial services. If these firms offer financial services today, can IBM and AT&T be far behind?

Not only are firm and industry demarcations no longer static; now the relationship between customers, firms, and suppliers is also fluid. A move by the electric power industry to incorporate fiberoptics into transmission lines suggests that a customer today may evolve into a rival tomorrow. Federal Express is employing satellites to diversify into electronic mail. Videoconferencing by the hotel industry indicates that there is rivalry not only within the telephone industry but with airlines as well. Both Kodak and Sears offer telephone service to the public.[44] And who dares to sort out the distinctions between publishing, radio broadcasting, the print media, television, and cable TV?

Given the pervasiveness of satellite relays and the information infrastructure, another area of market erosion is that of geography, because a terminal confers local, regional, and national coverage of, and access to, information. It is one thing to witness national distribution of newspapers, such as *USA Today, The Wall Street Journal* and *The New York Times* but global electronics now makes possible newspaper access to Europe and the Far East. Geographic pockets are no longer isolated. Technology feeds on an information infrastructure of terminals, networks, and services; there is literally no place to hide.

We are moving toward an economy with borderless markets. No one knows with certainty the precise content of this emerging economy, yet, several traits are visible. For one thing, the number of players is multiplying. As entry into the market gains momentum—as firm, industry, and geographic artifacts erode—competition, by definition, multiplies. This information environment obviously places a premium upon corporate flexibility and responsiveness. In 1977, a video-cassette recorder (VCR) priced at $1,300 was regarded as remotely competitive with an optical disc. In 1984, RCA had a $200 million tax write-off as the price of its VCR plunged to $300.[45] One can expect to see more of such substitutes in the years ahead.

Second, innovation is critical to corporate strategy. AT&T is essentially making the transition from an engineering to a market-oriented company. Corporations will also be forced to adapt to shorter product life cycles and faster obsolescence, and therefore must learn how to manage change.

Third, as decision making is reassigned to individuals in the corporate trenches, corporate organizations become flattened. IBM has formed 18 separate business units, which must acquire the traits of the small, start-up firm. And many firms acknowledge that they can no longer integrate blindly into manufacturing, research, marketing, and distribution. Make/buy decisions invite greater scrutiny than in the past.

As technology assaults market boundaries, it is evident that no one firm, and no one industry, possesses total control of expertise, talent, or resources. The joint venture in terminals, networks, and services is surfacing as a corporate strategy both in the U.S. and abroad. Having said this, there is no guarantee that corporate alliances provide the optimal solution to managing innovation in an environment of global rivalry.

Finally, as an ongoing endeavor, corporations are attempting to translate ideas into products and products into services. In a borderless economy, both the entrepreneur and the venture capitalist possess unique and critical skills in the struggle for corporate survival. Indeed, intrapreneurship is providing a challenge to firms who must address the reality of an information economy.

What are the implications of technological change? First, information is not merely an end but a means for a firm to perceive and seize new opportunities and new markets, and to satisfy new needs.Information is vital to corporate survival; it is critical to an economy's viability.

Second, an information infrastructure is prompting a massive redefinition of major institutions in the U.S. What is the telephone company? What is a bank? What is a hotel? What is a manufacturer? What is a newspaper? What is an insurance company? Indeed, higher education is beginning to reassess the "marketing" of its own product as private companies, via satellite-relay, offer master's degrees in computer sciences.

Finally, the U.S. is beginning to reasses the role of basic economic incentives. What drives a company? What generates income? What stimulates employment? How can U.S. firms acquit themselves well in a world of global rivalry, where the ingredients of innovation and creativity are critical and essential factors? These questions are timeless, for they indicate a search for productivity, efficiency, and employment. Whatever the answer, economic incentives remain on the policy agenda not merely in theU.S., but in the Far East and in Western Europe.

Conclusion

At least two forces are at work in an information economy. With the genie out of the bottle, an infrastructure alters boundaries, changes our business environment, and places a premium upon innovation and entrepreneurship. Technology defines choices, enhances productivity, fosters jobs, generates services, and provides investment opportunity. Technology is the driving force behind corporate entry and market deconcentration. Technology breeds diversity; it focuses on individual creativity; it is the essence of the term *enterprise*.

Against this force are institutions that resurrect boundaries, inhibit entry, curtail choice, and throttle innovation. Primary among such institutions is state regulation. State public utilities commissions, which neither perceive nor acknowledge the imperatives of an information economy, have opposed virtually every attempt in the last twenty years to introduce diversity, change, and pluralism into U.S. telecommunications (Table 1). As electronics penetrates the office, the university, the factory, the hotel, and the bank, voice, data, video, and teleconferencing services are expanding. Yet state commissions view "smart" or "intelligent" buildings as a threat to universal telephone service. In some jurisdictions, "smart" buildings face the possibility of hostile public regulation. In the meantime, "intelligent" buildings are being erected in Toronto, Singapore, Hong Kong, London, and Japan.[46] As technology nibbles at geographic boundary lines, state public utility commissions are attempting to replicate a telecommunication world of total discretion and control.

The judicial system is another institution that is resurrecting boundary lines. The courts have ruled that the Bell operating companies enjoy a natural monopoly. Presumably, Bell regional companies must be committed to basic telephone service. Separate subsidiaries are permitted to exist, but they must limit themselves to 10 percent of the gross revenues of a carrier's assets; furthermore, diversification plans must be cleared by the Department of Justice.[47] In a subtle sense, the Department of Justice is being converted into

Table 1: Regulatory Policy—National Association of Regulatory Utility Commissioners

Issue	*Position*	*Reason*
Carterfone	Opposition	Jurisdiction Preempted
Equipment Certification	Opposition	Jurisdiction Preempted
MCI	Opposition	Jurisdiction Preempted
Specialized Carrier	Opposition	Jurisdiction Preempted
Value-Added Carrier	Opposition	Jurisdiction Preempted
Line Sharing	Opposition	Jurisdiction Preempted
Cellular Radio	Opposition	Jurisdiction Preempted
Multipoint Distribution System	Opposition	Jurisdiction Preempted
Xerox's X-10	Opposition	Jurisdiction Preempted
Private Radio Interconnection	Opposition	Jurisdiction Preempted
Deregulation of Dominant Carriers	Opposition	Jurisdiction Preempted
One-Way Paging	Opposition	Jurisdiction Preempted
Competitive Equipment Procurement	Silent	Unstated

Source: M. R. Irwin, *Telecommunications America: Markets Without Boundaries* (Westport, Conn.: Greenwood Press, 1984).

a public utility regulatory commission, sanctioning and approving the non-regulated diversification efforts of regional Bell companies.

Finally, the Department of Defense, though silent on issues of telecommunication efficiency, productivity, and innovation, had fought the breakup of the Bell System, and has opposed competitive bidding on telephone equipment. In the name of national security, Defense opts for monopoly over competition. And now the Pentagon is classifying robots, computer software, heart pacemakers, fiberoptics, MacIntosh computers, computer-aided design, and telephone switchboards as products subject to military oversight.[48] Firms that produce these products must seek export clearance from the Pentagon. Even Japanese robots and British telephone-exchange sales are under Pentagon scrutiny, and AT&T must request Department of Defense approval to build a semiconductor factory in Spain.[49] Licensing by the Pentagon erects market boundary lines as the U.S. moves toward knowledge-intensive products and services.

Because of this regulatory surveillance, the cost of lost opportunities is borne disproportionately by the small firm. This cost concentrates rather than diversifies the reach of venture capital, and diminishes the critical role of the entrepreneur. By employing due process of the law as a device to regulate telecommunication products, the Department of Defense is emerging as an international NARUC.

What will be the outcome of the dual forces of decentralization and centralization? Will information technology outpace government control? Will public policy "housebreak" technology? Today, no one knows the algebraic sum of these forces. Perhaps the answer depends on whether one is able to discern the difference between the short and the long run. Or perhaps the answer turns on whether one is an optimist or a pessimist.

NOTES

1. Robert Cono, *A Streak of Luck* (New York: Simon & Schuster, 1978), pp. 82–83.

2. Annette Frey, "The Public Must Be Served," Part No. 59, *Bell Telephone Magazine* (March–June 1975) p. 5.

3. *United States v. Western Electric Co.,* Civil Action No. 17-49 (DNJ 1949).

4. U.S. Congress, House, *Consent Decree Program of the Department of Justice,* Hearings Before the Antitrust Subcommittee (Subcommittee No. 5) Committee on the Judiciary, 85th Cong., 2nd sess., 1958, Part 2, Vol. 1, American Telephone and Telegraph, p. 38.

5. Alvin Von Auw, *Heritage and Destiny* (New York: Praeger, 1983) p. 163.

6. *Hush-a-phone Corporation v. American Telephone and Telegraph Co.,* 238 F 2d 266 (D.C. cir-1956).

7. S. Mathison and P. Walker, *Computers and Telecommunications: Issues in Public Policy* (Englewood Cliffs, N.J.: Prentice-Hall, 1970), p. 48.

8. Von Auw, op. cit., p. 141.

9. FCC, In the Matter of AT&T, The Associated Bell System Companies, Charges for Interstate Telephone Service, AT&T Transmittal Nos. 10989, 11027, 11657, Docket No. 19129 (Phase II) *Final Decision and Order,* March 1977. (Hereafter cited as FCC 19129, *Final Decision.*)

10. *Litton Systems, Inc. et al. v. American Telephone and Telegraph, Inc. et al.* Civil Action No. 1323-26, 1344 U.S. Ct. of Appeals, 2nd, February 3, 1983.

11. Von Auw, op. cit., p. 000.

12. FCC 19129, *Final Decision,* op. cit. Appendix.

13. "Final Shape of Big AT&T Settlement," *U.S. News and World Report* (Aug. 30, 1982), p. 36.

14. EFT in the United States, *The Final Report of the National Commission on Electronic Funds-Transfer,* October 28, 1977, Washington, D.C., p. 166; Also, Competition Among Vendors, Request for Comment, 1977, p. 28.

15. E. Holmes, "FCC Defines 'DP' as Difference Between Smart, Dumb Terminals," *Computerworld* (Feb. 28, 1977), p. 6; Also, "AT&T Dataspeed 40 Tariff Stayed," *Electronic News* (Feb. 2, 1976), p. 8.

16. *IBM v. FCC,* No. 77-4405, Second Circuit, January 4, 1977.

17. M. Nichols, "Bell, Tex PUC Did Irreparable Harm," *Management Information Systems News* (June 10, 1981), p. 6.

18. Von Auw, op. cit., p. 165.

19. M. Langley, "AT&T Breakup Brings Calls for Staff Cuts as Thousands are Asked to Retire Early," *The Wall Street Journal,* Nov. 3, 1983, p. 4.

20. Claudia Ricci, "Once Secure Phone Union Faces a Loss of Power from AT&T Split," *The Wall Street Journal,* March 12, 1984, p. 31.

21. Dale Hatfield, "Local Distribution—The Next Frontier," Ninth Annual Telecommunications Policy Research Conference, Annapolis, Md., April 29, 1981.

22. John E. Madrid, "Divestiture Revolution Means Progress Tomorrow," *Management Information Systems Week* (May 9, 1984), p. 29. Also, "The End of the Dinosaurs," *Teleconnect* (June, 1984), p. 88.

23. C. Ricci, "AT&T Asks to Use Faster Depreciation for Certain Assets," *The Wall Street Journal,* May 15, 1984, p. 10.

24. J. McConnaughey and M. R. Irwin, "Rate-Base Evaluation and Vertical Ingetration: Shifting Standards in Telephone Regulation," *Indiana Law Review* **2:**185 (1978–79).

25. FCC 19129, *Final Decision,* op. cit.

26. U.S. International Trade Commission, *"Changes in the U.S. Telecommunications Industry and the Impact of U.S. Telecommunication Trade,"* Report to the Committee on Finance, U.S. Senate, Investigation No. 332-172, Section 332 of the Tariff Act of 1930, June 1984, p. X.

27. Mark Frankel, "Foreign Manufacturers Stake 19% of CPE," *Management Information Systems Week* (June 27, 1984). Also, E. E. Mier, "A Big Bonanza in Little Switches," *Data Communications* (June, 1984), p. 68, and C. H. Farnsworth, "Big Telecommunications Trade Gap Seen," *The New York Times,* June 26, 1984, p. 17.

28. Von Auw, op. cit., p. 183.

29. "Deregulation Drags Bell Labs Out of Its Ivory Tower," *Business Week* (Dec. 3, 1984), p. 116. Also, Ian M. Ross, "AT&T Bell Laboratories: A Proven Resource, a New Mission," *Signal* (June 1984), p. 36.

30. "Ma Bell's Heirs Are Not Apparent," *Business Week* (March 21, 1984), p. 264.

31. "The Business of America in Small Business," *Financial Digest,* The Manufacturers Hanover Digest **19:**1 (May, 14, 1984).

32. Ibid., p. 2; See also, David Birch, "Who Creates Jobs," *The Public Interest,* **3:**65 (Fall 1981).

33. FCC, Docket 83-1147, In the Matter of Long-Run Regulation of AT&T's Basic Domestic Interstate Services, *Comments of American Telephone and Telegraph,* April 2, 1984, Appendix F, p. 1.

34. E. E. Mier, "Equal Access: The Long and the Short of It," *Data Communications* (July 1984), p. 71.

35. U.S. Congress, Joint Hearings, *The Universal Telephone Service Preservation Act of 1983,* Hearings Before the Committee on Commerce, Science and Transportation (Senate); Committee on Energy and Commerce (House); 98th Cong., 1st sess., 1983; Testimony of O. J. Wade, President of Illinois Bell Telephone Company, p. 206.

36. May Frankel, "Foreign Manufacturers Stake 19% of CPE," *Management Information Systems Week* (June 27, 1984), p. 23.

37. E. Meadows, "Japan Runs Into America, Inc." *Fortune* (March 22, 1982), p. 57.

38. Walter Wriston, "The Five I's will Maintain Citicorp's Industry Domination and Impact," *American Banker* (April 9, 1984), p. 31.

39. "Tracking the Transportation Transition to Telecom," *Telecom Times and Trends,* Frank Communications Group (May 1984), p. 4.

40. Ibid., p. 9.

41. "The McDonnell Douglas 'Grand Plan' to Become a Computer Giant," *Business Week* (May 21, 1984), p. 104.

42. *Telecom Times and Trends,* op. cit. p. 4; Also, Sears is diversifying into telecommunications. See J. Dix, "Sears' Ambitious Network Plans Won't Carry into Office," *Computerworld* (Nov. 12, 1984), p. 5.

43. "Toyota Motor May Join Telecommunications Project," *Financial Times* (July 12, 1984), p. 25.

44. "Kodak Will Enter Communication Field," *Boston Globe,* Nov. 21, 1984, p. 24.

45. B. Abrams, "CBS Will End its production of Video Disks," *The Wall Street Journal,* July 10, 1984, p. 6.

46. "Satellite Seen Linking Japanese Telecommunication Cities to U.S.," *The Asian Wall Street Journal,* Jan. 2, 1984, p. 15.

47. *U.S. v. AT&T,* op. cit., civ. No. 82-0192, Opinion, Judge H. Greene, July 26, 1984, p. 52.

48. Guy De Jonqueres and D. Buchan, "Ministers Split Over Bulgarian Phones Deal," *Financial Times* (March 24, 1984), p. 10.

49. M. Frankel, "Nynex Asks Justice Department Approval on Overseas Sales, Service Ventures," *Management Information Systems Week,* (Sept. 19, 1984), p. 51; Also, R. E. Taylor, "Ameritech and Nynex Bids to Broaden Telephone Services Are Opposed by U.S.," *The Wall Street Journal,* Aug. 29, 1984, p. 6.

SUGGESTED READING

Brock, Gerald W. *The Telecommunications Industry: The Dynamics of Market Structure.* Cambridge, Mass.: Harvard University Press, 1981.

Brooks, John. *Telephone: The First Hundred Years.* New York: Harper & Row, Pub., 1975.

Evans, David S. *Breaking up Bell: Essays on Industrial Organization and Regulation.* Amsterdam: North-Holland, 1983.

Irwin, Manley R. *Telecommunications America: Markets Without Boundaries.* Westport, Conn.: Greenwood Press, 1984.

Shooshan, Harry M., III (ed.) *Disconnecting Bell: The Impact of the AT&T Divestiture.* New York: Pergamon Press, 1984.

9

The "Banking" Industry

Arnold A. Heggestad
William G. Shepherd

I. INTRODUCTION

The banking industry, or more precisely, the depository financial services industry, plays a critical role in the American economy. It has a pervasive influence because virtually every other sector of the economy must rely on its services. Households, government units, and business firms hold deposit balances in these institutions, as either demand deposits or time and savings deposits. Demand deposits constitute the primary component of the money supply of the economy because they may be transferred at par to any other bank in the system. Without the demand-deposit payments system, the economy could not function. The demand and savings deposits that are entrusted to financial institutions are in turn lent to others in the economy. They serve as the primary sources of credit for investment by households, government, and business.

The importance of these services to the economy has led to extensive regulation of the industry. The major thrust of regulation has been to promote industry "soundness." The safety of deposits is guaranteed through government-provided deposit insurance. Soundness is also provided by comprehensive competition and financial regulations that limit the risk exposure of the industry. There are still other regulations, those that are intended to direct credit to certain sectors of society, and which seek to protect borrowers from exploitation and unfair practices. Finally, competition is controlled through restrictions on geographic charters and expansion.

In recent years, the industry has been going through a major transition. Long-standing limits on pricing, on asset management, and on geographic locations are being reduced or eliminated. Deregulation has changed the products that financial intermediaries may legally offer and has substantially increased the degree of competition in banking markets. Firms are now able to compete for deposits, with virtually no price limitations.[1] They are correspondingly free to offer a wide range of new products. Their geographic limitations have also been lifted, to some degree.

Deregulation has permitted much new entry as major quasi-banks have begun to offer deposit and loan services in direct competition with the depository institutions. These firms have experienced significant growth because they are not limited by the regulations placed on depository institutions.

Two key public policy issues now face the depository financial services industry. First, can the industry be deregulated further without leading to an increase in the overall concentration of financial resources, with adverse economic and political consequences? Second, would further deregulation expose the industry to too much risk?

This chapter addresses these broad issues. We first describe the basic nature of the (broadly defined) financial services industry. Second, we discuss the major elements of the industry, with particular emphasis on the commercial banking industry. Next, we evaluate performance in the industry. Finally, we evaluate, for their possible implications on performance, recent and prospective changes in public policy.

We will see that the rapid change and rising uncertainty facing the industry need to be brought under control. Congress and regulatory agencies need to decide on the appropriate structure of the industry, as well as the degree of public control that is necessary. Our emphasis will be on commercial banking, because of its size and importance to all sectors of the economy. However, the conclusions about commercial banks will be relevant for other types of depository institutions as well.

Financial Services Sector

Financial markets play a critical role in the functioning of the economy. Every element of society needs to have access to the payments mechanism in order to conduct its economic activity. In addition, most people need to have access to financial markets so that they can separate the timing of their spending decisions from the timing of their income.[2] This need arises because individuals and businesses seldom receive their income at a rate that coincides with their demand for services.

Early in their adult life, individuals tend to receive less income than they require for their desired consumption and for their required investment in education and housing. On the other hand, as they approach retirement, they typically have excess income relative to desired consumption. Consequently, younger people need to be able to borrow funds against future income in order to finance current expenditures. Older individuals need the opportunity to save for retirement (and other goals) at low risk, and to receive a reasonable compensation for their funds. Thus, most individuals need access to financial markets, as both borrowers and lenders, at different times in their lives.

Business firms face the same problem. They often are required to raise funds for investment prior to generating revenue from selling their goods and services. The farmer must be able to purchase seed and fertilizer. The manufacturing firm must invest in plant, equipment, and inventory of raw materials and finished goods before it can begin to sell its product. Consequently, the business firm must rely on financial markets as a source of short- and long-term funding. And at times it will have excess funds, and will desire to earn a competitive return on these funds.

State and local governments also must rely on financial markets. They are often required to provide basic public services prior to receiving tax revenues. They borrow against future tax revenues. Conversely, they will on occasion have excess funds, as revenues exceed current expenditures.

Individuals, business, and government must rely on financial markets to meet these basic credit needs as well as transaction balances. Because their requirements are very heterogeneous, there are many different types of financial instruments available, which are tailored to meet specific requirements. They vary in such critical parameters as maturity, risk, return, liquidity, and size.

The primary supplier of financial products to all but the largest corporations are *financial intermediaries*. Financial intermediaries simultaneously raise funds in credit markets and use the proceeds to advance credit to borrowers.

Figure 1 illustrates the process by which borrowers and savers may interact in the financial markets. Each relationship depicts cash flowing from a lender to the borrower, and some form of financial asset flowing from the borrower to the lender. Typical financial assets include loan agreements, bonds, stocks, and commercial paper. Cash flows to the right, in the diagram. Financial assets flow to the left.

Borrowers and lenders may deal directly with each other. Private placement of loans or stock and commercial paper when large companies borrow and lend to each other, are examples of these types of transactions. However, because of the specialized nature of the needs of borrowers and lenders, search costs—to match borrowers and lenders with comparable needs—are very high. Specialized financial intermediaries have been developed to serve these markets.[3]

Financial intermediaries create new financial products to fulfill the needs of borrowers and lenders. When their financial assets are sold in the market, they typically have more liquidity and less risk than the underlying or supporting assets. A saver no longer needs to find a borrower with the exact risk, maturity, and liquidity characteristics he or she needs. Instead, the saver purchases a financial asset at an intermediary, i.e., he or she makes a deposit. In turn, the financial intermediary pools the funds of many savers and lends money (provides capital) to borrowers.

Financial intermediaries may be divided into two major categories. Depository institutions are characterized by the provision of government insurance on all deposits under $100,000. In turn, they are subject to substantial regulation of their financial activities and their competitive environment. The major forms of depository institutions include commercial banks, savings banks, savings and loan associations, and credit unions.

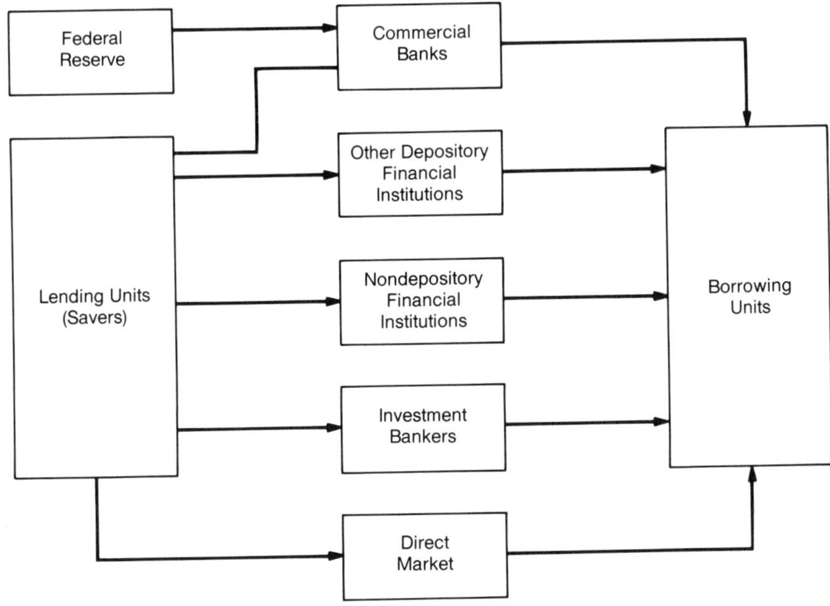

FIGURE 1. Financial markets flows of funds.

Nondepository financial intermediaries, including pension funds, insurance companies, and mutual funds, offer competing products but do not have government-protected deposits as a source of funds. Although this places them at a disadvantage, it is at least partially offset by the lack of regulations on other activities, which are imposed on depository financial institutions.

Investment bankers also play an important role in financial markets. They create a direct market for securities for business and government units. An organization wishing to raise funds may issue financial instruments, such as bonds or stock. The investment banker will purchase the instruments or guarantee a price. In turn, the investment banker will sell these instruments to investors. As an intermediary, investment bankers take the initial risk in obtaining funds. They do not, however, hold the securities on their own account or for depositors. Their profit is derived from the differential between the price they pay for the securities and the price they receive on the open market when they sell to the final investors.

The share of total financial activity held by nondeposit institutions has been growing in the past decade, because these companies have begun to offer deposit type services, in direct competition with commercial banks. As can be seen in Table 1, in a few years, the money market funds grew from virtually nothing to a size as large as the credit-union industry.[4] Their current size exceeds $200 billion.

In this chapter, our discussion will stress depository institutions, because public policy issues are focused on these firms. However, we will not ignore

Table 1: Private Financial Institution Ownership of Assets (in billions of dollars)

Institution	1946		1955		1965		1975		1979		Change Market Share 1946–79
	$	%	$	%	$	%	$	%	$	%	%
Savings & Loan Assn's	10.20	4.4	37.66	8.8	129.58	13.9	338.23	16.1	579.1	17.3	+12.9
Mutual Savings Banks	18.66	8.0	31.69	7.4	59.11	6.4	122.25	5.8	165.0	4.9	− 3.1
Credit Unions	.44	0.2	2.91	0.7	11.04	1.2	36.89	1.8	62.3	1.9	+ 1.7
Life Insurance Co.'s	47.46	20.3	87.85	20.5	154.20	16.6	279.67	13.3	420.5	12.6	− 7.7
Private Pension Funds	3.57	1.5	18.34	4.3	73.65	7.9	146.82	7.0	236.8	7.1	+ 5.6
State and Local Govt. Retirement Funds	2.87	1.2	10.83	2.5	34.08	3.7	104.80	5.0	178.9	5.3	+ 4.1
Other Insurance Co.'s	7.14	3.0	19.44	4.5	36.53	3.9	77.26	3.7	156.7	4.7	+ 1.7
Finance Co.'s	4.90	2.1	18.30	4.3	44.65	4.8	97.70	4.6	168.9	5.0	+ 2.9
Open-End Investment Co.'s	1.30	0.6	7.84	1.8	35.22	3.8	42.18	2.0	46.2	1.4	+ 0.8
Security Brokers & Dealers	3.42	1.5	5.91	1.4	10.34	1.1	18.43	0.9	30.6	0.9	− 0.6
REIT's	—	—	—	—	—	—	7.30	0.3	7.0	0.2	+ 0.2
Money Market Funds	—	—	—	—	—	—	3.70	0.2	45.2	1.3	+ 1.3
Total Private Nonbank Financial Institutions	99.97	42.7	240.77	56.2	588.40	63.3	1275.23	60.7	2079.2	62.6	+19.9
Commercial Banking*	134.20	57.3	187.44	43.8	340.71	36.7	825.91	39.3	1252.7	37.4	−19.9
Total Private Financial Institutions	$234.17		428.21		929.11		2101.14		3349.9		–

*U.S. bank holding company affiliate asset data are not reflected in U.S. commercial banking asset figures but are included in various financial sectors.
Source: Federal Reserve Flow of Funds Accounts, 1946–75, Board of Governors of the Federal Reserve System (Washington, D.C., Dec. 1976, Dec. 1979, and Feb. 1980). Totals may not add to 100% because of rounding. Adapted from Harold C. Nathan, "Nonbank Organizations and the McFadden Act," *Journal of Bank Research,* Vol. 11, No. 2 (Summer 1980).

the nondepository institutions, because their rapid growth has brought about much of the pressure for deregulation in recent years. Further, their continued growth and prosperity raises the critical issue facing the financial services industry: How much can the industry be deregulated to bring about the benefits of the free market, without risking financial chaos? If we do not deregulate depository institutions, can they survive under the new competition pressures?

Depository Institutions

The depository institutions differ primarily in the types of financial products they offer. Table 2 shows the products offered by commercial banks and the change in the nature of these products over time, as evidenced in the sources of funds and in their investment portfolios. Tables 3 and 4 show the products of the other major type of depository financial intermediary—savings banks and savings and loan associations.

The commercial bank may be thought of as a firm that produces various forms of credit. In its production process, its inputs are the funds entrusted to it by its depositors, as well as labor and equipment. However, for now we will focus on one financial input—deposits.

The commercial bank offers to the retail and wholesale markets a broad array of deposit services in order to obtain funds. Retail deposits include

Table 2: Assets and Liabilities of All U.S. Commercial Banks, 1950–1983

	(In Billions of Dollars)			
Assets	*1950*	*1960*	*1970*	*1983*
Cash Assets	$ 40.4	$ 52.2	$ 94.0	$ 341.8
Securities				
U.S. Government	62.3	61.1	59.3	244.6
State and Local Government	8.2	17.6	67.9	158.4
Federal Funds Sold	0.0	0.0	16.3	93.5
Loans (Total)	53.2	120.5	300.4	1,299.7
Commercial and Industrial	22.0	43.4	113.4	574.7
Real Estate	13.7	28.8	73.3	336.1
Individuals	10.2	26.5	66.3	218.1
Other	7.3	21.8	47.4	220.8
Other Assets	6.4	9.3	43.6	204.1
Total Assets	170.5	260.7	581.5	2,342.1
Liabilities and Equity				
Deposits	156.1	230.5	485.5	1,534.1
Demand	118.8	156.8	249.0	389.5
Time and Savings	37.3	73.7	236.5	1,144.6
Other Liabilities	2.7	9.1	52.8	667.5
Capital	11.7	21.1	43.2	140.5
Total Liabilities and Equity	170.5	260.7	581.5	2,342.1

Source: Board of Governors of the Federal Reserve System, *Federal Reserve Bulletin* (Washington, D.C., selected issues).

Table 3: Assets and Liabilities in Mutual Savings Banks, December 31, 1982 (in Millions of Dollars)

Assets	
Cash	$ 6,920
U.S. Government Obligations	9,685
State and Local Obligations	2,500
Mortgage Loans and Securities	108,633
Corporate Bonds and Stock	12,105
Other Loans	16,876
Other Assets	7,486
Total Assets	$174,204
Liabilities and Capital	
Savings Deposits	46,969
Time Deposits	105,766
Other Deposits	2,490
Borrowings	7,159
Other Liabilities	2,583
Total General Reserve Accounts	9,238
Total Liabilities and Capital	$174,204

Source: Annual Report of the President, National Association of Mutual Savings Banks, May 1983, p. 5.

Table 4: Assets and Liabilities of Savings and Loan Associations, December 31, 1982 (in Millions of Dollars)

Assets		
Mortgage Loans Outstanding		$482,234
Cash and Other Liquid Investments		70,179
Insured Mortgages and Mortgage-Backed Securities		63,030
Mobile Home and Home Improvement Loans		8,818
Other Loans		11,726
Other Investments		14,588
All Other Assets		55,470
Total Assets		$706,045
Liabilities and Capital		
Savings Deposits		$566,189
Earning Regular Rate or Below	$ 95,912	
Earning in Excess of Regular Rate	470,277	
Federal Home Loan Bank Advances		63,861
Other Borrowed Money		34,118
Other Liabilities		15,720
Net Worth		26,157
Total Liabilities and Capital		$706,045

Source: 1983 Savings and Loan Source Book, United States League of Savings Associations, p. 41.

demand deposits, savings deposits, time deposits, money market accounts, and NOW accounts. Each product offers a different combination of services and returns. Because all deposits under $100,000 are fully insured by the FDIC, most of a commercial bank's liabilities have no risk of default.

The demand deposit provides transaction balances and access to the payments mechanism. Because of regulation, banks are not permitted to pay interest on these funds. Competition for demand deposits consists of offering services and convenience to depositors. The interest payments are indirect. The availability of these funds to commercial banks has been sharply curtailed. In 1950, 70 percent of all funds available for commercial banks came from demand-deposit balances. By 1983, the demand-deposit share had fallen to 17 percent. Whereas the industry's assets grew at an annual rate of 12.1 percent since 1951, its demand deposits grow by only 5.3 percent. Therefore, it was forced to seek other sources of funds to finance its growth.

Passbook savings funds require no minimum balance and may be withdrawn on demand. Regulation *Q* limits the rate that may be paid on these accounts to very low levels. The ability of banks to keep low-cost passbook savings accounts has also been sharply curtailed as bank customers have chosen forms of higher-return savings.

Time deposits provide higher returns but require larger minimum balances and a definite time commitment by the depositor. Finally, the money market deposit account, which has become very popular, pays competitive rates for large-balance accounts. Its rates are generally tied to an index of money market rates on instruments such as Treasury Bills.

The wide range of deposit accounts is a relatively new phenomenon. As recently as 1978, commercial banks were limited to demand deposits and passbook savings accounts for all deposits under $100,000. The rate of deregulation of these deposits is the most important trend in the industry, and has created new opportunities and risks. For a description of these changes, see Table 5. After 1986, the only account that will still have limitations on rates will be the demand deposit of commercial firms.

In addition to retail deposit markets, commercial banks have been forced to raise funds in the wholesale financial markets. They borrow in the money markets by issuing large, negotiable certificates of deposit. These accounts are not insured for amounts exceeding $100,000, but they have no limit on interest and may be sold in secondary markets. Commercial banks also rely on the Federal funds market, the Eurodollar market, and the commercial paper market. Commercial banks have been forced to rely extensively on nondeposit sources of funds to finance their growth. In 1983, over 28 percent of their funds came from nondeposit sources. This compares with under 2 percent in 1950.

The primary product of the commercial bank is its loan portfolio. Deposits serve as an input to produce loans. Other assets are held to complement the loan portfolio, either by providing liquidity or diversification to the entire portfolio. Approximately 55 percent of commercial bank funds are lent to

Table 5: Major Actions to Deregulate Deposits Since 1978

Instrument	*Description of instrument and action*	*Effective Date*
Money market certificates (MMCs)	Nonnegotiable time deposits, with minimum denominations of $10,000 (reduced in Jan. 1983 to $2,500) and original maturities of exactly 26 weeks; ceiling rate of interest on new MMCs determined by the recently issued 6-month Treasury bill.	June 1978
Small-saver certificates (SSCs)	SSCs were 4-year or longer variable-ceiling accounts (with ceilings based on the Treasury coupon yield), having no minimum-denomination requirements. Since Oct. 1985, ceilings on all time deposits with maturities of 32 days or longer have been removed.	July 1979
Nationwide NOW accounts*	Interest-bearing checking accounts. Rates on all NOW accounts were subject to a fixed-rate ceiling.	December 1980
Ceiling-free time deposits	Negotiable or nonnegotiable time deposits with original maturities of 3-½ years or more were offered between May 1, 1982 and March 31, 1983; 2-½ year and longer time deposits were offered from April 1, 1983 to Sept. 30, 1983.	May 1982
7–31-day money market certificates	Nonnegotiable time deposits that required a minimum balance of $20,000 (reduced in Jan. 1983 to $2,500) and had an original maturity of at least 7 days but no more than 31 days. Before Jan. 1983, the ceiling rate was tied to the discount yield on the most recently issued 91-day Treasury bill, and thereafter it was removed.	September 1982
Money market deposit accounts	Deposits with a $2,500 initial and average balance requirement; no required minimum maturity; no restrictions on the amount of interest that may be paid unless the average balance falls below $2,500 (in which case the NOW account rate-ceiling applies); up to six transfer per month.	December 1982
Super NOW accounts	NOW accounts on which rate ceilings do not apply, provided a $2,500 minimum balance is met.	January 1983

Table 5: continued

Instrument	*Description of instrument and action*	*Effective Date*
Deregulated time deposits	Interest-rate ceilings and minimum-denomination requirements on all time deposits, with original maturities of 32 days or more, were removed (and rate ceilings on time deposits with 7–31 day maturities in denominations of $2,500 or more were lifted); such accounts can be issued in negotiable or nonnegotiable form.	October 1983

*NOW accounts were first authorized in 1974 for federal insured depositories in Massachusetts and New Hampshire. Authority to offer NOW accounts was extended to institutions in the rest of New England in 1976, New York in 1978, and New Jersey in 1979.

Source: T. D. Simpson and P. M. Parkinson, "Some Implications of Financial Innovations in the United States," *Staff Study*, Federal Reserve Board, September, 1984.

private borrowers, including individuals and small and large business firms. Business firms borrow to finance the purchase of fixed assets and to provide working capital; individuals borrow for many reasons, most often to purchase real estate or consumer durables. The most common consumer purchase funded by commercial banks is an automobile. Automobile-purchase credit constitutes over 30 percent of all consumer credit extended by commercial banks. Credit cards constitute an additional 20 percent.

There are significant variations in loan portfolios among commercial banks. Differences are related primarily to the demand for loans in the market area, and to the bank's strategic plans. Retail-oriented banks hold proportionally more consumer and mortgage loans. Wholesale-oriented banks concentrate more on commercial and industrial loans or on loans to other financial institutions. The remaining bank funds are kept in assets that complement the lending function, including cash to provide liquidity and government securities to provide secondary reserves and income.

The proportion of total loans to total assets has not changed significantly over time. However, the financial characteristics of loans have changed dramatically as a result of the changes in deposit sources and interest-rate volatility in the economy.[5] Virtually all commercial and industrial loans are now made at indexed interest rates. Loan rates are not fixed over the term of the loan. Rather, they are tied to an index that varies with money-market conditions. When interest rates increase, borrowers pay more, and when rates fall, borrowers pay less. Because the banks have a similar arrangement with depositors in short-term certificates of deposits, in money market accounts, and in their nondeposit sources of funds, they are able to use this type of loan to lock in a spread (or differential) between the borrowing and lending rate. If properly constructed, the spread will not change, irrespective of the level of interest rates. The bank can thus insulate itself from the risk of interest-rate fluctuations.

The risk of interest-rate fluctuations is borne by the borrower. If interest rates were to increase at a rate faster than the borrowers' income, there will be a higher probability of default. This has happened to several industries, including energy and agriculture. It has also happened to many foreign governments. In these cases, borrowers have been forced to default on loans, causing failures of financial institutions. Or the U.S. government and the World Bank must step in, and, with massive support, protect the banking sector.

A similar type of instrument has become very common in the mortgage markets. The fixed-rate 30-year mortgage, which was the standard for the past 40 years on residential property, has been replaced by adjustable rate mortgages of various types. Home owners, rather than the lending institutions now bear the risk of high interest rates. Of course, if interest rates fall, the borrower will have lower monthly payments. Just as in the case of variable-rate commercial loans, high-interest-rate periods have led to greater defaults.

Tables 3 and 4 present the balance sheets of savings and loan associations and savings banks. It can be seen that they differ significantly from commercial banks. However, the differential is narrowing. Savings institutions are increasingly developing portfolios very similar to bank portfolios, as their investment powers have been widened.

Savings banks and savings and loan associations have similar portfolios. Although they tend to differ in the states in which they operate, and in their primary regulatory authorities, the portfolios of both types of institutions are dominated by mortgage loans. The major source of their funds is consumer deposits.

The nature of savings institutions has changed dramatically in recent years. Their portfolio historically consisted of over 65 percent of total assets in fixed-rate mortgages. Since the mid-1970s deregulation and disintermediation shortened the maturity of their deposit base, which was used to fund the mortgages. They found themselves in the position of holding long-term fixed-rate assets with revenues that did not change over the interest-rate cycle. However, their liabilities were interest-sensitive. If the rate increased, their costs increased, and if rates fell, their costs fell.

The mismatch of long-term assets funded with short-term deposits creates vulnerability to interest-rate increases. The problem became evident in the late 1970s. As interest rates began to increase, savers began to withdraw their deposits from the savings and loan institutions (S&L) and looked for investments with higher yields. The S&Ls had little choice but to replace the funds by borrowing at money market rates, because they needed the funds to support their mortgage portfolios.[6] Alternatively, they developed deposits based on money market rates. As they substituted high-cost funds for low-cost deposits, the cost of input increased. However, their revenues did not increase correspondingly as holders of mortgages continued to pay the low rates negotiated at an earlier period. The net effect has been to place the industry in severe financial stress. In 1981, the return on assets for the industry was −.74. Losses at that rate would erode its capital base in a very short period of time. Regulatory agencies and the Congress have attempted to deal with this problem. One major approach has been to broaden the powers of S&Ls, so that they can offer loans with yields that are more sensitive to interest-rate changes, such as consumer and commercial loans. As this process has continued, the S&Ls have begun to compete directly with commercial banks.

The remaining type of depository institution is the credit union. Credit unions are chartered to raise funds by providing consumer savings deposits to their members. In turn, they make consumer loans to finance automobile purchases, home improvements, and other consumer purchases. Although deregulation has broadened their ability to offer a wider range of deposits and loans, their basic nature has not changed over the past decade. They generally play a less important role than the other depository institutions, because they are constrained by their cooperative form of organization, and by the requirement that their members must have a common bond.

Savings institutions are well on their way to competing directly with commercial banks. Both types of institutions must compete for the same deposits to fund their loans. The only way they will be able to offer competitive deposits will be if they earn comparable returns on their funds. That is, to be able to offer deposits of comparable return, liquidity, and maturity, their funds must be invested in similar assets. To generate these returns, the savings institutions will be forced to move increasingly into consumer and commercial lending. Federal and state legislation has been passed, giving them the option to offer virtually all products that commercial banks may offer. Indeed, in many states, they have considerably greater investment authority than banks. It remains to be seen if these changes will divert them from their original purpose—to provide funds to the housing sector.

The Regulatory Environment

Depository financial institutions are heavily regulated. Their industries are effectively defined by law and regulation. Banking and commerce is separated by law. Commercial banks cannot own nonfinancial firms, and nonfinancial firms cannot own commercial banks. They are limited in the extent to which they may branch within their state, and they are even more limited regarding the crossing of state lines. Their portfolios are restricted, to reduce risk. To prevent failures, regulators attempt to limit competition within the industry.

The commercial banking industry is subject to an extensive degree of regulation from several government agencies. The United States has a dual banking system—i.e. state banks and federal banks. A commercial bank may hold either a state or a Federal charter. If it is a state-chartered bank, it may also elect to stay out of the Federal Reserve System. These choices will

Table 6: Regulatory Structure, Commercial Banking Industry

Agency	*Regulatory Responsibilities*
Federal Reserve System	1. All state-chartered Federal Reserve member banks 2. All bank holding companies 3. Lender of last resort to all banks
Comptroller of Currency	1. All national banks
Federal Deposit Insurance Agency	1. Insures all banks 2. Regulates state nonmember banks
State Governments	1. All state nonmember banks

Source: Federal Reserve Bank of New York, *Depository Institutions and Their Regulators* (New York, Feb. 1984).

determine its primary regulators. The possible choices are illustrated in Table 6.

A state-chartered bank that belongs to the Federal Reserve is directly regulated by the state chartering agency and by the Federal Reserve System. In addition, if it has set up a bank holding company, the holding company is regulated by the Federal Reserve.[7] The Federal Reserve is the primary regulator of all bank holding companies. All banks must also meet the insurance requirements of the FDIC.

A state-chartered bank which does not belong to the Federal Reserve may evade regulation by the Federal Reserve unless it has a holding company. However, it then becomes directly regulated by the Federal Deposit Insurance agency, along with the state agency.

National banks avoid state control, but they come under the domain of the Comptroller of the Currency, and the Federal Reserve, the latter through their holding companies which are required to be members of the Federal Reserve.

The regulatory control of these various agencies is extensive. They set broad portfolio requirements for liquidity, diversification, and leverage. They periodically perform direct audits or examinations on the companies that are under their direct regulatory control. They regulate expansion activity, that is, branching or obtaining new charters. They also control merger activity. Applications for new branches, for charters, or for mergers must be approved by the appropriate regulatory agency. And they monitor compliance with consumer-protection laws.

Periodically, federal and state task forces have investigated the possibility of reorganizing the Federal regulatory agencies, making them a single entity, thereby reducing the wasteful overlap in the present system. The most recent investigation, that of the Bush Commission, will make recommendations to Congress in 1985. Proposed reorganization has been stymied by the industry and by the regulatory agencies. The industry prefers a system where it has some discretion regarding the appropriate regulatory agency. The agencies themselves, especially the state regulatory agencies, have served as a major force against any changes in the status quo.

Deregulation has become a major force in the industry. Virtually every regulation has been considered for revision or removal. However, the pendulum may be swinging the other way. Regulators and policy makers have become concerned that deregulation may have gone too far.

They have begun to ask what the proper role of commercial banks should be in the new financial environment. Are commercial banks unique in financial markets, as they have been considered for the past two hundred years, or are they simply another alternative provider of financial services, which should not have the regulatory attention they currently receive?

Perhaps the most thoughtful discussion of this question has been that of a senior Federal Reserve official, Gerald Corrigan, who currently serves as the President of the Federal Reserve Bank in New York. Corrigan argues that commercial banks provide three unique services, which makes them substantially different from other financial firms.[8] Of course, the same arguments apply to other depository institutions.

The first, and most important, is that they provide a transaction account, payable at par throughout the economy. By use of the banking system, an individual can transfer purchasing power instantaneously (through wire transfer) to any other individual. A portion of the liabilities of commercial banks, therefore, constitute the money supply of the U.S. Corrigan argues, correctly, that the economy could not function without this service.

Second, commercial banks provide backup liquidity for the remainder of the financial markets. Many financial markets rely on the commercial banking industry to provide liquidity in the event of a financial crisis. For example, the commercial paper market is backed up by lines of credit at commercial banks. Without this support, Corrigan argues, the markets could not function efficiently.

Finally, commercial banks offer safe consumer deposits throughout the society. This allows savers to defer consumption and earn a return on their savings. Corrigan argues that without risk-free deposits, the economy would lose a great deal of its current stability.

Thus, the discussion of regulation of banking raises several questions. First, is any regulation necessary? Without a doubt, the answer is yes. Second, have we overregulated to protect against failures? The answer is again yes. The overlap in regulation and regulatory agencies is expensive and too restrictive. The other questions are less obvious: How much can we deregulate, without destroying the essentially unique character of the banking system? At what level of regulation can the banking industry survive in a competitive world? The answers to the latter questions will be debated during the 1980s.

II. STRUCTURE OF THE INDUSTRY

The U.S. banking structure is characterized by a large number of banks. Banks in the United States are limited to operating within one state. Additionally, in many states, banks are limited to operating within restricted geographic areas, such as a county or perhaps a metropolitan area. Thus, most local customers generally do not have a large number of commercial banking options. Geographic deregulation, as well as growth of nonbank competitors, has significantly increased the options available to consumers in the past decade. In this section, we will discuss the U.S. banking structure at the national level, at the state level, and at the local market level.

The unusual skewed structure of the U.S. banking industry is described in Table 7. There are a very large number of commercial banks—over 14,500 in 1983. Most banks, however, are very small. Over 70 percent have assets under $50 million. A deposit base of $50 million is generally considered necessary to achieve the benefits of scale economies. Thus, 70 percent of the banks (10,000 in number) are too small to be efficient. These 10,000 banks, however, hold less than 16 percent of the total deposits of the commercial banking system. In contrast to the large number of very small banks, there are a few quite large banks. The largest 356 banks, which make up 2.5 percent of the banks in the U.S., hold 55 percent of all the deposits in the banking system. Thus, the U.S. banking system is widely varied in terms of the size of the firms.

To some extent these firms operate in different submarkets; the largest money-center banks serve a different set of customers than the smaller banks. However, this is not always true. Many large banks also compete for the smaller retail and small business customers, which are the primary customers of the small community banks. There has been considerable concern about the future of the small financial institutions in a highly deregulated environ-

Table 7: Asset Size Distribution of U.S. Commercial Banking Organizations (December 31, 1982)

Size Class (in Millions of $)	*Number of Organizations*	*Percent of Banks*	*Percentage of Total U.S. Commercial Bank Assets*
0–5	428	3.4	0.1
5–10	1,405	11.5	0.5
10–25	3,837	31.3	3.3
25–100	4,968	40.5	12.0
100–250	923	7.5	6.9
250–500	246	2.0	4.3
500–1000	170	1.4	5.9
1000–5000	225	1.8	25.3
5000+	56	0.5	41.8

Source: Board of Governors, Federal Reserve System. Banks reporting zero deposits, such as non-deposit trust companies, are eliminated.

ment. Most observers have argued that the vast majority of small institutions will do very well in serving specialized customers in local markets. Those institutions that cannot survive in this environment will generally be acquired by larger firms.

Overall Concentration

The concentration of deposits of the largest banks in the United States has remained fairly stable since at least 1955 (Table 8). In 1955, the top hundred banks had 49 percent of the total U.S. deposits. That number had fallen slightly to 45 percent in 1978. Similarly, the share of the top ten banks has dropped slightly, from 20.7 percent to 18.2 percent since 1955. This apparent stability, however, hides a shift in deposits bases for the institutions. Increasingly, the largest money-center institutions have relied on Eurodollars and large certificates of deposit for funds, rather than retail deposits from households and small businesses. Thus, if it were possible to calculate overall concentration of retail deposits, it is likely that concentration would actually be dropping. Mergers among the largest institutions, especially in an interstate banking environment, could reverse this trend.

The large U.S. banking firms are not large relative to large banks in

Table 8: Share of Domestic Deposits by Largest U.S. Banking Organizations, Selected Dates, 1934–78

Date	*100 Largest Banks*	*10 Largest Banks*
December 31, 1934	56.7	23.7
December 31, 1940	59.4	26.9
December 31, 1955	49.3	20.7
December 31, 1957	48.2	n.a.
December 31, 1960	49.5	21.2
December 31, 1961	49.4	n.a.
December 31, 1964	48.0	20.6
December 31, 1966	49.3	n.a.
December 31, 1968	49.1	20.4
June 30, 1970	49.9	19.9
June 30, 1972	46.8	19.1
December 31, 1973	47.0	n.a.
December 31, 1975	48.1	20.9
December 31, 1976	45.3	18.4
June 30, 1977	45.0	18.3
June 30, 1978	45.0	18.2

Source: This table is updated to 1978, from the original table in Cynthia A. Glassman and Robert A. Eisenbeis, "Banking Holding Companies and Concentration of Banking and Finance Resources," The Bank Holding Company Movement in 1978: A Compendium (Board of Governors of the Federal Reserve System, 1978, p. 246). Updated by Donald T. Savage and Elinor H. Solomon, "Branch Banking: The Competitive Issues," *Journal of Bank Research,* Vol. 11, No. 1 (Summer 1980), p. 112.

Table 9: Leading Banking Organizations in the World

Rank	*Name of Organization*	*Country*	*Total Assets (Millions of Dollars) 12/31/83*
1	Citicorp, New York	United States	125,974
2	Bank America Corp., San Francisco	United States	115,442
3	Dai-Ichi Kangyo Bank Ltd., Tokyo	Japan	110,451*
4	Fuji Bank Ltd., Tokyo	Japan	103,634*
5	Sumitomo Bank Ltd., Osaka	Japan	101,254*
6	Banque Nationale de Paris	France	101,191
7	Mitsubishi Bank Ltd., Tokyo	Japan	98,167*
8	Barclays Bank Plc, London	United Kingdom	94,111
9	Sanwa Bank Ltd. Osaka	Japan	91,355*
10	Credit Agricole Mutuel, Paris	France	90,365

*September, 1983

Source: American Banker (July 31, 1984).

other countries. In many other countries, banking is concentrated in the hands of only a few banks. In 1957, 270 of the largest 500 banks in the world were American. By 1967, the number of U.S. banks had fallen to 187 out of the top 500, and by 1983, only 95 banks of the top 500 in the world were American. As shown in Table 9, only two of the ten largest banks are American. In contrast, five are Japanese and two are French. This raises a problem with respect to takeovers of U.S. banks by foreign banks. Since U.S. banks are absolutely smaller than many large banks in Europe and Japan, takeovers are relatively easy for these large banks. The number of takeovers is becoming large enough to warrant public concern.

State Structures

The diffuse structure of banking nationally may not reflect the situtation within smaller geographic areas in which banks actually operate, because they are essentially limited to single states for their banking operations. Table 10 presents the concentration levels in states, and changes in concentration since 1955.

Under the U.S. dual banking concept, each state is free to determine how its banks may expand geographically within the state. States may choose a statewide branching system, whereby banks can branch throughout the state, or a limited branching network, where banks are allowed to branch within very limited geographic constraints. For example, banks may be allowed to branch within their own county, or perhaps, into contiguous counties. Finally, some states have elected to permit no branching whatsoever. Column 4 of Table 10 indicates the laws regarding branching within each state.

An analysis of Table 10 will show the role of branching with respect to statewide concentration. All of the states in the high-concentration ranges

Table 10: Percentage of Total Deposits at the Three Largest and Five Largest Banks, by State, 1970 and 1980 (States Ranked by Percentage at Five Largest Banks)

State	1970 5 Largest Firms	1980 5 Largest Firms	(Change) (Percentage Points) 5 Largest Firms	Branching Law	Interstate
Rhode Island	92.4	96.5	4.1	S	Y
Nevada	97.5	96.1	−1.4	S	
Arizona	96.8	94.2	−2.6	S	
Delaware	92.3	91.6	−.7	S	Y
Hawaii	89.8	90.8	1.0	S	
D.C.	86.1	87.9	1.8	S	
Idaho	88.0	86.1	−1.9	S	
Alaska	85.5	79.4	−6.1	S	Y
Washington	77.5	76.4	−1.1	S	Y
Maine	59.6	74.0	14.4	S	Y
Utah	73.7	73.6	−.1	S	Y
California	77.0	73.3	−3.7	S	
Oregon	86.4	72.8	−13.6	S	Y
N. Carolina	67.1	65.8	−1.2	S	Y
Massachusetts	64.1	65.3	−1.2	L	Y
Vermont	51.1	63.3	12.7	S	
Maryland	61.0	62.9	1.9	S	Y
S. Carolina	58.3	62.8	4.5	S	
Connecticut	61.3	61.4	.1	S	Y
Minnesota	59.1	56.9	−2.2	L	
Colorado	47.3	56.0	8.7	U	
New Mexico	54.2	54.8	.6	L	
Alabama	32.2	53.1	20.9	L	
Montana	58.4	51.7	−6.7	U	
Virginia	50.4	51.7	1.3	L	Y
Michigan	45.8	50.2	4.4	L	
S. Dakota	47.7	49.7	2.0	L	Y
New York	56.4	49.2	−7.2	S	Y
Georgia	43.8	47.1	3.3	L	Y
N. Dakota	50.5	47.0	−3.5	U	
Wyoming	36.4	46.7	10.3	N	
New Hampshire	42.8	46.7	3.9	S	
Missouri	31.1	40.6	9.5	U	
Tennessee	40.2	39.2	−1.0	L	
Illinois	39.4	38.3	−1.1	U	Y
Florida	28.0	36.9	8.9	L	Y
Texas	22.7	36.7	14.0	U	
Ohio	32.9	36.5	3.6	L	
New Jersey	24.6	35.8	11.2	S	
Mississippi	33.3	33.9	.6	L	
Wisconsin	33.9	33.2	−.7	L	
Pennsylvania	36.7	31.2	−5.5	L	

(continued)

Table 10: continued

	1970	1980	(Change) (Percentage Points)	Branching Law	Interstate
State	5 Largest Firms	5 Largest Firms	5 Largest Firms		
Kentucky	32.4	28.8	−3.6	L	Y
Nebraska	34.3	26.5	−7.8	U	Y
Oklahoma	32.6	26.1	−6.5	U	
Iowa	17.6	25.8	8.2	L	Y
Indiana	27.5	21.3	−6.2	L	
Louisiana	28.9	20.5	−8.4	L	
Arkansas	21.3	18.1	−3.2	L	
West Virginia	17.6	12.1	−5.5	L	
Kansas	15.4	12.0	−3.4	U	
AVERAGES (unweighted)	51.8	52.7	.9		

Source: Federal Reserve Bulletin, February 1982.

are states that permit statewide branching. Conversely, the bulk of the states that are least concentrated permit only unit banking.[9]

As Table 10 demonstrates, the range of concentration in states is quite substantial. Many states are highly concentrated, with the largest five banks holding as much as 95 percent of total deposits within the state. Alternatively, there are many states with a low concentration of banking resources. The general tendency in most states has been for concentration to fall at the state level. The increases in concentration have generally come in states such as Virginia, Maine, and Florida, which have liberalized their state branching laws, allowing banks to set up statewide organizations. Thus, the increase reflects not a change in the competitive situation as much as it reflects a change in the branching laws. Recent merger activity in many states is likely to further increase aggregate state concentration levels.

Just as state laws limit geographic expansion within the state, federal legislation prevents banks from operating branches or banking subsidiaries in more than one state, unless the state specifically permits interstate branching. Many states are considering, or have passed, legislation that permits some form of interstate banking within their borders. They are shown in Table 10. There is considerable variation in approach. Some states, such as Maine and Alaska, have opened their states to any bank from any other state. Others, such as South Dakota and Delaware, permit limited service interstate banks. Banks from other states may obtain a charter to run a credit-card business, for example. States such as New York have passed reciprocal arrangements in which they will grant charters in New York to banks from any states that permit New York banks to enter their state. Finally, states in New England and the Southeast have established regional interstate banking compacts that allow banks from neighboring states to enter. The general intent of the regional concepts is to allow banks to grow by merger from within the region, but to restrict entry by acquisitions by large money-center banks. The legality of the regional concept was decided by the U.S. Supreme Court in 1985.

Local Concentration

The most important dimension of structure is neither the national nor the state level of concentration. Concentration is most relevant in terms of its impact on the performance at the local market level. Banking is generally characterized as a local market industry.

Banks offer many products to different types of consumers. Depending on the size and type of the transaction, the geographic market for the bank product will differ considerably.[10] The market for consumer-demand deposits, where convenience is the most important factor, may be as small as a neighborhood or a section of a city. Conversely, the market for large commercial loans will cover the entire nation. Bank borrowers and lenders will find it is in their interest to arrange transactions irrespective of location. The bulk of commercial banking operations, however, including financial services sold to most households and small businesses, is limited to a fairly small geographic area, such as a city or a rural county.

Banking markets have been approximated in most studies of bank performance, and in most merger cases by a Standard Metropolitan Statistical Area (SMSA), or by a rural county, or by some combination of counties.[11] This may not be entirely appropriate. As Talley notes, "the bank regulatory agencies, the Department of Justice, and the courts frequently employ SMSA's and counties as approximations for banking markets, partly because deposit data on an office basis are readily available for these geographic areas."[12] If one recognizes these limitations, the SMSA will serve as a quite reasonable approximation.

The control of banking deposits by the largest banks in most metropolitan areas is highly concentrated. It is even higher in rural areas. Concentration levels for all U.S. metropolitan areas are presented in Table 11.

Two measures of concentration are given. The four-firm concentration ratio (CR4) indicates the share of deposits held by the largest four banks in the market. The second, and more precise, measure is the Hirschman-Herfindahl Index (HHI)[13] and its corresponding-numbers equivalent. The maximum HHI is 10,000, if one firm had 100 percent of the market. The HHI takes into consideration the relative size of all firms in the market, as well as the number of firms. Consequently, it provides an index of concentration which is less subject to error.

The metropolitan areas are arrayed on the basis of the number of banks operating in the market in 1982. Several facts are evident. First, even though most banking is retail-oriented, few markets have large numbers of banks.

Table 11: Concentration Levels in Metropolitan Areas 1982

Number of Banking Organizations in SMSA	*Number of SMSAs*	*Average CR4 (%)*	*Average HHI*
101 or more	7	54.4	1,103
61–100	7	52.0	907
41–60	14	58.4	1,257
31–40	15	64.8	1,483
26–30	16	67.5	1,602
21–25	22	61.1	1,320
18–20	26	68.1	1,708
15–17	32	69.9	1,615
12–14	44	74.0	1,908
9–11	60	80.7	2,163
6–8	57	89.1	2,732
5 or less	18	97.9	3,459

Source: Jim Burke, "Antitrust Laws, Justice Department Guidelines, and the Limits of Concentration in Local Banking Markets," *Staff Study,* Federal Reserve Board, 1983.

Only 52 out of 318 metropolitan areas have more than 25 banking organizations. Second, even those markets with a relatively large number of banks have high concentration levels. The seven markets with more than 100 banks have an average concentration ratio of 54.4 percent anda HHI of 1,103. This corresponds to a numbers-equivalent of 9.1. On average, these markets are as competitive as a market would be with nine banks of equal size.

Concentration levels have been used as proxy for monopoly power in banking markets. There have been numerous studies of the impact of market structure on performance in banking markets. The preponderance of evidence finds the existence of a statistical link between concentration and market performance.[14] Market performance is defined as profitability, prices relative to costs, and the provision of services to consumers. Although statistically significant, the economic effect of concentration on performance is relatively small.

Two major trends that have taken place in the industry make this approach questionable for structural analysis in the future. First, the granting of new powers to thrift institutions makes these institutions very comparable to commercial banks. If thrift deposits are included in the base, this will substantially change concentration levels. Further, because they compete directly with banks in many markets, market concentration of bank deposits becomes a less meaningful concept. The same concentration of bank deposits will have a different effect, depending on the strength of thrift institutions in the market. In addition, there has been a substantial increase in the intensity of competition from nonbank financial institutions in many, if not all, local markets. To the extent that nonbank competition varies across markets, it cannot be ignored when comparing and measuring market structures. For example, many banks have opened loan production offices (LPOs) in major markets across the country. Through their LPOs, they could be major competitors in the loan market; they would fund their loans from other liabilities. Deposit concentration measures totally ignore their presence.

The second factor that undermines the importance of deposit concentration as a predictor of performance is the deregulation of deposits. In the pre-1984 regulated world, with low-rate ceilings on deposits, managers basically treated deposits as outside of their control and invested these deposits to maximize profits. Deposits were an exogenous factor, at least in the short run. Deposits consequently represented lending capacity and were the appropriate measure of market power. However, with deregulated deposit markets, a firm may increase its deposit size at will by raising rates above the market rate. Consequently, even a bank with a small level of deposits in a market has the potential to become a dominant lending force rapidly, if it perceives profitable lending opportunities that are not being met in the market. It can simply outbid other financial institutions for the market deposits.

Banks have also become more aware of money markets as a source of funds (see Table 7). They may choose to raise funds for loans in a vast array of money markets, rather than in deposit markets. Consequently, the deposit base as a measure of concentration has far less significance.[15] Research is currently underway by economists and in the federal courts on how to describe the market structure of financial services in the current regulatory regime.

Economies of Scale

Economies of scale in the operations of financial intermediaries have been estimated often.[16] The consensus appears to be that the minimum efficient scale (where the average-cost curve is at its lowest point) is rather small, in the range of $50 million in deposits. Average costs may even turn up in banks with deposits above $50 million. Even if this estimate is too low by a factor of 10, it is possible to have viable competition even in the smaller cities, and far less concentration than is found in the larger ones.

The retailing function now can be done in microscopically small units, including automatic teller machines, which handle most transactions. Therefore, technology permits almost limitless branching for many of these operations. The more complex banking operations might, however, have major economics of scale. Thus, a large bank, with 500 loan officers, can include highly specialized experts (for example, engineers and geologists) on their staff. They, in turn, may improve the depth of knowledge about clients' prospects. Portfolio-management might also be done better by larger firms.

Economies of scale may be significant in banking relationships. To a slight extent, large firms need bankers that are also large. Large accounts can be divided among several banks, and indeed many of the largest firms do just that, through lending consortia. In the years prior to 1960, the links between banks and their clients were highly personal; they were usually on a one to one basis. The new, more profit-oriented banking involves a higher degree of objective evaluation, which any good medium-sized bank can do well. The riskier strategies of large firms need to be pooled among several banks—with independent evaluation—rather than borne by just one. This, too, has become common in the financing of actual loans.

There may be pecuniary advantages in large-scale banking relationships. Access to insider information may favor the larger banks and make their support and advice appear more valuable to clients. Also, their size and traditional status may permit the larger banks to provide cheaper capital by having access to more sources of funding. It remains a puzzle that studies find no economies of scale. Yet banks continue to merge and grow in the pursuit of perceived efficiency.

Mergers and Acquisitions

The banking industry has gone through a major merger movement in recent years. The number of mergers in 1983 exceeded the record in the previous year (Figure 2). The average size of acquisitions is also increasing each year (Figure 3). In 1983, over $40 billion in assets were acquired in less than 450 acquisitions. This contrasts with an average annual value of acquisitions of less than $10 billion throughout the 1960s and 1970s.

The releasing of the revised U.S. Department of Justice merger guidelines in 1982 had a major impact on the number and character of mergers in banking. These guidelines gave merging firms a stronger signal on the types of mergers that would be permitted by the regulatory agencies and the Justice Department.

The guidelines are couched in the form of the Hirschman-Herfindahl Index. The higher the concentration level of the merger, the more likely it is that a merger will be challenged. In unconcentrated markets, no mergers will be challenged. In highly concentrated markets, even relatively small mergers are likely to be challenged (see Table 12). Most banking markets are in the moderately concentrated levels.

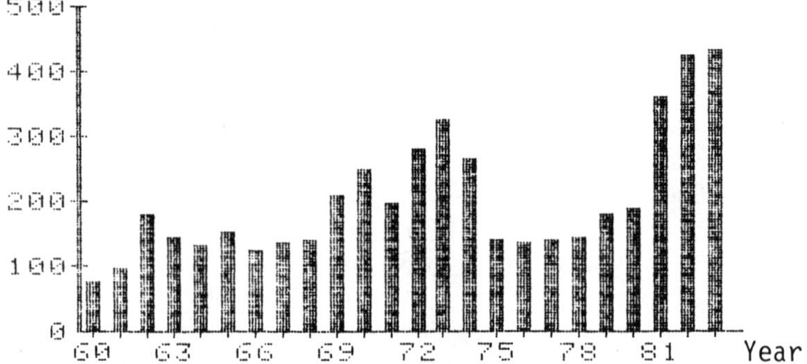

FIGURE 2. Number of bank acquisitions (1960–1983). *Source:* S. A. Rhoades, "Mergers and Acquisitions by Commercial Banks," *Staff Studies,* Board of Governors of the Federal Reserve System, 1985.

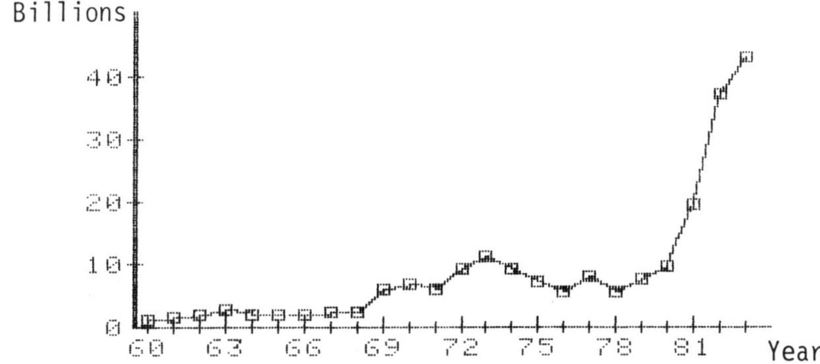

FIGURE 3. Value of acquired banks (1960–1983). *Source:* S. A. Rhoades, ibid.

Since the 1963 decision in *U.S.* v. *Philadelphia National Bank,* the Department of Justice has continually challenged horizontal mergers in commercial banking. Commercial banking was defined as *a line of commerce,* meaning that competition from savings and loan associations, credit unions, savings banks, and nondepository intermediaries was ignored in the determination of the legality of a merger, under the Bank Merger Act and the Celler-Kefauver Act. In a market in which the only financial-services firms were commercial banks, a merger of two banks was treated exactly as a merger of two banks in a market with a large number of other specialized financial intermediaries. Although the change in concentration of bank deposits would be the same in both mergers, the former merger is likely to have a more serious impact on competition.

The geographic market was considered to be local in nature. Market definitions often followed county or metropolitan-area definitions. Firm size was based on total deposits. The effect of the Court rulings, as well as the policy of the regulatory agencies, was that virtually any horizontal merger that increased concentration of bank deposits by even a small amount was illegal.

Most mergers were consequently not horizontal; they were of the market-extension type. Mergers were used to enter new geographic markets. The Justice Department was not highly successful in challenging these mergers, and a set of recent rulings has made it virtually impossible to challenge a market-extension merger.[17]

The guidelines on horizontal mergers, combined with the court decision on market-extension mergers, opened the door for significant expansion by larger institutions. At the same time, there was increased pressure on institutions to grow—in anticipation of interstate banking and because of the fear that their markets would be dominated by the large, money-center banks.

Mergers of bank holding companies have become more commonplace. Under the new rules, each holding company was allowed to have offices in

Table 12: Merger Guidelines U.S. Department of Justice

Market Structure	*Post Merger HHI**	*Change in HHI Due to Merger*	*Likely Department of Justice Action*
Unconcentrated	0–1,000	—	Will Not Challenge
Moderately Concentrated	1,000–1,800	0–100	Will Not Challenge
Highly Concentrated	over 1,800	0–50	Will Not Challenge
		Over 50	Likely to Challenge

*HHI is the sum of all market shares squared. It ranges from near *0* in a perfectly competitive market to 10,000 in a monopolistic market. A merger of two competitors with market shares of *x*% and *y*%, respectively, will increase the HHI by $2 \cdot x \cdot y$. For example, a merger of two firms with 10 percent at 5 percent of the market would increase the HHI by 100.

Source: Merger Guidelines of Department of Justice, 1982, 2 Trade Reg. Rep. (CCH), June 14, 1982.

many geographic markets. In markets where they did not have offices in common, it was unlikely that the merger would be challenged. In markets in which they both operated, they could use the Department of Justice guidelines. If they fell within the guidelines nothing was done. If the merger exceeded the guidelines the merged firm had two options. First, it could sell off the offices of either the acquired holding company or its own company, so as to transform the merger into a simple market-extension merger. Second, if the market was especially attractive, it could sell off enough branches to qualify under the guidelines. In either case, the way was open to consummate large, multimarket consolidations.

Mergers and Interstate Banking

If nationwide interstate banking is permitted, this merger process will continue, and it will increase in intensity. The existing antitrust laws will do little to stop major acquisitions by the largest U.S. banks, and this will lead to an overall concentration of resources, which would be unacceptable, from a public policy perspective. For example, if the largest U.S. bank had acquired the largest banking institutions in Florida and Texas, its share of 1982 U.S. deposits would have increased from 4.14 to 5.41 percent. This is certainly not enough of an increase to trigger a challenge and a denial under current Department of Justice standards.

Large interstate mergers in banking would not initially increase overall concentration ratios to very high levels, as compared with other industries. However, banking is a unique industry, and even small increases in the shares of the dominant firms should be subject to careful analysis.

A major acquisition movement by the largest commercial banks could impose sufficient social costs to warrant denial. Our national goal has always been to encourage a diffuse banking system, with many independent banks deciding on credit allocation within their own markets, and within the regions of the country. The feeling has been that, if control was increasingly held by a few large banks, potential borrowers could lose access to credit. Although there is no empirical evidence to substantiate this claim, it certainly is a possible consequence of high overall concentration of banking resources in the control of a few firms.

The greatest problem that would result from increases in concentration of control by the very largest banks would be an increase in the risk exposure of the banking system. It is extremely difficult to predict when (and which) banks will encounter major financial stress. They are all highly leveraged and therefore must take great risks in their normal business activities. In some periods, they may encounter financial stress owing to a mismatch of maturities in their balance sheets, e.g., lending long and borrowing short. In other cases, stress may be the result of other factors, such as large foreign loans, energy loans, losses on foreign-exchange transactions, or agricultural loans.

These kinds of risks occur almost at random and are not totally subject to management control. No matter how well it is managed, any bank could find itself in a financial crisis, unable to meet its liabilities. The larger the bank that is exposed, the greater the potential impact of its failure on public expectations regarding the soundness of the entire system. Because the system is basically run on public trust, we must be careful to keep banks to a size where we can tolerate their failures. A merger movement of the existing large banks would only make the economy more vulnerable.

The same situation would occur if banking were open to insurance companies, real estate companies, or investment banking. Major mergers of the dominant firms could take place without violating current antitrust standards. Moreover, these types of acquisitions are undesirable from a public policy viewpoint, because they could increase the actual or perceived risks of the banking system.

As commercial banking becomes increasingly deregulated, the failure rate of firms that offer banking services will undoubtedly rise. Their investment opportunities will broaden, and at least some of their activities will be riskier than their present activities. This would probably be in the public interest, and should be permitted. By maintaining some degree of diffusion in the banking structure, the possible impact of this increased exposure to risk is minimized.

III. PERFORMANCE

Because of the pervasive influence of the financial intermediaries on the U.S. economy, there has been a great deal of discussion regarding how well this sector performs. What does society require from the financial services sector? How can we guarantee this performance?

The most important element of performance is inherent in the nature of financial intermediaries and concerns its liabilities. We must have a safe, sound financial system. For the system to function effectively, the public must have confidence in the overall integrity of the system. If the public were to lose confidence in the soundness of financial intermediaries, there would be two major effects. First, there would be no demand deposits to fund banking transactions. Consequently, there would be a significant contraction in the money supply. Second, savers would begin to pull funds out of the weaker institutions. These institutions would not be able to obtain enough cash to meet the outflows without selling off assets at distress prices. Ultimately, even well-run conservative institutions could be forced into failure. To prevent both of these effects, public confidence in the stability of the system must be maintained.

The industry has performed very well in this regard, with the help of the regulatory agencies. The actual failure rate for commercial banks, savings and loan associations, and credit unions has been very small, averaging less than one per thousand per year, since the 1930s. Failing institutions have generally been merged with other institutions, protecting not only small depositors but also the large uninsured depositors. A panic—such as the one in the 1930s when depositors attempted to convert their funds into cash—has not developed.

For the regulatory agencies, the cost of this protection is at times very high. When a large bank is in financial trouble, the liability to the FDIC may be very high. In a recent bank failure, Continental Illinois cost the FDIC over $2 billion, to compensate for extremely high loan losses. Although it was sharply criticized for this form of bailout, the Federal Reserve has argued that there is no choice, because the failure of a very large institution, with its accompanying losses to uninsured depositors, would cause a panic in the national and international markets.

As the largest banking firms grow in size, the U.S. economy becomes even more vulnerable to this possibility. In an evaluation of the future performance of the industry, an important factor should be the ability of the economy to absorb a failure of its largest financial institutions.

The second most important element of performance—efficiency—is not unique to financial institutions, but it is perhaps more important because of their role in all transactions. We need an efficient system. We should minimize the real resources that must be spent to finance activity. An efficient system is innovative; it uses the best available technology; its firms are operating at peak efficiency, and they are charging competitive prices. In a system that is performing well, there should be no monopoly rents.

The third element of performance is related to resource allocation. It is the market that should allocate credit to the sectors of the economy and to the geographic areas where it is most needed. There should be mobile capital in the economy. However, there are additional credit-allocation goals, including the provision of funds for housing, student loans, and small business. Good performance requires that credit allocation meet these goals.

The final element of performance involves consumer protection. It is believed that there have been many abuses in the area of credit in past years. These have involved abusive collection practices, charging of usurious rates, and discrimination against women and minorities in the granting of credit. Good performance is not consistent with any of these practices.

As we have seen, bank performance has several particular components, but only a brief discussion of all of the elements of performance is possible here. In general, the industry has performed well. Increases in competition, as well as deregulation, have put considerable pressure on the industry to be efficient and innovative in the services it offers, as well as in the delivery of services. However, much of the current regulation is superfluous and creates inefficiency.

Profitability

Industry profitability has been stable and growing (see Figure 4). However, the levels of profit are not abnormally high. This factor is evident if one considers the returns to shareholders from 1956 to 1981, (shown in Figure 5). The return to owning a portfolio of many center bank stocks, or regional banks stocks, is below the return on the average market portfolio. Unless this is corrected, the industry will continue to find it difficult to raise capital.

Efficiency

There are various aspects of efficiency to consider. Internal efficiency had been mediocre, especially before 1965, according to the consensus among expert observers. The overriding concern for security induced a narrow, traditional range of activities. Liability management was largely by rote, and excellent profit opportunities were lost. Banks clung to their old clients, and neglected good alternative prospects. And, to take the most obvious surface indications, bank premises had traditionally displayed a degree of gold plating. There has also been a tendency to use certain other inputs, including staff

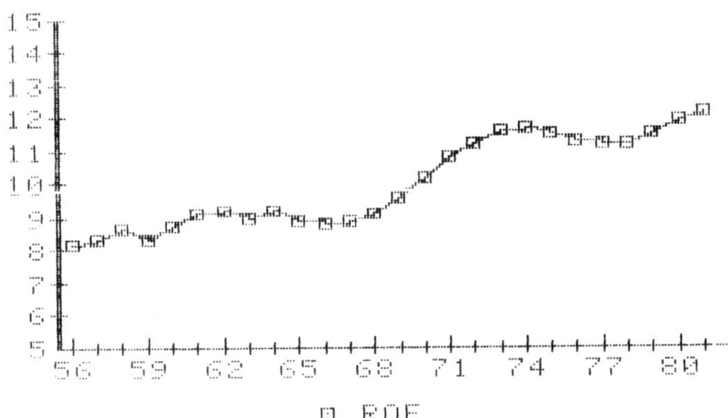

FIGURE 4. Return on equity, commercial banks (1956–1981). *Source:* Federal Reserve Bank of Minneapolis.

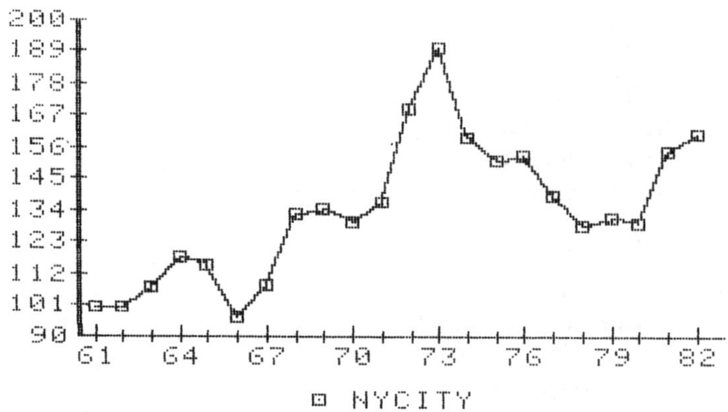

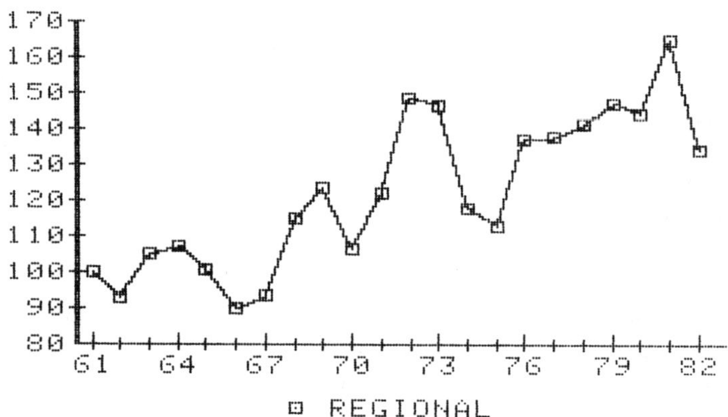

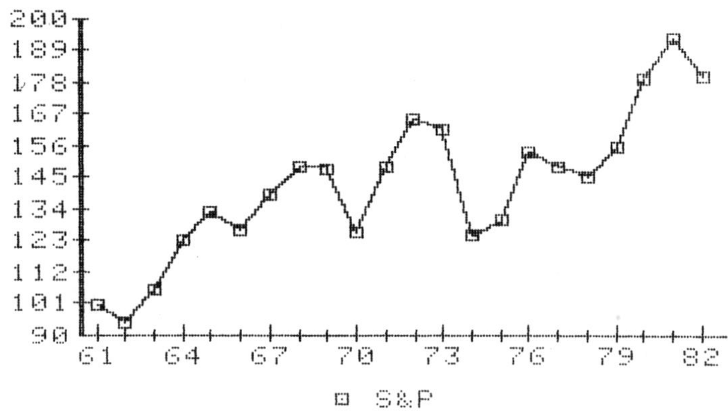

FIGURE 5. Return on shareholder investment, New York banks and regional banks (1956–1981). *Source:* Federal Reserve Bank of Minneapolis.

and managerial ranks, beyond efficient levels, especially in the more sheltered banks. This is rapidly changing, however, as competition is putting considerable pressure on less efficient firms.

Recently, a number of excesses have occurred with respect to dubious loans and unduly risky investments. The exposure of the large banks to high losses in foreign loans suggests deficiencies in management performance.

Allocation of Resources

The allocation of resources in banking operations had also been restricted, especially before 1965. This was most apparent in retailing operations. The open-for-business hours (9:30 A.M. to 2:30 P.M., weekdays only) were common, and there were few neighborhood branches. By 1961, many cities were clearly "underbanked"—as the rapid new entry, and branching, have since demonstrated. Improved services have coincided precisely with the rise in competition, and further improvements are to be expected in some areas. It may be that by 1985, markets were "overbanked," because of too much reliance on nonprice competition.

The allocation of capital has been restricted and distorted, in various degrees. In total, and especially for certain regions and groups of firms, the volume of credit has been smaller and has been made available at excessive prices. However, recent innovations in the capital markets, such as the development of a secondary mortgage market, are improving this situation dramatically.

The degree of inefficiency has been moderate rather than extreme, especially by international comparison; and its severity is probably receding, as the degree of competition and flexibility has risen.

Stability of Banks

The goal of public policy has been to promote stability in the banking system by the prevention of failures. The regulatory agencies, and the industry, have been extremely successful in this regard. Very few banks have failed. In the rare incidents in which a bank does fail, public confidence in the strength of the banking system has prevented a panic from developing in which depositors at other institutions seek to remove their deposits.

Strength and stability in the banking system has been achieved by a combination of restrictions on bank investment and loan policy, limitations on competition, by deposit insurance, and by the Federal Reserve standing as a lender of last resort to all banks. While this approach has worked, it may not have been the most effective means of achieving the desired objective, especially when other public policy goals for the banking industry are considered.

Throughout most of the period since the 1930's, there has been excessive soundness regulation. Competition and management behavior has been controlled to a degree that has limited competition and stifled innovation. Weak, poor performing management has been protected from failure and permitted to continue to operate.

The 1980's have brought an additional challenge to the stability of the banking system. Deregulation and increased competition in financial services have increased the opportunities for bankers to take risks and have also increased the pressure on them to earn high profits through increased risk. Large banks such as Continental Illinois in Chicago have been forced into bankruptcy. Many smaller banks have experienced large losses in real estate, energy, and agricultural loans that have led to their failures.

In this environment, there will be a need for the industry and for regulators to develop systems to limit the abuses that lead to failures. This must be accomplished without permitting a return to the policies of earlier periods that led to inefficiencies and poor performance due to excessive regulation.

Innovation

Innovation in banking traditionally has been slow, partly because of public-policy resistance. New services have been introduced and diffused slowly. New technology has also tended to be absorbed at a moderate-to-slow pace by the majority of banks. Almost all the technological changes have been prepared externally and injected by energetic outside firms, often against the considerable reluctance of bankers. Thus, computer handling was prepackaged by computer firms. Efficient portfolio management was an innovation that spread slowly among the older bankers. On the whole, and continuing even now, banking innovation has been slow, in line with inhibitions regarding entrepreneurship. Most innovation has been directed at evading regulations, rather than developing new products or new delivery systems.[18]

Equity

In appraising the defects of the banking system, one should bear in mind that the system as a whole is probably more efficient and more fair than the system in most other countries. Still, the defects are serious.

Fairness is affected by several of the conditions we have discussed. Exclusion and price discrimination affect both business and personal clients. Generally, the interest differentials against smaller borrowers exceed the differences in costs and intrinsic risk. Interest rates paid to savers are also biased against small customers, more than the costs would justify. Again, many small customers are flatly excluded from the more lucrative offerings (e.g., large certificates of deposit), and from many trust departments. Even minor service aspects, such as banking hours and location, have tended to put poorer citizens at a disadvantage. Is this the result of industry practice or of regulation?

Evaluating Regulation

Some policy actions—especially regulation—have been extensive and, in part, probably counterproductive. The regulatory patchwork is complex and costly; it is an industry in itself. Regulators go deeply into banks' affairs—usually quietly, but often spectacularly. The more thorough regulation is, the more it disrupts the banks' normal operations. The regulators must make thousands of complex judgments, about performance, new competition, applications for entry, and mergers. Some of the regulation is done superbly; other aspects of regulation, especially at the state level, are bureaucratic and passive.

Much of the banking regulation is excessive, considering its objective, that of optimum bank stability, which is already assured by deposit insurance and Federal Reserve support for the whole system. Especially when it is done thoroughly, regulation is most wasteful. Not only are the regulatory resources often used pointlessly, but regulation per se operates to suppress competition and discourage entrepreneurship. This is most evident in the state antibranching regulations, but it pervades the whole system of restraints.

Three possible benefits of regulation offset these costs. (1) Security is increased. (However, deposit insurance probably provides sufficient security.) (2) Regulation keeps banks and industrial firms on an arm's-length basis. The abuses and monopoly effects that mingling makes possible (abroad, and before 1937 in the United States) are avoided. Yet, much implicit mingling already occurs indirectly, in banking relationships and portfolio operations. And the separation is a simple matter of law: it does not require a small army of regulatory officials, bank examiners, and accountants to enforce it. (3) The local character of banking may be enhanced, but this, too, is the result of rules (for example, against bank branching), rather than regulation of operations. And "localness" often has led to inefficiency and restrictive behavior.

IV. PUBLIC POLICY

We have discussed most of the specific policy issues; however, many of these issues can be included in one basic question: What role should competition and regulation play in banking? Some observers suggest that competition should become universal, as in any "normal" industry. Others want public regulation and/or public banking to cover all essentials, in order to assure stability and meet overall social needs. During the 1970s, prior limits on banking were eroded, and competition (or, an overlapping of activities) increased. Should this shift go further? Should regulation be abolished, or at least reduced further?

1. Regulation should be further reduced—selectively. Deposit insurance should continue, but chartering should be liberalized, and most of the regulatory inspection of banks should cease. Under certain conditions, takeovers of banks should be permitted; but banking operations and accounts should be kept separate from nonbanking activities. The present salvaging of failing banks should continue (as in the Continental Illinois

Bank, in 1984), but there should be no official commitment to prevent bank failures at any cost.

2. A clear delineation of banking should be developed. Entry into banking should be opened further (perhaps phased in), in order to minimize disruptions. However, in terms of regulation, all firms that provide banking services should be treated equally.
3. Greater pressure should be developed to allow the private markets to control the risk exposure of banking firms. This can be accomplished by forcing the banks to go to uninsured-debt and to equity markets for some portion of their funds (e.g., those with high capital requirements), and by providing the public with more information on the banks.

Conclusion

There is much room for experimenting and learning as technology matures and external conditions change. Together, the aforementioned policies have a balance and depth that cover most of the apparent gaps in banking performance. More competition alone will not suffice, nor will a continuation of the present duplicative nonsystem of "regulation." All of the present standard policy tools—antitrust, regulation, and public enterprise—are appropriate, in varying degrees. But in a different form, and in a different balance, they could be optimally effective. We must see them for what they are, and then modify them, in order to make a good banking system an excellent one.

NOTES

1. Under the provisions of the Depository Institution Deregulation and Monetary Control Act of 1980, all limitations on rates on time and savings deposits will be removed by 1986.

2. For a thorough analysis of this concept, see James L. Pierce, *Monetary and Financial Economies* (New York: John Wiley & Sons, 1984).

3. For a discussion of these costs, see George Benston and Clifford Smith, "A Transactions Cost Approach to the Theory of Financial Intermediation," *Journal of Finance,* **31:** 215–231 (1976).

4. For an analysis of the growth of nondepository institutions, see H. Rosenblum and C. Pavel, "Banking Services in Transition: The Effects of Nonbank Competitors," in R. Aspinwall and R. Eisenbeis (eds.), *Handbook for Banking Strategy* (New York, John Wiley & Sons, 1985).

5. For a thorough discussion of these innovations, see Simpson and Parkinson, op. cit.

6. When a depositor removed $1,000 from a savings account, the S&L either had to sell a mortgage to obtain the $1,000, or it had to borrow the funds from elsewhere. Mortgages could only be sold at a substantial discount in the high interest-rate environment, therefore the only choice was to borrow in more expensive markets. For example, a $1,000 30-year mortgage, with payments set at 8 percent, would fall in market value to $625 if interest rates increased to 13 percent. If they were forced to sell their mortgage to meet the deposit outflow, they would be forced to accept a $375 capital loss, in this example.

7. By the end of 1982, there were 4,289 holding companies, which held 80 percent of total bank deposits. Consequently, the Federal Reserve, by controlling the parent holding companies, has some degree of regulatory control over virtually the entire industry.

8. See *Annual Report,* Federal Reserve Bank of Minneapolis, 1982.

9. This correlation does not imply that limitations on branching are in the public interest. In states that permit branching, customers at the local market level have more options than in a unit banking state. However, the result does not imply that one consequence of interstate banking will be an increase in overall concentration of banking resources as firms combine across the country. To minimize the concentrating effect, considerable attention must be directed to merger policy in an interstate banking environment.

10. For a thorough survey of local market concepts in commercial banking, see John Wolken, "Geographic Market Delineation: A Review of the Literature," *Staff Study,* Federal Reserve Board, November 1984.

11. This has been the judicial standard since *United States v. Philadelphia Nat'l. Bank,* 374 U.S. 321 (1963). In recent litigation, however, this simple approximation has been challenged. See *United States v. Connecticut Nat'l. Bank,* 418 U.S. 656 (1974).

12. Talley, "Recent Trends in Local Banking Market Structures," Staff Economic Studies, No. 89, p. 5 (Board of Governors of the Federal Reserve System, May 1977).

13. The Hirschman-Herfindahl Index is

$$H = \sum_{i=1}^{N} S_i^2$$

where S_i is the share of the market held by firm i, and where there are N firms in the market. The reciprocal of the Herfindahl Index is the "numbers equivalent," which is the number of equal-size firms that would give a Herfindahl Index of a given value. See Adelman, "Comment on the *'H'* Concentration Measure As a Numbers-Equivalent," *Review of Economics & Statistics* **51**:99–101 (Feb. 1969).

14. See R. A. Gilbert, "Banking Market Structure and Competition: A Survey," *Journal of Money, Credit, and Banking,* Vol. 16, No. 4, Part 2 (Nov. 1984), pp. 617–644, for a recent and critical survey.

15. For an elaboration, see Arnold A. Heggestad, "A Critical Appraisal of the Banking Structure and Performance Literature," *Journal of Money, Credit, and Banking* (Nov. 1984).

16. For a summary of this research, see David B. Humphrey, "Cost and Scale Economies in Bank Intermediaries," in Aspinwall and Eisenbeis (eds.), op. cit.

17. For a full discussion of the legal framework and history, see John D. Hawke, Jr., "Public Policy Toward Bank Expansion," in Aspinwall and Eisenbeis (eds.), op. cit.

18. See Edward Kane, "Accelerating Inflation, Technological Innovation, and the Decreasing Effectiveness of Banking Regulation," *Journal of Finance,* **36**:355–367 (May 1981).

SUGGESTED READINGS

Aspinwall, R. C., and R. A. Eisenbeis, (eds.) *Handbook for Banking Strategy.* New York: John Wiley & Sons, 1985.

Board of Governors, Federal Reserve System. *The Bank Holding Company Movement, to 1978: A Compendium*. Washington, D.C.: 1978.

Edwards, Franklin (ed.) *Issues in Financial Regulation*. New York: McGraw-Hill Book Co., 1979.

Heggestad, Arnold A. (ed.) *The Costs and Benefits of Public Regulation of Consumer Financial Services*. Cambridge, Mass.: Abt Associates, 1978.

U.S. Department of the Treasury. *Geographic Restrictions on Commercial Banking in the United States*. Washington, D.C.: 1981.

10

The Intercollegiate Athletics Industry

James V. Koch

I. INTRODUCTION

Intercollegiate athletics is one of the most interesting and rapidly changing industries in the American economy. This is true at least partially because intercollegiate athletics has often assumed a larger-than-life role in American society. The University of Notre Dame football team, for example, has traditionally benefited from a faithful group of "subway alumni" around the country—fans who root for the Irish, even though they have no visible connection with the University.

It is apparent that public attention to big-time intercollegiate athletics has grown in recent years. One measure of this attention is attendance at intercollegiate football games; 35 million fans attended games in 1983, an increase over 100 percent since 1955 (see Table 1). Yet, several other circumstances are even more indicative of why intercollegiate athletics now looms so large in the public imagination. A growing number of collegiate football coaches now earn more than the university presidents who are their nominal superiors. And reliable authorities now estimate that agile, seven-foot basketball players, such as Georgetown University's Patrick Ewing, are now worth as much as $3 million a year to their home institutions.[1] Much attention has been devoted to the high-stakes quarrel between the dominant intercollegiate athletic organization, the National Collegiate Athletic Association (NCAA), and some of its members, concerning who will control the financially lucrative right to televise intercollegiate football games.

Intercollegiate athletics has been in almost constant turmoil in recent years. The most important cause of this upheaval has been changes in fundamental economic relationships. We shall see that conventional economic analysis not only can explain most recent developments in intercollegiate athletics, but also that the structure-conduct-performance paradigm is an exceptionally useful foundation for that explanation.[2] The NCAA euphemistically talks about "the amateur student-athlete . . . who engages in a particular sport for the educational, physical, mental, and social benefits derived therefrom and to whom participation in that sport is an avocation."[3]

Table 1: Attendance at NCAA Football Games

Season	*Attendance, in millions*
1955	17.3
1960	20.4
1966	25.3
1971	30.5
1975	31.7
1980	35.5
1983	34.8
Division I–A	25.38
Division I–AA	4.89
Division II	2.70
Division III	1.85

Sources: Jack Falla, *NCAA: The Voice of College Sports*. Mission, Kan.: National Collegiate Athletic Association, 1981, Chap. 6, App. A; and the NCAA Central Office.

This view would no doubt come as a surprise to the male basketball players at a prominent southwestern public university, for not a single one of these individuals—who competed on this university's powerhouse teams between 1968 and 1982—ever received a baccalaureate degree from that university.[4] The NCAA's view might also come as a surprise to the University of Florida, a typical public university that operates a big-time intercollegiate athletics program. In 1983–1984, the University of Florida budgeted $8.77 million for men's intercollegiate athletics, and planned to collect $6.74 million from the operation of its football team. The Gator Boosters, Inc., an organization of financial supporters for University of Florida intercollegiate athletics, provided the University with $2.52 million during the same time period.[5]

The truth is that big-time intercollegiate athletics is an industry that can be examined in much the same fashion as any other industry. Far from being an exceptional, impossible-to-examine situation, big-time intercollegiate athletics is an industry that has exhibited surprisingly predictable behavior and development. Economic conditions, not euphemistic statements, have been the controlling factors in the evolution of big-time intercollegiate athletics in the United States.

II. STRUCTURE

Defining the Industry

A rough, but usable, definition of an industry is that it is a collection of firms, each of which is supplying to the same potential buyers products that have considerable substitutability. The firms in the intercollegiate athletics industry are the individual colleges and universities that field athletic teams (for example, Ohio State University). From an economic standpoint, these *university-firms* are primarily involved in the selling of athletic entertainment to potential fans and ticket purchasers. In addition, there is a belief that the university-firms (via their athletic teams) are supplying intangibles, such as pride and identification, to alumni, legislators, and friends of the institution, who might reward or support the institution.[6] In addition, the university-firms in recent years have also been actively engaged in selling to radio and television networks the right to broadcast or televise the intercollegiate athletics contests in which their teams compete.[7]

Some of the capital for this multiproduct productive process includes stadiums, equipment, and the like. But the most crucial element in the production of intercollegiate athletics is people—the coaches, athletic directors, and (especially) the student-athletes, who play on the teams that the university-firms field. The competition for, and use of, inputs such as student-athletes is the key to understanding the development of modern intercollegiate athletics. The development of the NCAA, which is the largest regulatory body in intercollegiate athletics, has largely come about because most university-firms have desired to limit competition between themselves concerning how they may hire and use their student-athlete inputs. The NCAA has written hundreds of detailed rules and regulations that circumscribe the conditions under which an individual university-firm (e.g., the University of California at Los Angeles) may contact, visit, compete for, hire, and eventually use student-athletes. The genesis of these rules has nearly always been the desire on the part of the university-firms to restrict the competition for, and use of, student-athletes. A review of the development of the NCAA demonstrates how and why this has taken place.

The Development of the NCAA

The NCAA is the most powerful organization concerned with intercollegiate athletics. The NCAA currently has almost 800 individual university-firms as members, in addition to almost 175 other organizations and conferences that are insitutional members. Table 2 indicates how NCAA membership has grown over time. The NCAA's only rival, the National Association of Intercollegiate Athletics (NAIA), is a much smaller and economically less significant entity, which caters to institutions that are usually small in size and do not seek to compete in big-time intercollegiate athletics. Since 1981, the NCAA has extended its dominance to include women's intercollegiate athletics, resulting in the demise of the one-time capstone organization in women's intercollegiate athletics, the Association of Intercollegiate Athletics for Women (AIAW).

The NCAA was founded in 1906, as a consequence of the efforts of President Theodore Roosevelt and others to reduce the unsavory violence and mayhem that characterized intercollegiate football contests at the time. Another concern of Roosevelt and others was the preservation of amateurism. One means of doing this was to define athlete eligibility; another was to

Table 2: Membership of the NCAA: 1905–1983

Year	*Number of Members*
1906	38
1909	67
1912	97
1924	135
1945	210
1949	302
1955	398
1968	609
1980	883
1983	971

Sources: Jack Falla, *NCAA: The Voice of College Sports*. Mission, Kan.: National Collegiate Athletic Association, 1981, Chap. 3, App. A; and *The NCAA News*, various issues.

develop common rules for conducting games and competition. These rules were used by the NCAA when it began to sponsor regional and national championships in a growing number of sports. (The NCAA currently sponsors over 80 national championships for men and women athletes.)

The post-World War I years were boom years to intercollegiate athletics. Rising consumer disposable incomes, along with increased public interest in intercollegiate athletic competition, spurred various sports-related developments, such as the designation of "All-American" teams by the media, the national ranking of teams by the press, and the expressed desire of radio networks to broadcast key intercollegiate athletic contests.[8] This led many university-firms to use intercollegiate athletics to attract enrollment and (in some cases) to augment their revenues.

Then, as now, most fans were not interested in paying to see losing teams compete. This led to increasingly fierce struggles between and among university-firms for the best student-athlete inputs. At this time, some colleges and universities decided that they would neither compete nor pay for student-athletes. Thus, the 1920s and 1930s saw the beginning of the membership dichotomy: small institutions (e.g., Rhode Island College) chose not to compete for players, and large institutions (e.g., the University of Notre Dame) decided to operate big-time intercollegiate athletic programs, and to compete both for student-athletes and ticket-purchasing fans.

The end of World War II, in 1945, brought with it a flood of military veterans into colleges and universities across the United States. This threatened to upset partially the status quo in intercollegiate athletics, because some university-firms fielded teams composed of individuals who were superb athletes but indifferent students. A series of scandals, concerning unethical practices, payoffs to student-athletes, altered grades, and the like, resulted in many cries for reform. The result was the NCAA-sponsored "Sanity Code," which sought to stop the many abuses. But compliance with the Sanity Code was voluntary, and the financial incentives to violate it were too great. The Code was abandoned by the NCAA in 1951.

Simultaneously, a new technological innovation, television, threatened to alter the intercollegiate athletic landscape even more. Many colleges and universities were convinced that the televising of intercollegiate football contests (the first televised contest was the Columbia–Princeton game, in 1939) would reduce attendance at their own games. The combination of adverse public attention (the aforementioned abuses) and the desire of most NCAA members to limit the effects of television upon their gate attendance, led to dramatic increases in the power and control of the central NCAA organization. Within a few years, the NCAA was transformed. It had been a coordinating organization that was largely confined to rule-making and sponsoring championships, and it became one that had considerable financial clout, because of the lucrative television contracts that it negotiated for its members, and because the punitive actions taken by the NCAA to enforce its rules often entailed significant financial penalties. It is generally conceded that individual NCAA members approved of these trends because the anticipated effect was to equalize competition and to harness what would have otherwise been a free market for televising intercollegiate football contests. The typical NCAA-member institution exhibited a much greater interest in protecting its share of the intercollegiate athletics financial pie than it did in promoting either amateurism in general or the academic progress of student-athletes in particular.

The NCAA has always controlled the television rights to its own sponsored championships (e.g., in men's basketball, each year); and, until 1983, it also controlled the right to negotiate, on behalf of its members, for the right to televise any intercollegiate football contest. These television rights turned out to be a gold mine for the NCAA. In the 1984–1985 academic year, for example, the NCAA expected to earn over $31 million solely from selling the rights to televise its Division I men's basketball championship.[9] Prior to 1984, the NCAA had in addition earned an average of over $65 million per year for itself and its members from its football television contracts. (See Table 3). A 1984 U.S. Supreme Court decision forced the NCAA to allow the individual university-firms to negotiate their own football television contracts, as they had always been able to do in other sports, such as basketball.[10] This threatened the financial stability of the NCAA and at the same time accentuated the existing inequality among the various university-firms. Some institutions (e.g., the University of Oklahoma) were more easily able to sell the television rights to their contests than others (for example, McNeese State University).

In sum, the history of intercollegiate athletics and its dominant organization, the NCAA, is one in which the financial bases for every decision

Table 3: Dollar Value of NCAA Television Contracts

Season	Annual Mean Value of Contract, in Millions	
1952	$ 1.1	
1953	1.7	
1955	1.3	
1959	2.2	
1960,1961	3.1	
1964,1965	6.5	
1966–1969	7.8	
1970,1971	12.0	
1972,1973	13.5	
1978–1981	30.0	
1982–1985	65.9	(This contract invalidated by U.S. Supreme Court in 1984.)

Sources: Jack Falla, *NCAA: The Voice of College Sports.* Mission, Kans.: National Collegiate Athletic Association, Chap. 6, App. A; and the NCAA Central Office.

and development have become increasingly obvious. The NCAA has consistently reacted to the commercialization of intercollegiate athletics in two ways. First, it has attempted to minimize costs of competition between and among its members by legislating rules that restrict competition, particularly for student-athletes. Second, it has attempted to control the most significant source of intercollegiate athletic revenue, the televising of contests between its members. Unfortunately for the NCAA, the behavior of the individual university-firms has made the accomplishment of these two goals exceedingly difficult to attain. We will now see why that has been true.

III. CONDUCT: NCAA CARTELIZATION

A cartel is an organization of firms that agrees to pursue joint policies with respect to key aspects of the environment in which the firms operate. The most common subjects of agreement are pricing policies, levels of output, market territories, sales quotas, use of input, and advertising expenditures. The NCAA is a reasonably effective, though somewhat unstable, cartel because it (1) sets the maximum price that can be paid for intercollegiate athletes; (2) regulates the quantity of athletes that can be purchased in a given time period; (3) regulates the duration and intensity of usage of those athletes; (4) occasionally fixes the price at which sports output can be sold; (5) periodically informs its members about transactions, costs, market conditions, and sales techniques; (6) occasionally pools and distributes portions of the organization's profits; and, (7) polices the behavior of its members and assesses penalties upon those deemed to have broken the organization's rules.[11]

What Motivates the NCAA?

Insofar as the university-firms are concerned, the NCAA exists to suppress and equalize competition between and among its members. Few, if any, NCAA members would admit openly to this motive. However, athletic competition works best and is most profitable when competition is relatively equal. It is worth noting that the major spurts of "reform" in the NCAA's history have usually occurred when there has been significant evidence of competitive imbalance among its members (for example, immediately after World War II). The effect of these and other "reforms" has nearly always been to suppress and equalize competition. Indeed, there is little evidence that in the long run the NCAA is truly interested in reforms that have the effect of enhancing academic standards. The NCAA and its members have seldom supported academic initiatives that will result in competitive imbalance or reduce the profitability of intercollegiate athletics. As one observer has stated, the NCAA and its members recognize only two things—money and bad publicity.[12] As a consequence, "big-time college sports programs are notorious for shortchanging athletes who are supposed to be receiving educational opportunities."[13]

It is important to differentiate between the motivation of the university-firms and that of the NCAA central organization. Whereas the members typically are interested in some form of joint profit maximization, designed to wring maximum revenues out of intercollegiate athletics, the NCAA central organization, like a typical bureaucracy, gives strong evidence of being interested in its own power, size, and permanence. Concern for abstract ideals such as amateurism and academic standards has seldom been in evidence among the NCAA leadership. *The Sporting News,* conventionally a strong spokesman for the sporting establishment, has in recent years frequently taken the NCAA central office and leadership severely to task for having overcommercialized intercollegiate athletics.[14] *The Sporting News* is correct in perceiving what the policies of the NCAA are, but has exhibited a bit of naïveté about the causes. Given the financial incentives of the NCAA's members, and given the structure of the intercollegiate athletics industry, different behavior on the part of the NCAA and its members could hardly be expected.

The NCAA's Structure and Its Effects Upon Conduct

Cartels succeed or fail primarily on the basis of the structure of the cartel and the environment in which the cartel operates. The most important facets of cartel structure and environment generally are the following: (1) the number of firms in the cartel; (2) the number of *points of initiative* in the cartel; (3) the knowledge that cartel members and outsiders have of the cartel's transactions; (4) the existence of barriers to entry; (5) the similarity of the interests of the cartel members, particularly where revenues and costs are concerned; and, (6) demand conditions in the cartel's markets. We will examine each of these facets in turn.

Number of Firms. Successful cartels seldom have a large number of member firms. A small membership allows the cartel to police member behavior more easily and to be able to impose effective discipline upon wayward cartel members. The NCAA now has almost 800 individual members; therefore it is very difficult to monitor the behavior of its members. If the NCAA's enforcement division were to visit one NCAA member daily, on each day of a five-day work week, and do so 52 weeks a year, it would take the enforcers over three years simply to visit each member. This helps explain why the NCAA's Walter Byers observed that "we are not keeping up . . ." with cheaters, even though in 1984 the NCAA deployed 10 full-time and 25 part-time investigators. The NCAA planned to spend almost $1.5 million on enforcement activities in 1985.

There is no magic number that we can decide is the answer to the question of whether a cartel has too many members to be effective. It recently has become evident that the Organization of Petroleum Exporting Countries (OPEC) has been unable to enforce price and output discipline upon its members, despite a reasonably small membership (about twenty countries). On the other hand, major league professional baseball (26 teams) and major league professional football (28 teams) have been relatively more successful in maintaining member discipline. Therefore, a small number of members is preferable, but this does not guarantee the success of a cartel.

Number of Points of Initiative. A point of initiative (in cartel jargon) is a place where one can buy, sell, exchange, or otherwise utilize the property rights to a resource. Successful cartels seldom have large numbers of points of initiative. The probability of cartel success increases if the cartel can restrict its members to undertaking their economic actions only at certain times and places.

The number of points of initiative is almost unlimited insofar as the NCAA and its membership are concerned. There are approximately 10,000 football players and 1,000 coaches in the NCAA's highest competitive division in football. In men's and women's basketball, the comparable numbers are approximately 45,000 players and 1,200 coaches. The number of alumni and camp followers of a team who might intrude is virtually infinite. There are also many professional agents, who seek to represent highly skilled players in their negotiations with professional sports teams.

The large number of points of initiative militates against the NCAA's effectiveness; however, when the NCAA can determine that a rule has been violated, it can impose truly impressive penalties upon violators. In 1983, for example, the President of the University of Southern California (USC), Dr. James Zumberge, estimated that an NCAA-imposed ban upon football television appearances by USC would cost USC several million dollars.[16]

The NCAA has in recent years changed its internal governance structure several times, in order to reduce the disparity between and among members and, at the same time, reduce the number of points of initiative. In football, for example, the university-firms are now grouped in four divisions; a particular institution's classification depends upon the level of its own financial commitment to intercollegiate football, as well as on the degree of fan interest, as indicated by attendance at football games. This had the effect of increasing homogeneity of university-firms inside a given division, and increasing the heterogeneity between the divisions. Division I–A football institutions, for example, now can legislate rules that apply only to them. This has allowed large university-firms, such as Pennsylvania State University, to go their own way, without being impeded by the wishes of smaller, less athletically oriented institutions.

Knowledge of Cartel Transactions. In effective cartels, all cartel members immediately learn of a transaction undertaken by a member, but noncartel members are kept in a state of ignorance about such transactions, and about the operation of the cartel as a whole. Individual cartel members find it difficult to cheat when other cartel members are quickly apprised of the cheater's actions. Consider once again OPEC, the oil cartel. The world oil market is so large and so diverse that it is relatively easy for the individual members (for example, Venezuela) to undercut the established cartel price without being observed.

Much the same situation exists in the case of the NCAA. Some of its members' actions—for example, the signing of a blue-chip athlete—are widely publicized. Other actions, for example, procuring a plush summer job for an athlete, are usually secrets that are kept from other NCAA members, as well as the public. Indeed, in 1984, Mike Rozier, the Heisman Trophy-winning running back for the University of Nebraska, revealed that he had received a steady series of cash payments from a professional agent while playing football for the Cornhuskers—a fact that had not been detected by the NCAA, by the University of Nebraska's competitors, or even (the University argued) by itself.[17]

Industries and markets that are characterized by competition are typically those in which any given competitor finds it extremely difficult to hide his actions from his competitors. One gasoline station cannot long hide from other stations the per gallon price that it charges for its gasoline. A supplier of microcomputer softwear finds it difficult to keep secret the features that it offers for sale in one of its floppy-disk programs. Quite the opposite is true of intercollegiate athletics. How can the NCAA keep track of all of the perquisites and concessions that might be offered to the parents and girl or boy friends of athletes, who are courted in locations far removed from the campus? How can the NCAA monitor the actual prices that supporters of a university-firm's basketball team pay the members of that team for the complimentary tickets that each player usually receives for each game? The answer, of course, is that the NCAA cannot do so effectively. And this is one of the most important reasons why the NCAA receives a relatively low grade on this aspect of cartelization behavior. Even the NCAA's Walter

Byers has joined those who admit that as many as 30 percent of the institutions that operate big-time intercollegiate athletic programs cheat consistently, and are not penalized.[18]

Barriers to Entry. A typical cartel strategy is to attempt to limit entry into its market, in order to enhance the chances of cartel members to earn economic rents. The NCAA has done so, but only in a limited sense. In theory, the NCAA is a voluntary organization, with only minimal barriers to entry. Any college or university that subscribes to the NCAA's stated purposes, and which agrees to abide by the NCAA's rules, may join the organization. Nonetheless, the NCAA has established strict requirements of admission into several of its divisions, for example, the big-time Division I–A in football. In order to be classified in Division I–A, a university-firm must sponsor a given number of intercollegiate sports, and then must satisfy requirements that relate to the size of the University's football stadium and the attendance at the University's football games. For example, to qualify for Division I–A status in football, a university-firm must have a home stadium that seats 30,000 or more spectators, and must have an average attendance of more than 17,000 at its home football games, at least once during a four-year period. This criterion immediately eliminates from consideration well over 80 percent of all university-firms in the NCAA.

The major reasons why the Division I–A institutions wish to limit entry into their division is so that they may fashion rules and regulations more to their own tastes. This typically tranlates into rules and regulations that recognize the profound economic bases of big-time intercollegiate athletics, and the strenuous competition that results. The university-firms in Division I–A recently passed legislation that would have established higher academic standards for those individuals who might receive the typical "full ride" athletic scholarship that the institutions offer. But the implementation of this proposal met with stiff opposition after it became known that the higher academic requirement would have eliminated a significant proportion of the high school athletes whom the Division I–A institutions usually court and recruit.[19] It remains to be seen whether any significant minimum academic requirements will ever be adopted by Division I–A institutions.

Until 1984, one of the significant incentives for Division I–A institutions to limit membership in their division was the apparent correlation of Division I–A status with increased access to the millions of dollars of football television revenues derived from the NCAA's contract with the television networks. The U.S. Supreme Court decision on that subject ended the NCAA's practice of preventing Division I–A members from negotiating their own football television contracts. Several coalitions of NCAA members now negotiate their own football television contracts (e.g., the College Football Association, an organization of over 60 Division I–A football powers).

The consequence of the U.S. Supreme Court decision has been a weakened NCAA, and more financial disparity among NCAA members. Predictably, a free market for football television has also increased the number of games seen by viewers, and more games of their choice. As long as the NCAA had the power to decide which games to include in its television "package," the networks were forced to accept a range of games that the NCAA agreed to supply. This was a form of "full-line forcing," a not uncommon industrial practice. (It means that a seller forces customers to buy less desirable products along with the very desirable products that they want to buy.) Thus, the NCAA would supply a low-demand game (for instance, the Appalachian State versus The Citadel) along with a high-demand game (for instance, the University of Oklahoma versus the University of Southern California). It is noteworthy that the NCAA offered television stations this choice for a Saturday in the fall of 1982. Four stations opted for the Appalachian State–Citadel game and over two hundred chose the Oklahoma–USC game.

Clearly, the NCAA television package violated the prescriptions of consumer sovereignty, especially when it placed arbitrary limits on the number of times that a given university-firm might appear on television, or when it forced the networks to televise games of marginal attractiveness. And the NCAA also engaged in price-fixing. The NCAA contract with the networks resulted in a single price being paid to any university-firm whose team appeared on a telecast, regardless of viewer interest, or the number of stations presenting the telecast. Thus, in the foregoing 1982 example, Oklahoma and USC received the same rights payment as did Appalachian State and The Citadel. This attempt by the NCAA to equalize the financial status of its members by means of price-fixing was specifically prohibited by the U.S. Supreme Court in its 1984 decision. The Court did not accept the argument of the NCAA, that its actions were an application of the famous Rule of Reason and thus were necessary in order to preserve an orderly market. The Court ultimately decided that this particular "orderly" market was synonymous with a cartelized market, which was not responsive to consumer tastes.

It should be noted, however, that many of the university-firms who had fought for the right to televise their own intercollegiate football games found that the newly instituted free market for football television actually decreased the total television revenues they received. The NCAA television package had strictly rationed the number of games that could be shown; hence, the price that the networks had paid for each game was higher than would have been the case in a free-market arrangement. The demand of networks for televising games was apparently price inelastic. Thus, when more games were televised, this drove down the average price the networks paid for each game. As a result, the total revenues collected by the university-firms because of football television declined by an estimated $42 million.[20] That the average price paid by the networks for a typical game would fall in a free market was predictable, because the university-firms were moving down the demand curve for televising their games. What the university-firms did not forecast was the extent to which free-market competition between and among university-firms would drive television prices downward.

Similarity of Interests. Successful cartels are characterized by their members' general similarity of interests. The most important aspects of similarity relate to classic economic variables: revenues, costs, levels of production, and the like. But it has been extremely difficult for the NCAA to rationalize the interests and needs of Clemson University, of the Atlantic Coast Conference, with those of a typical Prairie Conference member, such as Illinois College. Clemson University takes in more in revenues from a single one of its football games than all of the members of the Prairie Conference combined will take in, for all their sporting events, for a decade or more. It is hardly surprising, therefore, that members of the Atlantic Coast Conference often do not see eye to eye with members of the Prairie Conference when the NCAA formulates its rules and debates its future.

The amoeba-like division of the NCAA into more and more subdivisions has been a clear attempt to group together members who do have similar revenue, cost, and output circumstances. Some view these actions as presaging the imminent dissolution of the NCAA as an organization. However, dissolution is not likely to occur. The NCAA, or some other organization with a different name but with similar objectives, will almost surely continue to exist. There are two major reasons why this is so. First, even the NCAA's most vocal opponents confess that there is a need for a national organization to undertake both the regulatory and noneconomic functions of the NCAA (rule making, the sponsoring of championships, and the like). Second, there are significant financial disincentives deterring a single institution (or even a group of such institutions) operating a big-time program from leaving the NCAA. The latter point will be discussed later on in the chapter.

For secession from the NCAA to be successful, a large number of homogeneous university-firms would have to leave the NCAA at the same time. Only then could this group negotiate its own television contracts, conduct its own championship games, and provide its members with the considerable service that the NCAA currently provides. The NCAA's only visible competitor, the NAIA, is simply not a viable option if a university-firm wishes to field nationally prominent teams that attract media attention and ticket-purchasing fans. Consider also that some 170 institutions in the NCAA now field Division I men's basketball teams but are not classified Division I–A in football. If the University of Notre Dame (Division I–A in football) seceded from the NCAA, could it continue to schedule Marquette University (Division I in men's basketball, but not a football competitor) in men's basketball? What about women's competitions? Would there be multiple championships?

It is most likely, then, that the NCAA or a similar organization will continue to exist, but that even more segmentation of the NCAA's membership will take place. The degree of dissimilarity of members' interests will be the most important determinant of any new divisions that develop.

Walter Byers, the Executive Director of the NCAA, has recently talked candidly about the possibility of an openly professional division within the NCAA. It would pursue free-market intercollegiate athletic policies without reference to old norms, such as amateurism, or even academic standing on the part of the athletes involved.[21] This public discussion by the NCAA's powerful leader followed similar observations by academic leaders as diverse as Howard Swearer, President of Brown University, of the Ivy League,[22] and Barbara Uehling, Chancellor of the University of Missouri, in Columbia, Mo., a member of the Big Eight Conference.[23]

Demand Conditions. The economic success of a cartel is enhanced when it purchases its input from sellers who are small and unorganized. This is quite evidently the case with respect to most intercollegiate athletes; their ability to bargain is constrained by collusion between and among university-firms, and their ability to unite and organize is severely hampered by their ages and geographic dispersion. The result is that the university-firms often earn economic rents because they possess an input that is relatively limited in supply, but which is unable to negotiate for itself a price that approximates its market value.

As we mentioned before, a skilled basketball center such as Patrick Ewing has an incremental value of several million dollars to the institution that controls his services, Georgetown University. The approximate marginal value of Herschel Walker, the All-American football running back for the University of Georgia Bulldogs, has been estimated to be of the same magnitude. For an athlete of this caliber, who wishes to realize some or all of his marginal revenue, two options are available. First, he can accept illicit, under-the-table benefits and payments (as in the Rozier case mentioned earlier), or he can leave the university-firm and sign with a professional team, for whatever financial rewards his skills will command. Akeem Olajuwon, the All-American basketball center of the University of Houston, pursued this strategy after he had completed his junior year of eligibility, in 1983. Olajuwon signed for an estimated $6.3 million, spread over six years.[24]

Akeem Olajuwon left the University of Houston before he had exhausted all of his eligibility to play men's intercollegiate basketball there. This imposed potentially severe financial losses upon the University of Houston. It is for this reason that the NCAA traditionally attempted to prevent any intercollegiate athlete from leaving an NCAA member college and signing with a professional team before his intercollegiate eligibility has been exhausted. This was done under the guise of "protecting" the athlete, i.e., in order to increase the probability that the athlete would eventually earn a college degree. This self-serving rationale on the part of the NCAA and its members was transparent to most observers. It was clear that by propagating such a rule, the NCAA would derive great financial benefits. It was also apparent that the NCAA was not interested in whether or not an athlete ever obtained a baccalaureate degree. In any case, several courts have ruled that the NCAA violated the antitrust law by preventing athletes from signing professional contracts, and this NCAA rule has been effectively gutted. However, this development has significantly increased the financial incentives for individual university-firms to cheat (or to condone cheating by alumni and friends of the institution) to induce their exceptionally skilled athletes not to negotiate early contracts with professional teams.

When the NCAA "sells" its outputs, it confronts some customers who are not organized (that is, fans who purchase tickets to contests) and some who definitely possess some monopsony power (television networks). With respect to its network customers, the NCAA has exhibited considerable skill in getting them to bid against each other for the privilege of televising events such as the Division I men's national basketball championship (which brings over $30 million per year to the NCAA's coffers). The emergence of additional networks, such as the all-sports network (ESPN) and Ted Turner's Atlanta Superstation cable network, has strengthened the NCAA's bargaining position, because it has decreased the negotiating power of the three major networks, ABC, CBS, and NBC.

IV. PERFORMANCE: CURRENT INDUSTRY ISSUES

There are two current issues that continue to accelerate economic change in the intercollegiate athletics industry. These issues are the role and development of women's intercollegiate athletics and the perennially divisive problem of televised football games. The performance of the industry must be evaluated in light of these issues.

Women's Intercollegiate Athletics

Until the 1970s, the NCAA exhibited no interest in women's intercollegiate athletics. Indeed, in 1964 the NCAA specifically excluded women athletes from competition in the NCAA's men's championship events. Subsequently, in 1972, legislation, popularly known as Title IX, became law. Title IX prohibited discrimination in educational programs on the basis of sex. Although the implications of Title IX for intercollegiate athletics were ill-defined, the NCAA and its members soon sensed that individual university-firms might be required to expend funds in women's intercollegiate athletics that would be roughly equivalent to those being expended in men's intercollegiate athletics. This scenario sent shivers through the directors (almost all of whom were males) of intercollegiate athletics at the big-time football schools.

The NCAA, acting on the advice of its legal counsel, in 1973 eliminated its ban on women championship participants. Throughout the 1970s, the NCAA central office attempted to parry the impact of Title IX, in two ways. First, the NCAA supported legislative moves (none of which were successful) to remove intercollegiate athletics from the purview of Title IX. Second, beginning in 1975, a series of NCAA conventions were asked to approve the notion that the NCAA should regulate women's intercollegiate athletics as well as men's.

The NCAA's interest in women's intercollegiate athletics was strongly opposed by the Association of Intercollegiate Athletics for Women (AIAW), which had become the clearly dominant organization in women's intercollegiate athletics. The AIAW argued that the NCAA's attentions were unwanted, and that the NCAA's real interest in women's intercollegiate athletics was in controlling and capping the rising expenditures being made there. Expenditures on women's intercollegiate athletics rose from 1 percent of total intercollegiate athletic expenditures in 1972 to over 15 percent in 1978.[25] When, in addition, the AIAW negotiated its own television contract, many NCAA members sensed a growing threat to the financial security of their men's intercollegiate programs.

One financial argument raised by the NCAA at that time was that the growing expenditures made upon women's intercollegiate athletics required subsidization by the major men's "revenue" sports—football and basketball, at most institutions. A typical male athletic director would ask, Why should a women's field hockey team benefit from the ticket and television revenues raised by the men's football team?

In any event, the NCAA entered women's intercollegiate athletics with its own set of women's championships in the 1981–1982 academic year. The NCAA held its championship events on the same dates as the AIAW championships. Hence, each member was forced to choose between the NCAA and the AIAW. The AIAW lost this battle, at least partially, because it was NCAA policy to reimburse nearly all of the travel expenses of athletes and teams competing in NCAA championship events. The AIAW, which lacked the lucrative football television contract that the NCAA had, could not pay such expenses.

The AIAW eventually halted operations in 1983, but only after it had filed suit and charged the NCAA with monopolization and predatory conduct. The AIAW noted that the NCAA would spend some $3 million on women's intercollegiate athletics, but would generate only about a half million dollars from the same programs. The AIAW charged that the NCAA was exercising what industrial organization economists usually call "the power of the long purse." This hypothesis, for which there is only limited empirical evidence, suggests that a large firm will use its superior resources to enter a market, will subsequently drive out smaller and less well-heeled competitors by predatory actions, and ultimately exploit the new market by raising prices.

A United States District Court ultimately rejected the AIAW's monopolization argument, despite the fact that this case covered some of the same economic ground as the football television case, which the NCAA lost.[26] Despite the District Court's decision, strong superficial similarities exist between the behavior of the NCAA and the behavior of a multiproduct monopolist who engages in cross-subsidization and price discrimination in order to (1) deter entry, and (2) protect profits. The United States Postal Service and American Telephone and Telegraph often have been accused of this kind of behavior in the past. Those who subscribe to this view see the NCAA as having taken preventive action in women's intercollegiate athletics in order to minimize the drain on its members' profits, which might occur if women's intercollegiate athletics were to go its own way. As one observer has said, "It is hardly blasphemy to suggest that the NCAA would have no more interest in women's intercollegiate athletics than it does in random pick-up basketball games on urban asphalt if it were not for the increasingly important financial considerations involved.[27] In recent years, the NCAA rarely has undertaken any important action in which financial considerations have not buttressed or even determined the final outcome.

Football Television

On June 27, 1984, the United States Supreme Court ended the NCAA's three-decade reign over the televising of intercollegiate football games. By a vote of 7 to 2, the Court agreed with two lower courts that the NCAA's activities in football television constituted output restriction and price-fixing, and thus violated the Sherman Antitrust Act. The Court commented that "it is undeniable that these practices share characteristics of restraints that we have previously labeled unreasonable." The Court also labeled the NCAA a "classic cartel," and stated that "there can be no doubt that the challenged practices of the NCAA constitute a 'restraint of trade.' " By its decision, the Court clearly established that the property rights to the televising of intercollegiate football games belong to the individual university-firms, and not to the NCAA.[28] The Court's decision voided over $280 million of football television contracts that the NCAA had negotiated for its members.

A major consequence of the Supreme Court decision on football television was a period of frantic negotiations by individual university-firms, and by select groups of these firms, with various local television stations and with national networks. The most lucrative contract was negotiated with ABC-TV by the College Football Association (CFA), an organization of 63 Division I–A football superpowers. Another contract was negotiated with CBS-TV by university-firms that are members of the Pacific Ten and the Big Ten conferences. (None of the institutions in the CFA are members of the Pacific Ten or Big Ten conferences.) Still other, less significant contracts were negotiated by individual institutions and athletic conferences.

The NCAA was initially prohibited from participating in the football television market. However, in November 1984, the U.S. District Court Judge who had rendered the original decision in the case, Judge Juan G. Burciaga, ruled that the NCAA could participate in future football television negotiations provided two conditions were met: (1) participation by NCAA members was voluntary, and (2) the NCAA did not once again attempt to "restrict output or stifle competition."[29] Because there has been no strong move on the part of its members to push it in the direction of football television participation, the NCAA apparently will no longer negotiate football television contracts.

But Judge Burciaga did allow the NCAA to reimpose television bans upon university-firms that violate NCAA rules. The television ban is an extremely powerful tool in the hands of the NCAA, because a single football television appearance might be worth a million dollars. Therefore, the NCAA can once again deny such revenues to members who violate its rules, even though the NCAA will not have negotiated the television contract. It is this little-noticed stipulation on the part of Judge Burciaga that has substantially rehabilitated the NCAA's power as it deals with the university-firms that operate big-time intercollegiate athletic programs. As William B. Hunt, the NCAA's assistant director of enforcement said, the "decision will assist in the effort to implement an effective enforcement program."[30] Indeed, no cartel can succeed if it is unable to discipline its members. Effective disciplinary power once again resides with the NCAA. Although the operation of the NCAA as a cartel will never run smoothly (because of the structure of the intercollegiate athletic market), the revived ability of the NCAA to impose significant financial penalties upon selected members will enable it to survive, and even prosper.

It is noteworthy that the football television contracts negotiated by the CFA and by the Pacific Ten–Big Ten Conference coalition have been challenged by legal suits sponsored by television cable companies and independent television stations. These suits charge that, by restricting competition, the new contracts violate antitrust law, in part because the new contracts prevent the cable networks and independent stations from televising football games during certain time periods on Saturday. Furthermore, the new contracts are designed to discourage "cross-televising," for instance, when a CFA would televise a home game against an opponent from the Big Ten Conference (a non-CFA member). Such interferences in the market, the plaintiffs argue, are precisely what Judge Burciaga sought to prevent in his original decision.[31]

If the newest round of suits is successful, then it is unlikely that there will ever be a football television agreement that is national in scope. Individual university-firms and specific intercollegiate athletic conferences would freely and independently negotiate their own individual contracts. However, this would not introduce anarchy, because precisely this situation has existed in men's basketball and all other sports for many years. Although the NCAA has often looked longingly at the lucrative prospect of controlling all television for men's basketball, it has never claimed to control the property rights to that televising. Hence, individual university-firms have proceeded independently in men's basketball.

V. PUBLIC POLICY CONSIDERATIONS

The National Collegiate Athletic Association (NCAA) is the dominant organization in modern big-time intercollegiate athletics. Unbeknownst to most of its members, the NCAA has in recent decades acted as an economic cartel. Prices have been fixed, output controlled, and extensive rules and regulations have been promulgated concerning the use of the primary input to intercollegiate athletics—the student-athletes.

The cartelized behavior of the NCAA was never a matter of great import to either its own members, or to the public, until the revenues involved reached impressive dimensions. The NCAA's budget now approaches $40 million annually; and until it was thwarted by the United States Supreme Court, the NCAA controlled television contracts worth well over a quarter of a billion dollars. Furthermore, the annual revenues realized by Division I–A university-firms (from all phases of their football operations) approached a half billion dollars in 1983 and 1984. Hence, whereas the economic impact of big-time intercollegiate athletics was a *de minimus* consideration in 1950, this is not the case in the 1980s.

In 1950, big-time intercollegiate athletics was substantially noncartelized, and the plethora of rules and regulations that now exist in the industry were unknown. Many of the most important actions and decisions of the day were made in a nonmarket context. There was much less reference to purchasing inputs and selling outputs. Rather, intercollegiate athletic events were often sponsored by a university, without reference to the teams' market acceptance, or lack thereof.

In the decades since 1950, there has been an obvious emergence of economic motives in intercollegiate athletics. Now, big-time intercollegiate athletics is an identifiable industry, in which approximately one hundred university-firms compete in football and approximately two hundred compete in men's basketball. In women's intercollegiate athletics, particularly women's basketball, there is increasing evidence of a similar evolution. The NCAA has accelerated the emergence of these developments by cartelizing the industry, and by consistently advocating policies that have increased economic incentives. The NCAA, then, is both a cause and a reflection of powerful forces that have resulted in the emergence of big-time intercollegiate athletics as an industry.

What reasonable public policy alternatives exist today with respect to the NCAA and intercollegiate athletics? One current proposal advocates that the university-firms that operate big-time intercollegiate athletic programs acknowledge openly that they are really in the entertainment business, and, although a certain amount of such peripheral activity is acceptable for a college or university, it should be kept separate from their primary academic activities. Under this "professionalization" arrangement (which has been gaining public support), college athletes might be students, but, for them to compete as athletes this status would not be necessary. Universities would be free to pursue whatever policy they wished in the area of intercollegiate athletics, much as they now do in other activities, such as collegiate theater and music. Universities interested in intercollegiate athletics would voluntarily group themselves with peer institutions which espouse the same values and which would make roughly the same financial commitment.

A much different position is advocated by those who seek the reform, renewal, and strengthening of the amateur student-athlete model, which has been the focus of the NCAA's rhetoric for so many years. Proponents of this approach (which continues to have the most adherents) argue for more regulations, stiffer penalties for rules violators, and a return to the NCAA's founding ideals and spirit.[32] These individuals argue that intercollegiate athletics constitutes a legitimate extracurricular activity for students, but that it must be undertaken in light of the university's overriding academic purposes.

One manifestation of the regulatory-reform approach is the NCAA's Proposition 48, which would require new freshmen athletes to satisfy each of three criteria in order to be eligible for intercollegiate athletic competition: (1) have a high school grade-point average of at least 2.0 on a 4.0 scale; (2) have a high school grade-point average of at least 2.0 in a specified curriculum of 11 core academic courses, such as English, mathematics, and the like; and, (3) have a combined score of at least 700 on the Scholastic Aptitude Test (SAT), or 15 on the American College Test (ACT). The stated purpose of Proposition 48 is to ensure that universities admit student-athletes who have a realistic chance to achieve educational progress, and eventually to graduate. Nevertheless, although this purpose has been generally applauded, the reliance of Proposition 48 on standardized test scores has generated strenuous opposition. For example, it has been pointed out that about half of all black students who take either the SAT or the ACT score below the respective 700 and 15, the suggested cut-off points for athletic eligibility. It is not clear whether Proposition 48 will be implemented as originally scheduled on August 1, 1986.

So long as significant economic incentives exist within big-time intercollegiate athletics, the effectiveness of the regulatory-reform approach will be in doubt. For example, if a highly successful football or basketball team is ultimately worth several million dollars to a university-firm, then even the noblest sentiments and goals are unlikely to prevent the increasing commercialization of intercollegiate athletics, rule-breaking and cheating, and the consequent general ineffectiveness of the regulatory-reform model. The key, then, is to devise rules that reduce economic incentives without violating antitrust laws. One such possibility involves television revenue-sharing. Suppose all television revenues earned by the NCAA or its members were divided equally among all the members. Then, only modest advantages would accrue to any single university-firm that would deliberately choose to lower its academic standards or to cheat in order to produce a winning team.

NCAA members who have operated big-time intercollegiate athletic programs have previously rejected a "divide-the-revenues" approach, which is a modern-day application of Robin Hood philosophy. This rejection implies that the current economic incentive structure in intercollegiate athletics is likely to continue, and that the progressive commercialization and segmentation of intercollegiate athletics will proceed apace. Cries for reform will go unheeded because, given current institutional arrangement, big-time intercollegiate athletics is an industry, with firms that behave much like firms in any other industry. Those who expect noneconomic or uneconomic behavior from universities in this context are guilty of naïveté, and would be well advised not to hold their collective breaths as they wait for their ideal amateur-athletic millenium to appear.

NOTES

1. "The Biggest Men on Campus," *The Sporting News,* **198:**6 (April 23, 1984).

2. Detailed presentations of this analysis may be found in James V. Koch, "A Troubled Cartel: The NCAA," *Law and Contemporary Problems,* **38:**135–150 (Winter–Spring, 1973); and, Koch, "Intercollegiate Athletics: An Economic Explanation," *Social Science Quarterly,* **64:**360–374 (June 1983).

3. National Collegiate Athletic Association, *1983–1984 Manual of the National Collegiate Athletic Association.* Mission, Kan.: The National Collegiate Athletic Association, 1983, p. 9.

4. For a recent commentary on the nature of this problem see Frederick C. Klein, "Do College Jocks Graduate?" *The Wall Street Journal,* Nov. 11, 1984, p. 26.

5. Joe Marcin, "The Milch Cow," *The Sporting News,* **196:**26 (Sept. 19, 1983).

6. For a more lengthy discussion of the nature of the production function in intercollegiate athletics, see James V. Koch, "The Economics of 'Big-Time' Intercollegiate Athletics," *Social Science Quarterly,* **52:**248–260 (Sept. 1971).

7. The first All-American team was actually selected by Walter Camp in 1889. Grantland Rice subsequently assumed the leadership in the selection process. In 1936, the Associated Press initiated its own national ranking of football teams.

8. *NCAA News,* **21:**1 (Sept. 11, 1984).

9. *Board of Regents v. National Collegiate Athletic Association,* 546 F. Supp. 1276 (WD Okla. 1982), 707 F. 2d. 1147 (CA10, 1983), affirmed 464 U.S. 1 (1983).

10. See Koch (1983), *Supra,* Note 2.

11. Dan Stormer, as quoted in an editorial, "New Day for Athletes?" *The Sporting News,* **198:**6 (Aug. 8, 1984).

12. This is the view of *The Sporting News,* as found in *supra,* Note 11.

13. See, among many, Joe Marcin, "NCAA Postpones Improving Academic Standards," *The Sporting News,* **198:**53 (Oct. 29, 1984).

14. Walter Byers, as quoted in Charles S. Farrell, "NCAA Admits Difficulty in Catching Violators of Recruiting and Financial-Aid Regulations," *Chronicle of Higher Education,* No. 24 (Sept. 5, 1984), pp. 29, ff., at p. 29.

15. President Zumberge anticipated that there would be two or three television appearances, at approximately one million dollars each.

16. Mr. Rozier admitted that he received $600 per month from his agent, and that he had signed a professional contract with the Pittsburgh Maulers, of the United States Football League, prior to the end of the intercollegiate football season. George Vecsey, "Colleges Go With a Winner," *The New York Times*, Oct. 19, 1984, p. 24.

17. "Rise in Cheating by Colleges Seen," *The New York Times*, Aug. 1, 1984, p. 24. Mr. Byers' views have been recorded in "Why Is This Man Saying the Things He's Saying?" *Sports Illustrated*, **61:**11 (Sept. 17, 1984).

18. The effects of Rule 48 would have been differentially severe with respect to Black athletes, because the rule contained a requirement that a freshman athlete receiving financial aid would have to have scored at the 700 level or above on the combined verbal and quantitative sections of the SAT examination. Fully 69 percent of black male athletes, and 59 percent of black female athletes, would have been disqualified if such a rule were in existence. "Research Forecasts Effects of 'No. 48,' " *NCAA News*, **21:**1, ff. (Sept. 29, 1984).

19. "Colleges May Find TV's Golden Egg Is Tarnished," *The New York Times*, Aug. 26, 1984, p. 27.

20. Byers, as quoted in *Sports Illustrated, supra,* Note 16.

21. Howard Swearer, "An Ivy President Looks at College Sports," *The New York Times*, Feb. 21, 1982, Sec. 5, p. 2.

22. Barbara S. Uehling, "Athletics and Academe: Creative Divorce or Reconciliation?" *Educational Record*, **64:** 13–15 (Summer 1983).

23. *The New York Times*, Aug. 9, 1984, p. 18.

24. Data obtained from the NCAA and AIAW.

25. *Association of Intercollegiate Athletics for Women v. National Collegiate Athletic Association*, 558 F. Supp. 487 (D.D.C. 1983), affirmed, 735 F.2d 577 (D.C. Cir. 1984).

26. Koch (1983), *supra,* Note 2, p. 372.

27. Linda Greenhouse, "High Court Ends NCAA Control of TV Football: Restraint of Trade Cited," *The New York Times*, June 28, 1984, pp. 1, ff., at p. 1.

28. Gordon S. White, Jr., "NCAA to Pass Up TV Role for Now," *The New York Times*, Nov. 2, 1984, p. 28.

29. "Judge Clears Way for NCAA to Play Role in TV Pacts," *Chronicle of Higher Education*, No. 24 (Nov. 7, 1984), pp. 1, ff., at p. 34.

30. Judge Burciaga will have ample opportunity to make clear what he did mean, because the case involving the CFA will be heard in his courtroom. "Burciaga to Hear Suit Against CFA," *NCAA News*, **12:**1 (Nov. 12, 1984).

31. Robert H. Atwell, "Keeping the Amateur in Athletics," *Educational Record*, **64:**16–17 (Summer 1983).

SUGGESTED READINGS

Atwell, Robert H. "Keeping the Amateur in Athletics." *Educational Record*, **64:**16–17 (Summer 1983).

Falla, Jack. *NCAA: Voice of College Sports*. Mission, Kan.: National Collegiate Athletic Association, 1981.

Koch, James V. "Economics of 'Big-Time' Intercollegiate Athletics." *Social Science Quarterly*, **52:**248–260 (Sept. 1971).

——— "A Troubled Cartel: The NCAA." *Law and Contemporary Problems,* **38:**135–150 (Winter–Spring 1973).

——— "Intercollegiate Athletics: An Economic Explanation." *Social Science Quarterly,* **64:**360–370 (June 1983).

Leonard, W. L., Jr. *A Sociological Perspective of Sport,* 2nd ed. Minneapolis: Burgess Publishing Company, 1984, Chap. 10.

Uehling, Barbara. "Athletics and Academe: Creative Divorce or Reconciliation?" *Educational Record,* **64:**13–15 (Summer 1983).

11

Conglomerates: A "Nonindustry"

Willard F. Mueller

The large modern corporation typically is not confined to a single industry but embraces many lines of business, and its operations extend to all parts of the earth. We call such a firm a *conglomerate enterprise*.

Business organizations of this type are not new.[1] Sixty years ago, before they were stopped by the Department of Justice, the major meatpackers of the nation were assembling large commerical empires that spanned many industries and many countries.[2] Now, in much of the economy, conglomerate enterprise is no longer the exception but the rule.

This transformation of the corporation into the conglomerate is no less significant than the replacement of many highly fragmented industries by oligopolistic industries in the great merger movement that occurred around 1900. Economists responded to the new industrial structure of that era by developing the theory of *oligopoly*. This theory, which explains market power created by the structure of a particular industry, is not adequate to explain many features of an economy that is increasingly dominated by conglomerate firms. The power that conglomerates have within a particular industry (that is, the degree of influence they have regarding prices, output, new entry, and innovation) depends on their market position, not just in that one industry but in all their other lines of business, at home and abroad. When the same huge firms are among the leading producers in separate industries—for example, coal and petroleum—the industry lines themselves may become blurred. This does not mean that traditional industrial organization theory and research are meaningless, but rather, that conglomeration should be considered an additional structural variable when explaining behavior in many contemporary industries. This view is shared by Joan Robinson, whose 1933 work, *The Economics of Imperfect Competition,* is one of the pillars of modern oligopoly theory. In the preface to the 1969 edition of this seminal work, Robinson observes that growing conglomeration had largely made obsolete her theory of imperfect competition: "My old-fashioned comparison between monopoly and competition may still have some application to old-fashioned restrictive rings [cartels] but it cannot comprehend the great octopuses of modern industry.[3]

Because all huge firms are conglomerates to varying degrees, Corwin Edwards coined the term, *conglomerate bigness*.[4] Because bigness and conglomeration are correlated, increasing centralization of the economy in a relatively few vast corporations is one index of the growing importance of conglomerate bigness in the economy.[5] We therefore begin our discussion of conglomerate bigness by examining the growing centralization of the economy, and especially the unique role that conglomerate mergers have played in this process in recent years.

I. INDUSTRIAL CENTRALIZATION AND CONGLOMERATE BIGNESS

The great merger movement, around 1900, centralized control over much of manufacturing, which, at the time, represented a relatively small part of the economy. Whereas income originating in agriculture, around 1900, almost equaled income originating in manufacturing, income originating in manufacturing is today ten times greater than that in agriculture.

Moreover, compared with today's industrial elite, the early twentieth-century business monarchs ruled very modest domains. With combined sales of $181 billion in 1984, today's two largest manufacturing corporations have greater sales (even after adjusting for inflation) than did all manufacturing companies conbined, in 1900.

The leading corporations have not only grown larger in an absolute sense but in a relative sense as well. Since the mid-1920s, they have expanded substantially their share of the total assets held by corporations engaged primarily in manufacturing. This share increased primarily during periods of rapid growth by mergers: first, during the frenzied—although relatively brief—movement of 1926–1931, and again, during the accelerating merger activity since 1950.

The sharpest increase in the assets of the largest corporations during the postwar years occurred from 1966 to 1968, when the share held by the top 200 industrials jumped from 57 percent to 61 percent.[6] Indeed, by 1968, the top 100 industrial corporations held a larger share of assets (48 percent) than had been held by the top 200 industrials in 1950, an increase that is attributable primarily to mergers.[7] Although merger activity ebbed in 1971–1972, it continued thereafter at a heady pace, with the result that share of industrial assets of the top 200 corporations has risen above the merger-achieved highs of the late 1960s.[8] Based on the author's best estimates, the top 500 manufacturing and mining corporations' share of the total assets of all such corporations rose from 62 percent in 1964 to 75 percent in 1981.

Some economists suggest that no problem of industrial centralization and conglomeration exists unless the share of assets held by the top 100 or

200 firms increases continually. But this misses a crucial point. The most relevant measure of conglomerate bigness is the share held by all very large corporations. One such index is the share held by industrial corporations in manufacturing, mining, and trade, with assets of $1 billion or more. After adjusting for inflation, in 1929 there were about 70 corporations of this size, whereas in 1984 there were 339.[9] The share of industrial assets held by these large corporations grew from 18 percent in 1929 to 61 percent in 1984.[10] Thus, by 1984, only a few hundred huge corporations controlled more than one half of all manufacturing assets.

The trend toward growing centralization and conglomerate bigness is even greater because corporate decision making is, in many instances, further centralized by numerous corporate joint ventures among the large corporations. For example, leading petroleum companies operate hundreds of joint ventures with other large corporations as well as with numerous smaller ones. These joint ventures involve the partial merging of the parties involved. By forming new communities of interest and by strengthening existing ones, joint ventures create the capacity to reduce both actual and potential competition among their large corporate parents.

The enormous merger movement in manufacturing since World War II was part of a broader picture of centralization in the American economy. Increasingly, manufacturing corporations acquired large nonmanufacturing concerns. Firms engaged in distribution, insurance, newspapers, and finance also were caught up in the movement. Even the holding company returned to prominence as a vehicle by which nonindustrial corporations, especially railroads and banks, extended their control and influence over major industrial activities.[11]

II. MERGERS AND INDUSTRIAL CONGLOMERATION

One of the most important characteristics of recent merger activity is that, as it intensified, the share of horizontal and vertical mergers declined sharply, at the same time that more and more mergers were of the conglomerate type. Horizontal mergers are mergers between companies that produce identical or nearly identical products, e.g., two manufacturers of steel products. Vertical mergers are those between companies in a buyer-seller relationship, e.g., a shoe manufacturer and a shoe retailer. Conglomerate mergers are those between companies that are neither direct competitors nor in a buyer-seller relationship with one another. Conglomerate mergers may be subdivided into three classes: (1) geographic-market-extension mergers, which combine companies that produce identical products but sell in separate geographic (economic) markets, e.g., a fluid-milk processor in Chicago who merges with a fluid-milk processor in New York; (2) product-extension mergers, which combine companies that are functionally related in production and/or distribution but sell products that are not in direct competition with each other, e.g., a fluid-milk company that merges with an ice cream company; and (3) pure conglomerate mergers, which combine companies that fall in none of these categories, e.g., a railroad and a tire manufacturer.

In the period 1948–1955, most mergers were horizontal or vertical. As the laws that applied to such mergers become more stringent, and as merger activity accelerated, a growing share of mergers were of the conglomerate variety. The results were further enhancement of the absolute and relative size of many already large corporations, and the creation of many new ones. Twenty large corporations, whose growth was accelerated sharply by mergers (primarily conglomerate mergers) are listed in Table 1. This list is restricted to corporations ranking among the 100 largest industrials in 1983. Many of these corporations already were substantial firms in 1960, when 8 ranked among the top 100 industrials and 17 ranked among the top 500. Whereas the sales of the 500 largest industrial corporations increased by 724 percent from 1960 to 1983, these 20 corporations grew by 2,183 percent. All of these

Table 1: Twenty Large Corporations That Made Extensive Acquisitions During 1961–1983

	Sales[a] *(millions)*		*Growth*	*Rank Among Industrials*	
Corporation	*1983 ($)*	*1960 ($)*	*1960–1983 (percent)*	*1983*	*1960*
Mobil	54,607	3,718	1,618%	3	6
DuPont	35,378	2,143	1,551	7	13
Atlantic Richfield	25,147	561	4,383	12	77
Occidental Oil	19,116	3	—	14	[b]
Phillips Petroleum	15,249	1,200	1,171	16	31
Sun Oil	14,353	750	1,864	17	59
United Technologies	14,669	988	1,385	18	41
Tenneco	14,353	535	2,583	19	85
ITT	14,155	811	1,645	20	51
Union Oil	9,984	427	2,238	28	107
Philip Morris	9,466	330	2,768	35	140
Beatrice Foods	9,188	443	1,974	36	105
McDonnell-Douglas	8,111	437	1,756	42	110
Rockwell International	8,098	116	6,881	43	353
Consolidated Foods	6,573	126	5,117	49	[c]
Georgia Pacific	6,469	222	2,814	51	213
TRW	5,493	420	1,208	63	113
Gulf & Western	5,072	24	—	67	[b]
Litton Industries	4,719	188	2,410	74	249
LTV	4,578	148	2,993	78	285
Total 20 corporations	285,155	12,489	2,183%		
Fortune 500 Corporations	$1,686,698	$204,723	724%		

[a]Sales for consolidated subsidiaries.
[b]Not among the 1,000 largest industrials in 1960.
[c]Not primarily an industrial corporation in 1960.

20 corporations grew by more than 1,000 percent during the period. Each of these corporations had annual sales of more than $4 billion in 1983, and all increased their ranks among the top industrial corporations.

But mergers did much more than increase the absolute size of the acquiring corporations. Today, each of these corporations operates in many geographic and product markets, and most of them have extensive foreign as well as domestic holdings. In a word, they are huge conglomerate enterprises.

Because the boundaries of such enterprises extend far beyond particular industries and even nations, their economic significance cannot be comprehended by traditional analyses, which focus on individual industries. To capture the unique and multifaceted dimensions of corporate conglomeration requires an in-depth examination of individual enterprises. We therefore examine in some detail the growth and current scope of International Telephone and Telegraph Corporation (ITT), the most pervasive conglomerator of the 1960s.

III. ITT: THE ANATOMY OF A CONGLOMERATE

In 1960, International Telephone and Telegraph Corporation embarked on an ambitious diversification-through-merger program to transform itself from what its chairman, Harold S. Geneen, characterized as "primarily a one-product company."[12] Although it had not yet become a household word, ITT already was a substantial enterprise in 1960; it had sales of $811 million and ranked fifty-first among the nation's largest industrials. In the four decades following its founding in 1920, it had become a large international manufacturer of telecommunication equipment and an operator of telephone communication systems.

From 1960 to 1983, ITT's sales grew by 1,645 percent, making it twentieth among the nation's industrial firms. But even this understates ITT's actual size. Its total 1983 consolidated assets of $14 billion did not include the Hartford Fire Insurance Company and other unconsolidated corporations, with combined assets exceeding $20 billion; nor did they include the many government-owned facilities that it operated. In 1970, ITT operated 13 NASA and Department of Defense installations and manufacturing plants, with combined assets of $527 million.[13] (Current figures are not available.)

Like many other new conglomerates, ITT is a leading defense-space company. But unlike most other conglomerates, ITT also has a vast international organization that, according to an ITT annual report, "operates in more than 80 countries around the globe" extending to seven continents, "making ITT one of the few companies able to claim 'pole to pole' operations."[14]

During 1961–1968, ITT acquired 52 domestic and 55 foreign corporations, and the acquired domestic companies alone held combined assets of about $1.5 billion. During 1969, alone, ITT's board of directors approved 22 domestic and 11 foreign acquisitions. The three largest—Hartford Fire Insurance Company, Grinnell Corporation, and Canteen Corporation—added more than $2 billion, which brought ITT's acquisitions total for the decade to near $4 billion, far ahead of any other company. Significantly, most of ITT's acquired assets came not from small, ailing companies but from profitable corporations that were already leaders in their fields. Since 1969, ITT has acquired more than 100 domestic and foreign firms, although in 1971 it signed a Consent Decree with the Department of Justice, which placed partial restraints on its future acquisitions.[15]

Part of each American's tax dollars spent on defense and space programs goes to ITT, which is one of the nation's prime defense contractors. ITT maintains Washington's "hot lines" to Moscow, mans the Air Force Distant Early Warning System (DEW) and the giant Ballistic Missile Early Warning System (BMEWS) sites in Greenland and Alaska, and produces navigation equipment for the NAVSTAR satellites.

With its numerous foreign operations, ITT is an important force in international economic affairs. Some ITT officials have been better known in circles of national and international diplomacy than they were in business. They have included such notables as former U.N. Secretary-General Trygve Lie, as director of ITT Norway; one-time Belgium Premier Paul-Henri Spaak, as a director if ITT Belgium; two members of the British House of Lords; and a member of the French National Assembly. At home, they have included John A. McCone, former director of the CIA, and Eugene R. Black, who is widely known in international economics and political circles. Eugene Black has held such important posts as the special financial advisor to the secretary-general of the United Nations, and financial advisor to the sheik of Kuwait, and he has been a board member of dozens of large corporations. It is not unfair to ask whether these men were placed on ITT's board because of their business acumen or because of their power and prestige in domestic and international politics.

Nor is concern with these matters based on mere speculation or conjecture. Public exposés in the 1970s documented corporate misconduct in foreign affairs by ITT. The Senate Foreign Relations Subcommittee on Multinational Corporations documented ITT's efforts to overthrow the Allende government in Chile, including efforts to fund subversion by the CIA.[16] Nor was this intervention in the affairs of other nations a unique incident.[17] In a "sensational Belgium trial," the managing director of ITT-Belgium was found guilty of bribing a high official of the Belgium state telephone service.[18]

IV. CONGLOMERATE MERGERS: MOTIVES

Just what do these developments augur for the future of our economic and political institutions? It is well to begin by appreciating that they do not promise to usher in a new era of productive efficiency or technological advance. Although our knowledge is far from complete, it is clear that recent merger activity was not propelled primarily by the technological imperatives of large scale. Rather, most large mergers were motivated by special factors that, although conferring advantage and privilege on the private parties involved, did not necessarily promise corresponding benefits to society. Space permits only a brief review of the evidence.

Perhaps no concept so rapidly captured the imagination of so many as that conglomeration yields the benefits of *synergism*, i.e., the notion that combining separate substances produces an effect greater than that resulting from using the substances separately. In the popular trade parlance, synergism results in two plus two equaling five.[19] The synergism thesis held that the explanation for the conglomerate merger wave of the 1960s was to be found in the new management techniques of the merger makers. The Jimmy Lings (LTV) and Tex Thortons (Litton Industries) were viewed as a new breed of business manager, omniscient men who could make dynamic firms out of lethargic ones, who could make two blades of grass grow where others struggled to grow one.

For a time, there was superficial evidence that the new conglomerates could, indeed, outperform other corporations by relying primarily on internal growth. A number of conglomerates showed spectacular increases in their profit performance. This apparent superior profit performance was reflected in seemingly ever-rising stock prices. Few of the new conglomerates were praised more highly than Litton Industries, whose top management team, headed by Tex Thorton, had been schooled in the systems-analysis approach that was so popular at the Pentagon. During 1958–1969, Litton acquired at least 97 relatively small companies in such diverse fields as military and commercial ships, medical X-ray equipment, frozen foods, textbooks, store fixtures and refrigeration equipment, office calculators, typewriters, power-transmission equipment, microwave ovens, and education systems.

In what seemed indisputable evidence of synergism, Litton management had a magical record of earnings growth. Earnings per share of Litton common stock doubled from 1960–1962, more than doubled again from 1962–1965, and very nearly doubled again from 1965–1967. This profit performance was reflected in the astronomical rise in the value of its common stock which rose from a low of $6 per share in 1960 to $104¾ in early 1968. Then a precipitous decline set in. The first blow to the synergism mystique surrounding Litton came when its profits declined in 1968, the first annual earnings decline in its history. The initial reaction was one of guarded disbelief. As one financial analyst put it, "So hallowed had Litton's name become that, presumably, it was unthinkable among its disciples that the company could ever have anything but one banner year after another, ad infinitum."[20] In the face of a generally ebullient stock market, Litton's common stock tumbled to a low of $68 in 1968. But then the unthinkable happened: 1968 did not prove to be an exception but the beginning of a long downward slide in Litton's fortunes, as its common stock ultimately fell to a low of $2 ½ in 1974. Over the past decade, Litton's fortunes improved; in September 1985, its common stock was selling near $70.

Nor was Litton an exception among the leading conglomerates. LTV's common stock rose from an average price of $21 in 1960 to $108 in 1968; thereafter it declined steadily, reaching a low of $5 ¼ in 1978. In September 1985, LTV's stock was still selling around $7 per share.

How were some conglomerates able for so long to conceal from their stockholders the truth about their financial health? The answer is that some managements are able to "manage" profit performance by exploiting a host of accounting and tax gimmicks that are available to firms that expand by merging with other companies. The new conglomerate managers did not discover new management techniques; they developed a seemingly endless number of tax, accounting, and financial gimmicks that favored merger over internal growth. Events in the coal industry show how the discovery of a tax gimmick by one firm triggered other mergers and drastically restructured an industry almost overnight. In 1966, Continental Oil Company acquired Consolidation Coal Company, the country's largest coal producer. According to a Treasury Department report, the merger involved a complicated transaction that permitted Continental to save more than $175 million in taxes.[21] Shortly thereafter, Kennecott Copper Company, using the same tax gimmick, acquired Peabody Coal Company, the nation's second largest coal company. In 1968, the nation's third largest coal producer was purchased by Occidental Petroleum. Thus, in just three years, the three largest coal companies in the United States merged into other large corporations, which resulted in private gains of hundreds of millions of dollars at the taxpayer's expense.

This is only one of many examples. Consider the effects of the tax-loss carry-forward provisions of the Internal Revenue Code. After the merger that created the Penn Central railroad, the Penn Central Corporation was able to establish a tax-loss carry-forward of between $500 and $600 million. *The Wall Street Journal* reported that "Working under [its] tax shelter . . . the new company could acquire many profitable ventures and still pay no taxes for 5 or 6 years."[22] Not suprisingly, Penn Central subsequently became an active acquirer of profitable companies. Its holdings included two big real estate developers, as well as Buckeye Pipeline Company, Southwestern Oil & Gas Company, Royal Petroleum Company, and a large interest in the Madison Square Gardens Corporation. The last acquisition gave Penn Central an interest in New York's professional basketball and hockey teams, the Knickerbockers and the Rangers. Such helter-skelter growth certainly did not contribute to economic efficiency. Indeed, Penn Central's purchases of nontransportation businesses helped to exhaust its working capital, which created the liquidity crises that forced the company into bankruptcy proceedings in June 1970. This experience illustrates that the economy would have been better off had Penn Central management devoted more time to running the trains on time than to making mergers that reduced its tax obligations.

Perhaps the most notorious device used by a merger-active company to accelerate its earnings per share of common stock without increasing real earnings is pooling-of-interest accounting in which the book values of merging companies are combined. This permits the acquiring company to list the value of assets at less than their real costs. Abraham J. Briloff demonstrated how Gulf & Western was able to increase greatly its reported earnings, following its 1967 acquisition of Paramount Pictures.

> In its 1967 statement, Gulf & Western asserted that its earnings had more than doubled—from $22 million the previous year to $46 million. While this was certainly dramatic, supplemental data furnished by the report were even more euphoric. They revealed that companies acquired during 1967 contributed a whopping $22 million to the conglomerate's 1967 income, although these companies had earned only $2.6 million during 1966.
>
> Whether this extraordinary increase in earnings was attributable to the special brilliance and genius of Gulf & Western's management depends on how one defines billiance and ingenuity. The enormous profit inflation was triggered by Gulf & Western's wholesale disposition of television rights to the Paramount Pictures library. Gulf & Western simply disposed of properties which they had acquired in the acquisition of Paramount.
>
> By using the pooling-of-interest method of accounting, the conglomerate was able to pay out over $184 million for its 1967 acquisitions, while reflecting only a cost of less than $100 million on its books. It accomplished this by equating the cost of the 1967 acquisitions with the written down (or written off) amounts shown on the books of Paramount and the other acquired companies—that is, $100 million. The other $84 million was free to be used to bolster reported earnings and, as asserted above, a good part of it was so used.[23]

The numerous mergers of ITT offered it a seemingly limitless variety of ways to increase *reported* earnings per share without any real improvement in operating efficiency. Most important was its exploitation of the opportunities of those accounting rules that permit merging companies to pool their interests. As noted previously, the accounting procedure permits a company to pay well above the market price of another company and yet show only the book value of the acquired company on its books. A little-publicized Staff Report of the House Antitrust Subcommittee shows how ITT's use of pooling-of-interest accounting permitted ITT to greatly overstate its earnings from 1964 to 1968. During that period, ITT paid $1,278 million in stock for companies with a net worth of $534 million. If this excess payment for "goodwill" had been amortized during a 10-year period, ITT's actual reported net income for 1968 would have been overstated by 70.4 percent.[24] This is only one of several methods used by ITT to increase its profits on common stock. It also increased the company's leverage by increasing the ratio of debt capital and preferred stock to common stock.[25] After acquisition, ITT frequently changed the acquired firm's depreciation policy. Changes in accounting procedures by ITT-Sheraton, Continental Baking, and Rayonier increased ITT's profits by $7.2 million in 1968; this accounting change alone accounted for 11.8 percent of the increase in ITT's earnings from 1967 to 1968.[26] None of these changes was reported in the notes to ITT's financial statements in 1968.[27]

The failure of ITT to disclose the true source of its ever -growing earnings per share came under increasing fire from financial analysts. For example, Mr. David Norr, partner of First Manhattan Company and a member of the Accounting Principles Board, severely criticized ITT's 1970 annual report for not reflecting retroactively the results of the many companies it had acquired. Norr thought that this omission was sufficient grounds for the New York Stock Exchange to halt trading in ITT securities.[28] The Exchange did not, however, see fit to discipline one of its leading members.

Other financial analysts have reported their frustrations in seeking to learn the true source of ITT's rising earnings. In an "Alert for Portfolio Managers," investment analysts Scheinman, Hockstin, and Trotta warned, "ITT continues its financial advertising blitz in the financial media with the eye-catching caption, 'Here's the story again—in case you missed it in the press.' "[29] But after a careful study of ITT's financial statements—and with no help from ITT—these analysts found that, in 1968 and 1969, 34 percent of ITT's increased earnings per share were the result of such nonrecurring sources of income as sale of securities and plants.[30] The report added that it had "good reason to believe that similar or analogous transactions of even greater magnitude took place in 1970."[31] It concluded that "the key to ITT's 'growth' in 1970 share earnings (ex. Hartford Fire) lies in the undisclosed elements which were responsible for the 1970 increase in deferred taxes—equivalent to 40 cents a share of ITT earnings in 1970."[32]

Fortune magazine reported that, in 1971, ITT again reaped large capital gains from its Hartford Fire Insurance Company acquisition, and that it was likely to continue to do so for many years to come:

> Last year Hartford netted a total of $105 million. The fact that $36 million of this amount came from capital gains was not recorded. Hartford's unrealized capital gains amounted to about $270 million at the end of last year and, barring a major stock market crash, should for years be available to supplement the steadily growing stream of interest and dividend income that rolls out of the company's portfolio.[33]

Hartford is a deep well from which ITT apparently can pump increased reported earnings for years to come. Little wonder an ITT executive described it as "a gold mine."[34]

It appears that ITT has not abandoned its propensity to shore up its lagging operating earnings through "paper transactions." According to financial analyst Thornton O'Glove, ITT's reported profits during the first nine months of 1984 came from gains from selling securities, reserves, tax credits, changes in inventory reserves, foreign currency transactions, and asset sales. O'Glove concluded that such items exceeded ITT's reported earnings, which means "ITT has had no operating earnings this year."[35]

Its past financial wizardry seems to have caught up with ITT in recent years, as the company became plagued with operating and financial problems. Even its "cash cow, Hartford Insurance, has been having severe problems."[36] There is now much talk of corporate retrenchment, because ITT has sold off ailing divisions.[37] And as its profits have plunged, the value of its stock has fallen so sharply that ITT has been named as a probable takeover target.

As in past merger movements, banks and investment companies were leading promoters of mergers in recent decades. One Wall Street investment banker, commenting on the shenanigans involved in many merger deals said: "I suppose you could call some of it dirty. But it's so much fun. How can anything that much fun be dirty?" However, even some conservative financiers became increasingly concerned lest these questionable tactics ultimately backfire on the business community. Paul Costman Cabot, the dean of the Boston financial community, long-time director of J. P. Morgan & Company, and one-time treasurer of Harvard University, gave this warning:

> It shocks me that so many investment companies are playing the game too. It works like this: A take-over guy comes to them and says, 'I'm going to take over such-and-such at a price 50 percent over the current market price. Why don't you buy 5 percent of the stock and tender it to me when my offer comes out?' So the take-over guy gets a block of stock in friendly hands and the investment company gets an assured, easy profit. Even if the take-over fails, the raped company marries someone else and the investment company still makes out. This is a game that's going to give the whole investment company business a bad name.[38]

Cabot has observed: "It seems that each generation is cursed with problems all born of greed and a lust for power." After recounting various adverse effects flowing from these developments, Cabot concluded, "Possibly the most objectionable feature is the concentration of control and power in so few hands."

The aformentioned are some of the most obvious gimmicks and motivations that often make mergers a preferred method of corporate growth. Several studies document how various tax and accounting rules and practices encouraged mergers for reasons unrelated to economic efficiency.[39] A 1969 FTC report concluded, "The balance of evidence so far available lends little support to the view that the current merger movement reflects, in substantial measure, efforts to exploit opportunities to improve efficiency in resource allocation. On the contrary, there are abundant indications that certain institutional arrangements involving tax and accounting methods, aided by speculative developments in the stock market, have played a major role in fueling the current merger movement."[40]

The accounting and tax gimmickry pursued by some conglomerates ultimately caught up with them, and, as we have mentioned, their stock fell from the dizzy heights of the late 1960s. But it would be a mistake to conclude from this that market forces may ultimately punish some conglomerates (or, more correctly, their stockholders) for their past financial manipulations, thereby somehow dissipating any undesirable effects resulting from industrial conglomeration and centralization. Students of industrial history are familiar with many cases in which firms with merger-achieved market power performed inefficiently after they became very large, and yet continued to present a serious public policy problem. U.S. Steel, a classical example of this, was created in 1901 by "a combination of combinations," and on a foundation of watered stock. Shielded from competition by its tremendous market power, U.S. Steel nevertheless was very inefficient and had a lackluster research and development program.[41] It presented one of America's most intractable public policy problems for more than half a century. The lesson to be learned from this is that once huge corporations are formed they seldom wither away.

None of this is meant to imply that all, or even most, mergers are promoted to exploit accounting and tax gimmicks, or for purposes of greed or personal aggrandizement. Although a variety of factors may promote mergers, a consensus is emerging among economic researchers as to what mergers accomplish, or more correctly, what they do not accomplish. In 1970, Thomas F. Hogarty conducted a comprehensive review of fifty years of research on the question of whether mergers are more profitable than alternative investments. He concluded: "A host of researchers, working at different points of time and utilizing different analytical techniques and data, have but one major difference: whether mergers have a neutral or negative impact on profitability."[42]

During the 1970s, Dennis C. Mueller conducted a similar review of research findings. Perhaps the most important of these findings was that conglomerate mergers generally do not enhance the profitability or stock values of acquiring firms.[43] Among the important conclusions flowing from this finding is that the management of acquiring firms apparently are pursuing "corporate growth or other objectives not directly related to stockholder welfare and economic efficiency." Dennis Mueller believes that this explains "why managers of acquiring firms undertake mergers providing no benefits for their stockholders; why managers of acquisition targets vigorously resist bids which would greatly enrich their stockholders."[44]

A corollary of this finding is that acquired companies generally are not less efficient than the acquiring companies. This destroys another frequently used rationale for justifying all large conglomerate mergers (like Henry Manne's theory of "the market for corporate control,"[45] which asserts that conglomerate mergers are not to be condemned but praised). Manne believes that mergers promote economic efficiency, as Adam Smith's invisible hand leads efficient corporations to acquire those that are inefficiently managed. In this theoretical world, the most efficient always win takeover contests. However, this theory has been repudiated by much experience. It is not necessarily the most efficient who win a takeover contest, but those with the biggest bankrolls.

In sum, the best research evidence indicates that considerations other than efficiency motivate most large conglomerate mergers. But a question still remains: Even though large conglomerate mergers generally do not promote efficiency, are there reasons for placing restraints on such mergers?

Research studies suggest that there are at least two kinds of adverse effects of conglomerate mergers. First, some studies conclude that when management becomes preoccupied with growth by mergers, such growth is accomplished at the expense of more socially productive forms of growth, e.g., capital investment in research and development (R&D).[46] Second, conglomerate mergers result in greater overall concentration of economic resources, with a concomitant increase in corporate political power. Dennis C. Mueller observes that, whereas in earlier times economists were inclined to dismiss such concerns as unsubstantiated, "the age of innocence regarding corporate power is now over. Large corporations both have and utilize political power. And it seems reasonable to assume that this power is positively related to company size."[47] We now turn to the events of the 1970s that were responsible for ending "the age of innocence" regarding the interplay of corporate economic power and political power.

V. CONGLOMERATE BUSINESS AND THE POLITICAL PROCESS

The recent wave of very large mergers has not been motivated primarily by a quest for economic efficiency. This fact alone would not necessarily cause a serious public policy problem if it were not for the fact that our economic system is becoming increasingly centralized in ways that may transform adversely both our political and economic institutions. Corwin Edwards, in his seminal article on the conglomerate enterprise, spelled out how conglomerates are able to parlay their economic power into political power:

> The political strength of the great concern is an aspect of its ability to spend. . . . The campaign contributions of large companies and the occasional case of direct or indirect bribery are probably the least significant source of the large company's political power. More important, the large company spends whatever money is needed to argue effectively on behalf of its interest where a particular issue affects it. . . . The work of many people may be required in assembling facts and preparing persuasive arguments relevant to these decisions. . . . Large concerns are increasingly skilled in these processes, primarily because they take such work seriously and do it on a large scale.[48]

Edwards made the foregoing observations just before merger activity began accelerating between 1954 and 1955. Since then, vast conglomerate mergers have increasingly centralized the economy and transformed our economic-political order. Simply put, this centralization process is eroding our pluralistic political processes, which rest on a tradition of diffused, dispersed, heterogeneous pattern of industrial ownership. Justice William O. Douglas articulated well the traditional American view regarding centralized economic power when he observed

> Power that controls the economy should be in the hands of elected representatives of the people, not in the hands of an industrial oligarchy. Industrial power should be decentralized. It should be scattered into many hands so that the fortunes of the people will not be dependent on the whim or caprice, the political prejudices, the emotional stability of a few self-appointed men. The fact that they are not vicious men but reasonable and social-minded is irrelevant.[49]

Historians may record that the 1970s was the decade when the political power of large corporations was unmasked. First came revelations of improper domestic political conduct. International Telephone and Telegraph employed its considerable power in a well-orchestrated drive to receive a favorable antitrust consent decree.[50] The Watergate investigations uncovered numerous illegal political contributions by large corporations. In April 1974, George M. Steinbrenner, chairman of the board of American Shipbuilding Corporation and owner of the New York Yankees, became the first corporate executive ever indicted on felony charges in connection with illegal corporate political contributions.[51] The numerous disclosures of domestic corporate misconduct in political affairs soon were overshadowed by evidence of massive corporate bribery and political intervention in the affairs of other nations. The ITT efforts to overthrow the Allende government in Chile have been documented by the Senate Foreign Relations Committee.[52] United Brands admitted that it made a $1.3 million payment to an official of the Honduras government to reduce that country's banana tax; it subsequently admitted making payments of $750,000 to officials of the Italian government.[53]

Northrop Corporation paid $30 million in agents' fees to influence sales of its aircraft to foreign countries. Of this, $450,000 was paid to two Saudi Arabian generals. Northrop subsequently told the Securities Exchange Commission (SEC) that it made improper commission payments to five countries.[54] Gulf Oil disbursed $4 million to the ruling political party in South Korea, $110,000 to the president of Bolivia, and $350,000 to the president's political party. The SEC charged Gulf with falsifying financial reports to conceal $10.3 million in contributions to politicians at home and abroad, from 1960 to 1972.[55] Tenneco, Inc., the huge conglomerate, admitted that it made payments to state and local officials in the United States, as well as payments to foreign "consultants" to acquire "properties or materials from foreign governments."[56]

It was also revealed that Lockheed Aircraft Corporation paid sizable amounts to foreign officals and political organizations to influence aircraft sales to foreign governments. In Saudi Arabia, alone, Lockheed had paid or committed $106 million in "commissions" since 1970, millions of which were funneled to Saudi officials through numbered accounts in Liechtenstein and Geneva. Lockheed subsequently disclosed that it had given even larger bribes to government officials in Japan and Italy. It admitted making a $1.1 million payment to a "high Dutch official," whom the Dutch government identified as Prince Bernhard, husband of Queen Juliana.[57]

Perhaps no observer of the large modern corporation was surprised to learn that America's largest industrial corporation apparently was also one of the top corporate contributors to foreign elections. From 1965 to 1975, Exxon Corp. contributed more than $59 million to various political parties in Italy, alone.[58] Inexplicably, Exxon even contributed $86,000 to the Italian Communist party. It also has admitted making political contributions in Canada, as well as payments in three unnamed countries, to government officials and to officials of government-owned companies.

These are not isolated cases of corporate bribery and illegal political activities. In 1976, the Securities Exchange Commission (SEC) issued a special report on *Questionable and Illegal Corporate Payments and Practices*.[59] The SEC's interest in these matters was triggered by the work of the special prosecutor, who was appointed to investigate the illegal activities in the so-called "Watergate scandals." In 1973, several corporations and executive officers were charged with the illegal use of corporate funds for domestic political activities. After investigating these matters, the SEC found that "violations of the federal securities laws had indeed occurred." These investigations resulted in injunctive action against nine corporations during the years 1974 to 1975. Thereafter, additional cases were brought, totalling 14 cases filed as of May 10, 1976. In all cases, the corporations consented to the entry of a judgment of permanent injunction, which prohibited future violations of the federal securities laws.

As its investigations progressed, the SEC realized that more was involved than a few isolated violations of the federal securities laws and other laws. The violations included illegal or improper political contributions to domestic politicians, various activities in foreign affairs, and dubious accounting practices. The SEC therefore adopted a policy whereby all corporations subject to its jurisdiction were encouraged to make voluntary disclosure of questionable or illegal activities.

As of April 21, 1976, the SEC received 97 disclosures regarding illegal or questionable practices. The two most frequently represented industries were drug manufacturing and petroleum refining. Most of the corporations that engaged in the questionable activities were very large corporations: 49 had sales exceeding $1 billion in 1974, and 86 had sales exceeding $100 million. About one third of the 97 reporting companies had made illegal domestic political payments, and all 97 companies reported a total of 183 questionable or illegal practices.

Though cautious about drawing conclusions of wrongdoing, the SEC stated:

> [T]he problem of questionable and illegal corporate payments is, by any measure, serious and sufficiently widespread to be a cause for deep concern. Unfortunately, the Commission is unable to conclude that instances of illegal payments are either isolated or aberrations limited to a few unscrupulous individuals.[60]

The SEC report expressed concern about the extent of past illegal activities, but ended on this optimistic note:

> Thus, in the Commission's view, while the problem of questionable or illegal corporate payments is both serious and widespread, it can be controlled and does not represent an inherent defect in our economic system.[61]

One reason for the commission's optimism was that many corporations had issued directives ordering the cessation of questionable conduct, and adopted written corporate policies prohibiting similar practices in the future. However, four companies told the SEC that they intend to continue the practice of making "questionable" payments, particularly in foreign trade.

In 1980, *Fortune* magazine examined the extent of "crime in the executive suites" of large corporations, in a feature article entitled, "How Lawless Are Big Companies?"[62] In *Fortune's* words, "A look at the record since 1970 shows that a surprising number of them have been involved in blatant illegalities."[63] The *Fortune* study was "limited to five crimes about whose impropriety few will argue—bribery (including kickbacks and illegal rebates); criminal fraud; illegal political contributions; tax evasion; and criminal antitrust violations. The latter consist entirely of price fixing . . . and exclude the vaguer [areas of antitrust]."

The study examined 1,043 major corporations; 117, or 11 percent, of these had, during 1971–1978, committed at least one of the crimes listed in the *Fortune* study. Some corporations were multiple offenders, which means that there was a total of 163 crimes. This number is the minimum, because *Fortune's* list included only instances that involved actual conviction on federal criminal charges, or that that resulted in consent decrees during 1971–1978. The list of companies involved reads like a "Who's Who" of large conglomerates: Allied Chemical; American Airlines; Beatrice Foods; Bethlehem Steel; Borden; Du Pont; Firestone; Goodrich; Goodyear; Gulf Oil; ITT; Occidental Petroleum; Penn Central; Phillips Petroleum; R. J. Reynolds; Tenneco; a subsidiary of Time, Inc. (publisher of *Fortune*); TWA; and U.S. Steel.

Fortune observed that "eleven percent of major American corporations involved in corrupt practices is a pretty startling figure."[64] But the 11 percent figure understates the relative extent of illegal activity by the largest U.S. corporations. For example, the *Fortune* list of offenders included 39 percent of the 100 largest, 30 percent of the 200 largest, and 17 percent of the 500 largest U.S. industrial corporations of 1979. Therefore, of the corporations cited by *Fortune* as having committed white-collar crimes, the majority were very large corporations.

The following are three examples of the crimes reviewed by *Fortune*.

1. Gulf Oil "used a subsidiary in Nassau to launder funds sent from the U.S., ostensibly to be used to prospect for oil. At least $4.5 million returned to these shores to be distributed as political handouts." Gulf was also cited for bribing an IRS agent and for price-fixing.

2. General Tire and Rubber Co. doled out illegal political contributions, from at least 1967 through 1973.
3. Bethlehem Steel was fined $325,000 for laundering "hundreds of thousands of dollars" in Europe and returning them to the United States for distribution as bribes. Said *Fortune*, "Such sleazy goings-on by a company as prestigious as Bethlehem indicate that big-business crime hasn't been swept away in a tide of post-Watergate morality."

How can the pervasive illegal activity of large corporations be explained? *Fortune* believes that "Simple economic incentives explain much illegal behavior: corruption seems to pay, at least in the short term."[65] Perhaps the search for higher profits is the basic force that stimulates such behavior, but if it is, should it be condoned—any more than crimes committed by individuals who hope to improve their personal economic lots?

To Marshall B. Clinard, the leading expert on the sociology of corporate crime, the answer is an obvious no. Clinard states:

> Perhaps the strongest argument to be made for criminal sanctions against individual corporate offenders is the effect unequal justice has on the rest of society. When criminal responsibility is negated under the notion that only a "lack of proper managerial control" is involved and no "deliberate disregard for human welfare" is evinced, many persons in society conclude that "the rich get richer, and the poor get poorer" and the law is deliberately ineffective.[66]

We must emphasize, however, that many corporations, even very large ones, have not been cited for any violations since 1970. This is persuasive evidence that illegal corporate behavior is not endemic to American capitalism. Corporate behavior can be influenced by the codes of conduct set by top management. Moreover, the fact that most large corporations succeed without engaging in such conduct demonstrates that corporate success does not require illegal conduct.

The preceding discussion has dealt with evidence of corporate misconduct by the nation's largest corporations. Smaller corporations certainly violate the law, as well. The reason for special concern with crime by the largest corporations is that these enterprises account for the bulk of all business in most industries. These corporations symbolize the American economic system, both at home and abroad. Their conduct is thus frequently used to gauge the basic character of our economic and political system. This is why all Americans have a stake in the behavior of the huge corporations that run much of the American economy at home, and carry our flag abroad.

VI. CONGLOMERATE MERGERS AND THE COMPETITIVE PROCESS

Economists have identified a variety of ways in which mergers may injure competition. The most obvious injury occurs when merging companies are direct competitors. One example is the attempted merger of Bethlehem

Steel with Youngstown Steel in 1956. Horizontal mergers such as these injure competition by eliminating a significant direct competitor. After the court decision that prohibited the Bethlehem-Youngstown merger,[67] and after several Supreme Court decisions, the number of horizontal mergers among large companies declined sharply.

Although many economists during the 1950s would have taken a tolerant attitude toward a horizontal merger of this magnitude,[68] nearly all now applaud the Bethlehem-Youngstown decision, and many applaud the even stricter rules of law on horizontal mergers, which were spelled out in subsequent cases. Merger-enforcement policy regarding horizontal mergers represents a great victory for antitrust policy.[69] Had it been otherwise—if public policy had permitted mergers of the Bethlehem-Youngstown variety—concentration levels in many industries would have increased greatly in the postwar years.

Similarly, there are discernible anticompetitive effects in mergers among companies in buyer-seller relationships. For example, vertical mergers may foreclose part of the market to competitors, perhaps triggering a series of defensive mergers by companies which fear the loss of their markets.[70]

But the economic effects are less evident in the case of so-called *conglomerate mergers,* that is, mergers between companies that are neither horizontally nor vertically related. Some economists reason that competition is not injured so long as the merging companies are not direct competitors. In other words, they reason that there is no link between growing, *overall* industrial concentration and conglomeration, on the one hand, and the quality of competition in *particular* markets, on the other. As M. A. Adelman is fond of reciting, whenever growing conglomeration is discussed, "absolute size is absolutely irrelevant." Indeed, Adelman argues that "a truly conglomerate merger cannot be attacked in order to maintain competition, because it has no effect on any market structure."[71]

This view is based on the simplistic assumption that competition is determined solely by the structure of a particular market. But it overlooks the fact that the multimarket nature of many large industrial corporations enables them to engage in practices that are peculiar to conglomerate firms. It also ignores the fact that the organizational characteristics of the large conglomerate give it a unique capacity to alter the structures of the markets in which it operates.[72] Hence, the conglomerate may not only possess traditional market power—that is, power vis-à-vis customers or suppliers—but power vis-à-vis actual or potential rivals. The nature and extent of such power depends on the relationship between the conglomerate firm's structure, that is, its relative size, diversification, and profit capabilities in its individual markets, and that of its rivals, customers, and suppliers.[73]

Specifically, business conglomeration enlarges two lines of conduct that are unavailable to single-market firms, i.e., cross-subsidization and reciprocity. It also widens the scope of mutual interdependence among large firms, which leads to greater competitive forebearance among them. Conglomeration by merger accelerates the development of conglomerate options and mutual interdependence and allows such conduct characteristics to become significantly more pervasive than they would be if conglomeration were achieved by internal growth alone.

This is not meant to imply that conglomerate power always has anticompetitive consequences. Indeed, there are special market settings in which conglomerate power is used to inject new competition into the market. Specifically, in industries in which there are conglomerates, a conglomerate firm may increase competition by entering the industry by internal growth, or by acquiring a small firm in such a market and subsequently expanding it.[74] But competition may be injured when a conglomerate merger eliminates a significant *potential* competitor. Economic theory teaches that when industries are already highly concentrated, a major restraint on the oligopolists' market power is the threat of new entry. Often, the leading potential entrant into an oligopolistic industry is a firm in another industry. In this case, competition may be injured when a firm within an oligopolistic industry acquires one of the leading potential entrants into the industry. The most famous antitrust case involving this kind of conglomerate merger was the Federal Trade Commission's challenge of Procter & Gamble's (P&G's) acquisition of the Clorox Corporation, which had a 50 percent share of the household bleach industry. Although P&G did not sell household bleach, the U.S. Supreme Court upheld the FTC's finding that the merger threatened competition because P&G was a leading potential entrant into the household bleach industry.

Cross-Subsidization

An important fact about large conglomerate corporations is that the great majority operate across many industries and hold prominent positions in the most concentrated manufacturing industries.[75] In addition to being especially prominent occupants of concentrated industries, the largest corporations hold leading positions in many industries.

Because the large conglomerate generally enjoys abnormally high profits in at least some of its markets, it may expand its power by coupling noncompetitive profits with an ability to "shift marketing emphasis and resources among its various markets."[76] If a conglomerate firm earned a competitive rate of return in each of its product markets, it would have no "excess" profits with which to subsidize particular product lines. But, as we have seen, when a firm operates in many markets, it generally has market power in one or more of its important markets, and, hence, secures noncompetitive long-run profits. The amount of such profits depends not only on the degree of market power that the conglomerate firm has in its various markets but also on its total sales in markets where it has market power.

When a firm enjoys large noncompetitive profits, it has the *option* of engaging in special competitive tactics that are not available to the firm that earns only a competitive return. Conglomeration is an instrument through which these options can be exercised. By operating in many markets, the conglomerate can use excess profits in some markets to subsidize losses in other markets, either by price cuts or by incurring a substantial increase in costs—for example, by abnormally large advertising outlays. If the subsidized markets are small, compared with the overall operations of the firm, subsidization may have very little impact on overall profitability. When a firm undertakes this policy after a rational investment decision, it expects to enhance its long-run profits by virtue of the effects of subsidization on the structure of the subsidized markets, and because of the firm's relative position in these markets.

Not only may such practices have a direct impact on industrial concentration, one conglomerate merger may beget others. Nonconglomerate firms within an industry may respond defensively to the entry of a conglomerate with the capacity to employ cross-subsidization tactics. The reaction of an official of the Sunshine Biscuit Company (itself a sizable firm) to a proposed merger between its leading competitor, National Biscuit Company (NBC) and Coca Cola, illustrates that even substantial enterprises may respond defensively to mergers that promise to increase the market power of their rivals. One of Sunshine's directors stated:

> While there has been a tendency toward lack of interest in proposals of consolidation in the past, the recent reports of NBC and Coca Cola, although now called off, would in my opinion justify our careful consideration of this offer [from American Tobacco]. . . .
>
> It seems definitely certain that if our competitor with an already larger advertising fund than ours should join with someone with similar advantages—*that we could be snowed under in this field, much to the detriment of our future sales and profits.*[77]

The following year Sunshine sold out to American. This illustrates the essentially contagious nature of conglomerate mergers, as less powerful firms feel obliged to merge with others, lest they "be snowed under" by the superior power of their conglomerate rivals. Corwin Edwards summarizes aptly the advantages conferred by this dimension of conglomerate power:

> It can absorb losses that would consume the entire capital of a smaller rival . . . Moment by moment the big company can outbid, outspend, or outlose the small one; and from a series of such momentary advantages it derives an advantage in attaining its large aggregate results.[78]

Many case studies have demonstrated how large corporations have used their conglomerate-derived power to engage in cross-subsidization.[79] Here we review briefly recent events in the beer industry, in which conglomerate merger appears to have played an important role in increasing concentration.[80]

There was a persistent decline in the numbers of brewers following World War II, from 404 companies in 1947 to about 75 in 1970, reflecting in part economies of large-scale production and advertising. But whereas the *number* of local and regional brewers dropped sharply between 1947 and 1970, the total sales of all regional brewers remained about the same, which meant that the surviving regionals were getting a larger share of the market. This was especially true of the 13 regionals with sales exceeding 1 million barrels in 1970; until the early 1970s, they had enjoyed a barrelage increase nearly every year. Economists who analyzed the industry during the 1960s and early 1970s commented optimistically on its competitive future. Ira and Ann Horowitz concluded:

> it appears unlikely that concentration in the brewery industry, at least with regard to the leading five firms, will increase to any great extent in the near future, though we might anticipate that concentration for the leading 25 firms, say, will enjoy appreciable gains.[81]

Similarly, Kenneth Elzinga concluded, in 1973:

> Unlike Shakespeare's empty tigers and roaring seas, giantism in brewing is not exorable. There is no evidence [that] there are significant multiplant economies of scale. Consequently, given the size and estimated expansion of the national beer market, and allowing even a generous estimate of the minimum optimum size plant, the industry could support at least 30 efficient and independent firms.[82]

Seldom have the predictions of prominent economists been proven wrong so quickly. The reasons for their errors are to be found in events which were not impacting on the industry when they were examining it.

In 1973, a critical change occurred in the evolving structure of the beer industry. In that year, the sales growth of the national brewers began to accelerate at the expense of locals and regionals. In 1975, the regionals experienced the first drop in combined annual volume since 1961. The share of the surviving regionals and local brewers fell from 48 percent in 1972 to 20 percent in 1983. By 1984, Anheuser-Busch and Philip Morris-Miller had a combined share of 57 percent. Only two of the other 15 top brewers of 1972 increased their shares after 1975, and both of these, Stroh and Heileman, accomplished this by acquiring other brewers. Since 1972, seven of the top 15 brewers have been acquired—Schlitz, Pabst, Schaefer, Carling, Hamms, Rheingold, and National. In 1984, a mere 10 brewers made 98 percent of all U.S. brewed beer, a far cry from Elzinga's 1973 observation that the industry could "support at least 30 efficient and independent firms."

Because of these dramatic events, it is natural to raise this question: What happened after 1972 to bring about so concentrated an industry structure, which was contrary to what the experts had predicted only a few years earlier. The poor showing of the other national and large regional brewers, which had been prospering until 1973, suggests that more than economies of scale were involved. Much of the answer is probably to be found in Philip Morris' acquisition in 1969–1970 of the Miller Brewing Company, for $229 million.

Prior to its acquisition, Miller was the eighth largest U.S. brewer, with only 4.5 percent of sales in 1969. Miller was a financially successful company, whose operating income during 1967–1969 roughly equaled that of the three other national brewers. But in comparison with its acquirer, Philip Morris, Inc., Miller was a financial midget. Philip Morris is a huge, powerful conglomerate firm which overshadows all other U.S. brewers, except for Anheuser-Busch. In 1984, Philip Morris had total sales of $10.1 billion, advertising outlays of $527 million, and net profits of $889 million; it had a 35 percent share of the highly concentrated U.S. cigarette industry and a 20 percent share of worldwide cigarette sales. Philip Morris has substantial expertise and resources with which to promote consumer-type products that are readily transferable to the merchandising of beer. In late 1985, by acquiring the General Foods Corp., with 1984 sales of $8.6 billion and net profits of $291 million, Philip Morris became the world's largest consumer products company.

The picture that emerges from these comparisons is that of a huge and profitable Philip Morris-Miller (PM-Miller) towering over other firms in the beer industry. Its 1984 net profits of $889 million were greater than the combined net profits of all other brewers. The significance of this dominance is magnified because of the specialized nature of other brewers.

Over 25 years ago, economist John M. Blair emphasized the potential anticompetitive consequences that may follow when a conglomerate enters an industry composed of "single-line" firms. According to Blair, "The danger to competition posed by cross-subsidization, whether actual or anticipated, is at a maximum in unconcentrated industries populated largely by single-line firms." The key here is that "What had been a 'symmetrical' oligopoly, with each of the oligopolists having about the same position, might be transformed into an 'asymmetrical' oligopoly, with the new entrant assuming a position of dominance and leadership."[83]

Because Blair's comments are especially germane to a powerful conglomerate's entrance into the beer industry, we quote his comments in full:

> In the forms of rivalry to which oligopolists typically limit themselves, i.e., advertising, sales effort, services and other types of nonprice competition, the advantages tend to go to the firm with the greatest resources, not the lowest costs. Hence the conglomerate because of its greater resources, may be expected to improve its position over time at the expense of the other oligopolists. Ultimately the strength of the latter may be so reduced as to render them unable to pursue an independent course of conduct, even when they are so inclined. . . . Temporary financial stringency, dissatisfaction with their share of the market, the coming into power of a more aggressive management, a new technological development—all of the inducements which in the past have from time to time led other oligopolists to break away from the accepted *modus vivendi* and become industrial mavericks could not be implemented. The strength to do so would have eroded away.[84]

When a conglomerate acquires a small factor in a market, it has a strong incentive to engage in cross-subsidization to expand its position. But as its market share grows, the industry leaders are unlikely to stand idly by while their positions are usurped by the conglomerate intruder. All of the largest single-line firms would not succeed in maintaining their market positions, but, in the escalating price and nonprice rivalry triggered by the entering conglomerate's strategies, the leaders would fare better than the small firms caught in the resulting struggle for survival.

In view of the foregoing, it is not surprising that in 1971, Philip Morris initiated a policy of subsidizing the expansion of Miller, with the aim of becoming number one in the beer industry. To accomplish this, PM-Miller launched an aggressively orchestrated strategy of demand creation and capacity expansion, which prompted one financial analyst to characterize PM-Miller as the "juggernaut" of the beer industry.[85]

PM-Miller used what has been called a *market segmentation strategy,* that is, developing separate brands through advertising. Although it continued to expend the bulk of its advertising on its "flagship" brand, Miller High Life, it experimented with a variety of other brands. In doing so, Philip Morris was following the strategy that had proved so successful in the cigarette industry.

In 1972, Philip Morris acquired the Meister Brau and Lite brands of Meister Brau, Inc., of Chicago, one of the top three brands in the Chicago area. Immediately, PM-Miller began accelerating advertising outlays for the Meister Brau Lite brand. Measured media advertising expenditures for this brand accelerated, from $525,000 in 1973 to $53 million in 1983. *Business Week* characterized "Lite's heavy advertising program as a classic example of a company identifying a market segment and then blitzing its way into it, discouraging competition from others."[86]

The Lite success story represents the ultimate achievement of advertising-created product differentiation—being able to sell a lower-cost product at a higher price: "Despite the fact that the product is cheaper to produce, due to lower raw material usage and lower physical capacity requirements, Miller priced the beer above 'premium' levels in most markets . . . Miller correctly perceived that the consumer would be unaware of manufacturing costs and would pay a premium price for perceived quality or benefit."[87]

PM-Miller did the same with its "domestic import," Lowenbrau. In 1976, after spending $1.7 million to advertise Lowenbrau, it mounted an enormous advertising blitz in 1977, spending $11.3 million, or $18.80 per barrel; in 1979, its advertising expenditures for Lowenbrau reached $17 million, or about $17 per barrel.

PM-Miller's total expenditures on subsidized brand-creation through advertising were substantial: in 1970, these expenditures amounted to $9.4 million; by 1983, they totaled $161 million, an increase of 1,613 percent. This was well above the increase of other major brewers.

Paralleling its enormous outlays for brand creation, Philip Morris poured enormous amounts of money into expanding its existing plant facilities and building new ones. Immediately after acquiring 100 percent of Miller's stock in 1970, Philip Morris expanded its brewing capacity from about 5 million barrels in 1972 to 54 million in 1983. Over a six-year period, 1972–1979, Philip Morris's cumulative capital investment in Miller grew from about $228 million to over $1 billion.

PM-Miller's policy has forced other leading brewers to follow its lead. Regional brewers, which historically have spent relatively little on advertising, also have substantially increased their advertising outlays. Even Coors, long credited with being able to grow successfully with very little advertising, increased its advertising expenditures twenty-seven-fold between 1975 and 1983, from $1.1 million to $30.5 million.

Schlitz's experience in introducing its Light brand illustrates the high costs of failure. It introduced Schlitz Light in 1975, with outlays of $483,000. It accelerated these outlays to $9.3 million in 1976 and $12.5 million in 1977. Because the sales of this brand did not grow correspondingly, Schlitz's measured media costs in the third year of promotion for this brand were $9.61 per barrel. By 1984 Schlitz had virtually abandoned advertising its Light brand.

With the largest brewers spending heavily on light beers, the smaller brewers found it increasingly difficult to carve out a segment in this market. For example, during 1977, Olympia gambled $2.2 million or over one-quarter of its advertising budget on its Light brand. But despite a substantial increase in Olympia's *total* advertising after 1977, its market share continued to decline, which suggests that it did not have the financial and advertising muscle to keep pace in the new environment. In 1981 Pabst acquired Olympia.

This is the environment in which other brewers are now struggling for survival. As PM-Miller and Anheuser-Busch further segment the market with new brands, supported by enormous advertising outlays, competing brewers will be crowded out of the market unless they can strengthen their brands and increase their offerings. Regional brewers have been especially disadvantaged in the new environment because of the heavy emphasis on television advertising, where regional brewers are unable to obtain equal access to the television media.[88]

Miller's record expansion after 1970 was made possible by Philip Morris's ability and willingness to engage in deep and sustained subsidization of Miller's operations. Unlike other brewers, it could do this because of its conglomerate character. According to Emanuel Goldman, a senior financial analyst with Sanford C. Berstein & Co., "Miller does not have to make any return on its invested capital near term. *The thing that all the other brewers have in common is that they have to make a decent return on investment; for now, that is not the case with Miller.*"[89]

The extent and significance of PM-Miller's cross-subsidization can be best appreciated if Miller is viewed as an autonomous profit center. This lays bare the financial prerequisites of Miller's expansion in the face of deep and sustained losses. According to my estimates, Philip Morris's Miller division incurred losses every year during 1971–1975, totaling $120 million. In 1976 and 1977, Miller earned very modest profits. Since then its profits have continued to be submarginal. Although it is impossible to determine from public records, its profitability, Philip Morris's Annual Report for 1984 indicates that during 1981–83 the operating profits (profits before payment of interest expense and corporate overhead) of the Miller division were only 4 percent of beer sales; in contrast, the operating profits of its tobacco operations averaged 22 percent.[90] This strongly suggests that Philip Morris continues to receive very low returns from its beer operations. Moreover, Philip Morris built an enormous 10-million-barrel capacity brewery in Ohio, at a cost of about $450 million. Because it has not yet used this plant, Philip Morris took a $140 million write-down on the plant in the fourth quarter of 1984.[91] At Miller's current rate of improvement in operating income, Philip Morris may not recoup its accumulated losses and earn an average return on its investment before 1990. Thus, after years of subsidized expansion, causing massive structural reorganization in the beer industry, Phillip Morris will have converted Miller into a profitable operation; it will have moved Miller from its position in eighth place in a relatively unconcentrated industry to second place in a highly concentrated one.

This discussion makes explicit how an autonomous firm would have been forced to perform in the capital market to accomplish a similar result. Most important, it shows that during 1971–1976, an independent Miller would have sustained losses of $120 million at the same time that it was borrowing $480 million for capital expansion. It would have been forced to borrow an additional $394 million during 1976–1977, years in which it just barely covered its existing debt burden.

It is extremely unlikely that an autonomous firm of Miller's size and earnings record could have borrowed the huge funds needed for expansion at any rate of interest—much less at the market rate it paid after it became part of Philip Morris. Thus, the advantage that Miller enjoyed from Philip Morris's ability to cross-subsidize is only partially measured by the deep losses absorbed by Philip Morris during 1971–1976. Miller drew upon the great financial strength flowing from Philip Morris's profitable conglomerate operations to tap the debt-capital market in order to subsidize Miller's unprecedented expansion.

The PM-Miller conglomerate merger triggered an inexorable trend toward shared monopoly, in which price competition is replaced by escalating promotional competition and higher prices, an environment in which survival and success often depend on market power, not efficiency.

The case-study evidence of the impact of conglomerate power on market concentration is reinforced by recent statistical analyses in food retailing, where conglomerate acquisitions by large corporations were found to increase concentration in the acquired firm's market.[92]

Reciprocal Selling

We now turn to another competitive strategy that is available to conglomerate firms, *reciprocal selling*. Simply defined, this practice involves taking your business to those who bring their business to you. It becomes a potentially harmful competitive strategy under two conditions: (1) when the market structure creates special *incentives* in the promotion of a firm's sales; and (2) when the product and organizational characteristics of a business create extensive *opportunities* for engaging in the practice. In short, both the incentive and the opportunity are prerequisites to the successful use of reciprocal selling.[93]

A firm has an incentive to engage in reciprocity when doing so promises to increase its profits. In purely competitive markets there would be no incentive. In the absence of product differentiation, price alone would govern sales and purchases. But, in markets of relatively few firms, sellers recognize their interdependence. Each, knowing that it may influence the price level by its decisions, avoids price competition. Firms in these markets, therefore, have an incentive to engage in various nonprice strategies to promote sales, for example, by advertising, innovation, promotion, and tying arrangements. Reciprocal selling is another such nonprice strategy.

In markets in which firms sell a specialized product to firms similarly organized, generally there are few opportunities to practice reciprocity. The opportunity arises only when each firm produces something that is required in the operations of the other. An enterprise must purchase goods or services from companies that are potential customers for its products in order to make possible the arrangement, "You buy from me and I'll buy from you."

The volume of sales that may be influenced by reciprocal trading depends on the number, volume and type of products that are bought and sold. A single-line producer will have relatively few opportunities for reciprocal dealings, whereas a firm that buys and sells a large variety and volume of products has the best opportunity to engage in reciprocal dealing. It is in the large conglomerate enterprise that reciprocal dealing develops into a major strategy for expanding sales.

Some economists, relying on a simple theoretical model, contend that reciprocity is an insignificant anticompetitive problem. This position is most categorical among economists of the Chicago School, who reason thus: (1) in perfectly competitive markets reciprocity can have no adverse effects; (2) firms with monopoly power can exploit their own power without resorting to reciprocity; and (3) reciprocity is prompted primarily by a desire to increase efficiency by eliminating selling costs. After dismissing reciprocity on these theoretical grounds, members of the Chicago School usually close their argument by echoing George Stigler's observation that, in any event, "reciprocity is probably much more talked about than practiced and is important chiefly where prices are fixed by the state or a cartel."[94]

This problem is too complex to be disposed of with such simplistic logic. Analysis of reciprocity must begin with the recognition that most contemporary markets, although falling short of monopoly, are sufficiently concentrated so that price competition already is somewhat muted. As noted, in such markets oligopolists have an incentive to resort to a variety of nonprice strategies to promote their sales. Reciprocity is such a strategy, but, unlike most other sales strategies, the capacity to practice it depends on the overall size and conglomeration of the firm, not its position in an individual market.

In the real world, reciprocity is found in the broad spectrum of markets falling between the polar extremes of perfect competition and monopoly. Stigler et al. fail to explain adequately the competitive process in such markets, and therefore minimize the potential market power that reciprocity may confer on its users. They find some "frictions" in imperfectly competitive markets, but conclude that, "A plausible explanation for reciprocity under effectively competitive conditions is the desire to minimize costs of searching and selling."[95] Thus, they believe it is "plausible" that most reciprocity is merely a means of cutting the costs of locating and persuading customers, something to be applauded rather than condemned. The only exceptions they find to reciprocity that is motivated by the quest to minimize selling costs are in markets in which firms have monopoly power, or in markets that are subject to regulation. But here, again, they see reciprocity mainly as having a beneficial influence, because reciprocity either reduces the producers' surplus that would go to the monopsonistic buyer or it enables the market to approach a more optimal allocation of resources in regulated markets.

This analysis is wrong because of the unrealistic assumptions concerning the structural environment in which reciprocity is practiced. The analysis greatly underrates the capacity and propensity of large conglomerate firms to practice reciprocity. These economists apparently have not looked at, or have ignored, the considerable evidence showing that in imperfectly competitive industrial markets—covering a wide range of competitive structures—reciprocity is a pervasive, and often decisive, factor in determining the allocation of sales.[96] It can restructure markets by increasing concentration and by raising entry barriers to new competitors, and it can make prices more rigid.

Significantly, the firm that engages in reciprocity to expand its market share need not have a monopoly or monopsony, in the conventional sense. Indeed, as a buyer, it may have relatively modest market shares, which certainly fall far short of monopsonistic dominance. The classic *Waugh Equipment* case, frequently cited by the Chicago School, illustrates this point.[97] *Waugh* was the first reciprocity case brought by the antitrust authorities.[98] Briefly, the facts are these. In 1924, three officials of Armour & Company became affiliated with the Waugh Equipment Company. Because one of these individuals was an Armour vice president in charge of traffic, he was in a position to work out reciprocity arrangements with the railroads by promising to route Armour business on railroads that agreed to buy draft gears from Waugh. As a result, Waugh increased its share of the draft-gear market from about 1.5 percent in 1924 to nearly 50 percent by early 1930. During the period, Waugh sold to nearly every railroad in the country.[99]

It is important to know that Armour did not have monopsony power in the traditional sense; that is, it did not have a dominant share of the market. Armour did not hold a commanding position as a purchaser of freight cars; it accounted for less than 2 percent of all railroad freight shipments in 1929. Armour derived its bargaining advantage because, through the Waugh Equipment Company, it was the *only* meatpacker tied in with a draft-gear supplier to railroads. This enabled Armour to exchange favors with the railroads.[100]

Nor is the answer that competition was not injured because the draft-gear industry was quite oligopolistic prior to these developments. Before reciprocity was introduced, the draft-gear industry was relatively easy to enter, but thereafter new entrants faced much more formidable entry barriers: to compete on an equal footing with Armour-Waugh, they would have to be conglomerates capable of practicing reciprocity.

It is a mistake to assume that reciprocity forecloses entry of only small firms. As documented by the FTC *Merger Report,* entry into an industry by even a billion-dollar corporation can be prevented by reciprocity-created entry barriers when the market has become tied up by larger rivals. For example, in the 1960s the Cities Service Corporation found that its entry into the rubber-oil market was blocked because the major tire companies had developed extensive reciprocity arrangements with other large petroleum companies.[101]

Nor is there legitimate basis in fact for the argument expressed by Stigler: that reciprocity generally "restores flexibility of prices" in oligopolistic markets.[102] Logic and industrial experience show that the reverse is more likely to be the case. When firms become associated as reciprocity partners, "outsiders" soon learn that it is futile for them to compete for such accounts; doing so promises to "spoil" the open portion of the market (that not covered by reciprocity agreements) and fails to divert business from reciprocity partners, who, at most, simply renegotiate transaction prices. Indeed, once reciprocity becomes pervasive in an industry, reciprocity partners tend to minimize price as a factor in their transactions.

This is not idle speculation. The available evidence demonstrates that reciprocity creates tight trading bonds among practitioners. And, whereas reciprocity partners often claim that they only deal with one another on an "all-other-things-being-equal" basis (and, indeed, this is often the case), reciprocity partners often short-circuit the market so completely that they do not adequately test it to discover their lowest-price alternatives. In fact, it is not uncommon for reciprocity partners to pay prices above the going market price, although not for the reasons Stigler assumes (i.e., to grant secret price concessions to customers); rather, they do so in order to not rock the boat in an otherwise stable market. This is illustrated by an Atlantic-Richfield Trade Relations Manual, dated July 1, 1966, which outlined buyers' procedures for selecting vendors. The manual directed Atlantic-Richfield buyers to place business with bidders offering the lowest cost, "unless other factors, *including trade relations,* make it advisable to pay a higher price.''[103] This is not an isolated incident. Not only do firms frequently pay higher prices to their reciprocity partners, at times, they even accept lower-quality products in their drive to maintain an equitable balance of payments.[104] Such facts cannot be reconciled with the Chicago School's statements that, in oligopolistic markets, reciprocity (1) is practiced mainly as a device to discover new customers; (2) erodes price rigidity; and (3) generally improves the allocation of resources.

The manner in which conglomerate mergers enhance the reciprocity opportunities of already huge corporations was documented in the case of several of ITT's major acquisitions. For example, when ITT was considering its acquisition of Avis, Inc., the second largest car rental company, the ITT board was informed by its staff of the reciprocity opportunities that would be created by the merger: ''As one of the largest purchasers and renters of automobiles from two of the major manufacturers, the Avis relationship can possibly develop additional markets for our manufacturing operations that would otherwise not be available to use, especially for our components business.''[105] In 1967, the ITT-Avis purchases from Chrysler totaled $28 million, and its purchases from General Motors amounted to $23 million.[106] It is hardly surprising, therefore, that ITT anticipated that Avis's purchasing power might ''develop additional markets [with GM and Chrysler] that would not otherwise be available to us . . .''[107] A merger of ITT and Avis promised not only to increase ITT's sales but Avis's as well. Robert Townsend, Avis's president at the time it was acquired by ITT, immediately recognized the great reciprocity potential inherent in a merger with ITT. Even before the merger was consummated, Townsend asked ITT to use its business relations with ITT suppliers to increase Avis's business.[108]

The record in the ITT-Grinnell case shows many instances of reciprocal dealing by ITT. For example, ITT-Sheraton purchased Philco-Ford TV sets in return for Ford's use of Sheraton hotel rooms and services.[109] The ITT-Lamp Division explored ways of increasing its sales potential by virtue of ITT-Continental Baking Company's purchases of equipment.[110] The record further demonstrated that the Grinnell Corporation had practiced reciprocity prior to its merger with ITT, and that that merger greatly increased its potential use of the practice.[111] The record of the ITT-Canteen case documented how ITT promoted reciprocity with banks. The Justice Department discovered more than thirty identical letters written by ITT to banks, which said, in part, ''It is a pleasure being a customer of your bank and perhaps a member of our corporate family can likewise do business with you.''[112] In this case, ITT was using reciprocity to sell insurance to banks. Although the government never completed its discovery efforts in the ITT-Hartford Fire Insurance case (the case was settled before the final trial) substantial evidence of actual reciprocity and reciprocity opportunities was developed in the preliminary injunction proceedings.[113]

Chairman Harold Geneen testified in the ITT-Hartford preliminary injunction hearing that ITT had a long, well-established antireciprocity policy. Yet the record in the ITT-Grinnell case demonstrates that Geneen himself had engaged in reciprocity arrangements.[114] Indeed, Geneen admitted that the only ITT personnel ever reprimanded for violating this policy were those whose reciprocity activities were uncovered in the antitrust suits.[115] As the House antitrust staff study of ITT concluded:

> A major consideration in ITT's merger program was the acquisition of companies that would reinforce marketing efforts of other ITT subsidiaries. This cross-fertilization of total system effort was expected to confer desirable heft in particular markets and to increase the competitive strength of the individual subsidiaries in their business activities with outsiders.[116]

Although the ITT case ultimately was settled by a controversial Consent Decree,[117] Richard McLaren, head of the Antitrust Division, maintained, even after he had settled the cases, that the challenged ITT aquisitions involved "systematic reciprocity and the power to develop further reciprocity arrangements through interrelationships of the different companies . . . I think a strong economic case can be made against those mergers."[118]

A 1980 decision of the Federal Communications Commission provides an illustration of flagrant reciprocal trading by a huge conglomerate—General Tire and Rubber Company. General Tire has acquired numerous companies, and by 1979 had sales of $2.9 billion. Not only was General Tire one of the world's largest tire makers but it also controled Frontier Airlines; it was the world's largest producer of tennis balls, and controled many operations, including RKO General Inc., which operated 13 radio and television stations, mostly in large cities. Its large size and conglomerate operations enabled General Tire to develop pervasive reciprocal trading arrangements. The FCC found that General Tire carried on "an intensive trade relations program" whereby "companies were induced to advertise on RKO stations as a condition of doing business with the General Tire family."[119] The FCC concluded that "the purpose and effect of this scheme was, in part, to obtain advertising customers for RKO stations, not on the basis of those stations' advertising rates and demographics, but, instead, on the basis of the General Tire conglomerate's large-scale buying power."[120] Because of this and other misconduct,[121] the FCC concluded that RKO General was not qualified to serve as the licensee of television stations in Boston, New York, and Los Angeles.

Continued conglomerate expansion—both by merger and internal growth—promises to increase reciprocity opportunities, thereby threatening to result in closed-circuit markets from which medium and small businesses are excluded. Oligopoly in individual markets would be magnified by circular integration, in which purchases of the leading firms would be tied to sales, thus precluding the opportunities of firms without substantial reciprocity opportunities to gain access to the inner circle of firms. As stated in *Fortune:*

> trade relations between the giant conglomerates tend to close a business circle. Left out are the firms with narrow product lines; as patterns of trade and trading

> partners emerge between particular groups of companies, entry by newcomers becomes more difficult.[122]

Indeed, *Fortune* concludes that "the United States economy might end up completely dominated by conglomerates happily trading with each other in a new kind of cartel system."[123]

Conglomerate Interdependence and Competitive Forbearance

We have seen how the current merger movement is contributing to the creation of a dual economy, in which a few hundred enormous corporations are expanding their control over the bulk of industrial activity, leaving the literally thousands of smaller businesses to share the remainder. We also have seen how the conglomerate mergers, which propel this centralization, have greatly increased the reciprocity opportunities of large corporations as they expand their product lines, thereby increasing the potential buyer-seller linkages with other corporations.

But growing reciprocity opportunities are only the most obvious manifestation of the changed competitive environment. Reciprocity is but a symptom of the larger problems of conglomerate interdependence and competitive forbearance, which is the inevitable concomitant of an economy in which most commerce is controlled by a relatively few huge corporations.

It is now well recognized in economic theory and industrial experience that, in a market of few sellers, firms tend to behave interdependently. That is, each seller takes into account the direct and indirect consequences of its price, output, and other market decisions. This is called *oligopolistic interdependence*.

The theory of oligopoly explains the behavior of firms operating in a single market in which their discretion in pricing is constrained by certain structural characteristics of the market. Especially relevant characteristics are market concentration, product differentiation, and barriers facing would-be entrants.

The competitive conduct characteristics of particular markets may be influenced not only by these three traditional structural characteristics but also by the conglomerate character of some of the firms operating in the market. We have just seen that a conglomerate enterprise possesses a unique capacity to practice reciprocal selling. In addition, however, the multimarket characteristics of firms may result in what we will call *conglomerate mutual interdependence and competitive forbearance*[124] among actual and potential competitors—an interfirm relationship that differs from *oligopolistic interdependence* as it is traditionally viewed.

Conglomerate interdependence and forbearance can arise because (1) the same or related decision makers have simultaneous access to both firms, or (2) the firms share contact points in input-output markets, which creates an awareness of common interests. Interlocking directorates, intercorporate stockholdings, and joint ventures represent the first set of factors that facilitates coordinated relationships among firms. A *firm's* structure—that is, its size and conglomerateness—constitutes the second set of factors that create a commonality of interest. All of these factors determine the number and nature of the contact points that the firms will share. By increasing both size and diversification, the conglomerate merger increases the number of contacts shared with competitors, suppliers, and customers, thereby increasing the mutual awareness of common interests among firms. Simply put, growing conglomeration and overall industrial concentration greatly broaden and extend traditional "communities of interests" among key industrial decision makers.

The continuing merger movement of recent decades has greatly increased the contact points among large corporations, and, therefore, the likelihood that conglomerates will exercise forbearance in their competitive confrontations.[125] Table 2 shows how mergers increased the number of actual or potential contact points among 113 of the largest corporations during three years of extensive merger activity—1966–1968.[126] The table shows that in 1968, these firms had 15,579 horizontal contact points, or an average of 138 each. This means that on the average, each corporation met firms from among the 112 others—as actual competitors—138 times. The potential vertical contact points were much more numerous, because each of these firms had an average of 642 potential buyer-seller relationships. From 1965–1968, the number of horizontal contact points among these corporations increased by

Table 2: Number of Horizontal and Vertical Contact Points Among 113 Large Manufacturing Corporations and Between ITT and 112 Other Firms, 1965 and 1968

	Number of Instances		
Type of Contacts	*1965*	*1968*	*Change 1965–1968 (Percent)*
Horizontal	12,552	15,579	+24.1
Vertical	59,044	72,579	22.9
Total	71,596	88,158	23.1
Contacts Between ITT and 112 Other Corporations			
Horizontal	369	499	35.2
Vertical	2,113	2,816	33.3
Total	2,482	3,315	33.6

Source: The sample consisted of all corporations among the 100 largest manufacturing corporations in 1965 and 1968. The analysis was made by Leonard Weiss and I. Curtis Jernigen, Jr., "Changes in Corporate Interdependencies Between 1965 and 1968," Appendix 7 of the prepared testimony of Willard F. Mueller in *U.S. v. ITT and Grinnell Corporation,* Civil No. 13319.

24.1 percent, and the potential vertical relationship rose by 22.9 percent. The increase of such linkages involving ITT, leading acquirer during the period, rose more rapidly than for all other companies. By 1968, ITT had 499 horizontal and 2,816 potential vertical contact points with the other 112 firms. Practically all of this increase was the result of ITT's numerous large mergers during this brief three-year period.

Perhaps the simplest form of conglomerate interdependence is related to price decisions. Firms which meet as competitors in many markets are likely to regard each other with greater deference than if their pricing decisions were constrained solely by structural conditions in particular markets.

But conglomerate interdependence may take more subtle forms, as conglomerates accomodate and harmonize their behavior. Although they are generally ignored or overlooked by many economists, antitrust proceedings provide rich evidence of such behavior, which goes back more than half a century. This evidence demonstrates the inherent logic of conglomerate power: to possess such power inevitably invites its use.

For example, after Du Pont became a large, diversified corporation in the early 1920s, it developed a community of interest with other leading national and international corporations. The evidence demonstrates that when these corporations met as actual or potential competitors, they often exercised mutual forbearance. As early as 1923, a Du Pont vice president explained his company's policy toward Imperial Chemical Industries of Great Britain (ICI), the world's second largest chemical firm, which Du Pont met in many international markets:

> It is not good business sense to attempt an expansion in certain directions if such an activity is bound to result in a boomerang of retaliation. It has been the Du Pont Company's policy to follow such lines of common-sense procedure . . . [127]

Du Pont's philosophy of self-restraint in dealing with ICI was summed up succinctly:

> This was done on the broad theory that cooperation is wiser than antagonism and that in the matter of detail the chances in the long run were that the boot was just as likely to be on one leg as on the other.[128]

Irenée Du Pont pointed out, in 1927, that it was his company's policy to encourage the establishment of esprit de corps among the country's "great corporations." As he put it, the Du Pont company felt "that the great corporations of the country, especially those that are leaders in business ethics and in service to the economic structure, should stand together without fear of veiled threats from companies which are more predatory."[129]

"Standing together" may sometimes prove to be a euphemism for avoiding actual or potential competition with one another. For example, Union Carbide and Carbon, in 1931, purchased rights to a process for manufacturing a transparent wrapping material which Carbide thought might be competitive with Du Pont's cellophane. Lammot Du Pont reported a conversation on this topic with Carbide officials:

> They assured me repeatedly they did not wish to rush into anything; most of all a competitive situation with DuPont. Their whole tone was most agreeable . . . . In the course of the conversations, various efforts at cooperation between Carbide and DuPont were referred to and in every case assurances of their desire to work together.[130]

There also is evidence that, in recent times, DuPont has continued the "common-sense procedures" it embraced earlier in its history as a conglomerate enterprise.[131]

A well-documented example of conglomerate confrontation and swift accommodation involved a large conglomerate food manufacturer and food retailer, Consolidated Foods Corporation, and a large multimarket food retailer, National Tea Corporation.[132] As a manufacturer of many food products as well as a food retailer, Consolidated met National on two fronts, as a supplier and as a competitor in food retailing. In early 1965, Consolidated attempted to expand its supermarket sales in Chicago by initiating an aggressive "miracle prices" campaign, claiming "price levels slashed on over 5,000 items." Because National had annual supermarket sales of around $250 million in Chicago, its profit margins were threatened by Consolidated's move. National responded quickly by having its president warn that the next day there would be fewer Consolidated lines on National shelves. Consolidated got the word. It not only stopped its price campaign immediately, but it further accommodated National by selling its Chicago stores.

The lesson to be learned from this confrontation is clear. Conglomerate "interdependence" and "forbearance" eliminated Consolidated as an aggressive rival in food retailing. Because Consolidated was a food manufacturer as well as a food retailer, the competitive strategies it followed in one market boomeranged, because it invited retaliation in another. Had National not been one of its customers, Consolidated could have behaved independently of National in expanding its food-retailing in Chicago, and consumers would have benefited from its aggressive price campaign.

This and other evidence[133] demonstrate how shared contact points can induce forbearance and interdependence among potential competitors. The exchange of reciprocal favors among conglomerate corporations involves shared contact points, but the contemplated consequences of such sharing need not be limited to reciprocal buying. The interfirm structural framework characterized by the shared contact points leads to the consideration, proposal, and possible realization of acts of conglomerate interdependence and forbearance that can affect market shares, entry, and pricing practices. It may well represent the most serious threat to competition resulting from the growing merger-achieved centralization of economic resources among a relatively few conglomerates, which meet as actual or potential competitors or customers in many markets. The ultimate result is a closed economic system in which price and other business decisions by vast conglomerates become largely immune from the disciplining influence of the market. Such a system smacks of the pre-World War II Zaibatsu system in Japan, in which a handful of huge financial-industrial conglomerates, working in concert with the state, exercised great control over many key economic and political decisions. Such a system runs counter to the basic assumptions of a free, competitive enterprise system that relies on the market to discipline the use of private economic power.

Conglomeration by merger accelerates the development of such a system, and, when it involves large firms, it widens the market power differential between the largest firms and other firms in the economy. There thus exists a causal relationship between the growing merger-achieved centralization of control over American industry and the competitive structure and behavior found in particular markets occupied by giant conglomerate enterprises. It is extremely difficult to quantify how growing aggregate concentration and conglomeration change the structure and behavior of particular markets. However, the available case studies of cross-subsidization, reciprocity, and conglomerate interdependence provide important evidence of the effects. This case-study evidence is reinforced by several statistical analyses. One study found a significant positive relationship between the share of an industry held by the nation's 200 largest industrial corporations and increases in concentration within the industry. This finding supports the hypothesis that the more extensive the presence of very large corporations in an industry, the greater is the likelihood that market concentration will rise.[134] Another recent statistical analysis found that the presence of conglomerate firms in an industry raised entry barriers.[135]

These findings have rich implications for public policy concerning conglomerate mergers. They may provide an important bridge between the concern with overall centralization of economic power, as it was expressed by the Congress when it enacted the Celler-Kefauver Act, and the language of the Act that focuses on competition in specific markets. We turn now to the question of whether existing legislation and its enforcement are adequate to cope with the problems created by the increasing conglomeration of American industry.

VII. PUBLIC POLICY

Public policy must begin with the premise that large conglomerate enterprises will not wither away. Even very inefficient large corporations do not disappear from the economic landscape. Because of anticipated catastrophic consequences to stockholders, employees, and entire communities when a large corporation's survival is threatened, either the government bails it out—for example, Lockheed Aircraft[136] and Chrysler—or permits it to merge with another large corporation, even a direct competitor—for example, the merger of McDonnell Co. and Douglas Aircraft.[137]

Adequate Antitrust Funding

The federal antitrust agencies have always been seriously underfunded. If cost-benefit analysis were used to determine appropriate funding levels, a sound case could be made for providing substantial increases in funds for these agencies. For example, the plantiffs who brought treble damage suits against General Electric and other members of the "great electrical conspiracy" of the 1950s received awards exceeding $500 million. This is greater than the combined antitrust budgets for the FTC and the Antitrust Division between 1890 and 1960. In addition, the prices of electrical equipment subject to the conspiracy fell 10 percent or more following the government's case.

Without adequate funding, the antitrust agencies are hopelessly undermanned and outgunned in most litigation against the large corporations. An order of magnitude is given to this mismatch by noting that AT&T reportedly budgeted at least $50 million to "defend" itself in the recent suit brought against it by the Antitrust Division. This is greater than the *total* annual budget of the Antitrust Division.

Quite clearly, unless the antitrust laws are to remain a paper tiger, the antitrust agencies must receive adequate funding.

Strengthening the Merger Law

More vigorous antitrust enforcement alone will not deal effectively with conglomerate mergers and the problems resulting from existing levels of conglomeration. New legislation is required to overcome these problems.

If the traditional case-by-case antitrust approach is used, it could take a decade or more to explore the outer boundaries of the existing antitrust laws. Indeed, since the ITT case was settled in 1971, few big conglomerate cases have been brought. Moreover, during the 1970s the U.S. Supreme Court has become increasingly tolerant of mergers, which led one student of the Court to charge that the Burger majority harbors an "anti-antitrust bias."[138] The standards established by "the new antitrust majority," as Justice White has labeled it,[139] have made it virtually impossible for the government successfully to challenge conglomerate mergers. During 1973–1979, the Justice Department has lost nine consecutive conglomerate merger cases, and the Federal Trade Commission and private parties have lost eleven cases.[140] Since 1980, the Reagan Administration, as part of its overall policy of weakening antitrust enforcement, has not seen fit to challenge conglomerate mergers.[141]

Quite clearly, existing law, as interpreted by the Burger Supreme Court, is not capable of preventing undesirable conglomerate mergers. A more direct approach is called for: legislation that applies special legal standards to very large mergers. This legislation should recognize explicitly that such mergers pose serious economic and political dangers, which transcend the economists' narrow preoccupation with a merger's competitive impact on an isolated market.

In 1979, Senator Edward Kennedy intoduced a conglomerate merger bill, S.600, aimed at mergers among large corporations and acquisitions of firms holding large market shares. Specifically, this bill called for the prohibition of mergers among companies where each had sales of $350 million or more, or where a company with sales of $350 million acquired a company with a market share of 20 percent or more in any significant market. The bill provided that a merging company could provide the following affirmative defenses: (1) the merger "will have the preponderant effect of substantially enhancing competition"; (2) the merger "will result in substantial efficiencies"; or (3) within one year before the merger the parties shall have divested one or more viable businesses with revenues at least equal to revenues of the smaller merger partner. (These affirmative defenses would not apply where each of the merging companies had revenues exceeding $1 billion.) When introducing the bill, Senator Kennedy expressed his concern about the inability of existing laws to deal with conglomerate mergers, which, in his view, are antithetical to our system, on political, social, and economic grounds.[142]

Such strict restraints on large conglomerate mergers would prevent much merger-induced conglomeration and would contribute to the erosion of existing market concentration. By preventing large corporations from entering new industries by acquiring other large corporations, especially those holding large market shares, these firms would be encouraged to enter other industries—by building new capacity or by acquiring small concerns. Then, instead of merely being substitutes for an already large competitor in an industry, they would increase the number of significant competitors, thereby eroding the market position of entrenched firms.[143]

Legislation Requiring Restructuring of Concentrated Industries

Vigorous enforcement of existing and new-merger legislation may effectively prevent further conglomerate centralization, but it will do little to erode existing centralization. History suggests that widespread and expeditious divestiture in an industry requires direct legislation. Perhaps the most familiar instance of this type of legislation was the Public Utilities Holding Company Act of 1935, which specified massive divestiture. However, there are other instructive examples. The direct legislative approach also has been used in order to divest conglomerate-like centralizations of power. The Banking Act of 1933, which separated investment banking from commercial banking, succeeded in restructuring numerous large and medium-sized banks. The result was the spin-off of such large investment bankers as First Boston Corporation and Morgan Stanley & Company. Many of todays leading regional brokerage firms also had their genesis in the massive divestiture required by the 1933 Act. As a result, the American banking structure is much less centralized than it would otherwise be. Similarly, the McKellar-Black Air Mail Act of 1934 forced General Motors to relinquish its interest in various air carriers and airline manufacturers. These various legislation-mandated divestitures accomplished more industrial decentralization than all the decentralization that has been achieved under the Sherman Act since its enactment in 1890.

These experiences should teach us that the direct legislative route would be far preferable to antitrust action to divest existing conglomerations of power, especially in those areas that the Congress views as being particularly troublesome. A likely target is the energy industry, in which vast multinational petroleum corporations have come to control large shares of alternative energy sources, especially crude oil and natural gas, coal, uranium, oil shale, and tar sands. To achieve an even modest degree of deconglomeration in these areas, all of the resources of the antitrust agencies would be consumed—for decades. Congress, on the other hand, could spell out guidelines that would restructure the energy industry in a relatively few years. Although the legislative approach probably should be used sparingly, there doubtless are other areas in which legislative action would be far more effective and less time-consuming than conventional antitrust enforcement. Unless the legislative approach is used, the antitrust agencies will remain hopelessly mired down in a few big cases, and will have no real impact on existing levels of industrial conglomeration.

Proposals to deconcentrate some industries are not merely the creation of academic economists. Some persons who are intimately involved in business affairs are also outspoken advocates of such policies. For example, Arthur Brock, who spent most of his business career in promoting mergers and acquisitions, argues forcefully that deconcentration is essential to the restoration of economic efficiency and progress in industries now shielded from competition. Brock acknowledges that his current views may seem heretical, coming as they do from someone who has contributed to the present state of affairs: "If there is irony that one who has spent most of his lifetime in merging activities now promises de-merging as the salvation of the free enterprise system, so be it."[144]

Eliminating Corporate Secrecy via Federal Chartering

Even at best, the aforementioned measures will not bring about sufficient industrial restructuring to ensure that conglomerate power will be disciplined by the marketplace. Because of the enormous economic and political power of modern conglomerate corporations, it should be made very clear that conglomerates are not purely *private* institutions. Congress should explicitly declare that the large conglomerate corporation's business is very much the *public's* business. Simply put, the huge conglomerate enterprises that control most industrial resources are quasipublic institutions, because they have been granted the privilege—but not the explicit responsibility—of running the American economy. Former ITT chairman, Harold Geneen, acknowledged this when he said, "Increasingly, the larger corporations have become the primary custodians of making our entire system work."[145] This quite naturally raises questions of legitimacy—i.e., whether these powerful corporations are running the economy in the public interest.

Justice William O. Douglas identified the problem more than three decades ago, when he observed: "Enterprises . . . which command tremendous resources . . . tip the scales on the side of prosperity or on the side of depression, depending on the decisions of the men at the top. This is tremendous power, tremendous responsibility. Such men become virtual governments in the power at their disposal. In fact, if not in law, they become affected with a public interest."[146]

An appropriate first step toward recognizing that the large corporation is not a purely private enterprise is to require that all very large corporations receive a corporate charter from the federal government rather than from individual states.[147] In the more than one hundred years since New Jersey amended its constitution (1875) to liberalize greatly the incorporation process, state chartering statutes have become increasingly framed to suit the interests of corporate enterprises. The whole thrust of this development has been to confer on the corporation the rights and privileges of private citizens. Yet, during that period, as more and more of the economy has become the domain of enormous corporate enterprises, corporations increasingly have taken on the characteristics of public enterprises, in that they influence, directly and indirectly, the livelihood of all Americans.

A federal chartering statute should spell out a set of corporate *responsibilities* as well as *rights*. A major purpose of such a charter should be to remove the veil of secrecy covering much corporate decision making that is vital to the public interest. It should be restricted to only the very largest corporations, perhaps those controlling assets of $1 billion or more. (The 282 manufacturing corporations of this size controlled about 67 percent of all manufacturing assets in 1984). Among the possible provisions of such a charter are the following:

1. Extensive visitation privileges for the chartering agency, to insure it ready access to relevant corporate information.
2. Much more extensive public reporting of the sources of investment, revenues, and profits than is now required by the SEC.
3. Extensive public disclosure of the volumes of all products manufactured and sold, including such information that corporations currently supply to the Bureau of the Census, under strict rules of confidentiality.
4. Public disclosure of corporate federal income tax returns.
5. Disclosure of certain social costs.
6. Disclosure of publicly owned facilities operated or leased by private corporations.
7. Disclosure of various details of a corporation's foreign operations, and prohibitions against political intervention in the affairs of other nations.
8. Publicly appointed representatives on the board of directors, who would

obtain relevant information on corporate affairs, thereby providing the public a window into the affairs of the giant conglomerate.

This, in skeletal form, is a program for providing greater public disclosure of corporate affairs. It clearly is not an attack on our market economy, but an effort to perfect it. Although federal chartering is not a panacea, it is an essential first step in recognizing the large modern corporation for what it is—an essentially public institution.

Nor is this proposal a substitute for a vigorous program to make competition more effective wherever possible, or for the other reforms mentioned in this chapter. On the contrary, it complements such efforts. It recognizes that giant conglomerate corporations enjoy great discretion in making numerous decisions that affect our social, cultural, political and economic welfare. Therefore, more complete disclosure by large corporations would serve the dual objective of aiding natural market forces and of providing the broader benefits to society that flow from more complete information of corporate affairs. The belief in the elimination of unnecessary corporate secrecy is based on what Justice Louis Brandeis emphasized as being "the essential difference between corporations and natural persons."

The author holds no illusions that any of these proposals will be adopted in the near future. Proposals to restrain conglomerate mergers have received little support in recent years, and they are not likely to be enacted into law in the near term. President Ronald Reagan is on record as opposing such restraints as "arbitrary, unnecessary, and economically unsound,"[148] and the new chairman of the Senate Committee on the Judiciary has eliminated that Committee's Subcommittee on Antitrust and Monopoly, which had been the leading Congressional body concerned with conglomerate mergers. Both antitrust agencies, the Antitrust Division and the Federal Trade Commission, are now headed by individuals who are hostile to the basic tenets of the antitrust laws as articulated by the authors of these laws and by judicial precedents.[149] But those concerned with shaping public-policy alternatives that would improve our economic system must not be swayed by the popular moods of the times. To do so would silence all voices of reform.

NOTES

1. Even the economic power of the old Standard Oil Trust, which economists often cite as an early example of horizontal power, might better be explained in the context of conglomerate power. See S. Loescher, "A Sherman Act Precedent for the Application of Antitrust Legislation to Conglomerate Mergers, Standard Oil, 1911," in J. W. Markham and G. F. Papanek (eds.), *Industrial Organization & Economic Development* (Boston: Houghton, 1970), pp. 154–215.

2. See the report to President Wilson by the newly created Federal Trade Commission, FTC, *Report on the Meat-packing Industry* (Washington, D.C.: U.S. Government Printing Office), June 24, 1919.

3. Joan Robinson, *The Economics of Imperfect Competition,* 2nd. ed. (London: Macmillan & Co., 1969), p. IX.

4. Corwin D. Edwards, "Conglomerate Bigness As a Source of Power," in *Business Concentration Price Policy* (Princeton, N.J.: Princeton U. P., Conference of National Bureau of Economic Research, 1955), pp. 346–347.

5. In 1968, 181 of the 200 largest industrials manufactured ten or more products; in 1960, only 149 of the 200 largest made ten or more products. FTC, Staff Report, *Economic Report on Corporate Mergers* (Washington, D.C.: U.S. Government Printing Office, 1969), p. 224. (Hereafter referred to as FTC, *Merger Report*).

6. Ibid., p. 173.

7. The top 200 corporations' share of total industrial assets is even larger than the preceding estimates suggest. Many corporations hold large investment interests in other domestic and foreign corporations. Additionally, large corporations operate numerous facilities that actually are owned by the federal government. Although data are incomplete, in 1967, government-owned property operated by private corporations had assets of $14.7 billion. See U.S. Congress, Joint Economic Committee, Subcommittee on Economy in Government, *Economy in Government Procurement and Property Management,* 90th Cong., 2nd sess., April 1968, p. 7.

8. W. F. Mueller, *The Celler-Kefauver Act; The First 27 Years,* A Study prepared for the Subcommittee on Monopolies and Commercial Law of the Committee on the Judiciary, House of Representatives (Washington, D.C.: U.S. Government Printing Office, 1978), pp. 76, 81.

9. The wholesale price index was used to adjust for inflation since 1929.

10. Inflation-adjusted estimates were made for 1929, based on Norman Collins and Lee Preston, "The Size Structure of the Largest Industrial Firms, 1909–1958," *American Economic Review,* **51**:1005–1011(Dec. 1961); 1984 estimates from FTC, *Quarterly Financial Report for Manufacturing Corporations* (Second Quarter, 1984).

11. FTC, *Merger Report,* op. cit., pp. 65–67.

12. ITT, *Annual Report,* 1967, p. 3.

13. Prepared testimony of W. F. Mueller, in *United States v. ITT and Grinnell Corporation,* Civil no. 13319, App. 5.

14. ITT, *Annual Report,* 1979, p. 14.

15. W. F. Mueller, "The ITT Settlement: A Deal With Justice? " *Industrial Organization Review,* 1:80 (1973).

16. U.S. Congress, Senate, Committee on Foreign Relations, Subcommittee on Multinational Corporations, *International Telephone and Telegraph Company and Chile,* 1970–1971, *Report,* 93rd Cong., 1st sess., June 21, 1973, pp. 4–6.

17. See Morton Mintz and Jerry Cohen, *America, Inc.* (New York: Dial, 1971) pp. 330–337, who document ITT's political power in Great Britain, Canada, Denmark, Iceland, and the United States.

18. *The New York Times,* July 27, 1975, Sec. 3, p.1.

19. See "Wall Street: The Lure of 2 + 2 = 5," *Newsweek* (May 8, 1967), p. 82. This theme echoed the contemporary explanations given for the great merger wave that peaked in 1929, when journalists also "discovered" that merger makers of that day were making "business history by adding two and two to make five." *Business Week* (Nov. 27, 1928), p. 27.

20. *Financial World,* 129:12(Feb. 14, 1968).

21. U.S. Treasury Department, *Tax Reform Studies and Proposals,* Joint Publication of the House Committee on Ways and Means and the Senate Committee on Finance (Washington, D.C.: U.S. Government Printing Office, Feb. 5, 1969), Part 2, pp. 268–269.

22. *The Wall Street Journal,* April 17, 1968, p. 25.

23. Abraham J. Briloff, "Financial Motives for Conglomerate Growth," *St. John's Law Review* (Spring 1970), p. 877.

24. U.S. Congress, House, Antitrust Subcommittee of the Comittee on the Judiciary, *Investigation of Conglomerate Merger, Staff Report,* 92nd Cong., 1st sess., June 1, 1971, p. 414.

25. Ibid., p. 140.

26. Ibid., p. 139.

27. Ibid.

28. "Accountant Urges Better Reporting Practices," *The New York Times,* July 24, 1971.

29. Scheinman, Hochstin and Trotta, "Alert for Portfolio Managers," Supplement P, July 1971, p. 1.

30. Ibid., p. 1.

31. Ibid., p. 3.

32. Ibid.

33. *Fortune,* op. cit., p. 216.

34. Ibid., p. 212.

35. "Irv Jacobs' Raid Could Force a Breakup of ITT," *Newsweek* (Dec. 24, 1984), p. 31.

36. "The Trouble that Led to ITT's Dividend Shocker," *Business Week* (July 23, 1984), p. 77.

37. "ITT Indicates it May Reduce Company's Size," *The Wall Street Journal,* Aug. 1984, p. 5; and "ITT: The Giant Slumbers," *The New York Times,* July 1984, pp. 1, 21.

38. Prepared statement of P. C. Cabot before the U.S. Congress, House, Committee on Ways and Means, *Hearings on Tax Reform,* 91st Cong., 1st sess., March 12, 1969.

39. A. Briloff, op. cit., pp. 872–879; Henry B. Reiling, "EPS Growth from Financial Packaging: An Accounting Incentive in Acquisitions," *St. Johns Law Review* (Spring 1970), pp. 880–894; and Roger Sherman, "How Tax Policy Induces Conglomerate Mergers," *National Tax Journal* (Dec. 1972), pp. 521–529.

40. FTC, *Merger Report,* op. cit., p. 159; cf. Samuel R. Reid, *Mergers and the Economy* (New York: McGraw-Hill, 1968).

41. George W. Stocking, *Basing Point Pricing and Regional Development* (Chapel Hill, N.C.: U. of North Carolina P., 1954), p. 140; Edwin Mansfield, "Size of Firm, Market Structure, and Innovation," *Journal of Political Economy,* **71:**556–576(Dec. 1963); Walter Adams and Joel Dirlam, "Big Steel, Invention and Innovation," *Quarterly Journal of Economics,* **80:**169(May 1966).

42. T. F. Hogarty, "Profits from Mergers: The Evidence of 50 Years," *St. Johns Law Review,* special ed., **44:**389(Spring 1970).

43. D. C. Mueller, "The Effects of Conglomerate Mergers: A Survey of the Empirical Evidence," *Journal of Banking and Finance,* **1:**339(1977).

44. Ibid.

45. H. Manne, "Mergers and the Market for Corporate Control," *Journal of Political Economy,* **73:**110–120(1965).

46. S. R. Reid, *Mergers, Managers and the Economy* (New York: McGraw-Hill, 1968). W. Sichel, "Conglomerateness: Size and Monopoly Control," *St. Johns Law Review,* special ed., **44**:354–377(1970).

47. D. C. Mueller, op, cit., p. 342.

48. Edwards, op. cit.

49. *United States v. Columbia Steel Company et al.,* 334 U.S. 495(1948).

50. W. F. Mueller, "The ITT Settlement: A Deal With Justice?" op. cit., pp. 67–86.

51. "Before and After the Felony," *The New York Times,* Sept. 7, 1975, sec. 3, p. 1. Steinbrenner and the corporation subsequently pleaded guilty to reduced charges and were fined $15,000 and $20,000, respectively.

52. *The International Telephone and Telegraph Company and Chile, 1970–71,* op. cit., pass.

53. *The Wall Street Journal,* Aug. 19, 1975, p. 7.

54. "U.S. Company Payoffs Way of Life Overseas," *The New York Times,* May 5, 1975, p. 1. "Northtrop Uncovers $861,000 That Unit Paid in 5 Countries," *The Wall Street Journal,* Feb 23, 1976, p. 2.

55. "Gulf's Accounts of Political Gifts Abroad Stir Anger Overseas, Questions at Home," *The Wall Street Journal,* May 19, 1975, p. 2.

56. "Tenneco, Inc. Discloses to SEC Payments of Public Officials in U.S. and Overseas," *The Wall Street Journal,* Feb. 17, 1976, p. 2.

57. "Lockheed Data Payoffs in L-1011 Sales Overseas Is Sent to Senate Unit by Mistake," *The Wall Street Journal,* Feb. 17, 1976, p. 2.

58. "Exxon Concedes That Donations In Italy Were for Promoting 'Business Objectives,' " *The Wall Street Journal,* July 17, 1975, p. 2; "Exxon Says Donations in Italy Exceed $46 Million; Communists Got $86,000," *The Wall Street Journal,* July 14, 1975, p. 10; "Exxon Discloses More Foreign Payments in Filing, says SEC May Demand Details," *The Wall Street Journal,* Sept. 26, 1975, p. 6.

59. SEC, *Questionable and Illegal Corporate Payments and Practices* (Washington, D.C.: U.S. Government Printing Office, 1976).

60. Ibid., p. 54.

61. Ibid., p. 56.

62. "How Lawless Are Big Companies?" *Fortune* (Dec. 15, 1980), p. 57.

63. Ibid.

64. Ibid.

65. Ibid., p. 62.

66. M. B. Clinard and P. C. Yeager, *Corporate Crime* (New York: Macmillan, 1980), p. 298.

67. *United States v. Bethlehem Steel Corporation, 168 F. Supp. 576 (1958).*

68. Several prominent economists testified on behalf of Bethlehem, arguing that the merger would actually enhance competition because Bethlehem would not otherwise enter the Midwest market, a prediction subsequently proved false.

69. W. F. Mueller, *The Celler-Kefauver Act: The First 27 Years of Enforcement,* op. cit. Since 1950, the antitrust agencies have challenged more than one thousand mergers, practically all of which involved horizontal and vertical mergers.

70. See W. F. Mueller, "Public Policy Toward Vertical Mergers," in J. Fred Weston and Sam Peltzman (eds.), *Public Policy Toward Mergers* (Pacific Palisades, Calif.: Goodyear, 1969), pp. 150–166.

71. M. A. Adelman, "The Antimerger Act, 1950–1960," *American Economic Review,* **51:**243(May 1961).

72. FTC, *Merger Report,* op. cit., pp. 225–230. The following discussion of the sources of conglomerate power draws heavily on the FTC report, which was prepared under the author's direction. I wish particularly to acknowledge Professor Robert E. Smith, now of the University of Oregon, for helping to develop the ideas presented in this section of the report.

73. For a discussion of other ways in which business conglomeration may enlarge the conduct options of firms, see Edwards. op, cit., pp. 334–352. Bradburd has demonstrated theoretically that a conglomerate firm may have power even though it does not possess market power in any of its markets. R. M. Bradburd, "Conglomerate Power Without Market Power," *American Economic Review,* **70:**483–487(June 1980).

74. Howard H. Hines, "Effectiveness of 'Entry' by Already Established Firms," *Quarterly Journal of Economics,* **171:**132–150(Feb. 1957).

75. FTC, *Merger Report,* op. cit., pp. 214–215. These structural characteristics of conglomerates have been particularly well documented for the largest food manufacturing firms. J. M. Connor, R. T. Rogers, B. W. Marion, and W. F. Mueller, *The Food Manufacturing Industries: Structure, Strategies, Performance and Policies*(Lexington, Mass.: Lexington Press, 1984), pp. 69–193, 241–274.

76. John Narver, *Conglomerate Mergers and Market Competition* (Berkley: U. of California P., 1967), p. 105. See Chap. 4 in Narver for a discussion of other sources of economic power possessed by a conglomerate enterprise.

77. FTC, *Merger Report,* op. cit., p. 444. (Italics supplied.)

78. Edwards, op. cit., pp. 334–335.

79. FTC, *Merger Report,* op. cit., pp. 406–457; John Blair, *Economic Concentrations* (New York: Harcourt, 1972), pp. 43, 51, 363–367, and 594.

80. The following discussion of the beer industry is based in part on W. F. Mueller, testimony before the Subcommittee on Antitrust and Monopoly, Committee on the Judiciary, U.S. Senate, the 95th Cong., 2nd sess., May 12, 1978, pp. 78–124 Hereafter cited as Mueller testimony (1978).

81. I. Horowitz and A. R. Horowitz, "Firms in a Declining Market: The Brewing Case," *Journal of Industrial Economics,* No. 152 (March 1965). In a subsequent article, these authors concluded that "the 4 majors will ultimately claim about 40.3 percent and the widely marketed regionals 23.6 percent of the market." See, "Entropy, Markov Processes and Competition in the Brewing Industry," *Journal of Industrial Economics,* No. 205 (March 1967–68).

82. K. G. Elzinga, "The Restructuring of the U.S. Brewing Industry," *Industrial Organization Review,* **1:**114(1973).

83. J. Blair, "The Conglomerate Merger in Economics and Law," *Georgetown Law Journal,* (Summer 1958), p. 693.

84. Ibid., p. 693.

85. Emanuel Goldman, partner at Sanford C. Berstein & Co., "Beverage Industry: A Round Table Discussion." *The Wall Street Transcript,* New York (May 24, 1976), p. 106.

86. *Business Week* (Oct. 13, 1975), p. 117.

87. J. M. Weingarten and Y. P. Hentic, Research Department, Investment Recommendation, Anheuser-Busch, Inc., Wertheim & Co., Dec. 30, 1975, p. 15.

88. See W. F. Mueller. Paper submitted to the Department of Justice, January 15, 1979: "Competitive Significance for the Beer Industry of the Exclusive Advertising Rights Granted National Brewers in Major Network Sport Events." (Available from the author.)

89. Mueller testimony (1978), op. cit., p. 100.

90. *Philip Morris Incorporated, Annual Report:1984,* p. 30.

91. "Philip Morris, Inc. Cuts Book Value of Ohio Brewery," *The Wall Street Journal,* Nov. 29, 1984, p. 8.

92. R. W. Cotterill and W. F. Mueller, "The Impact of Firm Conglomeration on Market Structure: Evidence for the U.S. Food Retailing Industry," *The Antitrust Bulletin,* **22:**119–129(1977).

93. For further elaboration of the conditions necessary to practice reciprocity, see George W. Stocking and Willard F. Mueller, "Business Reciprocity and the Size of Firms," *Journal of Business of the University of Chicago* (April 1957); and FTC, *Merger Report,* op. cit., pp. 323–332.

94. See George Stigler, "Reciprocity," Working Paper IV, Nixon Task Force on Productivity and Competition, February 18, 1969, reproduced in *Antitrust Law & Economics Review* (Spring 1969), p. 52. These arguments are also made by James M. Ferguson, "Tying Arrangements and Reciprocity: An Economic Analysis," *Law and Contemporary Problems,* **30:**552–580(Summer 1965).

95. J. H. Lorie and P. Halpern, "Conglomerates: The Rhetoric and Evidence" *Journal of Law and Economics,* **13:**149–166(April 1970).

96. For an extensive discussion of the scope and practice of reciprocity, see FTC, *Merger Report,* op. cit., pp. 332–297.

97. See Ferguson, op. cit., and Lorie and Halpern, op. cit.

98. *Waugh Equipment Company,* 15 FTC 232 (1931).

99. FTC, *Merger Report,* op. cit., pp. 338–340.

100. Similarly, the facts disclosed in the Consolidated Foods case, *FTC v. Consolidated Foods, Inc.,* 380 U.S. 592 (1965), demonstrate that, although the Consolidated Food Corporation was a large (measured in absolute terms) grocery wholesaler and retailer, it made a very small share of total grocery product purchases, on the order of 1 percent. Nor is market concentration high in the purchase of food products by food retailers; the top twenty chains control about 31 percent of food store sales. Moreover, grocery product manufacturing firms with which Consolidated Foods practiced reciprocity, covered a broad spectrum of industrial structures, ranging from low to highly concentrated. Yet the record in the Consolidated Foods case demonstrates that firms in these various industries had an incentive and, indeed, did engage in reciprocity with Consolidated Foods. The 1963 four-firm concentration ratios for industries with which Consolidated was proven to have practiced reciprocity varied considerably: meatpacking, 24 percent; pickles and other pickled products, 29 percent; canned vegetables, 38 percent; canned baby foods, 93 percent; canned soups, 83 percent. U.S. Department of Commerce, *Concentration Ratios in Manufacturing* (Washington, D.C.: U.S. Government Printing Office, 1967).

These examples, plus other evidence, demonstrate that firms have both the incentive and capacity to practice reciprocity in imperfectly competitive markets covering a wide range of structural settings. As shown in the FTC, *Merger Report* (op. cit., pp. 332–386), reciprocity has been practiced in a broad spectrum of industrial settings including even the service industries, although there are fewer opportunities to practice it there than in industrial settings.

101. FTC, *Merger Report,* op. cit., pp.383–384.

102. Stigler, op. cit., p. 3.

103. FTC, *Merger Report,* op. cit., p. 387.

104. Ibid., pp. 392–393.

105. U.S. Congress, House, Antitrust Subcommittee, House Committee on the Judiciary. *Investigation of Conglomerate Corporations: Hearing, 91st Cong., 1st sess., Part e, 1969, p. 371*

106. Ibid., p. 601.

107. Ibid.

108. *United States v. International Telephone & Telegraph Corporation,* Civil Action No. 13319, PX 125 and PX 126. (Hereafter cited as *ITT-Grinnell* case).

109. Ibid., PX 136–137, Tr. 1877–1879.

110. Ibid., PX 180.

111. Ibid., Government's "Proposed Findings and Conclusions of Law" cites many examples, pp. 53—59.

112. U.S. Congress, Senate, Committee on the Judiciary, *Hearings on the Nomination of Richard G. Kleindienst,* 92nd Cong., 2nd sess., March and April 1972, p. 1252. (Hereafter cited as *Kleindienst Hearings.*)

113. See "Memorandum in Support of Government's Motion for Preliminary Injunctions, "*United States v. International Telephone & Telegraph Corporation and the Hartford Fire Insurance Company,* undated.

114. *ITT-Grinnell* case, op. cit., PX 123–126.

115. Ibid., Tr. 1651–1655; Geneen deposition, p. 48.

116. U.S. Congress, House, Antitrust Subcommittee of the Committee on the Judiciary, *Investigation of Conglomerate Mergers,* 91st Cong., 1st sess., June 1, 1971, p. 125.

117. Mueller, "The ITT Settlement," op. cit.

118. *Kleindienst Hearings,* op. cit., pp. 121–122.

119. Federal Communications Commission, In Re Applications of RKO General, Inc., Memorandum and Opinion, released November 26, 1980. (p. 2.)

120. Ibid.

121. In addition to its reciprocal trading, the FCC found that RKO General had engaged in "a pattern of misconduct, including improper domestic political contributions, schemes which defrauded its affiliates, improper foreign payments, and improper secret accounts designed to avoid foreign tax and currency exchange laws." Ibid., p. 3.

122. *Fortune,* **71:**194(June 1965).

123. Ibid.

124. Edwards first identified this problem. Op. cit., p. 376 ff.

125. FTC, *Merger Report,* op. cit., pp. 198–224.

126. A horizontal contact point is assumed to exist where each of a pair of firms produced the same four-digit product. A vertical contact point is assumed to exist where a pair of firms manufactured a product required as a significant input by the other firm.

127. Cited in Willard F. Mueller, *DuPont: A Case Study of Firm Growth* (Ph.D. dissertation, Vanderbilt University, 1955), p. 393.

128. Ibid.

129. Ibid.

130. Ibid., p. 202.

131. FTC, *Merger Report,* op. cit., pp. 463–476.

132. Ibid., pp. 468–470.

133. Ibid., pp. 458–471.

134. FTC, *Merger Report,* op. cit., pp. 230–234. For an analysis of this study, see Leonard Weiss, "Quantitative Studies of Industrial Organization," in M. D. Intriligator (ed.), *Frontiers of Quantitative Economics* (Amsterdam: North Holland, 1971), pp. 378–379.

135. L. L. Deutsch, "Entry and the Extent of Multimarket Operations," *Journal of Industrial Economics,* **32:** 477–487 (June 1984).

136. When Lockheed faced bankruptcy, the federal government guaranteed $195 million of its debt.

137. When Douglas Aircraft encountered serious financial difficulties, the Antitrust Division approved its acquisition, in 1967, by one of its leading competitors, McDonnell Company.

138. H. R. Lurie, "Merger Under the Burger Court: An Anti-Antitrust Bias and Its Implications," *Villanova Law Review,* **23:**214(Jan. 1978).

139. *Marine Bancorporation,* 418 U.S. at 644. Justices Brennan and Marshall concurred in Justice White's dissent.

140. "Justice Department Won't Appeal Loss on Merger Theory," *The Wall Street Journal,* Dec. 3, 1980, p. 12.

141. Willard F. Mueller, "Antitrust in the Reagan Administration," *Revue Française D'Éstudes Americaines,*"(Nov. 1984), pp. 427–434.

142. E. Kennedy, comments on S. 600. *Congressional Record–Senate,* March 8, 1979, pp. S. 2417–2419.

143. W. G. Shepherd, "Leading-Firm Conglomerate Mergers," *Antitrust Bulletin* (Winter 1968), pp. 1361–1382.

144. A. Brock. "Why Auto Companies Are Too Big," *Business Week* (Nov. 17, 1980), p. 19.

145. Quoted in A. Sampson, *The Sovereign State of ITT* (New York: Stein & Day, 1973), p. 125.

146. William O. Douglas, *Democracy and Finance* (New Haven, Conn.: Yale U. P., 1940), p. 15.

147. For a more detailed discussion of this writer's views on federal chartering, see W. F. Mueller, "Corporate Disclosure: The Public's Right to Know," in A. Rappaport and L. Revsine (eds.), *Corporate Financial Reporting* (Evanston, Ill.: Northwestern U. P., 1972), pp. 67–94, May 22, 1975.

148. "Government May Abandon Fight to Stem Conglomerate Takeovers," *The Wall Street Journal,* Nov. 23, 1980, p. 23.

149. Mueller, *supra,* note 155.

SUGGESTED READINGS

BOOKS

Blair, R. D. and R. F. Lanzillotti. *The Conglomerate Corporation*, Cambridge, Mass.: Oelgechlager, Gunn, & Hain, 1981.

Clinard, M. B., and P. C. Yeager. Corporate Crime. I New York: The Free Press, 1980.

Connor, J. M., R. T. Rogers, B. W. Marion, and W. F. Mueller. *The Food Manufacturing Industries: Structure, Strategies, Performance and Policies*. Lexington, Mass: D.C. Heath Co., 1984.

Goodrich, R. M. *Public Policy Toward Corporate Growth: The ITT Merger Cases*. Port Washington, N.Y.: National University Publications, 1978.

Mintz, Morton, and Jerry Cohen. *America, Inc.*, New York: Dial Press, 1971.

Mueller, D. C. (ed.) *The Determinants and Effects of Mergers*. Cambridge, Mass,: Oelgeschlager, Gunn & Hain, 1980.

Winslow, John F. *Conglomerates Unlimited*. Bloomington: Indiana University Press, 1973.

JOURNAL ARTICLES

Bradford, Ralph M. "Conglomerate Power Without Market Power." *American Economic Review*, **70:**483–487(June 1980).

Briloff, Abraham J. "Financial Motives for Conglomerate Growth." *St. John's Law Review*, **44:**872–879(Spring 1970).

Cotterill, Ronald W., and Willard F. Mueller. "The Impact of Firm Conglomeration on Market Structure: Evidence for the U.S. Food Retailing Industry." *The Antitrust Bulletin*, **15:**557–582(Fall 1980).

Deutsch, Larry L. "Entry and the Extent of Multiplant Operations," *Journal of Industrial Economics*, **32:**477–487 (June 1984).

Edwards, Corwin D. "Conglomerate Bigness As a Source of Power," in *Business Concentration and Price Policy*. Conference of National Bureau of Economic Research. Princeton, N.J.: Princeton University Press, 1955, pp. 346–347.

Geneen, Harold S. "Conglomerates: A Businessman's View." *St. John's Law Review*, **44:**723–742 (Spring, 1970).

Mueller, Willard F. "The ITT Settlement: A Deal with Justice?" *Industrial Organization Review*, **1:**80(1973).

——— "Antitrust in the Reagan Administration." *Revue Française D'Études Americaines* (Nov. 1984), pp. 427–434.

Siegfried, John J. "Market Structure and the Effect of Political Influence." *Industrial Organization Review*, 3:1–17(1975).

GOVERNMENT PUBLICATIONS

Federal Trade Commission, Staff Report, *Economic Report on Corporate Mergers*. Washington, D.C.: U.S. Government Printing Office, 1969.

U.S. Congress, House, Antitrust Subcommittee, Committee on the Judiciary. *Investigation on Conglomerate Mergers*, 92nd Cong., 1st sess., June 1, 1971.

U.S. Congress, Senate, Subcommittee on Multinational Corporations. *The International Telephone and Telegraph Company and Chile*, 1970–1971, 93rd Cong., 1st sess., June 21, 1973.

U.S. Congress, Senate, Committee on the Judiciary. *Acquistion and Mergers by Conglomerates of Unrelated Businesses, Before the Subcommittee on Antitrust and Monopoly*, 95th Cong., 2nd sess., 1978.

12

Public Policy in a Free Enterprise Economy

Walter Adams

When Congress passed the Sherman Act of 1890, it created what was then—and has largely remained—a uniquely American institution. Heralded as a *magna carta* of economic freedom, the Sherman Act sought to preserve competitive free enterprise by imposing legal prohibitions on monopoly and restraint of trade. The objective of the act, according to Judge Learned Hand, was not to condone *good* trusts or condemn *bad* trusts, but to forbid *all* trusts. Its basic philosophy and principal purpose was "to perpetuate and preserve, for its own sake and in spite of possible cost, an organization of industry in small units which can effectively compete with each other." In elaborating on the goals of the Sherman Act, Judge Hand stated: "Many people believe that possession of unchallenged economic power deadens initiative, discourages thrift, and depresses energy; that immunity from competition is a narcotic, and rivalry is a stimulant, to industrial progress; that the spur of constant stress is necessary to counteract an inevitable disposition to let well enough alone. Such people believe that competitors, versed in the craft as no consumer can be, will be quick to detect opportunities for saving and new shifts in production, and be eager to profit by them. . . . True, it might have been thought adequate to condemn only those monopolies which could not show that they had exercised the highest possible ingenuity, had adopted every possible economy, had anticipated every conceivable improvement, stimulated every possible demand. . . . Be that as it may, that was not the way that Congress chose; it did not condone 'good' trusts and condemn 'bad' ones; it forbade all. Moreover, in so doing it was not necessarily actuated by economic motives alone. It is possible, because of its indirect social or moral effect, to prefer a system of small producers, each dependent for his success upon his own skill and character, to one in which the great mass of those engaged must accept the direction of a few. These considerations, which we have suggested only as possible purposes of the Act, we think the decisions prove to have been in fact its purposes."[1]

THE ANTIMONOPOLY LAWS

Specifically, the Sherman Act outlawed two major types of interference with free enterprise: collusion and monopolization. Section 1 of the act, dealing with collusion, states: "Every contract, combination . . . or conspiracy, in restraint of trade or commerce among the several States, or with foreign nations, is hereby declared illegal." As interpreted by the courts, this made it unlawful for businesses to engage in such collusive action as agreements to fix prices; agreements to restrict output or productive capacity; agreements to divide markets or allocate customers; agreements to exclude competitors by systematic resort to oppressive tactics and discriminatory policies—in short, any joint action by competitors to influence the market. Thus, Section 1 was, in a sense, a response to Adam Smith's warning that "people of the same trade seldom meet together even for merriment and diversion, but the conversation ends in a conspiracy against the public, or in some contrivance to raise prices."[2]

Section 2 of the Sherman Act, which deals with monopolization, provided that: "Every person who shall monopolize or attempt to monopolize, or combine or conspire with any other person or persons to monopolize any part of the trade or commerce among the several States, or with foreign nations, shall be deemed guilty . . . and . . . punished." This meant that businesses were deprived of an important freedom, the freedom to monopolize. Section 2 made it unlawful for anyone to obtain a stranglehold on the market either by forcing rivals out of business or by absorbing them. It forbade a single firm (or group of firms acting jointly) to gain a substantially exclusive domination of an industry or a market area. Positively stated, Section 2 attempted to encourage an industry structure in which there are enough independent competitors to assure bona fide and effective market rivalry.

As is obvious from even a cursory examination of the Sherman Act, its provisions were general, perhaps even vague, and essentially negative. Directed primarily against *existing* monopolies and *existing* trade restraints, the Sherman Act could not cope with specific practices that were, and could be, used to effectuate the unlawful results. Armed with the power to dissolve existing monopolies, the enforcement authorites could not, under the Sherman Act, attack the *growth* of monopoly. They could not nip it in the bud. For this reason Congress passed, in 1914, supplementary legislation "to arrest the creation of trusts, conspiracies and monopolies *in their incipiency and before consummation*."[3] In the Federal Trade Commission Act of 1914, Congress set up an independent regulatory commission to police the industrial field against "all unfair methods of competition." In the Clayton Act of the same year, Congress singled out four specific practices that past experience had shown to be favorite weapons of the would-be monopolist: (1) price discrimination—that is, local price-cutting and cut-throat competition; (2) tying contracts and exclusive dealer arrangements; (3) the acquisition of stock in competing companies; and (4) the formation of interlocking directorships between competing corporations. These practices were to be unlawful whenever their effect was to substantially lessen competition or to create tendencies toward monopoly. Thus, price discrimination, for example, was not made illegal per se; it was to be illegal only if used as a systematic device for destroying competition—in a manner typical of the old Standard Oil and American Tobacco trusts.[4] The emphasis throughout was to be on prevention rather than cure. The hope was that—given the provisions of the 1914 laws to supplement the provisions of the Sherman Act—the antitrust authorities could effectively eliminate the economic evils against which the antitrust laws were directed. The thrust of the Celler-Kefauver Anti-Merger Act of 1950 was aimed at the same objectives.

THE CHARGES AGAINST MONOPOLY

What those evils were never has been clearly stated, and perhaps, never has been clearly conceived, by the sponsors of antitrust legislation. In general, however, the objections to monopoly and trade restraints—found in literally tons of antitrust literature—are of ancient vintage and can be summarized as follows:

1. *Monopoly affords the consumer little protection against exorbitant prices.* As Adam Smith put it, "the price of monopoly is, upon every occasion, the highest which can be got. The natural price, or the price of free competition, on the contrary, is the lowest which can be taken, not upon every occasion indeed, but for any considerable time taken together. The one is upon every occasion the highest which can be squeezed out of the buyers, of which, it is supposed, they will consent to give; the other is the lowest which the sellers can commonly afford to take, and at the same time continue their business."[5] The consumer is, under these conditions, open prey to extortion and exploitation—protected only by such tenuous self-restraint as the monopolist may choose to exercise because of benevolence, irrationality, concern over government reprisals, or fear of potential competition.

The monopolist generally can charge all the traffic will bear, simply because the consumer has no alternative sources of supply. The consumer is forced to pay the monopolist's price, turn to a less desirable substitute, or go without. His freedom is impaired, because his range of choice is artificially limited. (See Figure 1.)

An example, while admittedly extreme, serves to illustrate this point. It involves tungsten carbide, a hard-metal composition of considerable importance in such industrial uses as cutting tools, dies, and so on. In 1927, tungsten carbide sold in the United States at $50 per pound; but after a world monopoly was established by General Electric (GE) and Friedrich Krupp A. G., of Germany, under which GE was granted the right to set prices in the American market, the price promptly rose to a maximum of $453 per pound. During most of the 1930s the price fluctuated between $225 and $453

FIGURE 1. Free competition versus price fixing. *Source:* Thurman W. Arnold, *Cartels or Free Enterprise?* Public Affairs Pamphlet No. 103, 1945. Reproduced by courtesy of Public Affairs Commission, Inc.

per pound, and not until 1942—when an indictment was issued under the antitrust laws—did the price come down. Thereafter, it fluctuated between $27 and $45 per pound.[6]

2. *Monopoly causes a restriction of economic opportunity and a misallocation of productive resources.* Under free competition, it is the consumer who, through his dollar votes in the marketplace, decides how society's land, labor, and capital are to be used. Consumer tastes generally determine whether more cotton and less wool, more cigarettes and less pipe tobacco, or more aluminum and less steel shall be produced. Under free competition, the consumer is in this strategic position because businesses must, if they want to make profits, do as the consumer demands. Because a business, under competition, is free to enter any field and to produce any type and quantity of goods it desires, the tendency will be for it to do those things that the consuming public (in its wisdom or ignorance) deems most valuable.

In short, under a truly competitive system, the business can improve itself only by serving others. It can earn profits only by obeying the wishes of the community as expressed in the market.

Under monopoly, by contrast, the individual business finds its freedom of enterprise limited. It cannot do as it pleases, because the monopolist has the power of excluding newcomers or stipulating the terms under which newcomers are permitted to survive in an industry. The monopolist can interfere with a consumer-oriented allocation of resources. It, instead of the market, can determine the type and quantity of goods that shall be produced. He, and not the forces of supply and demand, can decree who shall produce what, for whom, and at what price. In the absence of competition, it is the monopolist who decides what *other* businesses shall be allowed to do and what benefits the consuming public shall be allowed to receive.

A good illustration of this is the Hartford-Empire Company, which once was an undisputed monopolist in the glass-bottle industry. Through its patent control over glass bottling machinery, Hartford-Empire held life and death power both over the producers already in the industry and those attempting to enter it. As one observer described the situation,[7] Hartford had become benevolent despot to the glass container. Only by its leave could a firm come into the industry; the ticket of admission was to be had only upon its terms; and from its studied decision there was no appeal. The candidate had to subscribe to Hartford's articles of faith; he could not be a price cutter or a troublemaker. It could not venture beyond its assigned bailiwick or undermine the market of its partners in the conspiracy. Each concern had to accept the restrictions and limitations imposed by Hartford. Thus, the Buck Glass Company was authorized to manufacture wine bottles for sacramental purposes only. The Sayre Glass Works was restricted to producing "such bottles, jugs, and demijohns as are used for vinegar, ciders, sirups, bleaching fluids, hair tonics, barber supplies, and fluid extracts." Knox Glass Bottle Company was allowed to make only amber-colored ginger ale bottles. Mary Card Glass Company could not make products weighing more than 82 ounces. Baurens Glass Works Inc. was licensed to provide bottles for castor oil and turpentine, but none to exceed 4 ounces in capacity. Here, indeed, was a shackling of free enterprise and a usurpation of the market—a private government more powerful than that of many states. Here, indeed, was a tight little island, where the law of the monopolist was supreme and unchallenged. Only through antitrust prosecution were the channels of trade reopened and the Hartford dictatorship dissipated.[8]

3. *Monopoly often restrains technological advances and, thus, impedes economic progress.* As Clair Wilcox points out, "the monopolist may engage in research and invent new materials, methods, and machines, but he will be reluctant to make use of these inventions if they would compel him to scrap existing equipment or if he believes that their ultimate profitability is in doubt. He may introduce innovations and cut costs, but instead of moving goods by price reduction he is prone to spend large sums on alternative

methods of promoting sales; his refusal to cut prices deprives the community of any gain. The monopolist may voluntarily improve the quality of his product and reduce its price, but no threat of competition compels him to do so."[9]

Our experience with the hydrogenation and synthetic rubber processes is a case in point. This, one of the less illustrious chapters in our industrial history, dates back to 1926, when I. G. Farben of Germany developed the hydrogenation process for making oil out of coal—a development that obviously threatened the entrenched position of the major international oil companies. Soon after this process was patented, Standard Oil Company of New Jersey concluded an agreement with I. G. Farben, under which Farben promised to stay out of the world's oil business (except inside Germany) and Standard agreed to stay out of the world's chemical business. "By this agreement, control of the hydrogenation process for making oil outside Germany was transferred to the Standard Oil Company in order that Standard's petroleum investment might be fully protected. In the United States, Standard licensed only the large oil companies which had no interest in exploiting hydrogenation. Outside the United States, Standard . . . proceeded to limit use of the process so far as the threat of competing processes and governmental interest [of foreign countries] permitted.[10] As a result, this revolutionary process was almost completely suppressed, except in Germany, where it became an effective tool for promoting the military ambitions of the Nazi government.

The development of synthetic rubber production in the United States was similarly retarded by the Farben-Standard Marriage of 1928. Because Buna rubber, under the agreement of 1928, was considered a chemical process, it came under the exclusive control of I. G. Farben—both in and outside Germany. Farben, however, was not interested in promoting the manufacture of synthetic rubber anywhere except in Germany, and proceeded, therefore—both for commercial (that is, monopolistic) and nationalistic reasons—to forestall its development in the United States. Farben had, at least, the tacit support of its American partner. As a result, the outbreak of World War II found the United States without production experience or know-how in the vital synthetic rubber field. In fact, when the Goodrich and Goodyear tire companies attempted to embark on synthetic rubber production, the former was sued for patent infringement and the latter formally threatened with such a suit by Standard Oil Company (acting under the authority of the Farben patents). This happened in November 1941, one month before Pearl Harbor. Not until after our formal entry into World War II was the Farben-Standard alliance broken, under the impact of antitrust prosecution and the production of vital synthetic rubber started in the United States. Here, as in the case of hydrogenation, monopolistic control over technology had serious implications not only for the nation's economic progress but also for its military security.[11]

4. *Monopoly tends to impede the effectiveness of general stabilization*

measures and to distort their structural impact on the economy. Monopolistic and oligopolistic firms, as John Kenneth Galbraith suggests, may insulate themselves against credit restrictions designed to curb investment and check inflation. They may do so by raising prices to offset higher interest costs, by raising prices to finance investment out of increased profits, or by resorting to the capital market rather than to banks for their supply of loanable funds. Competitive firms, by contrast, cannot raise prices to compensate for higher interest charges. They cannot raise prices to finance investment out of higher profits. They cannot readily turn to the capital market for funds. Their lack of market control makes them the weakest borrowers and poorest credit risks, and they must, therefore, bear the brunt of any "tight money" policy. In short, monopolistic and oligopolistic firms not only can undermine the effectiveness of monetary control in their sector of the economy, but also shift the burden of credit restrictions to the competitive sector and, thus, stifle its growth. The implications for concentration need not be belabored.[12]

5. *Monopoly threatens not only the existence of a free economy, but also the survival chances of free political institutions.* Enterprise that is not competitive cannot for long remain free, and a community that refuses to accept the discipline of competition inevitably exposes itself to the discipline of absolute authority. As Mutual Security Administrator Harold Stassen once observed, "world economic history has shown that nationalization and socialization have come when there has been complete consolidation and combination of industry, not when enterprise is manifold and small in its units. . . . We must not permit major political power to be added to the other great powers that are accumulated by big business units. Excessive concentration of power is a threat to the individual freedoms and liberties of men, whether that excessive power is in the hands of government or of capital or of labor."[13] The enemy of democracy is monopoly in all its forms, and political liberty can survive only within an effective competitive system. If concentrated power is tolerated, giant pressure groups will ultimately gain control of the government or the government will institute direct regulation of organized pressure groups. In either event, free enterprise will then have to make way for collectivism, and democracy will be superseded by some form of authoritarianism.

This objection to monopoly, this fear of concentrated economic power, is deeply rooted in American traditions—the tradition of federalism, the separation of church and state, and the tripartite organization of our governmental machinery. It is the expression of a sociopolitical philosophy of the decentralization of power, a broad base for the class structure of society, and the economic freedom and opportunity for new firms, new ideas, and new organizations to spearhead the forces of progress. It stands in stark contrast to the older European varieties of free enterprise, which merely involve curbs on governmental powers without similar checks on excessive private power.[14] The seriousness of a danger is not easy to evaluate. "Who can say whether any particular warning is due to overcautiousness, timidity, or even superstition or, on the other hand, to prudence and foresight? . . . It is, of course, possible that 'monopoly' is merely a bugbear frightening the believers in free enterprise and free society; but it is equally possible that we have underestimated the danger and have allowed the situation to deteriorate to such a degree that only a very radical effort can still save our social and political system."[15]

THE CHALLENGE OF ECONOMIC DARWINISM AND THE NEW LAISSEZ-FAIRE

In recent years, it has become fashionable to deprecate the traditional philosophy underlying the antitrust laws and to urge its replacement by a latter-day Economic Darwinism. The leaders of this movement—primarily members of the Chicago School–treat property rights and freedom of contract as near-absolutes, and believe that untrammeled laissez-faire will assure a natural selection of what is best and most worthy–a survival of the fittest.

Professor Robert H. Bork, probably the most incisive and sophisticated exponent of the *nouvelle vague,* sees a striking analogy between a free market system and the Darwinian theory of natural selection and physical evolution.[16] Says Bork: "The familiarity of that parallel, and the overbroad inferences sometimes drawn from it, should not blind us to its important truths. The environment to which the business firm must adapt is defined, ultimately, by social wants and the social costs of meeting them. The firm that adapts to the environment better than its rivals tends to expand. The less successful firm tends to contract—perhaps, eventually, to become extinct. The Stanley Steamer and the celluloid collar have gone the way of the pterodactyl and the great ground sloth, basically for the same reasons. Since coping successfully with the economic environment also forwards consumer welfare (except in those cases that are the legitimate concern of antitrust), economic and natural selection has normative implications that physical natural selection does not have. At least there seems to me more reasons for enthusiasm about the efficient firm than about the most successful physical organisms, the rat and the cockroach, though this view is, no doubt, parochial."[17]

There is little justification, Professor Bork argues, to interfere with the "natural" operation of a free market system. Laissez-faire, he says, can be trusted to produce optimum results in the operation of the system: "It is a common observation of biologists that whenever the physical environment provides a niche capable of sustaining life, an organism will evolve or adapt to occupy the place. The same is true of economic organisms, hence the fantastic proliferation of forms of business organization, products, and services in our society. . . . To expand, or even to survive, every firm requires a constant flow of capital for employees' wages, raw material, capital investment, repairs, advertising, and the like. When the firm is relatively inefficient over a significant time period, it represents a poorer investment and greater credit risk than innumerable alternatives. If the firm is dependent upon outside capital, the firm must shrink, and, if no revival in its fortunes occurs, die."[18] Monopoly or market power, according to Bork, are of little social concern because neither is endowed with significant durability: "a market position that creates output restriction and higher prices will always be eroded if it is not based upon superior efficiency."[19] Of course, if it is based on superior efficiency, Bork would say that it serves the best interest of consumers and should, therefore, be immune from public attack.

In this view, then, a firm achieves market power or giant size because of superior efficiency, and it would be wrongheaded for public policy to punish such a firm for its success. The winner of the race deserves the prize—the right to take all he can get. He won the race because he was the best, and punishing him would deprive others of incentives to excel. Punishing industrial success, the Darwinists argue, would not only lessen competition, but would inevitably result in a diminution of consumer welfare. Besides, the successful firm will retain its dominance only as long as its performance remains superior. As soon as it becomes slothful, lethargic, inefficient or unprogressive, it will surely be replaced by greedy newcomers aspiring to preeminence and leadership.

This doctrine of Economic Darwinism, which seems to have become official U.S. government policy during the 1980s, suffers from several defects:

1. It is based on the *post hoc ergo propter hoc* fallacy. It assumes that a monopolist, oligopolist, or conglomerate giant has achieved its market position exclusively or predominantly because of superior performance. This is no more than an assertion—devoid, more often than not, of any empirical substantiation.

2. Although Economic Darwinism makes superior economic performance the centerpiece of its policy position, its supporters concede that economic performance is difficult, if not impossible, to measure scientifically. Professor Bork, for example, concedes that "the real objection to performance tests and efficiency defenses in antitrust law is that they are spurious. They cannot measure the factors relevant to consumer welfare, so that after the economic extravaganza was completed we should know no more than before it began. In saying this I am taking issue with some highly qualified authorities. Carl Kaysen and Donald Turner proposed that 'an unreasonable degree of market power as such must be made illegal,' and they suggested that all the relevant dimensions of performance be studied. Their idea, essentially, is that a court or agency determine, through a litigation process, whether there exists in a particular industry a persistent divergence between price and marginal cost; the approximate size of the divergence; whether breaking up, say, eight firms into sixteen would reduce or eliminate the divergence; and whether any significant efficiencies would be destroyed by the dissolution."[20] Bork seems to despair about the possibility of measuring performance even though he posits superior performance as the ultimate goal of economic activity.

3. The new Darwinism is concerned primarily with static, managerial

efficiency rather than with dynamic social efficiency. It thus falls victim to the sin of sub-optimization. The relevant policy question is not whether General Motors produces automobiles powered by the internal combustion engine at the lowest possible cost, but whether it should be producing such automobiles at all. The relevant policy question is whether the tight oligopoly which presently controls the U.S. automobile industry is more likely to "reinvent the automobile"—a safer, more-fuel-efficient, more pollution-free prototype—than a competitively structured automobile industry.

4. The new Darwinism assumes that any firm that no longer delivers superior efficiency will automatically be displaced by newcomers. This underestimates the ability of established firms to build private storm shelters—or to induce the government to build public storm shelters for them—to shield them from the Schumpeterian gales of creative destruction. It ignores the difference between legal freedom of entry and the economic realities barring the entry of potential newcomers to concentrated industries. It underestimates the ability of powerful firms in concentrated industries to parlay economic power into political power to insulate their dominance from competitive erosion. Here, as elsewhere, the Economic Darwinists are so wedded to formal logic that they carry their logic one step beyond the realm of realistic applicability.

5. Economic Darwinism fails to make the crucial distinction between individual freedom and a free economic *system*. As Bentham pointed out, it is not enough to shout laissez-faire and oppose all government intervention: "To say that a law is contrary to natural liberty is simply to say that it is a law: for every law is established at the expense of liberty—the liberty of Peter at the expense of the liberty of Paul."[21] If individual rights were absolute and unlimited, they would mean license to commit the grossest abuses against society, including license to curb the freedom of others. Moreover, as Lord Robbins suggests, public policy must "distinguish between [government] interventions that destroy the need for intervention and interventions that tend to perpetuate it."[22]

Viewed in this light, Professor Bork's admonition not to penalize the winner of the race is quite irrelevant for policy purposes. The relevant policy problem is how to reward the winner without including in his trophy the right to impose disabling handicaps on putative competitors, or the power to determine the rules by which future races shall be run, or the discretion to terminate the institution of racing altogether. The policy challenge is how to maximize a *bundle* of freedoms and opportunity, not only at a point in time but over the long run as well.

6. Finally, the new Economic Darwinism fails to appreciate the linkage between industrial structure and market behavior and the consequences, ultimately, for economic performance. As John Bates Clark warned, more than half a century ago, "In our worship of the survival of the fit under free natural selection we are sometimes in danger of forgetting that the conditions of the struggle fix the kind of fitness that shall come out of it; that survival

in the prize ring means fitness for pugilism, not for bricklaying nor philanthropy; that survival in predatory competition is likely to mean something else than fitness for good and efficient production; and that only from strife with the right kind of rules can the right kind of fitness emerge. Competition is a game played under rules fixed by the state to the end that, so far as possible, the prize of victory shall be earned, not by trickery or mere self-seeking adroitness, but by value rendered. It is not the mere play of unrestrained self-interest; it is a method of harnessing the wild beast of self-interest to serve a common good—a thing of ideals and not of sordidness. It is not a natural state, but like any other form of liberty, it is a social achievement, and eternal vigilance is the price of it.''[23]

The fundamental objective of antitrust is not only—as the Economic Darwinists contend—to promote efficiency and consumer welfare. These are ancillary benefits which are expected to flow from economic freedom. The primary purpose of antitrust is to perpetuate and preserve, in spite of possible cost, a *system of governance* for a competitive, free enterprise economy. It is a system of governance in which power is decentralized; in which newcomers with new products and new techniques have a genuine opportunity to introduce themselves and their ideas; in which the ''unseen hand'' of competition instead of the heavy hand of the state performs the basic regulatory function on behalf of society.

Antitrust, like the political system prescribed by our Constitution, calls for a dispersion of power, buttressed by built-in checks and balances, to protect individuals from potential abuse of power and to preserve not only individual freedom but, more importantly, a free system. According to antitrust precepts—to paraphrase Justice William O. Douglas—power which controls the economy should not be in the hands of an industrial oligarchy. Since all power tends to develop into a government in itself, industrial power should be decentralized. It should be scattered into many hands so that the fortunes of the people will not be dependent on the whim or caprice, the political prejudices, the emotional stability of a few self-appointed men. The fact that they are not vicious men but respectable and social minded is irrelevant. That is the philosophy and the command of the antitrust laws. They are founded on a theory of hostility to the concentration in private hands of power so great that even a government of the people can be trusted to have it only in exceptional circumstances.[24]

Antitrust, then, is—above all—a *system of governance*. It is a system for distributing and harnessing economic power. It is a traditional and peculiarly American response to the perennial questions of social organization: Who shall make what decisions on whose behalf at what cost and for whose benefit? To whom shall the decision makers be accountable, and what safeguards shall be built into the system to guard against abuse?

The competitive market, of course, is the prime instrument for implementing the antitrust philosophy. It is to make social decisions. It is to function as the regulatory mechanism in the economy. It is to serve as the safeguard of the public interest. But the competitive market is not an academic model-builder's abstraction adumbrated in basic economic tests. Nor is it—contrary to the preachments of the Chicago School—a gift of nature. It is a social artifact which must be nurtured by constant vigilance and shielded from private subversion (i.e., collusion, predation, exclusion, and concentration) as well as governmental subversion (i.e., the public storm shelters built to protect special interests from the Schumpeterian gales of creative destruction). In short, the competitive market can perform its social role only under certain structural and behavioral preconditions. And the maintenance of these preconditions is the function of antitrust.

THE CHALLENGE OF NEO-MERCANTILISM

Perhaps, an even greater challenge to competition as the central regulatory mechanism in the American economy is the virulence of an emerging neomercantilism. This consists of an effort by various industries to insulate and immunize themselves from competition by utilizing the coercive power of the State to serve their protectionist objectives.

For analytical purposes, the Schumpeterian framework is probably most useful in explaining this phenomenon. It was Professor Schumpeter who argued that the capitalist process is rooted not in classical price competition, but rather the competition from the new commodity, the new technology, the new source of supply, the new type of organization—competition which commands a decisive cost or quality advantage and which strikes not at the margin of the profits and outputs of existing firms, but at their very foundations and their very lives. The very essence of capitalism, according to Schumpeter, is the perennial gale of creative destruction in which existing power positions and entrenched advantage are constantly displaced by new organizations and new power complexes. This gale of creative destruction is not only the harbinger of progress, but also the built-in safeguard against the vices of monopoly and privilege.[25] Needless to say, this process of creative destruction can function effectively only so long as no obstacles are interposed to attenuate its force.

But, alas, powerful firms and special interests were as keen as Professor Schumpeter in grasping the implications of the creative destruction process. Instinctively, they understood that storm shelters had to be built to protect themselves against this destructive force, because the mechanism which is of undoubted public benefit carries with it exorbitant private costs. And so they built private storm shelters wherever possible within the parameters of benign neglect by the antitrust authorities; and, where private monopolies and cartels were patently unlawful, unfeasible, or inadequate, they increasingly turned to the government for succor and support. Those who possessed entrenched power did not need to be told that manipulating the state for private ends is perhaps the most felicitous instrument for insulating themselves against, and immunizing themselves from, the Schumpeterian gales.

And so they proceeded to do precisely what seemed so obviously in their self-interest.

Our experience with the regulated industries, on the one hand, and import restrictions, on the other, illustrates this perversion of the state into an instrument for the creation of private privilege.

The Regulated Industries

Ideally, competition and regulation are opposite sides of the same coin. In theory, both are directed at the same objectives: efficient use of resources and protection of the consumer against exploitation. The means to these ends, however, are different. To be effective, competition requires rivalry among many sellers and freedom of entry into markets. It envisions a regulatory scheme in which the operation of autonomous market forces obviates the need for detailed government supervision. This is the philosophy embodied in the Sherman Act of 1890.

Regulation, as originally conceived, was to be both a supplement to and substitute for competition. It was to be applied in those industries where the cost of entry was so great or the duplication of facilities so wasteful that some degree of monopoly was considered unavoidable. Here, the visible hand of public regulation was to replace the invisible hand mentioned by Adam Smith, in order to protect consumers against extortionate charges, restriction of output, deterioration of service, and unfair discrimination. This was the rationale of the Interstate Commerce Act of 1887.

In many respects, the Sherman Act and the Interstate Commerce Act were generically different. One was cast in terms of negative prohibitions on certain types of conduct. The other was aimed at detailed and direct supervision of individual firms. One sought to protect the public by preserving competition, the other by regulating monopoly. Nevertheless, both hoped to protect the public against the agressions of private interests rather than to shield these interests from the bargaining power of the public.

The policy of regulation, originally founded on the "natural monopoly" or "public utility" concept, was first eroded and then extended, because the firms under regulation came to recognize that the better part of wisdom was not to abolish regulation but to use it for furthering their selfish interests. In 1892, for example, Attorney General Richard Olney was asked by his friends in the railroad industry to spearhead a drive to repeal the Interstate Commerce Act which had been passed five years earlier. In his classic reply, Olney wrote:

> My impression would be that looking at the matter from a railroad point of view exclusively it would not be a wise thing to undertake. . . . The attempt would not be likely to succeed; if it did not succeed, and were made on the ground of inefficiency and uselessness of the Commission, the result would very probably be giving it the power it now lacks. The Commission, as its functions have now been limited by the courts, is, or can be made, of great use to the railroads. It satisfies the popular clamor for a government supervision of the railroads, at the same time that that supervision is almost entirely nominal. Further, the older

such a commission gets to be, the more inclined it will be found to take the business and railroad view of things. It thus becomes a sort of barrier between the railroad corporations and the people and a sort of protection against hasty and crude legislation hostile to railroad interests. . . . The part of wisdom is not to destroy the Commission, but to utilize it.[26]

In 1911, when U.S. Steel came under antitrust attack, its president, Elbert Gary, told a Congressional Committee that he would not object to public utility style regulation (like that to which the railroads were subjected under I.C.C. auspices):

I realize as fully, I think, as this committee that it is very important to consider how the people shall be protected against imposition or oppression as the possible result of great aggregations of capital, whether in the possession of corporations or individuals. I believe that is a very important question, and personally I believe that the Sherman Act does not meet and will never fully prevent that. I believe we must come to enforced publicity and governmental control, even as to prices, and, so far as I am concerned, speaking for our company, so far as I have the right, I would be very glad if we had some place where we could go, to a responsible governmental authority, and say to them, "Here are our facts and figures, here is our property, here our cost of production; now you tell us what we have the right to do and what prices we have the right to charge." I know this is a very extreme view, and I know that the railroads objected to it for a long time; but whether the standpoint of making the most money is concerned or not, whether it is the wise thing, I believe it is the necessary thing, and it seems to me corporations have no right to disregard these public questions and these public interests.

'Your idea then,' said Congressman Littleton of the committee, 'is that cooperation is bound to take the place of competition and that cooperation requires strict governmental supervision?'

'That is a very good statement,' replied the Judge.[27]

Theodore Vail, president of AT&T during this era, repeatedly expressed similar views in support of regulation by government commissions. Obviously, these industrial leaders understood the value of regulation as a protective device against the much more exacting regulation to which they would be subject under effective competition.

Not surprisingly, therefore, the public utility concept was gradually transformed from consumer-oriented to industry-oriented regulation. The process was brilliantly analyzed by Horace Gray: "the policy of state-created, state-protected monopoly became firmly established over a significant portion of the economy and became the keystone of modern public utility regulation. Henceforth, the public utility status was to be the haven of refuge for all aspiring monopolists who found it too difficult, too costly, or too precarious to secure and maintain monopoly by private action alone. Their future prosperity would be assured if only they could induce government to grant them monopoly power and to protect them against interlopers, provided always, of course, that government did not exact too high a price for its favors in the form of restrictive regulation."[28]

Once this "new mercantilism" had taken root, it was extended to important segments of the economy. Between 1934 and 1940, Congress subjected radio, television, motor carriers, water carriers, freight forwarders, air carriers, and natural-gas transporters to the certification requirements of independent regulatory commissions. To mitigate the debilitating effects of depression, the role of competition was substantially curtailed. New commissions were created, and "public convenience and necessity" became the shibboleth of the day.

Most indefensible, perhaps, was the Motor Carrier Act of 1935, which brought the trucking industry under control of the Interstate Commerce Commission. Here was an industry that, at the time, comprised more than 20,000 interstate carriers and came as close as any American industry to meeting the structural prerequisites of "perfect" competition. There were no allegations—nor was there any evidence—that the industry charged exorbitant rates; indeed, the contention (advanced by the railroads) was quite the reverse: that the industry's rates were too "low," i.e., too competitive. Nor were there any allegations that product quality, i.e., service to shippers, was substandard. In other words, there was no economic justification for imposing a comprehensive regulatory framework on this industry in order to promote the public interest. The only rationale behind the enactment of the Motor Carrier Act was to protect the railroads against the competition of an effectively competitive trucking industry, and to protect established trucking firms from effective intra-industry competition.

Whatever the Congressional motivation, the ICC interpreted the legislation as a mandate for administrative protectionism of established transportation interests. In enforcing regulations, the Commission imposed an almost insurmountable burden on applicants for new operating authority, extension of existing authority, and alternative route privileges. It seemed quite unconcerned with implementing the avowed objective of the National Transportation Policy to promote efficient, economical, and flexible transportation service for the public. Thus, the Commission chose to measure shipper need in physical rather than economic terms; i.e., so long as existing carriers were physically capable of performing a particular service, prospective competitors were denied entry—even if their service was cheaper, better, and more efficient. In its decisions, the Commission emphasized repeatedly that "where existing carriers have expended their energy and resources in developing facilities to handle all available traffic and where their service is adequate, they are entitled to protection against the establishment of a new, competitive operations."[29] In other words, the Commission embraced what might be called the "going-concern" theory of regulation, a reluctance to subject existing firms—especially large firms—to competitive pressure. The test throughout was the physical adequacy of existing service, not the promotion of better and cheaper service.

With respect to rates, the Commission not only tolerated private collusion in rate making (pursuant to the infamous Reed-Bulwinkle Act), but continually emphasized "the need for as much stability of rates as is practicable"—in the belief that rate stability took precedence over rate competition. It almost never exercised its *maximum* rate powers in the Trucking Act, but, as the Brownell Committee found, consistently used its *minimum* rate powers "both to protect the railroads from motor carrier competition as well as to safeguard the motor carrier industry from 'destructive' competition within its own ranks. Indeed, from the inception of motor carrier regulation to the present day, the power to fix minimum rates has been more significant than the authority to fix maximum charges."[30] Under the circumstances, intermode competition could hardly contain the upward pressure on the entire rate structure. It could not neutralize the combined impact of minimum rate fixing by government and private rate fixing by trade associations. Other regulatory commissions pursued similarly restrictionist and protectionist policies.

Their record over the last half-century indicates that the experiments in public regulation have, as a rule, been singularly unsuccessful. What started as regulation—perhaps, inevitably—ended up as protection. The power to license entrants became the power to exclude; the regulation of rates, a system of price supports; the surveillance of mergers, an instrument of concentration; and the supervision of business practices, a pretext for harassing the weak, unorganized, and politically underprivileged. Given the power of the commissions to dispense and protect private privilege, competition was systematically curtailed. Indeed, the commissions seemed to behave as if their role was to protect the regulatees from competition rather than to protect the public from exploitation. The result was, as Lewis Engman, a former FTC chairman, observed that the regulated industries became "federal protectorates, living in the cozy world of cost-plus, safely protected from the ugly spectres of competition, efficiency, and innovation."[31]

Clearly, sound public policy militates toward total deregulation plus antitrust enforcement in inherently competitive industries like trucking. It also calls for massive deregulation plus strict antitrust enforcement in industries like communications, where increased competition is made possible by an explosive technology and where protection of the public interest, therefore, can be entrusted to institutional arrangements other than traditional regulation. Sound policy would certainly preclude the granting of antitrust immunity to firms engaged in collective action with respect to rates and service under a regulatory umbrella.

Recently, some regulatory commissions have begun to ease entry restrictions and to encourage limited rate competition. Congress has also moved in the same direction by authorizing deregulation of the airline industry (1978) and substantial deregulation of the trucking industry (1980). However, much remains to be done in removing neomercantilist protectionism and privilege creation from the regulated sector of the American economy.

Import Restraints

With the internationalization of markets and the progressive liberalization of world trade, the threat of foreign competition has revived the age-old cry for protectionism: to protect the nation's balance of payments; to protect domestic labor from import-induced unemployment; to protect domestic industry from the unfair competition of low-wage countries. These arguments are especially appealing in times of recession, and political office seekers are not loath to embrace them, especially in election years.

To an industry constrained to live in a free-trade environment, and striving for survival, profitability, and growth, foreign competition is a serious challenge. It is a disruptive force which undermines the market control of oligopolized industries and the cartel-like price maintenance schemes prevalent in many competitive industries. It causes instability by undermining "mutual dependence recognized," by promoting defection among cartel partners, and by encouraging entry. Foreign competition is the nemesis of "orderly marketing" and hence becomes a prime target for neo-mercantilist governments and the interest groups that manipulate them.

In recent years, import quotas—mandatory or voluntary, imposed unilaterally, or after bilateral or multilateral negotiations—have become a favorite tool of protectionism. The scenario is roughly as follows: imports increase and capture a growing share of the domestic market. The industry affected, exercising coalescing (rather than countervailing) power, is joined by its trade union in demanding protection from foreign competition. Complaints are filed under the antidumping, escape clause, countervailing duty, or similar statutes. In case of failure, which is more common than not, legislative action is then requested to impose mandatory restraints on the "injurious" or "potentially injurious" imports. Diplomatic channels are used to advise exporting countries that such mandatory restraints are likely to be imposed, unless they practice "voluntary" self-limitation. The typical result is the "voluntary" quota, which, however, rarely constitutes a final solution. If the quota applies to cotton textiles, the import problem will shift to wool or man-made fibers. If the quota applies to steel, the product mix of the imports will shift from lower-priced to higher-priced steel products. If the quota restrains one country (e.g., Japan), new producers (e.g., Hong Kong, Taiwan, or Korea) will enter the protected (high-price) market. Bilateral negotiations then yield to multilateral negotiations. Global import controls over an entire industry or an industry segment must be refined and rendered increasingly specific. Moreover, exporting countries, responsible for monitoring their side of the bargain, are obliged to reorganize their export trade—to encourage collective action among competing companies and to promote the formation of export associations (i.e., export cartels). These newly formed producer groups must allocate quotas and divide markets and, in the process, they inevitably raise prices to the importing country. They are also constrained to negotiate with counterpart associations in other exporting countries to develop a *modus vivendi* for competition in the import market. Finally, under the auspices of their respective governments, and under the threat of legislated trade restrictions, the exporting firms and the domestic industry are encouraged to work out "orderly marketing agreements," designed to prevent "injury" or "potential injury" to industry and labor in the importing country. These orderly marketing agreements, of course, are little more than a euphemism for international cartels organized and operated by special-interest groups with the connivance of governments. They are the politico-economic prototype of neo-mercantilist statecraft. They create a private government, an *imperium in imperio,* immunized from the disciplinary control of competition, and yet not subject to public regulation aimed at insuring acceptable (not to say, progressive) performance.[32]

Two bellwether industries in the American economy—steel and automobiles—illustrate the public policy challenge posed by import restraints. For at least three decades, both these industries have been afflicted by the typical maladies of a tight oligopoly. Entry has been at a minimum or nonexistent. Innovation has been slow, hampered by the bureaucratic dry-rot which tends to accompany monopoloid giantism. Price policy has been directed at uniformity and inflexibility, except in an upward direction; and, although the leadership role has on rare occasions rotated among the oligopolists, the level of product prices has been anything but market-determined. Moreover, until the 1960s, these industries had little to fear from foreign competition, so that their close-knit, co-fraternal members felt it safe to follow concerted, tacitly collusive, and consciously parallel price and product policies. Occasional mavericks might from time to time disturb the industry's quiet life but, like others before them, they eventually became members of the club. It is not surprising, therefore, that both industries, when faced with burgeoning foreign competition turned to the government in order to protect their accustomed market shares and market control.

Nor is it surprising that both industries were supported in these efforts to stifle competition by their respective trade unions. After all, steel and automobile workers seemed to have succeeded—through free, industry-wide, collective bargaining—in obtaining a "fair" share of their industry's monopoly largesse. In 1970, according to the Bureau of Labor Statistics, the hourly wages of steel workers were 28 percent higher than the average wage of U.S. production workers. By 1980, although employment in the industry had dropped nearly 20 percent and imports claimed more than 16 percent of the domestic steel market, steel workers were getting hourly wages 74 percent higher than the average in U.S. manufacturing. The same was true in automobiles. In 1970, hourly wages were 22 percent higher than the average for U.S. production workers. By 1980, they were 53 percent higher—in spite of the fact that some 200,000 auto workers were on long-term layoff and that the industry was faced with a sharp recession, astronomical interest rates, higher gasoline prices, and the loss of roughly 27 percent of the domestic market to imports. Both the United Steel Workers and the United Automobile Workers, it seems, supported the import restraints advocated by their respective industry leaders—convinced that the attenuation of import competition was the best guarantee for preserving their privileged positions. It was an exercise of coalescing power—in sharp contrast to the countervailing power once posited by John K. Galbraith—to use the combined political influence of industry and labor to serve their common protectionist economic objectives.[33]

The basic rationale advanced to justify import restraints was essentially the same in both the steel and automobile industries. It was a curious perversion of Friederich List's infant industry argument, i.e., to give these mature, lusty oligopolies a "breathing spell" to get themselves into shape to meet the increasingly stringent standards of international competition. Given "temporary" protection from import competition, it was argued, these industries could raise prices and bolster profits so as to finance badly needed investment in new plants, and to replace antiquated, obsolete facilities. Given such "temporary" relief from import competition, these industries would then be in good enough shape to "stand on their own feet" and compete on equal terms with the Western world's industrial frontrunners, especially the Japanese.

These cheerful prospects have not been realized. In steel—in spite of the "voluntary" quotas for carbon steel (1969–74), the quotas on specialty steel (1976–1980), the trigger price system (1978–1983), and the Reagan "voluntary" quota system (1984–)—the outstanding consequence of trade restraints has been to undergird the industry's wage-price escalation practices rather than to achieve a dramatic improvement in the industry's performance.

Thus, in the four years between January 1969 and December 1972, while the "voluntary" quotas were in effect, the composite steel price index rose at an annual rate 14 times greater than the annual average during the nine previous years, when imports were free to exercise their moderating effect on domestic steel prices. The cost burden of these "voluntary" quotas has been variously estimated at $500 million to $1 billion annually.

The *trigger price mechanism,* a thinly veiled scheme to put a floor under the price of imported steel, had roughly the same effects. In 1978, during the trigger price mechanism's first year of operation, the U.S. Government raised trigger prices by 10.63 percent. In 1980, it raised trigger prices 12 percent between the first and fourth quarters of the year. The cost burden of the trigger price mechanism has been variously estimated to fall in a range between $1 and $6 billion annually.

The Reagan "voluntary" quota system, which by the end of 1985 included bilateral trade restraint agreements with some 17 steel-exporting countries, has provided a similar cushion for domestic steel producers and imposed a similar cost burden on domestic steel users. In 1985, U.S. steel prices were some 20 percent above world levels, but if President Reagan succeeds in his efforts to cartelize steel exports to the United States, this differential will become even greater—to the detriment of domestic steel users such as the automobile and agricultural equipment industries. More ominous yet, if the Congressional Steel Caucus has its way, and imports are restricted to 15 percent of apparent steel supply in the United States, the annual cost to U.S. consumers, according to the Congressional Budget Office, would be between $4.3 and $5.9 billion (in 1983 dollars).[34]

Unfortunately, however, there is little evidence that these import restraints have had a noticeably beneficial effect on the steel industry's overall performance. They did not significantly spur technological progressiveness. Nor did they significantly stimulate the badly needed modernization of anachronistic facilities or the building of new plants. Nor did they provide a competitive discipline to curb the industry's proclivity for constant price escalation. Nor did they give the government, in exchange for its protectionist measures, the ability to exact "good performance" as a *quid pro quo* for the abandonment of competitive markets. A cynic might suggest that import restraints in steel had two principal consequences: an increase in steel prices and the reinforcement of cost-push inflation in the U.S. economy, on the one hand, and the diversification of steel producers into nonsteel industries, on the other. (Note, for example, the expenditure by U.S. Steel of $6.3 *billion* to buy Marathon Oil.) Import restraints certainly did little, if anything, to encourage an "infant" steel industry to develop into a mature, self-reliant, effectively competitive organism in world markets. It would appear that, as *The Economist* suggests, the only lasting remedy both for America's private-sector disasters and for Europe's state-owned dinosaurs is "more surgery and innovation, not more protection from reality."[35]

In the automobile industry, import restraints are of more recent vintage than in steel, and, although the evidence of their effects is less definitive, their ultimate impact is likely to be similar. During the 1974–75 recession, for example, the United Automobile Workers (with the tacit support of the industry) filed antidumping charges against foreign automobile manufacturers who had increased their U.S. market share from 15.2 percent in 1970 to 20.3 percent in the first half of 1975. In commenting on these charges, the Council on Wage and Price Stability observed that the most important factors explaining the increased market share of foreign automobiles "are the pricing policies of domestic producers and the inability of domestic manufacturers to respond rapidly to changing market conditions." The Council cautioned that the imposition of special dumping penalties "would likely result in an immediate increase in the price of automobiles to the American consumer. Moreover, such penalties, or even the threat of penalties, could substantially check what has been perhaps the single most effective spur to competition in this highly concentrated industry. This, in turn, could lead to less competitive prices and a reduced level of innovation."[36] These findings to the contrary notwithstanding, the U.S. Government ultimately resolved the complaint by obtaining assurances from five foreign manufacturers that they would *raise* their prices in the U.S. market, by warning fourteen other manufacturers that their prices would be monitored for two years, and by dismissing the charges with respect to five other manufacturers.

In 1981, again during a major recession, the coalition of Big Business,

Big Labor, and Big Government struck again—this time persuading the Japanese to accept a "voluntary" quota on their auto exports to the United States. Under the provisions of the agreement, negotiated by a Washington administration ostensibly committed to "getting government off the backs of business," the Japanese promised to reduce their exports from 1.82 million vehicles (1980) to 1.68 million annually, starting in April 1981, and to take no more than 16 percent of the *growth* (if any) in U.S. domestic consumption in the following year. Predictably, the big three car-makers—anticipating the successful conclusion of these quota negotiations—promptly terminated their various rebate plans and raised prices. General Motors announced its *fourth* increase in 1981 model prices, bringing the total for the year up to $900 per car and the average sticker price (including options) up to $10,200. Its fellow oligopolists, protesting impotence to do otherwise, dutifully followed suit. The overall cost of this "voluntary" quota on Japanese cars was substantial. The International Trade Commission calculates that over the four years during which the quota was in effect (1981–85), American consumers paid $15.7 billion in higher auto prices. The ITC also reports that the quota saved 44,000 auto worker jobs, but at a cost $357,000 per job.[37]

The fact that the quota imposed on the Japanese was "voluntary" rather than mandated by Congressional action was hardly reassuring. As *The Wall Street Journal* correctly observed, "a quota is a quota, whether legislated or negotiated. . . . In both cases, a limit on Japanese imports would reduce consumers' opportunities to buy the cars they want. In both cases, it would take away the pressure on the U.S. auto industry to lower labor costs and boost production efficiencies—in short, to regain international competitiveness. In both cases, it would raise prices and lower the quality of customer service, by reducing the intensity of competition . . . Indeed, in some ways, a voluntary export restraint might even be worse. For it to work—and . . . for it to comply with U.S. antitrust law—the Japanese Ministry of International Trade and Industry (MITI) would have to form some kind of cartel to divvy up U.S. market shares among Japanese car-makers. So not only would GM, Ford, Chrysler and Volkswagen be spared the full force of Japanese competition. Honda, Toyota, Nissan (Datsun), Fuji (Subaru) and Toyo Kogyo (Mazda) would also stop struggling so vigorously with *each other* for U.S. sales."[38]

Moreover, there is, of course, no assurance that import quotas are an efficacious mechanism to help an industry overcome the consequences of self-inflicted injury.[39] In theory, the restraints on Japanese automakers should enhance the *ability* of U.S. producers to finance the necessary conversion of domestic facilities from large-car to small-car production and thus hasten the adjustment of their product mix to prevailing patterns of consumer demand. At the same time, however, the quota reduces the *competitive pressure* on the companies to undertake such conversion or to proceed with it as rapidly as possible. ("Take away the pain," says *The New York Times* editorially, "and the patient forgets he is ill.")[40] The quota does not *compel* the companies to do what the unfettered operation of the market already indicates they must do. It does not exact a *quid pro quo* for government protection from competition. It offers no assurance that the additional funds, generated by higher prices and profits, will indeed be invested in new production facilities within the U.S., thus increasing *domestic* production and reducing *domestic* unemployment—the very objectives for which the quota was ostensibly imposed to begin with. Finally, it does not moderate the sometimes exorbitant demands by organized labor in the protected industry.

Alas, the record in steel and automobiles, as well as other industries sheltered from import competition by neo-mercantilist government policies, would seem to indicate that such restraints, more often than not, reflect a perversion of the political process to serve special-interest ends. Import restraints—whether "voluntary" or mandatory—tend to perpetuate rather than cure the very structural and conduct imperfections that were the original cause of an industry's need for protection. The prospects for improving performance in such an industry, as well as achieving ancillary benefits for the economy as a whole, would seem closer to realization under a regime of competition than under a system of restrictions. As Fred C. Bergsten, formerly Assistant Secretary of the Treasury, observed: "The benefits of an open trading system in holding down the rate of inflation extend across our entire economy. But competition from abroad is especially important in industries dominated by a few large firms, since these are the industries which may be least responsive to market pressure. In such industries, imports help to brake price increases and can provide critically important incentives for diversification of production in response to new market trends."[41] Perhaps, as Gottfried Haberler once suggested, in such industries, free trade may be the best antitrust policy.

SOME CONCLUDING OBSERVATIONS

A few final comments are in order with respect to public policy proposals for arresting the decline in the productivity of American industry by dispensing with our traditional concern about concentrated economic power.

The U.S. economy, so the argument runs, is in decline and its international competitive position is eroding. In the last decade, some two million jobs have been lost in U.S. manufacturing, and the U.S. share of world markets for manufactured goods had declined by nearly 25 percent during the period. Our domestic markets are being flooded, not only by foreign steel and automobiles, but by an almost endless list of such items as hand calculators, cameras, sporting equipment, motorcycles, stereo equipment, watches, tires, video components, pianos, and footwear. In 1970, it is argued, productivity (measured as real output per hour of work) was rising at an annual rate of 2.9 percent, whereas since 1977 it has been declining at .04 percent a year.[42] We are now said to have the highest percentage of obsolete plants, the lowest percentage of capital investment, and the lowest growth in productivity of any major industrial nation other than Great Britain.

Part of the solution offered for this malaise is to reindustrialize America; to emulate Japan's success by transcending the adversarial posture between business, labor, and government; and to provide entrepreneurs with incentives for efficiency and technological progress by relieving them of the shackles imposed by antimonopoly and antimerger laws.

These proposals emanate not only from ideological supply-siders in the Reagan Administration, but from leading economists identified with the "liberal" camp. Lester Thurow, for example, argues that "the time has come to recognize that the antitrust approach has been a failure"; that the "costs it imposes far exceed any benefits it brings"; that the message of some of the government's antimonopoly cases seems to be "it does not pay to be too efficient." Thurow concludes, therefore, that, "Given our modern economic environment, antitrust regulations should be stripped back to two basic propositions. The first would be a ban on predatory pricing. Large firms should not be allowed to drive small firms out of business by selectively lowering their prices in submarkets while they maintain high prices in other submarkets. The second proposition would be a ban on explicit or implicit cartels that share either markets or profits. *Firms can grow by driving competitors out of business or by absorbing them,* but they cannot agree not to compete with each other."[43] In this view, there is an inevitable trade-off—one that antitrust cannot successfully resolve—between (1) firms of the most efficient size but operating under conditions where there is inadequate pressure to compel firms to continue to be efficient and pass on to the consumer the benefits of efficiency; and (2) a system in which the firms are numerous enough to be competitive but too small to be efficient. According to this view, our choice is between monopoloid bigness and efficiency, on the one hand, and competition and relative inefficiency, on the other hand.

How valid is this alleged trade-off in any program for reindustrializing America? Are giant mergers, especially conglomerate mergers, the necessary means toward that end? If, for example, we posit increased oil and gas production and energy independence as a national goal, how is that objective served by Mobil's acquisition of Montgomery Ward; Arco's acquisition of *The London Observer* and Anaconda; Exxon's acquisition of Reliance Electric; Standard Oil of Ohio's acquisition of Kennecott Copper; Getty's entry into home box office television; Sun Oil's purchase of Seagram's *old* oil and gas properties; or the use of the Hunt brothers' oil fortune to speculate in silver? Incidentally, none of these actions was challenged under the antitrust laws.

After the experience of the last two decades, does anyone have the temerity to suggest that LTV's acquisition of Jones & Laughlin, or Lykes' purchase of Youngstown Sheet and Tube, or the subsequent merger between LTV and Lykes, or the more recent merger between LTV and Republic—all of them combinations among steel giants—promoted efficiency or injected competitive vigor into a somnolent steel oligopoly? Would anyone claim that ITT's acquisition of Avis, or NBC's purchase of Hertz enhanced competition or increased managerial efficiency in the car rental industry? Is there any evidence that the acquisition by ITT, once a quiet international public utility, of Continental Baking Company (the largest bread company in the United States), Sheraton (the largest hotel/motel chain), Levitt Brothers (the largest home builders), Hartford Insurance, and so on, contributed a synergistic *elan vital* to American manufacturing? Do such mergers create new capital values, new productive facilities, new jobs, new technology, new markets?

This kind of corporate empire building, it would seem, is little more than an entrepreneurial ego trip. It indicates that corporate managers—goaded by merger specialists in Wall Street's investment banking houses—are spending energy on increasing their companies' short-term profits through financial manipulation rather than increasing operating efficiency, enhancing productivity, and promoting technological progress. It should not come as a surprise that, in recent years, U.S. corporations have spent more on their acquisitions and mergers than they have chosen to invest in research and development. They engaged in high-stake games of financial razzle-dazzle, virtually untouched by the antitrust laws, largely devoid of socially redeeming advantages, and hardly calculated to accelerate the reindustrialization of America.

Giant size, especially when it is the product of a helter-skelter merger spree, is not automatically conducive to the kinds of investments and innovations necessary to increase a nation's capacity to generate wealth. The miraculous performance of the Japanese economy since World War II, for example, underscores rather than refutes this proposition. Japanese industry has achieved its enviable productivity and international competitiveness, not because it is populated by giant firms, nor because it is immune from stringent antitrust inhibitions, nor because it benefits from an allegedly symbiotic relationship with labor and government, nor because of peculiarly felicitous cultural traditions unlike those prevailing in the United States and Western Europe. The Japanese "miracle," I submit, is attributable to the fact that Japanese industry was compelled to export in order to survive and prosper, and that it was constantly subject to the ruthless discipline of an exogenous, competitive, international market mechanism that it could neither manipulate nor control. Whatever the rules of the game that Japanese industry had to obey at home, success was possible only if it could produce products wanted by consumers in competitive world markets, and sell those products at prices which consumers with competing alternatives were willing to pay. In short, the reward and punishment system confronting Japanese industry was that associated with competitive markets. No sweetheart relationship with labor and government, no immunity from antitrust prohibitions, could insulate Japanese producers from the restraints that international competition systematically imposed on them.

Therefore, size per se guarantees neither efficiency nor technological progressiveness. However, this does not mean that industrial giantism is benign. The fact is—though this may not be stressed in elementary economics courses—that today's giant corporation is as much a political as an economic institution. Without necessarily exercising market power in the diverse industries in which it may operate, it possesses the political power, by virtue of its absolute (rather than relative) size, to influence the rules by whch the competitive game is played. It tends to spend almost as much energy manipulating government policies for its own benefit as it does competing in the marketplace, improving productivity, or planning technological breakthroughs. It seeks governmental favors, subsidies, and privileges. It pleads for relief from "onerous" burdens like clean air, pure water, industrial safety, and energy conservation regulations. Above all, it expects the government to compensate it for its own mistakes which, given the firm's giant size, are likely to be of gigantic proportions.

These government bailouts—whether in the form of protection from import competition or in the form of protection from bankruptcy—are becoming standard operating procedure. The Chrysler bailout is a dramatic, but not unique, case in point. The tenth largest U.S. corporation on Fortune's list of the 500 Largest Industrials, with assets of some $6.6 billion, with more than 130,000 employees, and operations scattered over several states, Chrysler felt that the government could not "afford" to let it fail. It was a corporation of preeminent rank not only in the automobile industry, but a significant factor in the national economy, and it wielded sufficient political power—in conjunction with its powerful trade union, its suppliers, its dealers and distributors, and the states and municipalities dependent on its tax revenues—to persuade the federal government that bailout was preferable to bankruptcy.

Industrial giantism, whether or not accompanied by monopoly power in specific markets, is not benign and therefore cannot be ignored. At the very least, it breeds an arrogance of power and tends to divert entrepreneurship from risk-taking, investment, research and development, productivity enhancement and market expansion into efforts to manipulate the state for protectionist ends. It transforms the firm from an economic organism, which seeks to maximize profits by excelling in the marketplace, into a quasipolitical institution which seeks the quiet life in an *Ordnungswirtschaft* guaranteed by the state.

Therefore, the basic question, posed earlier, remains, especially in a democratic society: Who shall make what decisions, on whose behalf, at what cost, and for whose benefit? It is a question, not for economics, but for political economy. Throughout, the challenge is to design an exogenous control mechanism, largely immune from manipulation by special-interest groups, with built-in safeguards against abuse by concentrated power clusters, so that the system will operate not only to *permit* but rather *compel* decisions in the public interest. (See Figure 2.)

Thomas Jefferson and the founding fathers believed that "it is not by the consolidation or concentration of powers, but by their distribution, that good government is effected."[44] It is a proposition applicable to the organ-

FIGURE 2. Public policy alternatives: the road ahead. *Source:* Thurman W. Arnold: *Cartels or Free Enterprise?* Public Affairs Pamphlet No. 103, 1945. Reproduced by permission of Public Affairs Commission, Inc.

izational structure of economic as well as political institutions. The alternative, as Stocking and Watkins observed three decades ago, is "to accept some collectivistic alternative that may give more short-run basic security, but in the long run will almost certainly provide less freedom, less opportunity for experiment, less variety, less economic progress, and less total abundance."[45]

NOTES

1. *United States v. Aluminum Company of America,* 148 F.2d 416 (C.C.A. 2d, 1945).

2. *The Wealth of Nations,* Book 1, Chap. 10. Here it should be pointed out that businessmen engage in trade restraints and organize monopolies not because of any vicious and antisocial motives, but rather because of a desire to increase personal profits. As George Comer, former chief economist of the Antitrust Division, once observed, monopolies are formed "not because businessmen are criminals, but because the reports from the bookkeeping department indicate, in the short run at least, that monopoly and restraints of trade will pay if you can get away with [them]. It will pay a large corporation to agree with its competitors on price fixing. It pays to operate a basing point or zone price system. If patent pools can be organized, especially with hundreds or thousands of patents covering a whole industry, the profits will be enormous. If an international cartel can be formed which really works, the very peak of stabilization and rationalism is reached. If the management of all the large units in an industry can get together with the labor unions in the industry, a number of birds can be killed with one stone. And, finally, if the government can be persuaded to legalize the restrictive practices, the theory of 'enlightened competition' is complete." "The Outlook for Effective Competition," *American Economic Review, Papers and Proceedings,* **36:**154 (May 1946).

3. U.S. Congress, Senate, Committee on the Judiciary, S. Rep. 695, 63rd Cong., 2nd sess., 1914, p. 1 (Italics supplied.)

4. A congressional committee explained the background of the price discrimination provision of the Clayton Act as follows:

"In the past it has been a most common practice of great and powerful combinations engaged in commerce—notably the Standard Oil company and the American Tobacco Company, and others of less notoriety, but of great influence—to lower prices of their commodities, oftentimes below the cost of production in certain communities and sections where they had competition, with the intent to destroy and make unprofitable the business of their competitors, and with the ultimate purpose in view of thereby acquiring a monopoly in the particular locality or section in which the discriminating price is made.

"Every concern that engages in this evil practice must of necessity recoup its losses in the particular communities or sections where their commodities are sold below cost or without a fair profit by raising the price of this same class of commodities above their fair market value in other sections or communities.

"Such a system or practice is so manifestly unfair and unjust, not only to competitors who are directly injured thereby but to the general public, that your committee is strongly of the opinion that the present antitrust laws ought to be supplemented by making this particular form of discrimination a specific offense under the law when practiced by those engaged in commerce."

U.S. Congress, House, Committee on the Judiciary, H. Rep. 627, 63rd Cong., 2nd sess., 1914, pp. 8–9.

5. Smith, op. cit., Book 1, Chap. 7.

6. See C. D. Edwards, *Economic and Political Aspects of International Cartels,* Senate Committee on Military Affairs, Monograph, No. 1 (Washington, D.C.: U.S. Government Printing Office, 1946), pp. 12–13.

7. See W. H. Hamilton, *Patents and Free Enterprise,* TNEC Monograph, No. 31 (Washington, D.C.: U.S. Government Printing Office, 1941), pp. 109–115.

8. See *United States v. Hartford-Empire Co., et al.,* 323 U.S. 386 (1945).

9. Clair Wilcox, *Competition and Monopoly in the American Economy,* TNEC Monograph No. 21 (Washington, D.C.: U.S. Government Printing Office, 1941), pp. 16–17.

10. Edwards, op. cit., p. 36. For a popular discussion of the I.G. Farben-Standard marriage, see also G. W. Stocking and M. W. Watkins, *Cartels in Action* (New York: Twentieth Century Fund, 1946), Chap. 11, especially pp. 491–505.

11. See W. Berge, *Cartels: Challenge to a Free World* (Washington, D.C.: Public Affairs Press, 1944), pp. 201–214; G. W. Stocking and M. W. Watkins, *Cartels or Competition* (New York: Twentieth Century Fund, 1948), pp. 114–117; J. Borkin and C. A. Welsh, *Germany's Master Plan* (New York: Duell, Sloan, 1943). For a contrary view, see F. A. Howard, *Buna Rubber* (New York: Van Nostrand, 1947).

12. "Market Structure and Stabilization Policy," *The Review of Economics and Statistics,* **39:**131, 133 (May 1957). For further discussion of sellers' inflation, administered price inflation, and inflation in the midst of recession—in short, the relation between market structure and general price stability—see also U.S. Congress, Senate, Judiciary Committee, *Hearings on Administered Prices Before the Subcommittee on Antitrust and Monopoly,* Part 1, 1957, and Parts 9 and 10, 1959; and U.S. Congress, Joint Economic Committee, *The Relationship of Prices to Economic Stability and Growth,* 85th Cong., 2nd sess., 1958.

13. Address reprinted in *Congressional Record,* Feb. 12, 1947, p. A545. See also H. C. Simons, *Economic Policy for a Free Society* (Chicago: U. of Chicago P., 1948); F. A. Hayek, *The Road to Serfdom* (Chicago: U. of Chicago P., 1945); R. A. Brady, *Business as a System of Power* (New York: Columbia U. P., 1943); G. W. Stocking, "Saving Free Enterprise from Its Friends," *Southern Economic Journal,* 19:431 (April 1953). Also relevant in this connection are the repeated warnings by the FTC to the effect that "the capitalist system of free initiative is not immortal, but is capable of dying and dragging down with it the system of democratic government. Monopoly constitutes the death of capitalism and the genesis of authoritarian government." *The Basing Point Problem,* TNEC Monograph, No. 42 (Washington, D.C.: U.S. Government Printing Office, 1941), p. 9.

14. This point was well made by Senator Cummins, in 1914, when he pressed for adoption of the Federal Trade Commission Act and the Clayton Act:

"We have adopted in this country the policy of competition. We are trying to preserve competition as a living, real force in our industrial life; that is to say, we are endeavoring to maintain among our business people that honorable rivalry which will prevent one from exacting undue profits from those who may deal with him. . . . We are practically alone, however, in this policy. . . . England long ago became indifferent to it; and while that great country has not specifically adjusted her laws so as to permit monopoly they are so administered as to practically eliminate competition when the trade affected so desires. France has pursued a like course.

"Austria, Italy, Spain, Norway, Sweden, as well as Belgium, have all pursued the course of permitting combinations and relations which practically annihilate competition, and Germany, our most formidable rival, so far as commerce is concerned, not only authorized by her law the formation of monopolies, the creation of combinations which restrain trade and which destroy competition, but oftentimes compels her people to enter into combinations which are in effect monopolies. We are, therefore, pursuing a course which rather distinguishes us from the remainder of the commercial world.

"I pause here to say, and I say it emphatically and earnestly, that I believe in our course; I believe in the preservation of competition, I believe in the maintenance of the rule that opens the channels of trade fairly and fully to all comers. I believe it because it seems to me obvious that any other course must inevitably lead us into complete State socialism. The only monopoly which civilized mankind will ever permanently endure is the monopoly of all the people represented in the Government itself." *Congressional Record,* June 30, 1914, p. 11,379.

Since World War II, the contrast between the American and European approaches to the monopoly problem has been considerably reduced. Several nations in Western Europe have enacted restrictive practices legislation that, although not as far-reaching as the American prototype, nevertheless reflects a growing awareness of the problem. See European Productivity Agency, *Guide to Legislation on Restrictive Business Practices,* 2 vols. (Paris: Organization for Economic Cooperation and Development, 1960).

15. F. Machlup, *The Political Economy of Monopoly* (Baltimore: Johns Hopkins U.P., 1952), pp. 77–78. See also Walter Adams and Horace M. Gray, *Monopoly in America* (New York: Macmillan, 1955).

16. A somewhat less sophisticated version is offered by George Gilder, who assures us that monopoly positions "are not at all unlimited, because they are always held—unless government intercedes to enforce them—under the threat of potential competitors and substitutes at home or abroad. To the question of how many companies an industry needs in order to be competitive, economist Arthur Laffer answers: one. It will compete against the threat of future rivals. Its monopoly can be maintained only as long as the price is kept low enough to exclude others. In this sense, monopolies are good. The more dynamic and inventive an economy, the more monopolies it will engender." *Wealth and Poverty* (New York: Basic Books, 1981), pp. 37–38.

17. Robert H. Bork, *The Antitrust Paradox,* New York: Basic Books, 1978 p. 118.

18. Ibid., p. 119.

19. Ibid., p. 133.

20. Ibid., pp. 124–125.

21. *The Works of Jeremy Bentham* (J. Bowring, ed.), vol. 3., p. 185.

22. Lord Robbins, *Politics and Economics* (London: Macmillan & Co. 1963), pp. 50–51.

23. John B. Clark, *The Control of Trusts* (New York: Macmillan, 1912), pp. 200–201.

24. *U.S. v. Columbia Steel Corp.,* 334 U.S. 495 (1948).

25. Joseph A. Schumpeter, *Capitalism, Socialism and Democracy,* (New York: Harper, 1943), pp. 79ff.

26. Quoted in Matthew Josephson, *The Politicos* (New York: Harcourt, 1938), p. 526.

27. Quoted in Walter Adams and Leland E. Traywick (eds.), *Readings in Economics* (New York: Macmillan, 1948), p. 223.

28. Horace M. Gray, "The Passing of the Public Utility Concept," *Journal of Land and Public Utility Economics,* **16:**1–20 (1940).

29. Walter Adams, "The Role of Competition in the Regulated Industries," *American Economic Review* **48:**257 (May 1958).

30. Attorney General's National Committee to Study the Antitrust Laws, *Report* (1955), p. 265.

31. Address to the Financial Analysts Federation, Detroit, Michigan, Oct. 7, 1974.

32. For an elaboration of this thesis, see Walter Adams and Joel B. Dirlam, "Import Quotas and Industrial Performance," in A. P. Jacquemain and H. W. DeJong (eds.), *Welfare Aspects of Industrial Markets* (Leiden: Martinus Nijhoff, 1977), pp. 153–81.

33. Walter Adams and James W. Brock, "Countervailing or Coalescing Power? The Problem of Labor/Management Coalitions," *Journal of Post Keynesian Economics,* **6:** 180–197 (Winter 1983–84).

34. U.S. Congress, Congressional Budget Office, *The Effects of Import Quotas on the Steel Industry* (Washington, D.C., July 1984), pp. xv–xix.

35. "Should Steel Be Helped?" *The Economist* (Feb. 9, 1985), p. 12.

36. Quoted in Adams and Dirlam, op. cit., p. 177.

37. U.S. International Trade Commission, *A Review of Recent Developments in the U.S. Automobile Industry Including an Assessment of the Japanese Voluntary*

Restraint Agreements, U.S.I.T.C. Publication 1648 (Washington, D.C., Feb. 1985), pp. v–x.

38. *The Wall Street Journal,* March 20, 1981.

39. Among the important causes of the problems of U.S. auto manufacturers, none is more significant that the persistent failure by the big three companies to recognize that the era of the gas-guzzler had come to an end, and that small, fuel-efficient cars were what the market would demand. Thus, in spite of the dramatic economic transformation precipitated by the Arab oil embargo of 1973, auto manufacterers chose *not* to concentrate on the development and production of small cars and to continue to rely on "intermediate" and "standard" cars as the mainstay of the do domestic industry. Whatever the reasons for this decision—whether it was to avoid competition in the small car-field, where foreign producers were strong, or to capitalize on the higher profit margins on "full-sized" care (in accordance with Henry Ford II's maxim that "mini-cars mean mini profits"), or to profit from the more costly options (power steering and brakes, more powerful engines, automatic transmissions, etc.) required by large cars—the decision had seriously adverse consequences for the U.S. manufacturers and ultimately for their employees.

The statistics tell the story. Table I shows that U.S. producers' shipments of subcompact and compact cars not only held their own between 1975 and 1980, but substantially increased their share of apparent U.S. consumption. By contrast, the percentage of large cars, after peaking in 1977, declined dramatically during the same period.

Table I: Passenger Automobiles: Ratio of U.S. Producers' Shipments and Imports to Apparent Consumption, by Class of Vehicle, 1975–79, January-June 1979, and January-June 1980. (In percent)

		U.S. Producers' Shipments	
Period	*Imports*	*Small Cars*	*Large Cars*
1975	26.0	26.5	47.6
1976	25.1	24.6	50.2
1977	25.2	20.7	54.1
1978	26.2	26.1	47.7
1979	27.1	31.5	41.4
January-June			
1979	24.7	28.2	47.1
1980	34.5	36.3	29.2

Source: U.S. International Trade Commission

40. *The New York Times,* March 20, 1981. How, for example, did the U.S. auto industry use its four years of quota protection? Did it take the necessary steps to enhance its productivity and its international competitiveness? According to John B. Schnapp, vice president of a Massachusetts consulting firm, "General Motors made the following decisions during those four years: It abandoned previously made plans to produce its small S-car, now called Corsa, in the U.S., instead confining its production to Spain. It transformed the concept for its P-car, or Fiero, from an economy commuter vehicle to a pricey sports model. It undertook equity investment in Isuzu, Suzuki and Daewoo, the first two relatively small Japanese auto makers and the latter a Korean company, as elements of agreements under which those firms would supply vehicles to General Motors specifications for its Chevrolet and Pontiac divisions. And it established its joint venture with Toyota, called NUMMI, at its abandoned assembly plant in Fremont, Calif.

"During the same period Ford continued selling its import-fighter, Escort, but made no significant investment in even cosmetic updating, leaving Escort virtually unchanged since its introduction in 1980. And Chrysler, rather than replacing its own aged import-fighter, Omni/Horizon, with a U.S.-made counterpart, opted instead for increased equity investment in Mitsubishi Motors, its Japanese affiliate, and increased imports from that company." ("When a U.S. Industry Got Chance to 'Catch Up' " *The Wall Street Journal,* Sept. 25, 1985, p. 26.)

41. Testimony before the U.S. Senate Antitrust and Monopoly Subcommittee, *Hearings,* Washington, D.C., 1977.

42. "Reindustrialization," *Business Week* (June 30, 1980), pp.55ff.

43. Lester C. Thurow, *The Zero-Sum Society* (New York: Basic Books, 1980), pp. 146, 149, 150 (emphasis supplied).

44. Paul L. Ford (ed.), *The Writings of Thomas Jefferson* (New York: Putnam, 1904), vol. 1, p. 122.

45. G. W. Stocking and M. W. Watkins, *Monopoly and Free Enterprise* (New York: Twentieth Century Fund, 1952), p. 526. We might profit from British experience, which the conservative London *Economist* has summarized as follows: "The fact is that British industrialists, under the deliberate leadership of the Tory Party in its Baldwin-Chamberlain era, have become distinguishable from British Socialists only by the fact that they still believe in private profits . . .If free, competitive, private-enterprise capitalism is to continue to exist, not throughout the national economy, but in any part of it, then it needs rescuing from the capitalists fully as much as from the Socialists." *The Economist*, **139:**22 (June 29, 1946). Copyright *The Economist*. Reprinted by permission of the publishers.

SUGGESTED READINGS

BOOKS

Adams, W., and H. M. Gray. *Monopoly in America: The Government as Promoter*. New York: Macmillan Publishing Company, 1955.

Argyris, C. *Regulating Business*. San Francisco: Institute for Contemporary Studies, 1978.

Bain, J. S. *Barriers to New Competition*. Cambridge, Mass.: Harvard University Press, 1956.

Blair, J. M. *Economic Concentration*. New York: Harcourt Brace Jovanovich, 1972.

Bork, R. H. *The Antitrust Paradox*. New York: Basic Books, 1978.

Caves, R. E. *American Industry: Structure, Conduct, Performance,* 3rd ed. Englewood Cliffs, N.J.: Prentice-Hall, 1972.

———, and M. Uekusa. *Industrial Organization in Japan*. Washington, D.C.: Brookings Institution, 1976.

Dirlam, J. B., and A. E. Kahn. *The Law and Economics of Fair Competition: An Appraisal of Antitrust Policy*. Ithaca, N.Y.: Cornell University Press, 1954.

Edwards, C. D. *Maintaining Competition*. New York: McGraw-Hill Book Co., 1949.

Galbraith, J. K. *The New Industrial State*. Boston: Houghton Mifflin Company, 1967.

Goldschmid, H. J., H. M. Mann, and J. F. Weston (eds.). *Industrial Concentration: The New Learning*. Boston: Little, Brown and Company, 1974.

Greer, D. F. *Industrial Organization and Public Policy*, 2nd ed. New York: Macmillan Publishing Company, 1984.

Herman, E. S. *Corporate Control, Corporate Power*. New York: Cambridge University Press, 1981.

Kahn, A. E. *The Economics of Regulation*. 2 vols., New York: John Wiley & Sons, 1971.

Kaysen, C., and D. F. Turner. *Antitrust Policy*. Cambridge, Mass.: Harvard University Press, 1959.
Lindblom, C. E. *Politics and Markets*. New York: Basic Books, 1977.
Machlup, F. *The Political Economy of Monopoly*. Baltimore: The John Hopkins University Press, 1952.
Mansfield, E. (ed). *Monopoly Power and Economic Performance*, 4th ed. New York: W. W. Norton & Co., 1978.
Phillips, A. (ed.). *Promoting Competition in Regulated Markets*. Washington, D.C.: Brookings Institution, 1975.
Reid, S. R. *The New Industrial Order*. New York: McGraw-Hill Book Co. 1976.
Rosen, S. M. *Economic Power Failure*. New York: McGraw-Hill Book Co. 1975.
Scherer, F. M. *Industrial Market Structure and Economic Performance*, 2nd ed. Chicago: Rand McNally & Co., 1980.
Schultze, C. L. *The Public Use of Private Interest*. Washington, D.C.: Brookings Institution, 1977.
Schumpeter, J. A. *Capitalism, Socialism and Democracy*. New York: Harper & Row, 1942.
Shepherd, W. G. *Market Power and Economic Welfare*. New York: Random House, 1970.
———. *The Treatment of Market Power*. New York: Columbia University Press, 1975.
——— and Associates. *Public Enterprise: Economic Analysis of Theory and Practice*. Lexington, Mass.: Heath-Lexington Books, 1976.
Simons, H. C. *Economic Policy for a Free Society*. Chicago: University of Chicago Press, 1948.
Stigler, G. J. *The Organization of Industry*. Homewood, Ill.: Richard D. Irwin, Inc., 1968.
Stocking, G. W., and M. W. Watkins. *Cartels in Action*. New York: Twentieth Century Fund, 1946.
——— *Cartels or Competition?* New York: Twentieth Century Fund, 1947.
——— *Monopoly and Free Enterprise*. New York: Twentieth Centuty Fund, 1951.
Weidenbaum, M. L. *Business, Government, and the Public*, 2nd ed. Englewood Cliffs, N.J.: Prentice-Hall, 1981.
Wilcox, C., and W. G. Shepherd. *Public Policies Toward Business*. Homewood, Ill.: Richard D. Irwin, Inc., 1975.
Williamson, O. E. *Markets and Hierarchies*. New York: The Free Press, 1975.
Wilson, J. Q. (ed.), *The Politics of Regulation*. New York: Basic Books, 1980.

GOVERNMENT PUBLICATIONS

FTC, *Economic Report on Corporate Mergers*. Washington, D.C.: U.S. Government Printing Office, 1969.
Hamilton, W. H. *Antitrust in Action*. Temporary National Economic Committee Monograph No. 16. Washington, D.C.: U.S. Government Printing Office, 1940.
U.S. Congress, Congressional Budget Office, *The Effects of Import Quotas on the Steel Industry*, July 1984.
U.S. Congress, Senate, Committee on Banking, Housing, and Urban Affairs, *Chrysler Corporation Financial Situation, Hearings*, 96th Cong., 1st sess. 1979.
U.S. Congress, Senate, Subcommittee on Antitrust and Monopoly, Judiciary Committee, *Hearings*, Parts 1–10, 85th and 86th Congresses, 1957–1960.
U.S. Congress, Senate, Subcommittee on Antitrust and Monopoly, Judiciary Committee, *Economic Concentration*, Parts 1–8A, 88th–91st Congresses, 1964–1970.
U.S. Congress, Senate, Subcommittee on Antitrust and Monopoly, Judiciary Committee, *The Industrial Reorganization Act, Hearings on S*. 1167, 93rd–94th Congresses, Parts 1–9, 1973–1975.

U.S. Congress, Senate, Subcommittee on Antitrust and Monopoly. *Mergers and Industrial Concentration, Hearings,* 95th Cong., 2nd sess. 1978.

U.S. Congress, Senate, Committee on the Judiciary, *Federal Restraints on Competition in the Trucking Industry, Report,* 96th Cong., 2nd sess., 1980.

U.S. Congress, Senate, Subcommittee on Multinational Corporations, Foreign Relations Committee, *Multinational Corporations and U.S. Foreign Policy, Hearings,* 93rd–94th Congresses, Parts 1–11, 1973–1975.

U.S. Congress, Joint Economic Committee, *Federal Subsidy Programs, A Staff Study,* 93rd Cong., 2nd sess., October 18, 1974.

U.S. International Trade Commission, *A Review of Recent Developments in the U.S. Automobile Industry including an Assessment of the Japanese Voluntary Restraint Agreements,* U.S.I.T.C. Publication 1648, Washington, D.C., Feb. 1985.

JOURNAL AND MAGAZINE ARTICLES

Adams, W. "Dissolution, Divorcement, Divestiture: The Pyrrhic Victories of Antitrust." *Indiana Law Journal,* **27** (Fall 1951).

———. "The Military-Industrial Complex and the New Industrial State." *American Economic Review,* **58** (May 1968).

Adams, W. and J.W. Brock, "Countervailing or Coalescing Power? The Problem of Labor/Management Coalitions," *Journal of Post Keynesian Economics,* **6** (Winter 1983–84).

Adams, W. J. "Firm Size and Research Activity: France and the United States." *Quarterly Journal of Economics,* **84** (Aug 1970).

——— "Market Structure and Corporate Power." *Columbia Law Review,* **74** (Nov. 1974).

Comanor, W. S., and T. A. Wilson. "Advertising and the Advantages of Size." *American Economic Review,* **59** (May 1969).

Keezer, D. (ed.). "The Antitrust Laws: A Symposium." *American Economic Review,* **39** (June 1949).

Mason, E. S. "Current Status of the Monopoly Problem." *Harvard Law Review,* **62** (June 1949).

Scherer, F. M. "Firm Size, Market Structure, Opportunity, and the Output of Patented Inventions." *American Economic Review,* **55** (Dec. 1965).

Shepherd, W. G., " 'Contestability vs. Competition," *American Economic Review,* **74** (Sept. 1984).

Stigler, G. J. "The Case Against Big Business." *Fortune,* **45** (May 1952).

Name Index

Subject Index